D1570386

MACROECONOMICS
Selected Readings

MACROECONOMICS
Selected Readings

EDWARD SHAPIRO
The University of Toledo

Harcourt, Brace & World, Inc.
New York Chicago San Francisco Atlanta

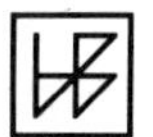

ISBN: 0-15-551207-2

Library of Congress Catalog Number: 72-124416

Printed in the United States of America

PREFACE

The most spectacular explosion in economics in recent decades has been in the body of knowledge that we call macroeconomics. From its relatively modest dimensions in the early 1930's, the literature encompassing this body of knowledge has grown to the point at which a one-volume book of readings in macroeconomics can offer at best no more than a sampling of selections from a sampling of the broad range of subject areas covered by the field.

The present compilation has drawn three or more papers from each of eight subject areas. The papers chosen and their distribution by subject area obviously reflect the editor's judgment on what is most relevant to the student to whom the book is directed. Although each article selected had to meet one or more of such obvious criteria as interpretative excellence, theoretical contribution, and empirical significance, these criteria were regarded as necessary but not sufficient. Another, and controlling, criterion has been the frequently neglected one of comprehensibility. This collection is intended specifically as a supplement to texts in the intermediate macroeconomics course and is thus intended for use by students whose total background in economics may include little more than the first year of introductory work. Therefore, for each of the many articles considered for inclusion, the first question was whether or not it was an article that could be mastered or at least firmly grasped and not merely "read" by these students. And it is because each article finally included did meet this as well as one or more other criteria that this book of readings may succeed in doing what it is intended to do: take the undergraduate student beyond his textbook to a manageable introduction to the professional literature of macroeconomics.

This book's sequence of subject areas and of articles within the subject areas follows as closely as possible the sequence of subject matter in most of the intermediate macroeconomics textbooks. Each article in this volume, of course, stands independent of the others, and any combination of articles can be profitably studied. However, in selecting articles for each part, another criterion that was met to the degree possible was to have the successive articles follow one another in a logical order. Thus, if more than one article in any part is to be studied, there is some reason for tackling those chosen in the order given. The reasons for the particular ordering of the articles in each part and the relationships within each group of articles are discussed in the introduction that precedes each part.

The editor is indebted to William J. Baumol, Edgar Feige, and John J. Klein for their detailed comments on successive lists of selections and for their suggestions as to alternatives and additions. The major indebtedness is, of course, to the authors and publishers of the articles and books that appear in the final list for their kind permission to reprint their work.

EDWARD SHAPIRO

CONTENTS

I

Income and Consumption

From the time of Keynes's *General Theory,* economists have emphasized the primacy of income among the many variables that influence consumer expenditures or saving. As long as one states this in the form of a very general proposition, there is hardly room for disagreement. However, as soon as one begins to specify the precise nature of the relationship, the doors are opened wide to disagreement. Actually, in the first years following the appearance of the *General Theory* there was little of this disagreement; the relationship between income and consumption specified by Keynes was quite generally accepted. Then, over the following years, rival hypotheses of the relationship were developed. Although the total number of such hypotheses is now greater than three, most, if not all, involve variants of what are generally recognized to be three basic hypotheses on the income-consumption relationship, usually identified as the absolute income, relative income, and permanent income hypotheses.

The first selection in this part provides a concise statement of these three hypotheses, surveys the empirical research on each, and shows how the two latter hypotheses developed out of dissatisfaction with the previously existing theory. Thus, the relative income hypothesis emerged during the forties as a rival to the absolute income hypothesis. The name most closely associated with the relative income hypothesis is James S. Duesenberry, and the second selection in this part is his major article on the subject. The third and final selection in this part is a modest empirical study that places side by side the three hypotheses discussed in the first selection and submits them to similar empirical tests based on a single body of data.

1

GENERAL THEORIES OF SPENDING OR SAVING BEHAVIOR

ROBERT FERBER

Three general theories currently exist on the determinants of total consumer spending: the *absolute income hypothesis,* the *relative income hypothesis,* and the *permanent income hypothesis.* Though radically different in interpretation, they nevertheless possess certain properties in common. One such property is their purported generality. Each has been used on time series as well as on cross-section data and to derive macro- as well as micro-relationships.[1] Each was advanced originally in terms of individual behavior and then generalized to aggregate behavior, sometimes with explicit recognition of the aggregation problem, and at other times largely ignoring it on the apparent presumption that nonlinearities or distributional effects are relatively unimportant.

Each hypothesis postulates a relationship between consumption and income, though the concepts underlying these terms may vary substantially. In other words, the primary concern is to isolate the influence of income, and occasionally of wealth, on consumer spending, holding constant the effect of other possibly relevant, less important variables—age, family composition, location of residence, education, etc. Each is the subject of wide controversy, receiving support from some empirical studies but not from others. Finally, each when first presented appears deceptively simple, at least in theory, but

[1]In the latter case, the application has often been to groups of households rather than to individual households, particularly in the case of the permanent income hypothesis, on the ground that the importance of erratic factors is so great for individual households as to obscure more basic relationships.

Reprinted from Robert Ferber, "Research on Household Behavior," Part I, *American Economic Review* (March 1962), pp. 20–32, by permission of the author and publisher. Robert Ferber is a professor at the University of Illinois.

when it comes to implementation, proponents of the same hypothesis often disagree with each other on appropriate definitions and approaches. This will become clear from a consideration of each hypothesis in turn.

A. Absolute Income Hypothesis. ". . . men are disposed, as a rule and on the average, to increase their consumption as their income increases, but not by as much as the increase in their income" [27, p. 96]. Whether or not this is the original statement of the absolute income hypothesis, there is no doubt that this statement by Keynes stimulated much empirical work to test this hypothesis and to derive "the consumption function." Many of these studies were carried out on time series, the general practice being to correlate aggregate consumption expenditures over time with aggregate disposable income and various other variables. They need not concern us here except to note that invariably they "corroborated" the hypothesis, producing very high goodness of fit (adjusted correlation coefficients of .98 or more), with current income accounting for the bulk of the variation in consumption, the average and marginal propensities being less than unity, and with the marginal propensity less than the average propensity.[2]

One early modification of the absolute income hypothesis was brought about by a theoretical controversy regarding the existence of any automatic force to assure full-employment equilibrium. Keynes took a negative position, but others showed that a full-employment equilibrium position could exist if consumption expenditures depended on wealth as well as on income, the "Pigou real balance effect" [41].[3] It was only in the postwar period that data became available to test the relevance of a wealth variable. Such tests as were made did tend to show that aggregate consumption was influenced by this variable, though nowhere to the extent of the influence of current income [23][29]. It is pertinent to note, however, that the early postwar years were characterized by high asset-income ratios, low stocks of durables, and relatively little debt.

At the micro level, many studies had been carried out prior to the advent of *The General Theory* but their focus invariably was on ascertaining budget relations for different groups of families or deriving Engel curves for particular components of expenditure.[4] In retrospect, such of these studies as were applicable appeared to corroborate the absolute income hypothesis. Indeed, it was this hypothesis that served as the basis for the derivation of estimates of aggregate expenditures for different population groups in 1935–

[2]For a summary of these studies to 1950, see Ferber [11]. An extensive bibliography of these earlier studies has been compiled by Orcutt and Roy [39].

[3]For a somewhat different interpretation, see Hansen [25].

[4]These are reviewed in Stigler [45]. A fairly comprehensive listing of these studies will be found in Williams and Zimmerman [50].

36, namely, by "blowing up" average consumption observed at each income level in the 1935–36 Consumer Purchases Study [48].[5] The absolute income hypothesis also served as a basis for the derivation of aggregate forecasts of postwar consumption patterns, particularly the consumption patterns that might be expected under full employment [4].

In its empirical applications the absolute income hypothesis has generally followed one of two forms. One form has been to express the level of saving, or of consumption expenditures,[6] as a function of income and of other variables, i.e.:

$$S = a + bY + cZ + u \tag{1}$$

where S represents saving, Y is income, Z is a conglomeration of other variables, u is a stochastic term, and the other letters represent parameters.[7]

The second form involves expressing the saving *ratio* as a function of the same independent variables, i.e.:

$$\frac{S}{Y} = a' + b'Y + c'Z + u' \tag{2}$$

Each of these forms has advantages and limitations. Thus, in equation (1) the marginal propensity is a constant and, if logarithms of the variables are used, the income elasticity is also constant, namely, b. Equation (2) does not possess this convenient property but may be more realistic for this reason. Parameter estimates based on equation (1) are subject to the danger of bias from two sources: the parameter estimates may be dominated by extreme values, and u is not likely to be independent of S. Expressing dollar variables in logarithms (assuming absence of negative values) removes this tendency somewhat, but not altogether. In actual practice, both forms have been used.[8]

Questions about the adequacy of the absolute income hypothesis arose because of its apparent inability to reconcile budget data on saving with observed long-run trends. Estimates of national saving and other aggregates derived by Kuznets [32] [33] and later by Goldsmith [22, Vol. 1, pp. 75–87] indicated that the aggregate saving ratio had remained virtually constant since the 1870's. Yet budget studies showed that the saving ratio rose

[5] The actual aggregation procedure was more complicated, but was based on this principle.

[6] It is perhaps needless to note that consumption functions and saving functions are the same, in theory, one being the complement of the other. However, substantial differences can be obtained in empirical work according to which term is being measured.

[7] We shall follow the usual distinction between *saving* and *savings*, the former representing a flow, that is, the difference between income and consumption during a particular period, and the latter representing a stock as of a certain point in time. Unless otherwise specified, saving is defined as the amount set aside out of current income rather than as the net increment in wealth.

[8] For applications of these functions at the microeconomic level, see Mendershausen [34], Klein [28] [30], Fisher [13].

substantially with income level. Since incomes have risen tremendously since the 1870's by almost any standard, this would suggest, according to the absolute income hypothesis, that the aggregate saving ratio should have moved up noticeably over time.

B. Relative Income Hypothesis. An answer to this apparent inconsistency is provided by the relative income hypothesis, which seems to have been first propounded by Dorothy Brady and Rose Friedman [3]. Its underlying assumption is that the saving rate depends not on the level of income but on the *relative position* of the individual on the income scale, i.e.:

$$\frac{s}{y} = a + b\frac{y}{\bar{y}} \tag{3}$$

where s and y represent individual saving and income, respectively, and $\bar{y}$ represents average income.

Much additional theoretical and empirical support of this hypothesis was provided by the work of Modigliani and of Duesenberry, carried out at about the same time [36] [7]. On a theoretical level, Duesenberry supplied psychological support for this hypothesis, noting that a strong tendency exists in our social system for people to emulate their neighbors and, at the same time, to strive constantly toward a higher standard of living. Hence, once a new, higher standard of living is obtained, as at a cyclical peak, people are reluctant to return to a lower level when incomes go down. In other words, people seek to maintain at least the highest standard of living attained in the past.

On the basis of this reasoning, Duesenberry inferred that from an aggregate time-series point of view the relative income hypothesis could be transformed into one expressing the saving rate as a function of the ratio of current income to the highest level previously reached, i.e.:

$$\frac{S}{Y} = a + b\,\frac{Y}{Y_0} \tag{4}$$

where Y_0 represents the highest level of income previously attained (after deflation for changes in prices and population).

The implication of this hypothesis is that the saving ratio in the long run is constant, independent of the absolute level of income, although in the short run (from one cycle to another) the rate depends on the ratio of current income to previous peak income.

One variation of this approach has been the suggestion by Davis: that previous peak consumption be substituted for previous peak income [6]. The rationale for this suggestion is that people become adjusted to a certain standard of *consumption,* rather than to a certain level of income, so that it is past spending that influences current consumption rather than past income. An additional argument for the substitution of consumption for income is that current income, referring to a period of one year or less, is likely to be less stable and less representative of a family's living standard than is current consumption [49, pp. 280–95].

The empirical support for the relative income hypothesis has proceeded along two lines. One consisted of showing that the aggregate relations of a form similar to (4) provide at least as good explanations and statistical "fits" to fluctuations in national personal saving over time as the various forms of the absolute income hypothesis [6] [7, pp. 89–92] [36, pp. 379–99]. Noteworthy in this respect was the finding of an independent evaluation that these functions yielded greater predictive accuracy outside of the period of observation than did various forms of the absolute income hypothesis [12].[9] In addition, of course, there was the constancy of the aggregate saving ratio over time which fitted in with the relative income hypothesis.

Second, a number of instances were demonstrated in which the relative income hypothesis was, and the absolute income hypothesis was not, able to explain differences in saving or consumption patterns observed in budget data. Thus, Brady and Friedman by this approach were able to reconcile the higher saving rates of village than city families at the same levels of income in 1935–36, and again in 1941; the similarly higher saving rates of farm families than nonfarm families in 1935–36, and also in 1941; and various geographic differences in saving rates in 1935–36 [3]. Duesenberry used this hypothesis to reconcile the fact that dissaving at a given level of income was less frequent in 1941 than in 1935–36, that Negro families saved more than white families in 1935–36 at the same level of income, as well as to explain geographic differences in savings rates [7, Ch. 4, 5]. Brady showed that family saving varied not only with family income but also with the income level of the community in which it resided [3].

Findings such as these do not necessarily serve to rule out the absolute income hypothesis, and it is still very much of an open question whether the facts do indeed conflict with the absolute income hypothesis or whether the hypothesis has been misinterpreted. A basic tenet of the hypothesis is the *ceteris paribus* assumption for all variables other than (current) income. Yet, data availability in empirical studies has been too restricted to allow other principal relevant variables to be held constant; and if such variables are indeed not constant, failure of saving, or the saving rate, to fluctuate with income may represent simply the effects of these omitted variables. Thus, Tobin shows that the apparent failure of the absolute income hypothesis to

[9]However, the most accurate predictions of all were obtained when the functions were transformed into first-difference form, and it was then of little consequence which functional form was used.

explain Negro-white saving differentials at the same level of income can be reconciled if allowance is made for the smaller financial resources available to Negro families than to white families. Because of this difference in wealth, Negro families are unable to dissave as frequently or as much as white families at the same income level, and therefore require extra financial reserves to tide them over emergencies [46, pp. 145–49].

In a similar manner Tobin shows that wealth differentials may explain geographic differences in saving rates, and even the historical constancy of the saving ratio. The latter is based on the presumption that the substantial growth in asset holdings over time may have reduced the need for saving out of current income and contributed to raising the propensity to consume as real income increased. Admittedly, the evidence is rather sketchy, as noted by Tobin [46, pp. 154–56] and is stressed by Milton Friedman [15, pp. 173–82]. However, if a variable such as wealth could be shown to have influenced the secular propensity to consume, the absolute income hypothesis could be vindicated.

C. The Permanent Income Hypothesis. This most recent hypothesis on consumer behavior grew out of the rising concern regarding the adequacy of current income as the most appropriate determinant of consumption expenditures.[10] Particularly among nonwage-earner families income receipts vary substantially from period to period, while consumption outlays exhibit much greater stability. This led to the belief that people geared their expenditures to average actual and anticipated income over a number of periods rather than only to income received in the current period. The central idea is as follows [15, pp. 220]:

> Consider a large number of men all earning $100 a week and spending $100 a week on current consumption. Let them receive their pay once a week, the pay days being staggered, so that one-seventh are paid on Sunday, one-seventh on Monday, and so on. Suppose we collected budget data for a sample of these men for one day chosen at random, defined income as cash receipts on that day, and defined consumption as cash expenditures. One-seventh of the men would be recorded as having an income of $100, six-sevenths as having an income of zero. It may well be that the men would spend more on pay day than on other days but they would also make expenditures on other days, so we would record the one-seventh with an income of $100 as having positive savings, the other six-sevenths as having negative savings. Consumption might appear to rise with income, but, if so, not as much as income, so that the fraction of income saved would rise with income. These results tell us nothing meaningful about consumption behavior; they simply reflect the use of inappropriate concepts of income and consumption. Men do not adapt their

[10] For example, see Margaret Reid [42], Milton Friedman, and Simon Kuznets [18].

cash expenditures on consumption to their cash receipts, and their cash expenditures on consumption may not be a good index of the value of services consumed–in our simple example, consumption expenditures might well be zero on Sunday.

As is often the case with developments of this sort, a theoretical foundation for this hypothesis was developed more or less independently by two different people: by Milton Friedman and by Franco Modigliani, the latter with the collaboration of R. E. Brumberg and Albert Ando. The two versions are similar in principle, though different in certain respects. Whether it is because of its deceptively simpler formulation or because of its more provocative interpretations and assumptions, the Friedman form has gained wider attention. In what follows both forms are presented, with greater emphasis on the Friedman formulation.

The permanent income hypothesis of Friedman may be said to rest on three fundamental tenets. First, a consumer unit's measured (observed) income (y) and consumption (c) in a particular period may be segregated into "transitory" and "permanent" components, i.e.:

$$y = y_p + y_t \tag{5a}$$

$$c = c_p + c_t \tag{5b}$$

Permanent income, say, in a given year, is the product of two factors: the wealth of the consumer unit, estimated as the discounted present value of a stream of future expected receipts, and the rate, r (or weighted average of a set of rates), at which these expected receipts are discounted [16].

The second tenet is that permanent consumption is a multiple, k, of permanent income:

$$c_p = ky_p \tag{6}$$

where k depends only on the interest rate, i, the ratio of nonhuman to total (nonhuman plus human) wealth, w, and a catchall variable, u, of which age and tastes are the principal components. In other words, $k = f(i, w, u,)$, but k is independent of the level of permanent income. It should be noted that consumption here is defined in the physical sense rather than in the monetary sense, i.e., as the physical consumption of goods and services. Durables purchased in a current period are considered as saving to the extent that they are not used up in that period.

Third, transitory and permanent income are assumed to be uncorrelated, as are transitory and permanent consumption, and transitory consumption and transitory income:

$$r_{y_t y_p} = r_{c_t c_p} = r_{y_t c_t} = 0 \tag{7}$$

As a result, a consumer unit is assumed to determine its standard of living on the basis of expected returns from its resources over its lifetime. These returns are expected to be constant from year to year, though in actual practice some fluctuation would result over time with changes in the anticipated amount of capital resources. The expenditures of the consumer unit are set as a constant proportion (k) of this permanent level of income, the value of k varying for consumer units of different types and of different tastes.[11] Actual consumption and actual income deviate from these planned, or permanent, levels to the extent that transitory factors enter in, e.g., a crop failure in the case of farm family income or unexpected medical bills in the case of spending. However, these transitory factors are essentially random and independent of each other, with the primary result of serving to obscure the true underlying relationship between the permanent components of income and of consumption.

The Modigliani-Brumberg-Ando (MBA) formulation is essentially a "permanent wealth" hypothesis rather than a "permanent income" hypothesis, though in practice the two approaches converge. In its most recent formulation, the household or consumer unit is assumed to determine "the amount available for consumption over life, which is the sum of the household's net worth at the beginning of the period . . . plus the present value of its non-property income . . . minus present value of planned bequests" [37, p. 78]. The amount allocated to consumption (defined in the same manner as by Friedman) is a certain proportion of these resources. Actual consumption, however, differs from this allocated amount by transitory expenditures and by certain stochastic factors (v), i.e.:

$$c_r = k_r^* x_r + v_r \tag{8}$$

Thus, this relationship is essentially the same as that derived by Friedman [by substituting (6) into (5b), with k^* in (8) corresponding to the product of r and k]. Note, however, that the variables in equation (8) have time subscripts whereas those of Friedman's do not. In the MBA formulation, k^* is assumed to vary explicitly with the age of the consumer unit, as is x, and possibly with other factors, such as family size. In the Friedman formulation, k is a constant for the same consumer unit over time.[12]

The MBA formulation is also more flexible in that the possibility is considered that transitory income and transitory consumption may be related

[11] A very similar formulation is provided by William Hamburger [24]. He postulates total current expenditures of consumers to depend principally on tastes, the interest rate and the discounted value of lifetime resources, the last being determined by the sum of wealth and a multiple of his current wage rate.

[12] Although k may vary among consumer units, as noted previously, i.e., $k = f(i, w, u)$.

to each other. In that event, Modigliani and Ando show that equation (8) turns into the following form:

$$c_r = f(k'_r, x_r, y_r) \tag{9}$$

so that current income as well as permanent income enter into this relation as determinants of current (observed) consumption. In their empirical work, however, Modigliani and Ando do not seem to have tested this relation.

In either formulation the central tenet is the assumption that the proportion of permanent income saved by a consumer unit in a given period is independent of its income (or its resources) during that period, and furthermore that transitory incomes may have no (Friedman) or little (MBA) effect on current consumption.

Clearly, from an empirical point of view, this is a very difficult hypothesis to test, because of the difficulty of measuring permanent income and permanent consumption. Nevertheless, the permanent income hypothesis is analytically a very rich one and lends itself to a number of significant inferences regarding individual and aggregate behavior. This is not the place to develop these inferences, particularly since they have been developed elsewhere [15, Ch. 3, 7] [38] [37, esp. pp. 74–109]. However, one theoretical inference of this hypothesis deserves special mention because of its basic importance to the empirical tests. Under the permanent income hypothesis, the slope of the relation between observed consumption and observed income, namely (assuming linearity) b in: $c = a + by$, can be shown to be equivalent to kP_y, where P_y is the ratio of the variance of the permanent component of income to the total variance of income, i.e.:

$$P_y = \frac{\Sigma(y_p - \bar{y}_p)^2}{\Sigma(y - \bar{y})^2}$$

Since k is constant, by assumption, this means that fluctuations in the slope of measured income reflect fluctuations in the relative importance of the permanent component of income. Furthermore, P_y is equivalent to the income elasticity of consumption, if the elasticity is estimated at the sample means and if the transitory components of both income and consumption average zero. The significance of this becomes clear when we list the principal empirical results and observations advanced to support the permanent income hypothesis.

1. From time series aggregates, Friedman notes that the following findings are in accord with the hypothesis [15, Ch. 5]: (a) The marginal propensity to consume is invariably less than the average propensity to consume. (b) The ratio of permanent consumption to permanent income, k, appears to have

been constant since at least 1897, after allowance for variability in the observed consumption-income ratio due to transitory factors.[13] (c) The income elasticity of consumption tends to rise as the period of observation to which a consumption function is fitted increases, thus confirming that transitory factors become less important over longer time spans. (d) Marginal propensities estimated from data deflated for price or population changes are less than those estimated from the corresponding undeflated data: permanent components are more important in the latter case because of the general positive correlation among output, prices and population.

2. From cross-section budget data, Friedman notes that [15, Ch. 4]: (a) Despite observed inequality of income distributions on a cross-section basis, long-run trends indicate that the income distribution is becoming, if anything, more equal–thereby suggesting that measured income is not a valid measure of wealth. (b) The average propensity to consume has been relatively constant in budget studies covering different times and different groups. Furthermore, the stability in the average propensities, and the values of less than unity of the income elasticities, contradict the stability of these cross-section relations–suggesting that the consumption-income ratio declines as income rises, which is inconsistent with the time-series aggregates. (c) Income elasticities are less for the United States than for Great Britain or Sweden, suggesting that transitory factors are more important in the United States, as one might expect. (d) The income elasticity, as well as the marginal propensity and *k*, are all lower for farm families, and for nonfarm and own-business families, than for other nonfarm families, in accord with the hypothesis. (e) Consumption-income regressions for groups of families classified by income change have steeper slopes than the over-all regression: the transitory component is smaller for income-change classes.

3. Turning to work other than Friedman's, P_y estimated from income data for the same consumer units over time yields consistent results for different groups and different time periods. Such estimates also correspond with estimated income elasticities from budget data, which also estimate (independently) P_y [43].

4. Classification of families by income change appears to result largely in a manifestation of transitory income, rather than expenditure lags behind changes in permanent income; the consumption-income ratio varies most between years for families with substantial income change [44].

5. The estimated income elasticity for all households exceeds the weighted average of income elasticities for relatively homogeneous groups of house-

[13]The allowance is rather arbitrary–seeing whether most of the annual points fall within 5 percentage points of a line going through the origin of the consumption-income graph and the long-run average of this ratio, .877. On the other hand, as Friedman notes, secular constancy of *k* is not an integral part of the permanent income hypothesis.

holds—variation due to transitory factors is less important in the former case [10] [37, pp. 123–66].[14] Furthermore, no systematic association is apparent between mean income and the consumption-income ratio for most criteria; education is a notable exception.

6. Increasing the importance of transitory income by classifying families by current income categories reduces income elasticity estimates—transitory components are more important among these presumably homogeneous subgroups [9].

7. Groups with the more variable incomes have higher saving ratios [14, pp. 229–63].

8. The effect of age, or life cycle, is supported by the fact that the observed saving ratio is low for young age groups, highest in the later earning stages, and negative or very low in retirement [38].

Despite these seemingly impressive arguments, the permanent income hypothesis is by no means established. Indeed, the evidence to the contrary seems at least as impressive. This opposing evidence, like the arguments for the theory, covers both theoretical and empirical considerations. On a theoretical plane, question is raised regarding the validity of the two central tenets of the theory, namely, the independence of k of the level of income, and the lack of correlation between transitory consumption and transitory income. Thus, Friend and Kravis note that the permanent income hypothesis implies "that low-income families will have no greater preference for purchase of future goods than will high-income families" [19, p. 538] while Duesenberry makes a similar criticism [8]. Such a concept they find to be seriously deficient on purely deductive grounds because of the very different kinds of pressures and motivations acting on families at different income levels.

In a similar fashion, the assumption of a zero marginal propensity to consume out of transitory income is questioned, partly on the basis that low-income families are under strong pressures to spend any unexpected income to meet current needs [19, pp. 539–41], and partly because of the very unequal distribution of wealth which mitigates against dissaving by low-income families to maintain consumption in the face of temporary declines in income [47, p. 451].

Criticism of the permanent income hypothesis on empirical grounds has followed two lines. One line has been to note that much of the evidence advanced is either inconclusive or is not inconsistent with other principal hypotheses. Thus, under the absolute income hypothesis one would also expect the marginal propensity to consume to be less than the average

[14] "Relatively homogeneous groups" means households classified by characteristics unrelated to transitory factors, and for which permanent and transitory incomes are uncorrelated. Classifying criteria used were city size, education, occupation, age, tenure.

propensity, groups with more variable incomes to have higher saving ratios, and consumption-income regressions for groups of families classified by income change to have steeper slopes than the over-all regression. In addition, as was noted previously, Tobin has suggested how the constancy of the long-run propensity to consume might be reconciled with the absolute income hypothesis. Furthermore, the interpretation given by Friedman to many of his test results is not the only possible interpretation and is at times subject to considerable doubt [21] [26] [47], though some of the evidence can apparently be interpreted only in terms of it [43].

From a more direct point of view, various test results have been advanced as contradicting the permanent income hypothesis. Thus, Friend and Kravis show that the same variation in the saving rate occurs when families are classified by constancy of three-year income as by constancy of one-year income, based on recall data obtained in one-time interviews [19, pp. 544–45]. In addition, they show that saving rates of different occupational groups appear to be closely correlated with the average income of these groups [19, p. 546] [20, pp. 272–73].

To test the zero propensity to consume out of transitory income, Bodkin [1] analyzed by correlation methods the extent to which consumption expenditures were made out of unexpected dividends paid in early 1950 out of National Service Life Insurance. This study yielded not only a statistically significant propensity but a propensity to consume out of these dividends much higher than out of regular income.[15] On the other hand, Kreinin [31] obtained a low marginal propensity to consume out of restitution payments made by Germany to former citizens in Israel. However, these payments could hardly have been unexpected.

Admittedly, these negative findings are themselves subject to question. For example, the reliability and representativeness of budget data collected in a partial wartime period such as 1950 is a matter of doubt [40]. In any event, the permanent income hypothesis is far from proven. However, whether or not the permanent income hypothesis turns out to be valid, there is little doubt that, to quote Tobin, "This is one of those rare contributions of which it can be said that research and thought in its field will not be the same henceforth" [47, p. 447]. Most of all, it has led to widespread recognition of

[15] Friedman attempts to reconcile the results with the permanent income hypothesis, on the assumption that these dividend receipts might have been anticipated and/or they created expectations of future dividend receipts, so that this windfall becomes a proxy for permanent income [17, pp. 191–206]. In view of the circumstances surrounding the payment of these dividends, however, such an assumption is highly questionable. A more likely explanation is one offered by Margaret Reid (unpublished) that the receipts may have stimulated purchase of homes, thereby setting off a long-run program of saving but a short-run program of spending.

the possible effects of variability in income on consumption patterns and has provided a theoretical basis for measuring these effects as a springboard for a more realistic theory of consumer behavior.[16]

References

1. Ronald Bodkin, "Windfall Income and Consumption" (62, pp. 175–87).
2. D. S. Brady, "Family Saving in Relation to Changes in the Level and Distribution of Income," in Nat. Bur. Econ. Research, *Studies in Income and Wealth,* Vol. 15, New York, 1952, pp. 103–30.
3. ____and Rose Friedman, "Savings and the Income Distribution," in Nat. Bur. Econ. Research, *Studies in Income and Wealth,* Vol. 10, New York, 1947, pp. 247–65.
4. J. Cornfield, W. D. Evans, and M. Hoffenberg, "Full Employment Patterns, 1950," *Mo. Lab. Rev.,* Feb. 1947, *70,* 163–90.
5. J. S. Cramer, "Ownership Elasticities of Durable Consumer Goods," *Rev. Econ. Stud.,* Feb. 1958, *25,* 87–96.
6. T. E. Davis, "The Consumption Function as a Tool for Prediction," *Rev. Econ. Stat.,* Aug. 1952, *34,* 270–77.
7. James Duesenberry, *Income, Saving and the Theory of Consumer Behavior,* Cambridge, Mass., 1949.
8. ____, comments on "General Saving Relations," in Irwin Friend and Robert Jones, ed., *Proceedings of the Conference on Consumption and Saving,* Vol. 2, Philadelphia, 1960, pp. 188–91.
9. Marilyn Dunsing and M. G. Reid, "Effect of Varying Degrees of Transitory Income on Income Elasticity of Expenditures," *Jour. Am. Stat. Assoc.,* June 1958, *53,* 348–59.
10. Robert Eisner, "The Permanent Income Hypothesis: Comment," *Am. Econ. Rev.,* Dec. 1958, *48,* 972–90.
11. Robert Ferber, *A Study of Aggregate Consumption Functions,* in Nat. Bur. Econ. Research, Tech. Paper 8, New York, 1953.
12. ____, "The Accuracy of Aggregate Savings Functions in the Postwar Years," *Rev. Econ. Stat.,* May 1955, *37,* 134–48.
13. Janet Fisher, "Income, Spending, and Saving Patterns of Consumer Units in Different Age Groups," in Nat. Bur. Econ. Research, *Studies in Income and Wealth,* Vol. 15, New York, 1962, pp. 75–102.
14. M. R. Fisher, "Explorations in Savings Behavior," *Bull. Oxford Univ. Inst. Stat.,* Aug. 1956, *18,* 201–78.
15. Milton Friedman, *A Theory of the Consumption Function,* Nat. Bur. Econ. Research, Princeton, 1957.

[16]For an interesting application of the permanent income hypothesis to analyzing consumer behavior, see the study by Jacob Mincer relating labor activity to family income and consumption [34].

16. ——, *Windfalls, the "Horizon" and Related Concepts in the Permanent Income Hypothesis.* (Unpublished memorandum.)
17. ——, "Comments on Windfall Income and Consumption," in Irwin Friend and Robert Jones, ed., *Proceedings of the Conference on Consumption and Saving,* Vol. 2, Philadelphia, 1960, pp. 191–206.
18. —— and Simon Kuznets, *Income from Independent Professional Practice,* New York, 1945.
19. Irwin Friend and I. B. Kravis, "Consumption Patterns and Permanent Income," *Am. Econ. Rev., Proc.,* May 1957, *47,* 536–55.
20. —— and ——, "Entrepreneurial Income, Saving, and Investment," *Am. Econ. Rev.,* June 1957, *47,* 269–301.
21. ——, "Discussion of Milton Friedman's 'A Theory of the Consumption Function,' " in L. H. Clark, ed., *Consumer Behavior: Research on Consumer Reactions,* New York, 1958, pp. 456–58.
22. Raymond Goldsmith, *A Study of Saving in the United States,* Princeton, 1955.
23. William Hamburger, "The Relation of Consumption to Wealth and the Wage Rate," *Econometrica,* Jan. 1955, *23,* 1–17.
24. ——, "The Determinants of Aggregate Consumption," *Rev. Econ. Stud.,* No. 57, 1954–55, *22,* 23–35.
25. A. H. Hansen, "The Pigouvian Effect," *Jour. Pol. Econ.,* Dec. 1951, *49,* 535–36.
26. H. S. Houthakker, "The Permanent Income Hypothesis," *Am. Econ. Rev.,* June 1958, *48,* 396–404.
27. J. M. Keynes, *The General Theory of Employment, Interest, and Money,* New York, 1936.
28. L. R. Klein, "Estimating Patterns of Savings Behavior from Sample Survey Data," *Econometrica,* Oct. 1951, *19,* 438–54.
29. ——, "Assets, Debts, and Economic Behavior," in Nat. Bur. Econ. Research, *Studies in Income and Wealth,* Vol. 14, New York, 1951, pp. 195–227.
30. ——, "Statistical Estimation of Economic Relations from Survey Data," in George Katona, L. R. Klein, J. B. Lansing, and J. N. Morgan, *Contributions of Survey Methods to Economics,* New York, 1954, pp. 189–240.
31. M. E. Kreinin, J. B. Lansing, and J. N. Morgan, "Windfall Income and Consumption," *Am. Econ. Rev.,* June 1961, *51,* 388–90.
32. Simon Kuznets, *National Product Since 1869,* Nat. Bur. Econ. Research, New York, 1946.
33. ——, "Proportion of Capital Formation to National Product," *Am. Econ. Rev.,* May 1952, *42,* 507–26.
34. Horst Mendershausen, "Differences in Family Saving between Cities of Different Sizes and Locations, Whites and Negroes," *Rev. Econ. Stat.,* Aug. 1940, *22,* 122–37.
35. Jacob Mincer, "Labor Supply, Family Income and Consumption," *Am. Econ. Rev., Proc.,* May 1960, *50,* 574–83.
36. Franco Modigliani, "Fluctuations in the Saving-Income Ratio: A Problem in Economic Forecasting," in Nat. Bur. Econ. Research, *Studies in Income and Wealth,* Vol. 11, New York, 1949, pp. 371–443.

37. ____ and Albert Ando, "The 'Permanent Income' and the 'Life Cycle' Hypotheses of Saving Behavior: Comparison and Tests," in Irwin Friend and Robert Jones, ed., *Proceedings of the Conference on Consumption Saving,* Vol. 2, Philadelphia, 1960, pp. 49–174.
38. ____ and ____, "Tests of the Life Cycle Hypothesis of Savings," *Bull. Oxford Univ. Inst. Stat.,* May 1957, *19,* 99–124.
39. Guy Orcutt and A. D. Roy, *A Bibliography of the Consumption Function,* Cambridge Univ., Dept. of Applied Economics, 1949. (Mimeographed.)
40. A. R. Oxenfeldt, "Comments on the Article by Friend and Kravis," in *Am. Econ. Rev., Proc.,* May 1957, *47,* 571–74.
41. A. C. Pigou, "The Classical Stationary State," *Econ. Jour.,* Dec. 1943, *53,* 343–51.
42. M G. Reid, "Effect of Income Concept Upon Expenditure Curves of Farm Families," in Nat. Bur. Econ. Research, *Studies in Income and Wealth,* Vol. 15, New York, 1952, pp. 133–74.
43. ____, "The Relation of the Within-Group Transitory Component of Income to the Income Elasticity of Family Expenditure," 1952. (Unpublished paper.)
44. ____ and Marilyn Dunsing, "Effect of Variability of Incomes on Level of Income-Expenditure Curves on Farm Families," *Rev. Econ. Stat.,* Feb. 1956, *38,* 90–95.
45. G. J. Stigler, "The Early History of Empirical Studies of Consumer Behavior," *Jour. Pol. Econ.,* Apr. 1954, *42,* 95–113.
46. James Tobin, "Relative Income, Absolute Income, and Saving," in *Money, Trade, and Economic Growth, Essays in Honor of John Henry Williams,* New York, 1951, pp. 135–56.
47. ____, "Discussion of Milton Friedman's 'A Theory of the Consumption Function,' " in L. H. Clark, ed., *Consumer Behavior: Research on Consumer Reactions,* New York, 1958, pp. 447–54.
48. U. S. National Resources Planning Board, *Family Expenditures in the United States,* Washington, 1941.
49. W. S. Vickrey, "Resource Distribution Patterns and the Classification of Families," in Nat. Bur. Econ. Research, *Studies in Income and Wealth,* Vol. 10, New York, 1947, pp. 260–329.
50. F. M. Williams and C. C. Zimmerman, *Studies of Family Living in the United States and Other Countries,* U. S. Dept. of Agriculture, Misc. Pub. 223, Washington, 1935.

2

INCOME-CONSUMPTION RELATIONS AND THEIR IMPLICATIONS

JAMES S. DUESENBERRY

Of all the new ideas introduced by Keynes in *The General Theory,* the concept of the "consumption function" was the easiest to accept. Few wished to deny that consumption expenditures are primarily determined by income; Keynes' arguments for the stability of the relationship were cogent enough to convince a great number of economists. The opportunities for empirical work opened up by the introduction of the new concept were at once apparent. Here, for once, was a theoretical relationship which involved magnitudes which could be measured not merely theoretically but practically. Econometricians went to work with a will and their efforts were amply rewarded. They were not only able to find a relationship between income and consumption, but they found that virtually all of the variation in consumer expenditures was explained by variations in income.

Yet, in spite of these empirical successes, the consumption function is a more controversial subject today than it was ten years ago. For empirical investigation has yielded not one consumption function but many, and each of them explains all the variations in consumption.

Like most economic magnitudes the literature on the consumption function seems to grow according to the compound-interest law. This would be easy to understand if the literature appeared as the result of the discovery of new data. But no fundamental changes in our knowledge of the facts about income and consumption have occurred in the past five years.

Most of the articles on the consumption function present hypotheses about

Reprinted from *Income, Employment and Public Policy, Essays in Honor of Alvin H. Hansen* (W. W. Norton & Company, 1948), by permission of the publisher. James S. Duesenberry is a professor at Harvard University.

the relation between consumption, income, and some other variable such as time, the price level, or the degree of unemployment. The hypothesis is presented in the form of an equation which makes consumption a function of the other variables. The appropriate regression is fitted to the data, and the correlation between the observed and calculated values of consumption or saving is computed. The correlation is invariably high, and most writers seem to be satisfied that a high correlation coefficient provides an adequate test of their hypothesis. But a test which is passed by so many different hypotheses is not a very satisfactory one. Before any more consumption functions are introduced it seems desirable to give some consideration to our methods of testing hypotheses.

In Section I it is shown that aggregate hypotheses cannot be adequately tested by the use of correlation analysis. The general principles on which appropriate testing methods can be developed are then discussed. Section II is devoted to a consideration of the possibility that the relation between saving and income is different at different points of the trade cycle. A test based on the principles developed in Section I shows that we must reject the hypothesis that the saving-income relation is invariant with respect to measures of position in the trade cycle.

In Section III hypotheses which explain both cyclical and secular movements of savings are developed. It is shown that these hypotheses are consistent with: (1) the long-run data on income and consumption given by Kuznets, (2) the annual data on income and consumption in the period 1923–1940, (3) the budget study data collected in 1935–1936 and 1941. These hypotheses lead to the conclusion that aggregate saving out of disposable income can be estimated by the equation $s_t/y_t = .165(y_t/y_0) - .066$, where s_t = current savings, y_t = current disposable income, y_0 = highest disposable income ever attained, with all variables corrected for population and price changes.[1]

I. TESTS OF AGGREGATE HYPOTHESIS

When we deal with a problem in aggregate economics we usually seek for relationships which are, in some sense, invariant. By invariance we do not mean a historical invariance like the Pareto law. Rather, we mean that the relationship between a certain set of variables is unaffected by changes in some other variables. The concept of an invariant relationship is therefore a

[1]Part of this paper was presented at the meeting of the Econometric Society in January, 1947. At the same meeting Prof. Franco Modigliani presented a paper containing an almost identical income-saving relation.

relative one; a relation may be invariant with respect to one set of variables, but not with respect to some others. Indeed it might be said that hardly any economic relationship can be regarded as completely invariant. For no economic relation is likely to continue to hold good both before and after a fundamental change in social organization. In fact, one of the objects of economic policy is the modification of social organization in such a way as to produce relations of a desirable type among economic variables.

Our idea of invariance is somewhat as follows: We conceive that at any one moment certain variables within the control of households or firms are related in a definite way to certain other variables not within their control. For example, we suppose that the consumption expenditure of families depends on their income. The form of these relations is governed by the behavior characteristics of individuals and by institutional factors such as laws or customs. The relations we seek are invariant with respect to all variables except these psychological or institutional factors. A relation which satisfies that criterion may be said to be more or less stable according as these factors are more or less constant. We can make satisfactory predictions if we can find invariant relations of this type which are highly stable.[2]

If an invariant relation of this type holds for the variables associated with individual households or firms, then a corresponding invariant relation must hold among some functions (not necessarily sums) of all the household or firm variables of the same kind. If we can write $y_i = f_i(x_i)$ for every household (when x_i and y_i are variables applying to the ith household), then we can write $\phi(x_1, x_2 \ldots x_n, y_1, y_2, \ldots y_n) = 0$. The invariance of the second relation will depend on the constancy of the behaviour characteristics and

[2] Finding invariant relations of this sort actually helps in only one kind of policy problem. We may conceive of the "structure" of the economy as being described by a certain set of invariant relations. Then one kind of policy consists in fixing the values of certain of the variables which enter into these equations without otherwise disturbing any of the relations. Fixing an interest rate or tax rate is a policy of this sort. If we know all the invariant relations necessary to describe the structure, we can predict the effect of this sort of policy (at least in the sense that we can assign a probability to any values of any economic variable at each point in the future).

On the other hand, many of the most important policies involve changes in the structure. If a law is changed which has never been changed before, then we may know that certain structural equations will be changed, but we may not be able to foretell exactly what the new equations will be like. Or, to take a simple example, if the Treasury undertakes a campaign to get people to save more, it will be difficult to know what its effect will be. For this is an attempt to induce changes in behaviour patterns, and we have comparatively little experience with this kind of change. The kind of data with which economists deal is not likely to reveal anything about the possible effects of the Treasury's campaign. On the other hand, a sufficiently general theory of behaviour ought to make a prediction possible, but this would be entirely a question of social psychology.

As a matter of fact, it seems probable that most of the economic policies of really fundamental importance involve structural changes of this sort. To the extent that this is true, economists can be regarded as competent to judge the effect of these policies only by default on the part of the social psychologists.

institutional elements which determine the invariance of the original relations, and in some cases on the constancy of the distribution of the x's. Aggregate relations which can be deduced from household or firm relations, I shall call fundamental aggregate relations. (There are of course some additional fundamental aggregate relations which are definitional and need not be deduced from anything.)

Now consider a pair of such fundamental aggregate relations:

$$\phi_1(x_1 x_2 \dots x_n) = \psi_1(y_1 y_2 \dots y_n) \qquad (1)$$
$$\phi_2(x_1 x_2 \dots x_n) = \psi_2(z_1 z_2 \dots z_n) \qquad (2)$$

where the x's are exogenous variables.

It is clear that a further relation (3) $x_1(y_1\, y_2 \dots y_n) = x_2(z_1 z_2 \dots z_n)$ may be derived from the first two. Further, this relation will be invariant so long as (1) and (2) are invariant. This type of relation I shall call a derived aggregate relation.[3]

Now suppose that we observe the historical invariance of the relation (3) and conclude that it is a fundamental relation. We might then conclude that by changing the z's we could manipulate the y's. But we might find instead that we had merely invalidated the relation (2) without having any effect at all on the y's or x's. Derived relations like (3) may break down either as a consequence of policy changes or of structural changes in the economy. In addition there is an important class of derived relations which are likely to hold good only during the course of a single trade cycle. For example, a certain variable z may be partly dependent on the level of unemployment. Within the course of a single trade cycle, income is very closely associated with the level of unemployment. If we have data covering only a single trade cycle, we might conclude from the empirical evidence that z is determined by income. Actually we have a derived relation between z and income, which is bound to break up because the upward trend in income will ultimately change the association between income and unemployment. It is clear from these considerations that many of the relations observed empirically may be only derived relations which will break down because of a structural change in one of the fundamental relations on which they are based. This is particularly true of relations whose existence has been tested against the data of only a single trade cycle. Whether we are concerned with policy or with prediction, we shall often make errors if we treat derived relations as though they were fundamental ones. The difficulty of distinguishing between these

[3]Cf. T. Haavelmo, "The Probability Approach to Econometrics," *Econometrica*, July, 1944, Supplement.

two kinds of relations is one of the fundamental difficulties in testing economic hypotheses.

Let us now return to a consideration of the adequacy of correlation methods of hypothesis testing. Suppose we have a hypothesis which asserts that total consumer expenditure is dependent on disposable income. We can fit a regression to the data for income and consumption and compute the correlation coefficient. When we find a significant correlation, what, exactly, have we found? We have not shown that the "data are consistent with the hypothesis." We have merely disproved the null hypothesis. That is, we have shown that the association between income and consumption was too strong to allow us to ascribe it to chance. Then we should be reasonably confident in asserting that we have found either (a) a fundamental relation between income and consumption, or (b) a derived relation between them. We might exploit our results a little further. If it could be shown that the lower confidence limit on the correlation was (say) .95, we could assert that during the period income was linearly related to all the variables fundamentally related to consumption. But this is about as far as we can safely go. It can be argued, of course, that a derived relation will tend to produce lower correlations than a fundamental relation. But, when our data cover only short periods, the connections between economic variables may be so close that the differences in correlations between the two sorts of relations may be too small to be statistically significant. Moreover, if the variables in a derived relation have a lower observational error than those in the fundamental relations, the correlation in the derived relation may be the higher one.

A very simple example of a derived relation is that which appears to have existed between consumer expenditures in dollars and disposable income in dollars during the period 1929–1940. Just as good a correlation is obtained by using undeflated as deflated data. This can be true only because the price level was related to income during the period. If real consumption is fundamentally related to real income, the money relationship is a derived one and will break down in the postwar period. Conversely, if money consumption is fundamentally related to money income the relation between the real variables is a derived one and will break down. Now it is obviously of vital importance to know which is the fundamental relation, but the correlation test is not very helpful.

The difficulties we have just been discussing arise because of the existence of derived relations among aggregate variables. But, ordinarily, such derived relations will not hold for individual firms or households. This suggests that in testing hypotheses we ought to operate on the following principles. First, every hypothesis ought to be stated in terms of the behaviour of individual firms or households, even when we are only interested in aggregate results. This does not, of course, prevent us from considering interactions among individuals, any more than the use of the theory of the firm in analysis of monopolistic competition prevents us from dealing with interactions among firms. Second, in so far as it is possible, we ought to test our hypotheses against data which indicate the behaviour of individual households or firms. This does not mean that we ought to abandon statistical procedures. Nearly every hypothesis has to allow for random elements in behaviour so that in making tests we have to measure the average behaviour of groups. But by dealing with relatively small groups we may escape the net of interrelations which makes it impossible to test aggregate hypotheses.

Suppose we are faced with the following situation: One hypothesis asserts that saving varies with income and the price level, another asserts that saving depends on income alone. Aggregate income and the price level are related in the period for which data are available. Then, if one of these hypotheses is true, it will be impossible to disprove the other by means of aggregate data alone. But, while movements of aggregate income may have been correlated with those of the price level, there are certainly some individuals whose incomes moved in a different way. By studying the behaviour of those individuals it will be possible to disprove one of the hypotheses. When this has been done the parameters in the chosen relation may be fitted by the use of aggregate data (though in some cases this may still be difficult because of multi-collinearity).

Of course it will not always be possible to find the data necessary to test every hypothesis. But there is a great deal of microeconomic data, which has never been properly exploited because of the tendency of econometricians to emphasize parameter fitting rather than hypothesis testing. Actually it is much more important to work with a true hypothesis than to make extremely precise estimates of parameters.

II. CHANGES IN INCOME AND THE RATE OF SAVING

In this section we shall apply the method just suggested to some questions about the consumption function. In the view of a number of writers, notably Smithies and Mosak,[4] consumer expenditures are essentially dependent on the prevailing level of disposable income. The effect on consumption of an increase in income is supposed to be the same whether the increase comes about through a rise of employment during recovery from a depression or through a rise in productivity in a period of sustained full employment like

[4] "Forecasting Postwar Demand, I, III," *Econometrica,* January, 1945.

that of the twenties. Professor Hansen[5] and Professor Samuelson[6] have maintained for some time that the relation between income and consumption varies through the trade cycle. Mr. Woytinski[7] and Mr. Bean[8] have made similar statements and have tried to test them empirically. They obtained correlations just as good as the others but no better, and certainly cannot claim to have disproved the alternative hypothesis. There is, however, some evidence which proves nearly conclusively that the consumption function is cyclically variable though not quite in the ways suggested by Bean or Woytinski.

This evidence is provided by the budget studies made in 1935–36[9] and 1941.[10] One of the remarkable results of the Study of Consumer Purchases of 1935–36 was that a great number of families reported expenditures in excess of income for the year. The average deficit of the under $500 a year group amounted to 50 per cent of income, while the average deficit of the $500–$1000 group was 10 per cent of income.[11] The results of the 1935–36 study are not above criticism, of course, but the fact that deficits were reported in every city and every area, together with the independent evidence of studies like those of Gilboy, Clague, and Powell, makes it clear that very substantial deficits did occur during the depression.[12]

The total deficits of urban and rural non-farm families (who were white and not on relief) alone amounted to 593 million dollars for 1935–36. Since total net savings of consumers during the twenties and thirties varied from $7.6 to $2.0 billion, an explanation of the deficits can contribute a good deal to our understanding of variations in saving.

But the real significance of the deficits does not lie in their magnitude but in what they reveal about the relations between income and saving. We shall first show that the deficits arose largely because families whose income fell in the depression tried to preserve their pre-depression living standards. Families in the higher income groups did the same thing but accomplished it

[5] *Business Cycles and Fiscal Policy,* New York, W. W. Norton & Company, 1941, pp. 225–249.

[6] "Full Employment after the War," in *Postwar Economic Problems,* edited by S. E. Harris, New York, McGraw Hill, 1943.

[7] "Relationship between Consumer's Expenditure, Savings and Disposable Income," *Review of Economic Statistics,* January, 1946.

[8] "Relationship of Disposable Income and the Business Cycle to Expenditure," *Review of Economic Statistics,* November, 1946.

[9] Summarized by the National Resources Committee in *Consumer Expenditures in the United States,* Washington, 1938; *Consumer Incomes in the United States,* Washington, 1939; *Family Expenditures in the United States,* Washington, 1941.

[10] Bureau of Labor Statistics, Bulletins 723 and 724.

[11] *Family Expenditures in the United States,* p. 1.

[12] Elizabeth Gilboy, *Applicants for Work Relief,* Cambridge, Harvard University Press, 1940. E. Clague and W. Powell, *Ten Thousand Out of Work,* Philadelphia, University of Pennsylvania, 1933.

by reducing their rate of saving rather than by dissaving. The analysis of the deficits is important chiefly because it helps us to analyze variations in the positive savings of higher income groups.

Let us first consider what kind of people were in the low income groups in 1935–36. While there is little direct information about the low income families in 1935–36, a rough estimate of their composition can be made from the data on income and employment in 1939 contained in the Census of 1940. Table 1 shows the result of this estimate.[13]

Table 1. White Urban and Rural Non-Farm Families with Incomes under $1000 in 1935–36

	Relief	*Non-Relief*
Retired	600,000	600,000
Independent Business and Professional	100,000	600,000
Partially or Fully Unemployed	2,100,000	1,900,000
Fully Employed	–	2,400,000
Total	2,800,000	5,500,000

In the nature of the case this estimate can be only a rough one since it has to be based on a number of unverified assumptions. Yet there does not seem to be much doubt that the non-relief low-income families included a high proportion of families whose incomes were low because of unemployment and whose incomes were much higher in periods of full employment. Moreover, some of the families in the independent business and professional group would have higher incomes in more prosperous periods. Finally, some of the fully employed wage and salary workers were downgraded from higher wage jobs so that their normal incomes were higher than the incomes reported in 1935–36.

(1) Keeping these considerations in mind, let us now ask what is the significance of the deficits for the theory of saving. A supporter of the view that saving depends on real income would say, presumably, that $c/y = f(y)$ and that c/y exceeds 1 for some positive value of y (where y is in constant prices). When that value of y is reached, those who have assets or credit will have deficits; the others will have to be content with spending all of their income.

In its simple form this position is untenable, for the break-even point (the

[13]This estimate was obtained by reconciling the data given by the National Resources Committee on numbers of families with incomes under $1000 in 1935–36 with the data of the Census of 1940 on the family wage and salary income and employment in 1939. See *Family Expenditures in the United States,* pp. 123, 127, 130 and Census of 1940, *The Labor Force (Sample Statistics), Wage or Salary Income in 1939* and *Family Wage or Salary Income in 1939.*

income at which consumption just equals income) stood at about $800 in 1917 and $1500 in 1935–36, using 1941 prices in both cases.[14] If consumption were merely a function of current income the break-even level of income should have remained the same. To this the sophisticated Keynesian will reply by introducing a trend factor. Consumption at a given level of income can be changed by the introduction of new goods (this is about the only factor likely to cause a trend in the consumption of urban families, and these are the families included in the budget studies in question). For the sake of the argument let us agree that introduction of new goods in itself increases consumption at a given level of income. We know too that families in the low income groups were driving automobiles and using various recently introduced household appliances. This does not advance the argument much, however, for the families in question were for the most part using these things rather than buying them. We can turn to other new goods, movies and silk stockings (say), which were also consumed by the low-income groups in the thirties. Let us grant that a family with an $800 income did not buy these things in 1917 and did in 1935. Then it follows that at least part of the deficits in the thirties were due to the fact that low income families bought new goods which did not exist in the earlier period. But this is not the whole story. We can say on the one hand that families at an $800 income level in the thirties spent more than families with that income in 1917 because they had become used to a high standard of living (including silk stockings and movies) in the twenties and found it difficult to give up. Or we can say that even if income had remained constant from 1917 to 1935 the attraction of these new goods was so irresistible that they incurred deficits to get them (or at least that they would have done so if they had had the necessary assets or credit). The latter position seems to be a somewhat untenable one. But, if we argue that consumption depends on current real income and trend, that is the position which must be maintained in order to explain the facts. For, if we write $c/y = f(y,t)$, nothing has been said about the influence of past living standards on current consumption.

This does not disprove the proposition that consumption at a given moment is dependent on real income alone; but it does require the supporters of that proposition to subscribe to some very strong propositions about the influence of new products and similar trend factors.

(2) We can make a further test if we compare the deficits reported in 1935–36 with those reported in 1941. Deficits at given levels of income were much smaller in 1941 than in 1935–36. At every level deficits were less than one half as great in 1941 as in 1935–36. How is this shift to be explained?

[14]See G. Cornfield, W. D. Evans, and M. Hoffenberg, "Full Employment Patterns in 1950, Part I," *Monthly Labor Review*, February, 1947, p. 181.

Suppose the deficits, in both cases, were due to the fact that families whose incomes had fallen as a result of unemployment found it hard to reduce their living standards. Then the explanation is easy. The low income group consists primarily of two subgroups: families whose earners are normally fully employed at low wages, and families whose incomes have been reduced by unemployment. The second group will run deficits to protect the high living standard attained when they were fully employed. The first group balances its budget. Suppose now that we have complete data on families in the $1000 income group in two periods. Suppose that the situation is as follows:

	Number	*Deficit*
Fully Employed Families (with normal incomes)	5000	0
Partially Employed Families	5000	$300
Average		$150

Suppose that in a second period we obtain reports from the same group but that half of the families in the $1000 group have increased their incomes. The situation in the $1000 group now is as follows:

	Number	*Deficit*
Fully Employed Families	5000	0
Partially Employed Families	2500	$300
Average		$100

Now suppose that instead of subdividing the families in this way our report had shown only the average deficit of the $1000 income families. We would have observed a reduction in the average deficit from $150 to $100 per family without knowing why. The differences in the 1935–36 and 1941 studies seem to correspond very clearly to the examples just given. In 1935–36 there were about 8 million unemployed, in 1941 there were only 3 million. In 1935–36 a much higher proportion of families in the low income groups were there because of unemployment than in 1941. If, therefore, we accept the proposition that the deficits were due to unemployment, or to incomes low by comparison with previous ones, the difference between the two studies is easily explained.

If we try to support the view that consumption depends on absolute income, how shall we explain the difference? The trend explanation cannot be used in this case. For the break-even point moves in the wrong direction.

We can suppose that the families left in the low income groups would like to have run deficits but were unable to do so because they lacked the necessary assets or credits. But we have argued that a higher proportion of the low income group in 1941 were permanent members of that group than in 1935–36. It follows that the higher deficits in 1935–36 must have been incurred by the group whose incomes had fallen. For those permanently in the low income group were in more or less the same position in both years. Then we have to explain the differences in the reactions of the two groups. There are three possible explanations. (1) The families with temporarily low incomes were technically in a better position to have deficits. That is, they were not more willing to run deficits, but more able to get the resources to do so. (2) The families with temporarily low incomes had expectations of reemployment and higher income in the future. (3) These families had had higher living standards in the past and were therefore more willing to have deficits to protect their living standards.

If either of the last two factors is influential, then consumption must depend on past income (since this governs the expected level of income at full employment) as well as on current income. In this case a general rise in income to levels above the 1929 peak followed by a fall would bring about a recurrence of the deficits, for the standard of living and expectations of income would be based on the new peak. If income declined from this peak by the same percentage as 1935 income had declined from the 1929 peak, deficits of a relative magnitude as large as those of 1935 would occur. This would be true even if the absolute level of income were as high as the 1929 level. On the other hand if the break-even point is independent of past levels of income no deficits would occur unless income were absolutely low.

The budget study data do not tell us anything directly about which of the three factors just mentioned are actually relevant. We must leave the question open for the moment. However, it should be noted that the hypothesis that consumption depends on past as well as on current income is consistent with all the data discussed so far. The alternative hypothesis that consumption depends only on current income can be made consistent with the data only if we are willing to accept some rather doubtful subsidiary propositions.

(3) One further piece of evidence is available for testing these two hypotheses. The 1941 budget study reported income for the first quarter of 1942 as well as for 1941. Families at each income level were classified by the changes in their income. Savings for the first quarter of 1942 were separately reported for those whose incomes had changed less than 5 per cent, for those whose incomes had increased more than 5 per cent, and those whose incomes had decreased more than 5 per cent from the 1941 level. The results are shown in Table 2. Families whose incomes rose had about the same savings or deficits as those whose incomes stayed the same. On the other hand, families whose incomes fell had much smaller savings or larger deficits than

Table 2. Average Yearly Savings in 1942 for City Families by Income Change from 1941 to 1942

	Consumers whose incomes in 1942		
Money income class in 1942	*Decreased over 5 per cent*	*Changed less than 5 per cent*	*Increased over 5 per cent*
0 to $1000	−337	−35	−15
$1000 to $1500	−181	−34	62
$1500 to $2000	−81	126	157
$2000 to $3000	0	242	290
$3000 and over	143	1228	1059

Annual rate for 1942 based on first quarter.
Based on B.L.S. Bulletin 724.

those whose incomes stayed constant. Now these facts can be interpreted in two ways. On the one hand we can say that they show that a rate of change factor is important in the determination of saving. That is, we write $c/y = f(y,y')$ where y' is the rate of change of income. On the other hand we can say that saving is low when income is low relative to past income. The two explanations are not the same. In a year when income is declining, either explanation would lead to the same result. But suppose that income declines and then remains at a (more or less constant) low level. After the decline has stopped, the rate of change is zero but income is still low relative to its pre-depression level.

It is fairly easy to tell which of the two hypotheses is correct. If the rate of change of income is an important factor it should show up in regressions of aggregate data. But it is well known that when the equation $c = f(y,t,y')$ is fitted to aggregate data for the twenties and thirties the addition of the factor y' contributes very little to the correlation. In the face of the budget study data this is difficult to explain unless we accept relative income instead of rate of change as the explanation of the differences in saving at the same level of income.

The asymmetry in the results is also important. If we take the view that rate of change of income is a determinant of saving, then there are strong reasons for supposing that the adjustment lag works in both directions. On the other hand, if we argue that people whose incomes are low relative to their past incomes reduce saving to protect their living standard, the asymmetry is easy to understand. Those whose incomes rose were for the most part getting back to levels of incomes which they had previously experienced. In these circumstances they merely returned to the expenditure patterns of the past and no adjustment lag is involved.

The data just discussed seem to show fairly conclusively that consumption at a given level of income does depend on past income. This hypothesis is consistent with the existence of deficits in 1935–36 and 1941, with the changes in deficits (at given levels of income) from 1935–36 to 1941, with the upward movement of the break-even point from 1917 to 1935–36 and 1941, and with the differences in saving among families whose incomes had changed in different ways. It is difficult to explain all of these facts on any other hypothesis.

Psychological Foundation

So far our argument has been a strictly empirical one. But it must be clear that it also has a strong psychological foundation. The fundamental psychological postulate underlying our argument is that it is harder for a family to reduce its expenditures from a high level than for a family to refrain from making high expenditures in the first place. Consider two families who have incomes of $1000 per year at a particular time. Now suppose one of these families has an income of $1000 per year for ten years thereafter. Suppose the other family gets an increase in income from $1000 to $1500, retains this position for nine years, and then has its income reduced to $1000 so that in the last year it is in the same position as the other family. Initially both families might have exactly balanced their budgets at $1000, and the first family might continue in this way for the whole ten-year period. But when the second family had its income increased it would increase its consumption by (say) $400 and its saving by $100. When the reduction in income occurred it would certainly find it difficult to cut its consumption to the $1000 level. The first family had only to refrain from increasing its consumption expenditures to balance its budget. The second family had actually to give up consumption of $400 per year to achieve the same result. It would be surprising if a family in these circumstances succeeded in reducing its consumption sufficiently to balance its budget after the loss in income.

Since all of the data are consistent with the view that this does happen, there does not seem to be much doubt that past income has an influence on current consumption and saving.

The argument so far has been devoted to explaining the deficits reported in the budget studies. But the significant result of this argument is not the conclusion that deficits will occur when income falls below previously attained levels but the more general proposition that families are willing to sacrifice saving in order to protect their living standard. This proposition applies to all income groups who have suffered losses in income. We can argue in the following way. If a family has a certain income y_0 and this income is higher than any previously attained, it will save some amount. This amount will be a function of income $s_0 = f(y_0)$. If its income increases the same function will hold. But if after an increase income falls to the original level its saving will be less than $f(y_0)$. If the family's income and saving are low throughout, it will have a deficit after the fall in income. If the family is in a higher bracket it will simply save less after the fall in income than it did before the increase. This view is checked by the fact that savings in the last five years of the twenties averaged 10.2 per cent of disposable income while from 1936 to 1940 they averaged only 9.0 per cent. Real disposable income per capita was almost the same in the two periods.

A Base Year for Downward Adjustments of Consumption

We have now shown that consumption is dependent on current income relative to past income as well as on the absolute level of current income. The problem now is to find just which past incomes are relevant. In view of the argument just given we appear to be safe in supposing that past incomes lower than the current one are not very relevant. This is pretty well demonstrated by the 1941–42 budget figures cited above. Families whose incomes rose to a given level saved about the same amount as those whose incomes had been at that level in the previous year. At first glance then it would seem reasonable to suppose that current consumption depends on the ratio of current income to some weighted average of past higher incomes, with weights decreasing as the time interval involved grows longer. There are, however, some fairly strong arguments against this position. The declines in income which occur in the depression are not uniformly distributed even though the size distribution of income remains more or less unchanged.

Income losses will be of three kinds: (1) reductions in property incomes, (2) reductions in wage rates, (3) losses due to underemployment. Since real wage rates do not decline very much in the depression (and were even higher in the late years of the depression than in the twenties), losses of income are mostly of types (1) and (3). (A fourth class results from downgrading of workers either within or between industries, but for our purposes this can be regarded as underemployment.)

Let us first consider the effect of losses of income in the upper income groups. It is not important here whether the losses are due to reductions in property incomes or to salary reductions. It can be assumed, however, that unemployment among the upper income groups is not important. The upper 10 per cent of the income distribution produces almost all of the positive saving for the whole economy. Moreover, families in this group save a high proportion of their income. This means that they have a good deal of leeway in maintaining consumption standards without running into deficits; also they have more free (non-contractual) saving. When high income families suffer a loss in income, therefore, they continue to live in the same kind of neighborhoods and maintain their contacts with others of the same socio-economic status. In general they maintain the way of life which was established before the onset of the depression. They will, of course, cut expenditures on some lines, particularly on durable goods. But in view of the high rate of savings maintained in prosperity they can absorb a considerable reduction of income by reducing saving without cutting consumption too deeply. Moreover, there is no reason why they should not continue in this position for several years. Suppose now that income falls sharply from a cyclical peak and then remains constant for several years. The peak year's consumption sets the standard from which cuts are made (provided the peak did not represent a mere spurt in income). The higher the peak consumption, the more difficult it will be to reduce consumption to any given level. After the initial reductions are made the situation becomes static. The peak year does not lose its influence because the consumption of the following years depends on the peak consumption. Of course, if income began to fall again further consumption cuts would take place, and the intermediate level of income would be important in determining the extent of the cuts as well as the previous peak income. But if the depression consists in a fall of income lasting only a couple of years followed by a rise or a low plateau, the consumption of the peak year is likely to have very heavy weight in determining consumption in the depression. The influence of the peak consumption will not "fade away" unless income continues to fall steadily.

All of the above argument applies only to the upper income groups. Those who were in the lower 90 per cent of the distribution in prosperity are in a different situation. For this group, reductions in individual income are usually associated with unemployment. These people probably save very little even in prosperous times. In a depression they can only influence saving by having deficits. A considerable number of families in this group go nearly unscathed by the depression. Their real wages do not fall and they never have serious losses of employment. These we may leave out of account since their savings are simply zero throughout. The remaining families suffer serious loss of employment at some point during the depression. These may also be divided into two groups. Some will remain employed up to a certain point, then lose their jobs and never get steady employment again until a high level of prosperity is reached. These families will presumably run substantial deficits immediatley after they become unemployed, but as their assets become smaller they will have to adjust to the new situation and presumably balance budgets in which relief is the principal source of income. They may continue to have deficits for a long time, but in any case the influence of the prosperity living standard will certainly "fade away" as time passes. However, it should be noted that not all of the persons who will eventually constitute the "hard core" of unemployment get there at once. The result is that a certain number of families are going through the initial stages of long-term unemployment at any time during the depression. Presumably, however, there are rather more families in this position during the downturn in the early years than later on. We should expect, therefore, to find somewhat greater deficits and lower aggregate savings at a given income in the downturn than in the upturn. However, the total number of families in this group was not very large in the thirties, and the differences in the numbers entering cannot have been great enough to cause numerically important reductions in aggregate savings.

The remainder of the unemployment is widely spread so that a large number of workers "take turns" being unemployed. Families lose income through unemployment and accordingly cut consumption; they also run a deficit. When they get reemployed they may return to something very close to the prosperity consumption standard. Sometime later unemployment may reoccur and the process repeats. Those families who are very frequently in and out of employment will presumably gradually reduce consumption (even when employed) because of the decrease in their assets and the accumulation of debt. The influence of the peak standard will therefore gradually lose its effect. But a great part of the total unemployment can be accounted for by families who have only one or two stretches of prolonged unemployment during the depression. For these families the influence of the peak consumption standard will not fade away because it renews itself with each stretch of full employment.

We can conclude then that the income or consumption of the last cyclical peak will carry a special and very heavy weight in determining consumption at a given (lower) level of income during a depression. In principle a weighted average of all the incomes from the peak year to the current year ought to be used. But with only a few observations it would be impossible to estimate the weights. In what follows we shall consider the relation of current consumption to the ratio (current income/highest previously attained income) but the results are to be taken as an approximation to the true relation.

If the argument just given is correct, then there is a cyclical component in the explanation of saving. Savings at a given level of income, when income is the highest ever attained, as in the late twenties, will be higher than savings at a similar income level reached in a decline from a still higher level. I conclude, therefore, that in a general way at least the propositions of those who have argued that saving varies with the trade cycle as well as with income are supported by the evidence of the budget studies.

III. AGGREGATE INCOME-SAVING RELATIONSHIPS

So far it has been shown that saving depends on the level of current incomes relative to higher incomes in previous years. But saving also depends on the absolute level of income. We may write then, $s_t = f(y_t, y_t/y_0)$ where y_0 is the highest income attained previous to the year t. Then

$$\frac{ds_t}{dy_t} = \frac{df}{dy_t} + \frac{df}{d\left(\frac{y_t}{y_0}\right)} \cdot \frac{d(y_t/y_0)}{dy_t}$$

If we plot out the long period relation of saving and income considering only periods of approximately full employment, the term $d(y_t/y_0)/dy_t$ will be 0 so that $ds_t/dy_t = df/dy_t$. But, with data covering a trade cycle, $d(y_t/y_0)/dy_t$ will have a positive value, and, if we use cyclical data to estimate the secular marginal propensity to consume, our estimates will be too high.

If data covering a number of cycles were available, we could take the regression of saving on y_t/y_0 and y_t and estimate simultaneously the secular and cyclical components in saving. Unfortunately the period 1923–1940 covers only one major cycle, so that we are forced to estimate the influence of the two factors separately. First, it should be noted that there are strong grounds for supposing that (in the absence of cyclical fluctuations) aggregate saving remains a constant proportion of aggregate income.

This position can be best understood by a consideration of the apparent contradictions in the relations between saving and income. On the one hand, we have the Keynesian dictum that "apart from short period changes in the level of income, it is also obvious that a higher absolute income will tend to widen the gap between income and consumption. For the satisfaction of the immediate primary needs of a man and his family is usually a stronger motive than the motives toward accumulation, which only acquire effective sway after a margin of comfort has been attained. These reasons will lead as a rule to a greater proportion of income being saved as income increases."[15] This argument which, at first glance at any rate, appears very plausible, has had wide acceptance. Moreover, it seems to be supported by important empirical evidence. Every budget study supports the view that families with high incomes save a greater proportion of income than those with low incomes. It is also known that, in the period 1923–1940, saving fluctuated more than in proportion to income. On the other hand, the data given by

[15] J. M. Keynes, *The General Theory of Employment, Interest, and Money,* New York, Harcourt, Brace and Co., 1937, p. 97. Reprinted by permission.

Kuznets indicate that aggregate saving has been an approximately constant proportion of income for a long time.[16]

From a psychological viewpoint, Keynes' argument about the relative importance of saving and accumulation at different income levels does not throw much light on the situation to which it is supposed to apply. It is no doubt true that a family will not save when its income is so low that it cannot satisfy its immediate primary needs. But in the United States, at least, the problem of getting an income high enough to maintain physical existence has hardly existed (for families whose workers are employed) for many years. The problem is not one of saving vs. consuming enough to maintain existence. It is one of choosing between an immediate comfort and security. Any psychological theory of saving must give an explanation of the resolution of the conflict between the desire for security and the desire for comfort. When the problem is put in this way the conclusion that saving rises more than in proportion to income is not at all obvious. Moreover, in view of the paucity and ambiguity of the empirical evidence a psychological basis is necessary if an adequate theory of saving is to be constructed.

Such a theory already exists in the form of marginal utility and "indifference map" analysis, but it is hardly adequate for our purposes. The whole structure of preference analysis is based on the assumption that one individual's preferences are independent of the actual consumption patterns of another individual's. It is this assumption which permits us to add up the demand functions of individuals to get a market-demand function.

Yet consumption preferences can hardly be regarded as innate characteristics of individuals. Nor can they be regarded, in a society as dynamic as ours, as being determined by tradition. There is a great deal of evidence to show that consumer tastes are socially determined. This does not mean that consumer tastes are governed by considerations of conspicuous consumption. Rather, it means that any individual's desire to increase his expenditure is governed by the extent to which the goods consumed by others are demonstrably superior to the ones which he consumes. If we can assume that the degree of superiority of one set of goods over another is highly correlated with the relative costs of obtaining these goods, we are led to the following proposition. The strength of any individual's desire to increase his consumption expenditure is a function of the ratio of his expenditure to some weighted average of the expenditures of others with whom he comes in contact. The weights are determined by the social character of these contacts. If the distribution of income is constant (in the Lorenz curve sense) this weighted average can be regarded as a function of an individual's percentile

[16]Simon Kuznets, *Uses of National Income in Peace and War,* New York, National Bureau of Economic Research, 1942, p. 30.

position in the income distribution. The proportion of income saved is set by balancing the desire to increase current consumption against the desire to increase assets relative to current consumption (that is, to have a greater assurance of continued maintenance of the existing standard). We may therefore conclude that if the strength of the desire to increase consumption is a function of percentile position in the income distribution, the proportion of income saved will be a function of the same variable. It is also easy to see that it will be a rising function.[17]

This hypothesis leads to the following conclusions:

(a) At any one moment the proportion of income saved will be higher for the higher income groups than for low income groups.

(b) If income increases, while the proportional distribution remains constant, the ratio of aggregate saving to aggregate income will be constant.

Both of these conclusions are in accord with known facts.

If we accept the hypothesis just given, then secularly consumer saving will be a constant proportion of disposable income.

This hypothesis, together with the cyclical relation, considered in Section II, should give a complete explanation of variations in saving.

If the secular relation between savings and income makes for a constant income-saving ratio, the *proportion* of income saved will depend only on cyclical factors.[18] Then we may write $s_t/y_t = F(y_t/y_0)$. There is not much basis for selecting any particular functional form for $F(y_t/y_0)$. However, a linear approximation, which fits the data well, is always satisfactory, provided that we do not have to make predictions involving values of the variable outside the range of data used in fitting the approximation. In the period 1923–1940 values of y_t/y_0 ranged from about 1.1 to .5. It seems unlikely that income will ever decline to less than 50 per cent of full employment levels, so that we can be safe in using a linear form for $F(y_t/y_0)$ for prediction. When the relation $s_t/y_t = a(y_t/y_0) + b$ is fitted to the data for the period 1923–1940, we obtain $a = .165$, $b = .066$.[19] The correlation is .9, which is as good as that usually obtained for relations between savings and income.

[17] In a paper of this length it is impossible to go too deeply into the theory of consumer behaviour underlying the above propositions. This theory together with some empirical tests of its adequacy will be developed more fully in a forthcoming paper.

[18] If we accept the proposition that the high marginal propensity to consume indicated by linear income consumption relationships is largely due to cyclical factors, there is no *evidence* of the existence of any powerful trend in consumption. Various factors which might have caused either an upward or a downward trend can be cited. But when we have a hypothesis which explains all the data there is no point in introducing a trend unless some evidence of its operation can be given.

[19] The data used are those given by E. G. Bennion, "The Consumption Function Cyclically Variable," *Review of Economic Statistics,* November, 1946. Disposable income and savings are both corrected for price and population changes.

However, the correlation is not the test of the adequacy of the relation. The test is based on the fact that the secular average propensity to consume is predicted by the relation just given. In a period when income is slowly rising with only minor cyclical fluctuations, each year's income should be slightly above that of the preceding year. y_t/y_0 should be about 1.02 in each year. If we put $(y_t/y_0) = 1.02$ in the relation $s_t/y_t = .165(y_t/y_0) - .066$ we obtain $s_t/y_t = .102$ which is very close to Kuznets' estimate of the (stable) savings ratio in the period 1879–1919. Since the regression was based on the period 1923–1940 we may say that the regression "predicted" the Kuznets' results.

All three major sources of data about income and consumption are consistent with the two hypotheses, (1) that secularly an individual's propensity to consume is a function of his position in the income distribution (which implies that aggregate saving tends in the long run to be a constant proportion of income) and (2) that, cyclically, the aggregate propensity to consume depends on the ratio of current income to the highest income previously achieved. They are also consistent with the internal evidence of the budget studies and with the results of intertemporal comparisons of budget studies. So far as I am aware there are no data about saving and income which are inconsistent with these hypotheses.

There is, however, another important class of hypotheses which has not been considered here. These are the hypotheses which introduce variables other than income into the consumption function. In particular it has been suggested that saving may vary with the price level (when the price level is considered as a separate variable and not as a mere deflator) and with the value of assets. There is, of course, no real conflict between these hypotheses and the ones presented here. The two variables just mentioned are highly correlated with income, so that it is quite possible that they may be important contributors to the variance of saving, even though a high correlation can be obtained without considering them. These hypotheses will have to be tested by methods similar to those used in Section II of this paper.

The implications of the hypotheses developed here are fairly obvious. We may expect that, when the transition period is completed, consumer savings will fall to around 10 per cent of disposable income. This may be compared with the estimate of 14 per cent given by Smithies for consumer savings out of a disposable income of 158.2 billion dollars in 1943 prices.[20] The volume of offsets to savings required to maintain full employment is therefore considerably smaller than would be expected from estimates based on simple income-consumption regressions.

The relation $s_t/y_t = .166(y_t/y_0) - .066$ has the property that the marginal propensity to save out of disposable income is fairly high with respect to

[20] *Vide* A. Smithies, "Forecasting Postwar Demand," *Econometrica*, January, 1945.

cyclical movements of income, but the average propensity to save is much lower and does not tend to rise with secular increases in income. During the trough of a cycle (from the time income falls below the peak value for one cycle until it rises above that value in the next cycle) y_t/y_0 is dependent entirely on y_t (since y_0 is constant). We have then $s_t = (.166/y_0)y_t^2 - .066y_t$; then $ds_t/dy_t = .332(y_t/y_0) - .066$. The marginal propensity to save with respect to decreases in income is therefore about .26 at the peak of a cycle. As income declines ds_t/dy_t falls until it reaches zero at an income equal to one-fifth that of the last cyclical peak.

On the other hand, the average propensity to save does not rise as income rises secularly. For in the upswing of a cycle after full employment is reached, y_0 and y_t move together. If income increases steadily at an annual rate of 3 per cent, y_t/y_0 is constant at a value of 1.03. The long-run savings function is therefore $s_t = .166(1.03)\ y_t - .066y_t$ or simply $s_t = .102\ y_t$. Thus the cyclical marginal propensity to save is (in the relevant range) higher than the long-run propensity to save, and the use of cyclical data to estimate the long-period relationship leads to invalid conclusions.

3

AN EMPIRICAL EVALUATION OF THEORIES OF SAVING[1]

HAROLD W. GUTHRIE

The theories of saving presented by Keynes, Duesenberry, and Friedman use three different measures of income to explain saving, and each theory has been supported by empirical evidence. The evidence consists of tests of a wide variety of hypotheses contained within or derived from the theories. The tests use many different kinds of data. The objective of this paper is to submit the basic behavioral hypothesis of each theory to a common test on a single set of data. The results show that the theories are equally acceptable on empirical grounds.

DETERMINANTS OF SAVING OTHER THAN INCOME

Although income is the principal explanatory variable in all three theories, it is obvious that there are many other variables which affect the level of consumers' saving. Some of the more important non-income variables are

[1]The Cowles Foundation for Research in Economics at Yale University provided financial support for the research reported here. The Computing Center of the University of Kentucky gave access to computing equipment, and the Board of Governors of the Federal Reserve System and the Survey Research Center, University of Michigan, permitted use of data from the Surveys of Consumer Finances. The author is grateful to each of these institutions for invaluable assistance.

Reprinted from the *Review of Economics and Statistics* (November 1963), pp. 430–33, by permission of the author and publisher, Harvard University Press. Harold W. Guthrie is a professor at the University of Illinois.

those which differentiate consumers according to life cycle, asset holdings, entrepreneurial activity, and the stage of the business cycle at the time of observation. Since some of these variables (for example, age, asset holdings) are also correlated with income, it is convenient to estimate their effects on saving before testing hypotheses about income. When these effects have been removed from the original data, the residuals are relatively free of the effects of collinearity which would confound tests of the combined effects of income and non-income variables.

The following regression equation specifies, for the purpose of this study, a relationship between saving and some variables which describe the life cycle and balance sheet positions of the spending units observed:[2]

$$100\,\frac{S}{Y} = b_0 + b_1A + b_2N + b_3N^2 + b_4H + b_5(Y'L) + u_S \tag{1}$$

where S/Y = fraction of income saved,

A = age of head of spending unit in coded form:

1 = 18–24 4 = 45–54
2 = 25–34 5 = 55–64,
3 = 35–44

N = number of persons in the spending unit,
H = 1 if the spending unit owns its home,
0 if the spending unit does not own its home,
Y' = 1 if the spending unit's current annual income is less than the previous year's income by 25% or more,
0 if a decline in income of 25% or more did not occur,
L = amount of liquid assets held at the beginning of the current year,
u_s = residual term.

A similar equation (2) provides a basis for estimating the effects of non-income variables on the level of expenditures for durable goods (G):

$$100\,\frac{G}{Y} = b_0 + b_1A + b_2N + b_3N^2 + b_4H + b_5(Y'L) + u_g\,. \tag{2}$$

The residuals, u_s and u_g, become dependent variables below.

Equations (1) and (2) have been estimated for each of four groups of

[2]The data used in this paper were collected in the Surveys of Consumer Finances of 1950 and 1951. See [7] for a description of methods used in the Surveys.

Table 1. Summary of Regressions on Demographic and Balance Sheet Variables
Regression Coefficients

Independent Variable	*Durable Goods*				*Saving*			
	Entrepreneurs		*Non-Entrepreneurs*		*Entrepreneurs*		*Non-Entrepreneurs*	
	1949	*1950*	*1949*	*1950*	*1949*	*1950*	*1949*	*1950*
Intercept	14.75	41.43	118.19*	69.44*	28.97	15.23	–3.81	3.29
A	.85	–13.42	–19.77*	–9.55*	–2.59	–.83	–.93	–.36
N	59.51*	67.28*	25.08*	44.81*	–8.33	1.29	2.18	–2.09
N^2	–6.31*	–7.45*	–3.02*	–5.54*	1.05	–.15	–.28	.25
H	–14.70	–9.37	13.58	8.68	8.99	10.09*	10.90*	10.10*
$(Y'L)$	–.19	–.12	.38*	1.40*	–.19*	–.61*	–.15*	–.59*
R^2	.015	.039	.025	.024	.025	.153	.028	.026
F ratio	1.31	3.47*	11.30*	10.97*	2.18	13.56*	12.75*	11.91*
Sample size	436	442	2,264	2,288	436	442	2,264	2,288

*The null hypotheses are rejected at a significance level of 5% or less; the regression coefficients are at least twice their standard errors.

consumers. Spending units in which the principal source of income is the operation of a farm or an unincorporated business are defined as entrepreneurs. Other spending units are non-entrepreneurs. The Surveys for 1949, a recession year, and 1950, in part a war-boom year, provide an opportunity to contrast the effects of economic fluctuations. Table 1 shows the estimated regression coefficients for entrepreneurs and non-entrepreneurs in 1949 and 1950.[3]

The life-cycle variables contribute to an explanation of expenditures on durable goods but do not explain the saving ratio. The durable goods ratio varies with age among non-entrepreneurs but not among entrepreneurs. Home ownership and consequent repayments of mortgage principal contribute to an explanation of saving except among entrepreneurs in 1949. A reduction in saving, varying with liquid asset holdings, when income declines sharply, is indicated in both years and both groups. The effect of economic fluctuations shows up most clearly in the entrepreneur groups where the combined effects of all variables were significant in 1950 but not in 1949, for both saving and durable goods expenditures.

[3]The following spending units were excluded from the samples: (1) those for which the values of one or more of the variables used in this study were not ascertained; (2) those in which the head was sixty-five years of age or older.

THE EFFECTS OF ALTERNATIVE MEASURES OF INCOME ON SAVING

The residuals u_s from the regression equations indicated by the estimates in Table 1 are the dependent variables in hypotheses which are described in this section. The results of the tests are shown in Table 2.

Keynes' Theory

The absolute amount of income is the primary independent variable in the Keynesian consumption function. Thus the relevant hypothesis is that saving is positively related to absolute income (Y), and the test supports this hypothesis.

Duesenberry's Theory

Relative income, that is, "percentile position in the income distribution" [2, p. 45] is an important variable in the Duesenberry theory. Income deciles were used in the test instead of percentiles. Deciles have values ranging from one, for the lowest 10 per cent of spending unit incomes, to ten, for the highest 10 per cent of spending unit incomes. Results of the test support the hypothesis that saving is positively related to income decile (D).

Table 2. Summary of Simple Correlation Coefficients of Saving and Specified Measures of Income

	*Correlation Coefficients**			
	Entrepreneurs		*Non-Entrepreneurs*	
Income Variable	*1949*	*1950*	*1949*	*1950*
Y (Keynes)	.18	.28	.17	.18
D (Duesenberry)	.22	.33	.19	.17
$D' - D$ (Variant of Duesenberry)	−.25	−.31	−.17	−.16
$D - D_M$ (Friedman)	.27	.31	.11	.12
R^2	.13	.09	.04	.04
F ratio	16.63	10.69	24.79	21.19
Sample size	436	442	2,264	2,288

*The null hypothesis is rejected at a significance level of 5% or less for all correlation coefficients and all F ratios.

A Modification of the Relative Income Hypothesis

In presenting his theory Duesenberry noted that a person is impelled to increase his consumption by the fact that his associates consume goods which he does not consume. The demonstration effect therefore occurs among associated consumers. To make the effect occur among all consumers, it is assumed that they live in a classless society in which interdependence is diffused through the consumer sector in a fairly homogeneous fashion. This assumption justifies using relative income position to explain variation in consumption.

There are, nevertheless, socio-economic classes in the United States, and it is conceivable that the effect of interdependence may be stronger within subgroups of consumers than within the whole consumer sector. The sixty-five subgroups of consumers used to test this modification of the demonstration effect were obtained by classifying consumers according to race, region, occupation, education, and age.[4] Within each subgroup, the intensity of the demonstration effect is measured by the difference between the highest observed value of income decile (D') and the decile position of a particular spending unit (D).

The difference in decile positions ($D' - D$) tends to reverse the scale of measurement relative to D, that is, a spending unit with a high decile value (D) would have a low difference ($D' - D$). The sense of the modification is therefore expressed in the hypothesis that saving is negatively related to the difference between an individual spending unit's income decile and the highest observed decile within a group of associated spending units. Results of the test support this hypothesis. It should be noted, however, that the data do not suggest that the modification is superior to the original Duesenberry hypothesis.

Friedman's Theory

Two of the more provocative components of Friedman's theory are the postulate that consumption is not correlated with transitory income, and its corollary that saving is positively and highly correlated with transitory income. The latter is the hypothesis tested here.

Whether the test is appropriate to the theory or not is open to question. Short of detailed observations of a consumer unit over time there is no operational method of distinguishing permanent from transitory income. The method used here is at least distantly related to one of Friedman's examples

[4]The sixty-five subgroups are the same as those shown in [5, pp. 487–90] except that spending units in which the head was sixty-five years or older were omitted from the present analysis. A few small subgroups were collapsed into adjoining age groups.

[3, p. 21]. The sixty-five subgroups of consumers who are relatively homogeneous with respect to race, region, occupation, education, and age are regarded as containing spending units that have common levels of permanent income. The median income decile (D_M) within each subgroup is considered to be a measure of size of permanent income. The observed income decile (D) for an individual spending unit is considered to be a measure of size of total income. The difference between the two values ($D - D_M$) therefore measures, approximately, transitory income. Results shown in Table 2 are consistent with the hypothesis that saving is positively related to transitory income but the correlation coefficient is no higher than those obtained for other measures of income.[5]

THE EFFECT OF ALTERNATIVE MEASURES OF INCOME ON EXPENDITURES FOR DURABLE GOODS

The residuals u_g from the regression equations indicated by the estimates in Table 1 are the dependent variables for the analysis reported in this section. The results are shown in Table 3.

The amount of saving, as calculated in the Surveys of Consumer Finances, does not include an offset for depreciation of the spending unit's stock of durable goods. If it is assumed that the stock of durable goods remains constant over time, each item being replaced as it is worn out, purchases of durable goods could be used as a proxy measure of consumption. This disposition of durable goods becomes less tenable, however, if stocks increase over time or if expenditures tend to be "lumpy"; for example, the purchase of a house may entail unusually large expenditures for durable goods. Under the latter conditions, durable goods expenditures include some element of saving. Given the nature of the original data, there seems to be no satisfactory procedure for avoiding the ambiguity.

The parallel analysis of saving and expenditures for durable goods offers some prospect of resolving the ambiguity, but the results are not decisive. Table 1 shows marked differences among the non-income variables with respect to their effects on saving and durable goods. A similar sharp difference shows up in the effects of income on saving and durable goods expenditures. Table 2 shows statistically significant correlation between

[5]It is interesting to note that the formulation of the hypothesis and the results of the test are also consistent with the "New Suburbia Thesis": social pressure causes families to consume at the normal level for their class, regardless of their income [9].

Table 3. Summary of Simple Correlation Coefficients of Durable Goods Expenditures and Specified Measures of Income

	Correlation Coefficients			
	Entrepreneurs		*Non-Entrepreneurs*	
Income Variable	*1949*	*1950*	*1949*	*1950*
Y (Keynes)	–.05	–.07	.01	.00
D (Duesenberry)	–.02	–.05	.07*	.04
$D' - D$ (Variant of Duesenberry)	–.03	–.03	.03	.02
$D - D_M$ (Friedman)	.05	.11*	–.05	–.05
R^2	.03	.00	.01	.01
F ratio	2.86*	.56	3.93*	3.32*
Sample size	436	442	2,264	2,288

*The null hypothesis is rejected at a significance level of 5% or less.

saving and each measure of income. With only two exceptions, Table 3 indicates that differences in income do not affect expenditures for durable goods. If durable goods expenditures are regarded as consisting primarily of saving, the two significant correlation coefficients offer modest support to the Duesenberry theory and to the Friedman theory.

The joint effect of all four measures of income produces three statistically significant coefficients of determination. These results are consistent with Tobin's suggestion that the best empirical explanation of the relationship between saving and income may lie in combinations of different measures of income [8].

CONCLUSIONS

Three major theories of consumers' saving have been submitted to similar tests on a single set of data. The tests were applied in an unusually severe form in that the effects of the variables—age, size of spending unit, home ownership, and liquid asset holdings—were removed before alternative measures of income were compared with respect to their explanatory power. The results are consistent with each of the theories, and no single theory is obviously superior to the others on empirical grounds. If a choice among the theories must be made—and it is not clear that there must be a single correct theory—then the choice must be made on the basis of other empirical results or other criteria.

References

1. Bodkin, Ronald, "Windfall Income and Consumption," *American Economic Review,* XLIX (September 1959), 602–14.
2. Duesenberry, James, *Income, Saving and the Theory of Consumer Behavior* (Harvard University Press, 1949).
3. Friedman, Milton, *A Theory of the Consumption Function,* National Bureau of Economic Research (Princeton University Press, 1957).
4. Friend, Irwin, "Some Conditions for Progress in the Study of Savings," *Bulletin of the Oxford University Institute of Statistics,* 19 (May 1957), 165–70.
5. Guthrie, Harold W., "Consumers' Propensities to Hold Liquid Assets," *American Statistical Association Journal,* 55 (September 1960), 469–90.
6. Klein, L. R., and N. Liviatan, "The Significance of Income Variability on Savings Behaviour," *Bulletin of the Oxford University Institute of Statistics,* 19 (May 1957), 150–60.
7. "Methods of the Survey of Consumer Finances," *Federal Reserve Bulletin,* 36 (July 1950), 795–809.
8. Tobin, James, "Relative Income, Absolute Income, and Saving," *Money, Trade, and Economic Growth* (New York: Macmillan, 1951).
9. Whyte, William H., Jr., "The Consumer in the New Suburbia," *Consumer Behavior,* Vol. 1 (New York University Press, 1954).

II

Investment

One can state with some confidence that business investment behavior is influenced by expectations, managerial preference patterns, cash flow, market or competitive strategy, technological changes, capacity utilization rates, innovations, and many other considerations that together add up to a rather long list. There are economists who argue that a useful theory of investment behavior must necessarily incorporate a good number of the factors in such a list, because many of them do exert a significant influence on investment outlays. Of quite a different viewpoint are the economists who believe that there are one or two key factors that alone can provide the basis for an adequate explanation of business investment patterns.

Perhaps foremost among the key factors identified by this latter group is the acceleration concept in its many forms, each of which in one way or another makes investment outlays a function of the rate of change of output or of the degree of capacity utilization. Another of these key factors is the level of business profits and, through this, the volume of internally generated funds and related aspects on the side of finance.

Among these factors, the acceleration principle has long received the most attention, and the first selection in this part by A. D. Knox provides a thorough survey of the role played by this principle in the theory of investment. This is followed by Robert Eisner's nontechnical but nonetheless substantial paper in which he presents a case for the acceleration principle and against the level of profits as the key factor in the determination of investment outlays. The final selection, by W. H. Locke Anderson, takes issue with economists, like Eisner, who are designated as "accelerationists" and with others who, in their concentration on the level of profits, are in parallel fashion designated as "profiteers." In this article, Anderson attempts to show that both a capacity-utilization form of the acceleration concept and certain financial variables, such as retained earnings that flow from the level of profits, belong together in an adequate explanation of investment. This conclusion is reached partially on the basis of a regression study whose procedure and results are summarized in this article.

4

THE ACCELERATION PRINCIPLE AND THE THEORY OF INVESTMENT: A SURVEY[1]

A. D. KNOX

I.

Over the past two decades the acceleration principle has played an extremely important part in the theory of investment. Its history, however, takes us back to the early years of this century[2]; and a considerable literature exists on the uses to which it may be put and on the reliability of its explanation of the motives for investment in capital equipment.[3]

The main body of literature centres on the acceleration principle and the trade cycle. Here the popularity of the principle dates from the development of the multiplier and the realisation that neat models could be based on the interaction of these two theories. J. M. Clark drew attention to the possibili-

[1]I should like to express my thanks for helpful suggestions to Mr. A. W. Phillips, Professor Lionel Robbins, Dr. W. J. L. Ryan, and Mr. Ralph Turvey.

[2]The main early works on the acceleration principle are: A. Aftalion, "La réalité des surproductions générales," *Revue d'Economie Politique,* 1909, pp. 219-220, and *Les Crises Périodiques de Surproduction* (Paris, 1913), tôme II, pp. 356-370; C. F. Bickerdike, "A non-monetary cause of fluctuations in employment," *Economic Journal,* 1914; and J. M. Clark, "Business acceleration and the law of demand: a technical factor in economic cycles," *Journal of Political Economy,* 1917, and reprinted in American Economic Association, *Readings in Business Cycle Theory* (Philadelphia, 1944), pp. 235-260.

[3]Useful bibliographies are in: G. von Haberler, *Prosperity and Depression* (Geneva, 1941), p. 87; and *Readings, op. cit.,* pp. 460-462.

[4]J. M. Clark, "Additional note on 'Business acceleration and the law of demand'," in *Preface to Social Economics* (New York, 1936) and reprinted in *Readings, op. cit.,* pp. 259-260; and *Strategic Factors in Business Cycles* (New York, 1934), pp. 167-183. See also R. Frisch,

Reprinted from *Economica* (August 1952), pp. 269-97, by permission of the author and publisher.
A. D. Knox is an economist with the International Bank for Reconstruction and Development.

ties of such models,[4] but they were first fully developed by Lundberg[5] and Harrod.[6] Harrod's work, in particular, aroused considerable interest in the acceleration principle—or the relation, as he called it—for in it the principle was brought to the very forefront of the analysis of the cycle.

> It is a relation [wrote Mr. Harrod] which has, indeed, been noted by learned writers often enough. Nonetheless I have the impression that not nearly sufficient importance has, on the whole, been attached to it. Its simplicity, ineluctability, and independence of all special theories as to the workings of the cyclical process demand for it pride of place.[7]

Since 1936 the acceleration principle has been significant in a number of models of the cycle: the rigorous statement of the interaction of the multiplier and the acceleration principle presented by Samuelson,[8] and the later refinements of Bennion,[9] Baumol,[10] Hicks,[11] and Goodwin.[12]

The acceleration principle, as applied to the theory of investment in capital equipment, has been used in two other connexions. In part the theory of pump-priming rests upon it.[13] More recently the major use of the principle has been with regard to the problem of the long-run growth of an economy. As in the theory of the trade cycle, it has lent itself to the formulation of neat models.[14]

Finally the acceleration principle has also been used to explain investment

---

"Propagation problems and impulse problems in dynamic economics," in *Essays in Honour of Gustav Cassel* (London, 1933).

[5]E. Lundberg, *Studies in the Theory of Economic Expansion* (London, 1937), ch. 9.

[6]R. F. Harrod, *The Trade Cycle: an Essay* (Oxford, 1936), especially ch. 2.

[7]*Op. cit.*, pp. 53–54.

[8]P. A. Samuelson, "A synthesis of the principle of acceleration and the multiplier," *Journal of Political Economy,* 1939; and "Interactions between the multiplier analysis and the principle of acceleration," *Review of Economic Statistics,* 1939. The latter article has been reprinted in *Readings, op. cit.*, pp. 261–269.

[9]E. G. Bennion, "The multiplier, the acceleration principle, and fluctuating autonomous investment," *Review of Economic Statistics,* 1945.

[10]W. J. Baumol, "Notes on some dynamic models," *Economic Journal,* 1948.

[11]J. R. Hicks, "Mr. Harrod's dynamic theory", *Economica,* 1949; and *A Contribution to the Theory of the Trade Cycle* (Oxford, 1950).

[12]R. M. Goodwin, "Secular and cyclical aspects of the multiplier and the accelerator," in *Income, Employment and Public Policy: Essays in Honor of Alvin H. Hansen* (New York, 1948); and "The non-linear accelerator and the persistence of business cycles," *Econometrica,* 1951.

[13]E.g., J. M. Clark, *Economics of Planning Public Works* (Washington, 1935); International Labour Office, *Public Investment and Full Employment* (Montreal, 1946); and H. M. Somers, *Public Finance and National Income* (Philadelphia, 1949), ch. 5.

[14]Lundberg, *op. cit.*, p. 180; R. F. Harrod, "An essay in dynamic theory," *Economic Journal,* 1939, and *Towards a Dynamic Economics* (London, 1948), especially ch. 3; E. D. Domar, "Capital expansion, rate of growth and employment," *Econometrica,* 1946, and other articles; Baumol, *op. cit.;* Hicks, *op. cit.;* and S. S. Alexander, "The accelerator as a generator of steady growth," *Quarterly Journal of Economics,* 1949, and "Mr. Harrod's dynamic model," *Economic Journal,* 1950.

in stocks[15] and in durable consumers' goods.[16] These applications are not discussed in this survey.

When applied to the explanation of investment in fixed capital, the acceleration principle is said to tell us what will be the behaviour of that part of this investment which is net and induced. These two terms have never been clearly defined in the literature on the acceleration principle; and indeed they do not lend themselves to precise definition. In rough terms, therefore, by net investment is meant an expansion of productive capacity.[17] Induced investment is the portion of net that depends on current movements in output; and thus the acceleration principle relates to investment in existing firms that produce existing types of goods for existing markets.[18] The acceleration principle as applied to net induced investment in a *single firm* may be stated rigorously and *without qualification* by means of a simple equation:

$$C_t \equiv K_t - K_{t-1} = a(O_t - O_{t-1})$$

Output of capital goods	Increase in stock of capital goods	Increase in final output times the accelerator.

The symbols have the following meanings:

C	Current output of capital equipment employed by the firm to make a net increase in its capital stock. In what follows this is referred to simply as output.
K	The firm's stock of capital equipment.
O	The firm's output of finished products—referred to as final output.
a	The accelerator or the coefficient of acceleration. This is the ratio between the current increase in the stock of capital equipment and the current increase in the flow of final output produced with that equipment. The accelerator is assumed to be constant.
$t, t-1$, etc.	Time periods.

[15] M. Abramovitz, *Inventories and Business Cycles* (New York, 1950), pp. 19-26, and the literature mentioned there; and J. Tinbergen, "An acceleration principle for commodity stockholding and a short cycle resulting from it," in O. Lange *et al.* (eds.), *Studies in Mathematical Economics and Econometrics* (Chicago, 1942).

[16] There is a fairly extensive literature, but the main elements of the theory are outlined in Haberler, *op. cit.*, pp. 92-99.

[17] There is a discussion in part II of this paper on the possibility of distinguishing between net and replacement investment. But since the acceleration principle rests on the assumption that this distinction may be made, the validity of doing so is not questioned for the moment.

[18] The distinction is between induced investment on the one hand and spontaneous or autonomous investment on the other hand. Once expectations are introduced it becomes

It is useful to express the acceleration principle in this form, for its two parts may readily be seen. The first part—$C_t \equiv K_t - K_{t-1}$—is an identity which tells us the very obvious fact that the current output of capital equipment for net investment is equal to the current increase in the stock of equipment. The second part is a theory of investment. Because the accelerator is assumed to be constant, there is always a fixed connexion between the current growth of capital stock and the current rise in final output. The validity of the theory of investment depends upon whether we can really assume the accelerator to be constant.

Despite its tautological nature, the first part yields certain useful and important conclusions about the timing and the proportional amplitude of fluctuations in the stock of capital equipment and in the output of the capital goods industries. The identity $C_t \equiv K_t - K_{t-1}$ expresses the fact that because capital equipment is durable[19] the stock of it exceeds the current output.[20] This excess of stock over output has the effect that turning points appear in output before they appear in stock, despite the fact that attempts to change the latter cause movements of the former. The condition that must be satisfied if C_t is to fall just below C_{t-1} is that $(K_t - K_{t-1})$ is less than $(K_{t-1} - K_{t-2})$, but that K_t exceeds K_{t-1}. In other words, the stock of equipment is rising, but not at a sufficiently fast rate to prevent a decline in the output of the capital goods industries.

The excess of stock over output has a further effect in that a given percentage fluctuation in stock means a more than proportionate fluctuation in output; and the more durable the stock the greater is the relative violence of the movements in output. This relationship may be shown by means of a simple arithmetical example. Assume that in period 1 one hundred machines of a particular type exist[21] and that the rate of replacement of these machines is a function solely of age. If they have a lifetime of 10 years then 10 machines are produced each year, so long as the stock of machines remains constant. Now assume a rise in that stock to 110 in period 2, at which level it remains in period 3. Output rises from 10 to 20, and then falls again to 10. A 10 percent increase in stock has led to a 100 percent rise in output, which then returns to its former level.[22] If, on the other hand, the lifetime of these

---

increasingly difficult to maintain the distinction. But as will be pointed out at the beginning of part II, we cling to the distinction in order to restrict the scope of this paper.

[19]Durability can be adequately defined only with reference to some time period. If we take a sufficiently short period the stock of most goods is greater than the current output. Unfortunately the relevant period for the acceleration period is not clear and is likely to be variable. We must, therefore, fall back on common usage which defines durable goods as those which are not destroyed or transformed in the act of consumption or production.

[20]Were capital equipment not durable, then C_t would be equal to K_t: i.e., $K_{t-1} = 0$.

[21]Ten machines have been added to the stock in each of the past ten years.

[22]The increase in stock causes a rise in replacement investment only after a lag.

machines is only 2 years, the same 10 percent increase in stock causes in period 2 only a 20 percent rise in output, which in period 3 returns to its former level of 50.

The effects of this purely technical relationship in matters of timing and amplitude are very useful in the analysis of business cycles; and its validity is unquestionable. This paper, therefore, is concerned with the second part of the acceleration principle: the theory of investment. So long as the accelerator is constant, the conclusions about the relationship between K and C apply also, once due allowances have been made for lags, to the timing and amplitude of fluctuations in K and in O. The crucial problem of the acceleration principle is whether the accelerator is constant.

The equation

$$K_t - K_{t-1} = a(O_t - O_{t-1})$$

states the acceleration principle in its most uncompromising form: net induced investment is solely a function of the rate of growth of final output. Stating it in this way enables us to see the mechanism at work. But few writers use this unqualified acceleration principle; and some have rejected the principle outright. Moreover, there have been various attempts to test it statistically, and the results of most of these tests have been unfavourable.[23] The next section attempts three things: (*a*) to set out the contending arguments on the modifications that should be made in the simple acceleration principle; (*b*) to assess the relative merits of these arguments, or at least to circumscribe the area of dispute; and (*c*) to seek from this review of the arguments the reasons for the unfavourable results yielded by the statistical tests.[24]

Before passing on to the next section it is necessary to make clear certain assumptions that will be maintained in this paper. The exposition of the acceleration principle related the investment of the single firm to the rate of growth of its output. One assumption is maintained for most of this paper,

[23] T. Hultgren, *American Transportation in Prosperity and Depression* (New York, 1948), pp. 157ff.; S. Kuznets, "Relation between capital goods and finished products in the business cycle," in *Economic Essays in Honour of Wesley Clair Mitchell* (New York, 1935), pp. 248–267; J. Tinbergen, "Statistical evidence on the acceleration principle," *Economica*, 1938, and *Statistical Testing of Business Cycle Theories* (League of Nations, Geneva, 1938), vol. I, chs. 3 and 5, and vol. II, ch. 2; T. Wilson, *Fluctuations in Income and Employment* (London, 1948), pp. 114ff.

On the other hand, Clark's statistical test yielded quite favourable results for the acceleration principle: *op. cit., Readings*, pp. 245–49. A. S. Manne has argued that a slightly modified version of the principle can be sustantiated empirically: "Some notes on the acceleration principle." *Review of Economic Statistics*, 1945.

[24] Even with the advances in econometrics the tools available for empirical testing are still somewhat crude. There is something to be said for occasional "theoretical verifications" of the results of the statistical tests!

until it is explicitly abandoned. It is that inventories are ignored, together with such things as the lengthening or shortening of order books. Investment therefore depends equally well on the rate of growth of sales or of output. The second assumption, which is kept throughout, provides for the application of the acceleration principle to the whole economy. Strictly, we should trace the effects of the rate of growth of, say, the output of shirts on the investment of the shirt-makers; the effects of the rate of growth of demand for shirt-making machinery on investment in the firms producing that machinery; and so on. It is doubtful whether we can successfully do so. Therefore, whenever the subsequent analysis deals with the economy as a whole, the assumption to be made is that aggregate net induced investment is related to the rate of growth of national income.[25]

II.

Many writers have criticised the acceleration principle, but no general agreement has emerged from these discussions. The history of discussions on the acceleration principle accounts at least in part for this continuing diversity of opinion. While much has been written on its various potential weaknesses, there have been few controversies in which the contending arguments might be marshalled and set forth as a whole. Issues have been raised for the most part without reference to previous discussions. Further, most writers have restricted their attention to a narrow range of criticisms; and sometimes to only one.

In order to simplify the problem of presenting this scattered and varied material, it is preferable to arrange it analytically rather than chronologically. Further, we may exclude from our terms of reference part of the literature on the acceleration principle. Criticisms of the acceleration principle may roughly be divided into two categories: those that dispute whether the principle gives a true representation of the forces determining induced investment; and those that, by questioning the importance of induced investment, cast doubt upon some of the more ambitious claims made on behalf of the principle. To settle the issues raised by both types of criticism would require a discussion of the entire theory of investment. Prudence, therefore, suggests that we concentrate on the first group. The problems to be discussed relate to[26]:—

[25] For discussions on this point, see J. M. Clark, *op. cit., Readings,* pp. 252–253; Baumol, *op. cit.,* p. 514 fn.; Hicks, *Trade Cycle, op. cit.,* p. 38; R. M. Bissell, "The rate of interest," *American Economic Review,* supplement, 1938, p. 32. The fullest discussion of this problem is to be found in B. A. Chait, *Les Fluctuations Economiques et l'Interdependance des Marches* (Brussels, 1938).

[26] For a complementary approach to the acceleration principle, see S. C. Tsiang, "Accelerator, theory of the firm, and the business cycle," *Quarterly Journal of Economics,* 1951.

1. surplus capacity;
2. replacement investment; and
3. expectations about demand, and the related questions of prices and profits.

1.

It is not easy to find the rationale for the acceleration principle. It is often called the acceleration principle of derived demand. The theory of derived demand as applied to investment tells us that a rise in the stock of capital equipment will continue only if there is at some stage an increase in consumption.[27] But this is not the same as saying, with the acceleration principle, that a given percentage rise in consumption must be met by an equal percentage rise in the stock of capital equipment. There appeared very soon the qualification that where surplus capacity exists the acceleration principle is not valid. In other words, the necessary assumption for the acceleration principle is that firms should be working at full capacity. J. M. Clark in his first article on the acceleration principle made this assumption quite clear when he wrote:

> . . . the first increase in demand for finished products can be taken care of by utilising the excess producing capacity which an industry using much machinery habitually carries over a period of depression. Thus they do not need to buy more equipment the instant the demand begins to increase.[28]

Many subsequent writers have noted that full capacity is a prerequisite for the acceleration principle but not one that is likely to be satisfied in the early stages of a cyclical upswing. That the accelerator is asymmetrical as between upswing and downswing has been argued by Tinbergen:

> Very strong decreases in consumers' goods production must not occur. If the principle were right, they would lead to a corresponding disinvestment and this can only take place to the extent of replacement. If annual replacement amounts to 10 percent of the stock of capital goods, then a larger decrease in this stock than 10 percent per annum is impossible. A decrease in consumers' goods production of 15 percent could not lead to a 15 percent decrease in physical capital as the acceleration principle would require. It is interesting that this limit is sharper the greater the duration of life of the capital goods considered.[29]

[27]Cf. the lengthy discussion in M. Bouniatian, *Les Crises Economiques* (Paris, 1922), esp. pp. 234ff.
[28]*Op. cit., Readings,* p. 244.
[29]Tinbergen, *op. cit., Economica,* 1938, p. 165.

This criticism is generally accepted; and it is agreed that the acceleration principle can make but little contribution to the explanation of the lower turning point. Many writers, however, argue that surplus capacity is exhausted during the upswing.[30] On this view the principle is useful for the analysis of the downturn and of long-run growth.

The matter is allowed to rest there by most writers; but not by all. Tinbergen stresses that it is only when production has reached full capacity that "the necessity of the principle's action recurs;"[31] and he argues that statistical evidence shows that this condition is rarely, if ever, satisfied.[32] The arguments and assumptions that have been surveyed so far make this a challenging criticism. Two things, however, must be borne in mind:

(*a*) The terms "capacity" and "surplus capacity" (and its variants "excess" and "unused" capacity) are much bandied about in discussions of the acceleration principle, but they are not defined.

(*b*) It is true to say that full capacity is commonly taken as a prerequisite for the acceleration principle, and that this full capacity is apparently looked upon as some *ne plus ultra* beyond which output cannot be expanded without the addition of capital equipment. There are, however, some writers who have queried whether this assumption is consistent with some of the conclusions derived from the acceleration principle; and others who query whether it is a necessary assumption.

In its simplest form the acceleration principle postulates that an increase in the rate of growth of output is accompanied simultaneously by a rise in net

[30] E.g., F. A. Burchardt, "The causes of unemployment," in Oxford Institute of Statistics, *The Economics of Full Employment* (Oxford, 1947), p. 29.
Haberler, *op. cit.*, p. 96.
A. H. Hansen, *Fiscal Policy and Business Cycles* (New York, 1941), p. 282.
Hicks, *Trade Cycle, op. cit.*, ch. IV.
W. Röpke, *Crises and Cycles* (London, 1936), p. 104.
Somers, *op. cit.*, p. 102.
Wilson, *op. cit.*, pp. 45–46.
Perhaps a word should be devoted to Manne's treatment of this capacity problem. He seeks to get round the difficulties experienced by the accelerator by relating changes in output to variations in the amount of equipment actually employed. The results of his correlations are much better than those obtained by correlating changes in output with changes in the stock of equipment. This is an interesting way of looking at the principle, but one that smacks a little of tautology. This is particularly so if we take this approach to its logical conclusion and include in the dependent variable not merely variations in the amount of equipment used, but also in the intensity with which it is used. Cf. Manne, *op. cit.*, pp. 94–96.

[31] *Op. cit., Economica,* 1938, p. 166.

[32] *Ibid.*, p. 167, and "Critical remarks on some business cycle theories," *Econometrica,* 1942, p. 139. See also R. G. Hawtrey, review of Bouniatian, *Les Crises Economiques* (ed. 2), *Economic Journal,* 1932, p. 437: "The productive power of the community is *never* fully employed even at times of intense activity. It would seem to follow that the appearance of an increased demand for consumption goods does not in itself require additional capital equipment, but merely the fuller employment of that which already exists." (Hawtrey's italics.)

investment. In its more complex forms there are many variants of the lags involved, but they all agree that the rise in investment does not come first.[33] This is not possible when the economy is working at full capacity. Output cannot rise until additional capital equipment has been produced and installed; and in an economy where the process of production has become very roundabout this gestation period is long. Moreover, the problem is not restricted to one of lags. A long gestation period may cause variations in the accelerator; but this problem is left until II (3).[34]

The second doubt raised in (*b*) is whether full capacity is a necessary assumption for the acceleration principle. Tinbergen thinks so; Clark does not. He suggests that there is always some surplus capacity in the economy and that it is fully compatible with the acceleration principle.[35] Are we to interpret this as a real conflict of view or merely as a difference of definition? It is not possible to say, because no definitions are given. It will be useful therefore to outline the possible definitions of capacity and to inquire into their implications for the acceleration principle.

At least four principal definitions of capacity appear in various economic writings:

(*a*) In terms of the single firm, the point at which its average total cost curve becomes vertical. This definition is hardly realistic, for it implies that "all of the strategic factor (plant and machinery) is operated at maximum speed and none is strictly idle for any of the 168 hours in a week."[36]

(*b*) "Practicable" capacity: i.e., the output that a firm can maintain for a reasonable period with a given plant, making due allowance for such factors as seasonal fluctuations, repairs, obsolescence, and custom and regulations governing hours of work.[37] Capacity here is less than under (*a*). The definition is more realistic, but precision is lost.

(*c*) The output at a firm's minimum average total cost. "At that point the differential cost of added output will be equal to the average cost, including all overhead costs on account of the machine itself. Beyond that point it will pay to get more machines. This point might furnish a theoretical measure of capacity, but one that would be hard to apply."[38]

[33] For a summary, cf. Somers, *op. cit.*, pp. 77–80.

[34] Cf. pp. 71–72.

[35] "Additional note . . .", *Readings, op. cit.*, pp. 256–257. This is a later work than that quoted on p. 55.

[36] R. Noyes, "Certain problems in the empirical study of costs," *American Economic Review*, 1941, p. 482.

[37] The attempt was made to "limit our estimates to what would be practically attainable under conditions of 'sustained simultaneous operations'." E. G. Nourse *et al.*, *America's Capacity to Produce* (Washington, 1934), p. 23.

[38] J. M. Clark, *Studies in the Economics of Overhead Costs* (Chicago, 1923), p. 91. This definition may give the same result as (*a*) if the average total cost curve has the particular shape

(*d*) Where marginal cost equals marginal revenue. This is a useful supplement to the other definitions when imperfect competition is under discussion; but for present purposes it has serious drawbacks. So far as firms seek to maximise profits they will usually be operating at capacity in this sense; and an increased demand may lead to a rise in the stock of capital or—equally well if we are discussing the economy—in price. The definition can have little meaning for the acceleration principle and may be ignored.

So much for the definitions—what are their implications for the acceleration principle? When the firms of an economy are working at full capacity in the sense of definition (*a*) the common view is apparently that the acceleration principle is inexorably valid. As pointed out on page 57 this neglects some problems, which are being left until II (3). At the moment the point at issue is the doubt whether this capacity is often attained. Breakdowns may occur; single shift working may be customary; or the organisations of firms may not be as efficient as possible; and so on. For these same reasons, however, the presence of surplus capacity in the sense (*a*) does not necessarily invalidate the acceleration principle. There is in fact some *prima facie* reason for using definition (*b*); but this may be rejected in favour of (*c*).

The acceleration principle may be given a simple rational basis. It may be interpreted to mean that entrepreneurs will meet a rise in demand by expanding their plant, where the cost of producing the extra output with the existing plant exceeds the operating cost with the enlarged plant plus the costs of purchasing and installing it. If we assume with the acceleration principle that changes in output are the only forces making for investment, we may conclude that there is no incentive for investment before the least cost point is reached,[39] and an increasing incentive the further beyond that point output goes.[40] Definition (*c*) is the most useful.

This interpretation enables us to reach some tentative conclusions about capacity and the acceleration principle. It is possible to admit the existence of surplus capacity as defined by (*a*) or (*b*) and to argue that the acceleration principle is a useful theory. Some such difference on the rationale of the principle may lie at the basis of the divergent views held by Clark and Tinbergen. Even if this is the explanation of the conflict of conclusion,

attributed to it by some writers: i.e., falling to the point of least cost and then rising vertically. The validity of this hypothesis is questionable and it need not detain us here. Cf. W. J. Eiteman, "Factors determining the location of the least cost point," *American Economic Review*, 1947, and "The least cost point, capacity, and marginal analysis," *ibid.*, 1948; and W. H. Haines, "Capacity production and the least cost point," *ibid.*, 1948.

[39]Cf. C. D. Long, *Building Cycles and the Theory of Investment* (Princeton, 1940), pp. 59–60.

[40]It should be remembered that the acceleration principle deals with the investment of existing firms. Cf. p. 51.

Tinbergen's stress on the volitional nature of investment is justified. There is nothing inevitable about investment, as the simpler version of the acceleration principle would have us believe. Tinbergen, however, presses rather too far the conclusion he derives from the capacity argument.[41] The aspect of the acceleration principle that is challenged by the vagueness of full capacity is its usefulness in explaining the timing of investment. From the moment at which least cost output is passed there is a possibility of investment; but there is no knowing just when the decision to invest will be taken. On the other hand this conclusion does not question the aspect of the acceleration principle that apparently gives it its major appeal. It is only reasonable to expect that when an entrepreneur invests, the amount of his investment is governed in some measure by a comparison of the output he can most efficiently produce with his existing plant and the output at which demand conditions now justify him in aiming. The timing and volume of investment are not fully independent. But they are sufficiently so to justify this conclusion: provided that output does not fall below the least-cost points of the firms in an economy, we may query the validity of the acceleration principle in explaining the timing of investment but not the volume.

The inadequacy of the acceleration principle in matters of timing is emphasised by other considerations. If net investment is to be strictly a function of the rate of growth of output, then the units into which the stock of capital equipment is divisible must be the same as those into which output is divisible. This point has been developed by Kuznets. On the assumption of perfect foresight, and of a certain period within which plant cannot be varied, he shows that where demand alters during this period the entrepreneur maximises his profits by having a plant of such size that part of it stands idle for some of the time.[42] His analysis suffers, however, in that he does not clearly show what determines this period within which plant is not varied. There are three principal reasons:

(*a*) The technical factor. Capital equipment may be bulky, and the employment of additional plant is justified only when output has risen considerably.[43] This factor is all the more important because usually what is added is a complex of machines and not a machine.

(*b*) The extension of plant may interfere with current output directly and will almost certainly do so indirectly through a diversion of managerial energies.[44] There are thus likely to be lulls in investment.

[41] *Op. cit., Economica,* 1938, esp. p. 167.

[42] *Op. cit.,* pp. 231-236.

[43] Long, *op. cit.,* pp. 61-2: "For example, paper-making machines for the manufacture of newsprint paper come only in million dollar units capable of producing one-fourth the requirements of a good-sized plant and characterised by great durability."

[44] Hultgren, *op. cit.,* p. 167, who writes that as a result of such factors "no one railroad

(*c*) The addition of plant may enhance the entrepreneur's uncertainty. He is now faced with the development of new markets to absorb his expanded output.[45] This factor, however, is possibly unimportant when discussing purely induced investment.

There can be little doubt that investment in the single firm is essentially a discontinuous process. Whether similar lulls will occur in the investment activity of the entire economy is not readily apparent. The process of aggregation may smooth them over; but it is difficult to believe that the timing of investment will be that suggested by the acceleration principle.

The literature on capacity and the acceleration principle is rambling, and in setting out and weighing the various arguments we have rambled with it. Our conclusions may nevertheless be stated briefly. It is not possible to devise a definition of capacity that is both realistic and precise. The acceleration principle, therefore, is not precise; but it draws attention to a possible reason for investment so long as firms are operating along the rising segment of their average total-cost curves. The effects of this lack of precision may be summed up by saying that the acceleration principle is unsatisfactory as an explanation of the timing of investment. It suffers from a further weakness: it is not of much use for explaining the lower turning point. But a rider must be added to this earlier criticism: it is valid only where output in all firms has fallen below their least-cost points.

2.

In his first outline of the acceleration principle[46] Clark assumes that net investment is a function of the rate of growth of output, but that replacement depends on its level. The implications of this thesis about replacement have interested many writers; but largely the assumption itself has been accepted. Pigou notes that as net investment falls replacement may rise and offset the depressing effects of this fall.[47] Frisch attaches even more importance to this qualification. He shows that the extent to which replacement may offset net investment depends on (i) the speed with which the rate of growth of output is falling, and (ii) the sizes of the two categories of investment. It is in fact

typically buys cars in continuous driblets; or at any rate small repetitive purchases can hardly account for any large part of total orders." Cf. also W. W. Heller, "The anatomy of investment decisions," *Harvard Business Review,* March 1951, p. 102: "One of the unforeseen—and most interesting—investment barriers was the bottleneck in top engineering and management talent."

[45] Cf. G. L. S. Shackle, *Expectations, Investment, and Income* (London, 1938), pp. 99–100.

[46] "Business acceleration . . . ," *op. cit., Readings,* p. 238.

[47] A. C. Pigou, *Industrial Fluctuations* (London, 1929, ed. 2), p. 110.

quite conceivable that total capital production may approach some constant level.[48] Since Frisch's statement of the problem, the argument has waxed and waned. Hansen censors Harrod for his neglect of the movements of replacement.[49] Clark[50] and Somers[51] recognise the strict validity of Frisch's criticism, but doubt whether circumstances often arise to make it really important. Samuelson defends the neglect of replacement with an argument[52] that is ingenious but also somewhat spurious in that it equates replacement with depreciation.

No single conclusion emerges from this discussion. This uncertainty about the effects of replacement on the acceleration principle is heightened by the fact that it is not universally accepted that replacement is a function solely of the level of output. Haberler, for example, assumes that it depends on the age of equipment, and that therefore replacement cycles will reflect earlier fluctuations in investment.[53] Kuznets works out the various possible models in some detail.[54] Whether replacement cycles coincide with those in net investment depends on (i) the life of capital equipment, all of which is assumed to last for a constant period, and (ii) the behaviour of gross investment in the relevant past period that is indicated by (i). The importance of the resulting replacement cycles in determining the turning points of gross investment depends on the relative volume of replacement and of net investment: that is, on the past behaviour of gross investment and on the present rate of growth of output.

The age hypothesis has in its turn been qualified in a number of ways in the literature on the acceleration principle:

[48] R. Frisch, "The interrelation between capital production and consumer-taking," *Journal of Political Economy,* 1931, pp. 649–652, and subsequent articles in *ibid.,* April and October 1932. This criticism of replacement is the issue usually associated with these articles; but, emphasised though it was by Frisch, it was not his principal worry. He was mainly concerned to make quite clear that the acceleration principle did not provide a closed model of the cycle. Cf. also his "Propagation problems . . . ," *op. cit.*

[49] A. H. Hansen, *Full Recovery or Stagnation?* (London, 1938), p. 49.

[50] J. M. Clark, "Capital production and consumer-taking—a reply," *Journal of Political Economy,* 1931, and a later article in *ibid.,* October 1932.

[51] Somers, *op. cit.,* pp. 75–76.

[52] ". . . It would involve double-counting to include in the computation of the national income both consumption and the replacement expenditures imputable as costs of that consumption. Only net investment is "multiplied" to give the national income; as a first approximation Harrod was justified in neglecting replacement in the formal relation." *Op. cit., Journal of Political Economy,* 1939, p. 796. Long, *op. cit.,* pp. 78–82, presents the same argument at greater length.

[53] Haberler, *op. cit.,* p. 91.

[54] Kuznets, *op. cit.,* pp. 221–225. Kuznets reserves the Frisch-Clark assumption for such types of investments as traders' stocks. Cf. *ibid.,* pp. 217–218 and his comment on Frisch's analysis of replacement, p. 219 fn.

(*a*) Somers points out that replacement depends partly on the "extent to which capital goods are used to produce 'finished' products (in so far as depreciation is a function of use, i.e. through wear and tear or direct use in the process of production)."[55]

(*b*) Kuznets qualifies his assumption about the importance of the age of machines, and shows that, given a constant rate of obsolescence, it will pay to replace earlier at a higher level of output than at a lower.[56] He errs, however, in concluding that this substantiates Frisch's conclusions.[57] Durability and hence age have to be given some place in the theory, as Kuznets recognises when he writes that the level of output will influence the replacement of only those items of equipment as are "sufficiently near the end of their average period of life to be affected by the change in the prospective savings from the installation of new units . . ."[58]

(*c*) Finally, Hicks has adduced two factors on which many elaborate echo effects have been based[59]: (i) capital goods do not have the same life-span, and (ii) they do not even have precise life-spans. From these two qualifications of the age hypothesis he concludes that replacement cycles will after a time become so damped that they may be ignored.[60]

In sum, a survey of the literature on replacement and the acceleration principle yields a bewildering number of conclusions. As with other aspects of the theory of investment, this variety of results reflects the complexity of the subject and our lack of empirical knowledge. The most that we can hope for, therefore, is to narrow somewhat the area of doubt. In particular we may be able to resolve the question whether replacement does or does not falsify conclusions drawn from the acceleration principle, although we may not be able to state the precise extent of this falsification.

We must consider whether it is possible to distinguish clearly between net and replacement investment. What is relevant in determining whether a particular act of investment has added to or merely maintained the stock of capital is "whether a person maintains a stock of non-permanent resources which will secure him an increasing, constant, or decreasing income stream, not whether the stock itself increases, remains constant, or decreases in any of

[55]Somers, *op. cit.*, p. 74. It should be noted that, contrary to what Somers implies, this yields the same result as the Frisch-Clark hypothesis only by ignoring the age of equipment.

[56]Kuznets, *op. cit.*, pp. 238–243.

[57]*Ibid.*, p. 243.

[58]*Ibid.*, p. 241.

[59]The outstanding discussion of these echo effects is probably R. Frisch, "Sammenhengen mellem primaerinvestering og reinvestering" *Statsøkonomisk Tidsskrift*, 1927, pp. 117–152. Cf. also J. Tinbergen, "Annual survey: suggestions on quantitative business cycle theory," *Econometrica*, 1935, pp. 288–291.

[60]Hicks, *Trade Cycle*, *op. cit.*, pp. 41–42.

its directly measurable dimensions."[61] This being so we can assess the effects of investment only where it is possible to foresee with certainty the future income stream to be yielded by the new equipment. In the uncertain world of reality this cannot be done. Replacement and net investment cannot be clearly distinguished from one another. This conclusion may be supported by a second argument. By and large, firms when replacing machines install something larger or better.[62] The new equipment is both net investment and replacement. Even if it were possible to determine *ex post* what part of investment is net and what part replacement, the distinction would be artificial. At the same time, we must recognise that the distinction has not been adhered to by so many writers without good reason. It is useful in analysing the motives for investment. There are some motives that are peculiarly concerned with replacing equipment, and others with adding to it.[63] In discussing the rationale of gross investment it is necessary to consider both sets of forces and then the results of their interplay.

The acceleration principle errs in discussing net investment where it should discuss gross. For all that it can be condemned for concentrating on net only when it is shown that the result is a distorted theory of net investment. The problem of distinguishing between net and replacement is *prima facie* evidence that such a distortion exists. To test the adequacy of this conclusion we must now examine the nature of the factors that make for replacement. Is there such flexibility in the timing of replacement investment that entrepreneurs undertake it only when it is convenient to add to their plant? Or do they add to their plant when the time is suitable for replacement?

Assuming that firms seek to maximise profits, there is an incentive to replace when the present value of the anticipated stream of profits from the new machines minus that from the old is greater than the price of the new machine minus the "scrap" value of the old.[64] This may be written:

$$\pi_{1t} - \pi_{2t} > P_{1t} - S_{2t} \tag{1}$$

The subscript 1 refers to the new machines, while 2 refers to the old. The

[61] F. A. Hayek, *The Pure Theory of Capital* (London, 1941), pp. 300–301.

[62] Cf. R. P. Mack, *The Flow of Business Funds and Consumer Purchasing Power* (New York, 1941), pp. 251–52; and Heller, *op. cit.*, p. 100: "Replacement is seldom made without improvement. A worn-out piece of equipment is rarely replaced with an identical item".

[63] Cf. J. Tinbergen and J. J. Polak, *The Dynamics of Business Cycles* (London, 1950), p. 176; and M. Gort, "The planning of investment: a study of capital budgeting in the electric-power industry, I," *Journal of Business of the University of Chicago*, 1951, p. 85.

[64] This discussion of the motives for replacing equipment is based on:

J. Einarsen, *Reinvestment Cycles and their Manifestation in the Norwegian Shipping Industry* (Oslo, 1938), which contains a useful survey of the earlier literature; and his "Reinvestment cycles," *Review of Economic Statistics*, 1938.

Mack, *op. cit.*, ch. 8.

subscript t refers to the time period. π stands for aggregate profit. P is a composite of the purchase price of the new machines and of the total costs of installation. Lastly, S represents "scrap" value, where that is interpreted to mean (i) the price equipment can fetch on the second-hand market or as junk, and (ii) the alternative uses to which the firm may put it, either by holding it in reserve or by using it for some task requiring less precision.

Equation (1) may be rewritten in terms of operating costs:

$$\sum_{t}^{t+n} \frac{Y}{(1+i)^n}(c_2 - c_1) > P_{1t} - S_{2t} \qquad (2)$$[65]

Y is the anticipated stream of output over future periods up to period $t + n$. c_1 is the average cost of production with the new machines, and c_2 with the old. n should represent the economic life of the new equipment. The problem is how to determine *ex ante* this economic life. To do so properly we must bc able to foresee the future course of technical development of the equipment

J. Meuldijk, "Der Englische Schiffbau wahrend der Period 1870–1912 und das Problem des Ersatzbaues," *Weltwirtschaftliches Archiv,* 640.

National Bureau of Economic Research, *Cost Behavior and Price Policy* (New York, 1943), ch. VII, sections 3 and 4; and appendix C.

R. C. Blanchard, "A replacement policy that shares responsibility," *American Machinist,* 1931, pp. 729–740.

A series of articles by P. T. Norton, G. S. Tracey, R. F. Runge, H. K. Spencer, H. P. Bailey, J. H. Jackson, and D. S. Linton, *ibid,* 1935.

P. de Wolff, "The demand for passenger cars in the United States," *Econometrica,* 638.

G. Terborgh, *Dynamic Equipment Policy* (New York, 1949).

S. L. Horner, *et al, Dynamics of Automobile Demand* (General Motors Corporation, 1939).

Cf. also, J. S. Bain, "The relation of the economic life of equipment to reinvestment cycles," *Review of Economic Statistics,* 1939; and B. Caplan, "Premature abandonment of machinery," *Review of Economic Studies,* 640.

[65] The derivation of equation (2) from (1) is:

$$\pi_{1t} = \sum_{t}^{t+n} \frac{rY}{(1+i)^n} - \sum_{t}^{t+n} \frac{c_1 Y}{(1+i)^n}$$

$$\pi_{2t} = \sum_{t}^{t+n} \frac{rY}{(1+i)^n} - \sum_{t}^{t+n} \frac{c_2 Y}{(1+i)^n}$$

where r is the price at which output sells. Substituting for π_{1t} and π_{2t} in (1),

$$\sum_{t}^{t+n} \frac{rY}{(1+i)^n} - \sum_{t}^{t+n} \frac{c_1 Y}{(1+i)^n} - \sum_{t}^{t+n} \frac{rY}{(1+i)^n} + \sum_{t}^{t+n} \frac{c_2 Y}{(1+i)^n} > P_{1t} - S_{2t}$$

$$\therefore \sum_{t}^{t+n} \frac{Y}{(1+i)^n}(c_2 - c_1) > P_{1t} - S_{2t} \qquad (2)$$

over all time.[66] This degree of foresight is impossible, and it appears that in consequence firms fall back on rule-of-thumb methods. *n*, therefore, is arbitrary and also short. The bulk of equipment is expected to pay for itself in at most 5 years.[67] Lastly, *i* is the rate of interest used in discounting.

It is possible to draw some conclusions about the various hypotheses summarised on pp. 60–62 by examining how each of the items in equation (2) is likely to behave during the trade cycle. When we are thinking of the economy as a whole, *Y* must stand for gross national income. The influence of *Y* is then clear. It stimulates replacement in the upswing, and stimulates it the more the stronger is the upswing. Similarly *Y* makes for the postponement of replacement in the downswing. Its influence is possibly stronger than appears from equation (2). It is often difficult to know just when the saving on any machine or group of machines is sufficient to justify replacement.[68] The timing of replacement may be a matter of chance: when somebody in the plant or a visiting salesman happens to notice the possibility of lowering costs by replacing some equipment. More likely, attention is given to replacement when times are good and funds are available. Funds come primarily from gross profits. In so far as these vary with *Y*, the influence of *Y* on replacement is strengthened. The pull exerted on replacement by *Y* is at the basis of Kuznets's qualification of the age hypothesis[69]; and thus possibly, as he argues, underlies the assumption made by other writers that replacement depends solely on the level of output. Undoubtedly, *Y* has a powerful effect on replacement, but equation (2) also points to the other forces that are at work. We must, therefore, reject this assumption. At the same time, the fluctuations of *Y* persuade entrepreneurs to take advantage of the flexibility in the life of their plant[70] to put off replacement in the downswing and to concentrate it in the upswing. This suggests that we should reject Hicks's conclusion that replacement cycles are so damped that they may be ignored.[71]

$(c_2 - c_1)$ is subject to a number of influences. The arguments outlined early in section (1),[72] that equipment falls out of use in the downswing and that in

[66] We can decide how long to keep the new machine only when we know how soon a superior model will appear. But simply to know the time of appearance of the first superior model is not sufficient. It may pay to ignore it and wait for the second model, if, when the first appears, further developments are regarded as imminent. And so on for the third and subsequent models.

[67] The published evidence relates to American manufacturing industry and is summarised in Terborgh, *op. cit.*, Ch. XII.

[68] This point may be seen very clearly in the articles from the *American Machinist* referred to in fn. 64, p. 64. Cf. N.B.E.R., *op. cit.*, p. 326.

[69] Above, pp. 61–62.

[70] Above, pp. 61–62.

[71] Above, p. 62.

[72] Above, p. 55ff.

consequence Y can rise in the upswing faster than the stock of capital equipment, supports Somers's contention about variations in user cost.[73] User cost is likely to be greater at high levels of output than at low. There is, however, one factor that is likely to counteract the effects of the level of output on wear and tear. In general, maintenance and repairs are curtailed in the downswing, while efforts are bent towards making good the effects of neglect when output is rising.[74] One cannot say unequivocally that user cost will strengthen the tendency for replacement to rise and fall with Y. Moreover, there are forces that make $(c_2 - c_1)$ act in the opposite direction to Y. If replacement is postponed during the depression, c_1 falls relatively to c_2 for two reasons: (i) plant is getting older and therefore c_2 rises; and (ii) technical development is usually not hindered by depression and as a result the potential c_1 is always falling. It is impossible to say just how strong will be the effect of this increase in $(c_2 - c_1)$, for that depends on the rate at which Y is falling relative to the rate at which $(c_2 - c_1)$ is rising. There is no reason why the relation between these rates should be constant from cycle to cycle. It might happen that the increase in $(c_2 - c_1)$ is sufficient to cause a rise in replacement which would help to explain the lower turning point. It will certainly happen that this increase will hasten the revival of replacement when the upswing begins. On the basis of the factors considered so far, the movement of $(c_2 - c_1)$ will stimulate a considerable bunching of replacement in the early period of the upswing. If such a bunching occurs, $(c_2 - c_1)$ will offset Y in the later part of the upswing, just as it does in the later part of the downswing. This tendency to offset occurs because the early upsurge of replacement leaves industry with comparatively up-to-date equipment. That is to say, c_2 falls sharply and some time must elapse before the gradual fall in c_1 and the gradual rise in c_2 are sufficient to encourage replacement. A temporary lull in replacement is quite plausible, particularly as the other forces that lead to discontinuity of investment are effective here. But as with the upturn, one cannot say whether the fall in $(c_2 - c_1)$ will be soon enough or large enough to explain the downturn. It will help Y in inducing a postponement of replacement where once the downswing has begun. This stronger force making for postponement early in the downswing increases the possibility that $(c_2 - c_1)$ may rise sufficiently to explain the upturn, which in turn makes more plausible the argument that a fall in $(c_2 - c_1)$ accounts for the downturn. But that is all on the assumption that other things are equal; and it is more likely that other things change to at least some extent from cycle to cycle. It assumes, moreover, that the entrepreneur always knows just when replacement is worth while; and, as we have seen, this is by no means

[73]Above, p. 62.
[74]Cf. Hultgren, *op. cit.*, pp. 169–175.

always a valid assumption. Finally, it assumes that we are discussing firms that are not growing rapidly. In rapidly expanding firms the age distribution of equipment is likely to be so skewed that no bunching of replacement occurs early in the upswing.[75] For our present purposes this qualification may be neglected, because it is doubtful whether the acceleration principle has much significance for such firms anyhow.[76] All in all, we must view with caution the thesis that replacement explains the turning points; but it is interesting to note that the movements of $(c_2 - c_1)$ may yield the same effects as the echo theories[77] and without their special assumptions about the lifetime of machines. Indeed, a consideration of the various forces affecting $(c_2 - c_1)$ helps us to see that, while the age structure of equipment is important, replacement cannot be regarded as a simple function of age. Furthermore, $(c_2 - c_1)$ makes it quite clear why it is impossible to accept the thesis that replacement depends solely on Y. One implication of this conclusion is that we cannot accept Frisch's contention that gross investment may approach asymptotically some level and stay there.

The behaviour of P and S need not detain us for long. P consists of the prices of capital equipment and of the costs of installing it. Kalecki's index of the prices of capital goods shows that they do not change much, and that such changes as do occur show no consistent pattern *vis-à-vis* the cycle.[78] The costs of installation include both direct costs and also indirect costs in the form of interference with current production and the diversion of managerial energies. Their effects have already been discussed and the conclusion has been reached that generalisation is hazardous. So far as they may be significant they have already been allowed for in the discussion about $(c_2 - c_1)$. S probably supports the effects of Y. Both the second-hand market and alternative opportunities improve as Y rises and deteriorate as it falls. It is difficult, however, to assess the significance of S.

The general conclusion to be derived from this discussion is that we may point to certain factors that have a significant influence on replacement. Furthermore, the analysis shows that we must reject the various hypotheses outlined at the beginning of this section. We cannot regard replacement as a function solely of Y or of age; nor can we safely assume that replacement cycles gently die away. To go beyond this, however, is most difficult. This is so for two reasons: (*a*) we cannot say at what stage of the cycle replacement becomes profitable or unprofitable; and (*b*) even if we knew the answer to this question, we should still be unable to say much on the timing of

[75] Cf. Horner, *op. cit.*, chart 12, p. 49.

[76] Cf. p. 51.

[77] See Einarsen *op. cit.;* and Tinbergen, *op. cit.*, *Econometrica,* 1935.

[78] M. Kalecki, *Essays in the Theory of Economic Fluctuations* (London, 1938), p. 39, table 3. This index should, perhaps, be viewed with caution.

replacement. The major reason for the first difficulty is the problem of predicting the behaviour of $(c_2 - c_1)$ relative to that of the other forces in the cycle. To do this we should require a closed model, and one based on a more complete theory of investment than the fragment under discussion here. The second difficulty arises from the fact that equation (2) tells us when replacement becomes profitable, but not when the decision to replace is taken. We are thwarted in our attempt to state the behaviour of gross investment influenced by motives for expansion as well as those for replacement. We can say no more, therefore, than that it is difficult, if not impossible, to separate replacement from net investment; and that there are strong forces acting on the motive for replacement. It is in consequence unlikely that gross investment will slavishly follow the pattern suggested by the acceleration principle. It is a weak conclusion, and clearly we must pursue our inquiries further.

3.

In general the acceleration principle is expressed as a theory relating current output to current investment. Sometimes lags are introduced and investment is regarded as a function of the changes in output during a past period. A number of critics have made the pertinent comment that no satisfactory theory of investment can be constructed without some provision for expectations. Indeed even the simplest formulation of the acceleration principle contains an implicit assumption about the future behaviour of output: it is expected to remain at the level which it has just reached. There is no dispute whether the assumptions made about anticipations affect the acceleration principle. The difference of opinion turns on the nature of that effect. There are three main schools of thought.

Professor Tinbergen stresses the distorting effects of errors of judgment. The ideal at which the entrepreneur aims in the adjustment of his capital equipment may be "the adaptation as set out by the acceleration principle. But since the adaptation must always be directed towards an unknown future demand for consumers' goods, it is only natural that errors may be committed."[79] The consequence, Tinbergen argues, is that the acceleration principle cannot accurately depict the formation of investment decisions. Other writers take the view that the explicit introduction of expectations helps to explain why statistical studies have in general yielded such unfavourable results for the acceleration principle. Such studies have sought the degree of

[79]Tinbergen, *Econometrica*, 1942, p. 139; cf. also J. M. Clark, *Strategic Factors*, *op. cit.*, p. 40; and Pigou, *op. cit.*, p. 108, esp. footnote. Clark and Pigou do not find these errors in forecasting very harmful to the acceleration principle.

correlation between all changes in output and all changes in the stock of capital equipment. A. S. Manne has suggested that since the entrepreneur is gifted with a certain measure of foresight he will be able to distinguish, at least in part, between those changes in the demand for his product that are purely transitory and those changes that justify some extension or contraction of his plant.[80] If this is so, empirical research must make some distinction between these categories of movements in demand. It will be noted, however, that this attempt to shield the acceleration principle from one criticism reinforces the argument that investment is discontinuous.[81] *Prima facie* another attempt to show that the acceleration principle can be made more useful by the introduction of anticipations is that by Professor Wright. Wright, however, uses the phrase "acceleration principle" to refer to the purely technical relationship outlined on pages 51–53. His introduction of expectations results in a complete rejection of the principle that is being discussed here. "We can take the matter further," he writes, "and divorce [investment] altogether from consumption,"[82] making it depend on autonomous changes in entrepreneurial expectations or on innovations. His attitude, therefore, is more akin to Tinbergen's than to Manne's.

Many writers who refer to the effects of expectations on the acceleration principle are eclectic and recognise that there are valid elements in the arguments for and against the principle.

> The supposition which underlies the rigid application of the acceleration principle is that the present level of demand is assumed to rule in the future also. Now it is very doubtful whether it is possible to generalise as to the exact behaviour of producers in this respect. Fortunately for the broad result, however, it is sufficient to indicate a certain range of expectations as probable and to eliminate others as highly unlikely.[83]

There can be no doubt that the eclectic approach is the safest one in view of our very restricted knowledge of how expectations are formed. The position has been summed up very aptly by Bissell: only when we have a workable theory of expectations shall we know just how far the acceleration principle

[80]Manne, *op. cit.*, pp. 96–97. See also, J. W. Angell, *Investment and Business Cycles* (New York, 1941); "Regardless of the state of present demand, entrepreneurs will not increase present capacity unless their anticipations for the future warrant the step." (p. 89, fn.).

Kuznets argues, *op. cit.*, p. 229, that the more durable the capital equipment the more wary will the entrepreneur be before he installs additional equipment in response to a rise in demand. This is true, however, only on certain assumptions about the age structure of existing equipment.

[81]Cf. above, p. 60.

[82]D. McC. Wright, "A neglected approach to the acceleration principle," *Review of Economic Statistics*, 1941, p. 101.

[83]Haberler, *op. cit.*, p. 343; and also pp. 102 and 306. Cf. Somers, *op. cit.*, pp. 83–86 and Long, *op. cit.*, pp. 44–55.

must be qualified.[84] One or two comments, however, are possible in an attempt to limit somewhat the range of uncertainty about anticipations and the acceleration principle.

To some extent memories of the past affect reactions to the events of the present. Firms that have known violent fluctuations in the demand for their output are likely to be hesitant about expanding their plant in the face of a current growth in demand.[85] The result is that during the course of a trade cycle different firms will respond to market changes with differing speeds and to differing degrees; and their various reactions will depend on their past experiences.[86]

A second factor that delimits somewhat the applicability of the acceleration principle is that firms in their investment policy may be concerned with distant possibilities that are divorced from the current movements of markets.[87] Strictly, however, this takes us into the territory of those criticisms that query the importance of induced investment. This territory is out of bounds.

In the light of these two arguments we may say that the acceleration principle is fully applicable only to induced investment in firms that have not suffered too greatly from ups and downs of demand. With regard to the firms that have not so suffered, we seek here to discuss only one qualification to the acceleration principle. In a world of imperfect foresight what effect has the current level of profits on the confidence with which entrepreneurs view the future? This involves us in the arguments as to the relative merits of the profits principle and the acceleration principle. It is more convenient to consider the effects of profits on anticipations together with these other arguments.

[84]Bissell, *op. cit.*, p. 34.

[85]E.g., the policy of the United States Steel Corporation as recorded in S. D. Merlin, *The Theory of Fluctuations in Contemporary Economic Thought*, p. 117, fn. 54. Also, Heller, *op. cit.*, p. 100: "There has been some tendency to regard the 1946–1950 markets as 'too good to be true'. Productive capacity has been held below levels needed to meet peak demands because the long-run plateau was expected to be lower."

[86]In so far as the firms with the most unpleasant memories are in the capital goods industries, some such hesitation to invest even when faced by sharply rising demand must lie at the basis of the explanation of the downturn given by Goodwin, especially in *op. cit.*, *Econometrica*, 1951, and by Clark in *Overhead Costs*, *op. cit.*, pp. 393–394. Clark and Goodwin suggest that the rate of growth of income is slowed down by this reluctance of the capital goods industries to add to their equipment.

It will be noted that in this section we abandon the simplifying assumption that output and demand may be treated as one.

[87]D. H. Robertson, *Essays in Monetary Theory* (London, 1939), p. 179; and Lundberg, *op. cit.*, p. 254. For some empirical evidence that raises doubts about the importance of these long-range anticipations, cf. Gort, *op. cit.*, pp. 81–84. It will be noted, moreover, that the introduction of expectations makes it exceptionally difficult to maintain the distinction between autonomous and induced investment. It is not discussed here in order to limit the scope of this paper.

The case for the profits principle, which has been put most forcefully by Tinbergen,[88] rests on two arguments: (*a*) in the uncertain world of reality the entrepreneur falls back on rule-of-thumb methods in trying to evaluate the future, and the present level of profits provides that rule-of-thumb; and (*b*) firms prefer internal sources of finance and thus profits must have a dominating influence on investment. He supports his theoretical arguments with correlation analyses of a number of time series. The profits principle has more than one form. It is sometimes argued that the level of profits determines the level of investment; and sometimes that what is important is the rate of profit, where this "is determined *grosso modo* by the level of national income and the stock of capital equipment."[89] There are arguments in favour of both these theses, but they favour the second more than the first.

Let us examine first profits and their effect on expectations. It is not plausible to argue that expectations will be based solely on the rule-of-thumb provided by the current level of profits. If entrepreneurs are as uncertain as this implies about the future market they are unlikely to invest at all.[90] This argument is strengthened by the fact that some at least of the decisions on an investment project initiated in the present can be put off until the situation is clearer.[91] The most, therefore, that can be said of the effects of profits is that they may distort expectations. It is worth dwelling a little longer on this distortion. It is likely to be the more severe the longer is the gestation period. When the gestation period is long a rise in demand will be met by a rise in price rather than by an increase in output. The individual producer has to decide by how much demand has risen in real terms. It is reasonable to suggest that his vision is likely to be distorted.[92] We are now in a better position to see the two horns of the dilemma on which the acceleration principle finds itself.[93] On the one hand, firms may reach capacity in terms of definition (*c*).[94] Where this happens a case can be made for the acceleration principle, but one which leaves it weak in matters of timing. On the other hand, capacity in terms of definition (*a*) may be reached. Were the

[88]See in particular, his *Statistical Testing, op. cit., passim;* and Tinbergen and Polak, *op. cit.*, ch. 13.

[89]Kalecki, *op. cit.*, p. 133. Models based on both forms of profits principle are in Tinbergen and Polak, *op. cit.*, pp. 195–206.

[90]On the importance of market forecasts, see W. E. Wright, *Forecasting for Profit* (New York, 1947), pp. 2 and 10; and Heller, *op. cit.*, p. 99.

[91]Gort, *op. cit.*, p. 82; and A. G. Hart, "Anticipations, business planning, and the cycle," *Quarterly Journal of Economics,* 1937, p. 286.

[92]The effects of a long gestation period on expectations is developed at length in Aftalion, *op. cit.;* cf. also J. Tinbergen, "Ein Schiffbauzyklus?" *Weltwirtschaftliches Archiv,* 1931; T. C. Koopmans, *Tanker Freight Rates and Tankship Building* (Haarlem, 1939), pp. 165ff.; and J. A. Schumpeter, *Business Cycles* (New York, 1939), vol. II, pp. 533–535.

[93]Cf. above, p. 57.

[94]Cf. II (1), esp. p. 57.

adjustment of plant to changes in output instantaneous, the acceleration principle would explain both the timing and the amount of investment once this capacity was reached. But instantaneous adjustment is not possible. Moreover, the gestation period must grow if, during an upswing, more and more firms reach capacity (*a*). In short, where there is surplus capacity according to definition (*a*) the acceleration principle encounters one serious obstacle; and where such surplus capacity does not exist it encounters another.[95]

The above argument, so far as it supports the profits principle, favours the level of profits as a determinant of investment. The case for this variant of the profits principle can be strengthened. The acceleration principle assumes (*a*) that where a firm needs outside capital for an investment programme it has no hesitation whatever in seeking it, and (*b*) that the supply of credit is perfectly elastic. We are here concerned with (*a*).[96] It is an unwarranted assumption. There is some evidence that firms prefer internal sources of finance to borrowing either short or long.[97] Profits are a major source of internal finance. The level of profits is, therefore, a major factor in determining how much a firm can invest and when it invests. Profits exercise, therefore, over both the amount and the timing of investment, an influence that is permissive,[98] except in so far as the availability of funds stimulates some inquiry into the openings for investment[99] or distorts expectations about such openings.

We must not, however, press too far the argument in favour of the level of profits. Undoubtedly there are strong reasons for looking upon the level of profits as the determinant of investment, but only where the openings for investment exceed the funds available.[100] A particularly important weakness of this variant of the profits principle is that it assumes that so long as profits remain at a given level, investment will continue to be constant regardless of the effects of past investment on the stock of equipment. This is not a valid assumption. "Indeed, if in a given period there is a high level of profitability

[95]It was recognition of this obstacle that led J. M. Clark to suggest that there is always some "surplus capacity". Cf. above, p. 57, and *Readings, op. cit.*, pp. 256–257.

[96]For a discussion of (*a*) and (*b*) cf. Tsiang, *op. cit.*, pp. 331–335.

[97]See, e.g., the case studies in J. K. Butters and J. Lintner, *Effect of Federal Taxes on Growing Enterprises* (Boston, 1945); and Heller, *op. cit.*, pp. 101–102.

[98]"But as repeated references to reliance on internal funds have indicated, finance is more a barrier to capital investment than a 'thrust' towards new projects." Heller, *op. cit.*, p. 101. See also the answers to the question on the "effect of the abundance or scarcity of liquid resources on investment in fixed plant", in J. E. Meade and P. W. S. Andrews, "Summary of replies to questions on the effects of interest rates," *Oxford Economic Papers*, 1938, pp. 25–8.

[99]Cf. the discussion about replacement on p. 65 above.

[100]It will be noted that once again we encounter the difficulty of distinguishing between induced and autonomous investment. Presumably they are both financed from the same source and thus their movements cannot be fully independent.

which induces investment this will not continue for the subsequent period because all investment plans will have already been undertaken under the influence of high profitability in the initial period."[101] This defect can be avoided by taking the rate of profit as the determinant of investment, for then we allow for the stock of capital equipment.

Within the restricted limits of this survey the determinants of investment may be summed up. We may write:

$$I = \beta(K_D - K_A), \text{ where}$$

(*a*) β is the inverse of the gestation period. Hitherto we have been able to treat the decision to invest and the actual execution of investment as one. The introduction of the gestation period makes it necessary to have a distinction; and I here refers to the process of investment.
(*b*) K_D is, for want of a better term, the desired level of capital stock.
(*c*) K_A is that part of the existing equipment that is considered efficient enough to be kept in operation.

This equation differs in certain respects from the acceleration principle. In the first place, it allows for some form of gestation period. In the second place, it differs as regards the timing of the decision to invest and as regards the proposed volume of investment. Thus K_D depends, for timing and amount, not solely on the level of national income but also on profits, which affect it in the ways outlined above.[102] To some extent, the essential characteristic of the acceleration principle is preserved in the difference between K_D and K_A. But, whereas the principle neglects replacement and thus the movements of K_A, those movements are allowed for in $(K_D - K_A)$. Thus I refers to gross investment, the timing and amount of which are strongly influenced by profits. That this is so is plausible in view of the difficulties experienced in II (1) and II (2), where we were discussing the timing of net and replacement investment.

III.

The acceleration principle may be criticised on three counts. It purports to give a precise explanation of the timing of investment where in fact it is vague. This is the conclusion of II (1); and it is supported in some measure

[101] M. Kalecki, "A new approach to the problem of business cycles," *Review of Economic Studies*, 1949–50, p. 61.

[102] The case for the profits principle would be strengthened if costs vary cyclically as has been suggested, e.g., by W. C. Mitchell, *Business Cycles and their Causes* (Berkeley, 1951). The case for this theory is not considered here, as it does not fall within our terms of reference.

by II (2). This latter section also suggests the inadequacy of any theory of investment that is restricted to net investment. Finally, we argued on p. 59 that there is a strong element of truth in the acceleration principle: namely, that the amount of an entrepreneur's investment is governed in some measure by a comparison of the output he can most efficiently produce with his existing plant and the output at which demand conditions now justify him in aiming. II (3), however, presents the arguments in favour of profits as a determinant of investment, both in matters of timing and of amount. Thus the essential appeal of the acceleration principle is somewhat muted, but mainly in that the level of profits may curb the enthusiasm to invest engendered by the rate of growth of output.

In sum, there is an element of truth in the acceleration principle; but it is an element that is so heavily overlaid by other factors that the acceleration principle by itself is inadequate as a theory of investment. Unfortunately, it is not at all clear what theory we should put in its place. $I = \beta(K_D - K_A)$ meets the criticisms of the acceleration principle; but it is no more than a summary behind which lie some very complex relationships. It is certainly not neat and easy to handle. Much of the appeal of the acceleration principle has lain in these very characteristics, but it may be wondered whether they should always be regarded as commending a theory of investment. There is sufficient similarity in the factors that determine investment from one cycle to the next to enable us to pick out certain salient factors and decide that those are the ones we must watch. There is not sufficient uniformity to justify our attaching fixed coefficients to these factors. The precise theory is easier to handle, but its precision should make it suspect. The many qualifications with which our conclusions have been hedged are in part an admission of ignorance; in part also they spring from a desire to avoid placing undue emphasis on the constancy of economic life.

5

CAPACITY, INVESTMENT, AND PROFITS[1]

ROBERT EISNER

Have you ever wondered what would happen in a dog race if a dog were to catch the mechanical rabbit he chases? Or what would happen to a real rabbit chasing a similarly moving carrot if the rabbit were given the carrot?

In both cases, we may presume that it is the expectation of a gain–of a rabbit or of a carrot–which sets the pace. The dog stuffed with rabbit or the rabbit stuffed with carrot would have little incentive to run.

In our economy the carrot is profits. It is the expectation of profits which sets the pace for economic activity. Our business firms will run harder if by running harder they can expect to earn greater profits.

To complete the transition from our allegory, it is reasonable and useful to explain business behavior in terms of the maximization of profits. Thus, an enterprise will invest, that is, acquire more plant and equipment or add to inventories, if by doing so it can add to profits. It should refrain from investment, no matter how high the profits it is already earning, if such investment can be expected actually to reduce earnings in the future. A firm experiencing poor earnings, even suffering losses, should certainly invest if investment will increase its earnings or reduce its losses.

This, then, is our text. In a free enterprise economy in which firms endeavor to maximize their profits, investment is determined by the expectation of additional profits (or reduced losses) which would result from the

[1]This article is a slightly edited version of a paper delivered at the Seventh Annual Economic Conference of the National Industrial Conference Board in New York, May 21, 1964.

Reprinted from the *Quarterly Review of Economics and Business,* Vol. 4, No. 3 (1964), pp. 7-12, by permission of the author and publisher. Robert Eisner is a professor at Northwestern University.

acquisition of additional plant, equipment, or inventories. An increase in the expected profit from investment will tend to raise investment, but only so long as additional investment will add to profits. Thus, a 10 percent increase in expected profits from currently contemplated investment may justify only a 2 percent expansion in investment if any investment beyond a 2 percent increase would have the effect of reducing expected profits.

It is to be noted emphatically that this true proposition, that investment is related to the expected profitability of investment–in economists' jargon, the position of the marginal efficiency of investment schedule in relation to the cost of capital–is in no necessary way related to the proposition that higher profits will bring about higher investment. In fact, I will argue, painful as it may appear to some of the rabbits, that too many carrots, far from speeding the pace, may only bring on indigestion. If this is so, it has profound implications for the economic outlook of the rest of this decade as well as for the policies to be pursued to make that outlook as favorable as possible in the years ahead. Before turning to the immediate implications for our economy, however, let us consider further the conceptual issues we are raising and note the historical and statistical data that may be useful in resolving them.

I.

The facts are as follows. Profits and investment have been positively associated by almost every kind of direct measure. The periods in which profits have been higher for the entire economy have tended to be the periods in which the entire economy invested more. The more profitable industries in the economy have tended to be the industries that invested more. The more profitable firms in industries have tended to be the firms that invested more. Excellent economists have observed these facts and have reported them with varying degrees of statistical sophistication. Why consider all of these data suspect?

Here it is necessary to run counter to an unfortunate American prejudice that "the facts" as opposed to theory can readily tell us the truth. To soften your resistance for what may be an attack on long-cherished beliefs, I might ask you to contemplate the relationship between, say, human births and automobile registrations. If we were to check, city by city, county by county, or state by state, we would find a very positive correlation between the total number of automobile registrations, or the rate of new registrations, and the number of children born. We would probably even note that long periods of depressed demand in the automobile industry (such as during the Great Depression) were periods of reduced births. Should this lead to the conclusion that automobile registration increases the reproductive urge or that the reduction of taxes on automobile manufacturers or the subsidization of automobile ownership in order to increase registrations would raise the population? We would certainly be skeptical and, if pressed for an explanation, might suggest that after all the high correlation observed between the numbers of automobile registrations and the numbers of birth certificates relates to common associated factors of population and income rather than to any causal connection between automobiles and births. But what common factors may be found in profits and investment which would explain away the repeatedly observed correlations found by economic investigators?

The key to our explanation is to be found in the first term of the title of this article: capacity. In a complete discussion of investment I would, of course, consider in some detail the many factors affecting investment, such as technological change, the rate of interest and cost of capital, the real rate of depreciation, relative prices and wages, and the nature of competition. In our economy, however, it can quickly be made clear that both in itself and in its pervasive influence on many of the other factors, the single most important determinant of the rate of capital expenditures is our overall rate of economic growth. And this overall rate of economic growth expresses itself, in the experience of the individual firm, in the pressure of demand on existing capacity.

In crudest simplification, without technological change or other alterations within the structure of the economy, for any given rate of output or aggregate demand, profit-maximizing business firms would soon find an optimum-sized capital stock. Once having acquired their desired plant and equipment, business firms would make additional investment only to replace the plant and equipment wearing out. Motivation for *net* investment, that is, acquisition of plant and equipment in excess of the amount wearing out, would have to be found in an increase in the rate of output or in aggregate demand which would entail an increase in the optimum size of capital stock.

A notion of how great this investment might be may be found in the very rough, but not entirely unrealistic, assumption that the ratio of capital stock to annual output in our economy is about 2 to 1, that is, that a stock of $2 of plant, equipment, and inventories is necessary to produce $1 of output during a year. Then, an expansion in output or gross national product of, say, 2 percent of $600 billion, or roughly $12 billion, would entail an increase in the desired capital stock of $24 billion, that is, investment of $24 billion in the year. An increase in the rate of growth of gross national product from 2 percent to 3 percent, or from $12 billion to $18 billion a year, would bring about a rise in the rate of net investment from $24 billion to $36 billion a year.

Of course, if a great amount of excess capacity already exists, it may take increases in demand some time before they induce business firms to acquire still additional capacity. But surely if demand keeps growing, capacity will ultimately be pressed and investment will be stimulated.

What has this to do with profits? The point is simple. Companies operating close to capacity will tend to be companies operating at high rates of profit. Companies operating with considerable excess capacity will tend to be companies operating at low rates of profit or at a loss. Periods when the economy as a whole is utilizing a high proportion of its productive capacity will be periods when aggregate profits are high.

Now we can begin to see a possible explanation for the association between profits and investment. Business does indeed usually invest more when profits are high. But this is explained by the fact that when profits are high, business is usually operating a high proportion of its existing capacity and therefore considers additions to capacity profitable. For those who doubt this explanation, we shall have recourse to some more facts, after all.

II.

By way of preface to these facts I might point out that I have been engaged for quite some time in this game of trying to find out what determines business investment. A decade ago I interviewed business executives in a dozen or so large corporations in the Midwest and in the East and asked these executives to tell me what determined their investment. This was a personally interesting study but it confirmed my opinion that asking businessmen to search their own souls is not the best way to find out why they invest. It is rather like trying to find the causes of disease by asking patients for their explanations of what caused them to get sick.

The report of my interviews with businessmen was therefore accompanied by a beginning of detailed statistical examination of data indicating what businessmen actually had done rather than their explanations of why they did things. In particular, I have been working now for a number of years with data of McGraw-Hill capital expenditure surveys and related financial information, furnished on such a basis as to preserve the confidential nature of individual firm responses. These data have been used to relate capital expenditures and capital expenditure anticipations of individual firms and of industries to such variables as profits, previous sales changes, expected sales changes, and the ratio of existing to desired rates of utilization of capacity.

As may have been anticipated, profits were indeed positively correlated with investment. Firms with higher profits invested more. Industries with higher profits invested more. This has been true for all of the years analyzed thus far, from 1949 through 1958. No doubt it will continue to be true with the data from 1959 on.

However, the data also reveal that capital expenditures are positively correlated with the ratio of existing to desired rates of utilization of capacity, with expected changes in sales, and with previous changes in sales. Indeed, it turns out that investment is higher if sales increased more in the previous year, if they increased more two years previously, if they increased more three years previously, if they increased more four years previously and, to a certain extent, if they increased more as far back as seven years previously. All of these past gains in sales on up to the present add up, of course, to current sales. But to the extent that existing capacity has not adjusted to past increases in sales–and capacity cannot adjust immediately–these past increases generate current investment.

Now if capital expenditures are positively correlated both with profits and with previous changes in sales–a measure of pressure on existing capacity–and if these variables are correlated with each other, how can we tell what is really bringing on the capital expenditures? Fortunately, our statistical techniques, particularly with the aid of modern computers, are able to handle this problem very readily. What we do is simply to note the relation between capital expenditures and all of the other pertinent variables at the same time. In doing so we find that, for the large firms which account for most of the business investment in this country, what is called the partial correlation coefficient or regression coefficient of capital expenditures on profits is essentially zero. In nontechnical terms, we find that while more profitable firms and more profitable industries invest more, it is almost entirely because they are firms and industries in which sales and demand have been growing more rapidly. If we compare firms and industries whose changes in sales and demand have been the same, we find that differences in profits have virtually no effect on investment.

Each of the foregoing statements has been qualified with the words "essentially" or "virtually." The qualification stems from the fact that the data indicate thus far that while profits–always as contrasted with the lure of hoped-for additions to profits in the future–have no apparent effect on investment in the large firms which account for the major part of capital expenditures, there is evidence of some modest role for profits in relatively smaller firms. This may be significant in determining the timing if not the total of investment of such firms over a period of years. This finding, of course, makes some sense in terms of imperfection of capital markets or problems of availability of funds for relatively smaller firms. However, even though small businesses are much more numerous than large businesses and even though they may play an important economic and political role in our society which I certainly do not mean to disparage, it must be recognized that when we are considering the $44 billion of capital expenditures anticipated in the United States economy in 1964, and the still greater amounts we may hope for in the rest of this decade, we are contemplating overwhelmingly the investment of large American enterprises.

A fairly obvious corollary of the finding that it is changes in sales which generate investment is that an increase of investment beyond that anticipated is associated with a greater rise in sales than had been anticipated. This finding from data of a number of years has striking implications for the interesting anticipations of the months and years ahead which have been revealed recently in surveys by the United States Department of Commerce and the Securities and Exchange Commission and by the McGraw-Hill Publishing Company. Both of these surveys emphasize that the high level of anticipated investment is associated with a major emphasis on expanding capacity to meet increased sales. Both of these surveys also report that business has been revising its own anticipations of capital spending in an upward direction. This is associated clearly with corresponding upward revisions of expected demand.

III.

Where, finally, does all this leave us with regard to our view of the latter half of the sixties? To begin with, I see every reason to be optimistic about the period immediately ahead. In the light of this discussion, however, if we are to look forward to high investment in the rest of this decade, we must understand precisely what has contributed to our current gains and what, therefore, will be necessary to sustain and expand them in the future. For the lesson is that business investment is high and growing (although still far from its relative peak), in the particular light of the tax cut, because the growth in after-tax income of the American people is rapidly stimulating demand and not directly because of the increased after-tax profits now being earned by business. It may be added that while further analysis is still in order on these matters, there is similarly little clear evidence that the further real increase in after-tax corporate earnings occasioned by liberalized tax depreciation and the investment tax credit—however the accountants measure them—are contributing much to investment beyond the general effects on aggregate demand.

All of us are old enough to know that booms do not last forever. Since much of investment is geared to increases in demand, we can expect investment to taper off and decline once we have experienced all the stimulatory effects of the current tax-cut-induced burst of actual and expected general demand. It would be dishonest to claim that my crystal ball shows just when these effects will wear off. It might be in 1965. It might be in 1966. It might be still later. Of critical importance, indeed, will be what other forces impinge upon demand. If, as we all hope, we enjoy a general easing of the world situation and increased ability to cope with it, along with further progress of Mr. McNamara's efforts to run the biggest business in the world like an efficient business, we shall ironically have a depressing force on investment stemming from a tapering off and reduction of the major component of demand constituted by the United States defense establishment.

With a correct understanding of the forces determining investment, however, this should constitute not merely a challenge but a great opportunity. Once increases in demand and the consequent pressure of demand on capacity are recognized as a major and decisive determinant of business investment, the way is clear to achieving a rate of investment and a general level of prosperity in the latter half of this decade far exceeding anything we have known and most of what we have imagined in the past. That way must be paved by measures to bring about a great new increase in demand.

The particular measures may well depend somewhat on political taste. Many of us in academic halls would like to see a large new demand for goods and services in the field of education. We think that billions of dollars can usefully be spent in building schools, laboratories, and libraries and in securing the best brains to invest in the young human beings which are the most precious part of our nation's heritage. Many of us also see immense needs as well as immense opportunities in direct attacks on the urban congestion, slums, disease, and general poverty in large part associated with inadequate education. What great harvest may we not reap in national well-being as well as business investment if increases in aggregate demand are in these areas!

But for those of somewhat different political tastes, such direct attacks on our ills may be eschewed and we may stimulate demand in a now time-honored way—even if a time of but a few months. For we can in a year or two, or whenever it appears necessary, stimulate demand by means of another tax cut. Our economy can indeed be dismayingly neutral about politics. Investment is likely to be stimulated as much by increased private spending as by greater government spending, by a tax cut that enables individuals to buy more washing machines and television sets as much as by an increase in government subsidies or expenditures for college students and college buildings. And perhaps, to delight the politicians, I might say that we can and should have both.

In fact, I should like hopefully to prophesy both more socially desirable government expenditures and a further cut in taxes in the latter half of the sixties. Our potential in the years ahead is very great, greater by far than that of any other nation in the world, and there is much evidence that we are arriving at a broad consensus among the highest leaders of government and business that this potential can and must be realized.

The realization of that potential demands a full utilization of our growing resources and consequently a steady expansion of our economy. Faced with a prospect of such expansion, business will invest. But if in shortsighted fascination with reported earnings we endeavor to shift income and taxes so as to increase profits at the expense of greater general demand, we will soon have neither the increased profits nor the greater demand, and then we will not have the investment. Our rabbits, having stuffed themselves with carrots, will no longer eat and no longer run.

6

BUSINESS FIXED INVESTMENT: A MARRIAGE OF FACT AND FANCY

W. H. LOCKE ANDERSON

INTRODUCTION

Several years ago Robert Eisner wrote a paper entitled, "Investment: Fact and Fancy."[1] Despite the author's explicit denial of such intent, there seemed little doubt that in his mind fact was to be equated with the acceleration principle and fancy with what is often called the "residual funds" theory of investment.[2] Eisner's provocative title is characteristic of the long-standing controversy between the accelerationists and the profiteers, which has so often been a source of enjoyable acrimony and occasionally even a source of enlightenment.

The basic position of the accelerationists is that capital goods must be loved to be worth purchasing. The basic position of the profiteers is that capital goods cannot be bought for love, alas, but only for money. Given the

[1] Robert Eisner, "Investment: Fact and Fancy," *American Economic Review*, May 1963, pp. 237–46.

[2] This theory is first clearly spelled out in John Meyer and Edwin Kuh, *The Investment Decision*, Cambridge, Mass., 1957, and further developed in James Duesenberry, *Business Cycles and Economic Growth*, New York, 1958.

NOTE: This project was started when the author was on the staff of the Council of Economic Advisers and completed as a project of the Research Seminar in Quantitative Economics at Michigan, with support of the National Science Foundation.

Reprinted from R. Ferber, ed., *The Determinants of Investment Behavior*, National Bureau of Economic Research, (Columbia University Press, 1967), pp. 413–25, by permission of the author and the Columbia University Press. W. H. Locke Anderson is a professor at the University of Michigan.

utter reasonableness of both of these propositions, it is not surprising that in recent years we have been treated to a number of econometric studies in which both capacity utilization and cost of funds variables have been shown to influence investment.[3]

In this study I have developed additional evidence in support of compromise. In brief, the equations which I shall present show investment expenditures to be functionally related to capacity utilization, retained earnings, net balance sheet positions, interest rates, and equity yields. The data, which are drawn from a variety of sources, have a much broader industrial coverage than that of most studies, embracing nearly all of producer durables and "other construction" in the national accounts.[4] Thus the results may be fairly directly incorporated into aggregative models for policy and prediction.

Before proceeding, I feel that I ought to say a few words on behalf of the much-maligned construction of highly aggregative models. I grant that because of collinearity, simultaneity, aggregation bias, and shortage of data points, variables as aggregative as those in the national accounts are not a very rich testing ground for economic hypotheses. Nonetheless, there are two good reasons for continuing to use them.

The first is that the less aggregative the approach to hypothesis testing is, the greater are the dangers that model building will degenerate into particular explanations for particular cases and that description will masquerade as theory. Broadly aggregative data provide a useful check on the generality of propositions established from less aggregative data.

The second reason is that policy formulation and forecasting often require quick and dirty estimates of economic parameters. If a policy maker needs to know the size of the accelerator, it is little help to him to be told that it is one value for manufacturing, another for public utilities, and some wholly unknown value for the remainder of industry which no one has yet bothered to investigate. Without a complete disaggregative model which is set up to yield quick answers, aggregate models will continue to be very useful.

[3]See, for example: Frank de Leeuw, "The Demand for Capital Goods by Manufacturers," *Econometrica,* July 1962, pp. 407–23; Gary Fromm, "Inventories, Business Cycles, and Economic Stabilization," in *Inventory Fluctuations and Economic Stabilization,* U.S. Congress, Joint Economic Committee, 87th Congress, 2nd Session, Washington, 1962; John Meyer and Robert Glauber, *Economic Decisions, Economic Forecasting, and Public Policy,* Cambridge, Mass., 1964; W. H. Locke Anderson, *Corporate Finance and Fixed Investment,* Cambridge, Mass., 1964; Shirley Almon, "Investment Decisions: A Quarterly Time Series Analysis of Capital Appropriations in Manufacturing," unpublished; Robert Resek, "Investment by Manufacturing Firms: A Quarterly Time Series Analysis of Industry Data," unpublished.

[4]The coverage is approximately the same as that of Bert Hickman's study, *Investment Demand and U.S. Economic Growth* (Washington, 1965), to which the present study owes a considerable debt.

THEORETICAL RATIONALE

The starting premise of this investment model is the familiar profit-maximization assumption, whereby business carries its fixed investment to the point which equates the marginal rate of return to the marginal cost of funds. The operational problem in evaluating this premise is that neither the marginal rate of return (*mrr*) nor the marginal cost of funds (*mcf*) is directly observable. Hence it is necessary to evaluate the premise indirectly by conceptually specifying a model of the form:

$$mrr = f_1(I, Z_1), \tag{1}$$

$$mcf = f_2(I, Z_2), \tag{2}$$

$$mcf = mrr, \tag{3}$$

where Z_1 and Z_2 are the (vector) determinants of the positions of the *mrr* and *mcf* schedules as functions of investment (I). The two unobservables are eliminated from the system, which is solved for I, yielding:

$$I = g(Z_1, Z_2). \tag{4}$$

Measurements are made directly on (4), from which inferences about (1) and (2) are drawn.

As determinants of the position of the *mrr* schedule, I have used the level of output and the existing capital stock.

As Duesenberry has shown, one need not be a strict accelerationist to recognize the close link between utilization and investment.[5] If marginal costs rise with output along a schedule whose position is determined by the capital stock in existence, then the higher is output relative to the capital stock, the greater is the saving on variable cost to be obtained by shifting the marginal cost curve to the right through accumulating capital, and the higher is the rate of return on new capital.

As determinants of the position of the marginal cost of funds schedule, I have used the flow of retained earnings, the level of output, total outstanding liabilities, the value of assets other than fixed capital, the bond yield, and the dividend/price yield on equity.

The reason for including retained earnings is obvious. As for the balance sheet items, their inclusion is dictated by opportunity-cost considerations derived from the risks of illiquidity and indebtedness.[6] Other things equal, the higher noncapital assets are, the lower is the imputed cost of using funds for the accumulation of capital rather than noncapital assets, or the lower is

[5] Duesenberry, *Business Cycles,* Chap. 4.

[6] For a further development of the rationale for including the state of the balance sheet, see Anderson, *Corporate Finance,* Chaps. 3 and 5.

the cost of decumulating noncapital assets to buy capital. The higher liabilities are, the higher is the cost of using funds for capital accumulation rather than debt retirement, or the higher is the cost of incurring further liabilities to finance capital expansion.

Along with the levels of liabilities and noncapital assets, some measure of businesses' ability to bear liabilities and its need to carry noncapital assets is required to determine the position of the imputed cost schedules. In both cases the level of output is probably a suitable variable, or in any case an adequate proxy which can be justified on grounds of simplicity.

The rate of interest is included to measure the market cost of raising funds through debt issue, and the dividend/share price ratio to measure the cost to existing stockholders of raising funds through equity issue.[7]

Taking these considerations together, we get relationships of the following sort (neglecting lags for the moment):

$$mrr = f_1(I, Q, K); \tag{5}$$

$$mcf = f_2(I, R, A, L, Q, s, r); \tag{6}$$

where I is investment, Q is output, K is capital stock, R is retained earnings, A is noncapital assets, L is liabilities, s is dividend/price ratio, and r is interest rate. If we normalize the dollar magnitudes for scale by taking them all as ratio to the capital stock and then make linear approximations, we get:

$$mrr = a_1 + a_2\frac{I}{K} + a_3\frac{Q}{K}; \tag{7}$$

$$mcf = b_1 + b_2\frac{I}{K} + b_3\frac{R}{K} + b_4\frac{A}{K} + b_5\frac{L}{K} + b_6\frac{Q}{K} + b_7 s + b_8 r. \tag{8}$$

Equating these and collecting terms with I/K on the left, we get:

$$\frac{I}{K} = c_1 + c_2\frac{Q}{K} + c_3\frac{R}{K} + c_4\frac{A}{K} + c_5\frac{L}{K} + c_6 s + c_7 r. \tag{9}$$

This is the model whose measurement has been the principal task of this study.

[7]The cost to existing stockholders is actually some discounted earnings stream per share divided by the current price per share. Dividends are usually a better measure (except for scale) of normal earnings than current earnings are. Hence I use the dividend/price ratio rather than the earnings/price ratio.

THE DATA

The data used to fit regressions corresponding to equation (9) come from a variety of sources to be described below. All dollar magnitudes are in billion 1954 dollars. All flows are annual. All stocks are measured at the end of the year. Bond and stock yields are measured in percentage points.

First, K (capital stock) and I (investment): The data on stocks, depreciation, and net and gross investment are derived from those prepared by the Department of Commerce.[8] They cover all stocks of producer durable equipment and "other construction" corresponding to the national accounts investment data, except those of agriculture and nonprofit institutions. The series have been extended through 1963, taking account of the July 1964 revisions in the national accounts.[9]

The Commerce Department provides four stock series corresponding to four different depreciation methods: straight-line, *Bulletin F* lives; straight-line, *Bulletin F* lives shortened by 20 per cent; double declining-balance, *Bulletin F* lives; double declining-balance, *Bulletin F* lives shortened by 20 per cent. Since there is little a priori basis for choice among these,[10] I have used each in turn to see which one seems to give the best results.

If the rate of growth of the capital stock is poorly measured, it will have a serious distorting effect on the measured coefficients of equation (9). There are two likely sources of such measurement error. First, the depreciation rate may be either higher or lower than the rate at which capital wastage really occurs. Second, the investment deflator may not accurately reflect changes in the productivity of capital goods.[11] Since either of these is quite likely to be the case with the data at hand, I have added an explicit time trend to the variables already included in equation (9). Its coefficient can compensate for any systematic trend in the error of measurement of the capital stock.

Second, Q (output): These figures from the national accounts include GNP originating in nonfarm business less that originating in finance, insurance, and real estate.[12] Thus the coverage is quite close to that of the capital series.

[8]These series were originally published in the *Survey of Current Business,* November 1962.

[9]The author would like to thank Robert Wasson of the Commerce Department for assistance in updating the series and removing the investment of nonprofit institutions. The tedious calculations involved in this process were ably performed by Charles Bischoff, a summer intern at the Council of Economic Advisers.

[10]If there were, the Commerce Department presumably would not have hedged.

[11]This possibility is raised by Hickman in *Investment Demand,* which gives an interesting account of the interrelationships among depreciation, capital productivity, and embodiment on pages 39–41.

[12]The GNP originating in nonfarm business comes from Table 10 of the July 1964 *Survey of Current Business* and earlier issues. That originating in finance, insurance, and real estate comes from the series prepared by Martin Marimont and published in the *Survey of Current Business,* October 1962 and September 1964.

Third, R (retained earnings), A (noncapital assets), L (liabilities): With the exception of inventory stocks (which are unpublished stock series corresponding to the national accounts nonfarm inventory investment), all these figures come from the flow-of-funds accounts for nonfarm, nonfinancial business.[13] The retained earnings include noncorporate depreciation and proprietors' net investment plus gross corporate saving. The assets include inventories plus noncorporate and corporate financial assets. The liabilities include all corporate and noncorporate liabilities except one- to four-family mortgages. All financial variables are deflated by the investment deflator.

Fourth, s (equity yield) and r (bond yield): These are annual averages of Moody's industrial dividend/price ratio and Moody's industrial bond yield.[14]

SPECIFICATION

The specification of equation (9) is incomplete, for it fails to indicate the lag structure. Moreover, a constraint had to be placed on some of the coefficients because of collinearity and a shortage of degrees of freedom.

Two specifications were ultimately adopted for measurement:

$$i_t^n = d_1 + d_2\bar{u}_t + d_3 f_t + d_4 s_{t-1} + d_5 r_{t-1}; \tag{10}$$

and

$$i_t^g = d_1' + d_2'\bar{u}_t + d_3' f_t + d_4' s_{t-1} + d_5' r_{t-1}. \tag{10'}$$

The following is an explanation of the new notation employed:

$$i_t^n = \frac{I_t^N}{K_{t-1}} \text{ is the net investment rate;}$$

$$i_t^g = \frac{I_t^G}{K_{t-1}} \text{ is the gross investment rate;}$$

$$\bar{u}_t = 0.5\frac{Q_t + Q_{t-1}}{K_{t-1}} \text{ is the output-capital ratio;}$$

$$f_t = \frac{A_{t-1}}{K_{t-1}} - \frac{L_{t-1}}{K_{t-1}} + 0.5\frac{R_t + R_{t-1}}{K_{t-1}} \text{ is the financial position.}$$

[13] Board of Governors of the Federal Reserve System, *Flow of Funds Accounts, 1945–62, 1963 Supplement*, updated with more recent estimates from the *Federal Reserve Bulletin*.

[14] These are available in *Business Statistics*.

The following are the justifications for the particular specifications adopted.

First, if the average effective depreciation rate on existing capital were a constant, the choice of i^n or i^g as the dependent variable would affect only the intercept of the equation. Since it is not constant (even for the declining-balance stock versions) because of variations in the useful-life mix of the stock, I initially tried using the depreciation rate as an independent variable. Its measured coefficients were implausible and insignificant. Yet when no account is taken of depreciation, neither (10) nor (10′) is wholly satisfactory. Other things equal, higher depreciation ought to increase gross investment since it shifts the rate of return schedule, but it should lower net investment, since the supply of funds schedule is not infinitely elastic. Omitting the depreciation rate seemed the lesser of two evils, since its inclusion raised substantially the standard errors of the coefficients of other variables without contributing much to compensate for this.

Second, by averaging the output figures to approximate $Q_{t-1/2}$, the locus of final investment decision making is implicitly placed at the end of the year preceding the investment. Given that annual capital spending intentions surveys which are made before the preceding year's end are typically much poorer than those made soon after the beginning of the year, this seems like a good rough approximation.

Third, although the collapsing of the three internal cost of funds variables into a single variable was in part dictated by a shortage of data points and by the considerable collinearity which would otherwise occur, there are certainly analytical bases of justification. There is no reason to suppose that equal increments to noncapital assets (which are liquid) and liabilities should raise the imputed cost of funds for investment; if it did, firms could lower the cost by selling assets and buying back their liabilities. Hence the net position is what matters. Averaging R_t and R_{t-1} gives an approximation to the retained earnings flow at the end of $t - 1$. This is used as a proxy for the expected flow during t. When this is added to $A_{t-1} - L_{t-1}$, it gives a variable which can be interpreted as the potential net position at the end of t if no investment is undertaken during t and no shares are issued. Apart from any equity issue, then, the further that investment is carried, the worse will be the end-of-year position, and the higher will be the cost of funds.

Fourth, the bond and stock yields are lagged by a full year rather than the half year by which the other variables were lagged. This was done in the belief that decisions and arrangements to issue shares or long-term debt to finance capital spending are usually worked out quite far in advance of the spending undertaken.

It would be quite possible, of course, to quibble with the details of this specification. One might, for instance, prefer to have a nonadditive equation. I experimented with a log-linear form and got results which were not appreciably different from those of the linear form. Since a linear model lends itself to such ready economic interpretation and application, I preferred to stick with it. I also experimented with minor variations in the lag pattern, but these had little effect on the general characteristics of the results.

RESULTS

The investment models given by equations (10) and (10′) were first fitted to data for which the dependent variable ranged from 1948 through 1963.[15] The fits were not especially impressive; and the standard errors of most of the coefficients were quite large. However, about half of the unexplained sum of squares was attributable to a very large residual for 1957. Since I firmly believe that the continuation of the mid-1950's investment boom into 1957 was collective madness *ex ante,* not to mention *ex post,* I had little compunction about pulling the 1957 observation and refitting the equations without it. The object of this was to increase the accuracy of the parameter estimates and not, of course, to raise the R^2. Anyone who feels that it is reprehensible to throw out maverick data points may feel free to double $1 - R^2$ in his own copy of Tables 1 and 2. All of the numbers in the tables as printed are based on calculations omitting 1957.

The results presented in Table 1 are those for equation (10), in which i^n is the dependent variable. Those in Table 2 are for equation (10′), in which i^g is the dependent variable. Each equation is estimated for each of the capital stock variants, and for each variant it is estimated with and without the trend variable.

There are very few noticeable differences between the coefficients in the two tables, except of course for the intercepts. The differences between the two columns of intercepts are not far from what one should expect from the average depreciation rates, which range from .085 for series A to .144 for series D. The pairs of corresponding slope coefficients rarely differ from each other by any amount which looks remarkable, given the standard errors. Neither set of equations seems to give fits that are systematically better than those of the other.

Likewise, there is little basis for choice among the various capital stock series to be found in comparisons of either over-all goodness of fit or significance of the output-capital ratio. The only place where one can detect any important differences is in the net investment rate equations. For the two declining-balance stock equations the coefficients of the output-capital ratios

[15] These computations were ably and quickly performed by Wayne Vroman, a research assistant in the Research Seminar in Quantitative Economics, University of Michigan.

Table 1. Regression Results: Net Investment Rate

Capital Stock Series	*Intercept*	*Coefficient of* $\bar{u}_t$	f_t	s_{t-1}	r_{t-1}	t	$\bar{R}^2$
A	−.1001	.1392	.1395	−.0068	−.0168		.9716
		(.0332)	(.0298)	(.0013)	(.0024)		
	−.1076	.1493	.1257	−.0070	−.0155	−.0003	.9692
		(.0394)	(.0420)	(.0014)	(.0037)	(.0007)	
B	−.1835	.1335	.1680	−.0078	−.0097		.9810
		(.0258)	(.0217)	(.0012)	(.0023)		
	−.1864	.1368	.1629	−.0079	−.0091	−.0002	.9790
		(.0301)	(.0303)	(.0013)	(.0034)	(.0006)	
C	−.0369	.0925	.1148	−.0091	−.0273		.9678
		(.0301)	(.0314)	(.0017)	(.0030)		
	−.0553	.1240	.0716	−.0096	−.0226	−.0013	.9714
		(.0352)	(.0412)	(.0016)	(.0042)	(.0009)	
D	−.0712	.0835	.1307	−.0115	−.0243		.9696
		(.0263)	(.0257)	(.0017)	(.0032)		
	−.1078	.1157	.0856	−.0122	−.0179	−.0017	.9781
		(.0266)	(.0299)	(.0015)	(.0040)	(.0008)	

are noticeably increased by inclusion of the trend terms. This suggests that the declining-balance depreciation leads to an understatement of the growth in the capital stock, and hence to an understatement of the secular downdrift in u_t. When the time trend is explicitly included, the coefficients on u_t get larger and the trends have negative coefficients. The trend has the least effect on the coefficients of the equations using stock series B; this is the series with the highest growth rate of the four.

The output-capital ratio coefficients are all quite significant; in every case they are at least three times their standard errors. They give more explanatory contribution to the straight-line stock equations than to the declining-balance equations, which is what one should expect if these are in fact somewhat better stock series.

In almost all equations the financial position variable is also highly significant. Its significance level is reduced when the trend variable is included in the regression, however. Since both the profit rate and the net position have downward trends over the data period, the financial position is quite collinear with the trend.

The dividend yield variable is highly significant in every equation. Indeed, this consistent predictive contribution is something of a puzzle if the stock

Table 2. Regression Results: Gross Investment Rate

Capital Stock Series	Intercept	Coefficient of $\bar{u}_t$	f_t	s_{t-1}	r_{t-1}	t	$\bar{R}^2$
A	.0103	.1234	.1391	–.0077	–.0162		.9730
		(.0287)	(.0265)	(.0013)	(.0022)		
	.0036	.1323	.1268	–.0078	–.0151	–.0003	.9708
		(.0350)	(.0374)	(.0012)	(.0033)	(.0006)	
B	–.0072	.1379	.1261	–.0088	–.0184		.9748
		(.0323)	(.0273)	(.0015)	(.0029)		
	–.0126	.1439	.1169	–.0089	–.0174	–.0003	.9725
		(.0376)	(.0379)	(.0016)	(.0042)	(.0008)	
C	.0338	.1135	.1340	–.0093	–.0214		.9685
		(.0272)	(.0284)	(.0015)	(.0027)		
	.0230	.1255	.1176	–.0095	–.0197	–.0005	.9663
		(.0350)	(.0409)	(.0016)	(.0042)	(.0008)	
D	.0241	.1191	.1365	–.0114	–.0250		.9716
		(.0288)	(.0281)	(.0019)	(.0035)		
	.0092	.1322	.1181	–.0117	–.0224	–.0007	.9692
		(.0353)	(.0397)	(.0020)	(.0052)	(.0010)	

dividend yield measures only the cost of equity funds. Its effects are probably nonlinear (threshold) for individual firms and hence it ought not to be easily approximated in an aggregate linear equation. It seems likely therefore that it also measures expectational elements which influence both investment and stock prices, but are not adequately reflected in u_t.

The rate of interest is also highly significant in every equation. Since it has a marked upward trend over the data period, it is quite collinear with the trend variable. Nonetheless, its significance levels hold up well even when the trend is explicitly included.

The time trend itself is a positive explanatory nuisance in almost all cases. Except in capital stock variants C and D in the net investment equations, the inclusion of the time trend always reduces the adjusted R^2. In the two exceptions the adjusted R^2 is increased only slightly by the trend. These results give very little indication, therefore, that the Commerce Department's estimating procedures systematically and significantly distort the growth rate of the effective capital stock.

Incidentally, these results suggest that the recent findings of Hickman[16] may result in part from incomplete specification. He observes a significant negative trend in his flexible accelerator equations. This he attributes to a

[16]Hickman, *Investment Demand.*

downtrend in the amount of capital desired per unit of output, as capital is conventionally measured. However, his specification does not include adequate accounting for the factors which have led to a secular uptrend in the position of the marginal cost of funds schedule. Lacking this accounting, he is forced to infer from an actual downtrend in the net investment rate at a constant output-capital ratio that there has been a decline in the desired amount of capital per unit of output. The data used in this study also show a significant negative trend if the variables standing for the marginal cost of funds are omitted. However, as soon as they are included, the trend ceases to be significant.

CONCLUSIONS

On the strength of the results given in Tables 1 and 2, it seems fairly clear that both capacity utilization and financial variables belong together in an adequate explanation of investment. If these were the only results to support this contention, one could justifiably be skeptical because of the formidable problems of drawing reliable inferences from time series aggregates. However, given the weight of evidence derived from less aggregative studies (see footnote 3) and the confirmation found in these aggregates, it is hard to see how one can remain a celibate accelerationist.

On the strength of the parameters of these equations, it is tempting to advance some conclusions about the effects of monetary and tax policies. At this writing I shall resist these temptations because of the dynamic complexities of the relationships among the variables involved. Quite apart from the macroeconomic feedbacks from investment to output and profits, one cannot change any of the variables in the equations without affecting most of the others. Not only are they linked together through accounting identities, but they are also interrelated through decision-making processes which determine borrowing and equity issue and through a technical relationship between the utilization rate and the retained earnings rate. Until these are adequately spelled out, it will not be possible to make even a partial equilibrium analysis of the effects of policy changes. Hence it seems best to close this tale with the wedding and leave the story of its progeny to a sequel volume.

III

The Public Sector and Income Determination

The influence of the public sector on the aggregate demand for goods and services can be measured by the difference between the amount that this sector contributes to total demand via its own expenditures and the amount by which it reduces private demand via its collection of taxes. It may seem, on first consideration, that if the amount of taxes collected in a given time period were just equal to the amount of government expenditures for that time period, the governmental addition to private demand would be matched by the governmental subtraction from private demand and that equal increases in government expenditures and taxation would be offsetting in effect and thus neutral in terms of their influence on aggregate demand. To the uninitiated, the second of the preceding two sentences appears to follow quite logically from the first, but the first sentence in fact is essentially correct and the second is just as essentially incorrect. The fact that the expansionary effect of a dollar of government expenditures is not generally the same as the contractionary effect of a dollar of taxation accounts for the difference.

What is called a fact here has been clearly recognized as such only since the forties, for it was then that economists, in elaborating the Keynesian model, found that a balanced budget could not be expected to be neutral in its effect on aggregate demand. The general view held earlier was that a balanced budget (or a balanced change in an unbalanced budget) is neutral in this respect. During the forties and fifties, not only was it recognized explicitly that a balanced rise in government expenditures and receipts may have a net expansionary effect, but models were developed to show the net effect that was to be expected from a change in a balanced budget under various circumstances.

Models of this kind are developed in the second selection in this part, but the first selection, by Harold M. Somers, provides an illuminating approach to this question in purely literary form. Estimation of the expansionary or contractionary impact of any budget is shown to require an examination of the way in which each instrument of budgetary policy affects the economy's supply of what Somers calls income and capital funds. The effect of government expenditures and taxation on income funds leads to further effects on consumer spending, and the effect of government expenditures and taxation on capital funds leads to further effects on capital spending. In Somers' approach, the net expansionary or contractionary effect of the budget as a whole is thus evaluated by tracing through the combined effects of government expenditures and taxation and also of government borrowing and debt repayment on income and capital funds. In the particular case of a balanced budget, tracing through these effects leads to the conclusion that a balanced budget is not neutral, the conclusion that is the basis for the reference to "The Fallacy of the Balanced Budget" in the title of this article.

William A. Salant's article pursues the fallacy of the balanced budget via the "balanced budget theorem," a theorem which holds that under certain conditions a tax-financed change in government expenditures will lead to an exactly equal change in the level of income. This conclusion is developed through a simple algebraic income model. Then, in successive algebraic models, Mr. Salant varies the underlying conditions and examines the effect of each variation on the magnitude of the balanced-budget multiplier, a magnitude that is found to be greater or less than the value of unity that is found under the assumptions of the simple theorem.

As familiar as the now well-established proposition that a balanced budget is not neutral is the proposition that the expansionary effect of an increase in government purchases of goods and services is generally greater dollar for dollar than a reduction in taxes. Although this proposition is a staple in the basic textbooks, Svend O. Hermansen argues in his brief paper that under quite ordinary circumstances it need not hold true. Those who consider it necessarily true fail to allow for the fact that tax reduction almost invariably involves a lowering of the marginal propensity to tax. The model presented by Hermansen allows for a lowering of this marginal propensity and, for what are believed to be reasonable values of the parameters, shows that a tax cut can be more effective than an increase in government expenditures.

The final selection in this part, an excerpt from the Annual Report of the Council of Economic Advisers for 1963, presents the council's appraisal of the impact on output and employment that was to be expected from the massive tax-reduction program proposed by the Kennedy Administration early in 1963. The proposed tax cut, involving an annual reduction of over $13 billion in personal and corporate income tax liabilities based on then current income levels, did not win congressional approval until early 1964, but by early 1966 the program had generated an expansion in output and employment of the order of magnitude suggested by the council in these few pages.

7

FEDERAL EXPENDITURES AND ECONOMIC STABILITY: THE FALLACY OF THE BALANCED BUDGET

HAROLD M. SOMERS

There is a prevailing opinion in both lay and expert circles that a balanced budget is substantially neutral in its effects on the economy. This opinion is fallacious.

There are a great many things to be said in favor of a balanced budget. In particular, if we are fearful of a growing debt, a balanced budget, by definition, means a stable debt. This financial consequence of a balanced budget does not, however, mean that the balanced budget leaves the economy substantially unaffected. A balanced budget may be highly expansive in its impact on the economy and may cause inflation. A balanced budget may also be highly restrictive in its impact on the economy and may cause depression. Likewise a budget that shows a surplus–generally regarded as being restrictive in its effects on the economy–may in fact be inflationary. A budget that shows a deficit (hence requiring borrowing)–usually regarded as being expansive in its effects on the economy–may, in fact, be restrictive. It is necessary to examine the nature of the expenditures and the taxes (and the borrowing) before any conclusion can be drawn as to the impact of any budget on the economy, whether it is a balanced budget or shows a surplus or a deficit.

Reprinted from Harold M. Somers, "Federal Expenditures and Economic Stability: The Fallacy of the Balanced Budget," *Federal Expenditure Policies for Economic Growth and Stability,* Joint Economic Committee, Congress of the United States (November 1957), pp. 412–19. Harold M. Somers is a professor at the University of California at Los Angeles.

FEDERAL EXPENDITURE IN THE BUDGETARY CONTEXT

It is undoubtedly possible to discuss the relation between Federal expenditure and economic stability by treating the Federal expenditure in isolation. We would then ignore other aspects of the Government's fiscal operations, such as tax revenues and borrowing. As a practical matter, however, it is budgetary policy as a whole that is the concern of policymakers. If we set as our aim the achievement of economic stability we cannot evaluate the effects of any particular amount or type of Federal expenditure unless we know many things about the economy. One of the most important of these is the revenue side of the Federal budget. For instance, a large Federal expenditure may have a small expansive effect if there exist certain taxes which drain off the expenditure as quickly as it reaches the economy. Budgetary policymakers should, in fact, consider both expenditure policy and tax policy more or less simultaneously because of the fact that the impact of the one is determined in part by the nature and extent of the other.

For these reasons our discussion of Federal expenditure and economic stability is set up in the context of the Federal budget as a whole. We shall indicate the various consequences of a given amount and type of Federal expenditure under a variety of different assumptions as to the prevailing tax structure. Since our primary interest in this paper is with Federal expenditure, the references that are made to tax policy are in the nature of assumptions as to prevailing institutional conditions. Among other important institutional conditions are the nature of the banking system and the state of the money market as a whole.

THE STRUCTURE OF BUDGETARY POLICY

Most of the individual instruments of budgetary policy–expenditures, taxation, borrowing, and debt repayment–have been subjected to meticulous examination by economists. The multiplier theorist has explored the effects of expenditures, and the tax theorist has built up an enormous literature dealing with every nook and cranny of tax incidence and effects. Borrowing and debt repayment have not been studied quite so thoroughly but there is a substantial literature even on these subjects. Although the individual instruments of budgetary policy have been studied carefully, the theory of budgetary policy as a whole lacks integration. The terminology and interests of the tax theorist have not been the same as those of the multiplier theorist while the borrowing and debt repayment expert has busied himself with matters monetary and capital to which the others have, in the main, paid only passing attention. As a result, it is difficult to make adequate allowance for the effects of taxation, borrowing, and debt repayment in trying to determine the consequences of any particular volume of government expenditures. Instead of being an integral part of the analysis, these effects usually take the unsatisfactory form of "modifications" or "qualifications."

The immediate task is to study each instrument of budgetary policy on some comparable basis and then construct a comprehensive picture of the budgetary impact as a whole. In every case the same broad types of effects are considered. Printing of new money has economic effects only insofar as the money is spent, hence printing of new money is not considered separately. Credit creation for government expenditures forms part of borrowing, in this case from the banking system. Since we wish to see how budgetary policy influences consumption, investment, and national income as a whole, we must consider the extent to which each instrument of budgetary policy involves some impact on the Nation's supply of income and capital funds. The impact on income funds serves as a starting point for the study of subsequent effects on consumer spending and the impact on capital funds serves as a starting point for the study of subsequent effects on investment.

Expansive Effects of Federal Expenditure

An elementary approach to the problem of measuring government spending for the purpose of determining the effects on economic stability would be simply to look at the amount of spending. Government expenditures of $20 billion would be expected to have an expansive impact twice as great as government expenditures of $10 billion.

Brief reflection will show that this approach is inadequate. There is no doubt that it is necessary to break down the amount of government spending in order to get an accurate measure of the effects on economic activity. It is important to know who receives the money paid out by the Government. If the money is received by persons who will spend it immediately the impact is much more expansive than if it is received by people who will save most of it. Any amount that is saved may be assumed to be available for use on the capital market if suitable terms are available. Some items listed as Federal expenditures are in fact entirely capital items making available funds for loans, e.g. an appropriation to a Federal lending agency. In some cases the Government merely pays money to itself, leaving the economy unaffected.

Another distinction that should be made is that between government transfer payments and government income-producing payments. The former represents merely a transfer of funds from the government to individuals and does not in and of itself involve any employment or income creation. Government income-producing payments represent the purchase of goods or services by the Government and therefore in and of themselves result in employment and income. In the case of transfer payments we must wait for the spending of the money before there is any impact on the economy.

What is done with funds received from the Government is not fixed and invariable. It depends on the psychological climate, the state of expectations, which will in turn be affected by what the Government does and how it does it.

Through the medium of expenditures the Government induces both consumer spending and capital lending. For the most part, income-creation is involved, as in the case of administrative expenses, relief, public works, and most national defense items. By purchasing goods or services the Government directly transfers income funds to the firms and individuals concerned. As pointed out above, there has also grown up another type of government disbursement of funds whereby the Government merely lends its money (nominally, at least) and does not give it away or purchase outright any goods or services. The extension of credit tends to have the same sort of ultimate effects on national income as the outright purchase of goods and services by the Government, but the path taken by these effects is different. Government expenditures associated with lending activities augment the supply of capital funds and thus tend to ease the terms of private borrowing. The effects of this depend on the nature of the inducement to invest and on the possibility of obtaining funds from other sources, for instance, the banks. On the other hand, the direct purchase of goods and services by the Government means, in and of itself, that the community's supply of income funds in hand is augmented. Government expenditures that directly result in the production of income we shall call "release of income funds"; expenditures that result merely in making loanable funds available (although if invested they too will create income) we shall call "release of capital funds." Thus we carry over into our later discussion the two categories of government disbursement of funds—those which involve a release of income funds and those which involve a release of capital funds.

Restrictive Effects of Taxation

In the case of tax revenues we have an absorption of funds by the Government; and here again we may consider the funds involved to be of two types. To some extent, the process of taxation transfers to the Treasury funds which would have been spent on consumers' goods. This is true in some degree of sales taxes and of income taxes on low-income groups. But some taxes impinge on savings, which may have augmented the supply of capital funds. These two parts of taxation have different effects on the national income. The first part directly reduces consumers' expenditures and national income while the second has only an indirect effect operating through the availability of capital supplied by individual income recipients. As a result of this type of taxation the terms of borrowing for private investment may be less favorable than they would otherwise have been. Where bank credit is freely available the restrictive effects arising from the absorption of capital funds through taxation may be negligible. Taxation, then, involves both an absorption of income funds and an absorption of capital funds.

Restrictive Effects of Borrowing

When we turn to borrowing we again find an instance of government absorption of funds. It might seem that since the money is borrowed the funds involved must necessarily be capital funds. But if we are concerned with the use to which the funds would have been put if they had not been lent to the Government, then we can see, paradoxically perhaps, that not all funds lent to the Government need be capital funds. In the case of some bonds issued during the war and more clearly in the case of compulsory savings, the money lent to the Government would, to some extent at least, have been spent on consumption goods. If the borrowed money comes from a restriction of consumption as a result of public pressure accompanying the borrowing campaign, the effects are different from those which result when the borrowed money comes from credit expansion or from savings which would have taken place anyway. The ordinary multiplier analysis usually takes it for granted that the borrowing of the money in itself is completely innocent of any effects as far as expansion and contraction are concerned. But government borrowing might reduce private consumption and, depending on the state of the banking system, might discourage private investment. Hence, in the case of borrowing as in the case of taxation we should consider separately the absorption of income funds and the absorption of capital funds.

Expansive Effects of Debt Repayment

We should not leave out of account the release of funds through debt repayment which goes on even when a net increase in the debt is taking place. The repayment of the debt (interest payments being considered part of expenditures) might seem to involve solely a release of capital funds. For the most part, this is true, since the funds paid out by the Government in retiring debt will probably be put on the capital market for the purchase of securities. But in some cases, the Government bonds represent a definite savings program on the part of the individual, with the retirement of the bonds marking the culmination of the program and the spending of the money involved. The repayment of bonds sold in wartime through the use of public pressure or compulsion will also have the effect of stimulating consumer spending. Debt repayment may then be considered to involve a release of income funds as well as a release of capital funds.

OPERATION OF THE BUDGETARY MECHANISM

The several instruments of budgetary policy operate as a unit. Their respective releases and absorptions of income and capital funds combine to achieve the total budgetary impact on the national income. It is useful to consider the various income and capital funds elements separately and then analyze the relation between the two.

Net Government Release of Income Funds

Having completed the isolated examination of each instrument of budgetary policy we can obtain an estimate of the extent to which the Government adds directly to the community's income funds. It is generally considered a mistake to regard the whole of Government expenditures as a net addition to income funds because there are offsetting effects in the form of taxation. Hence the magnitude of the deficit, sometimes modified to take account of capital items within expenditures and taxation, is generally regarded as the appropriate indicator of the Government's net contribution to the community's purchasing power. The deficit (or some variant of the deficit) has been generally used as the appropriate multiplicand of the multiplier principle. But if the foregoing dissection of budgetary policy has any validity, the deficit (that is, the extent to which expenditures are financed out of borrowing) gives a misleading picture of the Government's contribution to the community's income funds. Nor should we regard the whole of taxation as being an item to offset expenditures; some taxes are completely innocent of any detrimental effects operating directly on consumption. Finally, we should take account of the debt repayment activities of the Government.

In short, we should add together those parts of expenditures and debt repayment which involve a release of income funds; and deduct those parts of taxation and borrowing which involve an absorption of income funds. In this way we can take account of the income effects of each instrument of fiscal policy and obtain a measure of the net Government release of income funds. This, not the expenditures nor the deficit, is the appropriate measure of the Government's direct contribution to the Nation's purchasing power and is the appropriate multiplicand of the multiplier principle. It may conceivably be negative in some circumstances, that is, there may be a net Government absorption of income funds.

Net Government Absorption of Capital Funds

The other effects of each instrument of budgetary policy must not be ignored. Government borrowing involves mainly (and, in ordinary times, entirely) an absorption of capital funds. Likewise, taxation almost invariably absorbs some capital funds. These elements which involve an absorption of capital funds should be added together, and from them should be deducted those parts of expenditures and debt retirement which constitute a release of capital funds. In this way we obtain a measure of the net Government absorption of capital funds. In other words, we obtain a measure of the net amount of funds the Government withdraws from the money and capital markets. To take only the amount of Government borrowing, as is usually done, is incorrect, because taxes also involve a withdrawal of capital funds to some extent, and, at the same time, the Government puts some of these funds back into the capital market through its expenditures and repayment of debt. There may be a net release rather than absorption of capital funds on the part of the Government in some circumstances.

In deriving the overall measure representing the net absorption or release of capital funds, we should not lose sight of the individual segments making up this overall measure. The overall measure must be treated with the care required wherever we deal with broad concepts and ignore qualitative considerations. In the case of capital funds, in particular, quality is a vital consideration; a plenitude of funds in the call-money market is of no use to a family desiring to build a house; nor need a scarcity of funds in the long-term capital market have a detrimental effect on a business seeking to renew a 30-day note.

Conversion of Capital Funds into Income Funds

Each instrument of budgetary policy may, then, be considered to have a consumption-funds element and a capital-funds element. Borrowing and taxation absorbs both income funds and capital funds, while expenditures and debt repayment release both income funds and capital funds. We may say that expenditures and debt repayment have expansive effects, while borrowing and taxation have restrictive effects. We have broken up each of the expansive and restrictive effects into two parts: the effect on income funds and the effect on capital funds. There is usually a net absorption of capital funds and a net release of income funds. Where there is no change in the government's cash balance and no government printing of money to finance expenditures, the net government absorption of capital funds is identically equal to the net government release of income funds.

The fisc is essentially a mechanism which converts capital funds into income funds. In determining the extent of this conversion, we must not confine our attention to deficit spending, as is so often done. Each instrument of budgetary policy—expenditures, taxation, borrowing, and debt repayment—affects the availability of both capital funds and income funds and plays a part in the Government's conversion of capital funds into income funds.

EFFECTS OF BALANCED AND UNBALANCED BUDGETS

It has been suggested above that the net government release of income funds rather than the deficit is the appropriate overall indicator of the direct expansive impact of budgetary policy. This emphasis on the net government release of income funds directs attention to the expansive effects of expenditures financed through certain types of taxes. Since it is possible to have a net government release of income funds when the budget is balanced, it is possible to have an expansive effect on consumption, and thus national income, when the budget is balanced. For instance, if expenditures are $70 billion, made up of $65 billion release of income funds and $5 billion release of capital funds, and if tax revenues are also $70 billion (thus balancing the budget), made up of $50 billion absorption of income funds and $20 billion absorption of capital funds, the net government release of income funds is $15 billion ($65 billion release through expenditures minus $50 billion absorption through taxation). At the same time, the indirect restrictive impact is potentially $15 billion in the form of a net absorption of capital funds ($20 billion absorption through taxation minus $5 billion release through expenditures). Whether this indirect restrictive influence is actually felt depends on the state of the banking system and the general availability of capital. In any case, there is a direct expansive impact of $15 billion, even though the budget is balanced.

The direct expansive impact of budgetary policy may be greater than that indicated by the size of the deficit. For instance, if tax revenues were only $50 billion in the above example, and borrowing were $20 billion, both involving solely an absorption of capital funds, the net government release of income funds would be $65 billion ($65 billion release through expenditures with no absorption through taxes and borrowing). Thus, there would be a direct expansive impact of $65 billion with a deficit of $20 billion. There may also be an off-setting restrictive impact of $65 billion absorption (50 plus 20 minus 5) of capital funds in a tight-money market.

There may be a direct expansive effect even with a budget surplus. For instance, if expenditures are only $50 billion, constituting solely a release of income funds, and tax revenues are $70 billion (making a budget surplus of $20 billion), constituting $30 billion absorption of capital funds and $40 billion absorption of income funds, the net government release of income funds is $10 billion ($50 billion release through expenditures minus $40 billion absorption through taxation). In this case, there is a direct expansive effect of $10 billion, even though there is a budget surplus of $20 billion.

On the other hand, the direct expansive effect may be less than that indicated by the size of the deficit, and there may even be a direct restrictive effect when there is a balanced budget or when there is a deficit. If expenditures are $70 billion, releasing $50 billion income funds and $20 billion investment funds; if tax revenues are $60 billion, absorbing $45 billion income funds and $15 billion capital funds; and if borrowing is $10 billion, absorbing capital funds of the same amount, the net government release of income funds is only $5 billion ($50 billion release through expenditures minus $45 billion absorption through taxation). Thus, we have a direct expansive impact of only $5 billion when there is a deficit of $10 billion.

If expenditures are the same as above and tax revenues are also $70 billion, absorbing $60 billion income funds and $10 billion capital funds, there is a net absorption of $10 billion income funds ($60 billion absorption through taxation minus $50 billion release through expenditures). Thus, there is a direct restrictive effect of $10 billion, even though there is a balanced budget.

If expenditures are again the same but tax revenues are $60 billion, absorbing $55 billion income funds and $5 billion capital funds, and borrowing is $10 billion, absorbing only capital funds, then the net absorption of income funds is $5 billion ($55 billion absorption through taxation minus $50 billion release through expenditures). Thus, we have a direct restrictive effect of $5 billion, even though there is a deficit of $10 billion.

In all cases, there is a net absorption (or release) of capital funds equal to the net release (or absorption) of income funds. If investment capital is plentiful, however, a release or absorption of capital funds by the Government will have little overall impact on the amount of investment that actually goes on. In a tight-money market, on the other hand, any release or absorption of capital funds will have a corresponding effect in stimulating or restricting actual investment.

SIGNIFICANCE OF FEDERAL RESERVE POLICY

It was indicated above that a balanced budget of $70 billion may involve a net release of consumption funds of $15 billion and a net absorption of loanable funds of $15 billion. Although these figures are hypothetical it is reasonable to assume that a balanced budget of large magnitude involves a net release of income funds and a net absorption of capital funds. The release of income funds is undoubtedly expansive. Whether or not the absorption of capital funds is restrictive depends on the state of the money market. In a sufficiently tight-money market the absorption of capital funds may be highly restrictive, offsetting completely the expansive effects of the release of income funds. In an easy-money market, however, the absorption of capital funds may have little effect. Then the balanced budget as a whole would be expansive and under conditions of full employment inflationary.

Federal Reserve policy can determine the state of the capital market, hence the effect of the balanced budget. The balanced budget will be substantially neutral if and only if the Federal Reserve System tightens the capital market so as to make fully felt the effects of the Government's absorption of capital funds and thus offset completely the effects of the Government's release of income funds. In an easy-money market or even a moderately tight-money market the balanced budget is expansive, hence inflationary under conditions of full employment.

CONCLUSION

Federal expenditure in itself is expansive, hence inflationary under conditions of full employment. Federal expenditure matched fully by Federal revenue—i.e., a balanced budget—also tends to be expansive unless capital funds are scarce. A balanced budget is thus generally not neutral. The balanced budget becomes neutral only if it is accompanied by a Federal Reserve policy of tight money.

8

TAXES, INCOME DETERMINATION, AND THE BALANCED BUDGET THEOREM

WILLIAM A. SALANT

The proposition that a tax-financed change in expenditure will lead to an equal change in income has been subjected to critical examination in two recent articles.[1] Both emphasize that the proposition, which has been christened the "balanced budget theorem," applies only when certain conditions are fulfilled, and they dismiss it as a special case of little interest because of the restrictive character of these conditions.

There is undoubtedly a danger that conclusions drawn from simplified models will be applied beyond the context in which they are valid and will be invested with the aura of universal truths. By defining and calling attention to the limitations on the validity of the balanced budget theorem, the articles cited serve as a useful corrective against this danger in this case. There is, however, some danger that in two respects they may be the source of confusion rather than clarification. In the first place, they concentrate attention on the limitations of the balanced budget theorem in such a way that the reader may easily lose sight of its essential core of truth. Second, they may create a somewhat inaccurate impression as to the exact location of

[1]Ralph Turvey, "Some Notes on Multiplier Theory," *American Economic Review,* XLIII (June 1953), 282–86; and W. J. Baumol and M. H. Peston, "More on the Multiplier Effects of a Balanced Budget," *American Economic Review,* XLV (March 1955), 140.

Reprinted from the *Review of Economics and Statistics* (May 1957), pp. 152–61, by permission of Walter S. Salant, executor of the author's estate, and the publisher, Harvard University Press.

William A. Salant, prior to his death, was an economic consultant in California.

those limits. The first danger is discussed in the succeeding paragraphs: the second in the later portions of the present paper.

It may well be that the balanced budget theorem has little direct application to the world of reality because the necessary preconditions to its validity are rarely fulfilled in that world. Nevertheless, it does not follow that the theorem is completely uninteresting and that it provides no insight whatever into the real world. In order to recognize its role in the evolution of income theory, it is only necessary to recall that, until the balanced budget theorem was advanced, it was generally believed that, under exactly the same general conditions that are assumed in the development of the theorem, a change in expenditures balanced by a change in taxes had no effect on income whatever. That is, it was believed that the multiplier for a balanced budget was zero. Whatever its limitations, the balanced budget theorem represents an important refinement of this earlier view.

That view followed from the assumption (or impression) that taxes could be treated simply as deductions from expenditure. In the balanced budget analysis, it was recognized that, while expenditures (on currently produced domestic goods and services) generate income directly, taxes do not directly reduce expenditure and income. Instead, they reduce the flow of funds available either for spending *or nonspending*. If this flow is subject to further leakages (after the taxes have been paid), such as through saving, the distinction becomes significant.

The balanced budget theorem can best be regarded as a corollary of this treatment of taxes. In a still more refined analysis, it is true, the effect upon spending of different kinds of taxes would be distinguished (and the substitution effect as well as the income effects of taxes might be considered, as Baumol and Peston have suggested). Nevertheless, it remains true that the first step was to introduce taxes explicitly as a distinct entity in the analysis and to formulate some hypothesis, however simple, as to their effect on the flow of income.

Turvey has pointed out that, in his model, the balanced budget multiplier is unity when household saving is the only leakage.[2] Does this mean, as he seems to imply, that the balanced budget multiplier will *not* be a unity if there are any other leakages, or, to put it more precisely, if there are any dependent variables other than household saving and consumption? Here we must distinguish between taxes themselves and other variables. The case in which taxes are a dependent variable, assumed to be a function of income, is considered in section III. In section IV, new dependent variables, such as induced investment, imports, and business saving are introduced, and the

[2]Turvey, loc. cit., 285–86.

effect of tax changes and balanced budget changes is considered in these enlarged systems. We shall find that the application of the balanced budget theorem is not limited to the simple model for which it was first developed.

Before we proceed to these enlarged systems, it will be useful to place the balanced budget analysis in perspective by reviewing briefly, in section I, the earlier treatment of taxes in the theory of income determination. In section II, the model from which the balanced budget theorem was originally deduced is presented.[3]

I. BACKGROUND

It is a paradoxical fact that, although Keynes's *General Theory* was highly influential in directing attention to the role of governmental fiscal operations in determining the level of income, government as such plays no explicit part in the formal Keynesian model. That model divides the economy into two sectors, firms and households. Expenditures of households (consumption) are regarded as a function of income, while net expenditures of firms for goods and services (i.e., output less sales to households, or investment) are taken to be determined by other factors. Thus, given the consumption function, income is determined by investment.

In discussions based on this formulation, deficit spending by the government was considered equivalent, in its effect on income, to investment.[4] Tax-financed expenditure was assumed by implication to have no effect on income. It was sometimes mentioned, perhaps as an after-thought, that tax remission was equivalent in its effect to deficit spending. Thus taxes were

[3]It may be noted at this point that Baumol and Peston characterize the balanced budget analysis as "misleading in that it appears by a feat of magic to be able to determine an empirical magnitude (the value of the multiplier) without the use of any empirical material" (loc. cit., 140). This complaint is difficult to understand. The balanced budget theorem is, in this respect, formally equivalent to (a) the proposition that *if* the numerator and denominator of a fraction are equal, the value of that fraction will be 1, regardless of the magnitude of numerator and denominator; or (b) the proposition that *if* the elasticity of demand for a commodity is unity, a change in supply will cause no change in the value of sales regardless of the magnitude of the shift in the supply function or the elasticity of supply. The validity of these statements is a matter of logic, not of fact. Whether either proposition is applicable to a particular situation, however, cannot be determined without the empirical knowledge, in the case of proposition (a), that the numerator and denominator of the fraction are in fact equal or unequal, or, in the case of proposition (b), that the demand function does or does not have unit elasticity. See also Prof. Alvin Hansen's comment on the Baumol and Peston paper in "More on the Multiplier Effects of a Balanced Budget: Comment," *American Economic Review,* XLVI (March 1956), 157; and the "Reply" by Baumol and Peston, *ibid.,* 160.

[4]In Robertson's phrase, the government deficit was regarded as "honorary investment." See "Mr. Clark, and the Foreign Trade Multiplier," *Economic Journal,* XLIX (June 1939), 354.

treated, again by implication, as equivalent to negative investment (or to saving).[5]

Subsequent refinement of the theory brought about two major changes in the treatment of taxes.

1. It was recognized quite early that it is unrealistic to treat tax receipts or collections as an autonomous or exogenous variable, since, with a given structure of tax rates, tax collection tend to vary with income. Consequently, tax receipts were treated as a function of income.

2. It was recognized, though considerably later, that taxes cannot correctly be treated as equivalent to negative spending (or to saving) in their effect on income. Tax remission does not in itself involve any change in income or expenditure. It merely reduces the receipts of government and puts additional disposable income into the hands of the private sectors, income which they are free to save or to spend. If government expenditure and investment are considered autonomous, tax remission can raise income only by inducing an increase in consumption. As a first approximation, particularly appropriate in the case of income taxes, it seemed reasonable to assume that decisions about the division of income between consumption and saving are based on income after taxes, that is, to regard consumption as a function of *disposable* income.

These two refinements meant the introduction into the Keynesian model of one new equation, the tax-income function, and the modification of an old one, the consumption equation, to make consumption a function of disposable income instead of national income. These changes in the model altered the conclusions that it yields as to (1) the effect on income of changes in investment, government, or consumption expenditure with a *given* set of tax rates, and (2) the effect of changes in the tax structure itself.

With respect to the effect of changes in investment or government expenditure, or shifts in the consumption function, the recognition of tax receipts as a function of income meant that an autonomous change in spending would cause an income-induced change in taxes. Thus an increase in government spending would cause taxes to rise, and the resulting deficit would be smaller than the spending itself.[6]

Moreover, the increase in tax receipts would be a leakage that reduces the multiplier effect of the spending. The multiplier adjusted to allow for the

[5] The only explicit reference to taxes in the *General Theory* is the observation that they might influence the aggregate consumption function by redistributing income among individuals or by affecting the net return on savings. See *General Theory of Employment, Interest and Money* (New York, 1936), 94–95.

[6] While this point was frequently mentioned in the late 1930's, especially by advocates of expansionist fiscal policies, it is interesting to note that it was also recognized in Kahn's original formulation of the theory of the multiplier. See R. F. Kahn, "The Relation of Home Investment to Unemployment," *Economic Journal,* XLI (June 1931), 171.

marginal tax-income ratio is smaller than the simple Keynesian multiplier which allowed only for the leakage into saving.[7]

When we consider the effect on income of autonomous changes in taxes themselves, we find that much of the discussion does not appear to incorporate the second refinement mentioned above, the treatment of tax receipts as a function of income. For example, the two most explicit algebraic statements of the balanced budget theorem treat taxes as an independent variable.[8] On that assumption, it was concluded that:

1. Dollar for dollar, changes in taxes have a weaker income-generating effect than changes in expenditures (for currently-produced goods and services). Specifically, if the multiplier applicable to expenditures is k, the (negative) tax multiplier is $(k - 1)$.

2. As a corollary of (1) it follows that a change in expenditure balanced by an equal change in taxes will have a multiplier of 1.[9]

Whether these conclusions apply when tax receipts are assumed to vary with income is, as indicated above, one of the questions raised by Turvey's discussion and is considered in section III.

[7]See Paul A. Samuelson, "Fiscal Policy and Income Determination," *Quarterly Journal of Economics,* LVI (August 1942), 581.

[8]See Trygve Haavelmo, "Multiplier Effects of a Balanced Budget," *Econometrica,* XIII (October 1945), 311; and Samuelson, "The Simple Mathematics of Income Determination," in Lloyd Metzler et al., *Income, Employment, and Public Policy, Essays in Honor of Alvin H. Hansen* (New York, 1948), 138.

[9]For early statements of the balanced budget theorem, see references cited in Samuelson, "Simple Mathematics," 140. While the application of the balanced budget theorem to the situation in which an increase in effective demand is considered desirable has often been discussed, the reasoning, of course, applies also to situations verging on inflation. Thus, in order to prevent an inflationary gap when government expenditures are rising, it is not enough for taxes to rise in step with expenditures and keep disposable income from rising. They must increase faster, in order to reduce disposable income and private demand as government demand increases. While this fact was clearly recognized in some wartime studies of the inflationary gap–see e.g. Walter S. Salant's and Milton Friedman's papers on "The Inflationary Gap," *American Economic Review* XXXII (June 1942), 309 and 318, respectively–it is interesting to note that it was not recognized in the British budget address of April 1941, which introduced the concept of the inflationary gap, and in which Keynes played a central role.

Note: This statement must be drastically amended in the light of R. S. Sayers, *Financial Policy, 1939–1945* (London, 1956), which the writer was able to consult only after the present article was in proof. In his account of the 1941 budget, which he describes as the cornerstone of British wartime financial policy, Professor Sayers quotes an internal memorandum written by Keynes in September 1940, which states that extra taxes of £300 million might reduce consumption by only £150–200 million, the remainder of the taxation falling on saving (op. cit., 71). To effect a £300 million cut in consumption, the additional taxes needed were of the order of £400 million. This is, of course, as clear a statement as could be asked of the principle underlying the balanced budget theorem. It was evidently regarded as a refinement which could be slurred over in the budget address itself, and the language of that address appears to imply that, in order to achieve a specified cut in consumption, it was necessary only to increase taxes by an equal amount.

While the treatment of taxes in the Keynesian system was refined along the lines just described, it was shown that the original simple model could be developed and enlarged in numerous other ways, by the addition of new variables, the disaggregation of old ones, and the introduction of new behavior hypotheses. For example, exports, imports, and induced investment could be introduced, or saving could be divided into a business and a household component.[10] What is the effect of these developments on the conclusions as to the income effects of tax changes? In particular, does the balanced budget theorem apply to such enlarged systems? Section IV is addressed to these questions.

II. CONSUMPTION THE ONLY DEPENDENT VARIABLE

The simple model from which the balanced budget theorem was derived contains only the definitional identities:

$$Y = C + I + G \tag{1}$$

$$X = Y - W \tag{2}$$

and the single behavior equation

$$C = a + bX \tag{3}$$

where Y denotes income, C consumption, I investment, G government expenditure on currently produced goods and services, X disposable income (income less taxes plus government transfer payments), and W tax receipts less government transfer payments,[11] all in real terms. Equation (3) is an aggregate consumption function, assumed to be linear.[12] Investment, govern-

[10] For an excellent summary of these developments, see Samuelson's article on "The Simple Mathematics of Income Determination," cited above.

[11] It will be noted that transfer payments are treated as negative taxes. This treatment implies that the income effect of transfer payments is equal and opposite to that of taxes. Specifically, it is assumed that, although transfer payments do not themselves respresent income, they do add to the disposable income available for consumption or saving. On this assumption, which is reasonable for simple models, it is easier to treat transfer payments as negative taxes than as a special category of expenditure. In the text below, we shall, for the sake of brevity, refer to tax receipts less transfer payments of government simply as "taxes" or "tax receipts." Similarly, G, government expenditures, always denotes expenditures for currently-produced goods and services. Thus it excludes transfer payments, purchases of existing capital assets, and purchases that result in disinvestment in inventories. Turvey has pointed out that the balanced budget theorem does not apply to expenditures for these purposes, and Baumol and Peston have dealt with the value of the balanced budget multiplier when part of the additional expenditure is for purposes other than purchase of newly-produced goods and services.

[12] In order to concentrate on the income effect of taxes, we rule out the possibility of a shift in the consumption function arising from redistribution of income by assuming that all individuals have linear consumption functions with identical marginal propensities to consume.

ment expenditures, and taxes less transfer payments are all assumed to be autonomous.[13]

Solving for income, we get:

$$Y = \frac{I + G + a - bW}{1 - b} \tag{4}$$

The multiplier relating a change in income to a change in one of the independent variables, investment or government expenditure (or for that matter a parallel shift in the consumption function denoted by the addition of an amount h to the parameter a), takes the familiar form

$$\frac{\Delta Y}{\Delta I} = \frac{\Delta Y}{\Delta G} = \frac{\Delta Y}{h} = \frac{1}{1 - b}. \tag{5}$$

The multiplier relating a change in income to a change in tax receipts is

$$\frac{\Delta Y}{\Delta W} = -\frac{b}{1 - b}. \tag{6}$$

Thus tax changes will have a weaker effect on income, dollar for dollar, than expenditure changes. The ratio of the tax multiplier to the expenditure multiplier is $(-b)$. The effect on income of a change in expenditure accompanied by an equal change in taxes is the algebraic sum of the multipliers (5) and (6):[14]

$$\frac{\Delta Y}{\Delta G} = \frac{\Delta Y}{\Delta W} = 1 \text{ when } \Delta G = \Delta W. \tag{7}$$

This is the balanced budget theorem. It means that the increment in income will be equal to the increment in government expenditure and will consist entirely of additional goods and services produced for the government. Consumption will remain unchanged.

The foregoing is familiar ground. Two comments are called for at this point.

1. The values of the expenditure, tax, and balanced budget multipliers

[13]In this model, and in those considered below, the only behavior relations considered are simple income effects. That is, the dependent variables are made functions either of aggregate income or of some component of income or expenditure. This treatment excludes the possibility, for example, that changes in marginal tax rates might alter the inducement to invest with unchanged prospective demand, or that government expenditure for a particular purpose might affect private spending for related purposes and thereby shift the consumption function.

[14]It should be noted that the expression ΔY in the lefthand side of (7) refers to the total (or net) change in income resulting from the combined effect of the tax change and the expenditure change, not to that resulting from the expenditure change alone.

follow from the hypothesis in (3) that consumption is a function of disposable income. If instead it had been assumed that taxes were paid entirely out of saving, consumption would be a function of income, Y, and taxes would play no part whatever in income determination. If, on the other hand, it had been assumed that taxes were paid entirely out of consumption, the consumption function would have the form $C = C(Y) - W$, and the effect of taxes on the level of income would be equal and opposite to that of government or investment expenditure. The hypothesis that consumption varies with income after taxes appears most applicable to personal income taxes. Thus the balanced budget theorem applies primarily to these taxes, rather than to indirect taxes or corporate income taxes.[15]

2. The balanced budget theorem can be deduced directly by solving the underlying equations (1), (2), and (3) for disposable income, without going through the intermediate stages of calculating the expenditure multiplier and the tax multiplier. The solution for disposable income is

$$X = \frac{a + I + G - W}{1 - b}. \qquad (8)$$

Since a, b, and I are unchanged, and the change in taxes offsets the change in government expenditure, disposable income must be unchanged. Hence the change in income must be equal to the change in the budget.[16] We shall find this short-cut proof useful later in dealing with more complicated models.

III. TAXES A FUNCTION OF INCOME

We shall now consider the case in which taxes less transfers are assumed to be a linear function of income:[17]

[15] Somers has considered all three possibilities mentioned above: taxes falling on saving, those falling on consumption, and taxes falling on income that leave the marginal propensity to consume (out of disposable income) unchanged. See Harold M. Somers, "The Impact of Fiscal Policy on National Income," *Canadian Journal of Economics and Political Science* (August 1942), 364, and *Public Finance and National Income* (Philadelphia, 1949), 500–503 and 507–12. E. Cary Brown has analyzed the effect of consumption taxes in "Analysis of Consumption Taxes in Terms of the Theory of Income Determination," *American Economic Review,* XL (March 1950), 74.

[16] This method of demonstrating the balanced budget theorem is due to Samuelson. See "The Simple Mathematics of Income Determination," op. cit., 142.

[17] The reader may, if he finds it convenient, think of this function as representing a proportional income tax levied at rate t along with a head tax s. Alternatively, he may think of s as a lump-sum transfer payment or tax exemption, in which case its value would be negative. The assumption of linearity rules out consideration of an income tax with rising marginal rates.

$$W = s + tY. \tag{9}$$

Solving for income, we now get

$$Y = \frac{I + G + a - bs}{1 - b(1 - t)} \tag{10}$$

With a given tax structure, the multiplier for changes in either investment or government expenditure, or for an increment h to the constant term in consumption, is:

$$\frac{\Delta Y}{\Delta I} = \frac{\Delta Y}{\Delta G} = \frac{\Delta Y}{h} = \frac{1}{1 - b(1 - t)}. \tag{11}$$

It should be noted that changes in any of these variables will alter tax receipts. In particular, an increment in G will not result in an equal change in the budget deficit.

Changes in the tax function may be caused by changes in either of the parameters s or t. The former correspond geometrically to parallel vertical shifts in the tax function, the latter to changes in its slope resulting from rotation around its intercept with the vertical axis. We shall consider first parallel shifts resulting from the addition of an increment, denoted by Δs to the term s. The multiplier will be:

$$\frac{\Delta Y}{\Delta s} = -\frac{b}{1 - b(1 - t)}. \tag{12}$$

The ratio of the tax multiplier to the expenditure multiplier is still $(-b)$, as it was in the first model. The sum of the multipliers, however, which indicates the effect on income of a change in expenditure accompanied by an equal change in the terms of the tax function, is now:

$$\frac{\Delta Y}{\Delta G} = \frac{1 - b}{1 - b(1 - t)} \quad \text{when} \quad \Delta G = \Delta s. \tag{13}$$

This quantity will be less than unity as long as the marginal tax rate t is positive. Consumption, instead of remaining constant, as it does when the marginal tax rate is zero, will decline. A balanced change in expenditure and in tax receipts *at the initial level of income* will not produce an equal change in income.

This however, is not the whole story. The ultimate change in tax receipts at the new equilibrium level of income (ΔW in our notation) will be greater than Δs, and therefore greater than ΔG. Instead of equal changes in expenditures and taxes, we have an expenditure change accompanied by a somewhat greater change in taxes. The multiplier in (13) can hardly be called a "balanced budget" multiplier.

In order to determine the balanced budget multiplier for this model, we must so adjust the shift in the tax function that, *at the new equilibrium position,* the tax change and the expenditure change are equal. One way to find this multiplier is to set $\Delta W = \Delta G$, solve for the required shift in the tax function Δs, and then for the resulting change in income ΔY. We can proceed more directly, however, by solving for disposable income as in (2) of section II above. Since the solution for disposable income is identical with that developed in section II, equation (8), we know at once that disposable income must remain unchanged if $\Delta G = \Delta W$. Thus the change in income again equals the change in expenditures and the ultimate change in tax receipts. The "balanced budget" multiplier is again unity even when tax receipts are assumed to vary with income, but "balance" in the budget change must be understood to refer to the equality of ΔG with ΔW, the *ultimate* change in tax receipts, rather than Δs, the initial change.[18]

We turn now to the effect of changes in the marginal tax rate t on income.[19] Denoting the original tax rate t' and the new rate t'' and the original level of income Y' and the new equilibrium level Y'', we first solve for the change in income resulting from a change in the marginal tax rate from t' to t''.[20] The result is a fraction, equation (16) is footnote 20, of which

[18]One loose end remains. While we have assumed a vertical shift, Δs, in the tax function just sufficient to insure that $\Delta W = \Delta G$, we have yet to determine how great this shift must be. Since we now know that $\Delta Y = \Delta G = \Delta W$, the calculation is simple. Substituting ΔG for both ΔY and ΔW in the tax equation (9), we get

$$\Delta s = \Delta G(1 - t). \tag{14}$$

[19]This case has been considered only in geometric terms, so far as I am aware, except for Turvey's article, loc. cit., 285. Geometric treatments include Robert L. Bishop, "Alternative Expansionist Policies: A Diagrammatic Analysis," in *Income, Employment and Public Policy,* 317; E. Cary Brown, loc. cit., 74, in which the effect of consumption taxes is compared to that of income taxes; and J. G. Gurley, "Fiscal Policy for Full Employment," *Journal of Political Economy,* LX (December 1952), 525.

[20]From equation (10) we obtain for the change in income the unwieldy expression

$$\Delta Y = Y'' - Y' = \frac{I + G + a - bs}{1 - b(1 - t'')} - \frac{I + G + a - bs}{1 - b(1 - t')} \tag{15}$$

which fortunately simplifies to

$$\Delta Y = -\frac{b(t'' - t')Y'}{1 - b(1 - t'')} \tag{16}$$

This result corresponds to Turvey's conclusion, loc. cit., 285.

the numerator represents the product of the change in tax yield at the *original* level of income and the marginal propensity to consume, while the denominator is the same expression that appeared in the denominators of the multipliers in equations (11) and (12) above, but calculated at the *new* tax rate t''.

Equation (16) is the first case in which the initial level of income Y' appears in the solution for ΔY. By dividing through by Y', we can find the *relative* change in income as a function of the marginal propensity to consume and the new and old tax rates. This result is in accordance with common sense; a given change in tax rates (as opposed to tax receipts) will produce a determinate relative change in income, rather than a determinate absolute change.

The conclusions with respect to the balanced budget theorem are similar to those reached above in the case of parallel shifts in the tax function. When the change in tax receipts at the *original* level of income is set equal to the change in expenditure, i.e., when $(t'' - t')\ Y' = \Delta G$, the resulting change in income will be less than the change in revenues and expenditures. When, however, the *ultimate* change in taxes is set equal to the change in expenditures, i.e., when $\Delta W = \Delta G$, an equal change in income will result. This conclusion can again be derived from inspection of equation (8), the solution for disposable income, which remains unchanged.[21] It might be added that, since the form of tax and consumption functions does not affect equation (8), this conclusion does not depend on the assumption of linear functions.

We have shown that the treatment of taxes as a dependent variable instead of an independent parameter does not alter the value of the balanced budget multiplier. Similar conclusions apply if government expenditure is treated as a dependent variable.

Up to this point, we have been concerned largely with balanced changes in expenditure and taxation. What can we say about the relative effectiveness of tax changes by themselves, as compared with expenditure changes, in inducing changes in income? The first problem is to decide on the appropri-

[21]The calculation of the change in the marginal tax rate required to preserve the original state of budgetary balance is somewhat more complicated than before. The change in tax receipts, ΔW, which results from both the change in rates and the change in income, can be expressed as

$$\Delta W = t''Y'' - t'Y'.$$

By assumption $\Delta W = \Delta G = \Delta Y$.
Manipulation of these expressions gives the following result for the required change in rates:

$$t'' - t' = \frac{\Delta G(1 - t')}{\Delta G + Y'}.$$

ate terms for comparison. We might compare the increase in income resulting from a dollar of expenditure with that resulting from a dollar of tax remission (either at the initial or at the new equilibrium level of income). This, however, does not seem an entirely appropriate comparison, because, in the present model, the expenditure will itself induce a change in tax receipts, and the change in the budget surplus or deficit will be less than the additional expenditure. It would appear to be more interesting to compare the increase in income resulting from one dollar of additional *deficit* caused by expenditure with the increase resulting from a dollar of deficit caused by tax remission.

The result of this comparison is that the increase in income per dollar of deficit resulting from increased expenditure bears a ratio to the increase in income per dollar of deficit caused by tax remission of $1/b(1 - t)$.[22] Since the quantity $b(1 - t)$ must be less than unity in a stable system,[23] we can conclude that, per unit of deficit, expenditure has a greater impact on income than tax remission, just as it did in the first model.

IV. ADDITIONAL DEPENDENT VARIABLES INTRODUCED

We have just considered a model in which tax receipts (or expenditures) are considered a function of income, and we have found that the value of the balanced budget multiplier is still unity, provided the "balanced" change in expenditures and taxes is understood to refer to the values of those variables at the new equilibrium position. In this section we shall see what happens to the balanced budget multiplier when new dependent variables (whether leakages like imports or business saving, or expenditures like investment),

[22]The increase in income ΔY resulting from an increment of expenditure ΔG is given by equation (11). The rise in tax receipts is $t\,\Delta Y$, and the change in the deficit (which we may denote as $\Delta G - \Delta W$, is therefore $\Delta G - t\,\Delta Y$. The ratio of the change in income to the change in the deficit is

$$\frac{\Delta Y}{(\Delta G - \Delta W)} = \frac{1}{(1 - b)(1 - t)} \text{ with } s \text{ and } t \text{ constant.} \tag{17}$$

This result agrees with Samuelson, "Simple Mathematics," 145, equation (11). The corresponding ratio for changes in the tax function, whether they result from changes in the constant term s or in the marginal tax rate t, is

$$\frac{\Delta Y}{\Delta W} = -\frac{b}{1 - b} \text{ with } G \text{ constant.} \tag{18}$$

The value of the ratio $\Delta Y/\Delta W$ is the same as in the first model considered, in which taxes were an independent variable—see equation (6) above. This equality has been pointed out by Thomas C. Schelling, *National Income Behavior* (New York, 1951), 100.

[23]See Schelling, op. cit., 85.

other than taxes and household saving, are introduced. To anticipate the results, the conclusions will be that (1) the balanced budget multiplier will be unity if the new dependent variables are made functions of disposable income $(Y - W)$ or of private expenditure $(Y - G)$, but not if they are functions of national income (Y); (2) in any event, the balanced budget multiplier will be greater than zero and may be greater or less than unity.

To simplify the analysis, we shall first consider tax receipts an independent variable, as in section II above. We introduce investment as a new dependent variable, which we shall assume initially to be a linear function of national income.[24]

$$I = u + vY. \tag{19}$$

Solving the new system of equations (1), (2), (3), and (19) for income, we obtain

$$Y = \frac{a + u + G - bW}{1 - b - v}. \tag{20}$$

It is readily seen that the multiplier for changes in government expenditures, assuming all other parameters constant, is

$$\frac{\Delta Y}{\Delta G} = \frac{1}{1 - b - v} \tag{21}$$

while the multiplier for tax changes alone is

$$\frac{\Delta Y}{\Delta W} = -\frac{b}{1 - b - v}. \tag{22}$$

While the ratio of the tax multiplier to the expenditure multiplier remains $(-b)$, as in the first model considered in section II, the balanced budget multiplier, which is equal to the sum of the separate multipliers, is no longer unity but rather $(1 - b)/(1 - b - v)$, which is greater than unity if v is positive.

Why does the introduction of induced investment affect the balanced budget multiplier? While there are differences between investment and consumption which are vital for other purposes, inspection of the system of

[24]Investment has been selected as the new dependent variable because its introduction requires less change in the system of equations than would that of, say, business saving or imports, and it serves equally well to illustrate the propositions with which we are concerned here.

equations shows that, in the present context, the only difference is that investment is assumed to be a function of national income (Y), while consumption is made a function of disposable income ($Y - W$). Thus, while a balanced change in G and W will initially (i.e., in the "first round") leave disposable income and hence consumption unchanged, it will affect Y, and hence investment, and will set in motion a multiplier process.

If induced investment were assumed to be a function of disposable income instead of national income, equation (19), the investment function, would be exactly similar in form to equation (3), the consumption function, and the balanced budget multiplier would be unity.[25] Alternatively, investment might be assumed, with equal plausibility, to be a function of private expenditure (i.e., of $C + I$ which equals $Y - G$). The balanced budget multiplier would still be unity (although the government expenditure multiplier would now be reduced to $(1 - v)/(1 - b - v)$.

More generally, when each of the individual dependent variables is treated as a function of either disposable income ($Y - W$) or private expenditure ($Y - G$), they will be uniquely determined by $G - W$ (assuming the parameters of the behavior equations, such as a, b, c, and u in the present system, and any other independent variables, constant). Since a balanced change in G and W means that $G - W$ remains unchanged, all these dependent variables will also remain constant. Government expenditure will be the only type of expenditure that changes, and ΔY will equal ΔG; the balanced budget multiplier will be unity.

If, however, some dependent variable is not uniquely determined by $Y - W$ or $Y - G$ and, in particular, if it is a function of Y, then it cannot be expressed as a unique function of $G - W$, and it will be affected by balanced changes in G and W.

These conclusions can be readily applied to an open system with foreign trade. If, for example, exports are considered an independent variable which remains constant for the present purpose, and imports are made a function of national income (or of total expenditure $C + I + G + E$ where E denotes exports), then the balanced budget multiplier will be less than unity (but greater than zero). If, however, imports were assumed to consist entirely of goods destined for private consumption and investment but not for government use, then the introduction of foreign trade would not affect a balanced budget multiplier which had a value of unity in a closed system.

If business saving is introduced, the "disposable income" available to households is now reduced by the amount of the business saving, and the consumption equation must be adjusted accordingly. Under most conditions,

[25] Smithies has treated investment in this way in his chapter on "Federal Budgeting and Fiscal Policy," in *A Survey of Contemporary Economics* (Philadelphia, 1948), 188.

the introduction of business saving reduces the value of the balanced budget multiplier. There is, however, a special case which illustrates the general conclusions stated above. If personal taxes, imports, and investment are all zero or constant, and if business saving is a function of national income less business taxes, then business saving, disposable income, and consumption will all be uniquely determined by national income less taxes. Under these conditions, a change in expenditure fully balanced by a change in business taxes will have a multiplier of unity.

All of the preceding discussion has been based on the assumption that taxes are an independent variable. How are the conclusions altered if taxes are allowed to vary with income? It can be shown that, as in section III above when a tax function was added, the value of the expenditure multiplier will change, but the balanced budget multiplier will not be affected.[26] It also remains true that, per dollar of deficit, the income-generating effect of expenditures is higher than that of taxes.

The foregoing conclusions may be compared with Turvey's remark that the balanced budget multiplier will be unity when "household saving is the only leakage; i.e., business saving, marginal rates of government expenditure, all marginal tax rates, and the marginal propensity to import are all zero."[27] In section III above we concluded that marginal rates of government expenditure (on goods and services) and on personal income tax need not be zero if the balanced budget condition is interpreted to refer to the ultimate rather than the initial change in the budget. We can now conclude that the other leakages need not be zero provided the relevant dependent variables are functions of disposable income (or of $Y - G$).[28]

[26]The calculation of the value of the balanced budget multiplier when taxes are a function of income, and the balanced budget multiplier is not unity, is rather complex. The difficulty lies in determining how much of a shift in the tax function is required to insure that the change in tax receipts balances the change in expenditure. It will be recalled that in section III above, where taxes were treated as a function of income, we deduced at once by inspection of the equations that the balanced budget multiplier must be unity. Knowing the change in income, we could easily compute the required shift of the tax function. If, however, the value of the balanced budget multiplier cannot be determined by inspection, then it is necessary to calculate the shift in the tax function *before* the change in income can be determined. For example, if a given change in expenditure ΔG is to be balanced by an equal change in taxes ΔW, achieved in part through a vertical shift in the tax function Δs, the determination of the resulting change in income requires the following steps: (1) calculate the change in income resulting from ΔG alone; (2) calculate the change in the budget surplus resulting from ΔG alone, by applying the marginal tax rate to the change in income calculated in (1), and subtracting the result from ΔG; (3) calculate the change in the parameter s required to offset the change in the deficit resulting from ΔG alone, as found in (2); and finally (4) calculate the change in income resulting from the change in s alone, and add it to that resulting from ΔG alone. The sum is the change in income resulting from the balanced change in expenditures and taxes.

[27]Loc. cit., 285–86.

[28]In the particular model used by Turvey, neither imports nor business saving satisfies this condition, but indirect taxes are considered a function of disposable income. For this reason,

V. CONCLUDING REMARKS

The foregoing analysis suggests the following general conclusions about the income effects of personal income taxes (or transfer payments) and of balanced changes in such taxes and government expenditures on goods and services:[29]

1. Per dollar of additional deficit, an increase in expenditures with unchanged tax rates will have a greater income-generating effect than a dollar of deficit arising from a reduction in tax rates.

2. It follows from (1) that an increase in expenditures fully offset by an equal increase in tax receipts will have *some* income-generating effect. The magnitude of this effect will vary in different models.

3. An increase in expenditure fully offset by an equal increase in tax receipts will generate an equal increase in income in a system in which all the income-determining dependent variables, such as consumption, induced investment, and imports, are functions of disposable income ($Y - W$) or of private expenditure less imports ($Y - G$), but not when they are functions of national income.

4. The foregoing propositions apply even when income taxes (or for that matter government expenditures) are themselves dependent variables, provided it is understood that the relevant changes in expenditures and tax receipts are the *ultimate* changes at the new equilibrium levels of income, rather than the initial or impact effects of shifts in the tax (or expenditure) function at the original income level.

The balanced budget theorem, in what we may call its strict form, states that a balanced change in taxes and expenditures has a multiplier of exactly unity. As (3) above indicates, this proposition is valid only under certain conditions. In particular, it applies to simple models in which consumption (and taxes themselves) are the only dependent variables (and the hypothesis about the behavior of consumption is that it varies with income after taxes). Nevertheless, as stated in (2) above, a balanced change in taxes (or transfer payments) and expenditures will always have *some* income-generating effect; the appropriate multiplier may be greater or less than one, depending on the model. The balanced budget theorem, while only an approximation to the truth (like any statement derived from simplified models), is a better

---

the balanced budget multiplier will be unity in Turvey's model even if the marginal rate of indirect taxes (which Turvey assumes to fall entirely on consumption) is not zero, as Peston has pointed out. See "A Note on the Balanced Budget Multiplier," *American Economic Review,* XLIV (March 1954), 129.

[29]These conclusions apply to models of the type considered in this paper, in which all functional relations involve only simple income effects. See fn. 13.

approximation than the view it superseded, that the income-generating effects of taxes (or transfer payments) are equal and opposite to those of expenditures on goods and services, and hence that the balanced budget multiplier is zero.

9

THE MULTIPLIER EFFECT OF AN INCREASE IN GOVERNMENT EXPENDITURES VERSUS A DECREASE IN TAX RATES

SVEND O. HERMANSEN

The current public discussion of how to stimulate a sluggish economy has largely been confined to arguments with respect to the size of the tax cut necessary to obtain a satisfactory level of employment (usually defined in terms of a level of unemployment of 4 per cent of the labor force). Little has been said about the possibility of increasing economic activity through a higher level of government expenditures on goods and services.

Economists generally agree that under usual circumstances a dollar reduction of taxes will increase income by less than a dollar increase in government expenditures on goods and services. It is the burden of this brief paper to show that under quite ordinary circumstances this proposition is not necessarily true. Models that lead to the result that dollar for dollar tax cuts are less effective than increases in government expenditures typically assume either that net taxes or withdrawals are invariant with respect to income[1] or, if tax revenue is assumed to be a function of income, only tax cuts resulting in a parallel downward shift of the tax function are considered, thus leaving the marginal propensity to tax out of income unchanged.[2] The lack of realism

[1]See, for example, Paul A. Samuelson, "The Simple Mathematics of Income Determination," in *Income, Employment and Public Policy* (New York: Norton, 1948), p. 140.

[2]See, for example, L. S. Ritter, "Some Monetary Aspects of Multiplier Theory and Fiscal Policy," *Review of Economic Studies*, Vol. 23, No. 61 (1955–56), pp. 126–31. Ritter incorporates monetary effects of a tax cut in his model, but he operates only with a parallel shift in the tax function.

Reprinted from the *Quarterly Review of Economics and Statistics* (September 1963), pp. 67–71, by permission of the author and publisher. Svend O. Hermansen is a professor at New Mexico State University.

of such models is apparent inasmuch as practically all conceivable tax reductions involve a lowering of the marginal propensity to tax, perhaps combined with a downward shift in the tax function.

THEORY

The following conventional static model[3] is introduced to investigate the effect on income of a tax cut.

Consumption, C, is assumed to be a linear function of net national product, Y:

$$C = a + bY. \tag{1}$$

Investment, I, is similarly related to Y:

$$I = -c + dY.^{4} \tag{2}$$

Government expenditures on goods and services, G, are autonomous:

$$G = \overline{G}. \tag{3}$$

Net tax revenue, W, is a function of Y:

$$W = -e + fY.^{5} \tag{4}$$

Equilibrium income, Y, is

$$\overline{Y} = \frac{a - c + \overline{G}}{1 - b - d}. \tag{5}$$

An increase in government expenditures on goods and services will increase income by ΔG times the multiplier, which is

$$\frac{1}{1 - b - d}. \tag{6}$$

[3]The model has the usual limitations inherent in a static model. Furthermore, the monetary effects of a tax cut are ignored, partly because a monetary policy that neutralizes these effects seems a priori just as probable as one that does not and partly because the main point the author wants to make is more easily presented without introducing monetary policy directly.

[4]To make investment autonomous seems too severe an abstraction from reality; to make it a function of changes in income would make the model dynamic. For a defense of the legitimacy of relating investment functionally to income, see Paul A. Samuelson, *loc. cit.*, p. 137.

[5]All the constants from a through f are taken as positive.

To analyze the effect of a tax cut, a parameter, α, and a constant, k, are introduced into the tax revenue function (4):

$$W = (-e - \alpha) + (f - \alpha k)Y. \tag{7}$$

Mathematically both α and k are numbers. Economically α is interpreted as a unit of money in the first part of equation (7), $(-e - \alpha)$, for example, $1 billion, while in the second part of (7), $(f - \alpha k)$, α multiplied by k is the percentage point deduction from the old marginal propensity to tax, f. To illustrate, if the constant, k, is chosen to be, for example, .02, then we are considering the family of tax cuts that are characterized by the fact that for every $1 billion the tax revenue function is lowered at the origin (brought about, for example, by an increase in transfer payments), the marginal propensity to tax with respect to net national product is lowered by 2 percentage points. Suppose Y happens to be $400 billion at the time of the tax cut, a value of $\alpha = 1$ would then mean a tax cut of 1 + 2 per cent of $400 billion – $9 billion, a value of $\alpha = 2$ would yield a tax cut of $18 billion, and so on.

α is chosen as the independent variable while the value assigned to k determines the family of tax cuts under consideration, that is, the relative weight given to a lowering of the tax revenue function at the origin and a flattening of the function. Suffice it to say that equation (7) covers tax increases (for $\alpha < 0$) as well as tax cuts. If k were assigned a negative value, we could analyze the effect of either a lowering of the tax revenue function at the origin combined with an increase in the marginal propensity to tax (for $\alpha > 0$) or an upward shift in the tax revenue function at the origin together with a decrease in the marginal propensity to tax (for $\alpha < 0$). In the following exposition k is assumed to be positive.

Equation (7) could have been given the following form: $W = (-e - \alpha)(f - \beta)Y$, but we would then have had to treat a function with two independent parameters (α and β) and the following analysis would have been greatly complicated. Equation (7) as it stands can be applied to any tax cut; it embodies an infinity of tax revenue functions (one for every value assigned to the constant, k).

As the marginal propensity to consume with respect to disposable income, b_D, is equal to $b/(1 - f)$, the consumption function (1) changes to

$$C = a + \alpha b_D + (b + \alpha k b_D)Y. \tag{8}$$

In equilibrium, by definition

$$Y = C + I + G. \tag{9}$$

Substituting (2), (3), and (8) into (9) and differentiating implicitly we get

$$\frac{dY}{d\alpha} = \frac{b_D + kb_DY}{1 - d - (b + \alpha kb_D)}, \tag{10}$$

which is the income multiplier with respect to a tax cut as determined by α (given k). Inspection of (7) shows that the magnitude of a tax cut[6] is proportional to α, that is,

$$\frac{\Delta W}{\Delta \alpha} = 1 + kY, \tag{11}$$

which is a constant at the given level of income, $\overline{Y}$, and for given k. Consequently,

$$\frac{\Delta W}{\Delta \alpha} = \frac{dW}{d\alpha}. \tag{12}$$

To compare the effectiveness of a dollar tax cut with a dollar increase in government expenditures on goods and services, we must relate the increase in income to the decrease in tax revenue measured in dollars; in other words we must find dY/dW.
But

$$\frac{dY}{dW} = \frac{dY}{d\alpha} \div \frac{dW}{d\alpha}. \tag{13}$$

Substituting (10), (11), and (12) into (13), and dividing through by 1 + kY we obtain

$$\frac{dY}{dW} = \frac{b_D}{1 - b - d - \alpha kb_D}. \tag{14}$$

Equation (14) shows that dY/dW is an increasing function of α; in other words a \$2 tax cut is more than twice as effective as a \$1 tax cut. If k = 0, dY/dW becomes the familiar tax cut multiplier for a parallel shift in the tax function.

To identify the conditions under which a \$1 tax cut is exactly as effective as

[6]By a \$1 billion tax cut is understood a change in the tax revenue function such that tax revenue at the current level of income declines by \$1 billion.

a \$1 increase in government expenditures we equate the government expenditures multiplier (6) to the tax cut multiplier (14):

$$\frac{1}{1-b-d}=\frac{b_D}{1-b-d-\alpha k b_D}, \tag{15}$$

$$\text{or } b_D = 1 - \frac{\alpha k b_D}{1-b-d}. \tag{16}$$

As $1 - b_D$ is the marginal propensity to save with respect to disposable income, s_D, we obtain:

$$s_D = \frac{\alpha k b_D}{(1-b-d)}, \text{ or} \tag{17}$$

$$\alpha k = \frac{s_D(1-b-d)}{b_D} = \frac{s(1-b-d)}{b}, \tag{18}$$

where s is the marginal propensity to save with respect to net national product.

From (18) we can now conclude that if the percentage point cut, αk, in the marginal propensity to tax is equal to the ratio between the marginal propensity to save and the marginal propensity to consume (out of net national product or disposable income) divided by the "ordinary" multiplier, then dollar for dollar tax cuts are just as effective with respect to increasing the level of income as increases in government expenditures on goods and services.

Working through equations (15), (16), (17), and (18) with inequality signs easily shows that if the percentage point tax cut is greater (smaller) than the ratio between the two marginal propensities mentioned above divided by the multiplier, then dollar for dollar tax cuts are more (less) effective than increases in government expenditures.

NUMERICAL ILLUSTRATION

Let equations (1) through (5) be:

$$C = 30 + .6Y, \tag{1}$$

$$1 = -20 + .2Y, \tag{2}$$

$$G = 80, \tag{3}$$

$$W = -20 + .25Y, \text{ and} \tag{4}$$

$$\overline{Y} = \frac{30 - 20 + 80}{1 - .6 - .2} = 450. \tag{5}$$

Choose k in (7) equal to .005:

$$W = (-20 - \alpha) + (.25 - .005\alpha)Y. \tag{7}$$

The consumption function (8) then becomes (b_D = .8):

$$C = 30 + .8\alpha + (.6 + .004\alpha)Y. \tag{8}$$

We shall distinguish between two cases (A and B).

(A) *Tax cut more effective than an increase in government expenditures.*

Choose α = 12, that is, the tax cut lowers the marginal propensity to tax from 25 per cent to 19 per cent (αk = .06) and shifts the tax revenue function downward by 12 at the origin.

Inserting α = 12 in the consumption function (8) we obtain

$$C = 39.6 + .648Y.^{7} \tag{8'}$$

Equilibrium income, $\overline{Y}$, is now:

$$\overline{Y} = \frac{39.6 - 20 + 80}{1 - .648 - .2} = 655.3.$$

The increase in income, ΔY, as a result of the tax cut is

$$\Delta Y = 655.3 - 450 = 205.3;$$

the decrease in tax revenue, ΔW (at the old level of income), is

$$\Delta W = 12 + 6 \text{ per cent of } 450 = 39;$$

consequently the tax cut multiplier, dY/dW, must have been

$$\frac{dY}{dW} = \frac{205.3}{39} = 5.3.$$

[7]Instead of using the "C + I + G" approach, the multiplier (10) could have been used.

The multiplier pertaining to an increase in government expenditures, dY/dG, however, is only

$$\frac{dY}{dG} = \frac{1}{1 - .6 - .2} = 5. \qquad (6')$$

We conclude that a tax cut of the magnitude and nature considered here is more effective with respect to its income generating ability than an increase in government expenditures of the same size.

(B) *Tax cut less effective than an increase in government expenditures.*

Choose $\alpha = 6$, that is, the tax cut lowers the marginal propensity to tax from 25 per cent to 22 per cent ($\alpha k = .03$) and shifts the tax revenue function downward by 6 at the origin.

The consumption function now is

$$C = 34.8 + .624Y, \text{ and}$$

$$\overline{Y} = \frac{34.8 - 20 + 80}{1 - .624 - .2} = 538.6. \qquad (8'')$$

The tax cut multiplier, dY/dW, is

$$\frac{dY}{dW} = \frac{538.6 - 450}{19.5} = 4.5$$

In this case the tax cut is less effective than a similar increase in government expenditures.[8]

CONCLUSION

Let us try, in a very rough manner, to relate the model developed above to the current situation using the following data from 1962: net national product, 506; consumption expenditures, 357; net private domestic investment, 29; and personal and corporate savings, 36.[9] From these figures we can estimate the following propensities: average propensity to consume with respect to NNP = .70; average propensity to save with respect to NNP = .07; and average propensity to invest with respect to NNP = .06.

[8]It is easily seen from (18) that a reduction in the marginal propensity to tax by 5 percentage points represents the borderline case between A and B.

[9]See *Federal Reserve Bulletin,* May, 1963.

Assuming that the marginal propensities to save and invest are greater than the corresponding average propensities while the opposite is the case with respect to the propensities to consume, we can perhaps assume that (in very rounded numbers): the marginal propensity to consume with respect to NNP, b, = .60; the marginal propensity to save with respect to NNP, s, = .10; and the marginal propensity to invest with respect to NNP, d, = .10. Inserting these values in (18) we get

$$\alpha k = \frac{.10(1 - .6 - .1)}{.6} = .05.$$

We conclude that if current tax rates are lowered such that the marginal propensity to tax out of net national product is decreased by more than approximately 5 percentage points, then dollar for dollar the tax cut would be more effective with respect to increasing net national product than an increase in government expenditures on goods and services.

10

TAX REVISION: IMPACT ON OUTPUT AND EMPLOYMENT

Tax reduction will directly increase the disposable income and purchasing power of consumers and business, strengthen incentives and expectations, and raise the net returns on new capital investment. This will lead to initial increases in private consumption and investment expenditures. These increases in spending will set off a cumulative expansion, generating further increases in consumption and investment spending and a general rise in production, income, and employment. This process is discussed in some detail in this section. Tax reduction may also have financial effects associated with the increased budget deficit that it will initially produce. Since these effects—in the first instance, at least—depend on the methods used to finance the deficit, they are left for discussion in a later section [not included in this reading] dealing with monetary and debt management policy.

INITIAL EFFECTS: CONSUMPTION

Effects on Disposable Income

The proposed reduction in personal income tax rates will directly add to the disposable income of households. In addition, the reduction in corporate tax rates will increase the after-tax profits of corporations as a result of which corporations may be expected to increase their dividend payments. The initial direct effect on the disposable income of households resulting from the entire program of tax reductions should be approximately $8½ billion, at current levels of income.

Reprinted from the *Annual Report of the Council of Economic Advisers* (January 1963), pp. 45–51.

Consumer Response to Increase in Disposable Income

The ratio of total consumption expenditures to total personal disposable income has in each recent calendar year fallen within the range of 92 to 94 percent. Although there are lags and irregularities from quarter to quarter or even year to year, the change in personal consumption expenditures has in the past, after a few quarters, averaged roughly 93 percent of any change in personal disposable income. On this basis, the initial addition to consumer expenditures associated with tax reductions would be on the order of $8 billion, although all would not be spent at once.

Additions to after-tax incomes resulting from tax reduction are likely to be spent in the same way as other additions to income. The largest part of the proposed tax reduction will be reflected in reduced withholding of taxes from wages and salaries, and therefore in larger wage and salary checks; thus, it will be indistinguishable from additional income arising from wage or salary increases, greater employment, or longer hours of work. Similarly, part of the reduced corporate taxes will be passed along to stockholders in increased dividend checks. Stockholders will not be able to identify the source of their additional dividends. Tax reduction dollars carry no identifying label, and there is no reason to expect recipients to treat them differently from other dollars.

Recent experience with tax reduction demonstrates clearly that additions to disposable income from this source are spent as completely as any other additions. Taxes were reduced by about $4.7 billion on May 1, 1948, retroactive to January 1, with resulting large refunds in mid-1949. Again taxes were cut, net, by about $6 billion, effective January 1, 1954, with further cuts later that year. Table 1 shows that the percentage of disposable income spent by consumers remained within the normal range of quarterly fluctuation during the periods following the enactment of each of these tax reductions.

Table 1. Personal Consumption Expenditures as Percent of Disposable Personal Income During Two Postwar Periods of Tax Reduction

1948–49		*1953–55*	
Quarter	*Percent*	*Quarter*	*Percent*
1948: I	97.3	1953: IV	91.5
II	94.0	1954: I	91.8
III	92.6	II	92.8
IV	93.2	III	93.0
1949: I	93.9	IV	93.2
II	95.2	1955: I	94.5
III	95.7	II	93.5

It is sometimes suggested that tax reductions which add only a few dollars to the weekly pay check of the typical worker would do little good even if the money was spent, since the amounts involved would not be large enough to permit major expenditures—say on washing machines or automobiles. Instead, the money would be "frittered away" on minor expenditures and would do little good for the economy. But all purchases lead to production which generates income and provides employment. Therefore, the purpose of tax reduction is achieved when the proceeds are spent on any kind of goods or services.

Actually, of course, tax reduction which expands take-home pay even by a relatively small amount each week or month may induce recipients to purchase durable goods or houses of higher quality, since the increased income would permit them to handle larger monthly installment payments. It may even induce a rearrangement of expenditure patterns and thus bring about purchases of durable goods that would not otherwise be made.

INITIAL EFFECTS: INVESTMENT

Investment is a more volatile element than consumption in national expenditure. The timing and magnitude of its response to tax changes is less predictable. But a cut in tax rates on business income will stimulate spending on new plants and new machinery in two ways. First, it will strengthen investment incentives by increasing the after-tax profits that businessmen can expect to earn on new productive facilities. Second, it will add to the supply of internal funds, a large part of which is normally reinvested in the business (though part of this effect may initially be offset by the proposed acceleration of corporate tax payments).

Since the largest part of business investment is made by corporations, the proposed cuts in the corporate income tax are especially significant. But investments of unincorporated businesses will also be encouraged by cuts in personal income tax rates, especially in the upper brackets.

Two important reforms affecting the taxation of business income designed to stimulate investment in plant and equipment were put into effect during 1962: the new depreciation guidelines and the investment tax credit.

Evidence to date clearly indicates that these measures are already stimulating some capital spending that would not otherwise have taken place. The impact of the 1962 actions and the 1963 proposals to reduce taxes on business will, of course, differ from company to company and industry to industry, depending in part on the adequacy of their internal funds and their levels of capacity utilization. Though the speed of response may vary, industry after industry will begin to feel pressure on its capital facilities and funds as markets for its products are expanded by the 1963 tax program.

Furthermore, there are many individual companies for which the supply of internal funds is a constraint on investment, and many others that do not have excess capacity. Moreover, it is estimated that some 70 percent of the investment in plant and equipment is for modernization and replacement rather than expansion, that is, it is designed to produce new or better products, or to reduce production costs rather than primarily to expand productive capacity. For this large segment of capital spending, the stronger inducement to invest provided by the business tax changes already adopted and those now proposed will translate much more readily into actual purchases of plant and equipment.

As production expands and existing capacity is more fully utilized, the depreciation guidelines and the investment tax credit and the new business tax reductions will provide an even stronger stimulus to investment.

CUMULATIVE EXPANSION: THE CONSUMPTION MULTIPLIER

Tax reduction will start a process of cumulative expansion throughout the economy. If the economy is already undergoing slow expansion, this cumulative process will be superimposed upon it. The initial increases in spending will stimulate production and employment, generating additional incomes. The details and timing of this process will vary from industry to industry. The first impact may be to draw down inventories rather than to expand production. But as inventories are depleted, retailers will quickly expand orders. As manufacturers' sales rise in response and their own inventories of finished goods decline, they will activate idle production lines, hire additional workers, place orders for materials and components. Thus the expansion will be spread to other industries, leading to further expansion of production, employment, and orders.

Expanded sales mean increased profits. Increased employment means greater wage and salary income. Each additional dollar's worth of gross production necessarily generates a dollar of additional gross income.

But expansion does not proceed without limit. A considerable fraction of the value of gross production is shared with governments or becomes part of corporate retained earnings and does not become part of consumers' after-tax income. Some of the increase goes to pay additional excise and other indirect business taxes. Typically, when GNP is rising toward potential, corporate profits increase by about one-fourth of the rise in GNP. But a substantial part of this increase in profits is absorbed by Federal and State corporate income taxes, and another part is ordinarily retained by the corporations. Only the remainder is passed on to the households in dividend payments.

Part of the additional wage and salary incomes associated with added production is absorbed by higher social security contributions. At the same time, increased employment means a drop in payments for unemployment insurance benefits.

When all of these "leakages" are taken into account, a little less than two-thirds of an additional dollar of GNP finds its way into the before-tax incomes of consumers in the form of wages, dividends, and other incomes. Part is absorbed by personal taxes, Federal, State, and local. The increase in personal disposable income is 50 to 55 percent. Of this amount a small fraction–about 7 percent–is set aside in personal saving, and the remainder–about 93 percent–is spent on consumption, as indicated earlier. Thus, out of each additional dollar of GNP, initially generated by the tax cut, roughly half ends up as added consumption expenditure. But the process does not stop here.

The additional expenditure on consumption that is brought about by the rise in GNP generates, in its turn, further production, which generates additional incomes and consumption, and so on, in a continuous sequence of expansion which economists call the "multiplier process." The "multiplier" applicable to the initial increase in spending resulting from tax reduction, with account taken of the various leakages discussed above, works out to roughly 2. If we apply this multiplier only to the initial increase in consumption (about $8 billion), the total ultimate effect will be an increase in annual consumption–and in production (and GNP)–of roughly $16 billion. Lags in the process of expansion will spread this increase in GNP over time, but studies of the relationships between changes in disposable income, consumption, and production of consumer goods suggest that at least half of the total stimulus of an initial increase in disposable income is realized within 6 months of that increase.

CUMULATIVE EXPANSION: THE INVESTMENT RESPONSE

Tax reduction will also have important cumulative indirect effects on investment in inventories and in fixed productive facilities. These effects are much more difficult to predict than the induced effects on consumption.

Inventory Investment

The stocks of goods that businessmen wish to hold depend upon current and expected rates of sales and production and the volume of new and unfilled orders, as well as on price expectations and other factors. An expansion of aggregate demand can be expected to raise business inventory targets. Production for inventory will generate further increases in demand and income over and above the multiplier effects discussed above, and will in turn induce further increases in consumption spending.

Inventory investment is volatile, and induced inventory accumulation can add significantly to the expansionary effects of tax reduction within a few months. At the same time, it should be recognized that inventory investment is exceedingly difficult to forecast. As the increase in production and sales tapers off, stocks and the rate of inventory investment will be correspondingly adjusted.

Business Investment in Plant and Equipment

A tax reduction large enough to move the economy toward full employment will also stimulate business investment in plant and equipment. General economic expansion will reinforce the initial stimulus to investment of cuts in business taxes. In the first place, narrowing the gap between actual and potential output–now estimated at $30–40 billion–will increase the utilization of existing plant and equipment. As excess capacity declines, more and more businesses will feel increasing pressure to expand capacity. At the same time, increases in the volume of sales and in productivity will raise corporate profits–in absolute terms, relative to GNP, and as a rate of return on investment. Internal funds available for investment will rise, while at the same time higher rates of return on existing capital will cause businessmen to raise their estimates of returns on new investment. When investment incentives are strengthened by rising demand, internal funds are more consistently translated into increased investment than when markets are slack.

Residential Construction

The demand for housing depends on growth in the number of families, on the existing stock of houses, and on the cost and availability of mortgage credit. But housing demand also responds, to some extent, to changes in disposable income. Thus, tax reduction will have some direct effect on residential construction. And as production, employment, and income generally expand, the demand for new homes can be expected to increase further. This increase will, in turn, reinforce the other expansionary effects of tax reduction.

STATE AND LOCAL GOVERNMENT EXPENDITURES

State and local government units have found it difficult to finance the needed expansion of their activities. Given the present importance of income and sales taxes in State and local tax systems, government revenues at the State and local level expand automatically as GNP rises. The additional State-local revenues generated by economic expansion will assist these governments to meet their pressing needs. Moreover, since Federal tax liabilities are deductible under many State income tax laws, reduction in Federal tax rates will automatically generate some further addition to State-local tax revenues. Finally, a reduction in Federal taxes will enlarge the tax base available to State and local government units and may make it easier for them to raise rates or impose new taxes.

Undoubtedly, some of the added State-local revenues will be used either to retire existing debt or to reduce current borrowing rather than to increase expenditures. Whether the net result will be expansionary will depend upon whether the proportion of additional tax revenues spent on goods and services by State and local government units is greater or smaller than the proportion which would have been spent by the taxpayers from whom they collect the additional taxes. But whether or not the response of State and local government units is such as to strengthen the aggregate impact of Federal tax reduction on income and employment, the Federal tax program will ease, to some extent, the problems of these units in obtaining revenues needed to finance urgent public activities, such as education, transportation facilities, and urban development.

SUMMARY OF EFFECTS ON GNP

Tax reductions for consumers will have initial direct effects on the demand for goods and services, as consumers raise their spending level to reflect their higher after-tax incomes. Corporate tax reductions and the lower tax rates applicable to the highest personal income brackets will stimulate investment directly, through raising the rate of return on new investments and providing additional funds for their financing. Some of the tax reforms will also have a directly stimulating effect on productive investment.

These direct or initial effects on spending would occur even if total output, employment, and incomes remained unchanged. But the increased spending cannot fail to increase total output, employment, and incomes. And as activity responds to the initially increased level of spending, cumulative impacts begin to develop in which the several elements interact to carry the expansion far beyond its initial point.

The higher incomes which consumers receive from the added production of both consumer and capital goods will lead to a further step-up in the rate of spending, creating further increases in incomes and spending. The same expansion process raises rates of capacity utilization, thereby interacting with the initial impact of tax reduction on business incomes to make investment both for modernization and expansion more profitable. This in turn generates higher consumer incomes and more spending, helping to provide the added demand which justifies the higher investment.

If there were no investment stimulus—either initially, or as a result of the cumulative process of expansion—we could expect that GNP would ultimately expand by about $16 billion. If the result were no more than this, the tax reduction would still be abundantly rewarding in terms of greater production, employment, purchasing power, and profits. What will really be given up to produce added output will be only unwanted idleness of workers (whose families have reduced neither their needs nor aspirations) and incomplete utilization of plant and machinery (which have continued to depreciate).

But the pay-off is much more than this purely consumption impact. There is also an investment impact, and each extra dollar of investment that is stimulated should bring roughly another dollar of added consumption and encourage still further investment.

A strong expansion can alter profoundly the whole climate within which investment decisions are made. If not at once, then somewhat later, subtle but significant changes in business attitudes occur in response to the trend in the economic outcome. We have referred earlier to the cautious investment attitudes that more than 5 years of slack markets have generated. This caution did not arise at once in mid-1957, when output first began to fall away from the track of potential expansion. It developed gradually, fed on itself, and in part helped to justify itself. The reverse can and will happen.

No one can pretend to estimate with precision the ultimate impact of a program so far-reaching as that which the President will propose: it would come into operation in stages extending from July 1, 1963 to January 1, 1965, and its effects would cumulate and spread into 1966 and beyond.

Our study of the program, and our tentative projections based upon it do, however, convince us that the program measures up to the challenge that the 1960's present to our economy: that it will surely set us on a path toward our interim employment target; and that it will lay the foundation for more rapid long-run growth.

IV

Money and Interest

What has come to be called the "simple" Keynesian model is usually understood to mean a model in which aggregate demand is made up only of consumption and investment expenditures and in which the influence of the stock of money and the rate of interest on these expenditures is disregarded. The models presented in the readings of Part III brought in government expenditures and taxation and thus represented a large step beyond the simple consumption and investment expenditure model, but they still did not make any allowance for the influence of money and interest. We now take this next step in a group of articles concerned with the theory of money and interest.

The first selection, by Lawrence S. Ritter, traces the differences between the simple Keynesian model, designated "Keynes without money," and the more complete Keynesian model, designated "Keynes with money." Bringing money into the Keynesian model amounts to bringing in the question of why people hold money and the determinants of the amount they wish to hold or, in other words, the question of the demand for money in general and the Keynesian innovation of the so-called speculative demand for money in particular.

The other three papers in this part are concerned with various aspects of the theory of the demand for money. The first of these is an excerpt from an article in which James S. Duesenberry discusses the supply of liquid assets, corporate demand for money and other liquid assets, and household demand for money and other liquid assets. The excerpt included here covers the discussion of household demand only. It provides an unusually clear statement of the motives underlying household holdings of money and other liquid assets and offers some empirical evidence on the relative importance of these various motives in the total of household demand.

The speculative motive for holding money was employed by Keynes to describe what he believed to be a systematic relationship between the rate of interest and the amount of money the public chooses to hold over and above the amount it needs to meet its day-by-day transactions requirements. After Keynes, economists showed that there is, apart from the speculative demand, also such a relationship between the rate of interest and the amount of money the public holds for transactions purposes. The systematization of the concept of an interest-elastic transactions demand for money is known as the Baumol-Tobin thesis, after the two economists who developed it during the fifties. The third selection in this part is the article by William J. Baumol in which he develops his inventory-theoretic approach to the subject.

The final article in this part, by Henry A. Latané, is a relatively early and quite modest empirical study of the relationship between the interest rate and the demand for cash balances that has come to be a short classic in monetary economics.

11

THE ROLE OF MONEY IN KEYNESIAN THEORY

LAWRENCE S. RITTER

In recent years it has frequently been asserted, primarily by Quantity theorists, that the main characteristic of Keynesian theory is that "money does not matter."[1] The view that "money matters" is held to be the exclusive province of the Quantity theory, and extensive statistical tests are thereupon conducted to demonstrate that the supply of money has had an important influence on the level of economic activity. On this basis, Keynesian theory is, *ipso facto,* declared fallacious.

The purpose of this essay is to examine carefully the role of money in Keynesian theory, in order to evaluate the thesis that in the Keynesian system "money does not matter." It turns out that the validity of this point of view depends in large part on which version of Keynesian theory one has in mind, just as the validity of many Keynesian criticisms of the Quantity theory depends on which version of the latter one has in mind.

[1]See, for example, Milton Friedman's statements in *Studies in the Quantity Theory of Money* (Chicago: University of Chicago Press, 1965), p. 3; *Employment, Growth, and Price Levels,* Hearings before the Joint Economic Committee, U. S. Congress, 1959, pp. 606–7; and *A Program for Monetary Stability* (New York: Fordham University Press, 1960), p. 1.

Reprinted from Deane Carson, ed., *Banking and Monetary Studies,* sponsored by the U. S. Comptroller of the Currency (Richard D. Irwin, Inc., 1963), pp. 134–50, by permission of the publisher. Lawrence S. Ritter is a professor at New York University.

I. KEYNES WITHOUT MONEY

The most familiar version of Keynesian economics, which we will call Model A, is the elementary simplification of Keynes in which the only determinants of the level of national income are the consumption function and a given volume of investment (including government) spending. Consumption spending is seen as depending mainly upon income, and investment spending is assumed to be given, determined autonomously. Occasionally, in order to include an accelerator effect, investment spending may also be made to depend partly upon income. Within this context, the equilibrium level of national income is found where realized income, resulting from consumption plus investment expenditures, equals anticipated income, on the basis of which spending decisions are made. Alternatively, equilibrium income is that level of income at which planned investment equals planned saving.

It is this simplified model which has been popularized by the widely known "Keynesian cross" diagram, in which either consumption and investment or saving and investment are plotted on the vertical axis, and anticipated income is plotted on the horizontal axis. Equilibrium income is determined where aggregate demand equals anticipated income or, alternatively, where planned investment equals planned saving. [2] This particular analytical system has also been the basis for the bulk of orthodox Keynesian multiplier theory: a sustained increase in autonomous spending is assumed to raise equilibrium income by a multiple of the initial increment in spending. The specific value of the multiplier is determined solely by the size of the marginal propensity to consume. Such an uncomplicated formula for the value of the multiplier can only be derived from an equally uncomplicated frame of reference, such as that outlined above.[3] For if the value of the multiplier depends solely on the size of the marginal propensity to consume, it must be assumed, implicitly or explicitly, that spending is insensitive to such increases in interest rates and tightening of credit availability as would normally accompany an expansion in income.

On the basis of this model, countless public policy recommendations, dealing almost exclusively with the implications of alternative fiscal policies, have been advanced over the years in the name of Keynesian economics. In this scheme of things, the Quantity theory's characterization of the Keynesian system as one in which "money does not matter" is quite accurate: national

[2]This has been a standard textbook diagram for well over a decade. See Paul A. Samuelson, *Economics* (5th ed.; New York: McGraw-Hill Book Co., Inc., 1961), chap. xiii, or Abba P. Lerner, *Economics of Employment* (New York:McGraw-Hill Book Co., Inc., 1951), chap. v.

[3]See Paul A. Samuelson, "The Simple Mathematics of Income Determination," in *Income, Employment, and Public Policy* (New York: W. W. Norton & Co., Inc., 1948),, pp. 133-55; and L. S. Ritter, "Some Monetary Aspects of Multiplier Theory and Fiscal Policy," *Review of Economic Studies,* Vol. XXIII, No. 2 (1956), pp. 126-31.

income is determined without any reference whatsoever to either the supply of or the demand for money, and public policy prescriptions are confined to the area of fiscal policy. Monetary policy is completely extraneous. That this model evidently commands considerable allegiance, even today, is attested to by the great amount of attention paid in 1962 and 1963 to alternative forms of tax reduction, and to the size of the resulting budget deficit, as compared with the relative lack of interest in how such a deficit should be financed, i.e., whether by monetary creation or otherwise.

II. KEYNES WITH MONEY

Although Model A is probably the most popular version of Keynesian economics, it is not the same economics to be found in Keynes' *The General Theory of Employment, Interest, and Money.* As far as Keynes himself was concerned, and as the title of his major work indicates, money plays a significant role in the determination of income and employment. Let us call the orthodox Keynesian system, as advanced in *The General Theory* and much subsequent literature, Model B.

Most important, Keynes did not assume that investment spending is exogenous, a given datum, but rather that it depends on relationships *within* the system, namely on comparisons between the expected rate of profit and the rate of interest. The rate of interest, in turn, depends on the supply of and demand for money. The demand for money, or liquidity preference, is viewed as consisting of two parts, the demand for idle money balances (with the amount demanded increasing as the rate of interest falls) and the demand for active or transaction balances (with the amount demanded increasing as the level of income rises).

In contrast to the partial Keynesian system, represented by Model A, the complete Keynesian system, Model B, requires that *two* conditions be fulfilled before income can be said to be in equilibrium. Not only must planned investment equal planned saving, as before, but in addition at any moment in time the amount of money people want to hold must equal the supply of money, the amount that is available for them to hold. If the second condition is not satisfied, the rate of interest will rise or fall, thereby altering the volume of investment and consequently changing the equilibrium level of income.[4]

If, at a given interest rate and income, planned investment equals planned

[4]The diagrammatics of the complete Keynesian system thus are not contained in the "Keynesian cross," but rather in Hicks' *IS* and *LM* curves. See J. R. Hicks, "Mr. Keynes and the Classics; A Suggested Interpretation," *Econometrica,* Vol. V (1937), pp. 147–59, reprinted in *Readings in the Theory of Income Distribution* (Philadelphia: The Blakiston Co., 1946), pp. 461–76 [also reprinted in this volume, Selection 15]. Also see Alvin H. Hansen, *Monetary Theory and Fiscal Policy* (New York: McGraw-Hill Book Co., Inc., 1949), chap. v, and his *A Guide to*

saving but the amount of money desired exceeds (falls short of) the supply, the interest rate will rise (fall), thereby reducing (increasing) investment spending and lowering (raising) the level of income. As the interest rate rises, the desired amount of idle balances contracts, and as income falls the desired amount of active balances contracts, until the amount of money demanded is reduced to the point where it is equal to the given supply. Thus, the equilibrium level of income eventually is reached, with both planned investment equal to planned saving and the demand for money equal to the supply, but the interest rate is now higher and income now lower than initially postulated.

Here there is room for monetary policy to operate: if the monetary authorities want to prevent upward pressure on the interest rate, and the consequent drop in income, they can increase the supply of money enough to satisfy the demand at the initial interest rate and income level. On the other hand, if they want to permit money income to fall, they can sit back and let nature take its course. Both of these are rather passive policies. More aggressive actions would call for increasing the money supply even more than enough to satisfy the initial demand, in order to stimulate an increase in income rather than merely prevent a decrease; or actually reducing the money supply, even though it is already less than the demand, to provide added impetus to the decline in income.

It is obvious that a policy of doing nothing is but one alternative among a spectrum of possibilities. The Federal Reserve at times seems to suggest that those changes in interest rates which occur when the central bank is passive are none of its doing. It is implied that changes in interest rates which take place when the central bank is holding the money supply constant are solely the result of "free market forces," and are in some sense preferable to changes which result from more active monetary policies. But as long as interest rates could be different if the central bank did something rather than nothing, it follows that interest rates are what they are in part because the central bank prefers them that way.

All this does not mean that the monetary authorities are omnipotent. In the orthodox Keynesian system, monetary policy is important but not always in the same degree. As a general principle, monetary policy is likely to be *less* effective the more interest-elastic the demand for idle balances (for then a change in the money supply will not succeed in altering the interest rate) and the less interest-elastic the investment and consumption schedules (for then a change in the interest rate will not induce a change in spending). This has typically been construed by most Keynesians to mean that monetary policy is likely to be less effective in combating depression than in stopping inflation.

Keynes (New York: McGraw-Hill Book Co., Inc., 1953), chap. vii. For a concise exposition see Joseph P. McKenna, *Aggregate Economic Analysis* (New York: Holt, Rinehart & Winston, Inc., 1955), chap. viii.

In a severe depression, the public may prefer to hold additional amounts of money at low interest rates rather than lend it out or buy securities, so that the rate of interest may reach a floor below which it will not fall; investment prospects may appear so bleak that reductions in interest rates become of negligible importance; and job prospects may appear so dismal that consumer spending on durable goods is severely inhibited, despite such additions to the public's wealth as are brought about by expanding the stock of money.

In formal Keynesian terms, during severe depressions the interest-elasticity of liquidity preference may become so great as to prevent increases in the supply of money from reducing the interest rate, as they normally would. And investment and consumer spending may become so unresponsive to changes in interest rates and in wealth as to preclude what would be expected to be their normal reactions. In terms of the equation of exchange, $MV = PT$, increases in the money supply would be offset by proportionate reductions in the velocity of money. Under such circumstances, money again "does not matter" in the Keynesian system, in the sense that increases in the money supply beyond a certain point will not affect the volume of spending, and for all practical purposes we are back in the world of Model A above.

It is important to realize, however, that severe depression is only a special case in the general Keynesian system. And even then, *decreases* in the money supply would not be looked upon as trivial. In other instances, the supply of money may be of crucial importance. From the beginning, for example, it has been a basic tenet of Keynesian doctrine that inflation cannot proceed very far without an increase in the supply of money. Rising incomes are seen as leading to larger demands for transactions balances, which in the absence of increases in the money supply must be drawn from formerly idle balances, inducing a rise in interest rates. This process can continue until idle balances are depleted, or perhaps somewhat further if there is some interest-elasticity in the demand for active balances at high interest rates. But, unless the money supply is increased, the expansion in spending is viewed as having to grind to a halt before too long, because rising interest rates and tightening monetary conditions in general will sooner or later choke off investment spending.[5] Indeed, so strongly has this position been held by some orthodox Keynesians that they have at times objected to the use of monetary policy to stop inflation because of the fear that it is likely to be *too* effective.[6] In brief,

[5]"A rise in prices and incomes leads to an increase in requirements for money balances in active circulation. This tends to reduce the amount available for inactive balances and so causes the rate of interest to rise, which checks investment. The rope which holds the value of money is a limitation on its supply. If the monetary authorities are compelled to increase the supply of money, the rope frays and snaps in their hands." Joan Robinson, *Essays in the Theory of Employment* (Macmillan, 1937), pp. 17–21 (spliced quotation). Also see J. R. Hicks, *op. cit.*

[6]See Alvin H. Hansen, *Monetary Theory and Fiscal Policy,* pp. 161–63. For a closely related view see Keynes, *op. cit.*, pp. 322–23.

in the orthodox Keynesian system sometimes the supply of money is not very important, sometimes it is critically important, and most of the time it is somewhere in between, depending in each instance on the circumstances at hand.

It is rather ironic that Keynes should be the target of a blanket charge by Quantity theorists that he is responsible for propagating the view that "money does not matter." For in Keynes' own mind he was enlarging the scope of monetary theory, not narrowing it.[7] Before Keynes, prevailing monetary theory in the form of the Quantity theory of money, had been concerned almost exclusively with the determination of the general level of prices, to the neglect of the influence of money on real output and employment. As expressed by Jean Bodin in 1569, through John Locke, David Hume, David Ricardo, John Stuart Mill, and Irving Fisher, the Quantity theory had always stressed that the supply of money determined primarily the absolute price level. The velocity of money was held to be an institutional datum and aggregate real output was assumed at the full employment level by virtue of Say's Law. In terms of the equation of exhange, $MV = PT$, V and T were assumed to be given so that changes in the money supply would result in proportionate changes in prices.[8]

The policy implications of the pre-Keynesian Quantity theory were simple and paralyzing. Increases in the supply of money, even in periods of substantial unemployment, could never achieve any permanent benefit. They could only be harmful, by raising prices proportionately–a view that is deeply imbedded in popular folklore to this day. It is this framework, rather than the Keynesian, which in a fundamental sense views money as unimportant. Here money is seen as "neutral," a veil behind which "real" forces work themselves out just about as they would in the absence of money. In the Keynesian approach, on the other hand, money also plays a role in the determination of real output. For the first time money becomes more than merely a veil, and a monetary economy is seen as behaving very differently from a barter economy.

III. NEW DEPARTURES

Model C is a lineal descendant of Model B, but comes to rather different conclusions. Although Model C uses most of the orthodox Keynesian apparatus, it is so unorthodox in its handling of selected parts of that apparatus as to make it debatable whether it should be classified as a version of Keynesian theory. Perhaps it should be given a category of its own and called Radcliffism, since it has been most closely associated with the work of

[7]See *The General Theory,* Preface, chap. xvii, and pp. 292–94. On this point see also Dudley Dillard, "The Theory of a Monetary Economy," in Kenneth Kurihara, ed., *Post-Keynesian Economics* (New Brunswick, N. J.: Rutgers University Press, 1954), pp. 3–30.

[8]As expressed by Irving Fisher, in the most widely accepted pre-Keynesian statement of the

the Radcliffe Committee and Professors Gurley and Shaw.[9] In any case, in this model changes in the money supply are seen as no more likely to be effective against inflation than they were against depression in Model B!

The analysis of Model C differs from both previous models in that it does not ignore the liquidity preference function, as A does, nor does it stress the significance of its interest-elasticity, as B does. Rather than being ignored, the liquidity preference function is an integral part of Model C, *but the demand for liquidity is no longer viewed as identical with the demand for money.* And rather than stressing the importance of the interest-elasticity of the demand schedule for money, attention is directed instead to the likelihood of *shifts* in that schedule. While the orthodox Keynesian literature has a great deal to say about shifts in the investment demand function, through the influence of changes in expectations, it tends to ignore the possibility of shifts in the demand for money, and instead concentrates almost exclusively on its interest-elasticity.

In the orthodox Keynesian system, Model B, the demand for liquidity is synonymous with the demand for money. The ready availability of interest-yielding money substitutes, however, destroys that equation. Such near monies as time deposits, savings and loan shares, and Treasury bills are virtually as liquid as cash and in addition yield an interest return. Thus, the demand for money (demand deposits plus currency) may contract even though the demand for liquidity broadly conceived remains stable. Liquidity preference, in other words, may be satisfied partially by holdings of money substitutes in place of money itself.

There are two reasons for the demand for money in the orthodox Keynesian system. In the first place, active money balances are needed for transaction purposes. The demand for active balances is assumed to bear a more or less constant ratio to income, so that an expansion in income will lead to a proportionate increase in the amount of active balances desired. In the second place, idle cash is demanded because of uncertainties regarding the future course of interest rates. Idle cash is held primarily because of the fear that interest rates might rise (bond prices fall), imposing capital losses on bondholders. This is the main reason why Keynes believed that the amount

---

Quantity theory: "Since a doubling in the quantity of money will not appreciably affect either the velocity of circulation or the volume of trade, it follows necessarily and mathematically that the level of prices must double. There is no possible escape from the conclusion that a change in the quantity of money must normally cause a proportional change in the price level." Irving Fisher, *The Purchasing Power of Money* (Macmillan, 1911), pp. 156–57 (spliced quotation).

[9] *Report* of the Committee on the Working of the Monetary System (London, 1959), and J. G. Gurley and E. S. Shaw, *Money in a Theory of Finance* (Washington, D. C.: The Brookings Institution, 1960). See also J. G. Gurley, *Liquidity and Financial Institutions in the Postwar Economy,* Study Paper 14, Joint Economic Committee, U. S. Congress (1960); R. S. Sayers, "Monetary Thought and Monetary Policy in England," *Economic Journal,* Vol. LXX, No. 280 (December, 1960), pp. 710–24; and A. B. Cramp, "Two Views on Money," *Lloyds Bank Review,* No. 65 (July, 1962), pp. 1–15.

of idle cash desired would increase as the rate of interest falls.[10] The lower the rate of interest, the more it is likely to drop below what are considered "safe" or "normal" levels, leading to the expectation that its future course is likely to be upward, with consequent losses in capital values. Under such circumstances, it is prudent to get out of bonds and into a more liquid asset. In *The General Theory* the only liquid asset available is cash.

The existence of short-term money substitutes, however, provides an alternative to holding money for both of these purposes. With respect to *active* balances, there is no reason to assume that these need be held solely in the form of money. For immediate transactions purposes, there is little alternative to possessing the medium of exchange itself. But for payments scheduled for several months in the future, there are many assets available which can serve as a substitute for holding cash without diminishing liquidity, and which at the same time provide an interest income. Firms with scheduled payments to make at particular dates in the future can hold Treasury bills, sales finance company paper, or repurchase agreements with government securities dealers, for example—all of which can be easily arranged to come due when the cash is needed. The very purpose of tax anticipation bills is to fill just such a need. Similarly, households can hold time deposits, paying interest from date of deposit to date of withdrawal, pending anticipated payments. For possible emergencies, lines of credit can be arranged on a standby basis in place of holding idle cash.

Many other methods exist through which both households and business firms can economize on their average holdings of transactions cash without impairing their liquidity positions. Indeed, there is ample evidence that high short-term interest rates in the postwar period have stimulated the expenditure of considerable ingenuity in the economical management of cash balances, with consequent reductions in the required ratio of active money balances to income. To the extent that this is accomplished, an expansion in income will not lead to a proportionate increase in the amount of transactions cash desired.

With respect to *idle* balances, the existence of short-term money substitutes also provides an alternative to holding cash when it is feared that long-term interest rates might rise (bond prices fall). If it is thought that long-term rates are too low (bond prices too high) for safety, investors need not increase their holdings of idle cash to get liquidity, but instead can purchase Treasury bills or other interest-bearing liquid assets. With highly liquid money substitutes, the concept of a "safe" yield level is almost meaningless and the chance of suffering a capital loss close to nil; indeed, the very definition of a liquid asset is one which can be turned into cash on short notice with little or no loss in dollar value.

[10]See *General Theory*, pp. 201–2. Also see Day and Beza, *Money and Income* (New York: Oxford University Press, Inc., 1960), pp. 17–20.

The concept of a "safe" yield level is crucial in decisions as to whether or not to buy *long-term* securities, because the existence of uncertainty regarding future long rates gives rise to the fear of taking substantial capital losses (or the hope of making capital gains). But the rationale behind buying *short-term* liquid assets is that if yields rise no loss need be suffered. The securities will mature shortly anyway, and thereby turn into cash at their face value. And, in any event, even if one has no choice but to dispose of them before maturity, the resulting capital losses (or gains) are likely to be small. Unlike long-terms, a rather large change in yields on short-term instruments involves but a small change in their price.[11]

In brief, the amount of money desired may not increase when the rate of interest falls, even though the amount of liquidity desired does increase. At least part of the accumulation of liquidity is likely to take the form of interest-bearing near monies instead of nonearning cash. In comparison with Model B, the demand for idle cash balances will have contracted throughout the range of interest rates, even though the liquidity preference function may have remained stable. Under these circumstances, with both segments of the demand for money susceptible to leftward shifts, monetary policies confined to regulating the supply of money are not likely to be as successful in stemming inflation as orthodox Keynesian theory believes. Since the significant variable is not the supply of money, per se, but rather the supply relative to the demand, the flexibility of demand makes control of the supply, alone, an unreliable instrument through which to affect the level of economic activity. These results do not depend, as in orthodox Keynesian theory, on the short-run interest-elasticity of the demand for money, but rather on shifts in that demand.

In Model B, for example, if the economy is initially in equilibrium with planned investment equal to planned saving and the demand for money equal to the supply, an exogenous increase in spending will raise money income and increase the amount of transactions cash desired proportionately. Limitation of the money supply–holding it constant–will then automatically

[11]A rise in yields from 4 percent to 5 percent on a $1000 face value 30-year bond bearing a 4 percent coupon involves a fall in price from $1000 to $845. A similar rise in yield on a 3-month security of similar coupon involves a fall in price from $1000 to only $997.

The point can be made even more dramatically. Assume, not too unrealistically, that at the extreme long-term yields on government securities might be expected to vary between 2 percent and 6 percent in the foreseeable future, and short-term yields between 1 percent and 7 percent. The holder of a $1000 30-year bond bearing a 4 percent coupon might then anticipate, at the extreme, that its price might possibly vary between the limits of $723 and $1450. For a 3-month security of similar coupon, however, the possible range of price variation would be only from $992 to $1008. In one case possible range of price variation is $727 on a $1000 security, and in the other case it is only $16. Safety of principal is tenuous in the former, and practically assured in the latter.

These figures can be calculated from any bond basis book. See also Burton G. Malkiel, "Expectations, Bond Prices, and the Term Structure of Interest Rates," *Quarterly Journal of Economics,* Vol. LXXVI, No. 2 (May, 1962), pp. 197–218.

result in an excess demand for money, which will raise interest rates, check investment, and thereby bring the expansion in income to a halt. There will probably be some slippage, as the rise in interest rates attracts some funds out of idle cash holdings into transactions balances, with the degree of slippage depending on the interest-elasticity of the demand for idle balances and the specific ratio between active cash and income. But that same rise in interest rates, and the related tightening of monetary conditions in general, will tend to discourage some expenditures. In any event, sooner or later idle balances will be depleted. If the monetary authorities want to accelerate the process, they can provide added impetus by actually reducing the money supply rather than merely holding it stable.

In the world envisaged by Model C, on the other hand, these results are not as likely to be realized. If the required ratio of transactions cash to income contracts as income rises, the expansion in income will not lead to a proportionate increase in the amount of active cash desired. It may not even lead to an absolute increase. Limitation of the money supply then may not produce very much of an excess demand for money, so that upward pressure on interest rates will be negligible, investment will not be checked, and the rise in spending will proceed unhindered. If, at the same time, the demand for idle balances has also shifted to the left, then—regardless of its interest-elasticity—formerly idle balances will become available for transactions use, again with minimal increases in interest rates. Instead of an excess demand for money, there might conceivably be an excess supply, with consequent *downward* pressure on interest rates. Even if the monetary authorities were to actually reduce the supply of money, they might be hard put to keep pace with the contraction in demand. And although idle balances must sooner or later be depleted, this will pose no obstacle to the continued rise in spending if the desired active cash to income ratio continues to contract.

Of course, the process need not be this straightforward. Models B and C need not be mutually exclusive, but may be combined over several cycles. Interest rates may indeed rise during periods of cyclical expansion, especially if the expansion is vigorous, as spending increases more rapidly than can be accommodated by contractions in the demand schedules for money. However, rising interest rates are likely to stimulate new financial techniques for economizing on cash balances.[12] These techniques of cash management, introduced during periods of tight money, are not likely to be abandoned when rates recede in the subsequent recession. As a result, the contraction in the demand for money may not be clearly evident until the *next* upturn in business conditions. When that upturn comes, the supply of money may be more than ample to finance it, even though, by past standards, it would

[12]See Hyman P. Minsky, "Central Banking and Money Market Changes," *Quarterly Journal of Economics*, Vol. LXXI, No. 2 (May, 1957), pp. 171–87; and L. S. Ritter, "The Structure of Financial Markets, Income Velocity, and the Effectiveness of Monetary Policy," *Schweizerische Zeitschrift für Volkswirtschaft und Statistik*, Vol. XCVIII, No. 3 (September, 1962), pp. 276–89.

appear to be less than adequate. In effect, liquidity is accumulated during the recession, in the form of money substitutes instead of money, and is then released when needed to finance expenditures when economic activity revives.

Presumably, the central bank could always reduce the money supply drastically enough to counteract the decline in the demand for money, and thereby produce the results it wants. But with business prospects cloudy, as they generally are, and with past guidelines unreliable indicators of the current adequacy of the money supply, the monetary authorities are usually not sure enough of where they stand to take decisive action in *any* direction. This inaction is then rationalized by the invocation of moral principles, as ethical values are attributed to the determination of interest rates by "free market forces" and to "minimum intervention" in general.

It is for these reasons that Model C shifts attention away from the money supply narrowly defined to the significance of liquidity broadly conceived. Traditional monetary policy, which is confined to the control of the money supply, is seen as having to give way to a more broadly based liquidity policy if it is to successfully influence economic activity within the context of the present-day financial environment.[13] It is thus Radcliffe monetary theory, rather than orthodox Keynesian theory, which poses the most fundamental challenge to the modern Quantity theory of money.

IV. SUMMARY AND CONCLUSIONS

The differences between orthodox Keynesian theory (Model B), Radcliffe theory (Model C), and the modern Quantity theory of money can be summarized most conveniently in terms of their implications for the behavior of velocity. This simultaneously affords a comparison of their respective evaluations of the effectiveness of monetary policy. For if monetary policy is to be effective—i.e., if changes in the money supply are to produce changes in aggregate spending, and thus in income—then velocity must either remain more or less stable or else move in the same direction as the money supply.

If the phrase "money matters" is to have any operational meaning, it must imply the existence of such conditions. In terms of the equation of exchange, if changes in M are to produce changes in MV and thus in PT, then V must necessarily remain rather stable or else reinforce the change in M. On the other hand, to the extent that velocity falls when the money supply is increased, or rises when the money supply is decreased, or changes in the absence of changes in the money supply, the effectiveness of monetary policy

[13] In the words of the Radcliffe Report (paragraph 981, p. 337): "The factor which monetary policy should seek to influence or control is something that reaches far beyond what is known as 'the supply of money.' It is nothing less than the state of liquidity of the whole economy."

is correspondingly reduced. If these offsetting changes in velocity are so great that the influence of monetary policy is negligible, then "money does not matter." In between these two extremes lies a continuum of possibilities.

It should be noted that the modern Quantity theory is not precisely the same as the pre-Keynesian Quantity theory. As presented by Milton Friedman, the present-day version of the Quantity theory is no longer strictly an explanation of what determines the price level. Friedman uses the Quantity theory to explain major depressions as well as inflations, so that it is now, like the Keynesian approach, essentially a theory of income determination.[14]

In addition, Friedman accepts variations in velocity as consistent with the Quantity theory. Unlike Irving Fisher, Friedman does not view velocity as an institutional datum, nor as a numerical constant, but rather as a functional relationship in which the demand for money is a function of a number of variables within the system, such as interest rates, income, wealth, and expected changes in the price level. Depending on movements in these variables, velocity may vary both cyclically and secularly. This also represents a major shift in emphasis by the Quantity theory in the direction of the Keynesian approach, wherein velocity has *always* been functionally related to such variables.

Nevertheless, the two are still rather far apart. In Friedman's view, under normal circumstances the demand-for-money function is so stable and inelastic that such changes in velocity as do occur will not be very bothersome. Velocity may fall somewhat when the money supply is increased, or rise somewhat when the money supply is decreased, or even change to some extent in the absence of changes in the money supply so as to produce minor fluctuations in income despite stability in the stock of money. But these changes in velocity are assumed to be small. Velocity is no longer seen as constant, but it *is* seen as fluctuating only very moderately.[15] Thus, changes in

[14] In terms of the equation of exchange, T is no longer assumed as given by virtue of Say's Law, so that changes in the supply of money can affect output and employment as well as the price level. See Milton Friedman, "The Quantity Theory of Money—A Restatement," in *Studies in the Quantity Theory of Money,* and Chapter 1 in *A Program for Monetary Stability.* Friedman prefers to view the Quantity theory as a theory of the demand for money rather than a theory of income determination, with the addition of the supply of money necessary before income can be determined. However, this is a purely semantic matter. In the same sense, neither is orthodox Keynesian theory a theory of income determination until the supply of money is given.

[15] In Friedman's words: "It is, of course, true that velocity varies over short periods of time. The fact of the matter, however, is that these variations are in general relatively small." *Monetary Policy and Management of the Public Debt,* Hearings before the Joint Economic Committee, U.S. Congress, 1952, p. 720. From the same source, p. 743: "Income velocity is a reasonably stable magnitude. It has been declining over the last century . . . however, the decline appears to have been rather gradual, and income velocity is relatively stable over short periods." From *Studies in the Quantity Theory of Money* (p. 21):

velocity are not likely to appreciably offset changes in the money supply, and major fluctuations in income are not likely to take place in the absence of major fluctuations in the stock of money. As a result, the modern Quantity theory views monetary policy as highly effective. Aside from minor short-run fluctuations in income, monetary policy is seen as both necessary *and sufficient* for the attainment of economic stability.

Radcliffe monetary theory, on the other hand, looks upon monetary policy in a rather different light:

> Though we do not regard the supply of money as an unimportant quantity, we view it as only part of the wider structure of liquidity in the economy. It is the whole liquidity position that is relevant to spending decisions, and our interest in the supply of money is due to its significance in the whole liquidity picture. The fact that spending is not limited by the amount of money in existence is sometimes argued by reference to the velocity of money. It is possible, for example, to demonstrate statistically that during the last few years the volume of spending has greatly increased while the supply of money has hardly changed: the velocity of money has increased. We have not made more use of this concept because we cannot find any reason for supposing, or any experience in monetary history indicating, that there is any limit to velocity.[16]

While the Quantity theory views traditional monetary policy as both necessary and sufficient, and Radcliffe views it as too narrowly conceived to be of much use, Keynesian theory lies in between these two extremes. Sometimes changes in velocity are seen as nullifying changes in the money supply, sometimes they are seen as reinforcing,[17] and most of the time they are seen as somewhere in between. The crucial determinants of the behavior of velocity in the orthodox Keynesian system are the interest and wealth-elasticities of the spending and liquidity preference functions, and these are likely to vary depending on the particular historical, institutional, and expectational circumstances at hand. Since velocity is not something the

---

> There is an extraordinary empirical stability and regularity to such magnitudes as income velocity that cannot but impress anyone who works extensively with monetary data. This very stability and regularity contributed to the downfall of the Quantity theory, for it was overstated and expressed in unduly simple form. The numerical value of velocity itself, whether income or transactions, was treated as a natural 'constant.' Now this it is not; and its failure to be so, first during and after World War I and then, to a lesser extent, after the crash of 1929, helped greatly to foster the reaction against the Quantity theory. The studies in this volume are premised on a stability and regularity in monetary relations of a more sophisticated form than a numerically constant velocity.

[16]Radcliffe, *Report,* pp. 132–33.

[17]"In conditions like those of the last decade, it seems unwise to expect that induced changes in V will largely undo the effects of central bank operations; at times they could be reinforcing. The Radcliffe Report seems to me to give misleading impressions in this regard, whatever its other merits." Paul A. Samuelson, "Reflections on Monetary Policy," *Review of Economics and Statistics,* Vol. XLII, No. 3 (August, 1960), p. 268.

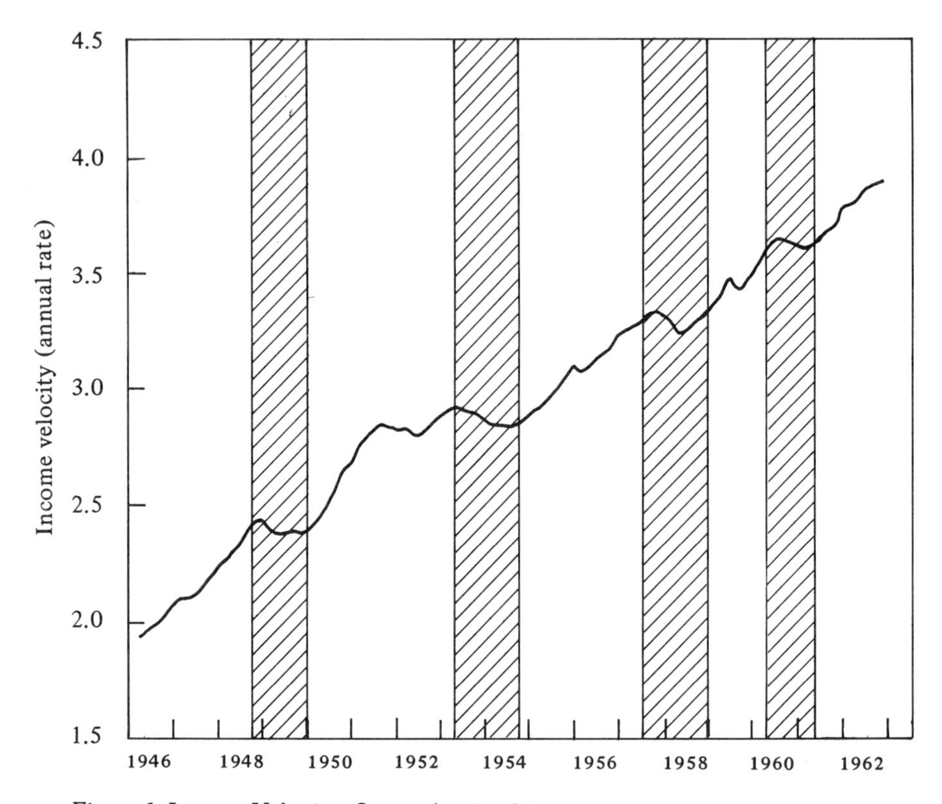

Figure 1. Income Velocity, Quarterly, 1946-1962.

Income velocity is the quotient of gross national product divided by the average money supply over the period, both seasonally adjusted. The money supply is defined as demand deposits, adjusted, plus currency outside banks. Shaded areas indicate periods of recession in general business conditions.

monetary authorities can depend upon, in the sense of being able to reliably anticipate its behavior, monetary policy emerges from the Keynesian system as usually necessary but rarely sufficient for the attainment of national economic objectives.

Although it is not the purpose of this paper to evaluate the implications of the empirical evidence, a brief look, in closing, at the postwar movements in velocity would not be inappropriate. As Figure 1 indicates, velocity has fluctuated between an annual rate of 1.93 in the first quarter of 1946 and 3.87

[18]In the first quarter of 1963, the latest data available at the time of writing, velocity reached a post-1929 high of 3.88. It should be noted that with our present money supply of about $150 billion, even so small an absolute change in velocity as 0.1 would correspond to a change in gross national product of $15 billion.

in the fourth quarter of 1962.[18] Over the period as a whole, velocity has shown a marked upward trend, with fluctuations about that trend coinciding with cyclical fluctuations in general business conditions. Each cyclical peak in velocity has typically been accompanied by rising interest rates and other signs of monetary stringency, leading observers to believe that velocity could not rise much further, that it was close to its upper limit.[19] But then, after a slight decline during recession periods, velocity has promptly resumed its upward climb as soon as business conditions have turned up again. Not only has velocity risen to successively higher peaks from cycle to cycle, but in each period of business recovery it has equaled or exceeded its prior-cycle peak *within only two quarters* after recovery has begun.

How much higher can velocity rise? Recent levels of velocity, approaching a turnover rate of 4 times per annum, are comparable to previous peaks of 4 reached in 1919 and again in 1929. This has once again revived speculation that velocity is approaching its upper limit. However, as of late 1962 and early 1963, liquidity has appeared to be ample throughout the economy, no upward pressure has been evident on interest rates, and the money and capital markets have been characterized more by ease than by tightness. There is thus less evidence today that velocity is approaching a ceiling than there was six years ago, when velocity was around 3.3. Recent increases in velocity would appear to stem from a decrease in the demand for money, rather than a scarcity of supply, indicating that there is probably considerable room for further advance still remaining.

The "extraordinary empirical stability" that Quantity theorists find in the behavior of velocity is revealed only to the disciples. But whether the Radcliffe Report is correct, that for all practical purposes velocity has no upper limit whatsoever, remains to be seen.

[19]See, for example, L. S. Ritter, "Income Velocity and Anti-Inflationary Monetary Policy," *American Economic Review*, Vol. XLIX, No. 1 (March, 1959), pp. 120–29.

12

HOUSEHOLD DEMAND FOR LIQUID ASSETS AND MONEY

JAMES S. DUESENBERRY

DEMAND FOR LIQUID ASSETS

Personal motives for holding liquid assets—transactions and precautionary motives, liquidity preferences, risk avoidance—are all so familiar that it is not necessary to discuss them in any detail. Just as in the corporate case, an individual who holds liquid assets takes a reduction in expected yield on his portfolio in return for a reduction in risk and inconvenience. The loss in expected yield depends on the price difference between the expected yields of variable assets—real estate, stocks, long-term bonds—and the yields on liquid assets. Just as in the corporate case, we expect that, other things equal, the amount of liquid assets an individual will wish to hold will decline as the cost of holding them increases. We also expect that increased confidence in the future stability of income will reduce the demand for liquid assets, and vice versa. An increase in the variance of the expected performance of variable price assets will increase the demand for liquid assets, while a decrease will reduce it.

Some of the reasons for holding liquid assets are related to uncertainties or unevenness in the flow of receipts and expenditures. On that account we might expect the demand for liquid assets to increase, other things equal, with the level of permanent income. But liquid assets are also required in an

Reprinted from James S. Duesenberry, "The Portfolio Approach to the Demand for Money and Other Assets," *Review of Economics and Statistics* (February 1963), pp. 16–23, by permission of the author and publisher, Harvard University Press. Copyright 1963 by the President and Fellows of Harvard College. James S. Duesenberry is a professor at Harvard University.

optimum portfolio even when there is no problem of income or expenditure variation. Other things equal, then, we should expect the demand for liquid assets to grow with both the level of income and the level of assets.

In individual portfolio management the size of the portfolio has an important influence on the proportion of assets held in liquid form. That is so for two reasons. Since borrowing is costly and inconvenient, most people wish to hold enough liquid assets to provide for short-term variations in income and expenditure. Persons whose total financial assets are small in relation to their incomes will find it advantageous to hold all their assets in liquid form. Second, asset management is an activity with decreasing costs to scale. The cost in terms of cash and effort of choosing assets subject to risk is much smaller per dollar invested for a large portfolio than for a small one. The net gain to be obtained from buying variable price securities as opposed to savings deposits of one type or another is not likely to be worth the trouble for the holder of a relatively small portfolio.

It seems probable that a substantial volume of liquid assets is held in connection with asset transfers. Individuals who sell marketable securities or real estate may hold funds pending reinvestment for periods ranging from a few days to several months. In some cases they may go liquid because they are bearish on variable price assets generally. But it is very common for people to sell a particular asset because they consider its net yield prospects unsatisfactory without having chosen another asset. They will hold liquid assets until they find a satisfactory alternative investment. We have no idea what volume of assets is tied up in this way but it may be very substantial.

Finally, there appears to be an interchange between strictly fixed-price assets–demand deposits, currency, savings deposits, and savings bonds–and assets with low credit risk and price variability, particularly high grade bonds. Individuals who have sufficient liquid assets to take care of short-term variations in income and expenditure may wish to have additional low-risk assets in their portfolio which they expect to hold for a fairly long time. The fact that savings deposits of various types can be converted to cash at any time with no transactions cost is of relatively little significance if one plans to hold an asset for a long time. Price variability is of some significance but those who plan to hold to maturity, anyway, need not give it a very heavy weight. Savings deposits of various types are therefore close substitutes for high quality bonds, particularly those with only moderately long maturities.

On that basis we should expect that, during periods when market yields on bonds are low relative to time-deposit rates, the flow of household funds into bonds would be relatively low and the flow into time deposits relatively high. Conversely, when bond yields rise relative to time-deposit yields, we should expect household bond purchases to rise relative to household takings of time deposits.

Of course the competitive relationship between time deposits and bonds is not just a cyclical phenomenon. The relative levels of time deposit yields and bond yields over the whole cycle will influence the division of individual portfolios. But because time deposit yields move slowly relative to market yields over the cycle (though linked in the long run to market yields), the cyclical influence of bond-time deposit substitution is much more apparent than any long-run substitution.

Liquid Assets and Expenditure

A number of writers have expressed the view that variations in household holdings of liquid assets have a strong influence on the rate of consumer expenditure. The rationale of that view has never been entirely clear to me.

It seems reasonable to expect that an increase in the real net worth of the household sector might tend to reduce saving and increase consumption. If people are saving in order to accumulate assets for some particular purpose, the desire to save may wane as they approach their goal. Of course, they may discover or recognize new goals for accumulation as they satisfy old ones, so it remains an empirical question whether an increase in net worth or in the ratio of net worth to income actually depresses saving.

But why should the possession of liquid assets, as distinguished from other assets, have a special effect on saving? One does not come any closer to any goal for accumulation by holding a deposit in a savings institution than by holding an equivalent amount of stocks and bonds.

The only difference seems to be that one can convert liquid assets into cash more easily and quickly than other kinds of assets. Consequently, one can give in to impulses to spend more easily if one holds liquid assets than if one holds other kinds of assets. There is some plausibility in that argument, but it obviously only applies to a limited part of the variation in liquid assets. The impulse consideration does not apply to persons who save regularly a substantial proportion of income or to persons who always have a substantial liquid position. For reasons which I will indicate below it seems likely that—except for the war and early postwar periods—most of the variation in liquid asset holdings is in the holdings of high income, high asset holders. In that case it is unlikely that cyclical variations in liquid asset holdings have much to do with variations in saving.

DEMAND FOR MONEY

In the last section we discussed the demand for liquid assets as a group without any distinction between money and other liquid assets. We must now turn to the question why people hold part of their liquid assets in noninterest-bearing demand deposits and currency. It should be noted at the outset that, in the literature, the reasons given in the last section for holding liquid assets are often given as reasons for holding demand deposits and currency. That may have been appropriate in periods when other forms of virtually riskless, readily marketable assets were not generally available. But it is not a satisfactory answer nowadays. The demand for currency and demand deposits must be analyzed, first, in terms of choices between liquid and nonliquid assets and, second, in terms of choices between currency and demand deposits and other forms of liquid assets.

Demand for Currency

The total amount of currency outstanding since the war has varied between $25 and $30 billion. Estimates made by the Federal Reserve Board of Governors suggest that about one-third of this amount is in business hands and the rest either in the hands of households, lost, destroyed, or gone abroad. It is fairly obvious that the bulk of the currency in nonbusiness hands is not being used for pocket money or being carried around by people who do not have bank accounts. The amount of currency not in business hands represents nearly a month's wages for the entire labor force. Over half of American families have checking accounts and some of the remainder deposit pay checks in savings accounts and withdraw currency and registered checks as needed. Moreover, the bulk of the families who do not use bank accounts receive wages weekly. A full week's wages for one part of the families and an average of a couple of hundred dollars for the rest–which seems a generous estimate even after allowing for travelers–will not account for as much as $10 billion of currency.

Some of the remainder is, no doubt, lost, destroyed, or gone abroad. The rest must be in hoards for some special reason. These would include currency used in illegal transactions or held by small businessmen and professionals who receive currency and hold part of it to evade taxes, and hoarded savings of farmers who saved during the war and distrusted banks.

The amount of currency outstanding nearly doubled during the depression and rose by a factor of about four during the war. After the war it fell slightly until 1950 and has risen slowly since then by nearly $5 billion. It should be noted that the amount of currency outstanding showed little trend in years from 1900 to 1914, rose sharply during World War I, and then remained more or less stationary during the twenties.

If currency were used only for transaction purposes, we should expect the amount outstanding to rise with income but at a slower rate because of the increasing use of checking accounts, registered checks, the spread of check-cashing facilities, and the increased use of credit cards. We might also expect that currency held for tax evasion and illegal activities would grow with the scale of the economy–if the incentives for tax evasion do not change much.

On the other hand, it is likely that special factors connected with war resulted in the generation of abnormally high levels of hoarding relative to income and tax rate levels. The gradual liquidation of some of those wartime hoards may be offsetting the other factors tending to make the currency outstanding to grow. That position gains some support from the fact that the currency grew rapidly during World War I and then leveled off during the twenties, even though income grew. The rate of liquidation of currency hoards other than those connected with tax evasion or illegal activities may have been speeded up by the rise in interest rates, but we have no real information on that point.

Household Demand for Demand Deposits

We can approach the analysis of the demand for demand deposits by asking why a man, given that he has some liquid assets, should hold them in a form which yields no interest. Certainly a major part of the answer lies in the fact that checking accounts are more convenient than other liquid assets and that funds left with savings institutions for short periods yield no return or a very small one.

Persons who hold liquid assets against a certain or fairly probable excess of payments over receipts in the near future will not find the return from savings deposits or savings bonds worth the trouble of converting from cash to earning assets and back again unless the amounts involved are very large. The income transactions demand for money will certainly account for some substantial amount of personal demand deposits. As the savings deposit interest rate rises, the proportion of "transient" liquid assets held in the form of demand deposits should decline.

The full theory of an optimum demand deposit inventory policy is just as complex as any other kind of inventory policy, but a simple example suffices to make the point in question. Suppose we consider only the disposition of liquid assets held against known lump-sum outpayments to be made at known dates and which cannot be financed out of expected net cash inflows in the intervening period. A sum of p dollars held for m months yields the holder $p \times (m/12) \times r$ dollars (when r is the yield on savings deposits neglecting compounding). If an individual requires a given dollar return to make worthwhile one round trip from cash to savings deposit and back to cash, the size of the payment p and the length of the interval m required to earn that amount of dollars obviously becomes shorter as r rises. When interest rates are low, savings deposits will be held only against large distant payments. As interest rates rise, people will hold savings deposits against smaller nearer-term payments which will produce a shift from demand balances to savings accounts.

It is unlikely, however, that the bulk of personal demand deposits are held for income transactions purposes. On January 31 (which is about the low point of the year for individual deposits), banks' records show that 85 per cent of personal demand deposit accounts had less than $1,000, but those accounts had only about 30 per cent of the total amount of personal demand deposits. Since the larger holders have more than one account, it is probable that the remaining 14 per cent of the accounts were held by no more than 10 per cent of the persons holding demand deposit accounts. And since nearly half of families have no demand deposit account it must be concluded that about 5 per cent of families own 70 per cent of personal demand deposits. Moreover, half the personal demand deposits are in accounts of over $5,000.

No doubt some part of the relatively large deposits is required for income transactions. But it seems probable that a large proportion of the larger personal demand deposit accounts is held in connection with financial transactions.

At a rough guess, individual purchases and sales of stocks, bonds, real estate, and other assets amount to something like $100 billion per year. An average holding period–between sale of one asset and purchase of another–of about four months would tie up over $30 billion. If half that sum were in demand deposits, $15 billion would be accounted for. I have no way of testing what amounts are tied up in asset float, but it seems probable that they are a significant part of personal demand deposits.

Now any individual who sells an asset and plans to reinvest in nonliquid assets, at a time some distance in the future or at an unspecified time, has the option of keeping his funds in a demand deposit or obtaining interest from a time deposit. Persons who plan to hold for periods less than a month cannot get interest from time deposits generally, and people in high tax brackets, who are interested only in capital gains, may not bother to try to get it. At low interest rates the proportion of people who will take the trouble to get time deposit interest in the circumstances under discussion is low. As rates rise, the proportion willing to take the trouble will rise and this will tend to shift funds (in relative terms) from demand deposits to time deposits.

A Summary and a Model

My conclusions on the relation of liquid assets to income, interest rate, and interest rate differentials may be summarized in the following way.

1. Composition of portfolios. Persons whose total financial assets are relatively small will tend to hold them all in liquid form because the differential return from other forms of financial assets is too small to make

the additional effort required worthwhile, and because the probability of occurrence of a situation requiring conversion of a large proportion of financial assets to cash is high.

Persons with larger portfolios of financial assets will divide them between liquid and nonliquid assets. The proportion held in liquid form will tend to increase if confidence in the stability of income deteriorates, if the differential between the expected net yield on nonliquid assets and that on liquid assets decreases, if the variance of the expected yield on nonliquid assets increases, if the ratio of total assets to income decreases. In particular, an improvement in confidence will tend to raise the value of stocks in relation to income and reduce the need for protective liquidity, thus tending to reduce the ratio of liquid assets to total financial assets. A change in the differential between mortgage and high-grade bond yields will–if it persists long enough to be reflected in savings institution yields–tend to cause a redistribution between holdings of savings deposits and near-liquid assets like high-grade bonds.

Since savings deposit yields move slowly, the differential between savings deposit yields and bond yields will reflect short-term movements of bond yields. A cyclical increase in bond yields tends to draw funds from liquid assets to bonds, and vice versa.

2. Liquid assets in relation to income. For a given state of confidence, relation of total financial assets to income, and given interest rate differentials, we should expect the liquid asset holdings of persons with relatively large financial assets to grow from cycle to cycle in rough proportion to income.

For persons with relatively small total financial assets, our expectation about the liquid asset-income ratio is less clear. If changes in the liquid asset-income ratio do not influence the savings ratio then, over a decade in which the growth rate of income is above average, the ratio of liquid assets to income for small asset holders should tend to fall. But, because the gross financial savings ratio varies not only with the total savings ratio but also with the amount of net investment in housing equity and the net flow of consumer credit, we cannot reach any very clear conclusion on the probable movements of the ratio of liquid assets to income for persons with small portfolios. We cannot, therefore, attach any great significance to observed movements in the ratio of liquid assets to income.

3. Money holdings versus liquid asset holdings. In general, we expect that as the yields on savings deposits rise, the proportion of liquid assets held in the form of demand deposits will decline. However, the relationship between interest rates and the distribution of liquid assets between demand and savings deposits will differ, as between different classes of people and as between assets held for different purposes. Finally, it should be noted that the yield on savings deposits should be interpreted to represent not only the rate

of interest or dividend paid, but also the whole complex of advertising and selling efforts which may induce people to shift from demand to time deposits.

The whole position may be summarized in terms of a few very simple equations. Let us first divide households into high-asset and low-asset households. Low-asset households hold all financial assets in liquid form. One part of their liquid assets is held for purposes directly related to income and these "transactions" holdings are proportional to income; the remainder is a residual. The proportion of transactions assets held in the form of demand deposits is a decreasing function of a moving average of savings deposit interest rates (strictly speaking, separate rates for different types of institutions and different locations should be used—a single rate is used only as a shorthand device). The proportion of the residual liquid assets held in demand deposit form is also a decreasing function of savings deposit rates. In general, since the residual balances are by definition not needed for near-term outlays, a smaller proportion of those balances will be held in demand deposit form than the proportion of transactions balances.

Thus $$DD^L = D^L(\bar{r}^s)Ay^L + D_2^L(\bar{r}^s)(L^L - Ay^L),$$ where

DD^L = demand deposits of low-asset holders

$\bar{r}^s$ = a moving average of savings deposit yields

y^L = the income of the low-asset group[1]

The change in liquid assets of the low-asset group over any time period equals the gross financial saving of the group during the period $L^L = GFS^L$.

For the high-asset group, the same considerations govern the division of liquid assets between demand deposits and others, except that we should add a factor to allow for the asset transactions demand for liquid assets and eliminate the residual element.

$$DD^H = D_2^H(\bar{r}^s)Ay^H + D_1^H(\bar{r}^s) \times D_3(r^M - r^s)W^{FH} + \phi(r^s)\sum_{i=1}^{M} F(r_{ti}^M - \bar{r}_t^s)GFS_{t-i}^H$$

DD^H = demand balances of high-asset holders

y^H = income of high-asset holders

W^{FH} = total financial wealth of high-asset holders

r^M = net expected yield on marketable securities.

[1]The question of permanent income arises here. When an individual's income declines and he remains a positive saver, he may keep his working cash balance unchanged, out of force of habit. If he becomes a negative saver (in cash-flow terms) he must draw down liquid assets and

The final term is really another kind of asset float which arises from the fact that persons who normally make little use of savings deposits will take some time to shift from demand deposits to savings deposits, if they should accumulate liquid funds as a result of a decline in the attractiveness of securities.

The variable W^{FH} will vary in proportion to income if the share of property income, valuation factors, and the concentration of income remain constant.

Gross financial saving for the higher-income groups should not be much influenced by variations in consumer credit or net investment in residential property but may show some tendency to rise when income rises rapidly. However, it would take us too far afield to discuss that point here.

MOVEMENTS OF HOUSEHOLD HOLDINGS OF LIQUID ASSETS AND MONEY IN THE POSTWAR PERIOD

It is clear that if (1) the ratio of wealth to income, (2) yields on nonliquid assets and on savings deposits and (3) the size distribution of wealth are all constant, the ratio of demand deposits to income will tend to be constant except for minor fluctuations resulting from variations in the ratio of gross financial savings to income.

If the other conditions are satisfied while savings deposit yields have an upward trend, there will be a downward trend in the ratio of demand deposits to income.

Now suppose that there are short-run variations in interest rates as a result of changes in monetary policy and changes in economic activity. A fall in investment activity will be accompanied by a decline in corporate retained earnings and a rise in government deficit. In mild depressions such as we have had in the postwar period, there is little decline in gross financial saving. Changes in required reserve ratios make it possible for banks to bid for securities and drive down interest rates to induce households to reduce their purchases of securities and increase holdings of both demand and time

---

I should be inclined to think he would draw down his cash balance because he holds it to absorb fluctuations in expenditure relative to income. If aggregate income falls, we shall have three groups of people: (1) those whose incomes are unchanged and who, other things equal, keep cash balances unchanged; (2) those whose incomes fall but who remain positive cash savers–if their cash balances do not fall, the ratio of cash balances to current income rises–the permanent income factor; (3) those whose incomes fall and who become negative savers, draw down cash balances absolutely and relatively to income. The buffer stock factors 2 and 3 affect the ratio of cash balances to income in opposite directions. For simplicity I have written the equation as though the two effects cancel out.

deposits. When disposable income remains constant, the residual liquid assets of those with small portfolios will also rise and some part of this will take the form of demand deposits.

Of course, households, who withdraw from or are pushed out of marketable securities, shift their funds into savings deposits as well as into demand deposits (indeed, in the postwar period the increase in the flow into time deposits in recession years has been considerably greater than the increase in the flow of household funds into demand deposits). Since savings institutions hold little cash (unless we count reserve absorption by commercial-bank time deposits as the equivalent of cash), these funds come right back into the market and draw securities away from households.[2] However, after a time, savings institutions begin taking mortgages on new houses and the increase in economic activity increases the transactions demand for cash.

Households go into cash and time deposits when interest rates fall, partly because bond yields are low relative to savings deposits yields, and partly because they expect a recovery and higher yields in the future. Some households, of course, speculate for a capital gain from a continued fall in interest rates, hoping to get out before the recovery. They, however, are usually bank financed and therefore merely supplement the demand for bonds generated by the expansion of bank reserves.

The process described above for the downswing works in reverse on the upswing, though not in an entirely symmetrical way. Rising levels of income will increase transactions balance requirements for liquidity, but a continued upward trend in the moving average of savings deposit rates works to lower the proportion of such balances held in demand deposit form. The same considerations apply to the effects of increasing total wealth. Thus, in the absence of a change in the level of yields on marketable securities, demand deposit holdings of households are likely to grow at a slower rate than income. A rise in household purchases of securities, associated with a rise in yields on marketable securities, may reduce both time and demand balances held as part of the asset float.

It seems to me that the analysis given above does conform fairly well to the actual experience of the postwar period. The ratio of total liquidity to personal income has shown no trend since 1952. Total liquidity (as defined here) has risen relative to income in recession years and fallen in booms. There has been a fairly obvious trade-off between time deposits and high-grade bonds–e.g., the "magic fives." The proportion of household liquidity in the form of currency and demand deposits has fallen steadily since 1952.

[2]Secondary market purchases of mortgages from FNMA reduce federal issues of securities and, therefore, reduce the amount available for households.

MOVEMENTS OF HOUSEHOLD LIQUIDITY AND DEMAND FOR MONEY IN THE PREWAR PERIOD

Total household liquidity remained a fairly constant proportion of personal income from 1922 to 1927 but fell rapidly during 1928 and 1929. The decline may be attributed to the large volume of new security issues floated and the general belief in the prospect of high net yields from investment in common stocks.

The level of liquidity in relation to personal income was lower (varying about a ratio of .6) than in the years since 1952 when the ratio of household liquid asset holdings to personal income has varied about a figure of .7. Some of the difference may be merely definitional since the treatment of high-grade bonds as an element in household liquidity is somewhat ambiguous. In addition, changes in income distribution have probably increased the share of financial saving by low-income groups who tend (for reasons given above) to hold all their financial assets in liquid form.

The most interesting and puzzling thing about the twenties is the steady reduction in the share of liquid assets held in the form of demand deposits and currency. In 1922, 38 per cent of household liquid asset holdings took the form of currency and demand deposits. By 1927 the proportion held in those forms had fallen to 30 per cent and by 1929 a further fall to 25 per cent had taken place. The sharp decline in household holdings of cash from 1927 to 1928 may be attributed to the rapid flow of household funds into common stocks. The furious pace of stock market activity resulted in a sharp reduction of the "asset float."

The decline in relative cash holdings in the earlier years is more difficult to explain. It was not due to rising yields on savings deposits because those yields were not rising. There is, however, some reason to believe that at least part of the shift resulted from changes in the competitive position of national banks with respect to time deposits. The establishment of differential reserve ratios for time deposits in 1914 and the widening of national bank mortgage lending powers, together with the strength of the demand for mortgages in the early 1920's, made time-deposit business attractive to commercial banks. It was generally believed during the 1920's that commercial banks encouraged customers to switch from demand to time deposits and even permitted checking against time deposits. It seems perfectly possible that increased nonprice competition for time deposits resulted in some redistribution of liquid assets between demand and time deposits. It is also possible that there was some shift from Liberty bonds to time deposits as a result of the decline in bond prices in 1920. Since we did not include those bonds in liquid assets, a switch from bonds to time deposits would reduce the ratio of demand deposits to the liquid assets included in the ratios quoted above.

Those explanations appear a little ad hoc and the possibility of other explanations cannot be ruled out.

During the decade of the thirties the ratio of household liquid assets to personal income reached the high figure of 74 per cent in 1932. The ratio then fell almost continuously until, by 1941, it had reached the 60 per cent level which ruled during the middle 1920's. It seems reasonable to attribute the variation to changes in confidence particularly in the early part of the period.

The share of liquid assets held in the form of demand deposits and currency rose throughout the 1930's, reaching 40 per cent by 1941. Since the yields offered for savings deposits declined throughout the period, there seems to be no special difficulty in explaining the rising share of demand deposits and currency in total liquidity.

CONCLUSIONS

The household demand for liquid assets and money is a complex matter which does not seem to have a simple explanation. Without repeating what has been said above we may conclude that, putting aside short cycle movements, the distribution of income and the extent of confidence in income stability are the major factors determining the demand for liquid assets in general. The distribution of liquid assets between demand and time deposits is significantly influenced by the efforts of savings institutions—through rate competition and other selling efforts—to obtain time deposits.

In the shorter cyclical movements, the volume of narrowly defined liquid assets held by households varies considerably with the variation in the difference between rate of return on time deposits and expected yield on marketable securities. Demand deposits holdings are also significantly affected by variations in expected yields on marketable securities.

Although demand and time deposits are competitive with one another, their short-run cyclical movements often tend to be positively correlated.

13

THE TRANSACTIONS DEMAND FOR CASH: AN INVENTORY THEORETIC APPROACH

WILLIAM J. BAUMOL

A stock of cash is its holder's inventory of the medium of exchange, and like an inventory of a commodity, cash is held because it can be given up at the appropriate moment, serving then as its possessor's part of the bargain in an exchange. We might consequently expect that inventory theory and monetary theory can learn from one another. This note attempts to apply one well-known result in inventory control analysis to the theory of money.[1]

A SIMPLE MODEL

We are now interested in analyzing the transactions demand for cash dictated by rational behavior, which for our purposes means the holding of those cash balances that can do the job at minimum cost. To abstract from

Reprinted from the *Quarterly Journal of Economics* (November 1952), pp. 545–56, by permission of the publisher, Harvard University Press. William J. Baumol is a professor at Princeton University.

[1]T. M. Whitin informs me that the result in question goes back to the middle of the 1920's when it seems to have been arrived at independently by some half dozen writers. See, e.g., George F. Mellen, "Practical Lot Quantity Formula," *Management and Administration*, Vol. 10 (September 1925). Its significant implications for the economic theory of inventory, particularly for business cycle theory, seems to have gone unrecognized until recently when Dr. Whitin analyzed them in *The Theory of Inventory Management* (Princeton, N.J.: Princeton University Press, 1963) which, incidentally, first suggested the subject of this note to me. See also, Dr. Whitin's "Inventory Control in Theory and Practice" *Quarterly Journal of Economics* (November 1952), p. 502, and Kenneth J. Arrow, Theodore Harris, and Jacob Marschak, "Optimal Inventory Policy," *Econometrica*, Vol. 19 (July 1951), especially pp. 252–55.

precautionary and speculative demands let us consider a state in which transactions are perfectly foreseen and occur *in a steady stream.*

Suppose that in the course of a given period an individual will pay out T dollars in a steady stream. He obtains cash either by borrowing it, or by withdrawing it from an investment, and in either case his interest cost (or interest opportunity cost) is i dollars per dollar per period. Suppose finally that he withdraws cash in lots of C dollars spaced evenly throughout the year, and that each time he makes such a withdrawal he must pay a fixed "broker's fee" of b dollars.[2] Here T, the value of transactions, is predetermined, and i and b are assumed to be constant.

In this situation any value of C less than or equal to T will enable him to meet his payments equally well provided he withdraws the money often enough. For example, if T is $100, he can meet his payments by withdrawing $50 every six months or $25 quarterly, etc.[3] Thus he will make T/C withdrawals over the course of the year, at a total cost in "brokers' fees" given by bT/C.

In this case, since each time he withdraws C dollars he spends it in a steady stream and draws out a similar amount the moment it is gone, his average cash holding will be $C/2$ dollars. His annual interest cost of holding cash will then be $iC/2$.

The total amount the individual in question must pay for the use of the cash needed to meet his transactions when he borrows C dollars at intervals evenly spaced throughout the year will then be the sum of interest cost and "brokers' fees" and so will be given by

[2]The term "broker's fee" is not meant to be taken literally. It covers all non-interest costs of borrowing or making a cash withdrawal. These include opportunity losses which result from having to dispose of assets just at the moment the cash is needed, losses involved in the poor resale price which results from an asset becoming "second-hand" when purchased by a non-professional dealer, administrative costs, and psychic costs (the trouble involved in making a withdrawal) as well as payment to a middleman. So conceived it seems likely that the "broker's fee" will, in fact, vary considerably with the magnitude of the funds involved, contrary to assumption. However, *some* parts of this cost will not vary with the amount involved—e.g., postage cost, bookkeeping expense, and, possibly, the withdrawer's effort. It seems plausible that the "broker's fee" will be better approximated by a function like $b + kC$ (where b and k are constants), which indicates that there is a part of the "broker's fee" increasing in proportion with the amount withdrawn. As shown in a subsequent footnote, however, our formal result is completely unaffected by this amendment.

We must also extend the meaning of the interest rate to include the value of protection against loss by fire, theft, etc., which we obtain when someone borrows our cash. On the other hand, a premium for the risk of default on repayment must be deducted. This protection obtained by lending seems to be mentioned less frequently by theorists than the risk, yet how can we explain the existence of interest-free demand deposits without the former?

[3]In particular, if cash were perfectly divisible and no elapse of time were required from withdrawal through payment he could make his withdrawals in a steady stream. In this case he would never require any cash balances to meet his payments and C could be zero. However, as may be surmised, this would be prohibitive with any b greater than zero.

$$\frac{bT}{C} + \frac{iC}{2}. \tag{1}$$

Since the manner in which he meets his payments is indifferent to him, his purpose only being to pay for his transactions, rationality requires that he do so at minimum cost, i.e., that he choose the most economical value of C. Setting the derivative of (1) with respect to C equal to zero we obtain[4]

$$-\frac{bT}{C^2} + \frac{i}{2} = 0,$$

i.e.,

$$C = \sqrt{\frac{2bT}{i}}. \tag{2}$$

Thus, in the simple situation here considered, the rational individual will, given the price level,[5] demand cash in proportion to the square root of the value of his transactions.

Before examining the implications of this crude model we may note that, as it stands, it applies to two sorts of cases: that of the individual (or firm) obtaining cash from his invested capital and that of the individual (or firm) spending out of borrowing in anticipation of future receipts. Since our problem depends on noncoincidence of cash receipts and disbursements, and we have assumed that cash disbursements occur in a steady stream, one other case seems possible, that where receipts precede expenditures. This differs from the first case just mentioned (living off one's capital) in that the individual now has the option of withholding some or all of his receipts from investment and simply keeping the cash until it is needed. Once this withheld cash is used up the third case merges into the first: the individual must obtain cash from his invested capital until his next cash receipt occurs.

We can deal with this third case as follows. First, note that any receipts exceeding anticipated disbursements will be invested, since, eventually, interest earnings must exceed ("brokerage") cost of investment. Hence we need only deal with that part of the cash influx which is to be used in making

[4]This result is unchanged if there is a part of the "broker's fee" which varies in proportion with the quantity of cash handled. For in this case the "broker's fee" for each loan is given by $b + kC$. Total cost in "brokers' fees" will then be

$$\frac{T}{C}(b + kC) = \frac{T}{C}b + kT.$$

Thus (1) will have the constant term, kT, added to it, which drops out in differentiation.

[5]A doubling of *all* prices (including the "broker's fee") is like a change in the monetary unit, and may be expected to double the demand for cash balances.

payments during the period between receipts. Let this amount, as before, be T dollars. Of this let I dollars be invested, and the remainder, R dollars, be withheld, where either of these sums may be zero. Again let i be the interest rate, and let the "broker's fee" for withdrawing cash be given by the linear expression $b_w + k_w C$, where C is the amount withdrawn. Finally, let there be a "broker's fee" for investing (depositing) cash given by $b_d + k_d I$ where the b's and the k's are constants.

Since the disbursements are continuous, the $R = T - I$ dollars withheld from investment will serve to meet payments for a fraction of the period between consecutive receipts given by $(T - I)/T$. Moreover, since the average cash holding for that time will be $(T - I)/2$, the interest cost of withholding that money will be

$$\frac{T-I}{T} i \frac{T-I}{2}$$

Thus the total cost of withholding the R dollars and investing the I dollars will be

$$\frac{T-I}{2} i \frac{T-I}{T} + b_d + k_d I.$$

Analogously, the total cost of obtaining cash for the remainder of the period will be

$$\frac{C}{2} i \frac{I}{T} + (b_w + k_w C)\frac{I}{C}.$$

Thus the total cost of cash operations for the period will be given by the sum of the last two expressions, which when differentiated partially with respect to C and set equal to zero once again yields our square root formula, (2), with $b = b_w$.

Thus, in this case, the optimum cash balance after the initial cash holding is used up will again vary with the square root of the volume of transactions, as is to be expected by analogy with the "living off one's capital" case.

There remains the task of investigating $R/2$, the (optimum) average cash balance before drawing on invested receipts begins. We again differentiate our total cost of holding cash, this time partially with respect to I, and set it equal to zero, obtaining

$$-\frac{T-I}{T} i + k_d + \frac{Ci}{2T} + \frac{b_w}{C} + k_w = 0,$$

i.e.,

$$R = T - I = \frac{C}{2} + \frac{b_w T}{Ci} + \frac{T(k_d + k_w)}{i},$$

or since from the preceding result, $C^2 = 2Tb_w/i$, so that the second term on the right-hand side equals $C^2/2C$,

$$R = C + T\left(\frac{k_w + k_d}{i}\right).$$

The first term in this result is to be expected, since if *everything* were deposited at once, C dollars would have to be withdrawn at that same moment to meet current expenses. On this amount two sets of "brokers' fees" would have to be paid and no interest would be earned—a most unprofitable operation.[6]

Since C varies as the square root of T and the other term varies in proportion with T, R will increase less than in proportion with T, though more nearly in proportion than does C. The general nature of our results is thus unaffected.[7]

Note finally that the entire analysis applies at once to the case of continuous receipts and discontinuous payments, taking the period to be that between two payments, where the relevant decision is the frequency of investment rather than the frequency of withdrawal. Similarly, it applies to continuous receipts and payments where the two are not equal.

SOME CONSEQUENCES OF THE ANALYSIS

I shall not labor the obvious implications for financial budgeting by the firm. Rather I shall discuss several arguments which have been presented by monetary theorists, to which our result is relevant.

The first is the view put forth by several economists,[8] that in a stationary

[6]Here the assumption of constant "brokerage fees" with $k_d = k_w = 0$ gets us into trouble. The amount withheld from investment then is never greater than C dollars only because a strictly constant "broker's fee" with no provision for a discontinuity at zero implies the payment of the fee even if nothing is withdrawn or deposited. In this case it becomes an overhead and it pays to invest for any interest earning greater than zero.

For a firm, *part* of the "broker's fee" may, in fact, be an overhead in this way. For example, failure to make an anticipated deposit will sometimes involve little or no reduction in the bookkeeping costs incurred in keeping track of such operations.

[7]If we replace the linear functions representing the "brokers' fees" with more general functions $f_w(C)$ and $f_d(I)$ which are only required to be differentiable, the expression obtained for R is changed merely by replacement of k_w, and k_d by the corresponding derivatives $f_{w'}(C)$ and $f_{d'}(I)$.

[8]See, e.g., Frank H. Knight, *Risk, Uncertainty and Profit* (Preface to the Re-issue), No. 16 in the series of Reprints of Scarce Tracts in Economic and Political Science (London: The London School of Economics and Political Science, 1933), p. xxii; F. Divisia, *Économique Rationelle* (Paris: G. Doin, 1927), Chapter 19 and the Appendix; and Don Patinkin, "Relative Prices, Say's Law and the Demand for Money," *Econometrica*, Vol. 16 (April 1948), 140–45. See also, P. N. Rosenstein-Rodan, "The Coordination of the General Theories of Money and Price," *Economica*, N. S., Vol. 3 (August 1936), Part 2.

state there will be no demand for cash balances since it will then be profitable to invest all earnings in assets with a positive yield in such a way that the required amount will be realized at the moment any payment is to be made. According to this view no one will want any cash in such a stationary world, and the value of money must fall to zero so that there can really be no such thing as a truly static monetary economy. Clearly this argument neglects the transactions costs involved in making and collecting such loans (the "broker's fee").[9] Our model is clearly compatible with a static world and (2) shows that it will generally pay to keep some cash. The analysis of a stationary monetary economy in which there is a meaningful (finite) price level does make sense.

Another view which can be reexamined in light of our analysis is that the transactions demand for cash will vary approximately in proportion with the money value of transactions.[10] This may perhaps even be considered the tenor of quantity theory though there is no necessary connection, as Fisher's position indicates. If such a demand for cash balances is considered to result from rational behavior, then (2) suggests that the conclusion cannot have general validity. On the contrary, the square root formula implies that demand for cash rises less than in proportion with the volume of transactions, so that there are, in effect, economies of large scale in the use of cash.

The magnitude of this difference should not be exaggerated, however. The phrase "varying as the square" may suggest larger effects than are actually

[9] It also neglects the fact that the transfer of cash takes time so that in reality we would have to hold cash at least for the short period between receiving it and passing it on again.

It is conceivable, it is true, that with perfect foresight the difference between money and securities might disappear since a perfectly safe loan could become universally acceptable. There would, however, remain the distinction between "real assets" and the "money-securities." Moreover, there would be a finite price for, and non-zero yield on the former, the yield arising because they (as opposed to certificates of their ownership) are not generally acceptable, and hence not perfectly liquid, since there is trouble and expense involved in carrying them.

[10] Marshall's rather vague statements may perhaps be interpreted to support this view. See, e.g., Book 1, Chapter 4 in *Money, Credit and Commerce* (London 1923). Keynes clearly accepts this position. See *The General Theory of Employment, Interest and Money* (New York 1936), p. 201. It is also accepted by Pigou: "As real income becomes larger, there is, prima facie, reason for thinking that, just as, up to a point, people like to invest a larger proportion of their real income, so also they like to hold real balances in the form of money equivalent to a larger proportion of it. On the other hand, as Professor Robertson has pointed out to me, the richer people are, the cleverer they are likely to become in finding a way to *economize* in real balances. On the whole then we may, I think, safely disregard this consideration . . . for a close approximation . . ." (*Employment and Equilibrium,* 1st ed. [London 1941], pp. 59–60). Fisher, however, argues: "It seems to be a fact that, at a given price level, the greater a man's expenditures the more rapid his turnover; that is, the rich have a higher rate of turnover than the poor. They spend money faster, not only absolutely but relatively to the money they keep on hand. . . . We may therefore infer that, if a nation grows richer per capita, the velocity of circulation of money will increase. This proposition, of course, has no reference to *nominal* increase of expenditure" (*The Purchasing Power of Money* [New York 1922], p. 167).

involved. Equation (2) requires that the average transactions velocity of circulation vary exactly in proportion with the quantity of cash, so that, for example, a doubling of the stock of cash will *ceteris paribus,* just double velocity.[11]

A third consequence of the square root formula is closely connected with the second. The effect on real income of an injection of cash into the system may have been underestimated. For suppose that (2) is a valid expression for the general demand for cash, that there is widespread unemployment, and that for this or other reasons prices do not rise with an injection of cash. Suppose, moreover, that the rate of interest is unaffected, i.e., that none of the new cash is used to buy securities. Then so long as transactions do not rise so as to maintain the same proportion with the square of the quantity of money, people will want to get rid of cash. They will use it to demand more goods and services, thereby forcing the volume of transactions to rise still further. For let ΔC be the quantity of cash injected. If a proportionality (constant velocity) assumption involves transactions rising by $k\Delta C$, it is easily shown that (2) involves transactions rising by more than twice as much, the magnitude of the excess increasing with the ratio of the injection to the initial stock of cash. More precisely, the rise in transactions would then be given by[12]

$$2k\Delta C + \frac{k}{C}\Delta C^2.$$

Of course, the rate of interest would really tend to fall in such circumstances, and this would to some extent offset the effect of the influx of cash, as is readily seen when we rewrite (2) as

$$T = C^2 i/2b. \tag{3}$$

Moreover, prices will rise to some extent,[13] and, of course, (3) at best is only an approximation. Nevertheless, it remains true that the effect of an injection of cash on, say, the level of employment, may often have been underestimated.[14] For whatever may be working to counteract it, the force making for

[11]Since velocity equals $(T/C) = (i/2b)C$ by (2).

[12]This is obtained by setting $k = Ci/2b$ in (3), below, and computing ΔT by substituting $C + \Delta C$ for C.

[13]Even if (2) holds, the demand for cash may rise only in proportion with the money value of transactions when all prices rise exactly in proportion, the rate of interest and transactions remaining unchanged. For then a doubling of all prices and cash balances leaves the situation unchanged, and the received argument holds. The point is that b is then one of the prices which has risen.

[14]But see the discussions of Potter and Law as summarized by Jacob Viner, *Studies in the Theory of International Trade* (New York 1937), pp. 37–39.

increased employment is greater than if transactions tend, *ceteris paribus,* toward their original proportion to the quantity of cash.

Finally the square root formula lends support to the argument that wage cuts can help increase employment, since it follows that the Pigou effect and the related effects are stronger than they would be with a constant transactions velocity. Briefly the phenomenon which has come to be called the Pigou effect[15] may be summarized thus: General unemployment will result in reduction in the price level which must increase the purchasing power of the stock of cash provided the latter does not itself fall more than in proportion with prices.[16] This increased purchasing power will augment demand for commodities[17] or investment goods (either directly, or because it is used to buy securities and so forces down the rate of interest). In any case, this works for a reduction in unemployment.

Now the increase in the purchasing power of the stock of cash which results from fallen prices is equivalent to an injection of cash with constant prices. There is therefore exactly the same reason for suspecting the magnitude of the effect of the former on the volume of transactions has been underestimated, as in the case of the latter. Perhaps this can be of some little help in explaining why there has not been more chronic unemployment or runaway inflation in our economy.

THE SIMPLE MODEL AND REALITY

It is appropriate to comment on the validity of the jump from equation (2) to conclusions about the operation of the economy. At best, (2) is only a suggestive oversimplification, if for no other reason, because of the rationality assumption employed in its derivation. In addition the model is static. It takes the distribution of the firm's disbursements over time to be fixed, though it is to a large extent in the hands of the entrepreneur how he will time his expenditures. It assumes that there is one constant relevant rate of interest and that the "broker's fee" is constant or varies linearly with the magnitude of the sum involved. It posits a steady stream of payments and

[15]See A. C. Pigou, "The Classical Stationary State," *Economic Journal,* Vol. 53 (December 1943).

[16]Presumably the "broker's fee" will be one of the prices which falls, driven down by the existence of unemployed brokers. There is no analogous reason for the rate of interest to fall, though it will tend to respond thus to the increase in the "real stock of cash."

[17]The term "Pigou effect" is usually confined to the effects on consumption demand while the effect on investment demand, and (in particular) on the rate of interest is ordinarily ascribed to Keynes. However, the entire argument appears to antedate Pigou's discussion (which, after all, was meant to be a reformulation of the classical position) and is closely related to what Mr. Becker and I have called the Say's Equation form of the Say's Law argument. See our article "The Classical Monetary Theory: The Outcome of the Discussion," *Economica* (November 1952).

the absence of cash receipts during the relevant period. It deals only with the cash demand of a single economic unit and neglects interactions of the various demands for cash in the economy.[18] It neglects the precautionary and speculative demands for cash.

These are serious lacunae, and without a thorough investigation we have no assurance that our results amount to much more than an analytical curiosum. Nevertheless I offer only a few comments in lieu of analysis, and hope that others will find the subject worth further examination.

1. It is no doubt true that a majority of the public will find it impractical and perhaps pointless to effect every possible economy in the use of cash. Indeed the possibility may never occur to most people. Nevertheless, we may employ the standard argument that the largest cash users may more plausibly be expected to learn when it is profitable to reduce cash balances relative to transactions. The demand for cash by the community as a whole may then be affected similarly and by a significant amount. Moreover, it is possible that even small cash holders will sometimes institute some cash economies instinctively or by a process of trial and error not explicitly planned or analyzed.

2. With variable b and i the validity of our two basic results–the non-zero rational transactions demand for cash, and the less than proportionate rise in the rational demand for cash with the real volume of transactions, clearly depends on the nature of the responsiveness of the "brokerage fee" and the interest rate to the quantity of cash involved. The first conclusion will hold generally provided the "broker's fee" never falls below some preassigned level, e.g., it never falls below one mill per transaction, and provided the interest rate, its rate of change with C and the rate of change of the "broker's fee" all (similarly) have some upper bound, however large, at least when C is small.

The second conclusion will not be violated persistently unless the "brokerage fee" tends to vary almost exactly in proportion with C (and it pays to hold zero cash balances) except for what may roughly be described as a limited range of values of C. Of course, it is always possible that this "exceptional range" will be the one relevant in practice. Variations in the interest rate will tend to strengthen our conclusion provided the interest rate never decreases with the quantity of cash borrowed or invested.[19]

[18] I refer here particularly to considerations analogous to those emphasized by Duesenberry in his discussion of the relation between the consumption functions of the individual and the economy as a whole in his *Income, Saving and the Theory of Consumer Behavior* (Cambridge, Mass. 1950).

[19] For people to want to hold a positive amount of cash, the cost of cash holding must be decreasing after $C = 0$. Let b in (1) be a differentiable function of C for $C > 0$ (it will generally be discontinuous and equal to zero at $C = 0$). Then we require that the limit of the derivative

It would perhaps not be surprising if these sufficient conditions for the more general validity of our results were usually satisfied in practice.

3. If payments are lumpy but foreseen, cash may perhaps be employed even more economically. For then it may well pay to obtain cash just before large payments fall due with little or no added cost in "brokers' fees" and considerable savings in interest payments. The extreme case would be that of a single payment during the year which would call for a zero cash balance provided the cash could be loaned out profitably at all. Cash receipts during the relevant period may have similar effects, since they can be used to make payments which happen to be due at the moment the receipts arrive. Here the extreme case involves receipts and payments always coinciding in time and amounts in which case, again, zero cash balances would be called for. Thus lumpy payments and receipts of cash, with sufficient foresight, can make for economies in the use of cash, i.e., higher velocity. This may not affect the rate of increase in transactions velocity with the level of transactions, but may nevertheless serve further to increase the effect of an injection of cash and of a cut in wages and prices. With imperfect foresight, however, the expectation that payments may be lumpy may increase the precautionary demand for cash. Moreover, the existence of a "broker's fee" which must be paid on lending or investing cash received during the period is an added

---

of (1) be negative as C approaches zero from above, where this derivative is given by

$$-b\frac{T}{C^2}+\frac{T}{C}b'+\frac{i+i'C}{2}. \tag{i}$$

Clearly this will become negative as C approaches zero provided b is bounded from below and b', i, and i' are all bounded from above.

The second conclusion, the less than proportionate rise in minimum cost cash holdings with the volume of transactions, can be shown, with only b not constant, to hold if and only if $b - b'C + b''C^2$ is positive. This result is obtained by solving the first order minimum condition (obtained by setting (i), with the i' term omitted, equal to zero) for T/C and noting that our conclusion is equivalent to the derivative of this ratio with respect to C being positive.

Now successive differentiation of (i) with the i' term omitted yields as our second order minimum condition $2(b - b'C) + b''C^2 > 0$ (note the resemblance to the preceding condition). Thus if our result is to be violated we must have

$$b-Cb' \leqq -b''C^2 < 2(b-Cb'), \tag{ii}$$

which at once yields $b'' \leqq 0$. Thus if b' is not to become negative (a decreasing *total* payment as the size of the withdrawal increases!) b'' must usually lie within a small neighborhood of zero, i.e., b must be approximately linear. However we know that in this case the square root formula will be (approximately) valid except in the case $b = kC$ when it will always [by (i)] pay to hold zero cash balances. Note incidentally that (ii) also yields $b - Cb' \geqq 0$ which means that our result must hold if ever the "brokerage fee" increases more than in proportion with C.

Note, finally, that if i varies with C the first order condition becomes a cubic and, provided $\infty > i' > 0$, our conclusion is strengthened, since T now tends to increase as C^2.

inducement to keep receipts until payments fall due rather than investing, and so may further increase the demand for cash.

4. The economy in a single person's use of cash resulting from an increase in the volume of his transactions may or may not have its analogue for the economy as a whole. "External economies" may well be present if one businessman learns cash-economizing techniques from the experiences of another when both increase their transactions. On the diseconomies side it is barely conceivable that an infectious liquidity fetishism will permit a few individuals reluctant to take advantage of cash saving opportunities to block these savings for the bulk of the community. Nevertheless, at least two such possible offsets come to mind: (a) The rise in the demand for brokerage services resulting from a general increase in transactions may bring about a rise in the "brokerage fee" and thus work for an increase in average cash balances (a decreased number of visits to brokers). If cash supplies are sticky this will tend to be offset by rises in the rate of interest resulting from a rising total demand for cash, which serve to make cash more expensive to hold. (b) Widespread cash economizing might require an increase in precautionary cash holdings because in an emergency one could rely less on the ability of friends to help or creditors to be patient. This could weaken but not offset the relative reduction in cash holdings entirely, since the increase in precautionary demand is contingent on there being some relative decrease in cash holdings.

5. A priori analysis of the precautionary and the speculative demands for cash is more difficult. In particular, there seems to be little we can say about the latter, important though it may be, except that it seems unlikely that it will work consistently in any special direction. In dealing with the precautionary demand, assumptions about probability distributions and expectations must be made.[20] It seems plausible, offhand, that an increase in the volume of transactions will make for economies in the use of cash for precautionary as well as transactions purposes by permitting increased recourse to insurance principles.

Indeed, here we have a rather old argument in banking theory which does not seem to be widely known. Edgeworth,[21] and Wicksell[22] following him, suggested that a bank's precautionary cash requirements might also grow as

[20] See Arrow, Harris, and Marschak, *op. cit.* for a good example of what has been done along these lines in inventory control analysis.

[21] F. Y. Edgeworth, "The Mathematical Theory of Banking," *Journal of the Royal Statistical Society*, Vol. 51 (1888), especially pp. 123–27. Fisher (*op. cit.*) points out the relevance of this result for the analysis of the cash needs of the public as a whole. The result was independently rediscovered by Dr. Whitin (*op. cit.*) who seems to have been the first to combine it and (2) in inventory analysis.

[22] K. Wicksell, *Interest and Prices* (London 1936), p. 67.

the square root of the volume of its transactions (!). They maintained that cash demands on a bank tend to be normally distributed.[23] In this event, if it is desired to maintain a fixed probability of not running out of funds, precautionary cash requirements will be met by keeping on hand a constant multiple of the standard deviation (above the mean). But then the precautionary cash requirement of ten identical banks (with independent demands) together will be the same as that for any one of them multiplied by the square root of ten. For it is a well-known result that the standard deviation of a random sample from an infinite population increases as the square root of the size of the sample.

[23]The distribution would generally be approximately normal if its depositors were large in number, their cash demands independent and not very dissimilarly distributed. The independence assumption, of course, rules out runs on banks.

14

CASH BALANCES AND THE INTEREST RATE—A PRAGMATIC APPROACH

HENRY A. LATANÉ

This paper is concerned with the interrelations of cash balances, that is, demand deposits adjusted plus currency in circulation (M), national income in current dollars (Y), and the long-term interest rates on high-grade obligations. In it we attempt first to set up hypothetical aggregative equations involving the two variables, cash balances as proportion of income (M/Y) and the interest rate (r); second, to select appropriate statistical series to measure the variables; and third, to test the equations. Quantitative relationships which have been statistically significant in the past are developed in this manner. Policy implications are discussed.

AGGREGATIVE EQUATIONS

We will test four equations:

1. The crude Cambridge version of the quantity theory of money may be expressed by the following equation:

$$M/Y = k. \tag{1.1}$$

This assumes that cash balances tend to be a fixed proportion of income whatever the interest rate. Equation (1.1) forms the basis for our first test.

Reprinted from the *Review of Economics and Statistics* (November 1954), pp. 456–60, by permission of the author and publisher, Harvard University Press. Henry A. Latané is a professor at the University of North Carolina.

2. Keynesian theory emphasizes the separation of money into its two functions as a store of value and as a medium of exchange. Following Modigliani in his "Liquidity Preference and the Theory of Interest and Money,"[1] we may use the following as a first approximation:

$$M = D_a(r) + D_T(Y) \tag{2.1}$$

where D_a is the demand for money as an asset and D_T is demand for money to spend. It is assumed as a first approximation that the demand for money as an asset is a function of the interest rate and the demand for money as a medium of exchange is a function of income. This assumption is open to question even as a first approximation because it ignores the effect of the interest rate on the opportunity cost of holding money for transactions,[2] and it also ignores the effect of the income level on the desire to hold money as an asset.

Equation (2.1) can be made operative by assuming linearity in Y and the reciprocal of r. We then have:

$$M = a/r + bY + c \tag{2.2}$$

which is based on the assumption that the demand for money as an asset varies inversely with the interest rate, and the demand for money as a medium of exchange varies directly with income.[3] We will test this form.

3. A modified quantity theory equation may be stated in the form:

$$M/Y = f_1(r). \tag{3.1}$$

[1] At the conclusion of an extensive discussion of the demand for money for transactions and as an asset, Modigliani says, "On the basis of these considerations we may, in a first approximation, split the total demand for money into two parts: the demand for money to hold, $D(r)$, and the demand for money to spend for transactions, $D(Y)$; and write . . . [our equation (2.1)]" (*Econometrica,* Vol. 12 [1944], 45–88).

[2] Keynes himself apparently believed that the opportunity cost of holding cash balances for transaction purposes was of some importance but could be ignored as a first approximation. The following quotation is taken from his article "The Theory of the Rate of Interest" included in *Lessons of Monetary Experience: Essays in Honor of Irving Fisher* (New York 1937), pp. 145–52: "So far as the active circulation is concerned, it is sufficiently correct as a first approximation to regard the demand for money as proportionate to the effective demand, i.e., to the level of money income; which amounts to saying that the velocity of the active circulation is independent of the quantity of money. This is, I say, only a first approximation because the demand for money in the active circulation is also to some extent a function of the rate of interest, since a higher rate of interest may lead to a more economical use of balances, though this only means that the active balances are under the same influence as the inactive balances." Lawrence Klein on page 194 of the technical appendix of his book *The Keynesian Revolution* (New York 1947) derives a somewhat similar formula to express the usual Keynesian liquidity preference function. It is his equation (20a) $M/p = f8 + f9r + f10Y/p$. It is to be noted, however, that he assumes a linear relation between M/p and r rather than $1/r$.

This states that the proportion of income which is held in cash balances is a function of the interest rate. There are several reasons for thinking that this form of the equation of exchange may be a reasonably satisfactory tool for exploring the interrelations of the three variables. It bypasses the major problem of separation of money by use. This seems fully justified as both types of monetary uses, that is, as a store of value and as a medium of exchange, clearly are influenced by both the interest rate and the level of income. As both types of monetary demand are affected in the same direction by the two forces under consideration, there seems to be no major reason to separate the two types in our equation.

Equation (3.1) can be made operative by changing to:

$$M/Y = c/r + d. \tag{3.2}$$

We will test it in this form.[4]

4. In equation (3.1) we have assumed that the interest rate was the independent, and the proportionate cash balances, M/Y, the dependent variable. That is, the direction of causation was assumed to flow from the interest rate to the size of the cash balances in proportion to the income. If it is assumed that the cash balances relative to income determine the interest rate, equation (3.1) becomes:

$$r = f_2(M/Y) \tag{4.1}$$

which can be converted to:

$$1/r = g(M/Y) + h \tag{4.2}$$

where g is a constant coefficient. This form also can be tested.

Statistical Data

We are dealing with aggregates and broad economic classes. Differing quantitative results will flow from differing selections of representative indexes. We know that there are many different types of monies and near-

[4]James Tobin in the *Review of Economics and Statistics,* Vol. 30 (November 1948), 315, in a rejoinder to Clark Warburton on "Monetary Velocity and Monetary Policy," shows a scatter diagram comparing Warburton's Circuit Velocity and the yield on U.S. bonds for the period 1919–45. In this comparison he is using different series measuring the reciprocals of the variables used in equation (3.2). In spite of the inclusion of time deposits in calculating velocity and the effects of income taxes on government bond yields, the scatter appears significant for the period covered. Tobin also shows a comparison of "idle balances" expressed in current dollars and the

monies which are held for many different reasons. Likewise, there is not one interest rate but a whole range of rates and yields. The income of one segment of the economy may have a far different effect on the demand for money and on interest rates than the income of another group. If we attempt to allow for all of these factors, we become lost in the web of interrelations. In spite of these qualifications, we believe that there are now available statistical data sufficiently accurate to permit broad tests of our equations. We use the following definitions and sources of data:

M: demand deposits adjusted plus currency in circulation on the mid-year call date (Federal Reserve Board data). We have limited money to this definition to avoid all the complexities of the near-monies, none of which is a final means of payment.

Y: Gross National Product–Department of Commerce series from 1929 to date; 1919–28 Federal Reserve Board estimates on the same basis (National Industrial Conference Board, *Economic Almanac,* 1952, p. 201); 1889–1919 from Kuznets, *National Product Since 1869,* p. 119, increased by 9.5% which is the average difference in the two series during the overlap from 1919–38.

r: interest rate on high-grade long-term corporate obligations. The U.S. Treasury series giving the yields on corporate high-grade bonds as reported in the *Federal Reserve Bulletin* is used from 1936 to date. Before 1936 we use annual averages of Macaulay's high-grade railroad bond yields given in column 5, Table 10, of his *Bond Yields, Interest Rates, Stock Prices.*

M/Y: the ratio of cash balances to income, as defined above, is used both as the independent and the dependent variable in our tests. We make no attempt to solve the problem of whether money is an exogenous or an endogenous variable in the system. In other words, we examine the stability and attempt to explain changes in the ratio M/Y, but do not attempt to determine whether this stability is brought about by adjustments in Y to a given level of M or whether M itself is determined by the level of income.

$1/r$: the reciprocal of the interest rate is also used either as the independent or the dependent variable. The reciprocal is used because theory calls for the demand for money to vary inversely with the interest rate and therefore directly with the reciprocal of the interest rate. The use of the reciprocal has another important justification in that the loss or gain in capital value to the holder of a perpetual obligation due to a change in interest rates, measured in time, is closely related to the change in $1/r$. For example, a .09 change in the interest rate from 3.00% to 3.09% would reduce $1/r$ by .9709 and would cost the holder of a perpetual bond a full year's interest through a decline in

yields on government bonds. This relationship clearly is open to the criticism outlined in the test of equation (2.2) which follows. A small change in interest rates from 1941 through 1945 is associated with a tripling of "idle balances."

capitalized value. Similarly, a change in the interest rate from 6.00% to 6.36% would cost the holder of a perpetual obligation a loss in capitalized value equivalent to one year's interest, and $1/r$ would decline .9434.

We have reasonably satisfactory annual data on the indicated series extending back to 1919. The period 1919–52 is used to make the basic tests of the models.

TESTS OF EQUATIONS

1. $M/Y = k$ (1.1)

It is apparent from the data for the past 33 years, shown in Figure 1, that M/Y is much more stable than either M or Y, but that, even so, it is subject to wide variations. Little is to be gained from assuming it a constant as is done in equation (1.1). The fit over various periods can be improved if time is introduced as a variable. For example, Lawrence Klein in *Economic Fluctuations in the United States 1921–1941* (Cowles Commission, 1950), p. 109, develops the equation

$$M = 8.45 + .24Y_1 + .03Y_1(t - 1931) - 1.43(t - 1931) + u \quad (1.2)$$

to fit the period 1921–41; Y_1 is the Net National Product in current dollars, t is time, and u is the error term. This equation fits the period for which it was designed, but cannot be extended and does not seem to have any justification in logic. If carried back to the 1904–13 decade, it gives an estimated value for M which is three times the actual. Likewise, if the estimate is carried through to 1952 it would give an estimate of M about three times larger than the actual. There seems to be no logic in the assumption, implicit in equation (1.2), that the demand for money as a percentage of the national income—$.03\,Y_1(t-1931)$—increases with time and the absolute demand for money—$1.43(t-1931)$—decreases.

2. $M = a/r + bY + c$ (2.2)

This equation (2.2) can be converted to the form

$$M/Y = a/rY + b + c/Y. \quad (2.3)$$

In this form it is clearly faulty. The fractions a/rY and c/Y will get smaller as Y increases if r remains relatively constant. In other words the cash balance as a proportion of income would get smaller as income increases if the rate of interest remains relatively steady. This assumption does not fit the data. For

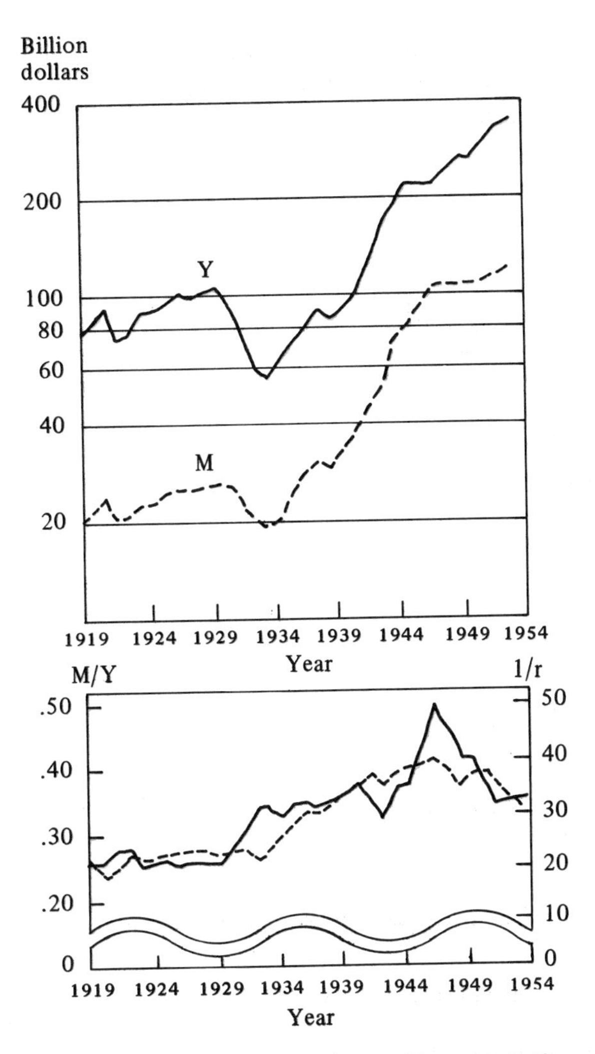

Figure 1. Data for Test of $M/Y = k$ (Equation 1.1), Annual Data

example, in the period 1938–52, Y quadrupled, yet M/Y and r were about the same at the end as at the beginning.

In *Economic Fluctuations in the United States 1921–1941,* p. 110, Klein tested for the effects of the interest rate on the demand for money, using an equation of the same general form as our (2.2). On the basis of this test, he concluded that the desire to hold demand deposits was not significantly affected by the interest rate in the period 1921–41. The test may have failed because (a) the type of equation is unsatisfactory in itself, as is indicated above, or (b) Klein assumed a linear relationship between demand for money and r rather than its reciprocal in making his calculations.

3. $M/Y = c/r + d$ (3.2)

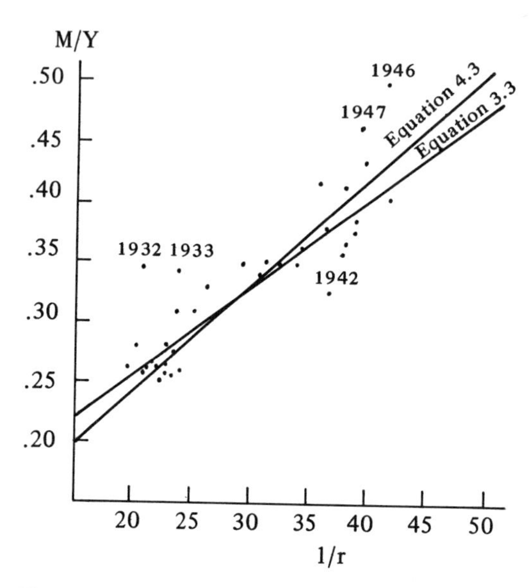

Figure 2. Data for Test of $M/Y = c/r + d$ (Equation 3.2), Annual Data, 1919-52.

The scatter diagram shown in Figure 2 was prepared to test equation (3.2). The regression line equation

$$M/Y = .0074328/r + .10874 \tag{3.3}$$

was derived by the least-squares method, excluding the data for the years 1932, 1933, 1942, 1946, and 1947 because they were not considered representative. The equation would be

$$M/Y = .00795304/r + .100418 \tag{3.4}$$

if the unrepresentative years are included. The coefficient of correlation is .87173 including the years affected by bank failures, mobilization, and demobilization; and it is .911 excluding the years so affected.

4. $1/r = g(M/Y) + h$ (4.2)

Equation (4.3) $1/r = 111.775M/Y - 7.233$ shows the least-squares fit for the same data with the same exclusions, assuming that M/Y is the independent variable and $1/r$ is the dependent variable. Including all years the equation is

$$1/r = 95.4M/Y - 2.44. \qquad (4.4)$$

From the data available, it is impossible to tell which is the independent and which the dependent variable. Consequently, it is impossible to choose between equation (3.3) and (4.3) on the basis of this test. Whatever the direction of causation, the correlation is high considering the number of observations, the few degrees of freedom sacrificed by the form of the equation, and the number of changes in trend involved.

If the relations derived from data in one period explain events in other periods their claim for recognition is increased. As is apparent from Figure 2 equations (3.3) and (4.3) do not differ substantially in the area of past experience. The formula

$$M/Y = .008/r + .09 \qquad (3.5)$$

or

$$1/r = 125M/Y - 11.25 \qquad (4.5)$$

falls between the two lines and is taken as a satisfactory approximation to a joint estimating equation. This formula was used in setting the scales for M/Y and $1/r$ in Figure 1. Similar comparisons are shown in Figures 3 showing (3a) ten-year averages going back to 1889 and (3b) quarterly data since 1947. The fit seems to indicate that the structural relations established from the 1919–52 data had some significance both over the longer period and currently.

IMPLICATIONS OF FORMULA

Based on the above, equation (3.5) seems to be a reasonable joint estimating equation for the relationship between cash balances as a proportion of income and the long-term interest rate. This relationship is linear between M/Y and $1/r$. In the past thirty years each 1.0% change in $1/r$ has tended to be associated with a change of .8% in gross national product held as currency and demand deposits.

The relationship between M/Y and r (rather than $1/r$) is shown in Figure 4. As is apparent from this chart, changes in interest rates have relatively

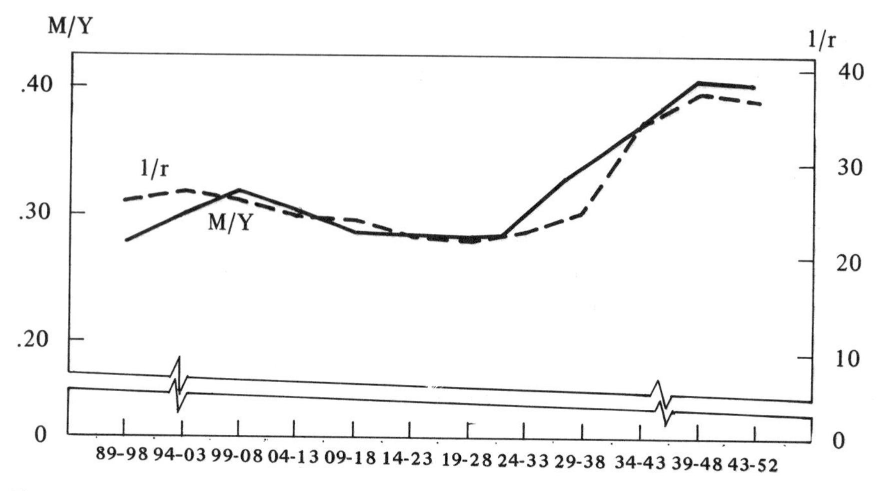

Figure 3a. Data for Test of $1/r = g(M/Y) + h$, Ten-Year Averages, 1889-1952.

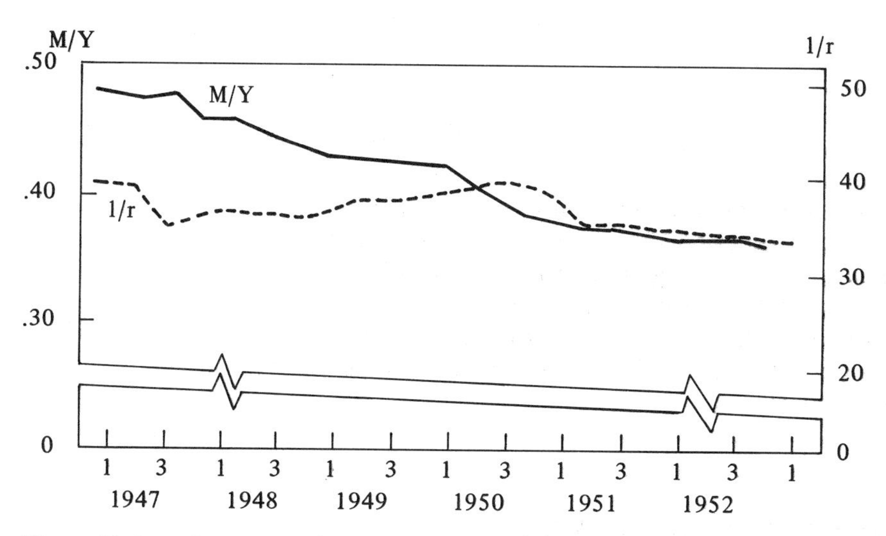

Figure 3b. Data for Test of $1/r = g(M/Y) + h$, Seasonally adjusted Quarterly Data at Annual Rates.

little absolute effect on the size of cash balances associated with given levels of income as long as the interest rate is relatively high, say above 5%. When rates are 3% or under, on the other hand, changes in interest rates have a substantial absolute effect on M/Y. When interest rates drop from 8% to 7% there is an increase in the associated M/Y of only 1.4 points from 19% to

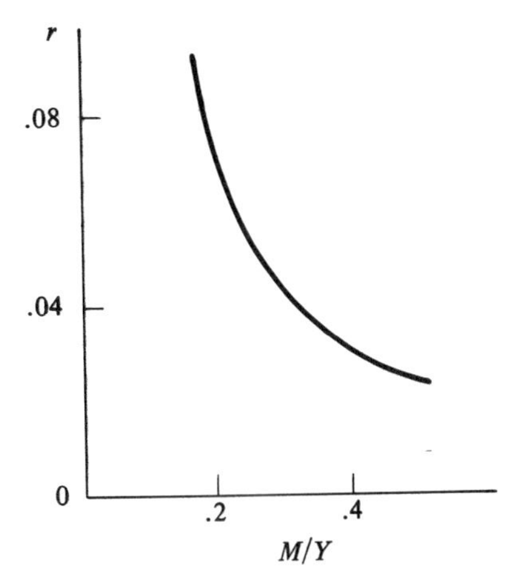

Figure 4. Data for Relationship of M/Y and r

20.4%. When rates drop from 3% to 2%, however, M/Y tends to rise from 35.7% to 49%.

On a proportionate basis the effects of a change in the interest rate are much more stable over the range of experience. When the interest rate drops by 10%, from 8% to 7.2%, we would expect the proportionate cash balances (M/Y) to increase 5.8%, from 19% to 20.1% based on past experience. Likewise, when the interest rate drops 10%, from 3% to 2.7%, M/Y should increase 8.2%, from 35.7% to 38.6%.

CONCLUSION

The policy implications of changes in long-term interest rates are especially important at this time of debt-funding. It is clear that a higher rate tends to be associated with a speed-up in the turnover of money. Conversely, a decline in rates has been associated with an increased demand for cash balances at a given level of income. Based on past experience an increase in the yield on long-term high-grade corporate bonds from 3.00% to, say, 3.30% would tend to be associated with a 7.5% expansion in income if cash balances remained constant. Whether this will prove true in the future, the effect is important enough to deserve careful consideration when formulating monetary and fiscal policy.

V

Money, Interest, and Income Determination

It has been said that to learn what Keynes was saying in the *General Theory,* the last place to look is the *General Theory*. The book is so badly written, so poorly organized, and so full of confusions that precious few of the many economists who undertook its study in the early days following its publication in 1936 really succeeded in finding out what it was about. Some of these economists, however, published their "interpretations" of the *General Theory,* and among these none was more successful in opening up the essence of the book to economists at large than John R. Hicks in a 1937 article, which appears in this part.

The *General Theory* itself opens with and maintains a running attack on what Keynes called the "classical" theory. As Hicks has pointed out, Keynes directed this attack against a long line of writers but focused particularly on certain writings of his fellow British economist A. C. Pigou, singling out Pigou's book *The Theory of Unemployment* as typical of classical economics. Inasmuch as this book by Pigou is very difficult, we are confronted in parts of the *General Theory* with an attack on a very difficult book by another very difficult book, so the latter's indigestibility is understandable enough. In contrast, Hick's article, in a few clear and sharp steps, sets up a more typical classical theory than Pigou's, sets Keynes's theory side by side with this classical theory, and reveals not the whole of the two theories, but at least what are the essentials of each in a form that all can comprehend. This article, which probably stands second only to the *General Theory* among the classics in this area of economics, is the first of the four selections in this part.

Hicks does so well what he sets out to do in this article by devising for the purpose what is now generally referred to as the *IS-LM* system, or tool, of analysis—a tool that has since become the most basic instrument in the macroeconomic kit. In the thirty-odd years since it was introduced by Hicks, the *IS-LM* tool has been elaborated, sharpened, and applied to a number of problems. One such application is found in the second selection in this part, in which Jerome L. Stein develops his "identifying" method. The level of money national income changes from year to year in response to a variety of exogenous disturbances, which Stein separates into "real," "monetary," and "liquidity" disturbances. The *IS-LM* system (together with the concept of the velocity of money) is then employed by Stein to identify whether each of the annual changes in money national income actually observed from 1919–1958 was mainly due to one or the other of the several types of exogenous disturbance.

The third selection in this part again involves the Hicksian *IS-LM* system, but the system is now supplemented in a way that permits the investigation of questions beyond the capacity of *IS-LM* alone. Among these questions is whether or not a system of flexible prices and wages tends automatically toward full employment, as was maintained by classical economists and denied by Keynes. This question was not investigated in Hicks's article, for that article assumes, as does the basic model of the *General Theory,* a system of rigid prices and wages and draws the conclusions that follow from this particular assumption. Suppose that we now ask in what ways these conclusions may vary according to whether both prices and wages are flexible, prices are flexible and wages rigid, or wages are flexible and prices are rigid. In the selection by Robert A. Mundell, an *IS-LM* framework supplemented by a production function and a labor supply function are used to investigate this question. In successive steps the author works out the conclusions that follow for income, employment, and other variables in the cases in which either wages or prices or both are flexible as well as the conclusions for the Keynesian or Hicksian case as they emerge from this expanded framework.

The issue of price flexibility that is met in the article by Mundell is examined in much greater detail by Don Patinkin in the final selection in this part. Writing in the forties, Pigou and other defenders of the classical theory had shown that, contrary to Keynes's conclusion, a system with flexible prices will tend automatically to generate full employment through the operation of what came to be known as the real balance, wealth, or Pigou effect. Through a remarkably lucid exposition and the use of the most elementary graphic apparatus, Patinkin manages to bring out in a most understandable way the dimensions of this major debate between the Keynesian and classical camps. Although this debate began in the forties and slowed in the fifties, it has remained alive in modified form in the sixties—a new book in support of the wealth effect appeared as recently as 1967.

15

MR. KEYNES AND THE "CLASSICS": A SUGGESTED INTERPRETATION[1]

JOHN R. HICKS

I.

It will be admitted by the least charitable reader that the entertainment value of Mr. Keynes' *General Theory of Employment* is considerably enhanced by its satiric aspect. But it is also clear that many readers have been left very bewildered by this Dunciad. Even if they are convinced by Mr. Keynes' arguments and humbly acknowledge themselves to have been "classical economists" in the past, they find it hard to remember that they believed in their unregenerate days the things Mr. Keynes says they believed. And there are no doubt others who find their historic doubts a stumbling block, which prevents them from getting as much illumination from the positive theory as they might otherwise have got.

One of the main reasons for this situation is undoubtedly to be found in the fact that Mr. Keynes takes as typical of "Classical economics" the later writings of Professor Pigou, particularly *The Theory of Unemployment*. Now *The Theory of Unemployment* is a fairly new book, and an exceedingly difficult book; so that it is safe to say that it has not yet made much

[1]Based on a paper which was read at the Oxford meeting of the Econometric Society (September, 1936) and which called forth an interesting discussion. It has been modified subsequently, partly in the light of that discussion, and partly as a result of further discussion in Cambridge.

Reprinted from *Econometrica,* (April 1937), pp. 147–59, by permission of the publisher and author. John R. Hicks is a professor at All Souls College, Oxford University.

impression on the ordinary teaching of economics. To most people its doctrines seem quite as strange and novel as the doctrines of Mr. Keynes himself; so that to be told that he has believed these things himself leaves the ordinary economist quite bewildered.

For example, Professor Pigou's theory runs, to a quite amazing extent, in real terms. Not only is his theory a theory of real wages and unemployment; but numbers of problems which anyone else would have preferred to investigate in money terms are investigated by Professor Pigou in terms of "wage-goods." The ordinary classical economist has no part in this *tour de force*.

But if, on behalf of the ordinary classical economist, we declare that he would have preferred to investigate many of these problems in money terms, Mr. Keynes will reply that there is no classical theory of money wages and employment. It is quite true that such a theory cannot easily be found in the textbooks. But this is only because most of the textbooks were written at a time when general changes in money wages in a closed system did not present an important problem. There can be little doubt that most economists have thought that they had a pretty fair idea of what the relation between money wages and employment actually was.

In these circumstances, it seems worth while to try to construct a typical "classical" theory, built on an earlier and cruder model than Professor Pigou's. If we can construct such a theory, and show that it does give results which have in fact been commonly taken for granted, but which do not agree with Mr. Keynes' conclusions, then we shall at last have a satisfactory basis of comparison. We may hope to be able to isolate Mr. Keynes' innovations, and so to discover what are the real issues in dispute.

Since our purpose is comparison, I shall try to set out my typical classical theory in a form similar to that in which Mr. Keynes sets out his own theory; and I shall leave out of account all secondary complications which do not bear closely upon this special question in hand. Thus I assume that I am dealing with a short period in which the quantity of physical equipment of all kinds available can be taken as fixed. I assume homogeneous labour. I assume further that depreciation can be neglected, so that the output of investment goods corresponds to new investment. This is a dangerous simplification, but the important issues raised by Mr. Keynes in his chapter on user cost are irrelevant for our purposes.

Let us begin by assuming that w, the rate of money wages per head, can be taken as given.

Let x, y, be the outputs of investment goods and consumption goods respectively, and N_x, N_y, be the numbers of men employed in producing them. Since the amount of physical equipment specialised to each industry is given, $x = f_x(N_x)$ and $y = f_y(N_y)$, where f_x, f_y, are *given* functions.

Let M be the *given* quantity of money.

It is desired to determine N_x and N_y.

First, the price-level of investment goods = their marginal cost = $w(dN_x / dx)$. And the price-level of consumption goods = their marginal cost = $w(dN_y / dy)$.

Income earned in investment trades (value of investment, or simply Investment) = $wx(dN_x / dx)$. Call this I_x.

Income earned in consumption trades = $wy(dN_y / dy)$.

Total income = $wx(dN_x / dx) + wy(dN_y / dy)$. Call this I.

I_x is therefore a given function of N_x, I of N_x and N_y. Once I and I_x are determined, N_x and N_y can be determined.

Now let us assume the "Cambridge Quantity equation"–that there is some definite relation between Income and the demand for money. Then, approximately, and apart from the fact that the demand for money may depend not only upon total Income, but also upon its distribution between people with relatively large and relatively small demands for balances, we can write

$$M = kI.$$

As soon as k is given, total Income is therefore determined.

In order to determine I_x, we need two equations. One tells us that the amount of investment (looked at as demand for capital) depends upon the rate of interest:

$$I_x = C(i).$$

This is what becomes of the marginal-efficiency-of-capital schedule in Mr. Keynes' work.

Further, Investment = Saving. And saving depends upon the rate of interest and, if you like, Income. $\therefore I_x = S(i, I)$. (Since, however, Income is already determined, we do not need to bother about inserting Income here unless we choose.)

Taking them as a system, however, we have three fundamental equations,

$$M = kI, \; I_x = C(i), \; I_x = S(i, I),$$

to determine three unknowns, I, I_x, i. As we have found earlier, N_x and N_y can be determined from I and I_x. Total employment, $N_x + N_y$, is therefore determined.

Let us consider some properties of this system. It follows directly from the first equation that as soon as k and M are given, I is completely determined; that is to say, total income depends directly upon the quantity of money. Total employment, however, is not necessarily determined at once from income, since it will usually depend to some extent upon the proportion of income saved, and thus upon the way production is divided between investment and consumption-goods trades. (If it so happened that the elasticities of supply were the same in each of these trades, then a shifting of demand between them would produce compensating movements in N_x and N_y, and consequently no change in total employment.)

An increase in the inducement to invest (i.e., a rightward movement of the schedule of the marginal efficiency of capital, which we have written as $C(i)$ will tend to raise the rate of interest, and so to affect saving. If the amount of saving rises, the amount of investment will rise too; labour will be employed more in the investment trades, less in the consumption trades; this will increase total employment if the elasticity of supply in the investment trades is greater than that in the consumption-goods trades—diminish it if *vice versa.*

An increase in the supply of money will necessarily raise total income, for people will increase their spending and lending until incomes have risen sufficiently to restore k to its former level. The rise in income will tend to increase employment, both in making consumption goods and in making investment goods. The total effect on employment depends upon the ratio between the expansions of these industries; and that depends upon the proportion of their increased incomes which people desire to save, which also governs the rate of interest.

So far we have assumed the rate of money wages to be given; but so long as we assume that k is independent of the level of wages, there is no difficulty about this problem either. A rise in the rate of money wages will necessarily diminish employment and raise real wages. For an unchanged money income cannot continue to buy an unchanged quantity of goods at a higher price-level; and, unless the price-level rises, the prices of goods will not cover their marginal costs. There must therefore be a fall in employment; as employment falls, marginal costs in terms of labour will diminish and therefore real wages rise. (Since a change in money wages is always accompanied by a change in real wages in the same direction, if not in the same proportion, no harm will be done, and some advantage will perhaps be secured, if one prefers to work in terms of real wages. Naturally most "classical economists" have taken this line.)

I think it will be agreed that we have here a quite reasonably consistent theory, and a theory which is also consistent with the pronouncements of a recognizable group of economists. Admittedly it follows from this theory that you may be able to increase employment by direct inflation; but whether or not you decide to favour that policy still depends upon your judgment about the probable reaction on wages, and also—in a national area—upon your views about the international standard.

Historically, this theory descends from Ricardo, though it is not actually Ricardian; it is probably more or less the theory that was held by Marshall.

But with Marshall it was already beginning to be qualified in important ways; his successors have qualified it still further. What Mr. Keynes has done is to lay enormous emphasis on the qualifications, so that they almost blot out the original theory. Let us follow out this process of development.

II.

When a theory like the "classical" theory we have just described is applied to the analysis of industrial fluctuations, it gets into difficulties in several ways. It is evident that total money income experiences great variations in the course of a trade cycle, and the classical theory can only explain these by variations in M or in k, or, as a third and last alternative, by changes in distribution.

(1) Variation in M is simplest and most obvious, and has been relied on to a large extent. But the variations in M that are traceable during a trade cycle are variations that take place through the banks–they are variations in bank loans; if we are to rely on them it is urgently necessary for us to explain the connection between the supply of bank money and the rate of interest. This can be done roughly by thinking of banks as persons who are strongly inclined to pass on money by lending rather than spending it. Their action therefore tends at first to lower interest rates, and only afterwards, when the money passes into the hands of spenders, to raise prices and incomes. "The new currency, or the increase of currency, goes, not to private persons, but to the banking centers; and therefore, it increases the willingness of lenders to lend in the first instance, and lowers the rate of discount. But it afterwards raises prices; and therefore it tends to increase discount."[2] This is superficially satisfactory; but if we endeavoured to give a more precise account of this process we should soon get into difficulties. What determines the amount of money needed to produce a given fall in the rate of interest? What determines the length of time for which the low rate will last? These are not easy questions to answer.

(2) In so far as we rely upon changes in k, we can also do well enough up to a point. Changes in k can be related to changes in confidence, and it is realistic to hold that the rising prices of a boom occur because optimism encourages a reduction in balances; the falling prices of a slump because pessimism and uncertainty dictate an increase. But as soon as we take this step it becomes natural to ask whether k has not abdicated its status as an independent variable, and has not become liable to be influenced by others among the variables in our fundamental equations.

[2]Marshall, *Money, Credit, and Commerce,* p. 257.

(3) This last consideration is powerfully supported by another, of more purely theoretical character. On grounds of pure value theory, it is evident that the direct sacrifice made by a person who holds a stock of money is a sacrifice of interest; and it is hard to believe that the marginal principle does not operate at all in this field. As Lavington put it:

> The quantity of resources which (an individual) holds in the form of money will be such that the unit of money which is just and only just worth while holding in this form yields him a return of convenience and security equal to the yield of satisfaction derived from the marginal unit spent on consumables, and equal also to the net rate of interest.[3]

The demand for money depends upon the rate of interest! The stage is set for Mr. Keynes.

As against the three equations of the classical theory,

$$M = kI, \ I_x = C(i), \ I_x = S(i, I),$$

Mr. Keynes begins with three equations,

$$M = L(i), \ I_x = C(i), \ I_x = S(I).$$

These differ from the classical equations in two ways. On the one hand, the demand for money is conceived as depending upon the rate of interest (Liquidity Preference). On the other hand, any possible influence of the rate of interest on the amount saved out of a given income is neglected. Although it means that the third equation becomes the multiplier equation, which performs such queer tricks, nevertheless this second amendment is a mere simplification, and ultimately insignificant.[4] It is the liquidity preference doctrine which is vital.

For it is now the rate of interest, not income, which is determined by the quantity of money. The rate of interest set against the schedule of the marginal efficiency of capital determines the value of investment; that determines income by the multiplier. Then the volume of employment (at

[3] Lavington, *English Capital Market,* 1921, p. 30. See also Pigou, "The Exchange-value of Legal-tender Money," in *Essays in Applied Economics,* 1922, pp. 179–181.

[4] This can be readily seen if we consider the equations

$$M = kI, \ I_x = C(i), \ I_x = S(I),$$

which embody Mr. Keynes' second amendment without his first. The third equation is already the multiplier equation, but the multiplier is shorn of his wings. For since I still depends only on M, I_x now depends only on M, and it is impossible to increase investment without increasing the willingness to save or the quantity of money. The system thus generated is therefore identical with that which, a few years ago, used to be called the "Treasury View." But Liquidity Preference transports us from the "Treasury View" to the "General Theory of Employment."

given wage-rates) is determined by the value of investment and of income which is not saved but spent upon consumption goods.

It is this system of equations which yields the startling conclusion, that an increase in the inducement to invest, or in the propensity to consume, will not tend to raise the rate of interest, but only to increase employment. In spite of this, however, and in spite of the fact that quite a large part of the argument runs in terms of this system, and this system alone, *it is not the General Theory*. We may call it, if we like, Mr. Keynes' *special theory*. The General Theory is something appreciably more orthodox.

Like Lavington and Professor Pigou, Mr. Keynes does not in the end believe that the demand for money can be determined by one variable alone—not even the rate of interest. He lays more stress on it than they did, but neither for him nor for them can it be the only variable to be considered. The dependence of the demand for money on interest does not, in the end, do more than qualify the old dependence on income. However much stress we lay upon the "speculative motive," the "transactions" motive must always come in as well.

Consequently we have for the General Theory

$$M = L(I,i), I_x = C(i), I_x = S(I),$$

With this revision, Mr. Keynes takes a big step back to Marshallian orthodoxy, and his theory becomes hard to distinguish from the revised and qualified Marshallian theories, which, as we have seen, are not new. Is there really any difference between them, or is the whole thing a sham fight? Let us have recourse to a diagram (Figure 1).

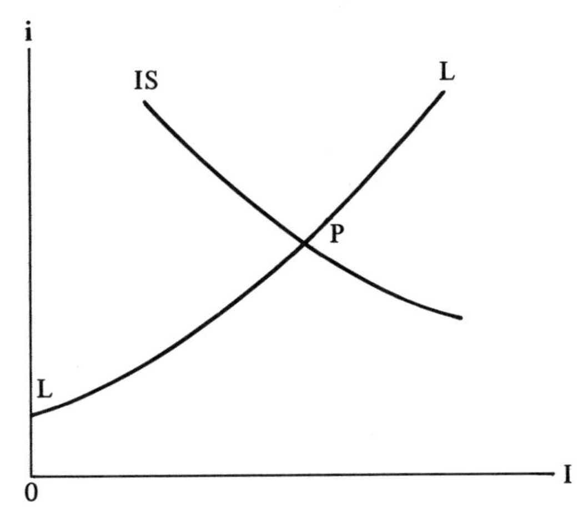

Figure 1.

Against a given quantity of money, the first equation, $M = L(I, i)$, gives us a relation between Income (I) and the rate of interest (i). This can be drawn out as a curve (LL) which will slope upwards, since an increase in income tends to raise the demand for money, and an increase in the rate of interest tends to lower it. Further, the second two equations taken together give us another relation between Income and interest. (The marginal-efficiency-of-capital schedule determines the value of investment at any given rate of interest, and the multiplier tells us what level of income will be necessary to make savings equal to that value of investment.) The curve IS can therefore be drawn showing the relation between Income and interest which must be maintained in order to make saving equal to investment.

Income and the rate of interest are now determined together at P, the point of intersection of the curves LL and IS. They are determined together; just as price and output are determined together in the modern theory of demand and supply. Indeed, Mr. Keynes' innovation is closely parallel, in this respect, to the innovation of the marginalists. The quantity theory tries to determine income without interest, just as the labour theory of value tried to determine price without output; each has to give place to a theory recognising a higher degree of interdependence.

III.

But if this is the real "General Theory," how does Mr. Keynes come to make his remarks about an increase in the inducement to invest not raising the rate of interest? It would appear from our diagram that a rise in the marginal-efficiency-of-capital schedule must raise the curve IS; and, therefore, although it will raise Income and employment, it will also raise the rate of interest.

This brings us to what, from many points of view, is the most important thing in Mr. Keynes' book. It is not only possible to show that a given supply of money determines a certain relation between Income and interest (which we have expressed by the curve LL); it is also possible to say something about the shape of the curve. It will probably tend to be nearly horizontal on the left, and nearly vertical on the right. This is because there is (1) some minimum below which the rate of interest is unlikely to go, and (though Mr. Keynes does not stress this) there is (2) a maximum to the level of income which can possibly be financed with a given amount of money. If we like we can think of the curve as approaching these limits asymptotically (Figure 2).

Therefore, if the curve IS lies well to the right (either because of a strong inducement to invest or a strong propensity to consume), P will lie upon that part of the curve which is decidedly upward sloping, and the classical theory

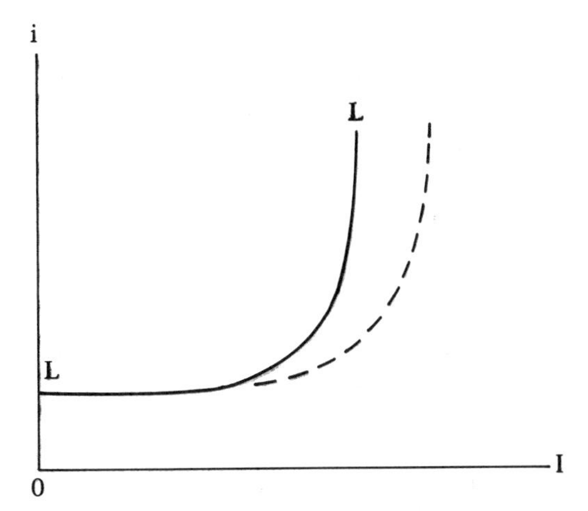

Figure 2.

will be a good approximation, needing no more than the qualification which it has in fact received at the hands of the later Marshallians. An increase in the inducement to invest will raise the rate of interest, as in the classical theory, but it will also have some subsidiary effect in raising income, and therefore employment as well. (Mr. Keynes in 1936 is not the first Cambridge economist to have a temperate faith in Public Works.) But if the point *P* lies to the left of the *LL* curve, then the *special* form of Mr. Keynes' theory becomes valid. A rise in the schedule of the marginal efficiency of capital only increases employment, and does not raise the rate of interest at all. We are completely out of touch with the classical world.

The demonstration of this minimum is thus of central importance. It is so important that I shall venture to paraphrase the proof, setting it out in a rather different way from that adopted by Mr. Keynes.[5]

If the costs of holding money can be neglected, it will always be profitable to hold money rather than lend it out, if the rate of interest is not greater than zero. Consequently the rate of interest must always be positive. In an extreme case, the shortest short-term rate may perhaps be nearly zero. But if so, the long-term rate must lie above it, for the long rate has to allow for the risk that the short rate may rise during the currency of the loan, and it should be observed that the short rate can only rise, it cannot fall.[6] This does not

[5]Keynes, *General Theory*, pp. 201–202.

[6]It is just conceivable that people might become so used to the idea of very low short rates that they would not be much impressed by this risk; but it is very unlikely. For the short rate may rise, either because trade improves, and income expands; or because trade gets worse, and the desire for liquidity increases. I doubt whether a monetary system so elastic as to rule out both of these possibilities is really thinkable.

only mean that the long rate must be a sort of average of the probable short rates over its duration, and that this average must lie above the current short rate. There is also the more important risk to be considered, that the lender on long term may desire to have cash before the agreed date of repayment, and then, if the short rate has risen meanwhile, he may be involved in a substantial capital loss. It is this last risk which provides Mr. Keynes' "speculative motive" and which ensures that the rate for loans of indefinite duration (which he always has in mind as *the* rate of interest) cannot fall very near zero.[7]

It should be observed that this minimum to the rate of interest applies not only to one curve *LL* (drawn to correspond to a particular quantity of money) but to any such curve. If the supply of money is increased, the curve *LL* moves to the right (as the dotted curve in Figure 2), but the horizontal parts of the curve are almost the same. Therefore, again, it is this doldrum to the left of the diagram which upsets the classical theory. If *IS* lies to the right, then we can indeed increase employment by increasing the quantity of money; but if *IS* lies to the left, we cannot do so; merely monetary means will not force down the rate of interest any further.

So the General Theory of Employment is the Economics of Depression.

IV.

In order to elucidate the relation between Mr. Keynes and the "Classics," we have invented a little apparatus. It does not appear that we have exhausted the uses of that apparatus, so let us conclude by giving it a little run on its own.

With that apparatus at our disposal, we are no longer obliged to make certain simplifications which Mr. Keynes makes in his exposition. We can reinsert the missing i in the third equation, and allow for any possible effect of the rate of interest upon saving; and, what is much more important, we can call in question the sole dependence of investment upon the rate of interest, which looks rather suspicious in the second equation. Mathematical elegance would suggest that we ought to have I and i in all three equations, if the theory is to be really General. Why not have them there like this:

$$M = L(I,i), \quad I_x = C(I,i), \quad I_x = S(I,i)?$$

[7]Nevertheless something more than the "speculative motive" is needed to account for the system of interest rates. The shortest of all short rates must equal the relative valuation, at the margin, of money and such a bill; and the bill stands at a discount mainly because of the "convenience and security" of holding money—the inconvenience which may possibly be caused

Once we raise the question of Income in the second equation, it is clear that it has a very good claim to be inserted. Mr. Keynes is in fact only enabled to leave it out at all plausibly by his device of measuring everything in "wage-units," which means that he allows for changes in the marginal-efficiency-of-capital schedule when there is a change in the level of money wages, but that other changes in Income are deemed not to affect the curve, or at least not in the same immediate manner. But why draw this distinction? Surely there is every reason to suppose that an increase in the demand for consumers' goods, arising from an increase in employment, will often directly stimulate an increase in investment, at least as soon as an expectation develops that the increased demand will continue. If this is so, we ought to include I in the second equation, though it must be confessed that the effect of I on the marginal efficiency of capital will be fitful and irregular.

The Generalized General Theory can then be set out in this way. Assume first of all a given total money Income. Draw a curve CC showing the marginal efficiency of capital (in money terms) at that given Income; a curve SS showing the supply curve of saving at that *given* Income (Figure 3). Their intersection will determine the rate of interest which makes savings equal to investment at that level of income. This we may call the "investment rate."

If Income rises, the curve SS will move to the right; probably CC will move to the right too. If SS moves more than CC, the investment rate of interest will fall; if CC more than SS, it will rise. (How much it rises and falls, however, depends upon the elasticities of the CC and SS curves.)

The IS curve (drawn on a separate diagram) now shows the relation between Income and the corresponding investment rate of interest. It has to be confronted (as in our earlier constructions) with an LL curve showing the

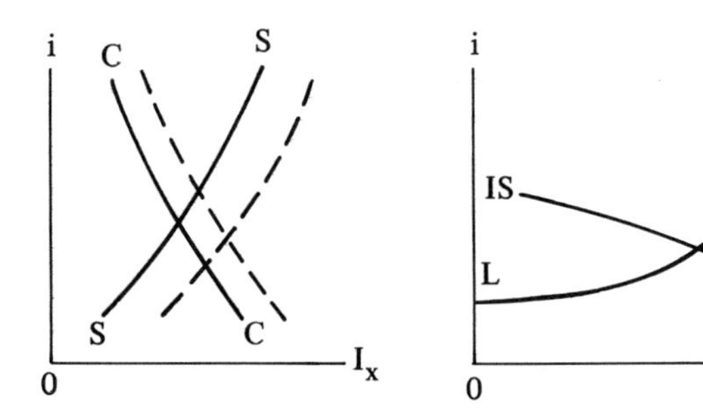

Figure 3.

by not having cash immediately available. It is the chance that you may want to discount the bill which matters, not the chance that you will then have to discount it on unfavourable terms. The "precautionary motive," not the "speculative motive," is here dominant. But the prospective terms of rediscounting are vital, when it comes to the *difference* between short and long rates.

relation between Income and the "money" rate of interest; only we can now generalize our *LL* curve a little. Instead of assuming, as before, that the supply of money is given, we can assume that there is a given monetary system—that up to a point, but only up to a point, monetary authorities will prefer to create new money rather than allow interest rates to rise. Such a generalized *LL* curve will then slope upwards only gradually—the elasticity of the curve depending on the elasticity of the monetary system (in the ordinary monetary sense).

As before, Income and interest are determined where the *IS* and *LL* curves intersect—where the investment rate of interest equals the money rate. Any change in the inducement to invest or the propensity to consume will shift the *IS* curve; any change in liquidity preference or monetary policy will shift the *LL* curve. If, as the result of such a change, the investment rate is raised above the money rate, Income will tend to rise; in the opposite case, Income will tend to fall; the extent to which Income rises or falls depends on the elasticities of the curves.[8]

When generalized in this way, Mr. Keynes' theory begins to look very like Wicksell's; this is of course hardly surprising.[9] There is indeed one special case where it fits Wicksell's construction absolutely. If there is "full employment" in the sense that any rise in Income immediately calls forth a rise in money wage rates; then it is *possible* that the *CC* and *SS* curves may be moved to the right to exactly the same extent, so that *IS* is horizontal. (I say possible, because it is not unlikely, in fact, that the rise in the wage level may create a presumption that wages will rise again later on; if so, *CC* will probably be shifted more than *SS*, so that *IS* will be upward sloping.) However that may be, if *IS* is horizontal, we do have a perfectly Wicksellian construction,[10] the investment rate becomes Wicksell's *natural rate*, for in this case it may be thought of as determined by real causes; if there is a perfectly elastic monetary system, and the money rate is fixed below the natural rate, there is cumulative inflation; cumulative deflation if it is fixed above.

[8]Since $C(I, i) = S(I, i)$,

$$\frac{dI}{di} = -\frac{\partial S/\partial i - \partial C/\partial i}{\partial S/\partial I - \partial C/\partial I}$$

The savings investment market will not be stable unless $\partial S/\partial i + (-\partial C/\partial i)$ is positive. I think we may assume that this condition is fulfilled.

If $\partial S/\partial i$ is positive, $\partial C/\partial i$ negative, $\partial S/\partial I$ and $\partial C/\partial I$ positive (the most probable state of affairs), we can say that the *IS* curve will be more elastic, the greater the elasticities of the *CC* and *SS* curves, and the larger is $\partial C/\partial I$ relatively to $\partial S/\partial I$. When $\partial C/\partial I > \partial S/\partial I$, the *IS* curve is upward sloping.

[9]Cf. Keynes, *General Theory*, p. 242.

[10]Cf. Myrdal, "Gleichgewichtsbegriff," in *Beiträge zur Geldtheorie*, ed. Hayek.

This, however, is now seen to be only one special case; we can use our construction to harbour much wider possibilities. If there is a great deal of unemployment, it is very likely that $\partial C/\partial I$ will be quite small; in that case *IS* can be relied upon to slope downwards. This is the sort of Slump Economics with which Mr. Keynes is largely concerned. But one cannot escape the impression that there may be other conditions when expectations are tinder, when a slight inflationary tendency lights them up very easily. Then $\partial C/\partial I$ may be large and an increase in Income tends to *raise* the investment rate of interest. In these circumstances, the situation is unstable at *any* given money rate; it is only an imperfectly elastic monetary system–a rising *LL* curve–that can prevent the situation getting out of hand altogether.

These, then, are a few of the things we can get out of our skeleton apparatus. But even if it may claim to be a slight extension of Mr. Keynes' similar skeleton, it remains a terribly rough and ready sort of affair. In particular, the concept of "Income" is worked monstrously hard; most of our curves are not really determinate unless something is said about the distribution of Income as well as its magnitude. Indeed, what they express is something like a relation between the price-system and the system of interest rates; and you cannot get that into a curve. Further, all sorts of questions about depreciation have been neglected; and all sorts of questions about the timing of the processes under consideration.

The *General Theory of Employment* is a useful book; but it is neither the beginning nor the end of Dynamic Economics.

16

AN EXPOSITION OF SOME SUBTLETIES IN THE KEYNESIAN SYSTEM

ROBERT A. MUNDELL

The introduction of supply conditions into the Keynesian system and their integration with the theory of income and interest rate determination pose one of the more formidable subjects for the student of income theory to master. Since Keynesian theory is often the student's first introduction to income theory, and since it is usually the point of departure for discussions of wealth effects and dichotomies in the pricing process, a simple, compact and generalized exposition might prove useful to the student of the subject. This paper attempts such an exposition although generalization is limited to the four cases in which (a) prices and wages are both flexible, (b) prices are flexible and wages are rigid, (c) wages are flexible and prices are rigid, and (d) prices and wages are both rigid. The distinction between the four cases hinges on whether or not firms are prevented from maximizing profit and whether or not workers are impeded in their pursuit of maximum utility.[1]

[1]For a discussion of some of these points the reader is referred to the standard works of J. R. Hicks, "Mr. Keynes and the 'Classics': A Suggested Interpretation", *Econometrica,* Vol. V, Menasha, Wis., 1937, pp. 147sqq., reprinted in: *Readings in the Theory of Income Distribution,* Selected by a Committee of the American Economic Association, Pref.: Howard S. Ellis, Repr., Blakiston Series of Republished Articles on Economics, Vol. III, Philadelphia and Toronto, 1949, pp. 461sqq.; Franco Modigliani, "Liquidity Preference and the Theory of Interest and Money", *Econometrica,* Vol. XII, 1944, pp. 45sqq., reprinted in: *Readings in Monetary Theory,* Selected by a Committee of the American Economic Association, Blakiston Series of Republished Articles on

Reprinted by permission of the publisher from *Weltwirtschaftliches Archiv* (December 1964), pp. 301–14. Robert A. Mundell is a professor at the University of Chicago.

I. INCOME AND INTEREST RATE DETERMINATION

To develop the more complex apparatus used later we first tread over some well-travelled ground, and develop the version of the Keynesian system made popular by Hicks.[2] The equations are based on two equilibrium conditions:

(1) $I(r) = S(y)$

(where I = real investment, S = real saving, r = the interest rate and y = real income),

(2) $L(r, y) = M$

(where L = the demand for money and M = the stock of money). In this simple version it is assumed that the price level is fixed. Equation (1) states that investment equals saving and gives the relation between r and y for output to be demanded. Equation (2) states that the demand for money equals the supply of money; for diagrammatical purposes, however, it will be convenient to split L into its transaction (L^T) and asset (L^A) components. The supply of money is assumed to be constant.

1. The IS Schedule

Equation (1) is developed in Figure 1. Quadrant IV graphs the propensity to save, $S = S(y)$, Quadrant II graphs the incentive to invest, $I = I(r)$, and Quadrant III depicts the condition of equilibrium, $I = S$. From these relations the IS schedule, $I(r) = S(y)$, can be derived in Quadrant I. For example, at the interest rate $r = r_1$ investment is $I = I_1$. For saving to equal investment $S = S_1$ is necessary. But $S = S_1$ only if income $y = y_1$. Hence, the

---

Economics, Vol. V, New York, Philadelphia and Toronto, 1951, pp. 186sqq.; and Don Patinkin, *Money, Interest, and Prices, An Integration of Monetary and Value Theory,* Evanston, Ill., 1956; see also Harry G. Johnson, "Una versione diagrammatica della teoria dell'interesse dei fondi prestabili", *Rivista internazionale di scienze economiche e commerciali,* Anno III, Padova, 1956, pp. 16sqq., for a diagrammatic exposition. The present paper was stimulated by my reading of a valuable paper by Edgar O. Edwards, "Classical and Keynesian Employment Theories: A Reconciliation", *The Quarterly Journal of Economics,* Vol. LXXIII, Cambridge, Mass., 1959, pp. 407sqq., whose analysis, however, is restricted to case (b) above. In the preparation of the present paper I have benefited from the helpful comments of Diana Dane and Wolfgang Rieke.

[2] Hicks, *op. cit.*—More generally, one could allow for wealth effects, a marginal propensity to invest, a responsiveness of saving to the interest rate, and some interest elasticity in the supply of money. But the present version is more in keeping with the spirit of the *General Theory*. It should also be mentioned that I ignore throughout the extreme cases associated with the "liquidity trap" (the situation in which interest rates are so low that the demand for money is supposed to be completely elastic) and full employment saving-investment equality at a negative rate of interest.

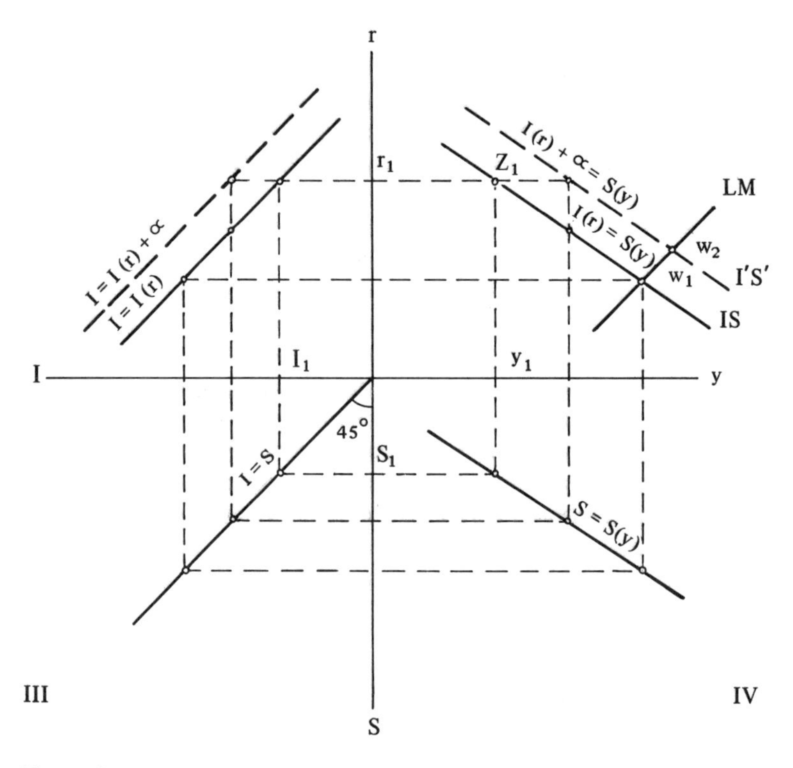

Figure 1.

income level $y = y_1$ must be associated with the interest rate $r = r_1$ in order that investment equal saving. The point Z_1 is therefore one point on the IS schedule. In a similar fashion every other point along IS can be established.

Note that IS is steeper the steeper is I(r) and the greater is the marginal propensity to save $S'(y)$. Note also that an upward shift in investment or a reduction in the propensity to save shifts IS upward and to the right. For example, an increase in investment of the amount α shifts IS to I′S′.

2. The LM Schedule

Equation (2) is developed in Figure 2. In Quadrant IV the line $L^T = L^T(y)$ plots the *transactions* demand for money which is a function of income, while in Quadrant II the line $L^A = L^A(r)$ plots the *asset* demand for money, which is a function of the interest rate. Quadrant III gives the equilibrium condition

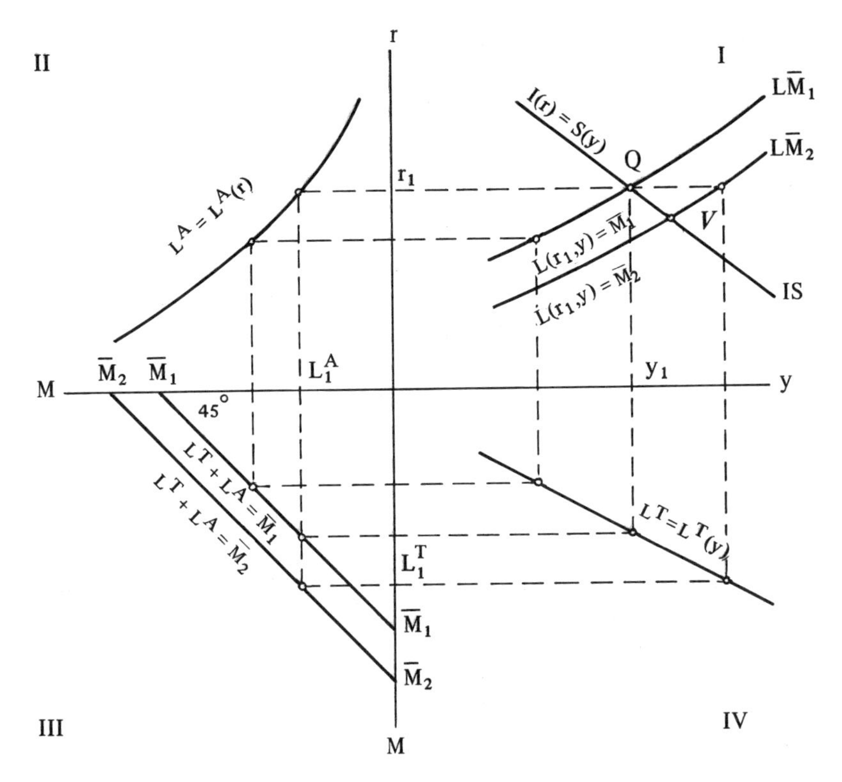

Figure 2.

that the supply of money, $\overline{M}_1$, must equal the sum of the demand for money for both asset and transactions purposes, $L^T + L^A$. The LM schedule can easily be derived from these relations.

For example, consider the interest rate $r = r_1$. At this interest rate the public wants to hold L_1^A of money for asset purposes and this leaves L_1^T of money left over from the given money stock for transactions purposes. But the public will want to hold L_1^T of money only if income is $y = y_1$. Therefore, the interest rate $r = r_1$ must be associated with the income level $y = y_1$ if the demand for money is to equal the supply of money. The point Q is then one point on the LM schedule, and all other points can similarly be derived.

Note that LM is flatter the less steep is $L^A(r)$ and the smaller is the marginal propensity to hold money for transactions purposes. It can also be shown that an increase in the money supply (which can be analyzed by shifting the $\overline{M}_1\overline{M}_1$ line to $\overline{M}_2\overline{M}_2$ in Quadrant III), or a reduction in the demand for money for either transactions or asset purposes, both work to shift LM down and to the right. For example, an increase in the money supply from $\overline{M}_1$ to $\overline{M}_2$ shifts LM from $L\overline{M}_1$ to $L\overline{M}_2$.

3. The Hicksian Diagram

Combining the two schedules in Quadrant I of Figures 1 and 2 gives a version of the Hicksian diagram. Thus, an increase in the incentive to invest (or a decrease in the propensity to save) will raise both income and the interest rate as equilibrium moves in Figure 1 from W_1 to W_2, or an increase in the supply of money (or a decrease in the demand for money) lowers the interest rate and raises income, as equilibrium moves in Figure 2 from Q to V.

II. SUPPLY CONDITIONS

The preceding analysis is unsophisticated because it does not explicitly account for supply conditions and because the price level and wage are assumed to be constant. It is not immediately obvious how important these assumptions are. A more complete system is necessary and it requires additional equations. If wages and prices are flexible the system is as follows:

(3) $I(r) = S(y)$ (Commodity Market)

This equation is the same as (1) because I, S, and y are all defined in real terms and are not, therefore, affected by the price level.[3]

(4) $L(r, y) = M/p$ (Money Market)

The *real* demand for money equals the *real* supply of money, with p = price level.

(5) $y = \phi(n)$ (Production Function)

This is the production function with one variable factor (n = employed labor) which implies $\phi'(n) > 0$, and $\phi''(n) < 0$ if there is diminishing returns.

(6,7) $\phi'(n) = w/p = \psi_l'(n)$ (Maximum Profit and Utility Conditions)

Firms are maximizing profits only if the marginal productivity of labor equals the real wage rate, w/p, where w = money wages; and labor is

[3]Implicit in (3) is the assumption that expenditure is independent of the distribution of income.

maximizing utility only if the real wage rate equals the marginal disutility of labor $\psi'(n)$.[4]

The five equations (3–7) suffice to determine the five unknowns r, y, p, w and n, given the nominal supply of money ($\overline{M}$). However, equations (6,7) alone suffice to determine both employment and the real wage rate, implying that these are independent of the quantity of money. Moreover, the real magnitudes of the system, w/p, n, y and r, can be determined without the aid of equation (4), which implies that the money equation simply determines absolute prices and wages and that changes in the quantity of money leaves unaltered the level of output and the interest rate.

The system can be analyzed graphically by deriving two schedules, EE and RR, relating the interest rate and the real wage rate. These schedules are shown in Quadrant I of Figure 3, and are derived on the basis of the schedules in the other quadrants. Quadrant II plots the IS schedule, equation (3); Quadrant III plots the production function, equation (5); and Quadrant IV plots the labor supply and demand conditions, equations (6,7). For the moment ignore the LM schedule, equation (4).

To derive RR, consider the interest rate $r = r_1$. At this interest rate the only level of output that will clear the market is $y = y_1$ in Quadrant II. To produce this output requires $n = n_1$ of labor (Quadrant III). But n_1 of labor will only be *demanded* if the real wage rate is $(w/p)_1$. Hence r_1 and $(w/p)_1$ are the coordinates of one point on RR. Another point is given by the coordinates of r_0 and $(w/p)_0$ so RR has a positive slope.

To derive EE, consider another interest rate $r = r_2$. At this interest rate the level of output at which saving equals investment is $y = y_2$, which requires $n = n_2$ of employment. But this amount of labor will only be *supplied* if the

[4]Alternatively, equations (6–7) can be written as

$$(6a, 7a) \quad \eta^d\left(\frac{w}{p}\right) = \eta = \eta^s\left(\frac{w}{p}\right)$$

where η^d represents the demand for labor and η^s represents the supply of labor. However (6, 7) is slightly preferable for present purposes insofar as the schedules, in certain cases of rigidities, are not precisely demand and supply curves; there are discontinuities.

The following points are worth noting:

(1) Edwards, *op. cit.*, has pointed out that the Keynesian case does not depend on money illusion on the part of labor; it is sufficient that labor *bargains* for a money wage.

(2) With one variable factor the condition (6) is equivalent to the condition that firms equate marginal cost and price since $w/\phi'(n)$ is marginal cost.

(3) The supply curve of labor may bend backward at some (high) real wage.

(4) In the following discussion I shall refer to any discrepancy between price and marginal cost as a "failure of profit maximization," and to any gap between the real wage and the marginal disutility of labor as a "failure of utility maximization," though this is a restricted use of the term "maximization."

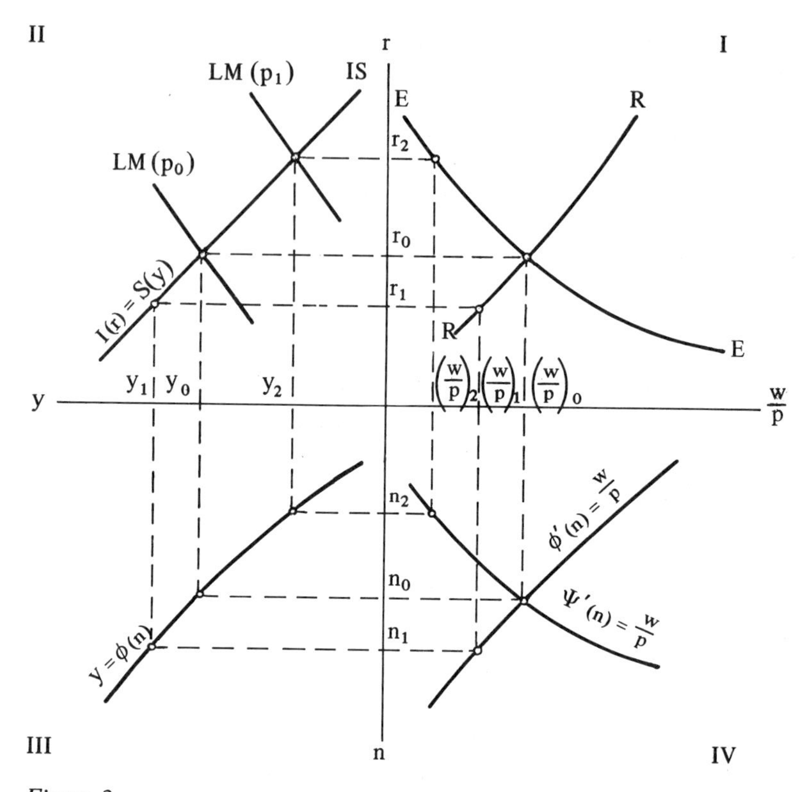

Figure 3.

real wage is $(w/p)_2$. Hence r_2 and $(w/p)_2$ are the coordinates of a point on EE. Another point is given by r_0 and $(w/p)_0$ so that EE has a negative slope in that range of the labor supply curve which has a normal slope.

The two schedules have precise interpretations. EE is the relation between the interest rate and the real wage rate at which *the employment levels which maximize labor's utility will produce outputs which can all be sold.* RR, on the other hand, is the relation between the interest rate and the real wage rate at which *the employment levels implied by profit maximization (under competition) will yield outputs which can all be sold.* On both EE and RR, therefore, the implied output can be sold, but only along EE is labor maximizing utility, and only along RR are firms maximizing profits. And only at the interest rate $r = r_0$ and the real wage $(w/p) = (w/p)_0$ are *both* utility maximization of labor and profit maximization of firms consistent with production which can exactly be sold.

The system will gravitate to the equilibrium interest rate r_0 and the equilibrium real wage rate $(w/p)_0$ whatever is the stock of money. This can be seen by noting that LM(p) (which shifts with the price level in view of (4)) can be inserted into Quadrant II. Suppose that, at the absolute price level, $p = p_1$, LM intersects IS at the interest rate $r = r_2$ and the output level $y = y_2$. To produce this output $n = n_2$ of labor is required. But at this employment level the demand price for labor is higher than the supply price. At the supply price of labor $(w/p)_2$ firms will want to produce an output greater than y_2 and will want to hire more labor than the amount $n = n_2$ forthcoming at that supply price. Hence money wages will rise to equilibrate the labor market and the price level will fall to equilibrate the commodity market. As the price level falls, the real value of money balances increases and the LM schedule shifts downward. Only when LM intersects IS at the interest rate $r = r_0$ and the output level $y = y_0$ will the system be in equilibrium. There is only one price level at which this position of LM is possible, the price level $p = p_0$, which is the equilibrium price level.

III. RIGIDITIES IN THE SYSTEM

The EE and RR schedules can now be used to interpret price and wage rigidities. When there are price or wage rigidities the real values of the system are no longer independent of the money supply. The authorities can alter the interest rate, the real wage rate, the level of employment and the level of output by adjusting the supply of money.

Consider Figure 4, which reproduces the EE and RR lines of Figure 3. As we have already noted, along EE workers, for any given wage rate, are offering the utility-maximizing employment and the ensuing output can all be sold at the corresponding interest rate; there is full employment. But above and to the right of EE the marginal disutility of labor is less than the real wage rate and there is involuntary unemployment, while below and to the left of EE there is involuntary overemployment.

Similarly (and as already noted), along RR the profit-maximizing output can all be sold. On the other hand, above and to the left of RR the marginal productivity of labor is greater than the real wage rate, which implies that price is greater than marginal costs (hence there is "underproduction") while below and to the right of RR price is less than marginal cost (hence there is "overproduction").

I. Rigid Money Wages and Flexible Prices

If the money wage rate is pegged the system (3–7) contains five equations in only four unknowns, r, y, n and p. It is therefore overdetermined and this means that one of the equations cannot be satisfied. Since a change in *money*

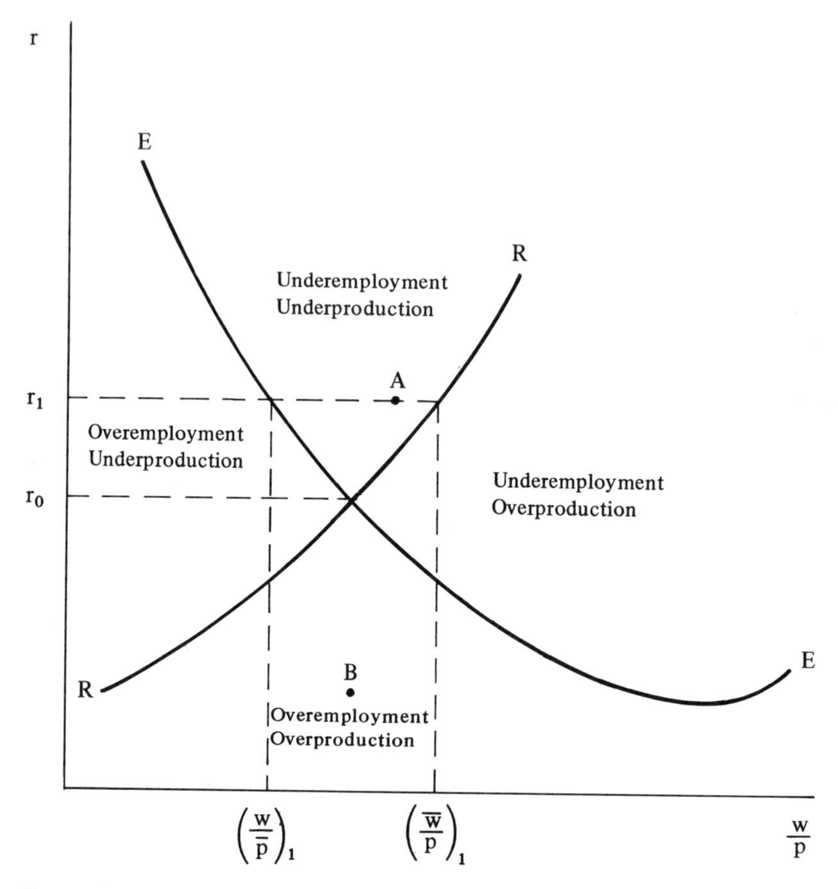

Figure 4.

wage rates is the instrument by means of which labor brings its marginal disutility of work into line with the real wage rate, the fixing of money wages means that equation (7), $\bar{w}/p = \psi'(n)$, will be frustrated. The system then is

(8) $I(r) = S(y)$ Commodity Market
(9) $L(r,y) = M/p$ Money Market
(10) $y = \phi(n)$ Production Function
(11) $\phi'(n) = \bar{w}/p$ Maximum Profit Condition

which is completely determined.

Consider, for example, the interest rate $r = r_1$ which, for simplicity, we can suppose to be maintained by the Central Bank by appropriate adjustments in the money supply. At this interest rate there is only one level of output at which supply will equal demand in the goods market, and there is, therefore, only one equilibrium level of employment. Now it should be clear that at this level of employment the real wage rate which is equal to the marginal disutility of labor must differ from the real wage rate which is equal to the marginal productivity of labor; this must be true at every interest rate except the equilibrium interest rate $r = r_0$. But the conflict will be resolved in favor of profit maximization of firms rather than utility maximization of labor, because output will respond whenever price differs from marginal cost (which is the same as marginal productivity differing from the real wage), and the change in output will immediately occasion an adjustment in the price level, altering the real wage. At the point A, for example, the real wage is less than the marginal productivity of labor, so firms attempt to increase employment and output, but this simply bids down the price level until the real wage has risen to a point on RR, corresponding to the real wage $(\overline{w}/p)_1$. Similarly, at points in the graph to the right of the RR line the real wage will tend to move downward.

With both wages and prices flexible, it will be remembered, the nominal quantity of money did not make any difference to the real equilibrium of the system. With money wages inflexible, however, one degree of freedom is lost; the money supply changes the equilibrium of the system. There is, therefore, only one level of the money supply which will yield a full employment equilibrium, given the level of wages, and that is the money supply necessary to effect the rate of interest $r = r_0$. At the point A, of course, there is general underemployment and underproduction.

2. *Flexible Wages and Rigid Prices*

Price rigidity may arise from monopoly or cartel arrangements or government control. If the price level is rigid but the wage rate is flexible, the general system of equations is again over-determined and one of them will be left unsatisfied. Since labor will always be willing to lower or raise money wages according to whether the marginal disutility of work exceeds or falls short of the going real wage rate, this equation must remain, and it is the marginal productivity equation which must be left unsatisfied. The system is then

(12) $I(r) = S(y)$ Commodity Market
(13) $L(r,y) = \overline{M}/\overline{p}$ Money Market
(14) $y = \phi(n)$ Production Function
(15) $w/p = \psi'(n)$ Maximization of Labor Utility

which is completely determined.

Consider again the interest rate $r = r_1$. Again, the level of output and employment at which investment is equal to saving will involve a difference between the real wage at which labor maximizes utility and the real wage at which firms maximize profits. But as long as money wage rates are flexible, the level of money wages and hence (with prices fixed) real wages will fall until the marginal disutility of labor is equal to the real wage rate. There is no provision for profit maximization of firms in the usual sense. At the interest rate $r = r_1$ the equilibrium real wage is $(W/\bar{p})_1$ which is a real wage consistent with full employment.

The implication that firms do not maximize profits seems at first puzzling. In the position under consideration in Figure 4 price exceeds marginal cost. Why is it that firms do not expand?

If firms expanded employment and output, the additional supply could not be sold at the given interest rate. Inventories would simply pile up. Thus, the additional output yields zero marginal revenue to firms. To put it another way, while the value of the marginal product exceeds the real wage, the marginal revenue product is less then the real wage–it is zero.

3. *Rigid Wages and Rigid Prices*

This means that two degrees of freedom are lost from the system (3–7) and that two equations cannot be satisfied. In this case both equations (6,7) must be dropped and the system becomes

$$(16)\quad I(r) = S(y) \quad \text{Commodity Market}$$
$$(17)\quad L(r,y) = M/p \quad \text{Money Market}$$
$$(18)\quad y = \phi(n) \quad \text{Production Function}$$

which suffices to determine r, y and n. The real wage is of course given once the price level and the wage rate are specified.

In Figure 4 any point on the diagram is a possible situation. Given the interest rate and the real wage the nature of the disequilibrium in the factor market is revealed. Thus, at the interest rate and real wage implied by the point B, price exceeds marginal cost and the marginal disutility of labor is less than the real wage rate. There is no mechanism, as in the other cases,[5]

[5]In addition to these cases, the reader may wish to experiment with situations in which there is excess supply of or excess demand for goods, i.e., situations where investment does not equal saving; or with situations in which money demand does not equal money supply. Those situations are, of course, more likely in the short run than in the intermediate run under consideration.

for ensuring either full employment (a point on EE) or profit maximization (a point on RR).

IV. CONCLUSIONS

The four cases can be summarized as follows:

(1) Flexible wages and prices imply profit maximization of firms and utility maximization of labor. The system settles at a full employment equilibrium in which the real values of the variables are independent of the quantity of money.

(2) Any rigidity in the system means that the interest rate, income, employment and the real wage rate are all affected by changes in the quantity of money. If money wages are rigid and prices are flexible, firms can maximize profits but there is full employment only at a unique level of the quantity of money.

(3) If prices are rigid and money wages are flexible, there is automatic full employment, but firms produce at outputs where marginal cost differs from the fixed price, except when the supply of money is at a unique equilibrium level.

(4) If both wages and prices are fixed, the general case is one where the marginal disutility of labor differs from the real wage, and marginal cost differs from the fixed price level.[6]

[6] This article was expository, rather than critical, but the reader is entitled to a reminder about some of the defects in the Keynesian system: (1) The savings function and the liquidity function cannot plausibly be separated completely since excess or deficient liquidity will itself affect spending. (2) The investment relation I(r) has a downward slope because interest rate changes alter the demand price for the stock of capital goods and hence the flow supply; but relative changes in the production mix of consumer and capital goods may also affect the marginal productivity of capital and hence the *position* of I(r), just as changes in employment, as D. Meiselman has observed, will affect the ratio of capital and labor and thus capital's marginal productivity. (3) The LM-IS configuration relates *stock* equilibrium of money and *flow* equilibrium of goods so that the intersection of the schedules gives equilibrium only if the rate of expansion of the monetary stock is not constant but instead equals the rate of growth; otherwise, as I show in a forthcoming paper in the *Journal of Political Economy*, there will be a gap at the point where the schedules intersect between the cost of holding money and the real rate of interest. See my "Inflation and Real Interest", *The Journal of Political Economy* (Chicago, Ill., June 1963) for a discussion of inflationary equilibrium in a full employment economy.

17

A METHOD OF IDENTIFYING DISTURBANCES WHICH PRODUCE CHANGES IN MONEY NATIONAL INCOME[1]

JEROME L. STEIN

This paper specifies a general model of income determination which can produce either the Keynesian or the classical results, depending upon the labor-supply equation employed. A variety of exogenous disturbances is permitted to affect the level of money national income in this model. A method is then proposed for inferring the nature of the dominant exogenous disturbance on the basis of observed behavior. The relative importance of each type of disturbance in producing changes in the level of money income is examined for the years from 1919 to 1958.

I *define* (this term is defined below) three distinct sets of exogenous disturbances which are capable of producing changes in money income in the context of my income-determination model. (1) A "real" disturbance is defined as an exogenous disturbance which changes the money demand for goods and services, given the level of real income, the price level, and the interest rate. A rise in the marginal efficiency of investment schedule as a result of innovations would be a "real" disturbance. (2) A "monetary" disturbance is defined as an exogenous disturbance which changes the quantity of money which is supplied at the given interest rate. Consider a supply curve of money, with the interest rate on the price axis and the stock of money on the quantity axis. Then a "monetary" disturbance reflects the

[1]I am grateful to George Borts and Phillip Cagan for helpful advice and criticism. I am solely responsible, however, for the views advanced here.

Reprinted from the *Journal of Political Economy* (February 1960), pp. 1-16, by permission of the author and The University of Chicago Press.
Jerome L. Stein is a professor at Brown University.

shift of the schedule. A change in Federal Reserve policy is an important example of a monetary disturbance. Suppose that the Federal Reserve System reduced the legal reserve requirement. Insofar as the resulting increase in excess reserves increased the willingness of the banking system to lend, this would be a "monetary" disturbance. (3) A "liquidity" disturbance is defined as an exogenous disturbance which changes the demand for money, relative to other forms of wealth, given the interest rate and the level of money income. Suppose that people lost confidence in United States government bonds and wished to convert these bonds into money, given the level of money income and the interest rate. This would be a "liquidity" disturbance.[2]

It is difficult to evaluate the relative importance of each type of disturbance without a general model which explicitly allows all three forces to operate. For example, suppose that the economy is at a trough in the business cycle and that two things happen simultaneously. There is a gold inflow into the United States as a result of political unrest abroad, and the government increases its expenditures in order to raise the level of money income. Money income then rises. Is the rise in money income from the trough the result of (what I have arbitrarily called) real or monetary factors? Surely, it is incorrect to claim that monetary factors were efficacious because money income and high-powered money moved in the same direction. It is also incorrect to claim that fiscal policy was effective because money income and government expenditures moved in the same direction. I specify an income-determination model which permits these different types of disturbances to occur. Although neither the real, monetary nor the liquidity disturbance is directly observable, each will produce different effects upon observed economic variables. I will therefore be able to infer (in the above example) which disturbance predominated in producing the rise from the trough.

For simplicity, I assume that the dynamic system is non-oscillatory and stable. If the equilibrium value of X rises to $\bar{X}$, then $X(t)$ will monotonically converge to $\bar{X}$. The economy is assumed to converge monotonically from one comparative static equilibrium to another. Obviously, this assumption prevents me from having an endogenous cycle theory. Downturns and upturns are caused, in my model, by the intrusion of exogenous real, monetary, and liquidity disturbances which I attempt to identify.

If the assumption that $X(t)$ converges monotonically to $\bar{X}$ is realistic, it has a great advantage for empirical research. I need only consider a comparative static model, where all endogenous variables are at the equilibrium levels. If the exogenous disturbance raises the equilibrium value of X to $\bar{X}$, then I

[2]The reader may prefer to call these effects *A*, *B*, and *C*, respectively, if he objects to the connotations of the terms "real," "monetary," and "liquidity."

claim that $X(t)$ will rise monotonically to $\overline{X}$. I then examine the data to see whether this has occurred.

The year-to-year changes in money income from 1919 to 1958 were examined. In 21 of 39 cases, real disturbances dominated in producing changes in money income. Every decline of money income from a peak was produced by real factors. There were seven troughs in money income in the period covered. Monetary factors dominated in producing a rise from three troughs: 1921, 1933, and 1938. Liquidity disturbances only dominated in six cases. From 1930 to 1931 and from 1931 to 1932, liquidity disturbances dominated in producing a fall in income. Liquidity disturbances occurred again in 1940–41 and 1949–50—the beginnings of World War II and the Korean conflict.

The conclusions depend upon the income-determination model employed. Although my model is quite general, it is just one possible type of model. It clearly is possible to construct a model where these results do not occur. For example, if the appropriate dynamic model were oscillatory, then the techniques used here would not permit an identification of the nature of the exogenous disturbances. The major contributions of this paper are (*a*) a tentative identification of the nature of the exogenous disturbances and (*b*) the formulation of a method of identification which may be applicable to a large set of models.

I. AN INCOME DETERMINATION MODEL

My model of income determination is compatible with either the Keynesian or the classical system.[3] This model is extremely flexible and permits real, liquidity, and monetary disturbances to affect the level of money income. This is a comparative static model, but I arbitrarily assume that the appropriate dynamic counterpart of this model is non-oscillatory and stable. Hence $X(t)$ converges monotonically to $\overline{X}$, the equilibrium value.

A. The General Model

The first equation equates the supply and demand for money:

$$M(B, r) = L^*(y, p, r, C)\,. \tag{1.0}$$

The quantity of money supplied $M(B, r)$ depends upon an exogenous variable B and the rate of interest r. The variable B reflects the ability and

[3] A classical system is defined as one in which the real wage is determined solely in the labor market.

eagerness of the banking system to increase the quantity of money at the given interest rate. B will include the legal reserves of the monetary system, the availability and price of discounts, the desired ratio of secondary reserves to deposits, etc. Changes in Federal Reserve policy are quite important in producing changes in B. The variable B is not observable and is precisely the set of monetary factors defined above. If one thinks of a supply curve of money, with the interest rate on the price axis and the stock of money on the quantity axis, the B reflects the shift of the schedule. M_1 is defined as strictly positive. (M_1 is the partial derivative of the M function with respect to B, the first variable.)

The quantity of money supplied depends also upon the rate of interest, $M_2 > 0$, for, the higher the rate of interest, the greater is the cost of holding excess reserves.

The quantity of money demanded, $L^*(y, p, r, C)$, depends upon the level of real income y, the price level p, the interest rate r, and a shift parameter C. Tobin has examined the logic of this function in detail, and the rationale need not be repeated here.[4] The variable C represents the expected risk attached to holding securities or the penalties involved in suffering a loss from holding securities. The variable C is precisely the set of liquidity disturbances mentioned above. L_4^* is taken as strictly positive. L_1^* and L_2^* are strictly positive due to the transactions motive and to the view that money is not an inferior good. L_3^* is strictly negative.

The second equation equates the money value of planned investment and government expenditures with planned savings and taxes.

$$I^*(p, y, r, A) = S^*(p, y)\,. \tag{2.0}$$

The exogenous variable A is precisely the non-observable set of "real" factors which is capable of producing variations in the level of money income. It represents the shift factor in the schedule relating the aggregate demand for goods and services with the interest rate. Changes in the height of the savings function or in the level of tax rates are subsumed under variations in the A variable. Alternatively, equation (2.0) could have been written as $X(p, y, r, A) = 0$, where X is the *ex ante* excess demand for investment and government expenditures over planned savings and taxes.

I_4^* is taken to be strictly positive. I_1^* and I_2^* and S_1^* and S_2^* are strictly positive. Moreover, assume that the marginal propensity to save out of real income S_2^* exceeds the marginal propensity to invest out of real income I_2^*

[4] James Tobin, "Liquidity Preference as Behavior toward Risk," *Review of Economic Studies*, No. 67 (February 1958); "The Interest-Elasticity of Transactions Demand for Cash," *Review of Economics and Statistics*, Vol. XXXVIII (August, 1956). Note that real wealth, y/r, is not excluded from the liquidity function defined above in the paper.

and that $\epsilon > (S_1{}^* - I_1{}^*) > 0$, where ϵ can take any strictly positive value.[5] $I_3{}^*$ is taken to be strictly negative.

(3) $Y \equiv py$, that is, the level of money income Y is defined as the product of the price level (p) and the level of real income (y).

(4.0) $y = f(N)$ is the production function. Since the capital stock is given in the static model, f is a function of N, the level of employment.

(5) $w = pf'(N)$ equates the money wage w with the value of the marginal product of labor.

The supply of labor in this model may be either a classical (6*a*) or a Keynesian (6*b*) function. Our subsequent analysis holds in either case.

$$N = N(w/p) \qquad (6a)$$

$$W = w^* . \qquad (6b)$$

In the Keynesian case the money wage is exogenously determined at w^*.[6] In the classical case employment depends solely upon w/p, the real wage.

B. A Specific Model

For purposes of exposition, I shall work with a specific version of the general model described above. The general model is not easily amenable to geometric analysis, whereas the specific model can easily be handled geometrically. No difference occurs in my results by using the specific rather than the general model, as is proved here and in the Appendix.[7]

For equation (1.0) substitute

$$M(B, r) = L(Y, r, C) ; \qquad (1.1)$$

$$L > 0, L_2 < 0, L_3 > 0 .$$

Y is money income. The M function is unchanged, but we have an L function instead of an L^* function.

For equation (2.0) substitute

$$I(Y, r, A) = S(Y) ; \qquad (2.1)$$

$$1 > S' > I_1 > 0 ,$$

$$I_2 < 0, I_3 > 0 .$$

The variables are defined as above. The remaining equations are kept unchanged.

[5] See Section B below for the reasons underlying the use of this assumption.

[6] A Keynesian model can be defined without (6*b*) if one fixes r at the floor, but this substitution would make the Keynesian model "depression economics."

[7] Except when y is fixed at y_0 and $S_1{}^* = I_1{}^*$. This is discussed later on in this section.

It is easily shown that in an "extreme" Keynesian model, where all supply curves are perfectly elastic, equations (1.0) and (1.1) and (2.0) and (2.1) are formally equivalent. Given $p = p_0$, equation (1.0) becomes

$$M(B, r) = L^*(Y/p_0, p_0, r, C) ,$$

and equation (2.0) becomes

$$I^*(p_0, Y/p_0, r, A) = S^*(p_0, Y/p_0) .$$

By fixing p at p_0, L^* is now a function of Y, r, and C. Write this new function of three variables as L. $\partial L^*/\partial Y$ is positive and so is $\partial L/\partial Y$. $\partial L^*/\partial r$ and $\partial L/\partial r$ are negative. Similarly, $\partial L^*/\partial C$ and $\partial L/\partial C$ are positive. Hence, when p is fixed at p_0, the L^* and L functions are equivalent.

Given $p = p_0$, equation (2.0) becomes

$$I^*(p_0, Y/p_0, r, A) = S^*(p_0, Y/p_0) .$$

I^* is now a function of Y, r, and A; and S^* is now a function of Y. Write these new functions as I and S, respectively. $\partial I^*/\partial Y > 0$ and $\partial I/\partial Y > 0$; $\partial I^*/\partial r < 0$ and $\partial I/\partial r < 0$; $\partial I^*/\partial A > 0$ and $\partial I/\partial A > 0$. Similarly, $\partial S^*/\partial Y > 0$ and $\partial S/\partial Y > 0$. We have therefore proved that, in an "extreme" Keynesian case, the general and the specific models are equivalent.

Consider the classical case where employment is determined in the labor market, equations (5) and (6*a*). The production function, equation (4), determines real income $y = y_0$. Hence equation (1.0) becomes

$$M(B, r) = L^*(y_0, Y/y_0, r, C) .$$

where y is fixed at y_0. The L^* function is equivalent to the L function (eq. [1.1]) because $\partial L^*/\partial Y > 0$ and $\partial L/\partial Y > 0$; $\partial L^*/\partial r < 0$ and $\partial L/\partial r < 0$; $\partial L^*/\partial C > 0$ and $\partial L/\partial C > 0$. Both $L^*$and L are functions of Y, r, and C when y is fixed at y_0.

Given $y = y_0$, equation (2.0) becomes

$$I^*(Y/y_0, y_0, r, A) = S^*(Y/y_0, y_0) .$$

Now the importance of the assumption, $\epsilon > (S_1^* - I_1^*) > 0$, becomes clear.

When y is fixed at y_0, I^* and I are both functions of Y, r, and A; and S^* and S are functions of Y. $\partial I^*/\partial Y > 0$ and $\partial I/\partial Y > 0$; $\partial I^*/\partial r < 0$ and $\partial I/\partial r < 0$; $\partial I^*/\partial A > 0$ and $\partial I/\partial A > 0$. Similarly, $\partial S^*/\partial Y > 0$ and $\partial S/\partial Y > 0$. However, the specific model claims that $\partial S/\partial Y - \partial I/\partial Y \equiv S' - I_1 > 0$. This follows from the general model, when y is fixed, only if $S_1^* - I_1^* > 0$. Hence the specific model is equivalent to the general model, in the classical case where y is fixed, only if $\epsilon > (S_1^* - I_1^*) > 0$. This exception is not important for my purposes, because I shall be examining Y and r over time. It is most unlikely that the level of y is fixed when year-to-year changes are examined, because N increases over time.

The Appendix proves that, when both p and y are variable, the use of the specific model does not change the results obtained from the general model. Intuitively, this seems reasonable. Except when $S_1^* - I_1^* = 0$, the general model and the specific model yield the same results in the two extreme cases: p fixed, y variable, and p variable, y fixed. Since neither partial derivative can change sign, an "intermediate" case (p and y variable) should not lead to different results.

In the subsequent discussion, we shall use the specific model and assume that $\epsilon > (S_1^* - I_1^*) > 0$.

II. EMPIRICAL PROPOSITIONS

A. Income and Interest-Rate Changes

Given this specific model of income determination, variables in A (the set of real factors), B (the set of monetary factors), and C (the set of liquidity factors) exert different effects upon observed variables. Although neither A, B, nor C is directly observable, their existence is manifested by changes in income, the rate of interest, and velocity.

Graphically, the specific model looks like the Hicks[8] model. Equation (1.1) is described by an LL curve which is the set of points (Y, r) such that equation (1.1) is satisfied. The slope of this schedule

$$\frac{\partial r}{\partial Y} = \frac{L_1(Y, r, C)}{M_2(B, r) - L_2(Y, r, C)}$$

is strictly positive; hence the LL curve is upward sloping. The LL curve will shift to the right when B increases and to the left when B decreases. Thus monetary factors shift the LL curve.

Liquidity factors also affect the LL curve. When C increases, the LL curve will shift to the left; when C decreases, the LL curve will shift to the right.

Equation (2.1) is described by the IS curve. This curve is the set of points (Y, r) such that equation (2.1) is satisfied. The slope of the IS schedule

[8]J. R. Hicks, "Mr. Keynes and the Classics," *Econometrica*, V (1937), 147–59; *The Trade Cycle* (Oxford: Oxford University Press, 1950), chaps. xi and xii.

$$\frac{\partial r}{\partial Y} = \frac{s - I_1(Y, r, A)}{I_2(Y, r, A)}; \qquad \frac{dS(Y)}{dY} \equiv s$$

is strictly negative by the assumptions made above. When A increases, the *IS* curve (Fig. 1*a*) will shift to the right and up.

The intersection of the two schedules gives the equilibrium level of income and interest rate. Money income Y will increase with an increase in A (reflecting a stimulating real disturbance), an increase in B (reflecting a stimulating monetary disturbance), or a decrease in C (reflecting a stimulating liquidity disturbance). Figures 1*a*, 1*b*, and 1*c* indicate the effects of a rise in A, a rise in B, and a rise in C.

When A rises, the *IS* schedule shifts to the right (Fig. 1*a*), producing a higher equilibrium level of money income. The equilibrium point rises from P_1 to P_2 as a result of this real disturbance. Since we assume that the dynamic system is non-oscillatory and stable, Y_1 converges to Y_2, and r_1 converges to r_2, monotonically. The expansion path of income and the interest rate lie along the *LL* schedule.

When B increases (reflecting a monetary disturbance), the *LL* curve shifts to the right and lowers the equilibrium point (Fig. 1*b*) from P_1 to P_3. Given the assumption concerning the dynamic nature of the economy, income rises monotonically from Y_1 to Y_3 and the interest rate falls monotonically from r_1 to r_3. The expansion path is along the *IS* schedule.

When C increases, reflecting a greater demand for liquidity, the *LL* curve shifts upward to the left. The equilibrium point (Fig. 1*c*) moves from P_1 to P_4. Given the assumption concerning the dynamic nature of the economy, income falls monotonically from Y_1 to Y_4, and the interest rate rises

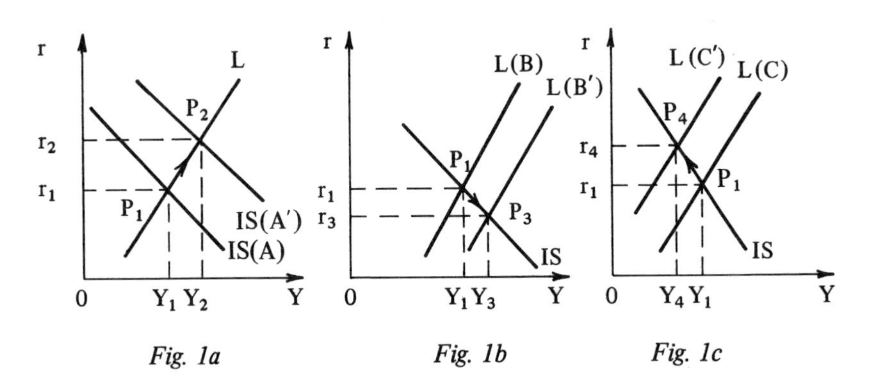

Fig. 1a. The effects of a real disturbance: rise in A.
Fig. 1b. The effects of a monetary disturbance: rise in B.
Fig. 1c. The effects of a liquidity disturbance: rise in C.

Table 1. The Impact of Exogenous Disturbances upon Money Income, Interest Rate, and Velocity

(1)			(2)	(3)	(4)
Type of Exogenous Disturbance			*Change in Y*	*Change in r*	*Change in V*
1. Real	A	+	+	+	+
	A	–	–	–	–
2. Monetary	B	+	+	–	–
	B	–	–	+	+
3. Liquidity	C	+	–	+	–
	C	–	+	–	+

monotonically from r_1 to r_4. The expansion path is along the *IS* schedule. If *A, B,* or *C* decrease, the whole process is reversed.

The resulting[9] empirical propositions concerning the effects of real, monetary, and liquidity disturbances upon the level of income Y and the interest rate r are presented in Table 1. In column (1) the nature of the exogenous disturbance is specified. The plus or minus sign indicates whether

[9]
$$\frac{\partial Y}{\partial A} = \frac{\begin{vmatrix} M_2 - L_2 & 0 \\ -I_2 & I_3 \end{vmatrix}}{\begin{vmatrix} M_2 - L_2 & -L_1 \\ -I_2 & s - I_1 \end{vmatrix}} > 0;$$

and

$$\frac{\partial r}{\partial A} = \frac{\begin{vmatrix} 0 & -L_1 \\ I_3 & s - I_1 \end{vmatrix}}{D} > 0$$

where D is the denominator of $\partial Y / \partial A$, the Jacobian of the specific model. $D \neq 0$, for $(M_2 - L_2)(s - I_1) - L_1 I_2 > 0$.

$$\frac{\partial Y}{\partial B} = \frac{\begin{vmatrix} M_2 - L_2 & -M_1 \\ -I_2 & 0 \end{vmatrix}}{D} = \frac{-M_1 I_2}{D} > 0 .$$

$$\frac{\partial r}{\partial B} = \frac{\begin{vmatrix} -M_1 & -L_1 \\ 0 & s - I_1 \end{vmatrix}}{D} = \frac{-M_1(s - I_1)}{D} < 0 .$$

$$\frac{\partial Y}{\partial C} = \frac{\begin{vmatrix} M_2 - L_2 & L_3 \\ -I_2 & 0 \end{vmatrix}}{D} < 0 ;$$

$$\frac{\partial r}{\partial C} = \frac{\begin{vmatrix} L_3 & -L_1 \\ 0 & s - I_1 \end{vmatrix}}{D} > 0 .$$

the value of the exogenous variable has increased or decreased. In column (2) the effect upon the level of money income is specified. Thus, when A decreases, Y will decrease. When C rises, Y falls. In column (3) the effect upon the interest rate is specified. When B rises, r decreases, etc. Column (4), which is discussed below, is presented here for completeness. It indicates the effect of changes in the exogenous variable upon the income velocity of money. Figures 1*a*, 1*b*, and 1*c* illustrate this graphically.

This table, and the entire paper, are based upon the assumption that the real economic system is non-oscillatory and stable.

B. Simultaneous Shifts of the Exogenous Variables

Suppose that A and B are simultaneously increased; that is, real and monetary disturbances simultaneously occur. Then the IS curve shifts to the right, and so does the LL curve, as described in Figure 2. The equilibrium point will rise from P_1 to P_5. Formally, this is equivalent to a movement from P_1 to P_2 to P_5 or from P_1 to P_3 to P_5. However, given our assumption concerning the dynamic nature of the economy, the expansion path goes directly from P_1 to P_5 along the dotted line. At P_5 the rate of interest and the level of income are higher than at P_1. The net effect of the simultaneous shift of A and B resembled a shift in A, with B constant. That is, the shift in A had bigger gross effects upon Y and r than did the shift in B, because both Y and r rose. Consequently, we say that the *main* or dominant disturbance was "real" rather than "monetary." All subsequent analysis will be concerned with the effects of simultaneous shifts in A, B, and C. The main or dominant disturbance will be defined as the disturbance which by itself would produce

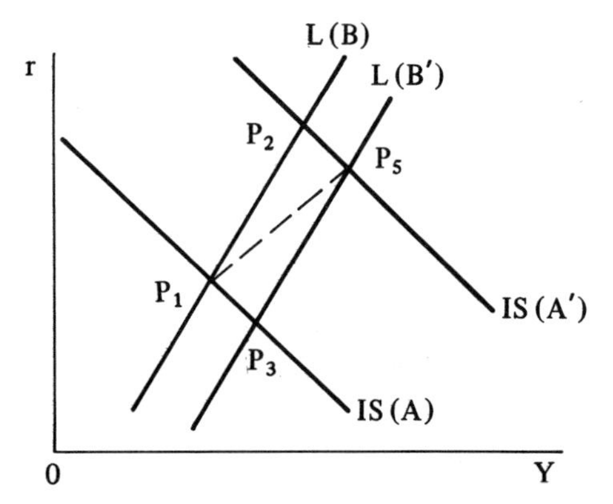

Fig. 2. The effects of changes in both A and B simultaneously.

the observed effects upon Y, r, and velocity. When the main disturbance was termed "real," it did not mean that the IS curve shifted by more than the LL curve—merely that the final result resembled a shift in A, with B and C constant.

On the basis of observed behavior it is easy to discern the difference between a mainly real and a mainly monetary disturbance. Suppose that money income rose. If the interest rate increased, then the disturbance was mainly real rather than mainly monetary. If the interest rate declined as the level of money income rose, then the disturbance was mainly monetary rather than mainly real. Similarly, on the basis of observed behavior, one can distinguish between a mainly real and a mainly liquidity disturbance. If the disturbance is mainly real, then money income and the interest rate rise or fall together. But if the disturbance is mainly a liquidity disturbance, then money income and the interest rate move in opposite directions.

However, one cannot distinguish between a mainly monetary and a mainly liquidity disturbance by comparing movements in money income and interest rates, for money income and the interest rate move in opposite directions when the disturbance is mainly a monetary or mainly a liquidity disturbance. For that reason, I examine the effects of each type of disturbance upon velocity. When the movement of velocity is examined in conjunction with changes in money income and the interest rate, it becomes possible to differentiate between a mainly monetary and a mainly liquidity disturbance.

C. Velocity Changes

If the disturbance is real,[10] then velocity will rise as the level of money income rises, and it will fall as the level of money income falls. On the other hand, if the disturbance is monetary, then velocity will fall if money income rises, and it will rise if money income falls.

The proof of these statements is given in a footnote,[11] but I shall give a verbal justification for these statements here. When money income rises as a

[10] Whenever the reader sees the terms "real," "monetary," or "liquidity," he should prefix them with *mainly*, which will not always be used in the subsequent discussion because of the resulting cumbersome expressions.

[11] Let V denote the money income velocity of money. Then, $\partial V/\partial A = (\partial V/\partial r)(\partial r/\partial A)$ and $\partial V/\partial B = (\partial V/\partial r)(\partial r/\partial B)$. I know that $\partial r/\partial A$ is positive and $\partial r/\partial B$ is negative. Hence $\partial V/\partial A$ and $\partial V/\partial B$ have opposite signs. We need only determine the sign of $\partial V/\partial A$ in order to determine the signs of $\partial V/\partial A$ and $\partial V/\partial B$.

$$\frac{\partial V}{\partial A} = \frac{\partial(Y/M)}{\partial A} = \frac{I_3}{MD}\,[(M_2 - L_2) - VM_2L_1]\ ,$$

where D is the Jacobian of the specific model as defined above. $\partial V/\partial A \gtreqless 0$ insofar as $(M_2 - L_2) \gtreqless VM_2L_1$; i.e., insofar as $1 - L_2/M_2 \gtreqless VL_1$. The quantity VL_1 is the money income elasticity of demand for money $(Y/M)\partial L/\partial Y$. L_2 is negative and M_2 is positive. Hence (1 –

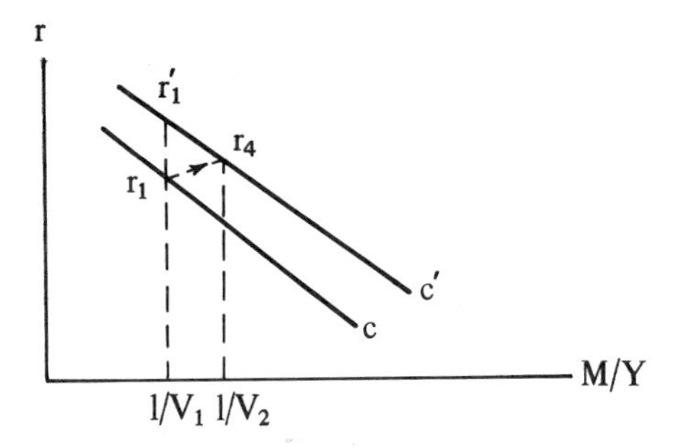

Fig. 3. The effect of a liquidity disturbance.

result of a real[12] disturbance, then we know (from Fig. 1) that the interest rate will rise. Given the demand for money equation, velocity rises with the interest rate; that is, the liquidity preference function L implies that the interest rate and equilibrium velocity move together. Since the equilibrium interest rate is higher, the equilibrium velocity must be higher.

When the disturbance is monetary, a higher level of money income is associated with a lower equilibrium interest rate (see Fig. 1*b*). Given the liquidity preference function L, a lower interest rate is associated with a lower equilibrium velocity. Hence velocity and money income change in opposite directions when a monetary disturbance has produced the change in money income.

When there is a liquidity disturbance (a change in C), then money income and velocity change in the same direction. A proof of this statement is given in a footnote,[13] but again I shall give a nonmathematical justification for this statement. When C rises, then a higher interest rate is required to maintain the same ratio of money to income; that is, an upward shift of the Keynesian liquidity preference schedule occurs. In equilibrium, there is a rise in the interest rate but not by the full amount that is called for by an increase in the demand for money. In terms of Figure 1*c* the interest rate rises by less than the full amount of the shift of the LL curve. Or, in terms of Figure 3, the interest rate does not rise to r'_1. Instead, it rises from r_1 to r_4. Since the

---

L_2/M_2) exceeds unity. Insofar as the short-run income elasticity of demand for money is not greater than unity, $\partial V/\partial A$ is positive. There is evidence that the short-run (money) income elasticity of demand for money does not exceed unity. This is deduced from the evidence that over the cycle (*a*) velocity and real income and (*b*) prices and real income move in the same direction. Hence VL_1 is not greater than unity; $\partial V/\partial A$ must be positive and $\partial V/\partial B$ is negative.

[12] Recall "mainly" should precede the terms "real," "monetary," and "liquidity."

[13] $\partial V/\partial C = (\partial[Y/M]/\partial C) \cdot D$ is the Jacobian of the specific model.

$$\frac{D}{L_3 V}\frac{\partial V}{\partial C} = \frac{I_2}{Y} - \frac{M_1}{M}(S' - I_1) \gtrless 0 .$$

interest rate rises to r_4, the velocity falls from V_1 to V_2. Consequently, velocity and interest rate move in opposite directions when a liquidity disturbance occurs; velocity and money income move in the same direction.

Column (4) in Table 1 summarizes these empirical propositions. It is now clear that a (mainly) monetary disturbance can be differentiated from a (mainly) liquidity disturbance. Money income and the interest rate will move in opposite directions if either a monetary or a liquidity disturbance occurs. However, if velocity and interest rate move in the same direction, a (mainly) monetary disturbance has occurred. But, if interest and velocity move in opposite directions, a (mainly) liquidity disturbance has occurred. These empirical propositions are based upon the assumption that the real economic system is non-oscillatory and stable.

III. AN EXAMINATION OF THE DATA

A. The Data Used

The empirical propositions derived from the model are concerned solely with the directions of the changes in three variables: money income, the interest rate, and velocity. On the basis of changes in these variables, described in Table 1, I infer the nature of the dominant exogenous disturbance. Since my concern is solely with the directions of changes, two measures of money income or interest rate are equally acceptable if they always move in the same direction.

1. *Money income.*—As my measure of money income Y, I used gross national product. Net national product would have given the identical results concerning the direction of change. From 1919 to 1929, Kuznets' data[14] were used; from 1929 to 1958 Department of Commerce data[15] were used, both series expressed in current dollars.

2. *Interest rate.*—The rate of interest relevant for liquidity preference is the rate of interest on safe securities. Hence the government-bond yield would appear to be the appropriate interest rate. The savings and investment equation would require that the long-term corporate-bond yield be used as the rate of interest. Fortunately, the series on long-term government-bond

Since D, L_3, and V are strictly positive, $\partial V/\partial C \gtrless 0$ insofar as $I_2/Y - M_1/M(S' - I_1) \gtrless 0$. That is, $\partial A/\partial C \gtrless 0$ insofar as $I_2 \gtrless VM_1(S' - I_1)$. We know I_2 is negative and $V, M_1 (S' - I_1)$ are positive. Therefore, $\partial V/\partial C < 0$.

[14]Simon Kuznets, *National Product since 1869* (New York: National Bureau of Economic Research, 1946), Table I-14, p. 51. The "wartime concept" was used, and it always moves in the same direction as the "peacetime concept."

[15]I used Table D-1 in the *Economic Report of the President*, January, 1959.

yields[16] concords extremely well with the series on corporate-bond yields.[17] In each year from 1919 to 1958 except 1942–43, 1943–44, and 1949–50, the two series moved in the same direction. As my measure of r, the rate of interest, I used the Aaa corporate-bond yield. I could have used the long-term government bond yield with practically identical results.[18]

3. *The money supply.*—I used the traditional definition of the money supply as demand deposits adjusted plus currency outside the banks. The former includes all demand deposits at commercial banks in the continental United States except interbank and United States government deposits, less cash items in the process of collection.[19] These figures represent the total volume of the means of payment outstanding.

In the model described above, velocity is simply the ratio of observed Y to observed M. Having defined Y and M, the velocity figure follows.

There is a reason for excluding government deposits from M but including the income produced by the government in Y. The liquidity-preference equation refers to the sectors which shift between money and securities to maximize the expected value of their utility. Since the government does not seem to operate this way, government deposits were excluded from M. On the other hand, the money income relevant for savings and investment decisions includes the government-generated money income.

4. *The use of annual data.*—Annual, rather than quarterly, data were used in order to allow changes in the supply of money to affect the rate of investment. A reduction in interest rates in the first quarter of the year need not produce a rise in investment in the second quarter. Some time is required to plan and implement the formation of new capital. On the other hand, a year was considered to be sufficient time for monetary changes to affect the level of money in income.

A period of time longer than a year could have been used. But, the longer

[16]For the years 1919–41, I used the long-term yields found in Board of Governors of the Federal Reserve System, *Banking and Monetary Statistics* (Washington, D.C., 1943), p. 468. A fuller explanation of these data, covering 1919–38, is found in *Federal Reserve Bulletin,* December, 1938, p. 1045. From 1942 to 1958, I used the data for long-term government bonds found in Table D-43 of the 1959 *Economic Report of the President.*

[17]For corporate bond yields, I used the yield on Aaa corporate bonds. For the years 1919–41 I used the data in *Banking and Monetary Statistics,* p. 468. This series is continued to 1958 in Table D-43 of the *Economic Report of the President.* These are yearly average figures.

[18]If the long-term government-bond yield were used instead of the corporate-bond yield, then three, rather than one, unexplained cases would occur over the 1919–58 period. One case would be changed from "liquidity" to "real." This is indicated in Table 3.

[19]From 1919 to 1929, the figures on demand deposits adjusted and currency outside of the banks were taken from p. 34, Table No. 9, in *Banking and Monetary Statistics.* The money supply is taken at June 30 of each of these early years. From 1929 to 1958, the data were taken from Table D-40 of the President's *Economic Report* where the figures are given as of December 31.

the time interval, the greater the number of exogenous disturbances that could have occurred. In order to minimize the number of exogenous disturbances that occurred during the time interval, but allow monetary effects to operate, year-to-year changes were used.

B. The Evidence

The empirical propositions summarized in Table 1 can be rewritten in a simpler form. This is done in Table 2. The columns indicate whether the exogenous disturbance has been mainly (1) real, (2) monetary, or (3) liquidity. Row (1) gives the sign of $\Delta Y \Delta r$, the change in money income ΔY multiplied by the change in the interest rate. If they change in the same direction, a (+) is scored, if they change in opposite directions, a (–) is scored. Row (2) gives the sign of $\Delta r \Delta V$, the change in interest rate multiplied by the change in velocity. A (+) means Δr and ΔV change in the same direction; a (–) means they change in opposite directions. Row (3) gives the sign of $\Delta Y \Delta V$, the change in income and the change in velocity. A plus (+) means ΔY and ΔV change in the same direction; a minus (–) means that ΔY and ΔV change in opposite directions. Column (4) should not occur if the model is stable, complete, and correct. In fact, this phenomenon does occur (see Table 3), but in no more than three out of thirty-nine cases.

Table 3 summarizes the data from 1919 to 1958 in terms of the cause of the exogenous disturbance. Column (1) records the change in money income from year $t - 1$ to year t. A plus indicates that income in year t was higher than it was in year $t - 1$.

Real factors were mainly responsible for 21 out of 39 year-to-year changes in money income. Monetary factors were mainly responsible for 11 year-to-year changes in money income; and liquidity factors were mainly responsible for 6 year-to-year changes. In one year, 1941–42, the variables moved in a manner unexplained by my model. If the long-term government-bond yield is used instead of the corporate-bond yield, 1942–43 and 1943–44 are also unexplained.

Table 2. Empirical Propositions Concerning the Dominant Exogenous Disturbance

Sign of	*(1) Real*	*(2) Monetary*	*(3) Liquidity*	*(4) Inconsistent with our model*
$\Delta Y \Delta r$	+	–	–	+
$\Delta r \Delta V$	+	+	–	–
$\Delta Y \Delta V$	+	–	+	–

Table 3. The Empirical Evidence Concerning the Nature of the Dominant Exogenous Disturbances, 1919–58

Year	(1) Change in Y	(2) Sign $\Delta Y \Delta r$	(3) Sign $\Delta r \Delta V$	(4) Sign $\Delta Y \Delta V$	(5) Disturbance
1919	....	....	....	....	....
1920	+	+	+	+	Real
1921	–	+	+	+	R
1922	+	–	+	–	Monetary
1923	+	+	+	+	R
1924	+	–	+	–	M
1925	+	–	+	–	M
1926	+	–	–	+	Liquidity
1927	–	+	+	+	R
1928	+	–	–	+	L
1929	+	+	+	+	R
1930	–	+	+	+	R
1931	–	–	–	+	L
1932	–	–	–	+	L
1933	–	+	+	+	R
1934	+	–	+	–	M
1935	+	–	+	–	M
1936	+	–	+	–	M
1937	+	+	+	+	R
1938	–	+	+	+	R
1939	+	–	+	–	M
1940	+	–	+	–	M
1941	+	–	–	+	L
1942	+	+	–	–	Unexplained
1943	+	–	+	–	M*
1944	+	–	+	–	M*
1945	+	–	+	–	M
1946	–	+	+	+	R
1947	+	+	+	+	R
1948	+	+	+	+	R
1949	–	+	+	+	R
1950	+	–	–	+	L†
1951	+	+	+	+	R
1952	+	+	+	+	R
1953	+	+	+	+	R
1954	–	+	+	+	R
1955	+	+	+	+	R
1956	+	+	+	+	R
1957	+	+	+	+	R
1958	–	+	+	+	R

Source: See Sec. IV, A.

*If the long-term government-bond yield is used instead of the corporate-bond yield, the unexplained (or inconsistent) phenomenon occurs.

†The dominant effect here is "real," if the long-term government-bond yield is used.

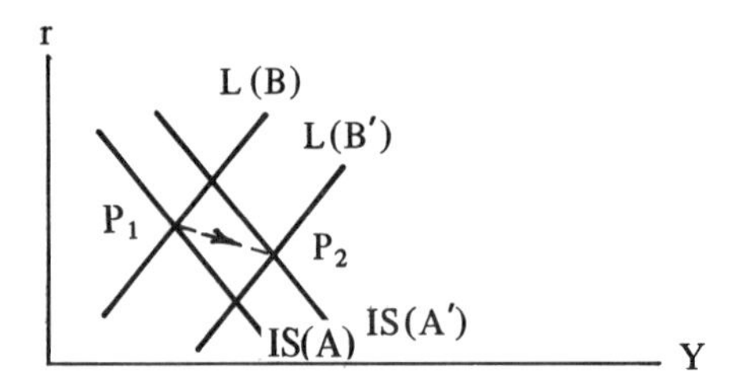

Fig. 4. A mainly monetary disturbance.

There were 15 turning points in money income from 1919 to 1958, when year-to-year changes are considered. There were eight peaks and seven troughs.

1. *Movements from troughs.*—There were seven troughs in money income: 1921, 1927, 1933, 1938, 1946, and 1954. (The 1959 data are not yet available; hence I do not use 1958 as a trough year.) Mainly monetary factors were associated with the recoveries from the serious troughs: 1921, 1933, and 1938. From the trough to the following year, interest rates and velocity declined; and investment expenditures increased as the interest rate fell.

From 1921 to 1922, interest rates and velocity fell as income rose. Net capital formation rose from 3.1 (billion dollars) to 4.5.

From 1933 to 1934, interest rates and velocity declined as income rose. Gross private domestic investment rose from 1.4 to 2.9. This rise in investment occured in all three categories of investment. New construction rose from 1.4 to 1.7; investment in producers' durable equipment increased from 1.6 to 2.3, and inventory investment went from −1.6 to −1.1.

From 1938 to 1939, interest rates and velocity declined as income increased. Gross private domestic investment rose from 6.7 to 9.3. New construction increased from 4.0 to 4.8, investment in producers durable goods increased from 3.6 to 4.2, and inventory investment rose from −0.9 to 0.4.

The recovery in the 1930's was dominated by monetary factors, as described in Figure 4. The recovery from 1933 or 1938 may have involved an increase in the *IS* schedule, representing a rise in the marginal efficiency of investment and government expenditures schedule. Nevertheless, the dominant effect was an increase in the *LL* curve which produced a decline from P_1 to P_2. The "Keynesian view" that monetary policy was ineffective during the 1930's seems questionable in light of the data adduced here.

The 1946 and 1954 recoveries from the trough were associated, on balance, with real factors. Interest rates and velocity rose as the level of money income increased. The movement of the *IS* schedule dominated whatever movements may have occurred in the *LL* schedule.

2. *Movement from peaks.*—There were eight peaks in money income: 1920,

1926, 1929, 1937, 1945, 1948, 1953, and 1957. Real factors dominated at each peak. As money income fell, interest rates and velocity also declined. At each peak, except 1945, the downward shift of the *IS* curve was probably the result of a fall in the marginal efficiency of investment schedule. For the declines in money income and interest rates coincided (on a year-to-year basis) with declines in investment. The only peak at which investment did not decline was 1945. Then the *IS* curve shifted downward as the result of the large fall in government expenditures. We conclude that on balance the monetary system has been a passive element in every decline in money income. That is, real factors have dominated whenever money income fell from a peak.

3. *Liquidity disturbances.*–Liquidity disturbances arise from shifts in the demand schedule for money, given the aggregate demand for goods and services. There were six cases where the change in money income was, on balance, the result of a liquidity disturbance.

From 1930 to 1931 and 1931 to 1932 there was a rise in our autonomous variable *C*, signifying an increase in liquidity preference. People desired to shift from securities to money and thus raised interest rates and decreased velocity. (See Table 1.) The rise in *C*, the demand for money, was probably the result of the greater risks involved in holding stocks and bonds. Thus we start with a decline in money income from 1929 to 1930 that resulted from a decline in the *IS* schedule. Then a liquidity crisis occurred from 1930 to 1932 which further caused income to fall.

Liquidity disturbances occurred again in 1940–41 and 1949–50. In these years our *C* variable declined, indicating a shift away from money into securities. Thus interest rates fell and velocity increased (see Tables 1 and 3). This shift away from money into securities occurred at the beginning of World War II (1940–41) and at the beginning of the Korean War (1949–50).[20]

Two other liquidity disturbances are found in the data: 1925–26 and 1927–28. Interest rates fell and velocity rose, and the level of income increased. This indicates a decline in the demand for money relative to securities. Common-stock prices did rise by 11 per cent from 1925–26 and by 27 per cent from 1927–28, as one would expect when *C* falls.

Finally, there is an unexplained observation for 1941–42, when *r*, *Y*, and *V* move in a manner not included in the list of possibilities covered in Table 1. This observation indicates that my theory can be disproved; certain phenomena can occur which are not contained in the theory.[21]

[20]The year 1949–50 shows "real" disturbances dominant if the long-term government-bond yield is used.

[21]Three unexplained, or inconsistent, cases arise if the long-term government-bond yield is used. They all occur from 1941 to 1944.

IV. CONCLUSION

This paper presents a method of identifying the exogenous factors which have dominated to produce changes in the level of money income. The empirical propositions derived are based upon the assumption that the real economic system is non-oscillatory and stable. When real or liquidity disturbances occur, the quantity of money and velocity will change to produce a different level of money income. The monetary system can be said to have played a "passive" role in producing the change in income when the supply curve of money has remained stable. However, when monetary disturbances occur, the quantity of money and velocity will also change to produce a new level of income; the monetary system can then be said to have played an "active" role in producing the change in income because the lower interest rates were caused by an increase in the supply curve of money.

If one is willing to accept these definitions of when the monetary system has played an "active" or a "passive" role in producing changes in income, then the data suggest that on balance the monetary system played a passive role in every downturn at a peak and that the monetary system played an active role in producing the recovery from the great depression.

APPENDIX

A. According to the specific model it was found that:

$$\frac{\partial Y}{\partial A} > 0 \text{ and } \frac{\partial r}{\partial A} > 0 . \tag{1}$$

$$\frac{\partial Y}{\partial B} > 0 \text{ and } \frac{\partial r}{\partial B} < 0 . \tag{2}$$

$$\frac{\partial Y}{\partial C} < 0 \text{ and } \frac{\partial r}{\partial C} > 0 . \tag{3}$$

$$\frac{\partial V}{\partial C} < 0 , \frac{\partial V}{\partial A} > 0 \text{ and } \frac{\partial V}{\partial B} < 0 . \tag{4}$$

In the body of the paper it was proved that (*a*) an extreme Keynesian version of the general model, where p is fixed and y is variable, is equivalent to the specific model. Moreover, (*b*), if we assume that $\epsilon > S_1^* - I_1^* > 0$, then an extreme classical version of the general model, where p is variable and y is fixed, is also equivalent to the specific model. We must now prove that the general and specific models both produce results $A(1)$ through $A(4)$ above in the intermediate case where both p and y are variable.

B. Proof

It is convenient to rewrite equation (4.0) in terms of its inverse. Hence, instead of (4.0) $y = f(N)$, write (4.1) $N = g(y)$. The inverse function g exists insofar as the marginal product of labor is not zero.

$$w^* = pf'(N) = p(f' o g)(y) = pF(y), \; F' < 0 . \tag{5.1}$$

Equation (5.1) states that the autonomous money wage w^* is equal to the value of the marginal product of labor. Instead of $f'(N)$, we write $F(y)$, where F is the composition of functions f' and g. Since f'' is negative (indicating declining marginal productivity), F' is also negative. Recall that the classical case, where the supply of labor depends upon the real wage, was proved in the body of the paper on the assumption that $\epsilon > (S_1{}^* - I_1{}^*) > 0$. We therefore only consider the case where w is exogenously given.

1. *Signs of* $\partial Y/\partial A$ *and* $\partial r/\partial A$.—Differentiate the general model consisting of equations (1.0), (2.0), and (5.1) with respect to A (the "real" disturbance)' For simplicity, drop the asterisks (*) from the L, I, and S functions but remember that we are working here with the *general* model. Moreover, $(S_1{}^* - Ii_1{}^*)$ and $(S_2{}^* - I_2{}^*)$ were assumed to be positive. Write s_1 for the former and s_2 for the latter expression, where s_1 and s_2 are positive.

$$L_1 \frac{\partial y}{\partial A} + L_2 \frac{\partial p}{\partial A} + (L_3 - M_2)\frac{\partial r}{\partial A} = 0$$

$$s_2 \frac{\partial y}{\partial A} + s_1 \frac{\partial p}{\partial A} \qquad - I_3 \frac{\partial r}{\partial A} = I_4$$

$$pF' \frac{\partial y}{\partial A} + F \frac{\partial p}{\partial A} \qquad = 0 .$$

The Jacobian of the system is clearly negative, given the assumed signs of the partial derivatives.

$$J = \begin{vmatrix} L_1 & L_2 & L_3 - M_2 \\ s_2 & s_1 & -I_3 \\ pF' & F & 0 \end{vmatrix} < 0 .$$

To find $\partial Y/\partial A = (\partial[py]/\partial A)$, we must find $\partial p/\partial A$ and $\partial y/\partial A$.

$$\frac{\partial y}{\partial A} = \frac{\begin{vmatrix} 0 & L_2 & L_3 - M_2 \\ I_4 & s_1 & -I_3 \\ 0 & F & 0 \end{vmatrix}}{J} > 0 .$$

$$\frac{\partial p}{\partial A} = \frac{\begin{vmatrix} L_1 & 0 & L_3 - M_2 \\ s_2 & I_4 & -I_3 \\ pF' & 0 & 0 \end{vmatrix}}{J} > 0 .$$

Since $\partial y/\partial A$ and $\partial p/\partial A$ are strictly positive, $(\partial[py]/\partial A) = \partial Y/\partial A$ is positive.

Solving for $\partial r/\partial A$, we find that

$$\frac{\partial r}{\partial A} = \frac{\begin{vmatrix} L_1 & L_2 & 0 \\ s_2 & s_1 & I_4 \\ pF' & F & 0 \end{vmatrix}}{J} > 0 .$$

Hence, we have proved that $\partial Y/\partial A > 0$ and $\partial r/\partial A > 0$ in both the general and specific models.

2. *Signs of* $\partial Y/\partial B$ *and* $\partial r/\partial B$.—By differentiating the equations (1.0), (2.0), and (5.1) with respect to B, and using the simplifications described above, we obtain the following system.

$$(J)\left(\frac{\partial y}{\partial B}, \frac{\partial p}{\partial B}, \frac{\partial r}{\partial B}\right) = (M_1, 0, 0) ,$$

where (J) is the matrix whose Jacobian is J.

$$\frac{\partial y}{\partial B} = \frac{\begin{vmatrix} M_1 & L_2 & L_3 - M_2 \\ 0 & s_1 & -I_3 \\ 0 & F & 0 \end{vmatrix}}{J} > 0 .$$

$$\frac{\partial p}{\partial B} = \frac{\begin{vmatrix} L_1 & M_1 & L_3 - M_2 \\ s_2 & 0 & -I_3 \\ pF' & 0 & 0 \end{vmatrix}}{J} > 0 .$$

Since $\partial y/\partial B$ and $\partial p/\partial B$ are positive $(\partial[py]/\partial B) = \partial Y/\partial B$ is strictly positive.

$$\frac{\partial r}{\partial B} = \frac{\begin{vmatrix} L_1 & L_2 & M_1 \\ s_2 & s_1 & 0 \\ pF' & F & 0 \end{vmatrix}}{J} < 0 .$$

Hence we have proved that $\partial Y/\partial B > 0$ and $\partial r/\partial B < 0$ in both the general and the specific models.

3. *Signs of* $\partial Y/\partial C$ *and* $\partial r/\partial C$.—When the general model is differentiated with respect to C, the "liquidity" disturbance, we obtain

$$(J)\left(\frac{\partial y}{\partial C}, \frac{\partial p}{\partial C}, \frac{\partial r}{\partial C}\right) = (-L_4, 0, 0).$$

$$\frac{\partial y}{\partial C} = \frac{\begin{vmatrix} -L_4 & L_2 & L_3 - M_2 \\ 0 & s_1 & -I_3 \\ 0 & F & 0 \end{vmatrix}}{J} < 0 .$$

$$\frac{\partial p}{\partial C} = \frac{\begin{vmatrix} L_1 & L_4 & L_3 - M_2 \\ s^2 & 0 & -I_3 \\ pF' & 0 & 0 \end{vmatrix}}{J} < 0$$

Consequently,

$$\frac{\partial Y}{\partial C} = \frac{\partial (py)}{\partial C} < 0 .$$

$$\frac{\partial r}{\partial C} = \frac{\begin{vmatrix} L_1 & L_2 & -L_4 \\ s_2 & s_1 & 0 \\ pF' & F & 0 \end{vmatrix}}{J} > 0$$

We have proved that $\partial Y/\partial C < 0$ and $\partial r/\partial C > 0$ in both the general and the specific models.

4(*a*). *Sign of* $\partial V/\partial C$.–

$$\frac{\partial V}{\partial C} = \frac{\partial(Y/M)}{\partial C} = \left(M\frac{\partial Y}{\partial C} - Y\frac{\partial M}{\partial C}\right)\frac{1}{M^2}$$

$$\frac{\partial M}{\partial C} = M_2\frac{\partial r}{\partial C},$$

which is clearly positive. $\partial Y/\partial C$ is clearly negative. Therefore, $\partial V/\partial C < 0$ in both the general and the specific models.

(*b*) *Signs of* $\partial V/\partial A$ *and* $\partial V/\partial B$.–By the reasoning in Section III, C, above $\partial V/\partial A$ and $\partial V/\partial B$ must have opposite signs. This is true because $\partial r/\partial A$ and $\partial r/\partial B$ have opposite signs. We must prove that $\partial V/\partial A$ is strictly positive, if the short-run money income elasticity of demand for money does not exceed unity. Then all our conclusions will apply to both the general and the specific models.

Show that $\partial V/\partial A > 0$ if $L_1 y/M < 1$ and $L_2 p/M < 1$. The latter two are the money-income elasticities of demand for money; in the first case p is constant, and in the second case y is constant.

$$\frac{\partial V}{\partial A} > 0 \text{ if } f\frac{M\partial Y}{\partial A} - \frac{Y\partial M}{\partial A} > 0. \tag{i}$$

$$M\left[y\frac{\partial p}{\partial A} + p\frac{\partial y}{\partial A}\right] > py\left[M_2\frac{\partial r}{\partial A}\right]? \tag{ii}$$

Substitute the value of $\partial p/\partial A$, $\partial y/\partial A$, and $\partial r/\partial A$ obtained from the general model. Simplifying, we obtain

$$Z - \frac{yF'}{F}(Z - n_p) > n_y?, \tag{iii}$$

where

$$Z = 1 - \frac{L_3}{M_2},$$

which is greater than unity, since L_3 is negative;

$$n_p \equiv \frac{L_2 p}{M} \leqslant 1 \text{ and } n_y \equiv \frac{L_1 y}{M} \leqslant 1.$$

F' is negative. Hence it follows that $\partial V/\partial A > 0$. This completes our proof.

18

PRICE FLEXIBILITY AND FULL EMPLOYMENT

DON PATINKIN

At the core of the Keynesian polemics of the past ten years and more is the relationship between price flexibility and full employment. The fundamental argument of Keynes is directed against the belief that price flexibility can be depended upon to generate full employment automatically. The defenders of the classical tradition, on the other hand, still insist upon this automaticity as a basic tenet.

During the years of continuous debate on this question, the issues at stake have been made more precise. At the same time, further material on the question of flexibility has become available. This paper is essentially an attempt to incorporate this new material, and, taking advantage of the perspective offered by time, to analyze the present state of the debate.

In Part I, the problem of price flexibility and full employment is presented

Reprinted from *Readings in Monetary Theory* (Irwin, 1951), pp. 252–83, by permission of the author and publisher. This is a revised version of an article that originally appeared in the *American Economic Review* (September 1948), pp. 543–64. The author made the following major changes in the revision: the addition of the latter part of the last paragraph of §5, as a result of discussions with Milton Friedman; the addition of paragraphs three and four of §6, as a result of comments by Donald Gordon, Franco Modigliani, and Norman Ture; the correction of the last paragraph of §6 and Table 1 of §11 in accordance with Herbert Stein's comment on the original article in the *American Economic Review,* XXXIX (1949), 725–26; and the addition of the last three paragraphs of §14, in the attempt to clarify some points left ambiguous in the original article. All significant additions are enclosed in brackets.

In the process of writing this paper the author acknowledges having benefited from stimulating discussions with Milton Friedman, University of Chicago, and Alexander M. Henderson, University of Manchester. The author is a professor at Hebrew University, Jerusalem, Israel.

from a completely static viewpoint. Part II then goes on to discuss the far more important dynamic aspects of the problem. Finally, in Part III, the implications of the discussion for the Keynesian-classical polemic are analyzed. It is shown that over the years these two camps have really come closer and closer together. It is argued that the basic issue separating them is the rapidity with which the economic system responds to price variations.

I. STATIC ANALYSIS

1. The traditional interpretation of Keynesian economics is that it demonstrates the absence of an automatic mechanism assuring the equality of desired savings and investment at full employment. The graphical meaning of this interpretation is presented in a simplified form in Figure 1. Here the desired real savings (S) and investment (I) are each assumed to depend only on the level of real income (Y). I_1, I_2, and I_3 represent three possible positions of the investment schedule. Y_0 is the full employment level of real income. If the investment desires of individuals are represented by the curve I_1, desired savings at full employment are greater than desired investment at full employment. This means that unemployment will result: the level of income will drop to Y_1, at which income desired savings and investment are equal. Conversely, if I_3 is the investment curve, a situation of overemployment or

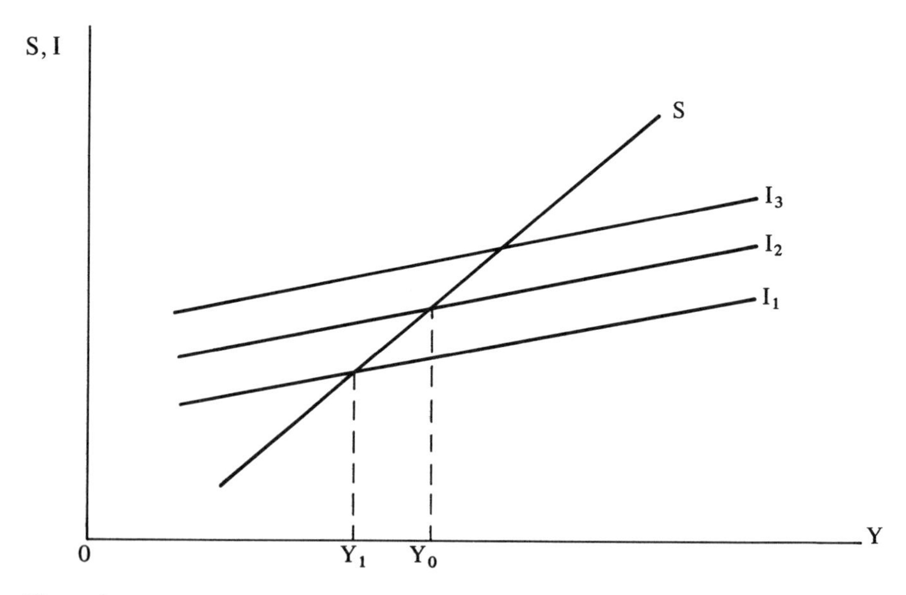

Figure 1.

inflation will occur: people desire to invest more at full employment than the amount of savings will permit. Only if the investment schedule happened to be I_2 would full employment, desired investment and savings be equal. But since investment decisions are independent of savings decisions, there is no reason to expect the investment schedule to coincide with I_2. Hence there is no automatic assurance that full employment will result.

2. The classical answer to this attack is that desired savings and investment depend on the rate of interest, as well as the level of real income; and that, granted flexibility, variations in the interest rate serve as an automatic mechanism insuring full employment.

The argument can be interpreted as follows: the savings and investment functions (representing what people desire to do) are written as

$$S = \Omega(r, Y)$$

$$I = \Psi(r, Y)$$

where r represents the rate of interest.

Consider now Figure 2. On this graph there can be drawn a whole family of curves relating savings and investment to the rate of interest—one pair for each level of real income. In Figure 2, these pairs of curves are drawn for the full employment income, Y_0, and for the less than full employment income, Y_1. On the assumption that for a given rate of interest people will save and invest more at a higher level of income, the investment curve corresponding to $Y = Y_0$ is drawn above that corresponding to $Y = Y_1$; similarly for the two savings curves. The curves also reflect the assumption that, for a given level of real income, people desire to save more and invest less at higher rates of interest.

Consider now the pair of curves corresponding to the full employment income Y_0. If in Figure 2 the interest rate were r_1, then it would be true that individuals would desire to save more at full employment than they would desire to invest. But, assuming no rigidities in the interest rate, this would present no difficulties. For if the interest rate were to fall freely, savings would be discouraged, and investment stimulated until finally desired full employment savings and investment would be equated at the level $S_0 = I_0$. Similarly, if at full employment desired investment is greater than desired savings, a rise in the interest rate will prevent inflation. In this way variations in the rate of interest serve automatically to prevent any discrepancy between desired full employment investment and savings, and thus to assure full employment.

This argument can also be presented in terms of Figure 1: assume for simplicity that desired investment depends on the rate of interest as well as the level of real income, while desired savings depends only on the latter.

Then downward variations in the interest rate can be counted on to raise the investment curve from, say, I_1 to I_2. That is, at any level of income people can be encouraged to invest more by a reduction in the rate of interest. Similarly, upward movements of the interest rate will shift the investment curve from, say, I_3 to I_2. Thus desired full employment savings and investment will always be equated.

3. The Keynesian answer to this classical argument is that it greatly exaggerátes the importance of the interest rate. Empirical evidence has accumulated in support of the hypothesis that variations in the rate of interest have little effect on the amount of desired investment. (That savings are insensitive to the interest rate is accepted even by the classical school.) This insensitivity has been interpreted as a reflection of the presence of widespread uncertainty.[1] The possible effect of this insensitivity on the ability of the system automatically to generate full employment is analyzed in Figure 3. For simplicity the savings functions corresponding to different levels of income are reproduced from Figure 2. But the investment functions are now represented as being much less interest-sensitive than those in Figure

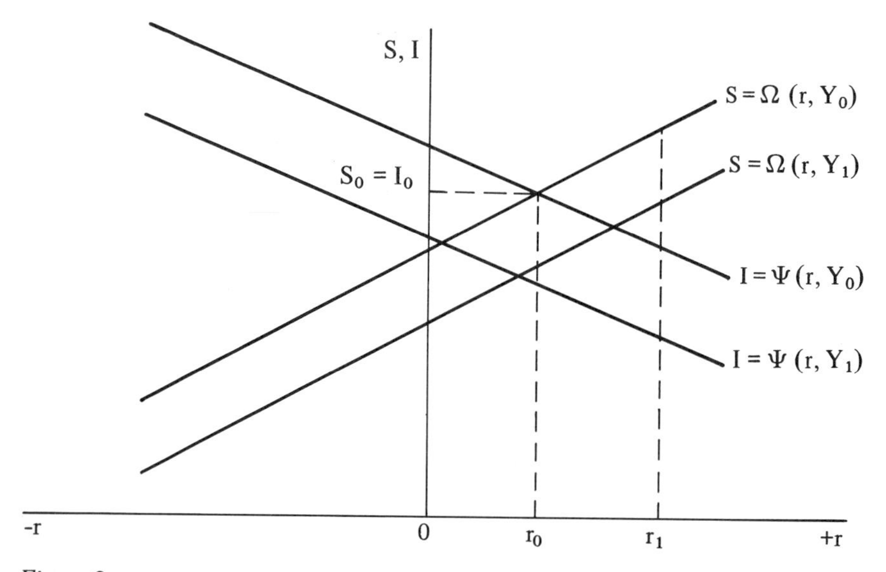

Figure 2.

[1] *Cf.* Oscar Lange, *Price Flexibility and Employment* (Bloomington, Indiana, Principia Press, 1945), p. 85 and the literature cited there. For an excellent theoretical discussion of this insensitivity, *cf.* G. L. S. Shackle, "Interest Rates and the Pace of Investment," *Economic Journal,* Vol. LVI (1946), pp. 1–17.

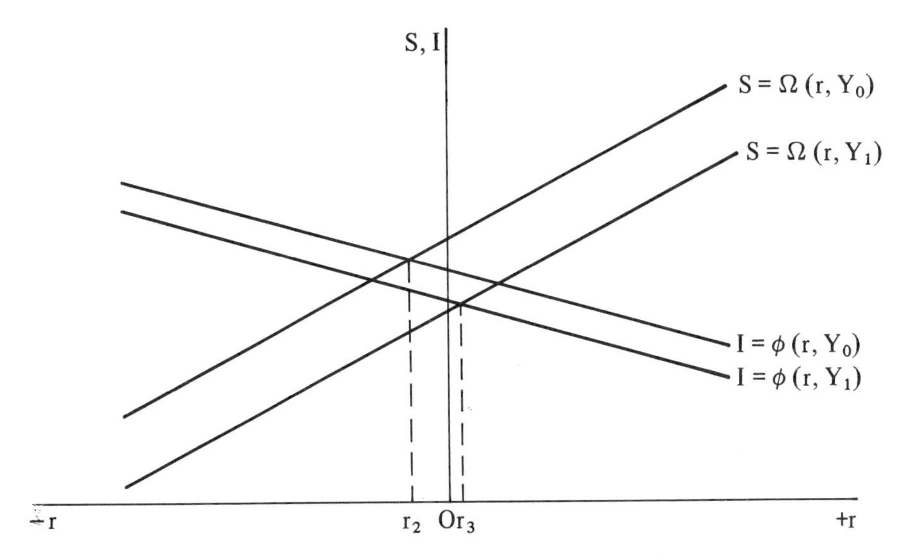

Figure 3.

2. If the situation in the real world were such as represented in Figure 3, it is clear that interest rate variations could never bring about full employment. For in an economy in which there are negligible costs of storing money, the interest rate can never be negative.[2] But from Figure 3 we see that the only way the interest rate can equate desired full employment savings and investment is by assuming the negative value r_2. Hence it is impossible for the full employment national income Y_0 to exist: for no matter what (positive) rate of interest may prevail, the amount people want to save at full employment exceeds what they want to invest. Instead there will exist some less than full employment income (say) Y_1 for which desired savings and investment can be brought into equality at a positive rate of interest, (say) r_3 (*cf.* Figure 3).

Thus once again the automaticity of the system is thrown into question. Whether the system will generate full employment depends on whether the full employment savings and investment functions intersect at a positive rate of interest. But there is no automatic mechanism to assure that the savings and investment functions will have the proper slopes and positions to bring about such an intersection.[3]

[2]Note that in a dynamic world of rising prices, the effective rate of interest may become negative. But even here the *anticipated* effective rate cannot be negative. For in that event there would again be an infinite demand for money.

[3][I have discussed this whole question of the contrast between the classical and Keynesian positions in greater detail elsewhere. *Cf.* "Involuntary Unemployment and the Keynesian Supply Function," *Economic Journal* LIX (1949), 376–78.]

4. Sometimes attempts are made to defend the classical position by arguing that the investment function is really higher (or the savings function lower) than represented by the Keynesians—so that desired full employment savings and investment can be equated at a positive rate of interest (*cf.* Figure 3). But this is beside the point. [The fundamental disagreement between Keynesian and classical economics lies in the former's denial of the automaticity of full employment posited by the latter.] Hence a successful restatement of the classical position must demonstrate the existence of some automatic mechanism which will always bring about full employment. Thus to argue that *if* the investment or saving function is at a certain level, full employment will be brought about is irrelevant; what must be shown is that there exist forces which will *automatically* bring the investment or saving functions to the required level. In other words, the issue at stake is not the *possible,* but the *automatic,* generation of full employment.

5. [To the Keynesian negative interest rate argument replies have been made by both Haberler and Pigou.[4] Just as the crude Keynesian argument of §1 was answered by introducing a new variable—the rate of interest—into the savings function, so the more refined argument of §3 is countered by the introduction of yet another variable—the real value of cash balances held by the individuals in the economy. Thus, denoting the amount of money in the economy M_1 (assumed to remain constant) and the absolute price level by p, Pigou's saving schedule is written as

$$S = \Gamma \left(r, Y, \frac{M_1}{p}\right).]$$

His argument is as follows: if people would refuse to save anything at negative and zero rates of interest, then the desired savings schedule would intersect the desired investment schedule at a positive rate of interest regardless of the level of income (*cf.* Figure 3). The willingness to save even without receiving interest, or even at a cost, must imply that savings are not made solely for the sake of future income (*i.e.,* interest) but also for "the desire for possession as such, conformity to tradition or custom and so on."[5] But the extent to which an individual wishes to save out of current income for reasons other than the desire of future income is inversely related to the real

[4] [G. Haberler, *Prosperity and Depression* (League of Nations, Geneva, 1941), 3rd ed., pp. 242, 389, 403, 491–503.]

A. C. Pigou, "The Classical Stationary State," *Economic Journal,* LIII (1943), 343–51; "Economic Progress in a Stable Environment," *Economica,* n. s. XIV (1947), 180–90. Although these articles deal only with a stationary state, their basic argument can readily be extended to the case in which net investment is taking place.

[In the subsequent text, I shall follow the exposition of Pigou; but the argument holds also with respect to Haberler.]

[5] *Ibid.,* p. 346.

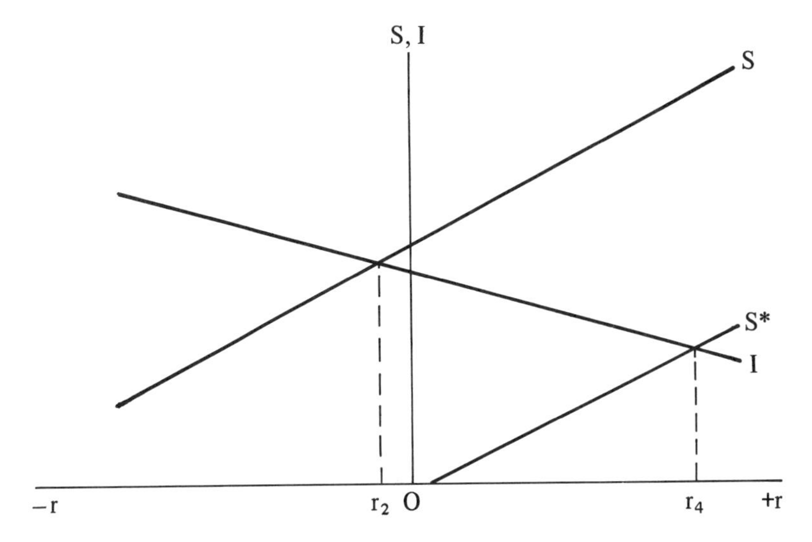

Figure 4.

value of his cash balances.[6] If this is sufficiently large, all his secondary desires for saving will be fully satisfied. At this point the only reason he will continue to save out of current income is the primary one of anticipated future interest payments. In other words, if the real value of cash balances is sufficiently large, the savings function becomes zero at a positive rate of interest, regardless of the income level.

A graphical interpretation of this argument is presented in Figure 4. Here S and I are the full-employment savings and investment curves of Figure 3 (*i.e.*, those corresponding to $Y = Y_0$), and r_2 is again the negative rate of interest at which they are equal. Pigou then argues that by increasing the real value of cash balances, the full employment savings curve shifts to the right until it is in such a position that no savings are desired except at positive rates of interest. This is represented by the savings curve S*, which becomes zero for a positive rate of interest. (In fact, S* shows dissaving taking place for sufficiently low rates of interest.) The full employment savings curve S* clearly intersects the full employment investment curve I at the positive rate of interest r_4. Thus by changing the real value of cash balances, desired full employment savings and investment can always be equated at a positive rate of interest.

[6] And all his other assets too. But the introduction of these other assets does not change Pigou's argument; while concentration on money assets brings out its (the argument's) basic aspect. *Cf.* below, §6.

How can we be sure that real cash balances will automatically change in the required direction and magnitude? Here Pigou brings in his assumptions of flexible wage and price levels, and a constant stock of money in circulation. If full employment saving exceeds investment, national income begins to fall, and unemployment results. If workers react to this by decreasing their money wages, then the price level will also begin to fall. As the latter continues to fall, the real value of the constant stock of money increases correspondingly. Thus, as the price level falls, the full employment saving function continuously shifts to the right until it intersects the full employment investment function at a positive rate of interest.[7]

This is the automatic mechanism on which Haberler and Pigou rely to assure full employment. It is essential to note that it will operate regardless of the interest-elasticities of the savings and investment functions—provided they are not both identically zero. [It should also be emphasized, as Haberler does, that although this argument has been presented above as an answer to Keynes, it is of much older origin. In particular, it is implicit in classical theorizing on the quantity theory of money. The crucial step in this analysis, it will be recalled, comes at the point where it is argued that as a result of increasing the amount of money in the economy, individuals' cash balances are larger than desired at the existing price level, so that they will attempt to reduce these real balances by increasing their money expenditures. The main

[7]The exact price level is determined when to our preceding four equations is added the liquidity preference equation, M_0 = (r, Y, p), where M_0 represents the given amount of money in the system. (As will be shown in the next section, the "stock of money" relevant for the liquidity equation is completely different from the "stock of money" relevant for the Pigou analysis of the savings function; hence the use of two different symbols—M_0 and M_1.) We then have the complete system of five equations in five variables:

$$I = \Phi(r, Y)$$

$$S = \Gamma\left(r, Y, \frac{M_1}{p}\right)$$

$$I = S$$

$$Y = Y_0$$

$$M_0 = \Lambda(r, Y, p) .$$

Under the Pigovian assumptions this system is consistent; its equations are satisfied for a positive rate of interest.

[The workings of a more general system of equations under the Pigovian assumption are described in detail in Parts IV and V of the reference cited in footnote 3 above. In this more detailed treatment, the full employment level, Y_0, is not arbitrarily defined—as is done in the present paper—but emerges instead from the economic behavior functions themselves.]

contribution of Haberler and Pigou is to show how this set of forces must, and can, be introduced into the Keynesian analytical apparatus.]

6. The inner mechanism and distinctive characteristic of the Pigou analysis can be laid bare by considering it from a larger perspective. It is obvious that a price reduction has a stimulating effect on creditors. But, restricting ourselves to the private sector of a closed economy, to every stimulated creditor there corresponds a discouraged debtor. Hence from this viewpoint the net effect of a price reduction is likely to be in the neighborhood of zero. The neatness of the Pigou approach lies in its utilizing the fact that although the private sector considered in isolation is, on balance, neither debtor nor creditor, when considered in its relationship to the government, it *must be* a net "creditor." This is due to the fact that the private sector always holds money, which is a (non-interest bearing) "debt" of government. If we assume that government activity is not affected by the movements of the absolute price level,[8] then the net effect of a price decline must always be stimulatory.[9] The community gains at the "expense" of a gracious government, ready, willing, and able to bear the "loss" of the increased value of its "debt" to the public.

More precisely, not every price decline need have this stimulating effect. For we must consider the effect of the price decline on the other assets held by the individual. If the decline reduces the real value of these other assets (*e.g.*, houses and other forms of consumer capital; stock shares; etc.) to an extent more than offsetting the increased value of real cash balances,[10] then the net effect will be discouraging. But the important point is that no matter what our initial position, *there exists* a price level sufficiently low so that the total real value of assets corresponding to it is greater than the original real value. Consider the extreme case in which the value of the other assets becomes arbitrarily small.[11] Clearly even here the real value of the fixed stock of money can be made as large as desired by reducing the price level sufficiently. Thus, to be rigorous, the statement in the preceding paragraph should read: "There always exists a price decline such that its effect is stimulatory." From this and the analysis of the preceding section, we can derive another statement which succinctly summarizes the results of the Pigou analysis: "In the static classical model, regardless of the position of the

[8] Pigou makes this assumption when he writes the investment function (which presumably also includes government expenditure) as independent of the absolute price level. *Cf.* footnote 7 above.

[9] It must be emphasized that I am abstracting here from all dynamic considerations of the effect on anticipations, etc. These will be discussed in Part II of the paper.

[10] A necessary (but not sufficient) condition for this to occur is that the price level of assets falls in a greater proportion than the general price level.

[11] I am indebted to M. Friedman for this example.

investment schedule, there always exists a sufficiently low price level such that full employment is generated." In any event, it is clearly sufficient to concentrate (as Pigou has done) on cash balances alone.[12]

[This analysis is subject to at least two reservations, neither one of which has been considered by Haberler or Pigou. First of all, we have tacitly been assuming that the depressing effect of a price decline on a debtor is roughly offset by its stimulating effect on a creditor; hence the private sector, being on balance a creditor with respect to the government, can ultimately be stimulated by a price decline. But allowance must be made for the possibility of a differential reaction of debtors and creditors. That is, if debtors are discouraged by a price decline much more than creditors are encouraged, it may be possible that there exists no price decline which would have an encouraging effect on expenditures. In brief, the Keynesian aggregative analysis followed by Pigou overlooks the possibility of microeconomic "distribution effects."

Secondly, we have so far considered only the effects of a change in real balances on household behavior; that is, on the consumption (or, its counterpart, the savings) function. It seems only natural to extend the analysis to include the influence of real cash balances on firms, and, hence, on the investment function as well. However, this extension cannot be made automatically, inasmuch as the respective motivations of firms and households are not necessarily the same. Neverthless, it does seem reasonable to assume that investment decisions of firms are favorably influenced by a higher level of real balances. Once we take account of firms, the differential reactions mentioned in the preceding paragraph become increasingly significant. If firms are, on balance, debtors with respect to households and government, then a persistent price decline will cause a wave of bankruptcies. This will have a seriously depressing effect upon the economy which may not be offset by the improved status of creditors. Furthermore, in most cases of bankruptcy the creditors also lose. For these reasons it is not at all certain that a price decline will result in a positive net effect on the total expenditures (consumption plus investment) function. On this point much further investigation–of a theoretical as well as an empirical nature–is required.]

From the preceding analysis we can also see just exactly what constitutes the "cash balance" whose increase in real value provides the stimulatory effect of the Pigou analysis. This balance clearly consists of the net obligation of the government to the private sector of the economy. That is, it consists

[12] *Cf.* above, footnote 6. Another possible reason for Pigou's emphasis on cash balances to the exclusion of other assets is that the relative illiquidity of the latter makes them less likely to be used as a means of satisfying the "irrational" motives of saving. Hence the inverse relationship between other assets and savings out of current income might not be so straightforward as that between real cash balances and savings.

primarily of the total interest- and non-interest-bearing government debt held outside the treasury and central bank, [plus the net amount owed by the central bank to member banks]. Thus, by excluding demand deposits and including government interest-bearing debt and member bank reserves, it differs completely from what is usually regarded as the stock of money.

These same conclusions can be reached through a somewhat different approach. Begin with the ordinary concept of the stock of money as consisting of hand-to-hand currency and demand deposits. Consider now what changes must be made in order to arrive at the figure relevant for the Pigou analysis. Clearly, government interest-bearing debt must be added, since a price decline increases its value. Now consider money in the form of demand deposits. To the extent that it is backed by bank loans and discounts, the gains of deposit holders are offset by the losses of bank debtors.[13] Thus the net effect of a price decline on demand deposits is reduced to its effect on the excess of deposits over loans, or (approximately) on the reserves of the banks held in the form of hand-to-hand currency [and deposits in the central bank]. Finally, hand-to-hand currency held by individuals outside the banking system is added in, and we arrive at exactly the same figure as in the preceding paragraph.

For convenience denote the stock of money relevant for the Pigou analysis by M_1. Note that this is completely different from M_0 of footnote 7: for M_0 is defined in the usual manner as hand-to-hand currency plus demand deposits. This distinction is of fundamental importance. [One of its immediate implications is that central bank open market operations which do not change the market price of government bonds affect the economic system only through the liquidity preference equation.] Since such operations merely substitute one type of government debt (currency) for another (bonds), they have no effect on M_1 and hence no direct effect on the amount of savings. [Even when open market purchases do cause an increase in the price of government bonds, the changes in M_0 and M_1 will not, in general, be equal. The increase in M_0 equals the total amount of money expended for the purchase of the bonds; the increase in M_1 equals the increase in the value of bonds (both of those bought and those not bought by the central bank) caused by the open-market operations.[14] Corresponding statements can be made for open-market sales.]

[13] *Cf.* M. Kalecki, "Professor Pigou on 'The Classical Stationary State'–A Comment," *Economic Journal,* LIV (1944), 131–32.

[14] [It might be argued that through its effect on the interest rate, open-market purchases affect the value of assets other than government securities; hence, this change in value should also be included in the change in M_1. This is a point which deserves further investigation. The main question is whether there exists an offset to this improvement in the position of bondholders of private corporations.]

7. How does the Pigou formulation compare with the original classical theory?[15] Although both Pigou and the "classics" stress the importance of "price flexibility," they mean by this term completely different things. The "classics" are talking about flexibility of relative prices; Pigou is talking about flexibility of absolute prices. The classical school holds that the existence of long-run unemployment is *prima facie* evidence of rigid wages. The only way to eliminate unemployment is, then, by reducing *real* wages. (Since workers can presumably accomplish this end by reducing their *money* wage, this position has implicit in it the assumption of a constant price level—[or at least one falling relatively less than wages].) Pigou now recognizes that changing the relative price of labor is not enough, and that the absolute price level itself must vary. In fact, a strict interpretation of Pigou's position would indicate that unemployment can be eliminated even if real wages remain the same or even rise (namely, if the proportionate fall in prices is greater than or equal to that of wages); for in any case the effect of increased real value of cash balances is still present.[16]

The Pigou analysis also differs from those interpretations of the classical position which, following Keynes, present the effect of a wage decrease as acting through the liquidity preference equation to increase the real value of M_0 and thereby reduce the rate of interest; this in turn stimulates both consumption and investment expenditures—thus generating a higher level of national income. To this effect, Pigou now adds the direct stimulus to consumption expenditures provided by the price decline and the accompanying increase in real balances. Consequently, even if the savings and investment functions are completely insensitive to changes in the rate of interest (so that the effect through the liquidity equation is completely inoperative), a wage decrease will still be stimulatory through its effect on real balances and hence on savings.

8. Before concluding this part of the paper, one more point must be clarified. The explicit assumption of the Pigou analysis is that savings are directly related to the price level, and therefore inversely related to the size of real cash balances. This assumption by itself is, on *a priori* grounds, quite

[15]Pigou, of course, introduces the absolute price level into the analysis of the real sector of the economy, whereas classical economics insists that this sector must be considered on the basis of relative prices alone. [As I have shown elsewhere, on this point classical economics is definitely wrong. For, in a money economy, the demand for any good must, in general, depend on the absolute price level, as well as on relative prices. This is a direct result of utility maximization. *Cf.* "Money in General Equilibrium Theory: Critique and Reformulation," *Econometrica,* XVIII (1950), and references cited there.]

[16]The role of real wages in Pigou's system is very ambiguous. At one point (p. 348, bottom) he assumes that reduced money wages will also decrease real wages. At another (p. 349, lines 20–38) no such assumption seems to be involved. "As money wage-rates fall . . . prices fall and go on falling." *Ibid.*

reasonable; [indeed, in a money economy it is a direct implication of utility maximization (above, note 15)]. But it must be emphasized that even if we disregard the reservations mentioned in the preceding sections, this assumption is insufficient to bring about the conclusion desired by Pigou. For this purpose he *implicitly* makes an additional, and possibly less reasonable, assumption. Specifically, in addition to postulating explicitly the direction of the relationship between savings and the price level, he also implies something about its *intensity.*

The force of this distinction is illustrated by Figure 5. Here S and I are the full employment savings and investment curves of Figure 3 (*i.e.,* those corresponding to $Y = Y_0$) for a fixed price level, p_0. The other savings curves, S_1, S_2, S_3, S_4, represent the full employment savings schedules corresponding to the different price levels p_1, p_2, p_3, p_4, respectively. In accordance with the Pigou assumption, as the price level falls, the savings function shifts over to the right. (That is p_1, p_2, p_3, p_4, are listed in descending order.) But it may well be that as the real value of their cash balances continues to increase, people are less and less affected by this increase. That is, for each successive increase in real balances (for each successive price level decline) the savings function moves less and less to the right, until eventually it might respond only infinitesimally, no matter how much prices fall. In graphical terms, as the price decline continues, the savings function might reach S_3 as a limiting position. That is, no matter how much the price level might fall, the savings function would never move to the right of S_3.[17] In such an event the declining price level would fail to bring about full employment. The validity of the Pigou argument thus depends on the additional assumption that the intensity of the inverse relationship between savings and real cash balances is such that it will be possible to shift over the savings function to a position where it

[17]Mathematically this may be stated as follows. Write the savings function as

$$S = \Gamma(r, p, Y).$$

(*Cf.* footnote 7, above.) Pigou's explicit assumption is

$$\Gamma_p(r, p, Y) > 0$$

where Γp is the partial derivative of S with respect to p. Let $Y = Y_0$ represent the full employment income. Then the argument here is that the savings function, Γ, may still be of a form such that

$$\lim_{p \to 0} \Gamma(r, p, Y_0) = \Gamma^*(r, Y_0)$$

for any fixed r—where Γ^* is any curve which intersects the investment curve at a negative rate of interest. (In the argument of the text, Γ^* is taken to be S_3 in Figure 5.) Pigou tacitly assumes that the savings function approaches no such limit; or that if it does, the limiting function intersects the investment function at a positive rate of interest.

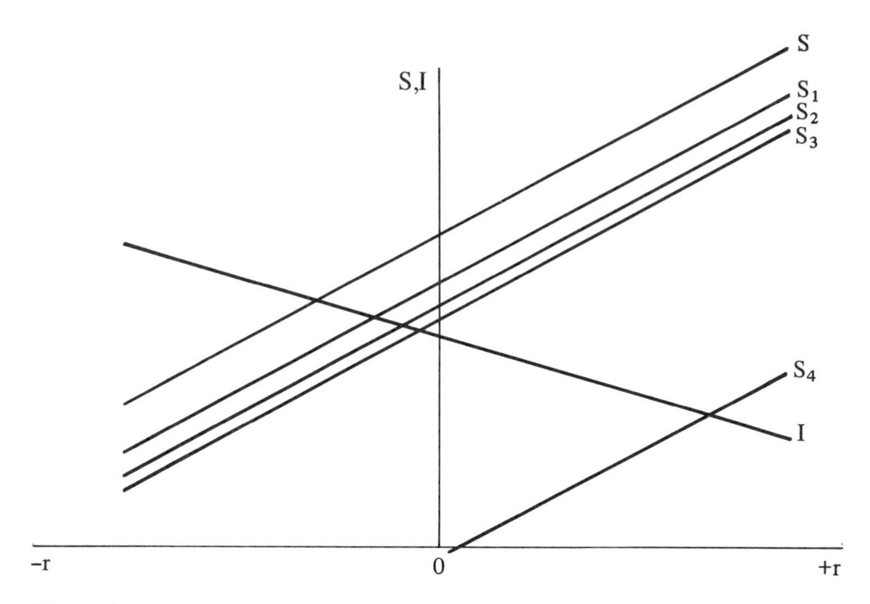

Figure 5.

will intercept the investment function at a positive rate of interest: say, S_4 (*cf.* Figure 5).

What is at issue here is the reaction of individuals with already large real balances to further increases in these balances. Consider an individual with a cash balance of a fixed number of dollars. As the price falls, the increased real value of these dollars must be allocated between the alternatives of an addition to either consumption and/or real balances.[18] How the individual will actually allocate the increase clearly depends on the relative marginal utilities of these two alternatives. If we are willing to assume that the marginal utility of cash balances approaches zero with sufficient rapidity relative to that of consumption, then we can ignore the possibility of the savings curve reaching a limiting position such as in Figure 5. That is, we would be maintaining the position that by increasing the individual's balances sufficiently, he will have no further incentive to add to these balances; hence he will spend any additional real funds on consumption, so that we can make him consume any amount desired. If, on the other hand, we admit the possibility that, for sufficiently large consumption, the decrease in the marginal utility of cash balances is accompanied by a much faster decrease in the marginal utility of consumption, then the individual will

[18]I am abstracting here from the possible third alternative, investment.

continuously use most of the additional real funds (made available by the price decline) to add to his balances. In this event, the situation of Figure 5 may well occur.

9. I do not believe we have sufficient evidence—either of an *a priori* or empirical[19] nature—to help us answer the question raised in the preceding paragraph. The empirical evidence available is consistent with the hypothesis that the effect of real balances on savings is very weak. But even granted the truth of this hypothesis, it casts no light on the question raised here. What we want to know is what happens to the effect of real balances on savings as these real balances increase in size. Even if the effect were arbitrarily small, but remained constant regardless of the size of real balances, there could be no convergence of savings functions like that pictured in Figure 5. In the face of this lack of evidence, we have to be satisfied with the conclusion that, subject to the [reservations of §§6 and 8, Haberler and Pigou have] demonstrated the automaticity of full employment within the framework of the classical static model[20]—the main mechanism by which this is brought about being the effect of a price decline on cash balances.

The statement of this conclusion immediately raises the interesting question of how this set of forces, [emphasized by Haberler and Pigou,] could have been overlooked by Keynesian economists, in general, and Keynes himself, in particular. Questions of this type can rarely be answered satisfactorily—and perhaps should not even be asked. Nevertheless, I think it is both possible and instructive to trace through the exact chain of errors in Keynes's reasoning which caused him to overlook these factors.

I submit the hypothesis that Keynes recognized the influence of assets on saving (consumption), but unfortunately thought of this influence only in terms of physical capital assets. This was his fundamental error.[21] From it immediately followed that in his main discussion of the (short-run) consumption function, where he assumed a *constant* stock of capital, the possible influence of assets was not (and could not) even be considered.[22] But as soon as Keynes discussed a period sufficiently long for noticeable capital growth,

[19]Empirical studies on the effect of real balances on savings have been made by L. R. Klein, "The Use of Econometric Models as a Guide to Economic Policy," *Econometrica*, Vol. XV (1947), pp. 122–25. Klein's procedure was incorrect in that he used a series for M_0, instead of M_1 in fitting his equations (*cf.* last paragraph of §6 above).

[20]It must be re-emphasized that this conclusion holds only for static analysis. The modifications that must be introduced once dynamic factors enter are discussed in Part II.

[21]Note that there are really two distinct errors involved here. The first is the obvious one of the exclusion of monetary assets. The second is that what is relevant for the influence on saving is not the *physical* asset, but its *real* value in terms of some general price level.

[22]J. M. Keynes, *The General Theory of Employment, Interest, and Money* (New York, Harcourt, Brace, and Co., 1936), Chap. 8. See especially pp. 91–5, where Keynes considers the possible influence of other factors besides income on consumption, and does not even mention assets.

the influence of assets on savings was immediately recognized.[23] Even here, Keynes could not come to the same conclusion as Pigou. For Keynes restricted himself to physical assets, and thus rightfully pointed out that it would be "an unlikely coincidence" that just the correct amount of assets should exist–*i.e.*, that amount which would push over the savings function to such a position where full employment could be generated. Compare this with the determinate process by which just exactly the "correct amount" of real cash balances is brought into existence in the Pigou analysis. (See above, §5, paragraph 4.)

This exclusion of physical assets from the short-run consumption function was subconsciously extended to all kinds of assets. Here was the last link in the chain of errors. For later when Keynes began to examine the effects of increased real cash balances (brought about either by price declines or increases in the amount of money), he did not even consider their possible influence on consumption. Instead, he concentrated exclusively on their tendency, through the liquidity function, to lower interest rates.[24] (*Cf.* above, §7, last paragraph.)

Looking back on the nature of these errors, we cannot but be struck by the irony that they should have emanated from the man who did most to demonstrate the fundamental inseparability of the real and monetary sectors of our economy.

II. DYNAMIC ANALYSIS: THE QUESTION OF POLICY

10. [The Haberler-Pigou analysis discussed in Part I makes two contributions. First, in its emphasis on the effects of a price on savings *via* its effects on real balances, it introduces into the Keynesian analytical apparatus a set of forces hitherto overlooked by the latter. (For convenience this will be referred to as the Pigou effect–though, as mentioned at the end of §5 above, it is of much older origin.) Secondly, it proceeds to draw the implications of this set] of forces for static analysis, and summarizes its results in the following theorem (*cf.* §§5 and 6): *There always exists a sufficiently low price level such that, if*

[23] *Ibid.*, p. 218, second paragraph.

[24] *Ibid.*, pp. 231-34, 266. The following passage is especially interesting: "It is, therefore, on the effect of a falling wage- and price-level on the *demand for money* that those who believe in the self-adjusting quality of the economic system must rest the weight of their argument; though I am not aware that they have done so. If the quantity of money is itself a function of the wage- and price-level, there is, indeed, nothing to hope for in this direction. But if the quantity of money is virtually fixed, it is evident that its quantity in terms of wage-units can be indefinitely increased by a sufficient reduction in money wages. . . ." (*Ibid.*, p. 266. Italics not in original.)

expected to continue indefinitely,[25] *it will generate full employment.*[26] (For convenience this will be referred to as the Pigou Theorem.) The purpose of this part of the paper is to accomplish a third objective: *viz.,* to draw the implications of the Pigou effect for dynamic analysis and policy formulation. It must be emphasized that the Pigou Theorem tells us nothing about the dynamic and policy aspects which interest us in this third objective. (This point is discussed in greater detail in §12.)

Specifically, consider a full employment situation which is suddenly terminated by a downswing in economic activity. The question I now wish to examine is the usefulness of a policy which consists of maintaining the stock of money constant, allowing the wage and price levels to fall, and waiting for the resulting increase in real balances to restore full employment.

At the outset it must be made clear that the above policy recommendation is *not* to be attributed to Pigou. His interest is purely an intellectual one, in a purely static analysis. As he himself writes: ". . . The puzzles we have been considering . . . are academic exercises, of some slight use perhaps for clarifying thought, but with very little chance of ever being posed on the chequer board of actual life."[27]

In reality, Pigou's disavowal of a deflationary policy (contained in the paragraph from which the above quotation is taken) is not nearly as thoroughgoing as might appear on the first reading. The rejection of a price decline as a practical means of combatting unemployment may be due to: (a) the conviction that dynamic considerations invalidate its use as an immediate policy, regardless of its merits in static analysis; (b) the conviction that industrial and labor groups, sometimes with the assistance of government, prevent the price flexibility necessary for the success of a deflationary policy. A careful reading of Pigou's disclaimer indicates that he had only the second of these alternatives in mind; *i.e.,* that he felt that the policy would not work because it would not be permitted to work. What I hope to establish in this part of the essay is the first alternative: namely, that even granted full flexibility of prices, it is still highly possible that a deflationary policy will not work, due to the dynamic factors involved.

Nevertheless, nothing in this part of the paper is intended (or even relevant) as a criticism of Pigou, since the latter has clearly abstained from the problem of policy formulation. If sometimes the terms "Pigou effect" and "Pigou Theorem" are used in the following discussion, they should be understood solely as shorthand notations for the concepts previously explained.

[25]This qualifying phrase incorporates in it the restriction of the Pigou argument to static analysis.

[26]I am overlooking here the reservations discussed in §§6 and 8 above.

[27]"Economic Progress in a Stable Environment," *Economica,* n. s. XIV (1947), 188.

11. The analysis of this section is based on the following two assumptions: (a) One of the prerequisites of a successful anti-depression policy is that it should be able to achieve its objective rapidly (say, within a year). (b) Prices cannot fall instantaneously; hence, the larger the price level fall necessary to bring about full employment *via* the Pigou effect, the longer the time necessary for the carrying out of the policy. (If no price fall can bring about full employment, then we can say that an infinite amount of time is necessary for the carrying out of the policy.)

There are at least two factors which act toward lengthening the period necessary to carry out a policy based on the Pigou effect. The first is the possibility that the effect of an increase in cash balances on consumption is so small, that very large increases (very great price declines) will be necessary. [Certainly there is a burden of proof on the supporters of a policy of absolute price flexibility to show that this is not so;] that the economic system is sufficiently responsive to make the policy practical. So far no one has presented the required evidence.

The second factor is a result of the price decline itself. In dynamic analysis we must give full attention to the role played by price expectations and anticipations in general. It is quite possible that the original price decline will lead to the expectation of further declines. Then purchasing decisions will be postponed, aggregate demand will fall off, and the amount of unemployment increased still more. In terms of Figures 1 and 3, the savings function will rise (consumption will be decreased) and the investment function fall, further aggravating the problem of achieving full employment. This was the point on which Keynes was so insistent.[28] Furthermore, the uncertainty about the future generated by the price decline will increase the liquidity preference of individuals. Thus if we consider an individual possessing a fixed number of dollars, and confronted with a price decline which increases the real value of these dollars, his uncertainty will make him more inclined to employ these additional real funds to increase his real balances, than to increase his expenditures.[29] In other words, the uncertainty created by the price decline might cause people to accumulate indefinitely large real cash balances, and to increase their expenditures very little if at all. [Finally, the bankruptcies caused by the inability of creditors to carry the increased real burden of their debt (above, §6) will strengthen the pessimistic outlook for the future. The simultaneous interaction of these three forces] will further exacerbate these difficulties. For as the period of price decline drags itself out, anticipations for the future will progressively worsen, and uncertainties further increase. The

[28]See his discussion of changes in money wages, *op. cit.*, pp. 260–69, especially p. 263. *Cf.* also J. R. Hicks, *Value and Capital* (Oxford, Oxford University Press, 1939), and O. Lange, *op. cit.*

[29]*Cf.* above, §8, last paragraph.

end result of letting the Pigou effect work itself out may be a disastrous deflationary spiral, continuing for several years without ever reaching any equilibrium position. Certainly our past experiences should have sensitized us to this danger.

Because of these considerations I feel that it is impractical to depend upon the Pigou effect as a means of policy: the required price decline might be either too large (factor one), or it might be the initial step of an indefinite deflationary spiral (factor two).

On this issue, it may be interesting to investigate the experience of the United States in the 1930's. In Table I, net balances are computed for the period 1929–32 according to the definition in §6. As can be seen, although there was a 19 per cent *increase* in real balances from 1930 to 1931, real national income during this period *decreased* by 13 per cent. Even in the following year, when a further increase of 19 per cent in real balances took place, real income proceeded to fall by an additional 18 per cent. For the 1929–1932 period as a whole there was an increase in real balances of 46 per cent, and a decrease in real income of 40 per cent.

It will, of course, be objected that these data reflect the presence of "special factors," and do not indicate the real value of the Pigou effect. But the pertinent question which immediately arises is: To what extent were these "special factors" necessary, concomitant results of the price decline itself! If the general feeling of uncertainty and adverse anticipations that marked the period is cited as one of these "special factors," the direct relationship between this and the decline in price level itself certainly cannot be overlooked. Other proposed "special factors" must be subjected to the same type of examination. The data of the preceding table are not offered as conclusive evidence. But they are certainly consistent with the previously stated hypothesis of the impracticability of using the Pigou effect as a means of policy; and they certainly throw the burden of proof on those who argue for its practicality.

12. The argument of the preceding section requires further explanation on at least one point. In the discussion of the "second factor" there was mentioned the possibility of an indefinitely continuing spiral of deflation and unemployment. But what is the relation between this possibility and the Pigou Theorem (*cf.* §10) established in Part I? The answer to this question may be expressed as follows:

On the downswing of the business cycle it might be interesting to know that there exists a sufficiently low price level which, if it were expected to continue existing indefinitely, would bring about full employment. Interesting, but, for policy purposes, irrelevant. For due to perverse price expectations and the dynamics of deflationary spirals, it is impossible to reach (or, once having reached, to remain at) such a position.

[*Table 1.*

Year	*Money in circulation outside Treasury and Federal Reserve System*	*Market value of government interest-bearing debt held outside government agencies and the Federal Reserve System*	*Member bank deposits in the Federal Reserve System*	*Nonmember bank deposits in the Federal Reserve System*	*Other Federal Reserve accounts*	*Reserve bank credit outstanding excluding that based on reserve bank holdings of U.S. government securities*	*Treasury deposits in member and nonmember banks*	*Postal savings*	*Net balances* (M_1) *(1) + (2) + (3) + (4) + (5) − (6) − (7) + (8)*	*Cost of living index (p)*	*Net real balances* $\frac{M_1}{p}$ *(9) ÷ (10)*	*Real national income*
	(1)	(2)	(3)	(4)	(5)	(6)	(7)	(8)	(9)	(10)	(11)	(12)
1929	4.5	14.5	2.4	0.0	0.4	1.3	0.4	0.2	20.2	1.22	16.6	89.9
1930	4.2	13.9	2.4	0.0	0.4	0.5	0.3	0.2	20.4	1.19	17.1	76.3
1931	4.7	15.1	2.3	0.1	0.4	0.6	0.4	0.6	22.1	1.09	20.3	66.3
1932	5.3	16.0	2.1	0.1	0.4	0.6	0.4	0.9	23.7	.98	24.2	54.2

All money figures are in billions of dollars.

Data for series (1), (3), (4), (5), (6) were obtained from *Banking and Monetary Statistics*, p. 368. On pp. 360–67 of this book their interrelationships are discussed. For (7) see *ibid.*, pp. 34–5. For (8) see *Statistical Abstract of the United States*, 1947, p. 419.

Being unable to find an official series for (2), I used the following procedure: Total outstanding government debt at face value was classified according to maturities (0–5 years, 5–10, and over 10) on the basis of *Banking and Monetary Statistics*, p. 511. These classifications were multiplied by price indexes for government bonds with maturities of more than 3 and less than 4 years, more than 6 and less than 9, and more than 10, respectively (Standard and Poor, *Statistics: Security Price Index Record*, 1948 edition, pp. 139–44). The sum of these products was used as an estimate of the market value of the total government debt. The ratio of this to the face value of the total debt was computed, and this ratio applied to the face value of government debt held outside the Treasury and Federal Reserve System (*Banking and Monetary Statistics*, p. 512) to yield an estimate of the required series.

Series (10): Bureau of Labor Statistics, cost of living index, *Survey of Current Business*, 1942, p. 16.

Series (12): National income in billions of 1944 dollars. J. Dewhurst and Associates, *America's Needs and Resources* (New York, The Twentieth Century Fund, 1947), p. 697.]

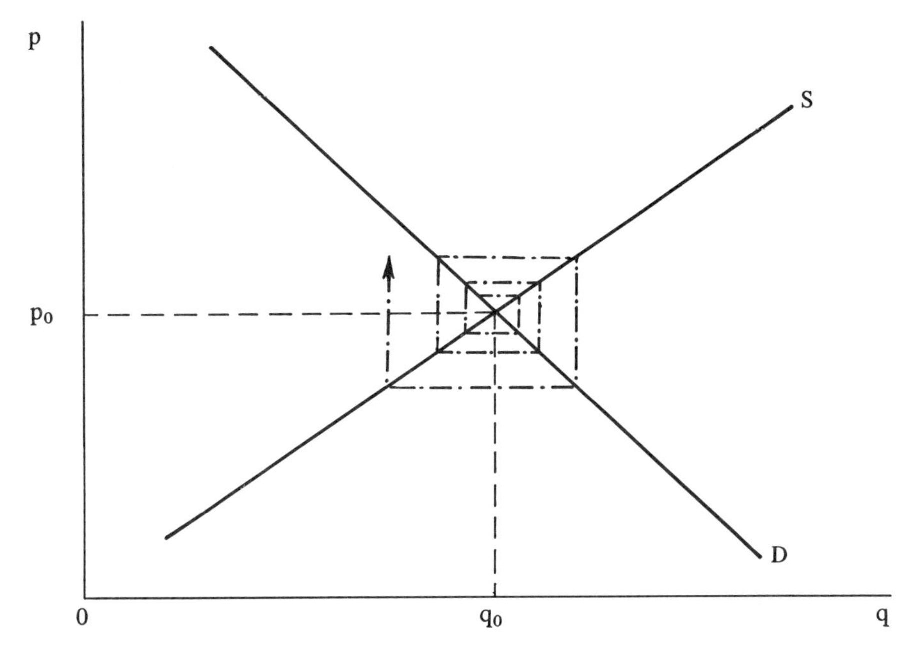

Figure 6.

The implication of these remarks can be clarified by consideration of the cobweb theorem for the divergent case. Assume that a certain market can be explained in terms of the cobweb theorem. It is desired to know whether (assuming unchanged demand and supply curves) the designated market will ever reach a stationary position; that is, whether it will settle down to a unique price that will continue indefinitely to clear the market. This question is clearly divided into two parts: (a) does there exist such a price, and (b) if it does exist, will the market be able to attain it. In the case of the cobweb presented in Figure 6 it is clear that such a price does exist. For if the price p_0 had always existed and were expected to exist indefinitely, it would continuously clear the market. But Figure 6 represents the case of a divergent cobweb; hence the market will never be able to reach the price p_0. In brief, even though p_0 exists, it is irrelevant to the workings of the market. The analogy to the argument of the preceding paragraph is obvious.[30]

[30]The distinction of this section can be expressed in rigorous mathematical form using the dynamic system which has become familiar through the work of Samuelson and Lange (P. A. Samuelson, "The Stability of Equilibrium: Comparative Statics and Dynamics," *Econometrica,* Vol. IX [1941], pp. 97–120; Lange, *op. cit.,* pp. 91 ff.). Consider a single market and let D, S, and p represent the demand, supply and price of the particular good, respectively. Let t represent time. Then we can write this system as

III. CONCLUSIONS

13. The conclusions of this paper can be summarized as follows: in a static world with a constant stock of money,[31] price flexibility assures full employment. (I abstract here again from the difficulties raised in §§6 and 8.) But in the real dynamic world in which we live, price flexibility with a constant stock of money might generate full employment only after a long period; or might even lead to a deflationary spiral of continuous unemployment. On either of these grounds, a full employment policy based on a constant stock of money and price flexibility does not seem to be very promising.

All that this means is that our full employment policy cannot be the fairly simple one of maintaining a constant stock of money and waiting for the economic system to generate full employment automatically through price declines. Other policies will be required. One possible alternative policy can be inferred from the Haberler-Pigou analysis itself: there are two ways to increase real balances. One is to keep the money stock constant and permit prices to fall. An equally effective way is to maintain the price level constant,

---

(a) $D = f(p)$ demand function

(b) $S = g(p)$ supply function

(c) $\frac{dp}{dt} = h(D-S)$ market adjusting function

The last equation has the property that

(d) $\text{sign}\ \frac{dp}{dt} = \text{sign}\ (D-S)$

i.e., price rises with excess demand and falls with excess supply. Consider now the static system identical with (a) – (c), except that it replaces (c) by

(e) $D = S$

As long as (e) is not satisfied, we see from (d) that the system will not be in stationary equilibrium, but will continue to fluctuate. Thus the existence of a solution to the static system (a), (b), (e) (*i.e.*, the consistency of (a), (b), (e)) is a *necessary* condition for the existence of a stationary solution for the dynamic system (a), (b), (c). But this is not a sufficient condition. For the static system (a), (b), (e) may have a consistent solution which, if the dynamic system is not convergent, will never be reached.

Thus Pigou has completed only half the task. Setting aside the difficulties of §8, we can accept his proof of the *consistency* of the *static* classical system. But that still leaves completely unanswered the question of whether the classical *dynamic* system will converge to this consistent solution. In this and the preceding section I have tried to show why such convergence may not occur in the real world. (I have discussed these issues in greater detail elsewhere. *Cf.* footnote 3, above.)

[31] Throughout Part III, unless otherwise indicated, "stock of money" is to be understood in the M_1 sense of the last paragraph of §6.

and increase the stock of money by creating a government deficit.[32] This method of increasing real balances has the added advantage of avoiding one of the difficulties encountered previously (§11), for a policy of stabilizing the price level by increasing money stocks avoids some of the dangers of uncertainty and adverse anticipation accompanying general price declines. Nevertheless, there still remains the other difficulty—that individuals may not be very sensitive to increases in real balances. If this turned out to be true, we would have to seek still other policies.

14. [On the basis of the analysis presented in this paper it is possible to re-examine the question which has been a favorite one of economists these past years: namely,] What is the distinctive characteristic of Keynesian analysis? It certainly cannot be the claim to have demonstrated the possibility of the coexistence of underemployment equilibrium and flexible prices. This, in its day, served well as a rallying cry. But now it should be definitely recognized that this is an indefensible position. For flexibility means that the money wage falls with excess supply, and rises with excess demand; and equilibrium means that the system can continue on through time without change. Hence, *by definition,* a system with price flexibility cannot be in equilibrium if there is any unemployment;[33] [but, like any other proposition that must be true by definition, this one, too, is uninteresting, unimportant, and uninformative about the real problems of economic policy].

[32] Considered from this perspective, the Pigou analysis presents in a rigorous fashion part of the theoretical framework implicit in the fiscal-monetary policy of the Simons-Mints position. *Cf.* the recently published collection of essays of Henry C. Simons, *Economic Policy for a Free Society* (Chicago, University of Chicago Press, 1948); and Lloyd W. Mints, "Monetary Policy," *Revue of Economic Statistics,* Vol. XXVIII (1946), pp. 60–9.

[33] This can be expressed mathematically in the following way: let N^S and N^D be the amounts of labor supplied and demanded, respectively; w, the money wage rate; and t, time. Then a flexible dynamic system will, by definition, contain an equation of the general type

$$\frac{dw}{dt} = f(N^D - N^S)$$

where

$$\text{sign}\,\frac{dw}{dt} = \text{sign}\,(N^D - N^S)\,.$$

If by equilibrium is meant a situation such that

$$\frac{dw}{dt} = 0$$

then clearly this system cannot be in equilibrium unless

$$N^D - N^S = 0$$

i.e., unless there is full employment.

Nor should Keynesian economics be interpreted as asserting that just as an underemployment equilibrium is impossible, so, too, in a static system may a full-employment equilibrium be impossible. That is, the static system may be at neither an underemployment equilibrium, nor a full-employment equilibrium. In other words, the static system may be inconsistent. (This is the negative interest rate argument of §3.) For Pigou's and Haberler's discussion of the effect of a declining price level on real balances shows how this inconsistency is removed. It is, of course, still possible to maintain this interpretation of Keynes on the basis of the reservations of §§6 and 8. But I think this is neither necessary nor advisable. For the real significance of the Keynesian contribution can be realized only within the framework of *dynamic* economics. Whether or not an underemployment equilibrium exists; whether or not full employment equilibrium always will be generated in a static system—all this is irrelevant. The fundamental issue raised by Keynesian economics is the *stability of the dynamic system:* its ability to return automatically to a full-employment equilibrium within a reasonable time (say, a year) if it is subjected to the customary shocks and disturbances of a peacetime economy. In other words, what Keynesian economics claims is that the economic system may be in a position of underemployment *dis*equilibrium (in the sense that wages, prices, and the amount of unemployment are continuously changing over time) for long, or even indefinite, periods of time.

But this is not sufficient to characterize the Keynesians. Everyone agrees that there exist dynamic systems which will not automatically generate full employment. What distinguishes one economic school from the other is the system (or systems) to which this lack of automaticity is attributed. If the Keynesian message is applied to an economic system with no monetary policy (if such a thing is possible to define), then it is purely trivial. For few would claim automaticity of full employment for such a system. Keynesian theory acquires meaning only when applied to systems with more intelligent monetary policies. Here an element of arbitrariness is introduced; for what is termed "Keynesian" depends entirely on the choice of the monetary policy to be used as a criterion.

On the basis of Keynes' writings, I believe it is clear that he was primarily interested in attacking the policy of assuring full employment by manipulation of the interest rate through open market operations.[34] But to Keynes, this policy was equivalent to one of wage flexibility;[35] for (he erroneously

[34]*Cf.* Keynes, *op. cit.*, pp. 231–34; 266–67.

[35]"There is, therefore, no ground for the belief that a flexible wage policy is capable of maintaining a state of continuous full employment;—any more than for the belief that an open market monetary policy is capable, unaided, of achieving this result. The economic system cannot be made self-adjusting along these lines." (*Ibid.*, p. 267.)

thought) the only effect of a wage decline was to increase the real value of the stock of money (in the M_0, not M_1, sense; *cf.* above, last paragraph of §6) and thereby decrease the rate of interest—just as in open market operations. As we have pointed out above (end of §§6 and 7), these policies are really not equivalent. For open market operations may change only M_0, whereas a wage and price decline change the real value of M_1 as well. Hence, open market operations may act only through the liquidity preference equation, whereas a policy of price flexibility acts also through the savings function (*cf.* above, footnote 7 and end of §§6 and 7).

Let us now assume that even if Keynes had recognized the distinction between open market and wage flexibility policies (*i.e.*, if he had recognized the Pigou effect) he still would have continued to reject the latter as a means of assuring full employment. This is not an unreasonable assumption; for most of the objections cited above (§11) against the use of a policy based on the Pigou effect, are the very same ones that Keynes uses in arguing against open market operations.[36]

Granted this assumption, I believe it is useful to identify the Keynesian position against one which maintains that full employment can be automatically achieved *via* the Pigou effect by maintaining a constant stock of money, and providing for wage and price flexibility. It is now possible to delineate three distinct theoretical formulations of the Keynesian position—differing in varying degrees from the classical one: (a) Most opposed to the classical position is the Keynesian one which states that even if there were no problem of uncertainty and adverse anticipations (that is, even if there were a static system), and even if we were to allow an infinite amount of time for adjustment, a policy of price flexibility would still not assure the generation of full employment. (This is the negative interest rate argument of §§3 and 8; [or the argument based on differential creditor-debtor responses of §6].)

(b) Then there is the position which states that, in a static world, price flexibility would always assure full employment. But in a dynamic world of uncertainty and adverse anticipations, even if we were to allow an infinite adjustment period, there is no certainty that full employment will be generated. That is, we may remain indefinitely in a position of underemployment disequilibrium. (c) Finally, there is the Keynesian position, closest to the "classics," which states that even with uncertainty full employment would eventually be generated by a policy of price flexibility; but the length of time that might be necessary for the adjustment makes the policy impractical.

Although these positions are quite distinct theoretically, their policy implications are very similar. (In what way would the policies of a man

[36] *Cf.* the passages cited in footnote 34, above.

advocating position (a) differ from those of a man advocating (c) and stating that the adjustment would take ten years?) The policies would in general be directed at influencing the consumption and investment functions themselves, in addition to manipulating the amount of money. Thus the policies may advocate tax reductions to stimulate consumption and investment (the Simons-Mints school); or may insist on direct government investment to supplement private investment (Hansen, *et al.*). In this way we could cross-classify Keynesian positions according to their advocated policies, as well as their theoretical foundations.

[Finally, it should be noted that none of the preceding three formulations of the Keynesian position is dependent upon the assumption of wage rigidities. This assumption is frequently, and erroneously, attributed to Keynesian economics as a result of two related misconceptions as to its nature. First of all, as we have seen, the attempt to interpret Keynes' analysis of unemployment within a static equilibrium framework makes it mandatory, by definition, to assume the existence of wage rigidities. The dynamic approach followed in this paper obviates this necessity.

A second implication of restricting ourselves to static equilibrium analysis is that *involuntary* unemployment can, *by definition,* exist only if there are wage rigidities. For if there were no wage rigidities, the wage level could assume any value; and for each such value there would be a corresponding, and presumably different, amount of labor supplied. Thus at the intersection point of the demand and supply curves–the only point of interest in static equilibrium analysis–workers are providing all the labor they wish to at the equilibrium wage. There can be no question of involuntary unemployment. Only if there are wage rigidities–a minimum wage w_0, below which workers refuse to go–can the situation be different. For then the supply curve of labor is parallel to the quantity axis at the height w_0 until a certain point (say) N_1, is reached; only afterwards does the curve begin to rise. If the demand curve is now assumed to intersect the supply curve in its horizontal portion at, say, the quantity N_0, then we can say that *involuntary* unemployment to the extent $N_1 - N_0$ exists; for at the equilibrium wage rate, w_0, workers desire to provide a maximum of N_1 units of labor, and are instead providing only N_0.

However, once we throw off the restrictions of static equilibrium analysis, we also free ourselves of the necessity of assuming wage rigidity as a necessary precondition of involuntary unemployment. For, during any given period of time, the dynamic workings of the system may well keep the workers at a point *off their supply curve.* In this departure from the supply curve lies the *involuntariness* of the unemployment. The important point here is that this situation can exist regardless of the shape of the supply curve; that is, even if wages are not rigid. One's view on the length of time such a situation can continue clearly depends on one's choice of the three alternative Keynesian positions delineated above. All this has been dealt with at length elsewhere,[37] and there is no need for any further repetition here.[38]]

[37] *Cf.* reference cited in footnote 3 above.

[38] It might be added that in the light of Chapter 19 of the *General Theory*–the chapter which provides the climax to Keynes' argument, and which explicitly examines the effects of wage flexibility–it is difficult to understand how wage rigidities can be considered a basic assumption of the Keynesian theory of unemployment. From this chapter it is quite clear that wage rigidities are *not* an *assumption* of Keynes' analysis, but rather a policy conclusion that follows from his investigation of the probable effects of *wage flexibility*.

Further explicit evidence that Keynes, in his theory of unemployment, was concerned with a regime of flexible prices is provided by the following passage from the *General Theory* (p. 191): "in the extreme case where money wages are assumed to fall without limit in face of involuntary unemployment . . . there will, it is true, be only two possible long period positions–full employment and the level of employment corresponding to the rate of interest at which liquidity preference becomes absolute (in the event of this being less than full employment)."

VI

Growth

In the late fifties and early sixties, probably no term was heard more often in discussions among economists in this country than "growth". The dismal growth record of the economy during 1953–60, a period marked by the two downturns of 1953–54 and 1957–58, was a subject deserving of the attention it received. It would not be correct to say that growth was the word heard least often in the late sixties, but the growth record produced over almost a decade of uninterrupted business expansion was so dramatically improved that by comparison growth hardly appeared as a problem any longer.

It may be argued that no matter how satisfactory the growth rate may be for any period, it is always desirable to raise it higher, if this can be done at an acceptably low cost. But when the growth rate is as low as it was during those years in the fifties, raising it becomes a matter of necessity, not simply desirability. The first selection in this part, by Edward F. Denison, was very relevant in 1962 and was one of a number of studies that preoccupied economists in their discussions of the then recent period of slow growth. In this article Denison submits a list of ways to increase the amount of inputs and to raise their productivity, the net result of which would be the one percentage point increase in the growth rate that is in the title of his selection. He does not refer to a more rapid rate of technological progress or technological advance as a contributor to his one percentage point increase, but something similar to this appears under the term "advance of knowledge."

Whether a writer speaks of technological progress, technological advance, advance in knowledge, or something similar, his intent is to refer to a factor long recognized as one of major importance to an economy's potential rate of growth. The second selection in this part focuses on the relationship between this factor and the growth rate. It is taken from Chapter 1 of the book, *Technology, Economic Growth, and Public Policy,* by R. R. Nelson, M. J. Peck, and E. K. Kalachek. The authors view technological advance as "an increase in knowledge relevant to economic activity" and in the first part of the chapter develop this concept in a way that helps one toward a clearer understanding of the meaning of technological advance—a term that is used with widely different meanings by various people. In the second part of the chapter the authors turn to the particular role played by technological advance in the growth process.

Neither of the first two selections of this part involves what may be called growth theory, or models of growth. Denison's examination of the factors involved in raising the growth rate and the Nelson, Peck, Kalachek discussion of the meaning of technological advance and its relation to the growth rate do not enter into such subjects as the functional relationships between the growth rate of output and the growth rates of the labor force and the capital stock or the determinants of the growth rate of these inputs, or the conditions under which the system will or will not follow an equilibrium growth path. These are all issues of growth theory—an area to which the third and fourth selections in this part provide some coverage.

The third selection, Evsey D. Domar's 1947 article, is one of a number of writings by Domar that, together with the contributions of Roy F. Harrod, are the basis for what is known as the Harrod-Domar growth model or theory, the approach that dominated the growth theory area in the early post-Keynesian period. Among the several branches along which growth theory, has developed in more recent years, the neoclassical has been the one most discussed. A basic difference between this branch and Harrod-Domar is found in the assumption made by each with respect to factor proportions. Harrod-Domar assumes a single production process that imposes a fixed ratio between capital and labor, while the neoclassical theory assumes an unlimited number of production processes, merging into one another in a way that permits any combination of labor and capital to be employed in the production process. This difference makes for two quite different theories, as will be evident from a study of the Domar selection and this part's final selection on neoclassical theory by Harry G. Johnson.

19

HOW TO RAISE THE HIGH-EMPLOYMENT GROWTH RATE BY ONE PERCENTAGE POINT

EDWARD F. DENISON

My assignment is to devise a package of proposals that can raise the growth rate over the next twenty years by one percentage point. The package was put together for this session, but my estimate of the contribution each ingredient of the package would make to growth rests upon a study which is about to be published by the Committee for Economic Development.

I was asked to talk about ways of altering the growth of the economy's productive potential, when success in maintaining fairly full utilization of labor and other resources is assumed. We must also find ways to validate the high-employment assumption, but that is outside the present discussion.

Next, I shall be concerned with ways to raise the growth rate of real national income or product as defined and measured by the Department of Commerce. Certain characteristics of these output measures somewhat limit the ways available to raise their growth rate. They preclude raising the growth rate by shifting resources so as to produce things that are more urgently wanted; for example, by eliminating distortions in the pattern of output introduced by excise taxes, monopoly or farm programs. Again, the treatment of quality change in the price indexes bars raising the future high-employment growth rate of measured output by developing new or better final products more rapidly.

I omit from my discussion steps that would increase the satisfactions derived from output without changing its amount as measured. However, I shall not consider shifts of resources that would increase measured output

Reprinted from the *American Economic Review, Proceedings,* (May 1962), pp. 67–75, by permission of the author and the publisher. Edward F. Denison is an economist with the Brookings Institution.

while leaving unchanged or reducing a "truer" output measure. Real national income or product may be thought of as an index with certain biases that may be fairly uniform over time so long as steps are not taken deliberately to "rig" the index.

The specific series I shall use to measure economic growth is the index of real national income, which is the same thing as the index of real net national product except that components are weighted by factor cost rather than market price. It is *net* income or product, not GNP, that economic policy properly seeks to maximize. Factor cost valuation is more appropriate and convenient than market price valuation for examination of changes in productivity or inputs. However, the conclusions I shall reach would be little changed if reference were to net or even gross national product.

Next, the assigned topic concerns means of changing the growth rate over a twenty-year period. This is a reasonable period to consider, but it should be understood that the length of the period greatly affects my results. Because most ways of changing output, and hence affecting the growth rate, are in the one-shot category, it is easier to raise the growth rate by a given amount for twenty years than for a hundred. Suppose, for example, some obstacle to efficient production costs us 1 per cent of the national income. If the obstacle were eliminated, which could be done only once, the level of national income thereafter would be 1 per cent higher than if the obstacle remained. The effect on the growth rate is approximately 1 per cent divided by the number of years over which the growth rate is computed. Thus elimination of the obstacle would raise the growth rate computed over a twenty-year period by one-twentieth of a percentage point, and the growth rate computed over a hundred-year period by one-hundredth of a percentage point. Some measures, on the other hand, would not have their maximum effect in a period as short as twenty years. Provision of additional education to the young and an increase in the saving rate are examples.

I shall use 1960 to 1980 as my twenty-year period, as if it were now 1960, because the calculations I draw on were based on those twenty years. But nothing would be changed materially by substituting 1961 to 1981, or 1962 to 1982.

Next, this paper is not directed to the question of how we can raise the growth rate from what it was in the past. The question posed for this session by Edward Mason is how the growth rate can be raised by one percentage point from "whatever the speaker thinks it will be" if unemployment is low, and in other respects we continue existing policies. I project a 1960–80 growth rate of 3⅓ per cent in potential national income, starting from a 1960 high-employment level. The amount by which this projected rate exceeds the actual rate in the past is not part of the one percentage point increment my prescription must provide. My task is to indicate how to raise the high-employment growth rate from 3⅓ per cent to 4⅓ per cent. Let me also stress that the topic is not whether 3⅓ percent is a correct projection given existing policies, but how the rate can be raised one percentage point from whatever it would be if we do nothing special to affect it.

So much for ground rules. Now for some general observations. First, the difference between a 3⅓ per cent rate and a 4⅓ per cent rate is big. One implies an increase in per capita income from 1960 to 1980 of 33 per cent, the other of 61 per cent. Thus, a prescription to raise the growth rate of total income by one percentage point must be powerful enough to nearly double the anticipated increase in per capita real income. This conclusion must be modified insofar as the growth rate is to be stimulated by more immigration.

Second, I can hardly stress enough that, as I use the term, economic growth refers only to output. Quite aside from defects in measures of output, aggregate output is anything but a complete measure of economic welfare or economic progress, even less of total welfare or progress. To talk about changing even economic welfare, we would have also to consider, at the very least, real costs of production and the distribution of income and output.

In the present context this is no small caveat. It is the heart of the matter. The output we get, aside from involuntary underuse of resources, is determined by individual and collective decisions as to what is or is not worth doing.

I stress that to accelerate growth requires that someone act differently than he would otherwise, that this action usually means higher costs as well as higher output, and that more output is never the only effect of any action we might take. To decide whether steps to accelerate growth are sensible requires comparison of costs, the size of the effect on growth, and side effects.

This leads to the first of two conditions I deem essential for any program to stimulate growth a great deal beyond what it will be if we have no such objective. It is that the public be persuaded that acceleration of growth must be made an overriding national goal. Moreover, it must probably be persuaded of this for reasons other than the increase in individual welfare—probably reasons related to the external situation facing the country. This is necessary because there is a presumption that the more important steps required impose costs that exceed the income benefits and thus reduce welfare. Otherwise they presumably would be taken anyway. Even where the benefits may exceed the costs for the country as a whole, we are usually dealing with some deep-seated condition, often of long standing, that is likely to be changed only for some new and overpowering reason.

The presumption that the costs of a proposed change exceed the benefits may be refuted in specific instances. We need not suppose that we now act rationally on the basis of full information in reaching all of our individual and collective decisions, so we need not assume that every step that would increase growth would reduce individual welfare. In putting together my own package of proposals, I try to stress those where I think the possibility is greatest—I do not mean that it is necessarily great—that present practices derive from ignorance and would be changed by greater knowledge and understanding. This may imply a certain arrogance on my part, but without some such approach this paper could not be written.

The second condition necessary for any large effort to stimulate growth is full utilization of resources. It will hardly be possible to obtain support for a broad program to increase our productive potential unless we use rather fully the potential that we do have. Indeed, if unemployment is persistently high, we can look forward to actions that will reduce growth, including greater public and private restrictions on efficient production, and reduction of hours intended to spread employment rather than to increase leisure.

To add one percentage point to the growth rate I shall suggest a thirteen-part program that seems to me to combine feasibility, in the sense of avoiding things no one knows how to do, with minimization of sacrifice. The expected contribution from each proposal to the growth rate over twenty years will be stated in hundredths of a percentage point. Thus we need means of adding 100 hundredths of a percentage point to the growth rate.

Let me now indicate the general approach I use to assess the effect of each proposal on the growth rate. To raise the growth rate over twenty years by one hundreth of a percentage point requires some action not now in prospect that would make the 1980 national income .2 per cent, or nearly 2 billion dollars, larger than it would be in the absence of that action. The action must serve either to increase the quantity or quality of labor, land, or capital going into the productive system, or else to increase their productivity.

Because of the presence of economies of scale, an increment of slightly less than .2 per cent to total factor input in 1980 would probably suffice to raise the 1980 national income .2 per cent. I assume the addition to output would exceed that in total input by one-eleventh. Hence an increase in total input of slightly over .18 per cent would raise output by .2 per cent. This could, in principle, be accomplished by increasing all kinds of input by .18 per cent or only one kind of input by a larger percentage. From national income data I estimate that labor comprises 77 per cent of total input, capital 20 per cent, and land 3 per cent. Hence we could raise total input by slightly over .18 per cent in 1980 if we could raise labor input alone by .24 per cent over what it would otherwise be, or capital input alone by .93 per cent, or land input alone by 6.10 per cent. My proposals would not change the ratio of capital to labor input very much, so the problem of diminishing returns is not acute.

I shall first suggest some ways to increase inputs, indicating the contribution expected from each and sketching the basis of the estimate, and then turn to ways of raising productivity.

1. Yearly net immigration currently equals .2 per cent of our population. As recently as 1911–15 it averaged .6 per cent. Immigration could be increased simply by changing the law. I assume the additional immigrants would make a per capita contribution of labor two-thirds as large, after adjustment for quality differences, as does the existing population. On this assumption, doubling the present immigration rate would raise labor input in 1980 by about 2½ per cent, enough to add .10 to the growth rate of national income. Extra immigration probably would not lower the per capita income of the existing population, but it would impose some other costs. It would also benefit our international relations. More immigration seems to me among the most sensible means of stimulating growth.

2. By working three hours a week, or about 8½ per cent, longer than we otherwise would in 1980, we could add .28 to the growth rate.

My projection of a 3⅓ per cent growth rate assumed that normal annual working hours will drop the equivalent of four hours a week from 1960 to 1980. This is about the rate at which they dropped during the fifties and much less than they dropped during the thirties and forties. Had I assumed a drop of only one hour instead of four, my projected growth rate would have been .28 higher. The calculation that we could add .28 to the growth rate by working three hours a week longer assumes that, in the range within which we will then be operating, more than three-fourths of the impact of shorter hours falls on output rather than being offset in labor efficiency. A decline of only one hour a week in twenty years would allow some leveling down where hours are especially long and some additional holidays, vacations, or coffee breaks, but no change in the standard forty-hour week.

Longer hours are in my list partly because it would be hard to obtain the desired total effect on the growth rate without them. But it is at least possible that we tend to arrive at a level of hours too short to maximize welfare. I say this partly because so little is known about the amount of income that actually is sacrificed for more leisure, and partly because hours have sometimes been shortened in order to spread employment.

Acceptance of this proposal requires employment opportunities so abundant that work spreading disappears as a reason for shortening standard hours, no reduction in legal standards for hours, and probably general acceptance by labor and employers of the need to maintain present hours. Since the AFL-CIO has already established the thirty-five hour week as an objective, this means a change in the present policy of labor.

3. I call upon additional education to raise the quality of labor enough to add .07 to the growth rate. I estimate that this requires addition of one year to the average amount of schooling that would otherwise be received by everyone leaving school between now and 1980. This estimate is derived from existing income differentials among groups with different amounts of

education, and the assumption that three-fifths of these differentials result from more education rather than reflect associated variables such as natural ability. It allows for the loss of work by those who will be in school in 1980 rather than working, on the assumption that if they were working their labor would be of half the average quality. Provision of the extra schooling would absorb .3 or .4 per cent of the national income.

My national income projection already assumes a considerable increase from the present age at which young people leave school. This trend can be confidently anticipated. To add still another year, without adversely affecting the quality of education, would place great strain on educational resources and require a major effort to secure teachers and facilities. Noneconomic benefits of extra schooling seem to me large, and this is another case where we might do more than we will be doing if the public had complete information on which to base decisions.

4. I estimate that we could add .03 to the twenty-year growth rate if we could cut in half structural unemployment and underemployment that results from long-term declines in labor requirements in individual areas and industries, including agriculture.

To contribute to growth in any real sense this must be done by speeding re-employment in expanding industries and areas, not by curtailing the displacement of workers that results from demand shifts or technological progress. If we have a bouyant economy in which unfilled jobs at least match the number unemployed, there ought to be ways to cut these types of structural unemployment in half. Swedish experience can be drawn upon in devising means.

5. I look to increased capital input for a contribution of .20 to the growth rate. This requires capital input in 1980 to be 19 per cent larger than it would be otherwise. Whereas my projection assumes a 64 per cent increase in capital input from 1960 to 1980, capital input must nearly double in the same period to provide this additional contribution to growth.

I look for this to be made possible by the other measures proposed to raise growth. I assume here that the crucial difficulty in accelerating growth by increasing the rate of capital formation concerns the possibility of providing attractive investment opportunities rather than of changing saving propensities. Hopefully, the other means of accelerating growth that I am suggesting would bring about the required broadening of investment opportunities. The capital-output ratio will be the same in 1980 if real national income increases 4⅓ per cent a year and capital input doubles or if national income increases 3⅓ per cent a year and capital input increases 64 per cent.

To raise capital formation this much requires a higher fraction of national income to be saved during the next twenty years, even though income would itself be larger with a higher growth rate. Hence it would require the sacrifice of consumption that could otherwise be made. If net private saving proves inadequate for so high a rate of net investment, as it may, additional saving could be provided by a surplus in the federal budget.

These five ways of increasing labor and capital input would provide 68 of the required 100 hundredths of a point in the growth rate. For the remaining 32 hundredths, I turn to ways of increasing output per unit of input.

6. From estimates by Gary S. Becker, it can be inferred that employment discrimination against Negroes, taking their qualifications as given, costs us .8 per cent of the national income. If discrimination could be abolished within twenty years by a concerted national effort, this would add .04 to the growth rate. To the extent that progress will be made anyway the economic costs of discrimination twenty years hence will be less than now, and the opportunity for further growth stimulation is overstated.

7. For nearly two centuries most economists have held that restrictions on international trade reduce output and living standards while most of the public has believed the exact opposite to be true. The economists are right, but I am not sure how they can become more persuasive in the future than in the past. The cost to us of misallocation of resources resulting from barriers to international trade is not easy to estimate, but I have put it at about 1½ per cent of the national income. My projection assumes this percentage will not change. A serious program to stimulate growth would sweep away all barriers to imports and use our willingness to do so as leverage to get foreign nations to eliminate barriers to our exports. If we could eliminate all barriers far enough in advance of our twenty-year deadline to allow basic readjustments in production and trading patterns to be made throughout the world, this would add .07 to the growth rate.

8. Resale price maintenance laws result in the use of more resources in trade than are required to perform the function. Their cost is very hard to estimate, but I believe it to be large. If, as I have guessed, fair trade costs us 1 per cent of the national income, repeal of fair-trade laws could add .05 to the growth rate.

9. Formal obstacles imposed by labor unions in some industries against the most efficient use of resources costs us output, although again it is very difficult to say how much. My guess is that the cost here might also be 1 per cent of the national income. It seems to me possible that a determined program to adopt better ways of meeting labor's needs might cut this cost in half. This would add .02 to the growth rate.

10. The effectiveness of labor incentives is important to productivity. Close correspondence between each employee's individual contribution to production and his individual reward, and employee awareness of the correspondence, are crucial. Shifts from time rates to piecework have sometimes been

accompanied by large increases in productivity. Greater use of incentive pay systems where they are or can be made feasible is the obvious way to obtain substantial improvement. Better evaluation of individual performance for use in setting pay differentials among salaried employees and others paid by time, and in promotion, and more honest letters of recommendation, would be helpful. Certain changes in the tax laws might also help. It strikes me as possible that an intensive effort to improve incentives along these lines could contribute .05 to the growth rate. This could be done, for example, if efficiency of one-tenth of the work force could be raised 11 per cent.

11. We could add to output by permitting consolidation in the regulated industries where this would mean greater efficiency. If claims that as many as 200,000 employees could be eliminated by railroad consolidation are correct and some minor economies are possible in other regulated industries, consolidation could add about .02 to the growth rate.

12. We could increase output by shortening the lag of average business practice behind the best known. My projection assumes that knowledge will be advancing fast enough to contribute .8 percentage points to the growth rate of real product, as measured, in the next twenty years. This exceeds my estimate of its rate of advance in the past. If we could shorten the lag of average practice behind the best known by nine months, which I consider a large reduction for the whole economy, output in 1980 would therefore be .6 per cent larger than otherwise and the twenty-year growth rate .03 higher. My projection of national product already assumes a reduction of nine months in the lag; thus I am calling for an additional nine-months reduction.

Sweeping away all barriers to international trade, aside from the benefits previously taken into account, would put pressure for modernization upon protected industries that are not now highly competitive, and some of the other steps I have suggested would be slightly helpful in this respect. For the rest, we should have to look to better means of disseminating information and alertness in adopting it. I may note in passing that there is nothing to be added on this account to the contribution of additional investment to growth that I have already computed.

13. For the final .04 required to reach my goal of a full point in the growth rate I look to the advance of knowledge itself. This requires that the state of knowledge in 1980 be where it would otherwise be in 1981. I would be uncomfortable in looking for a large contribution because we know too little about how to alter the rate at which knowledge relevant to production advances to feel sure we know how to get much more out of this source of growth. There is little evidence that the big postwar increase in research and development expenditures has had much effect on the rate of increase in measured productivity. Moreover, present prospects are that we shall absorb into research and development all the qualified personnel that will be

available and be expanding these human resources as fast as is likely to be fruitful. But something can probably be done about the distribution of effort. There is extreme concentration of research expenditures in a few product lines and industries. In 1956, industries accounting for only 31 per cent of the national income made 96 per cent of research and development expenditures. Moreover, most of the effort, by far, is devoted to development of new and better products rather than cost reduction. It seems likely that greater dispersion of research effort might get us ahead faster, and it is to steps to bring this about that I would look for the additional contribution to growth.

I suspect there are important possibilities of raising productivity in research. But in the absence of agreement even on whether we should move toward more or less organization and planning of research, I cannot very well recommend what should be done that would not otherwise be done.

This completes my prescription for raising the growth rate by one percentage point. The contributions to be obtained from the individual elements obviously are crude estimates, but with any luck overestimates will be offset by underestimates and the package should achieve the assigned target.

Many alternative packages of proposals could be put together to arrive at the same effect on the growth rate. The study from which this list is drawn tries to provide a rather complete menu of the choices available to stimulate growth. From that list anyone can make his own combination. This particular package is fairly concrete and practical in the sense that the principal steps required do not exceed our knowledge. I have tried to put together as attractive a package as I could. In my view it would not impose intolerable burdens. But this does not mean I am advocating it or think the country would necessarily be better off for adopting it. This depends mainly on a judgment as to how important it is to raise the rate at which output grows, and why.

20

TECHNOLOGICAL ADVANCE AND GROWTH OF POTENTIAL OUTPUT

RICHARD R. NELSON, MERTON J. PECK,
and EDWARD K. KALACHEK

Most contemporary analyses of economic growth focus on the relationship between output and inputs of various factors of production. Technological advance is treated as one factor shifting that functional relationship so as to increase productivity. Several recent studies have attempted to relate technological advances to research and development expenditures.[1] This approach, however, has the disadvantage of treating technological change implicitly. An effect is measured–an increase in the productivity of inputs. A possible cause is examined–R&D expenditure. But technological advance itself, which would seem to demand definition in terms of an increase in knowledge relevant to economic activity, is not treated explicitly.

Instead of emphasizing inputs and treating technological knowledge as a key factor determining their productivity, the authors have focused on technological knowledge with physical inputs as determinants of the extent to which knowledge is applied.

In a strict formal sense, it makes no difference whether an analysis of the determinants of output centers on technology or on physical inputs. In the

[1] Edwin Mansfield, "Rates of Return from Industrial Research and Development," *American Economic Review,* Vol.55, No. 2 (May 1965) and Zvi Griliches, "Research Expenditures, Education, and the Aggregate Agricultural Production Function," *American Economic Review,* Vol. 54 (December 1964), pp. 961–74.

Reprinted from Richard R. Nelson, Merton J. Peck, and Edward K. Kalachek, *Technology, Economic Growth, and Public Policy* (The Brookings Institution, 1967), pp. 7–21, by permission of the publisher. Richard R. Nelson and Merton J. Peck are professors at Yale University, and Edward K. Kalachek is a professor at Washington University (St. Louis, Missouri).

broader context of growth theory, the set of simultaneous equations is the same, although they are ordered and expressed somewhat differently. The restructuring is a matter of convenience, permitting a sharper focus on the principal topic of this book. The different focus, however, brings out more clearly the critical role of technological advance in economic growth.

KNOWLEDGE AND POTENTIAL OUTPUT

Knowledge is a protean concept. Although there have been many attempts to define and classify it, whenever a specific case of any complexity is examined the definitions and classifications do not quite apply. This is a problem that plagues any discussion of the general concept of knowledge.

The following discussion will be limited to technological knowledge which pertains predominantly to the production of goods and services in organized economic activity. The operational part of the body of technological knowledge is a set of techniques, each defined as a set of actions and decision rules guiding their sequential application that man has learned will generally lead to a predictable (and sometimes desirable) outcome under certain specified circumstances.[2]

The Stock of Technological Knowledge

The stock of known technique for achieving practical results is only part of the richer and deeper body of human knowledge which includes, as well, a comprehension of the properties of things under various conditions, relationships among and between objects and properties, and broad frameworks of interpretation. Much of this rich general background of understanding is called science, but part of it cannot be dignified by that term. Rather it simply is the result of experience and its rather straightforward generalization.[3]

In many cases technique can be derived from the general body of understanding. Thus, building and use of a ramp to extricate a car from a ditch is a technique. A person may be able to figure out how to build an

[2]Some technique, like that of turning the doorknob to open a door, is almost completely unintellectual and can only be dignified by the term knowledge because it is learned and can be taught—key attributes of anyone's definition of knowledge.

The stock of human techniques comprises a vast and heterogeneous lot. While almost all of it is applied in the production of economic goods and services—like the technique of opening doors, or of writing with a pencil—most of it is not what people have in mind when they discuss technology and technological advance in the process of economic growth.

[3]This treatment of the distinction between understanding and technique has much in common with the distinction between science and technology made by James B. Conant in his *Science and Common Sense* (New Haven: Yale University Press, 1951).

adequate ramp and use it properly from knowledge of the weight of a car, the strength of wood, and his grasp of the simple physics of inclined planes, even if he had no prior experience with or knowledge of ramps per se. A technique that can be derived in fine detail from more basic understanding can be called perfectly understood. Few techniques are perfectly understood in this sense. Generally there are at least a few fine points which go beyond understanding, and these significantly influence effectiveness. Indeed, in some cases understanding may even fall short of the rough outlines of known effective technique; the technique is almost completely empirical.[4] It is known through experience that something works in a predictable way, but it is not known why.[5]

The fact that technique can often be largely or partially derived from the more general body of human knowledge crucially affects the way many new techniques get discovered or invented, and has important implications for the way people learn to master known techniques. But while technique blends into the rest of human knowledge, it is a body of knowledge in its own right.

In theory any technique can be described by and communicated as a set of instructions—as a cookbook recipe or a computer program[6]—whether or not the technology is understood in terms of more fundamental knowledge.

Technology is the operational part of a production function. If used with the inputs it specifies, the result will be an output of specified characteristics.[7] Generally a technique or technology is not completely describable by a unique routine; usually there are options in the program. These options permit some choice of inputs and input proportions (a recipe may work with either whole or powdered eggs) and some flexibility with respect to operations (the eggs may be added before or after the sugar). The operations may be performed in different ways; for example, different degrees of mechaniza-

[4]For many years this was so for many chemical processes: thus iron was reduced from ore years before anyone really understood oxidation and reduction. For a general discussion see Rupert Hall, "The Scholar and the Craftsman in the Scientific Revolution," in M. Clagett (ed.), *Critical Problems in the History of Science* (Madison: University of Wisconsin Press, 1959).

[5]In terms of decision theory the distinction made is between knowledge required to structure the choice problem and knowledge of a good strategy. While good strategies often can be derived from logical manipulation of the general problem formulation, this is often hard to do. Further, good strategy may sometimes be discovered by trial and error.

[6]For a more general discussion of the use of the concept of a computer program to model human activity see H. A. Simon and Allen Newell, "The Simulation of Human Thought" (Santa Monica: The RAND Corporation, P-1734, June 1959).

[7]In the main line of economic theory the concept of a technology and the concept of a production function tend to be used synonomously; thus Tjalling Koopmans defines technology as the vector of inputs and outputs resulting from use of an activity at a unit level. See his "Analysis of Production as an Efficient Combination of Activities," in Tjalling Koopmans (ed.), *Activity Analysis of Production and Allocation* (New York: John Wiley and Sons, 1951). What is suggested here is that a vector of inputs, *plus* a vector of actions or operations, leads to an output. The vector of operations can be defined as the technology used in the production function which creates the output from the inputs.

tion may be employed (the mix may be beaten with a spoon, a hand beater, or an electric beater). Some variation in output specification may be possible (such as the shape of the cake or the kind of frosting).[8] These variations in processes or output determine the degree to which economic efficiency can be maintained in the face of varying circumstances (such as changing supplies of different primary inputs and of labor and machinery, and changing demand for different product variants).

The flexibility built into a technology also provides scope for errors without catastrophic results. (A recipe may produce a roughly adequate product if the cook puts in a little more, or a little less milk than is called for, although the cake may not have as good a texture, and if more milk is added than is optimal, there will be needless expense.) Thus a relative novice sometimes can operate the technology, but not as well as an expert, and his grasp of the technology may include only a small subset of the possible variations.

At any given time the stock of known technique defines the set of products which may be produced, and the known broad processes (and the range of variation within these processes) for making them.

The Embodiment of Technological Knowledge in the Labor Force

The use of technological knowledge in economic activity requires a labor force in whom that knowledge is embodied through education, training and experience. There is no unique relationship between the technologies used by a society and the specific pattern of labor force embodiment. Rather there are a wide range of alternatives, both for dividing up the knowledge requirements among the labor force, and for imparting that knowledge.

On the requirements side, the technology used in a particular activity is broken down into a set of subtechniques, plus a hierarchal set of coordinating programs. Correspondingly, activities are decomposed into a set of sub-activities which can be conducted largely independently, plus a set of management functions. Furthermore, for each of the sub-activities it is often possible to build a portion of the operations and their control into machines, making a further division of knowledge, between machine builders and machine operators. Thus to run an activity effectively it is not necessary that every, or even any, person know the full technology. Rather the operation of a technology is essentially a team or group problem.[9]

[8]The lines between variability within a technology and different technologies are blurred, but appear meaningful.

[9]The embodiment of technological knowledge in the minds of men has been stressed by Theodore Schultz, particularly in his *Transforming Traditional Agriculture* (New Haven: Yale University Press, 1964). Robert Solow, in contrast, has stressed the embodiment of technology in machinery in his "Investment and Technical Progress," in *Mathematical Methods in the Social Sciences, 1959* (Stanford: Stanford University Press, 1960). Of course, knowledge must be in the minds of men before it is in the design of machines.

Such a decomposition of activities into sub-activities permits a vast reduction in the amount any person must know in order to be an effective worker. All a single worker needs is the technique relevant to his job.

On the impartation side, there are a range of possible systems by which technology can be embodied in the labor force. It would be possible, of course, to have a specific self-contained training program for each job. However, if activities are appropriately divided, many jobs in different activities will have a great deal in common. A system of knowledge embodiment has been designed to capitalize on these common elements.

The techniques relevant to most jobs have a large common set of elemental building blocks. It greatly simplifies the teaching and learning of techniques if these more primitive elements are already learned—if a cake recipe can simply state "pour in a cup of milk" and not explain what milk is or describe how to measure and pour. General education imparts these general purpose skills, relations, data, and language.

In addition to these elemental building blocks, there are certain sets of higher order techniques and categories of general knowledge which are useful in mastering certain complex jobs common to a wide range of activities. Technique and knowledge tend to become associated with occupations and professions, and their impartation institutionalized in occupational and professional training.

Skillful decomposition of activities, and an education and occupational training system well tuned to the pattern of decomposition, permit a great reduction in the amount of knowledge that must be specific to any particular activity.[10] However, almost every job will have a few nuances, and most activities will require at least a few people with a considerable amount of specialized knowledge. This may be the case for certain operating jobs; thus a machinist involved in producing aircraft engines must have his general training as machinist, supplemented by special knowledge and instructions relevant to the parts of an aircraft engine with which he is concerned. And it almost always is true that the higher order coordinating programs are quite specialized; to manage the machinery operation of engine production requires considerable knowledge about aircraft engines in general, as well as the specific aircraft engine, beyond that which a production engineer or manager learns in his general professional training.

Therefore general and vocational education must be supplemented by

[10]Mary Jean Bowman, in several essays in C. A. Anderson and M. J. Bowman (eds.), *Education and Economic Development* (Chicago: Aldine Publishing Company, 1965), has presented a model of the education system and the returns to education very similar to the one presented here.

specific job training.[11] A considerable part of this training, like more general education and training, is formal. But in many cases the special knowledge required to operate a technique effectively cannot be taught fully in a formal training program. Often formal training and education provides enough knowledge to enable a person to perform the job or manage the operation crudely, but not enough to achieve the highest quality or the lowest cost. Formal training and education must be complemented by experience–the self-training and education that comes from doing.[12]

To acquire knowledge relevant to a specific technique, a considerable amount of redundant knowledge is picked up which may not pay off on a particular job. It may, however, facilitate the understanding and mastery of new jobs and techniques. Redundant knowledge pays off in terms of flexibility.[13]

Determinants of Potential Output

For a technology to be applied to economic activity, three things are needed: workers possessing the relevant knowledge; organization capable of effectively putting this knowledge into action; the required material inputs.

Economic activities differ intrinsically in their complexity. However, the fact that a technology is complex does not necessarily mean that a considerable amount of specialized training and experience is required of the work force. This depends largely on the nature of the sub-jobs into which the activity is decomposed. Jobs can require considerable specialized knowledge, or they can be automated or otherwise structured so as to demand only the kinds of knowledge imparted in general and occupational education pro-

[11] George R. Hall and Robert E. Johnson of the Rand Corporation make a related distinction–between general knowledge and activity specific knowledge–in their "Aircraft-Co Production and U. S. Procurement Policy." Unpublished manuscript.

[12] The relationship between what has already been learned in general and occupational education, and what remains to be learned in job specific training, has been discussed and analyzed by Gary S. Becker in *Human Capital,* National Bureau of Economic Research (New York: Columbia University Press, 1964).

[13] The other side of the coin is that knowledge specific to any job generally is picked up in pieces. Consider the self-education and training that a person would have to experience to build a television set. If this were his first attempt he would be likely to make some mistakes, but he would probably be able to muddle through, following published instructions. However, if he did not know how to solder a connection, for example, he would have to consult another source. If he did not know how to read and understand diagrams or understand the symbols describing the various components, he would have to study a more general electronics handbook, which in turn might well require that he know at least high school algebra. Further, he might find a knowledge of elementary physics essential to the instructions and certainly helpful in enabling him to decide how closely he must follow the details.

grams.[14] When much specialized knowledge is required to perform a job satisfactorily, special training and experience may be the key to work force competence. However, when a technology is automated or reduced to a set of sub-techniques matched to existing professional and occupational training, or when a technology is so new that specialized experience is scarce and special training programs have not been worked out, but is at least partially understandable within existing professional knowledge, the strength of the overall education system may be far more important in determining the supply of competent labor.

The effective operation of a technology also requires competent organization. If the activity involves a considerable division of labor and expertise, it may be no trivial matter to coordinate and organize the work. A decision making and control mechanism generally must be tailored to that particular technology.

Effective organization requires more than managerial knowledge, since the requirements for coordinating are beyond the scope of any one activity and the control of any particular manager. There must be effective links to organizations that provide the necessary equipment and other inputs, as well as links to customers. These links involve technical assistance (reflecting the division of knowledge) and the flow of physical products. The effectiveness of this wider organization depends in large part upon the laws and institutions that determine the kinds of communication, incentives, and constraints which can be used to inform or influence people and other organizations.

Finally, the material inputs must be available. If basic raw materials are ignored the availability of the necessary inputs—machinery, components, and materials—depends ultimately on whether organization and knowledge can be acquired to produce them. The rapid recovery of Germany and Japan from the damage to their physical capital inflicted during World War II, and the inability of many of today's underdeveloped economies to use equipment effectively, provide dramatic evidence of the primacy of technological knowledge and the organizational capabilities to bring this knowledge to fruition. These are the key factors determining the long run productive potential of an economy.[15] Considerable time and resources may be needed to produce machinery and equipment in sizeable quantities, however. In the short run, the existing stock of physical plant and equipment obviously is an important factor in determining the extent to which a technology can be applied.

[14]Alternative decompositions are the points along an isoquant of different possible sets of actions, and different possible mixes of required labor training.

[15]See K. C. Yeh's discussion of this point for Chinese industrialization in his "Soviet and Communist Chinese Industrialization Strategies" (Santa Monica: The RAND Corporation, P-3150, May 1965).

There are four principal constraints, then, to the kinds and quantities of goods that an economy can produce per worker:

(1) The stock of technological knowledge, which limits the kinds of products man knows how to produce, and the various processes he knows for producing them.

(2) The education, training, and experience of the work force, which determines the extent to which this knowledge is embodied in people.

(3) The organization of firms and of the economy as a whole, which determines the effectiveness with which this knowledge can be used.

(4) The stock of physical capital and the availability of natural resources.[16]

Within these limits—and given time to permit human and material resources to be reallocated—there is a considerable range for private and public choice concerning what and how much can be produced. Society can choose how much of its productive potential it will allocate to meet defense needs, produce automobiles, produce food, build hospitals, houses or roads, add to blast furnace capacity, teach children, or undertake research and development. Society has a choice between more production and more leisure. If voluntary leisure is considered a good, then potential output can be described by the outer boundary of the set of output possibilities open to a society over a period of time.[17]

DYNAMICS OF GROWTH

Economic growth is the shifting outward of this frontier of possibilities. Growth may occur fortuitously. A new and rich source of oil may be discovered accidentally, for example, but this happens only occasionally. Sometimes growth results from improved economic organization, but in a reasonably well organized economy the opportunities through this route are limited. The principal source of growth is investment—the employment of resources in building plants and equipment, roads and dams, and other physical capital; in providing training and education; in research and development, and in other activities which advance technology.

[16]This list of factors resembles most conventional analyses of growth process. See for example *The Annual Report of the Council of Economic Advisors,* January 1962 (Washington: Government Printing Office, 1962).

[17]Potential output has been defined as the possibilities open over a period of time, not at a specific moment. Along the production possibility frontier, choices of output composition reflect various choices in the allocation of resources. Time and often the utilization of resources are required to effect a change in allocation. Another way of defining the potential output frontier is in terms of the alternative output combinations the economy can be producing at some specific time in the future. In either case, the production possibility concept inherently involves future adjustments and reallocations over a period of time, not different allocations of resources at any one moment.

Catalytic Role of Technological Advance

Any analysis of economic growth must identify the functional relationships between growth of potential output and the quantities of different forms of investment, and discover how the magnitude and kind of investment are determined. The problem is made especially difficult because of the complexity of interaction among the many variables.[18]

The contribution of additional capital equipment and education, for instance, is strongly dependent upon the rate at which technological knowledge is advancing. At a constant level of technological knowledge, output per worker can be increased through more equipment, or through better training, but only to a certain extent. Equipping a worker with an even bigger shovel will be pointless. Giving him more training in the use of a shovel will yield little return, for there will be little left to learn. The rate at which returns diminish can be retarded by switching to known techniques that were unprofitable when capital was scarcer or the worker less educated, such as using a bulldozer. But in the absence of new technological knowledge, sooner or later these possibilities would be exhausted. As returns to additional capital and education declined, not only would their contribution to further expansion diminish; their rate of expansion probably would decline as well.[19]

With technological knowledge improving over time, new and more productive techniques will become available (for example, a radically new ditch digging machine). New physical capital will be needed to apply the new technology. Further, technological advance probably will permit growing quantities of capital per laborer to be compatible with high rates of return on capital. Thus, the growth of physical capital can proceed with high returns.

The contribution of and the returns to educated people also will be enhanced. With technology changing, the advantage to workers (and their employers) of an education beyond that which is needed for a particular job will be significantly greater. This is so not because the new technology is inherently more complex than the old, but because it is different. Consequently, there is a premium on the ability to learn new techniques rapidly and, sometimes, to work with those as yet unroutinized. The demand for well educated workers reflects the fact that they are relatively easy to train for a variety of jobs, and thus are particularly valuable when the composition of jobs changes. The assignment of a highly paid chemical engineer to a

[18]An earlier discussion of these interactions is contained in Richard R. Nelson's "Aggregate Production Functions and Medium-Range Growth Projections," *American Economic Review*, Vol. 54 (September 1964).

[19]It is assumed that the interest rate and the relative wages of educated workers tend to fall as capital and education become more plentiful.

production job during the installation of a new chemical process is made because the process is not routinized sufficiently to permit rapid training of workers without the relevant background understanding.

The effect is not just on the production work force. Technological advance changes the whole pattern of information that must flow between economic units. High remuneration of technically trained sales people in the electronics industry, for example, relates to their ability to communicate new developments to the potential market. Returns to trained management reflects their ability to assess new alternatives and to deal expertly and imaginatively with the problems created by new techniques. The economic advantage of education here extends far beyond the imparting of specific skills to deal with specific problems. It lies in the added flexibility to learn new things and understand new kinds of opportunities and problems that some types of education impart, and which rapid technical change make important.[20]

Rapid technological advance not only enhances the contribution of physical capital and education, but also spurs their expansion.

The interactions also exist in the other direction. If current technical advance creates high levels of demand for educated personnel, current investment in education affects the future cost of generating and diffusing technical change. The rate of advance of technical understanding in recent years has probably been closely related to the number of educated personnel engaged in R&D. And the speed of the diffusion process depends on the availability of people capable of evaluating and perceiving potential markets, communicating technical information, and dealing with the problems which invariably arise in the early stages of production before techniques become routinized.

While the development of new products and processes stimulates investment booms and permits capital-labor ratios to rise without depressing the profitability of new investment, at the same time new technology often needs new capital. It is also true that the extent to which average technique in use lags behind the most advanced technique depends on the rate of gross investment.[21] Further, rapid growth of and updating of the capital stock stimulates the advance of the frontier. Improvement and perfection is a sequential learning process. The rate of learning is dependent not only on the length of experience with a particular version of the technology, but also on the ability to try suggested improvements. If these improvements require

[20] Naturally this depends on the kind of education. Certain kinds of education, and attitudes toward education, can make a person less, not more, flexible.

[21] The embodiment effect has been stressed by Robert Solow, *op. cit.*, and W. E. G. Salter, *Productivity and Technical Change* (Cambridge: Cambridge University Department of Applied Economics, 1960).

embodiment, the rate of learning will be strongly affected by the rate of new physical investment.[22]

While an advance in any key element in the growth process tends to raise the productivity of and spur the advance of the others, technological advance is the key catalytic factor. If technology continues to advance, but the size and average age of the capital stock and the average level of education remain constant, per capita economic growth would slacken—but the slackening might well be moderate. Old workers die and new workers graduate from M.I.T., Michigan, and Central High. Old machines wear out and are replaced by new. Design improvements consequently could be embodied in new machinery and generalized advances in knowledge in new textbooks. Economic growth might be more closely bounded, but still vigorous. If technological advance dries up, however, the system soon would reach a limit in terms of per capita income.[23] It may be a different matter for those underdeveloped countries which can borrow technology; for them capital formation and education alone may have a more powerful independent thrust. But, as Schumpeter stated,[24] in advanced nations economic growth is best understood with technological advance playing the leading role, and capital formation and education providing the necessary support.[25]

[22]Learning by doing has been stressed by Kenneth J. Arrow in his "The Economic Implications of Learning by Doing," *Review of Economic Studies,* Vol. 29 (June 1962). There is a large literature on learning curves which we shall discuss subsequently.

[23]This is an implication of almost all growth models, not just the one proposed by the authors.

[24]Joseph Schumpeter, *The Theory of Economic Development* (Cambridge: Harvard University Press, 1934).

[25]Recent studies which have attempted to estimate the contribution of technological advance to growth of GNP have yielded significant underestimates. There are several sources of underestimation.

First, many of the studies have assumed a Cobb-Douglas production function. If, as is strongly suspected, the elasticity of substitution is significantly less than one for large increases in the capital-labor ratio (for a given technology), this should result in an overestimate of the contribution of growing capital per worker and, hence, an underattribution to other factors, including technological advance.

Second, to the extent that the returns to a particular factor are dependent on the rate of technological progress and this is not explicitly taken into account, some of the credit which should go to technological advance is attributed to these other factors. This is probably the case regarding the high returns to education—these returns would have been far less if technological advance had been slower. As another example, some authors have credited significant increases in output to reallocation of labor from low to high productivity jobs. Surely a large part of this reflects the exploitation of new technological knowledge which created the new jobs, and is the lagged effect of technological advance (and of education which permits labor to learn the new techniques) rather than an independent factor.

Third, the studies generally ignore the effect of an increase in one factor on the supply of the others. Supply interactions reduce the significance of attribution, but do not necessarily lead to bias. However, if technological advance is strongly catalytic, as suggested, one of its major effects is inducing increases in other factors. See Nelson, *op. cit.*

New Products

Technical change is emphasized here not only because of its role as a catalyst, but also because it endows economic growth with much of its capacity for satisfying human wants. This latter point is generally not fully appreciated, since the unique contribution of many new products is not adequately captured by the Gross National Product measure.

Certain technological advances, like the automatic loom and improved catalytic process equipment for producing gasoline, increased the ability of the economy to produce established private or public consumption goods, but did not introduce any new dimension to the available goods which determine the welfare of consumers. Similarly, from the viewpoint of the final consumer, hybrid corn (fed to livestock, not people) is not a new consumer good, but a more efficient way to produce beef and pork. Other technical changes create the possibility of producing substantially new or improved consumer goods. The airplane, penicillin, and television expanded the range of final goods and services, and permitted the satisfaction of wants which had not been satisfied before.[26]

The differentiation between new and established final products is not razor sharp. Final products are, after all, merely ways of satisfying consumer wants. New final goods are often simply more efficient processes–less costly ways of meeting needs that were met before.[27] While in some situations the airplane is simply a less costly way to travel (counting time) than a train, it made cross-country travel possible in a few hours–something which was previously impossible. Penicillin has made it possible–not just less costly–to save the lives of many people with certain infections.

When technological advance increases the productivity of existing goods and services, its contribution is not essentially different from that of any other investment. In terms of potential output, it makes no difference whether steel capacity is increased by providing more blast furnaces of existing design or by discovering how to make existing equipment more productive.

For enlarging the spectrum of choice, however, there is no substitute for technological advance. The dramatic increase in modern health standards could not have been achieved simply by allocating more men and equipment to meeting health needs. While this also has happened, the main improvements have been the advances in the quality of medicines and in medical knowledge. Improvements in transportation and communications likewise would have been impossible but for the invention and development of the

[26]Introduction of a new final good means the introduction of a new good for which no combination of older goods provides a perfect substitute.

[27]Kelvin Lancaster, "Change and Innovation in the Technology of Consumption," *American Economic Review,* Vol. 56 (May 1966), p. 22, presents a useful model.

radio and the airplane. These and other advancements represent the most treasured prizes of economic growth.

Stated another way, growth of economic potential has a direction as well as a rate. If production possibilities shifted outward uniformly, there would be little difficulty in providing a scalar measure of growth, and indeed potential GNP as it is calculated would provide a good measure. However, a better process for making aluminum will not shift outward beyond the frontier uniformly; rather it will primarily shift those productive possibilities which involve a large aluminum output. Creation of a new final product will actually introduce a new dimension to production possibilities.

Without new products, Americans still would have achieved a significant improvement in their standards of living, but the kinds of developments would have been different. The fourfold increase in measured GNP which has occurred since 1900 would have meant far less in terms of potential to meet needs. New products are measured in the GNP calculations by the amount people spend on them, but for many people the value of obtaining the new product far exceeds the total price. If airplane service were eliminated from the spectrum of final products, many consumers would require a significant increment of income to achieve comparable levels of satisfaction. For those who owe their lives to penicillin, the value of the new product is not measurable.[28]

The most prized aspects of increasing affluence are largely attributable to technological advance rather than to generalized economic growth. Real GNP per person is more than twice as large as in 1900, but technological change has so altered the nature of society and the quality of life that GNP comparisons over such long periods of time are meaningless. Man today has a life expectancy of 70 years, is much better protected from a wide range of

[28]It is not argued here that, because of the introduction of new products, growth of GNP underestimates growth of welfare: rather, that a given growth of measured GNP means more in terms of consumer satisfaction if it is accompanied by the availability of new products. It is clear that if a person is unable to buy a particular product he presently is purchasing, he is made worse off even if he can purchase other products at existing prices. The argument is reversible. People with a specific income and facing a set of product prices will be made better off if a new product is introduced—provided the product and its price are sufficiently attractive that they buy it.

Put another way, the consumer price index suggests that the prices of consumer goods and services in 1960 were approximately three times the 1900 level. Most people would probably be willing to settle for far less than three dollars to spend on goods available in 1960 at 1960 prices rather than one dollar to spend on goods available in 1900 at 1900 prices. But it is impossible to say how much less.

Of course, some people would not agree that the 1960 range of choice is better than that of 1900. A 1960 dollar buys far less personal service and housing space than did a 1900 dollar. For those whose tastes stress these things, it is possible that they would be willing to trade much more than three 1960 dollars for one 1900 dollar and the accompanying prices. This problem of values is the heart of the measurement problem.

devastating diseases, has teeth extracted with little pain, and has his view of the world expanded by cheap and rapid travel. Even without these developments, the growth of GNP would have helped to eradicate poverty and increase the enjoyment of life. But it would have been far less powerful a liberating force in a society restricted to the consumption possibilities of 1900–wider carriages, more coal for the kitchen stove, and more kerosene for the oil lamp.

21

EXPANSION AND EMPLOYMENT[1]

EVSEY D. DOMAR

"A slow sort of country," said the Queen. "Now, *here*, you see, it takes all the running *you* can do, to keep in the same place. If you want to get somewhere else, you must run at least twice as fast as that." Lewis Carroll: *Through the Looking Glass*

In these days of labor shortages and inflation, a paper dealing with conditions needed for full employment and with the threat of deflation may well appear out of place. Its publication at this time is due partly to a two-year lag between the first draft and the final copy; also to the widely held belief that the present inflation is a temporary phenomenon, and that once it is over, the old problem of deflation and unemployment may possibly appear before us again.

Our comfortable belief in the efficacy of Say's Law has been badly shaken in the last fifteen years. Both events and discussions have shown that supply does not automatically create its own demand. A part of income generated by the productive process may not be returned to it; this part may be saved and hoarded. As Keynes put it, "Unemployment develops . . . because

[1]This paper forms a sequence to my earlier article on "The 'Burden' of the Debt and the National Income," published in this *Review*, Vol. XXXIV, No. 5 (Dec., 1944), pp. 798–827. Though their titles seem different, the two papers are based on the same logical foundation and treat a common subject: the economic role of growth.

Reprinted from *The American Economic Review* (March 1947), pp. 34–55, by permission of the author and publisher. Evsey D. Domar is a professor at the Massachusetts Institute of Technology.

people want the moon; men cannot be employed when the object of desire (*i.e.*, money) is something which cannot be produced. . . ."[2] The core of the problem then is the public's desire to hoard. If no hoarding takes place, employment can presumably be maintained.

This sounds perfectly straight and simple, and yet it leaves something unexplained. Granted that absence of hoarding is a *necessary* condition for the maintenance of full employment, is it also a *sufficient* condition? Is the absence of hoarding *all* that is necessary for the avoidance of unemployment? This is the impression *The General Theory* gives. And yet, on a different plane, we have some notions about an increasing productive capacity which must somehow be utilized if unemployment is to be avoided. Will a mere absence of hoarding assure such a utilization? Will not a continuous increase in expenditures (and possibly in the money supply) be necessary in order to achieve this goal?

The present paper deals with this problem. It attempts to find the conditions needed for the maintenance of full employment over a period of time, or more exactly, *the rate of growth of national income* which the maintenance of full employment requires. This rate of growth is analyzed in Section I. Section II is essentially a digression on some conceptual questions and alternative approaches. It may be omitted by the busy reader. Section III is concerned with the *dual* character of the investment process; that is, with the fact that investment not only generates income but also increases productive capacity. Therefore the effects of investment on employment are less certain and more complex than is usually supposed. In Section IV a few examples from existing literature on the subject are given, and Section V contains some concluding remarks. The most essential parts of the paper are presented in Sections I and III.

As in many papers of this kind, a number of simplifying assumptions are made. Most of them will become apparent during the discussion. Two may be noted at the outset. First, events take place simultaneously, without any lags. Second, income, investment and saving are defined in the *net* sense, *i.e.*, over and above depreciation. The latter is understood to refer to the cost of replacement of the depreciated asset by another of *equal* productive capacity. These assumptions are not entirely essential to the argument. The discussion could be carried out with lags, and, if desired, in gross terms or with a different concept of depreciation. Some suggestions along these lines are made in Section II. But it is better to begin with as simple a statement of the problem as possible, bearing in mind of course the nature of assumptions made.

[2]John M. Keynes, *The General Theory of Employment Interest and Money* (New York, 1936), p. 235.

I. THE RATE OF GROWTH

It is perfectly clear that the requirement that income paid out should be returned to the productive process, or that savings be equal to investment, or other expressions of the same idea, are simply formulas for the retention of the income *status quo*. If underemployment was present yesterday, it would still remain here today. If yesterday's income was at a full employment level, that *income level* would be retained today. It may no longer, however, correspond to full employment.

Let yesterday's full employment income equal an annual rate of 150 billion dollars, and let the average propensity to save equal, say, 10 percent. If now 15 billions are annually invested, one might expect full employment to be maintained. But during this process, capital equipment of the economy will have increased by an annual rate of 15 billions–for after all, investment *is* the formation of capital.[3] Therefore, the productive capacity of the economy has also increased.

The effects of this increase on employment will depend on whether or not *real income* has also increased. Since money income has remained, as assumed, at the 150 billion annual level, an increase in real income can be brought about only by a corresponding fall in the general price level. This indeed has been the traditional approach to problems of this kind, an approach which we shall have to reject here for the following reasons:

1. The presence of considerable monopolistic elements (in industry and labor) in our economy makes unrealistic the assumption that a falling *general* price level could be achieved without interfering with full employment. This of course does not exclude *relative* changes among prices. As a matter of fact, if industries subject to a faster-than-average technological progress do not reduce their prices to some extent, a constant general price level cannot be maintained.
2. For an economy saddled with a large public debt and potentially faced (in peacetime) with serious employment problems, a falling price level is in itself undesirable.
3. A falling price level can bring about a larger real income only in the special case when prices of consumers' goods fall more rapidly than those

[3]The identification of investment with capital formation is reasonably safe in a private economy where only a small part of resources is disposed of by the government. When this part becomes substantial, complications arise. This question will be taken up again in Section II. Meanwhile, we shall disregard it and divide total national income, irrespective of source, into investment (*i.e.*, capital formation) and consumption.

The term "national income" is understood here in a broad sense, as total output minus depreciation, and does not touch on current controversies regarding the inclusion or exclusion of certain items. Perhaps "net national product" would be more appropriate for our purposes.

of investment goods. For otherwise (with a constant propensity to save) money income will be falling as fast or faster than the price level, and real income will be falling as well. To prevent money income from falling so rapidly, the volume of real investment would have to keep rising—a conclusion which will be presently reached in the more general case.

4. Finally, the assumption of a falling general price level would obscure—and I believe quite unnecessarily—the main subject we are concerned with here.

For these reasons, a *constant general price level* is assumed throughout this paper. But, from a theoretical point of view, this is a convenience rather than a necessity. The discussion could be carried on with a falling or a rising price level as well.

To come back to the increase in capacity. If both money and real national income thus remain fixed at the 150 billion annual level, the creation of the new capital equipment will have one or more of the following effects: (1) The new capital remains unused; (2) The new capital is used at the expense of previously constructed capital, whose labor and/or markets the new capital has taken away; (3) The new capital is substituted for labor (and possibly for other factors).

The first case represents a waste of resources. That capital need not have been constructed in the first place. The second case—the substitution of new capital for existing capital (before the latter is worn out, since investment is defined here in the net sense)—takes place all the time and, in reasonable magnitudes, is both unavoidable and desirable in a free dynamic society. It is when this substitution proceeds on a rather large scale that it can become socially wasteful; also, losses sustained or expected by capital owners will make them oppose new investment—a serious danger for an economy with considerable monopolistic elements.

Finally, capital may be substituted for labor. If this substitution results in a *voluntary* reduction in the labor force or in the length of the work week, no objections can be raised. Such a process has of course been going on for many years. But in our economy it is very likely that at least a part of this substitution—if carried on at an extensive scale—will be involuntary so that the result will be unemployment.

The tools used in this paper do not allow us to distinguish between these three effects of capital formation, though, as will appear later, our concepts are so defined that a voluntary reduction in the number of man-hours worked is excluded. In general, it is not unreasonable to assume that in most cases all three effects will be present (though not in constant proportions), and that capital formation not accompanied by an increase in income will result in unemployed capital and labor.

The above problems do not arise in the standard Keynesian system because of its explicit assumption that employment is a function of national income, an assumption which admittedly can be justified only over short periods of time. Clearly, a full employment income of 1941 would cause considerable unemployment today. While Keynes' approach—the treatment of employment as a function of income—is a reasonable first approximation, we shall go a step further and assume instead that *the percentage of labor force employed is a function of the ratio between national income and productive capacity*. This should be an improvement, but we must admit the difficulties of determining productive capacity, both conceptually and statistically. These are obvious and need not be elaborated. We shall mean by productive capacity the total output of the economy at what is usually called full employment (with due allowance for frictional and seasonal unemployment), such factors as consumers' preferences, price and wage structures, intensity of competition, and so on being given.

The answer to the problem of unemployment lies of course in a growing income. If after capital equipment has increased by (an annual rate of) 15 billions an income of 150 billions leaves some capacity unused, then a higher magnitude of income can be found—say 155 or 160 billions—which will do the job. There is nothing novel or startling about this conclusion. The idea that a capitalist economy needs growth goes back, in one form or another, at least to Marx. The trouble really is that the idea of growth is so widely accepted that people rarely bother about it. It is always treated as an afterthought, to be added to one's speech or article if requested, but very seldom incorporated in its body. Even then it is regarded as a function of some abstract technological process which somehow results in increasing productivity per man-hour, and which takes place quite independently of capital formation. And yet, our help in the industrialization of undeveloped countries will take the form not only of supplying technical advice and textbooks, but also of actual machinery and goods. Certainly the 80 odd billion dollars of net capital formation created in the United States in the period 1919–29 had a considerable effect on our productive capacity.[4]

A change in productive capacity of a country is a function of changes in its natural resources (discovery of new ones or depletion of others), in its labor force (more correctly, man-hours available), capital and the state of technique.[5] Since changes in natural resources and technique are very difficult concepts, we can express changes in total capacity via changes in the quantity and productivity of labor or of capital. The traditional approach builds around labor. The several studies of the magnitude of total output corre-

[4]This figure, in 1929 prices, is taken from Simon Kuznets, *National Income and Its Composition,* Vol. I (New York, 1941), p. 268. The actual figure was 79.1 billion dollars.
[5]Taking other conditions listed [earlier on this page] as given.

sponding to full employment, made in the last few years, consisted in multiplying the expected labor force (subdivided into several classes) by its expected average productivity.[6] This procedure did not imply that the other three factors (natural resources, technology and capital) remained constant; rather that their variations were all reflected in the changes in productivity of labor.

It is also possible to put capital in the center of the stage and to estimate variations in total capacity by measuring the changes in the quantity of capital and in its productivity, the latter reflecting changes currently taking place in natural resources, technology and the labor force. From a practical point of view, the labor approach has obvious advantages, at least in some problems, because labor is a more homogeneous and easily measurable factor. But from a theoretical point of view, the capital approach is more promising and for this reason: the appearance of an extra workman or his decision to work longer hours *only* increases productive capacity without, however, generating any income to make use of this increase. But the construction of a new factory has a *dual* effect: *it increases productive capacity and it generates income.*

The emphasis on this dual character of the investment process is the essence of this paper's approach to the problem of employment. If investment increases productive capacity and also creates income, what should be the magnitude of investment, or at what rate should it grow, in order to make the increase in income equal to that of productive capacity?[7] Couldn't an equation be set up one side of which would represent the increase (or the rate of increase) of productive capacity, and the other—that of income, and the solution of which would yield the required *rate of growth?*

We shall attempt to set up such an equation. It will be first expressed in symbolic form, and later (on p. 306) illustrated by a numerical example.

Let investment proceed at an annual rate of I, and let annual productive capacity (net value added) per dollar of newly created capital be equal on the average to s. Thus if it requires, say, 3 dollars of capital to produce (in terms of annual net value added) one dollar of output, s will equal one-third or 33.3 percent per year. It is not meant that s is the same in all firms or industries. It depends of course on the nature of capital constructed and on many other factors. Its treatment here as a given magnitude is a simplification which can be readily dispensed with.

The productive capacity of I dollars invested will thus be Is dollars per

[6] See for instance E. E. Hagen and N. B. Kirkpatrick, "The National Output at Full Employment in 1950," *Amer. Econ. Rev.*, Vol. XXXIV, No. 4 (Sept., 1944), pp. 472–500.

[7] This statement of the problem presupposes that full employment has already been reached and must only be maintained. With a small extra effort we could begin with a situation where some unemployment originally existed.

year. But it is possible that the operation of new capital will take place, at least to some extent, at the expense of previously constructed plants, with which the new capital will compete both for markets and for factors of production (mainly labor). If as a result, the output of existing plants must be curtailed, it would be useless to assert that the productive capacity of the *whole economy* has increased by Is dollars per year.[8] It has actually increased by a smaller amount which will be indicated by $I\sigma$.[9] σ may be called the *potential social average productivity of investment*. Such a long name calls for an explanation.

1. As stated above, σ is concerned with the increase in productive capacity of the whole society and not with the productive capacity per dollar invested in the new plants taken by themselves, that is with s. A difference between s and σ indicates a certain misdirection of investment, or—more important—that investment proceeds at too rapid a rate as compared with the growth of labor and technological progress. This question will be taken up again in Section II.

2. σ should not be confused with other related concepts, such as the traditional marginal productivity of capital. These concepts are usually based on a *caeteris paribus* assumption regarding the quantity of other factors and the state of technique. It should be emphasized that the use of σ does not imply in the least that labor, natural resources and technology remain fixed. It would be more correct therefore to say that σ indicates the increase in productive capacity which *accompanies* rather than which is caused by each dollar invested.

3. For our purposes, the most important property of σ is its *potential character*. It deals not with an increase in national income but with that of the *productive potential* of the economy. A high σ indicates that the economy *is capable* of increasing its output relatively fast. But whether this increased capacity will actually result in greater output or greater unemployment, depends on the behavior of money income.

The expression $I\sigma$ is the supply side of our system; it is the increase in output which the economy *can* produce. On the demand side we have the multiplier theory too familiar to need any elaboration, except for the emphasis on the obvious but often forgotten fact that, with any given marginal propensity to save, to be indicated by α, an increase in national income is not a function of investment, but of the *increment* in investment. If investment today, however large, is equal to that of yesterday, national

[8]These comparisons must of course be made at a full employment level of national income. See also pp. 308–310.

[9]We are disregarding here external economies obtained by existing plants from the newly constructed ones.

income of today will be just equal and not any larger than that of yesterday. All this is obvious, and is stressed here to underline the lack of symmetry between the effects of investment on productive capacity and on national income.

Let investment increase at an absolute annual rate of ΔI (*e.g.*, by two billion per year), and let the corresponding absolute annual increase in income be indicated by ΔY. We have then

$$\Delta Y = \Delta I \frac{1}{\alpha} \tag{1}$$

where $1/\alpha$ is of course the multiplier.

Let us now assume that the economy is in a position of a full employment equilibrium, so that its national income equals its productive capacity.[10] To retain this position, income and capacity should increase at the same rate. The annual increase in potential capacity equals $I\sigma$. The annual increase in actual income is expressed by $\Delta I(1/\alpha)$. Our objective is to make them equal. This gives us the fundamental equation

$$\Delta I \frac{1}{\alpha} = I\sigma \tag{2}$$

To solve this equation, we multiply both sides by α and divide by I, obtaining

$$\frac{\Delta I}{I} = \alpha\sigma \tag{3}$$

The left side of expression (3) is the absolute annual increase (or the absolute rate of growth) in investment—ΔI—divided by the volume of investment itself; or in other words, it is the relative increase in investment, or the annual percentage rate of growth of investment. Thus the maintenance of full employment requires that investment grow at the annual percentage rate $\alpha\sigma$.

So much for investment. Since the marginal propensity to save—α—is assumed to be constant, an increase in income is a constant multiple of an increase in investment (see expression [1]). But in order to remain such a constant multiple of investment, income must also grow at the same annual percentage rate, that is at $\alpha\sigma$.

[10] See note 7.

To summarize, the maintenance of a continuous state of full employment requires that *investment and income grow at a constant annual percentage* (*or compound interest*) *rate* equal to the product of the marginal propensity to save and the average (to put it briefly) productivity of investment.[11]

This result can be made clearer by a numerical example. Let $\sigma = 25$ percent per year, $\alpha = 12$ percent, and $Y = 150$ billions per year. If full employment is to be maintained, an amount equal to $150 \times (12/100)$ should be invested. This will raise productive capacity by the amount invested times σ, *i.e.*, by $150 \times (12/100) \times (25/100)$, and national income will have to rise by the same annual amount. But the relative rise in income will equal the absolute increase divided by the income itself, *i.e.*,

$$\frac{150 \times \frac{12}{100} \times \frac{25}{100}}{150} = \frac{12}{100} \times \frac{25}{100}$$

$$= \alpha\sigma = 3 \text{ percent} \tag{4}$$

These results were obtained on the assumption that α the marginal propensity to save, and σ, the average productivity of investment, remain constant. The reader can see that this assumption is not necessary for the argument, and that the whole problem can be easily reworked with variable α and σ. Some remarks about a changing α are made on p. 313.

The expression (3) indicates (in a very simplified manner) conditions needed for the maintenance of full employment over a period of time. It shows that it is not sufficient, in Keynesian terms, that savings of yesterday be invested today, or, as it is often expressed, that investment offset saving. Investment of today must always exceed savings of yesterday. A mere absence of hoarding will not do. An injection of new money (or dishoarding) must take place every day. Moreover, this injection must proceed, in absolute terms, at an accelerated rate. The economy must continuously expand.[11a]

[11] The careful reader may be disturbed by the lack of clear distinction between increments and rates of growth here and elsewhere in the text. If some confusion exists, it is due to my attempt to express these concepts in non-mathematical form. Actually they all should be stated in terms of rates of growth (derivatives in respect to time). For a more serious treatment of this point, as well as for a more complete statement of the logic of the paper, see my article "Capital Expansion, Rate of Growth, and Employment," *Econometrica,* Vol. XIV (Apr., 1946), pp. 137–47.

[11a] After this paper was sent to the printer, I happened to stumble on an article by R. F. Harrod, published in 1939, which contained a number of ideas similar to those presented here. See "An Essay in Dynamic Theory," *Econ. Jour.,* Vol. XLIX (Apr., 1939), pp. 14–33.

II. THE ARGUMENT RE-EXAMINED

The busy reader is urged to skip this section and proceed directly to Section III. The present section is really a long footnote which re-examines the concepts and suggests some alternative approaches. Its purpose is, on the one hand, to indicate the essential limitations of the preceding discussion, and on the other, to offer a few suggestions which may be of interest to others working in this field.

It was established in Section I that the maintenance of full employment requires income and investment to grow at an annual compound interest rate equal to $\alpha\sigma$. The meaning of this result will naturally depend on those of α and σ. Unfortunately neither of them is devoid of ambiguity.

The marginal propensity to save—α—is a relatively simple concept in a private economy where only a small part of resources is handled by the government. National income can be divided, without too much trouble, into investment and consumption, even though it is true that the basis for this distinction is often purely formal.[12] But on the whole it sounds quite reasonable to say that if marginal propensity to save is α then an α fraction of an increase in income is saved by the public and invested in income-producing assets.

When a substantial part of the economy's resources is disposed of by the government, two interpretations of the marginal propensity to save, or of savings and investment in general, appear possible. The first is to continue dividing the total output, whether produced by government or by private business, into consumption and investment. This method was implicitly followed in this paper. But a question arises regarding the meaning and stability of α. It makes sense to say that a person or the public saves, in accordance with the size of their incomes, their habits, expectations, etc., a certain, though not necessarily constant, fraction of an increment in their *disposable* (*i.e.*, after income and social security taxes) income, but can a similar statement be made regarding total national income, a good part of which is not placed at the disposal of the public? Also it is not easy to divide government expenditures into consumption and investment.

The other method would limit α to disposable income only, and then provide for government expenditures separately. It would be necessary then to find out the effects of these expenditures on productive capacity.

Depreciation raises another problem. Since all terms are defined here in the net sense, the meaning and magnitude of α will also depend on those of depreciation, irrespective of the choice between the above two methods.

[12] Thanks are due to George Jaszi for his persistent efforts to enlighten me on this subject. The division of national income into investment and consumption is really a more difficult task than my text might imply.

Depreciation has been defined here (see page 299) as the cost of replacement of a worn out asset by another one with an equal productive capacity. While this approach is about as bad or as good as any other, the difficulty still remains that businesses ordinarily do not use this definition, and therefore arrive at a different estimate of their net incomes, which in turn determine their propensity to save.

I do not have ready answers to these questions, though I do not consider them insurmountable. I am mentioning them here partly in order to indicate the limitations of the present argument, and also as obstacles which will have to be overcome if a more exact analysis is undertaken.

σ is even more apt to give rise to ambiguities. s, from which it springs, has been used, in one form or another, in economic literature before, particularly in connection with the acceleration principle.[13] Here it indicates the annual amount of income (net value added) which can be produced by a dollar of newly created capital. It varies of course among firms and industries, and also in space and time, though a study recently made seems to indicate that it has been quite stable, at least in the United States and Great Britain, over the last 70 years or so.[14] Whether s has or has not been relatively stable is not essential for our discussion. The real question is whether such a concept has meaning, whether it makes sense to say that a given economy or a plant has a certain capacity. Traditional economic thinking would, I fear, be against such an approach. Unfortunately, it is impossible to discuss this question here. I believe that our actual experience during the last depression and this war, as well as a number of empirical studies, show that productive capacity, both of a plant and of the whole economy is a meaningful concept, though this capacity, as well as the magnitude of s, should be treated as a *range* rather than as a single number.

In some problems s may be interpreted as the minimum annual output per dollar invested which will make the investment worth undertaking. If this output falls below s, the investor suffers a loss or at least a disappointment, and may be unwilling to replace the asset after it has depreciated.

All these doubts apply to σ even more than to s. As explained on page 304, σ differs from s by indicating the annual increment in capacity of the *whole economy* per dollar invested, rather than that of the newly created capital taken by itself. The possible difference between s and σ is due to the following reasons:

[13] See for instance Paul A. Samuelson, "Interactions between the Multiplier Analysis and the Principle of Acceleration," *Rev. Econ. Stat.,* Vol. XXI (May, 1939), pp. 76–79; also R. F. Harrod, *The Trade Cycle* (Oxford, 1936). These authors, however, used not the ratio of income to capital, but of consumption to capital, or rather the reciprocal of this ratio.

[14] See Ernest H. Stern, "Capital Requirements in Progressive Economies," *Economica,* n.s., Vol. XII (Aug., 1945), pp. 163–71.

1. The new plants are not operated to capacity because they are unable to find a market for their products.

2. Old plants reduce their output because their markets are captured by new plants.

As productive capacity has no meaning except in relation to consumers' preferences, in both of the above cases productive capacity of the country is increased by a smaller amount than could be produced by the new plants; in the limiting case it is not increased at all, and $\sigma = 0$, however high s may be. But it must be made clear that the test of whether or not σ is below s can be made only under conditions (actual or assumed) of full employment. If markets are not large enough because of insufficiency of effective demand due to unemployment, it cannot yet be concluded that σ is below s.

3. The first two cases can take place irrespective of the volume of current investment. A more important case arises when investment proceeds at such a rapid rate that a shortage of other factors relative to capital develops. New plants may be unable to get enough labor, or more likely, labor (and other factors) is transferred to new plants from previously constructed ones, whose capacity therefore declines. In its actual manifestation, case 3 can hardly be separated from cases 1 and 2, because to the individual firm affected the difference between s and σ always takes the form of a cost-price disparity. The reason why we are trying to separate the first two cases from the third lies in the bearing of this distinction on practical policy. The first two cases arise from an error of judgment on the part of investors (past or present) which is, at least to some extent, unavoidable and not undesirable. The struggle for markets and the replacement of weaker (or older) firms and industries by stronger (or newer) ones is the essence of progress in a capitalist society. The third case, on the other hand, may result from poor fiscal policy. It constitutes an attempt to invest too much, to build more capital than the economy can utilize even at full employment. Such a situation can develop if an economy with a high propensity to save tries to maintain full employment by investing all its savings into capital goods. But it should be made clear that the expressions "too much capital" or "high propensity to save" are used in a relative sense–in comparison with the growth of other factors, that is natural resources, labor and technology.

The use of σ certainly does not imply that these factors remain fixed. As a matter of fact, it would be very interesting to explore the use of a more complex function as the right side of expression (2) instead of $I\sigma$, a function in which the growth of labor, natural resources, and technology would be presented explicitly, rather than through their effects on σ.[15] I did not attempt

[15] Some work along these lines has been done by J. Tinbergen. See his "Zur Theorie der langfristigen Wirtschaftsentwicklung" in the *Weltwirtschaftliches Archiv*, Vol. LV (May, 1942), pp. 511–49.

it because I wished to express the idea of growth in the simplest possible manner. One must also remember that in the application of mathematics to economic problems, diminishing returns appear rapidly, and that the construction of complex models requires so many specific assumptions as to narrow down their applicability.

And yet it may be interesting to depart in another direction, namely to introduce lags. In this paper both the multiplier effect and the increase in capacity are supposed to take place simultaneously and without any lag. Actually, the multiplier may take some time to work itself out, and certainly the construction of a capital asset takes time. In a secular problem these lags are not likely to be of great importance, but they may play an essential rôle over the cycle. We shall return to this question on page 315.

Finally, it is possible to approach the problem of growth from a different point of view. It was established here that the rate of growth required for a full employment equilibrium to be indicated by r is equal to

$$r = \alpha\sigma \tag{5}$$

so that if α and σ are given, the rate of growth is determined. But the equation (5) can also be solved for α in terms of r and σ, and for σ in terms of r and α. Thus if it is believed that r should be treated as given (for instance by technological progress), and if it is also decided to keep σ at a certain level, perhaps not too far from s, then it is possible to determine $\alpha = r/\sigma$, as being that marginal propensity to save which can be maintained without causing either inflation or unemployment. This approach was actually used by Ernest Stern in his statistical study of capital requirements of the United Kingdom, the United States and the Union of South Africa.[16] I also understand from Tibor de Scitovsky that he used the same approach in a study not yet published.

It is also possible to treat r and α as given and then determine what $\sigma = r/\alpha$ would have to be. Each approach has its own advantages and the choice depends of course on the nature of the problem in hand. The essential point to be noticed is the relationship between these three variables r, α, and σ, and the fact that if any two of them are given, the value of the third needed for the maintenance of full employment is determined; and if its actual value differs from the required one, inflation in some cases and unused capacity and unemployment in others will develop.

III. THE DUAL NATURE OF THE INVESTMENT PROCESS

We shall continue the discussion of growth by returning to expression (2) on page 305,

[16]Stern, *op. cit.*

$$\Delta I \frac{1}{\alpha} = I\sigma$$

which is fundamental to our whole analysis. As a matter of fact, the statement of the problem in this form (2) appears to me at least as important as its actual solution expressed in (3). To repeat, the left part of the equation shows the annual increment in national income and is the demand side; while the right part represents the annual increase in productive capacity and is the supply side. Alternatively, the left part may be called the "multiplier side," and the right part the "σ side."

What is most important for our purposes is the fact that investment appears on both sides of the equation; that is, it has a *dual effect:* on the left side it generates income via the multiplier effect; and on the right side it increases productive capacity—the σ effect. The explicit recognition of this dual character of investment could undoubtedly save much argument and confusion. Unless some special assumptions are made, the discussion of the effects of investment on profits, income, employment, etc., cannot be legitimately confined to one side only. For the generation of income and the enlargement of productive capacity often have diametrically opposed effects, and the outcome in each particular case depends on the special circumstances involved.[17]

Analyzing expression (2) further, we notice that even though investment is present on both its sides, it does not take the same form: for on the σ side we have the *amount* of investment as such; but on the multiplier side we have not the amount of investment but its annual increment, or its absolute *rate of increase.*

The amount of investment (always in the net sense) may remain constant, or it may go up or down, but so long as it remains positive (and except for the rare case when $\sigma \leqq 0$) productive capacity increases. But if income is to rise as well, it is not enough that just any amount be invested: *an increase in income is not a function of the amount invested; it is the function of the increment of investment.* Thus the whole body of investment, so to speak, increases productive capacity, but only its very top—the increment—increases national income.

In this probably lies the explanation why inflations have been so rare in our economy in peacetime, and why even in relatively prosperous periods a

[17]The effects of labor saving machinery on employment of labor is a good case in point. Some economists, particularly those connected with the labor movement, insist that such machines displace labor and create unemployment. Their opponents are equally sure that the introduction of labor saving devices reduces costs and generates income, thus increasing employment. Both sides cite ample empirical evidence to prove their contentions, and neither side is wrong. But both of them present an incomplete picture from which no definite conclusion can be derived.

certain degree of underemployment has usually been present. Indeed, it is difficult enough to keep investment at some reasonably high level year after year, but the requirement that it always be rising is not likely to be met for any considerable length of time.

Now, if investment and therefore income do not grow at the required rate, unused capacity develops. Capital and labor become idle. It may not be apparent why investment by increasing productive capacity creates unemployment of labor. Indeed, as was argued on page 301, this need not always be the case. Suppose national income remains constant or rises very slowly while new houses are being built. It is possible that new houses will be rented out at the expense of older buildings and that no larger rents will be paid than before; or that the new houses will stand wholly or partly vacant with the same result regarding the rents.[18] But it is also possible, and indeed very probable, that the complete or partial utilization of the new buildings which are usually better than the old ones, will require the payment of larger rents, with the result that less income will be left for the purchase of, say clothing; thus causing unemployment in the clothing trades. So the substitution of capital for labor need not take the obvious form of labor-saving machinery; it may be equally effective in a more circuitous way.

The unemployment of men is considered harmful for obvious reasons. But idle buildings and machinery, though not arousing our humanitarian instincts, can be harmful because their presence inhibits new investment. Why build a new factory when existing ones are working at half capacity? It is certainly not necessary to be dogmatic and assert that no plant or house should ever be allowed to stand idle, and that as soon as unused capacity develops the economy plunges into a depression. There is no need, nor is it possible or desirable, to guarantee that every piece of capital ever constructed will be fully utilized until it is worn out. When population moves from Oklahoma to California, some buildings in Oklahoma will stand idle; or when plastics replace leather in women's handbags, the leather industry may suffer. Such changes form the very life of a free dynamic society, and should not be interfered with. The point is that there be no vacant houses while prospective tenants are present but cannot afford to live in them because they are unemployed. And they are unemployed because income and investment do not grow sufficiently fast.

The extent to which unused capacity, present or expected, inhibits new investment greatly depends on the structure of industry and the character of the economy in general. The more atomistic it is, the stronger is competition,

[18] It is worth noticing that in both cases the construction of the new houses represents a misdirection of resources, at least to some extent. But a complete avoidance of such misdirection is perfectly impossible and even undesirable.

the more susceptible it is to territorial, technological and other changes, the smaller is the effect of unused capacity on new investment. One firm may have an idle plant, while another in the same industry builds a new one; steel may be depressed while plastics are expanding. It is when an industry is more or less monopolized, or when several industries are financially connected, that unused capacity presents a particularly serious threat to new investment.

Strictly speaking, our discussion so far, including equation (2), was based on the assumption that α remained constant. If α varies within the time period concerned, the relation between investment and income becomes more involved. What the left side of the equation (2) requires is that *income* increase; and investment must grow only in so far as its growth is necessary for the growth of income. So if α declines sufficiently fast, a growing income can be achieved with a constant or even falling investment. But years of declining α have evidently been offset by others of rising α, because whatever information is available would indicate that over the last seventy years or so prior to this war the percentage of income saved was reasonably constant, possibly with a slight downward trend.[19] Therefore, in the absence of direct government interference, it would seem better not to count too much on a falling α, at least for the time being

In general, a high α presents a serious danger to the maintenance of full employment, because investment may fail to grow at the required high rate, or will be physically unable to do so without creating a substantial difference between s and σ. This difference indicates that large numbers of capital assets become unprofitable and their owners suffer losses or at least disappointments (see page 309). Space does not permit me to develop this idea at greater length here.[20] But it must be emphasized that what matters is not the magnitude of α taken by itself, but its relation to the growth of labor, natural resources, and technology. Thus a country with new resources, a rapidly growing population, and developing technology is able to digest, so to speak, a relatively large α, while absence or at least a very slow growth of these factors makes a high α a most serious obstacle to full employment.[21] But the problem can be attacked not only by lowering α, but also by speeding up the rate of technological progress, the latter solution being much more to my taste. It must be remembered, however, that technological progress makes it *possible* for the economy to grow, without guaranteeing that this growth will be realized.

[19]See Simon Kuznets, *National Product since 1869*, National Bureau of Economic Research (mimeo., 1945), p. II-89. I do not mean that we must always assume a constant α; rather that we lack sufficient proof to rely on a falling one.

[20]See my paper, *Econometrica*, Vol. XIV, particularly pp. 142–45.

[21]*Cf.* Alvin H. Hansen, *Fiscal Policy and the Business Cycle* (New York, 1941), particularly Part IV.

In a private capitalist society where α cannot be readily changed, a higher level of income and employment at any given time can be achieved only through increased investment. But investment, as an employment creating instrument, is a mixed blessing because of its σ effect. The economy finds itself in a serious dilemma: if sufficient investment is not forthcoming today, unemployment will be here today. But if enough is invested today, still more will be needed tomorrow.

It is a remarkable characteristic of a capitalist economy that while, on the whole, unemployment is a function of the difference between its actual income and its productive capacity, most of the measures (*i.e.,* investment) directed towards raising national income also enlarge productive capacity. It is very likely that the increase in national income will be greater than that of capacity, but the whole problem is that the increase in income is temporary and presently peters out (the usual multiplier effect), while capacity has been increased for good. So that as far as unemployment is concerned, investment is at the same time a cure for the disease and the cause of even greater ills in the future.[22]

IV. AN ECONOMIC EXCURSION

It may be worth while to browse through the works of several economists of different schools of thought to see their treatment of the σ and of the multiplier effects of investment. It is not suggested to make an exhaustive study, but just to present a few examples.

Thus in Marshall's *Principles* capital and investment are looked upon as productive instruments (the σ effect), with little being said about monetary (that is, income or price) effects of investment.[23] The same attitude prevails in Fisher's *Nature of Capital and Income,*[24] and I presume in the great majority of writings not devoted to the business cycle. It is not that these writers were unaware of monetary effects of investment (even though they did not have

[22] That income generating effects of investment are temporary and that new and larger amounts must be spent to maintain full employment has been mentioned in economic and popular literature a number of times. Particular use has been made of this fact by opponents of the so-called deficit financing, who treat government expenditures as a "shot in the arm" which must be administered at an ever increasing dose. What they fail to realize is that exactly the same holds true for private investment.

[23] Marshall was very careful, however, to distinguish between the substitution of a particular piece of machinery for particular labor, and the replacement of labor by capital in general. The latter he regarded impossible, because the construction of capital creates demand for labor, essentially a sort of multiplier effect. See *Principles of Economics* , 8th ed. (London, 1936), p. 523.

[24] Irving Fisher, *The Nature of Capital and Income* (New York, 1919).

the multiplier concept as such), but such questions belonged to a different field, and the problem of aggregate demand was supposed to be taken care of by some variation of Say's Law.

In the business cycle literature we often find exactly an opposite situation. The whole Wicksellian tradition treated economic fluctuations as a result of monetary effects of excessive investment. It is curious that all this investment did not lead to increased output which would counteract its inflationary tendencies. Indeed, as one reads Hayek's *Prices and Production*, one gets an impression that these investment projects never bear fruit and are, moreover, abandoned after the crisis. The σ effect is entirely absent, or at least appears with such a long lag as to make it inoperative. Prosperity comes to an end because the banking system refuses to support inflation any longer.[25]

σ fares better in the hands of Aftalion.[26] His theory of the cycle is based upon, what I would call, a time lag between the multiplier and the σ effects. Prosperity is started by income generated by investment in capital goods (the multiplier effect), while no increase in productive capacity has taken place as yet. As investment projects are completed, the resulting increase in productive capacity (the σ effect) pours goods on the market and brings prosperity to an end.

A similar approach is used by Michal Kalecki. The essence of his model of the business cycle consists in making profit expectations, and therefore investment, a function (with appropriate lags) of the relation between national income and the stock of capital. During the recovery, investment and income rise, while the accumulation of capital lags behind. Presently, however, due to the structure of the model, the rise of income stops while capital continues to accumulate. This precipitates the downswing.[27]

Space does not allow us to analyze the works of a number of other writers on the subject, among whom Foster and Catchings should be given due recognition for what is so clumsy and yet so keen an insight.[28] I am also omitting the whole Marxist literature, in which capital accumulation plays

[25] Friedrich A. Hayek, *Prices and Production* (London, 1931). I don't mean to say that Professor Hayek is not aware that capital is productive; rather that he did not make use of this fact in his theory of the business cycle. See, however, his "The 'Paradox' of Saving," *Economica*, Vol. XI (May 1931), pp. 125–69.

[26] Albert Aftalion, "The Theory of Economic Cycles Based on the Capitalistic Technique of Production," *Rev. Econ. Stat.*, Vol. IX (Oct., 1927), pp. 165–70. This short article contains a summary of his theory.

[27] Michal Kalecki, *Essays in the Theory of Economic Fluctuations* (New York, 1939). See particularly the last essay "A Theory of the Business Cycle," pp. 116–49. What Mr. Kalecki's model shows in a general sense is that accumulation of capital cannot proceed for any length of time in a trendless economy (*i.e.*, an economy with a secularly constant income). His other results depend upon the specific assumptions he makes.

[28] William T. Foster and Waddill Catchings, *Profits* (Boston and New York, 1925). This book is the most important of their several published works. It is interesting to note that they did

such an important role, because that would require a separate study. The few remaining pages of this section will be devoted to Hobson and Keynes.

Hobson's writings contain so many interesting ideas that it is a great pity he is not read more often.[29] Anti-Keynesians probably like him not much more than they do Keynes, while Keynesians are apt to regard the *General Theory* as the quintessence of all that was worth while in economics before 1936, and may not bother to read earlier writings. I may say that Keynes's own treatment of Hobson, in spite of his generous recognition of the latter's works, may have substantiated this impression.[30]

Even though both Keynes and Hobson were students of unemployment, they actually addressed themselves to two different problems. Keynes analyzed what happens when savings (of the preceding period) are not invested. The answer was–unemployment, but the statement of the problem in this form might easily give the erroneous impression that if savings were invested, full employment would be assured. Hobson, on the other hand, went a step further and stated the problem in this form: suppose savings are invested. Will the new plants be able to dispose of their products? Such a statement of the problem was not at all, as Keynes thought, a mistake.[31] It was a statement of a different, and possibly also a deeper problem.

Hobson was fully armed with the σ effect of investment, and he saw that it could be answered only by growth. His weakness lay in a poor perception of the multiplier effect and his analysis lacked rigor in general. He gave a demonstration rather than a proof. But the problem to which he addressed himself is just as alive today as it was fifty and twenty years ago.[32]

This discussion, as I suspect almost any other, would be obviously incomplete without some mention of Keynes's treatment of the σ and of the multiplier effects. Keynes's approach is very curious: as a matter of fact, he has two: the familiar short-run analysis, and another one which may becalled a long-run one.[33]

Keyne's short-run system (later expressed so admiringly by Oscar Lange[34])

---

come to the conclusion that ". . . as long as capital facilities are created at a sufficient rate, there need be no deficiency of consumer income. To serve that purpose, however, facilities must be increased at a constantly accelerating rate" (p. 413). This they regarded quite impossible.

[29] I am particularly referring to his *Economics of Unemployment* (London, 1922) and *Rationalization and Unemployment* (New York, 1930)

[30] See *The General Theory*, pp. 364–71.

[31] *Ibid.*, pp. 367–68.

[32] Contrary to popular impression, Hobson does not advocate a maximum reduction in the propensity to save. What he wants is to reduce it to a magnitude commensurable with requirements for capital arising from technological progress–an interesting and reasonable idea.

[33] This whole discussion is based on *The General Theory* and not on Keynes's earlier writings.

[34] Oscar Lange, "The Rate of Interest and the Optimum Propensity to Consume," *Economica*, n.s., Vol. V (Feb., 1938), pp. 12–32. This otherwise excellent paper has a basic defect in the

is based on " . . . given the existing skill and quantity of available labor, the existing quality and quantity of available equipment, the existing technique, the degree of competition, the tastes and habits of the consumer . . ." [35] Productive capacity thus being given, employment becomes a function of national income, expressed, to be sure, not in money terms but in "wage units." A wage unit, the remuneration for "an hour's employment of ordinary labor" (page 41), is of course a perfect fiction, but some such device must be used to translate real values into monetary and *vice versa,* and one is about as good or as bad as another. The important point for our purposes is the assumption that the amount of equipment (*i.e.,* capital) in existence is given.

Now, the heart of Keynesian economics is the argument that employment depends on income, which in turn is determined by the current volume of investment (and the propensity to save). But investment (in the net sense) is nothing else but the rate of change of capital. Is it legitimate then first to assume the quantity of capital as given, and then base the argument on its rate of change? If the quantity of capital changes, so does (in a typical case) productive capacity, and if the latter changes it can be hardly said that employment is solely determined by the size of national income, expressed in wage units or otherwise. Or putting it in the language of this paper, is it safe and proper to analyze the relation between investment and employment without taking into account the σ effect?

The answer depends on the nature of the problem in hand. In this particular case, Keynes could present two reasons for his disregard of the σ effect. He could assume that the latter operates with at least a one period lag, the period being understood here as the whole time span covered by the discussion.[36] Or he could argue that over a typical year the net addition (*i.e.,* net investment) to the stock of capital of a society, such as England or the United States, will hardly exceed some 3 or 5 percent; since this increment is small when compared with changes in income, it can be disregarded.[37]

Both explanations are entirely reasonable provided of course that the period under consideration is not too long. A five-year lag for the σ effect would be difficult to defend, and an increase in the capital stock of some 15 or 20 percent can hardly be disregarded. I am not aware that Keynes did present either of these explanations; but there is just so much one can do in four hundred pages at any one time.

---

assumption that investment is a function of consumption rather than of the rate of change of consumption.

[35] *The General Theory,* p. 245. See also pp. 24 and 28.

[36] This again is not quite safe unless some provision for investment projects started in preceding periods and finished during the present period is made.

[37] The second assumption is specifically made by Professor Pigou in his *Employment and Equilibrium* (London, 1941), pp. 33–34.

It would be perfectly absurd to say that Keynes was not aware of the productive qualities of capital. In the *long run* he laid great stress on it, possibly too great. All through the *General Theory* we find grave concern for the diminishing marginal efficiency of capital due, in the long run, to its increasing quantity.[38] There is so much of this kind of argument as to leave the reader puzzled in the end. We are told that marginal efficiency of capital depends on its scarcity. Well and good. But scarcity relative to what? It could become less scarce relative to other factors, such as labor, so that the marginal productivity of capital in the real sense (*i.e.*, essentially our σ) declined. But then on page 213 we read: "If capital becomes less scarce, the excess yield will diminish, without its having become less productive—at least in the physical sense."

Why then does the marginal efficiency of capital fall? Evidently because capital becomes less scarce relative to income.[39] But why cannot income grow more rapidly if labor is not the limiting factor? Could it be only a matter of poor fiscal policy which failed to achieve a faster growing income? After all we have in investment an income generating instrument; if investment grows more rapidly, so does income. This is *the* multiplier effect of investment on which so much of the *General Theory* is built.

I don't have the answer. Is it possible that, while Keynes disregarded the σ effect in the short-run analysis, he somehow omitted the multiplier effect from the long-run?

V. CONCLUDING REMARKS

A traveller who sat in the economic councils of the United States and of the Soviet Union would be much impressed with the emphasis placed on investment and technological progress in both countries. He would happily conclude that the differences between the economic problems of a relatively undeveloped socialist economy and a highly developed capitalist economy are really not as great as they are often made to appear. Both countries want investment and technological progress. But if he continued to listen to the debates, he would presently begin to wonder. For in the Soviet Union investment and technology are wanted in order to enlarge the country's productive capacity. They are wanted essentially as labor-saving devices which would allow a given task to be performed with less labor, thus releasing men for other tasks. In short, they are wanted for their σ effects.

[38] See for instance pp. 31, 105–106, 217, 219, 220–21, 324, and 375.

[39] There is a third possibility, namely that income is redistributed against the capitalists, but Keynes makes no use of it.

In the United States, on the other hand, little is said about enlarging productive capacity. Technological progress is wanted as the creator of investment opportunities, and investment is wanted because it generates income and creates employment. It is wanted for its multiplier effect.

Both views are correct and both are incomplete. The multiplier is not just another capitalist invention. It can live in a socialist state just as well and it has been responsible for the inflationary pressure which has plagued the Soviet economy all these years, since the first five-year plan. And similarly, σ is just as much at home in one country as in another, and its effect—the enlarged productive capacity brought about by accumulation of capital—has undoubtedly had much to do with our peacetime unemployment.

But what is the solution? Shall we reduce σ to zero and also abolish technological progress thus escaping from unemployment into the "nirvana" of a stationary state? This would indeed be a defeatist solution. It is largely due to technology and savings that humanity has made the remarkable advance of the last two hundred years, and now when our technological future seems so bright, there is less reason to abandon it than ever before.

It is possible that α has been or will be too high as compared with the growth of our labor force, the utilization of new resources, and the development of technology. Unfortunately, we have hardly any empirical data to prove or disprove this supposition. The fact that private investment did not absorb available savings in the past does not prove that they could not be utilized in other ways (*e.g.*, by government), or even that had private business invested them these investments would have been unprofitable; the investing process itself might have created sufficient income to justify the investments. What is needed is a study of the magnitudes of s, of the difference between s and σ which can develop without much harm and then of the value of α which the economy can digest at its full employment rate of growth.

Even if the resulting magnitude of α is found to be considerably below the existing one, a reduction of α is only one of the two solutions, the speeding up of technological progress being the other. But it must be remembered that neither technology, nor of course saving, guarantee a rise in income. What they do is to place in our hands the *power* and the ability of achieving a growing income. And just as, depending upon the use made of it, any power can become a blessing or a curse, so can saving and technological progress, depending on our economic policies, result in frustration and unemployment or in an ever expanding economy.

22

THE NEO-CLASSICAL ONE-SECTOR GROWTH MODEL: A GEOMETRICAL EXPOSITION[1]

HARRY G. JOHNSON

The neo-classical one-sector growth model has become a standard piece of equipment in the economic theorist's tool kit. Nevertheless, most of the available expositions of it are needlessly complicated and mathematical, and tend to obscure the simplicity of the central analytical propositions. This article presents a geometrical exposition of the model for the simplest possible case.[2] It then goes on to indicate how various relaxations of the assumptions of this case can be accommodated, and how the model can be used to illustrate various theories of the nature of the problem of economic development . . . .

[1]This article was written while the author was Visiting Professor at the London School of Economics.

[2]The simple model, and the use of it to establish the golden rule conditions, are due to A. L. Marty: see his "The Neoclassical Theorem," *American Economic Review*, vol. LIV (1964), pp. 1026–9.

For other geometrical expositions of growth theory, see R. M. Solow, "A Contribution to the Theory of Economic Growth," *Quarterly Journal of Economics*, vol. 70 (1956), pp. 65–94; T. W. Swan, "Economic Growth and Capital Accumulation," *Economic Record*, vol. 32 (1956), pp. 334–61; John Buttrick, "A Note on Growth Theory," *Economic Development and Cultural Change*, vol. 9 (1960), pp. 75–82; W. M. Corden, "A Brief Review of Some Theories of Economic Growth," *Malayan Economic Review*, vol. 6 (1962), pp. 1–12; J. E. Meade, *A Neo-Classical Theory of Economic Growth*, 1961; F. H. Hahn and R. C. O. Matthews, "The Theory of Economic Growth: A Survey," *Economic Journal*, vol. LXXIV (1964), pp. 779–902.

Reprinted from *Economica*, (August 1966), pp. 265–79, by permission of the author and the publisher. This reprinting omits Part IV, pp. 279–87, entitled "Extensions to a Monetary Economy." Harry G. Johnson is a professor at the University of Chicago and the London School of Economics.

I. THE SIMPLE MODEL

The simplest possible growth model assumes that production requires the use of two factors of production, labour and capital, which are employed in a production function that is subject to constant returns to scale and diminishing returns to increases in the ratio of one factor to the other; that capital is physically the same product as consumption goods, and that when output is used to add to capital stock, it lasts forever; that labour grows at a constant percentage rate (n); and that saving (equals investment) is a constant fraction of income.

On these assumptions–particularly that of constant returns to scale, which enables output per factor and the marginal products of factors to be expressed as functions of the ratios of factors–the economics of growth can be summarized in the diagram of Figure 1. The abscissa represents capital per worker (k) and the ordinate represents output (y) and other income magnitudes per worker. *O.y* graphs output per worker, as a function of capital per worker and *0.sy* graphs savings per head as a function (via income per head) of capital per worker. The line *O.kn,* with slope n (the rate of growth of population), graphs the investment required to supply the new additions to the labour force with the same capital per head as the existing labour force.

The first proposition to be established is that the economy will converge in the long run on a rate of growth equal to the rate of growth of the labour force, n. To prove this, it is sufficient to establish that the economy will converge on an equilibrium stock of capital per head and therefore output per head, since if output per head is constant, total output must grow at the

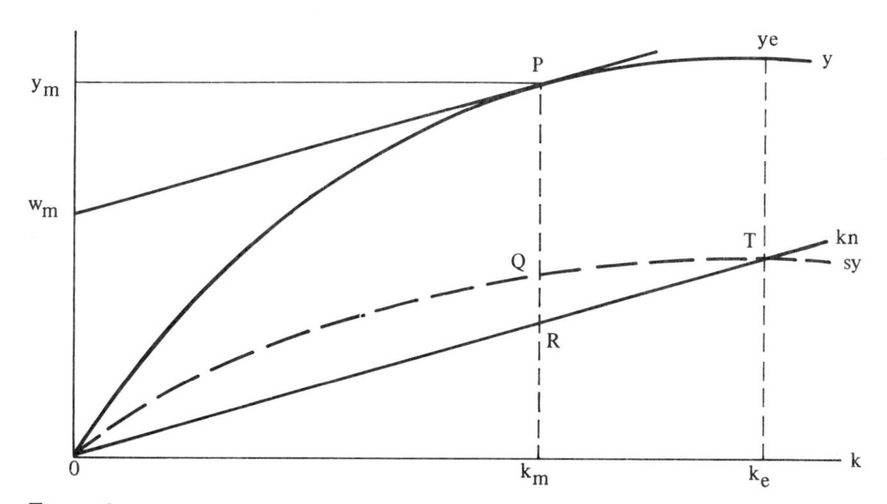

Figure 1.

same rate as the number of heads. As the diagram shows, there will be such an equilibrium stock of capital per head (capital–labour ratio in the economy), such that savings per head is just sufficient to equip the new workers with the same stock of capital per man as the pre-existing workers possess. This equilibrium stock (Ok_e) is indicated by the intersection of $0.sy$ with $O.kn$ at T. To prove that the economy's growth must converge on T, suppose that the economy began with the stock of capital per head represented by k_m less than the equilibrium stock k_e; with this stock, output would be k_mP and savings k_mQ, whereas k_mR would be sufficient to equip the additional workers with the same capital per man as existing workers, so that QR would be available to increase capital per head. Thus capital per head would increase above Ok_m,[3] and would continue to do so until it reached Ok_e. Similarly, if capital per head were above Ok_e, saving would be insufficient to equip the additional labourers with the same capital per head as existing labourers command, and capital per head would fall over time to Ok_e. T and k_e thus represent a stable equilibrium. Both the existence and the stability of this equilibrium derive from two assumptions implicit in the diagram; that there are sufficiently diminishing returns in production, and that at some output per head saving is more than sufficient to equip new workers with the capital per head available to existing workers. It should be noted that at T, $n = sy/k$, that is, the growth rate is equal to the savings ratio divided by the capital-output ratio. This is the familiar Harrod-Domar growth equation; but in this model the capital-output ratio adjusts to the growth rate, and not the other way around.

In the analysis just presented, income per head (y_ek_e) and consumption per head (y_eT) are determined, given the growth rate of the labour force, by the savings ratio s, and can be regarded as a function of that ratio. While income per head rises (by assumption) as capital per head rises, consumption per head (the vertical distance between $O.y$ and $O.kn$) first rises and then declines as capital per head rises. There is therefore obviously a savings ratio which will maximize consumption per head. This is the ratio for which the long-run equilibrium capital stock per head is such that the slope of the tangent to the $O.y$ curve at that point is equal to the slope of the $O.kn$ curve, so that a small variation of the capital-labour ratio in either direction does not alter consumption per head and a larger variation in either direction will reduce it. The maximum consumption per head situation in the diagram is represented by k_m, with consumption per head of PR, the savings ratio required to achieve it being Rk_m/Pk_m.

The behaviour requirements for achieving maximum consumption per

[3]The increase in capital per head would be something less than QR, approximately $QR/(1 + n)$.

head may be defined in two alternative ways, each economically illuminating. First, the slope of $O.kn$ is n, the equilibrium rate of growth of the economy; and the slope of $O.y$ at P is the marginal (gross and net) product of capital (owing to the assumption that capital lasts forever) and also the own-rate-of-return on capital (since units of output and capital are identical and exchange one for one on the market). Hence the condition for maximum consumption per head can be expressed as equality of the rate of return on capital with the growth rate. Second, the savings per head required to maintain the maximum consumption per head are measured by Rk_m, the savings ratio required being Rk_m / Pk_m; the income earned by the capital stock per head is $y_m w_m$ (the quantity of capital per head $O.k_m = y_m P$ multiplied by the marginal product of capital, the slope of the tangent at P, $w_m P$) and the share of capital in output is $y_m w_m / Oy_m$. Since (by the parallelism of $w_m P$ and $O.kn$ required for maximization of consumption) $y_m w_m = Rk_m$, the condition for maximum consumption can be expressed as equality of savings with the income of capital or of the savings ratio with the share of capital in income. This condition, it may be noted, will be fulfilled automatically if, as is assumed by a number of writers on growth theory, capitalists save all their income and workers consume all theirs.[4]

The condition for maximum consumption per head, expressed in the second form, has been designated as "the golden rule of accumulation". This designation, however, is misleading to the extent that it implies that some quality of optimality attaches to maximum consumption per head at all points of time. There is no reason to assume that maximum consumption per head would represent maximization of welfare in terms of social utility or consumers' preferences, and certainly no reason to assume that a society not on the golden rule growth path should set itself the objective of moving itself onto that path, or that a society on the golden rule path should stay on it, since to do either would involve re-arranging its pattern of consumption and saving over time, with effects on welfare falling outside the compass of the analysis. The conditions for maximum consumption per head apply only to alternative equilibrium growth paths of the economy, and are deduced entirely from consideration of supply factors—the exogenously given rate of growth of the labour force, and the production function, which determines the functional relation between output per head and capital per head. Utility and welfare considerations do not enter into the problem. The analysis is therefore most properly conceived as establishing the technical limits on the possibility of raising consumption per head by increasing capital per head in an expanding economy.

[4]Note that this assumption is not equivalent to assuming that the society is composed of workers and capitalists, the two classes having different savings ratios; that assumption raises the problem that as workers save and accumulate capital they merge into the capitalist class.

In conclusion to this section, it should be noted that there is nothing in the foregoing analysis to prevent the savings ratio from being such that the economy over-shoots the capital-labour ratio that maximizes consumption per head—in fact, this possibility rather than its more commonly assumed converse is illustrated in Figure 1. Nor is there anything to preclude a savings ratio implying, on the equilibrium growth path, a rate of return on capital that is negative, or less than some minimum demanded by capitalist investors. The problems raised by this possibility pre-suppose a monetary economy.

II. RELAXATION OF THE ASSUMPTIONS

(a) The Savings Assumption

The assumption that a constant proportion of income is saved is completely arbitrary and theoretically indefensible, an analytical relic of naive Keynesianism deriving no logical support from utility maximization theory. Nor can it be defended on the empirical argument of consistency with the observed secular constancy of the ratio of savings to income, since that observation pertains to an economy characterized by population growth and technical progress and is equally consistent with less naive theories of saving. Consequently little of theoretical advantage can be gained by complicating the model by assuming that aggregate saving is the sum of saving from capital income and saving from labour income, each being related to the total income of the relevant factor by a different but still fixed savings ratio, the savings ratio from the income of capital being assumed to be higher than that from labour income. The model can, however, readily be extended in this direction if so desired.

The modifications required relate only to the construction of the savings-capital per head relationship (*O.sy* in Figure 1) and take advantage of the fact that the distribution of income between the factors is uniquely related to the capital-labour ratio through the form of the production function. This relationship can be expressed in terms either of the elasticity of substitution between the factors in production, or of the elasticity of output per unit of labour with respect to the capital-labour ratio.

As is well known, if the elasticity of substitution is greater than unity, the share of capital will rise as the capital-labour ratio rises; and, consequently, so will the ratio of savings to income on the assumption of a higher savings ratio out of capital income than out of labour income. Conversely, if the elasticity of substitution is less than unity, the capital share and the saving ratio will fall as the capital-labour ratio rises; and if the elasticity of substitution is unity, the relative factor shares and the savings ratio will be constant. The first two of these possibilities will affect the relation between the curves representing saving per head and output per head, but the general lines of the analysis will not be affected (though the analysis will indicate the possibility of fulfilling the golden rule conditions by an appropriate transfer of income between the two factors).[5]

Alternatively, the share of capital can be identified with the elasticity of the curve depicting output as a function of capital per head at the point corresponding to each particular capital-labour ratio.[6] If the elasticity of the curve is constant, capital's share and the savings ratio are constant; if the elasticity increases as the capital-labour ratio rises, capital's share and the savings ratio rise with the capital-labour ratio, and conversely. Again, the general results are the same.

A step towards a more traditional theory of saving could be made by assuming that the savings ratio rises with income per head, and may either fall or rise as the rate of return on capital falls. On the first of the latter two alternatives, the savings ratio might either rise or fall with income per head, on the latter it would necessarily rise; in either case the possibility of unstable and multiple equilibrium would be present. The impression of orthodoxy would, however, be somewhat spurious, as the posited relationships between saving and its determinants implicitly assume a process of maximizing utility over time that is not specified by the model.

An approach more in keeping with the context of equilibrium growth would be to assume that saving is motivated by a desire to achieve a preferred ratio of wealth to income. This approach can be formulated in diagrammatic terms in two alternative but fundamentally equivalent ways, depending on whether one wishes to emphasize the desired ratio to income of wealth in the narrow sense of the value of material capital, or of wealth in the broad sense of the capitalized value of the productive services of both non-human and human wealth. Both exploit the fact that wealth in either sense is uniquely correlated with the level of output.

The first approach is illustrated in Figure 2. P_1 represents the initial situation, with capital-labour ratio Ok_1 and output per head of Oy_1, the initial

[5] It might appear that fluctuations in the elasticity of substitution as capital per head increased might, by producing fluctuations in the savings ratio, lead to multiple equilibrium. Robert Solow has shown me that this is not so, since regardless of the behaviour of the elasticity of substitution savings per unit of capital must fall as capital increases. Let $y = f(k)$; then the savings ratio $s = s_w[(f - kf')/y] + s_p(kf' /y)$ where s_w and s_p are the savings ratio from wages and rent of capital; and $sy/k = s_w(f/k) + (s_p - s_w)f'$. This must decline as k increases because an increase in k reduces both the average product (f/k) and the marginal product (f') of capital.

[6] The marginal product of capital is $y_m w_m / y_m P$; the average product is $Pk_m / Ok_m = Oy_m / y_m P$; the elasticity of output with respect to capital (marginal product divided by average product) is therefore $y_m w_m / Oy_m$, previously identified with the share of capital in output.

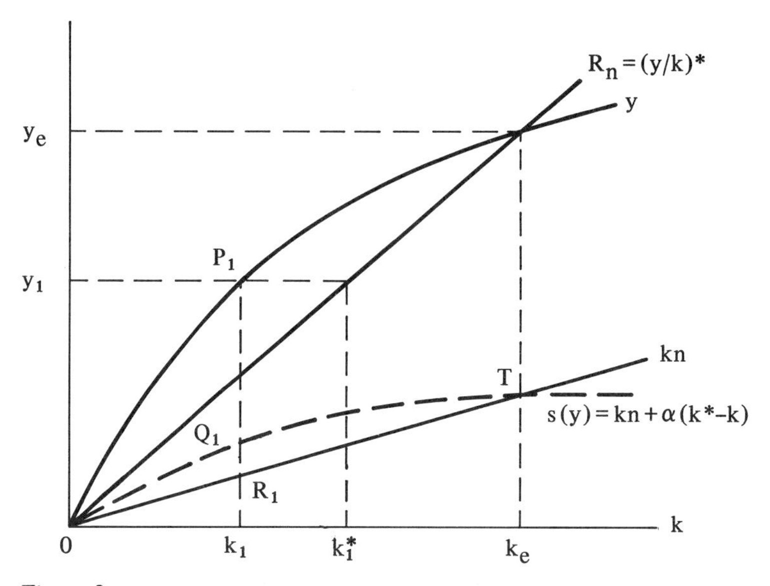

Figure 2.

ratio of output and income to non-human capital being represented by the slope of OP_1 and the non-human-wealth-to-income ratio by its reciprocal (slope with reference to the vertical axis). The desired ratio of non-human wealth to income is represented by the slope of OR_n with reference to the vertical axis. To achieve this ratio, the average individual is assumed to save from current income a fraction α of the difference between his desired and his actual non-human capital stock ($Ok_1^* - Ok_1$) over and above what must be saved to maintain the current non-human-capital-to-income ratio (R_1k_1); specifically his savings (Q_1k_1) are equal to $k_1n + \alpha(k_1^* - k_1)$. His savings behavior at other levels of income is derived in the same way to yield the savings curve $O.s(y) = \alpha(k^* - k) + kn$, the economy reaching growth equilibrium when the desired ratio of non-human capital to income is reached at the capital-labour ratio Ok_e and the output per head k_ey_e. In that equilibrium, the economy will be above or below the maximum-consumption-per-head level of capital, according as the rate of return on capital at the desired ratio of non-human capital to income is below or above the rate of population growth n.

The second approach is illustrated in Figure 3, where P_1 is again the initial situation, and the slope of OR_t with reference to the vertical axis represents the desired ratio of total (human and non-human) wealth to income. Non-human wealth is Ok_1. The value of total wealth (OK_1) is found by drawing

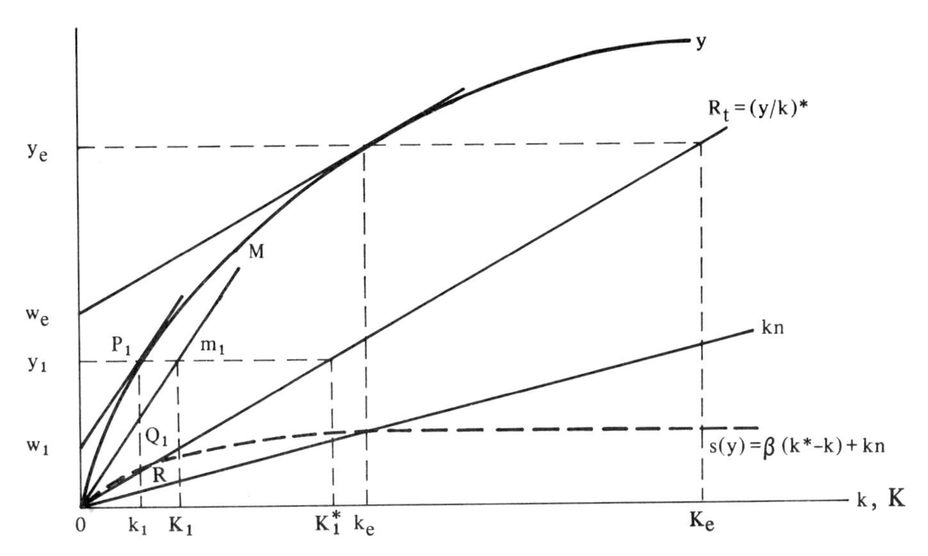

Figure 3.

OM parallel to w_1P_1 to intersect y_1P_1 produced, P_1m_1 being the value of labour income capitalized at the rate of return on capital ruling at P_1; the desired value of total wealth is OK_1^*. The individual is assumed to save a fraction β of the difference between his actual and his desired total wealth, over and above the amount (R_1k_1) he must save to maintain the current wealth-to-income ratio; his savings function is $O.s(y) = \beta(K^* - K) + kn$. These savings can only be invested in non-human capital; but accumulation of non-human capital raises the value of human capital in two ways, increasing the real wage and reducing the rate of interest at which it is capitalized. The economy reaches its equilibrium growth path when the actual ratio of total wealth to income is equal to the desired ratio: in the diagram, with income y_ek_e, capital-labour ratio Ok_e, and wealth-to-income ratio OK_e. Note that in this case the equilibrium output, non-human capital stock, and total wealth per head are defined by equality of the slope of *Oy* with the slope of OR_t, that is, by equality of the rate of return on non-human capital and the (average and marginal) desired ratio of income to total wealth.[7] In equilibrium, the economy will be above or below the level of capital per head yielding maximum consumption per head according as the

[7]This implies that the economy must come into equilibrium growth with a positive rate of return on capital, which is not necessarily the case with the Keynesian assumption of a constant propensity to save or the postulate that saving is motivated by a desired ratio of material capital to income.

reciprocal of the desired ratio of wealth to income (the desired ratio of income to wealth) is below or above the rate of population growth n.

The foregoing analyses have assumed for simplicity that the desired ratio of non-human or total wealth to income is fixed, independent of the level of income and wealth; there is no difficulty in extending the analysis to allow this desired ratio to vary with the level of income and wealth. *A priori*, one might be inclined to assume that the ratio rises as wealth and income rise.

(b) Depreciation

Relaxation of the assumption that capital once accumulated lasts forever raises no serious difficulties. It does, however, require drawing a distinction between gross and net output, gross and net saving and investment, and the gross and net marginal product of capital, the difference in each case corresponding to depreciation.

The simplest assumption is that capital depreciates by "evaporation", a certain fraction (d) of the existing stock disappearing at each moment of time. Thus replacement requirements are a constant fraction of the stock. This model is represented in Figure 4, where $O.kn$ as before represents the net saving required to equip the additional labour resulting from the growth of the labour force with the same capital per head as existing workers, $O.k(d + n)$ represents the gross saving required to make good depreciation of the existing stock and equip new workers with the same capital as existing workers, OY represents gross output as a function of the capital-labour ratio, and Oy $(= OY - dk)$ represents net output after allowance for depreciation. The savings curve $O.sy$ (not shown in the diagram) may be drawn either gross or net.

Since depreciation is rigidly tied to the current stock of capital, it is evident that the same demonstration of the convergence of the growth rate of the economy on the rate of growth of population will apply in this case as in the previous case; and that in equilibrium the Harrod-Domar equation will hold, again as a consequence of the adjustment of the capital-output ratio to the savings ratio and the rate of growth of population. More interest attaches to the conditions for maximization of consumption per head, which can be derived either by using the net output and net capital requirements curve, or by using the gross output and net-capital-requirements-plus-depreciation curves. (Because the two sets of gross and net curves both differ by the amount of depreciation, the parallelisms of the two gross and two net curves will occur at the same capital-labour ratio, Ok_m in the diagram.) The former approach yields, as alternative statements of the condition for the maximization of consumption, equality of the net marginal product of capital (the rate of interest) with the rate of population growth, and equality of the net

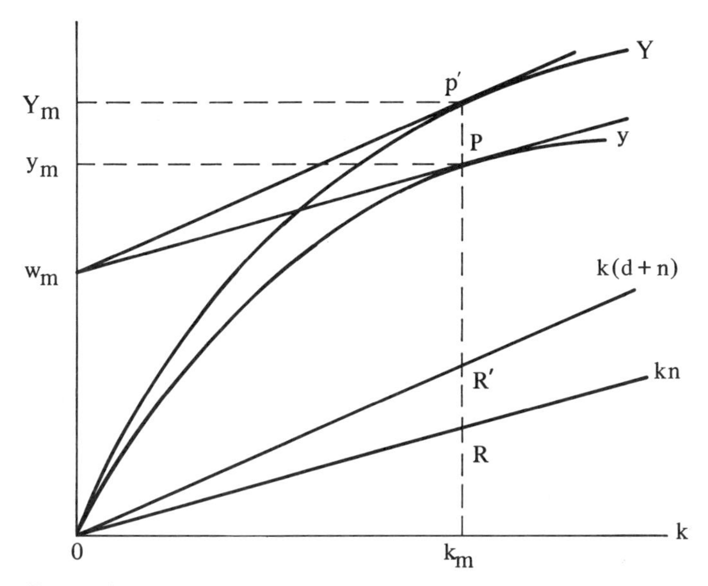

Figure 4.

income of capital (capital share in net income) with the amount of net investment (net savings ratio). The latter yields the alternative conditions, equality of the gross marginal product of capital (the sum of the rate of interest and the rate of depreciation) with the sum of the rate of population growth and the rate of depreciation, and equality of the gross income of capital (share of capital in gross output) with the amount of gross investment (share of gross investment in gross output). Since depreciation appears on both sides of these two equalities, it nets out to yield the same conditions as previously stated.

An alternative assumption about depreciation is the "one-hoss-shay" assumption, according to which capital equipment lasts with unchanging efficiency for a fixed period of time and then collapses into worthlessness. On this assumption, the ratio of depreciation to the existing stock is a variable and not a constant, since it depends not only on the fixed life of capital equipment but on the rate of growth of the economy. (The faster the rate of growth, the smaller is the amount of capital installed in the part that is now collapsing, relative to the size of the current stock.) Since, however, the capital requirements curve is drawn for the rate of growth of population, which is exogenously determined, this feature of depreciation requires only the incorporation in that curve of the value for d (the ratio of depreciation to existing stock) appropriate to the value of n. The demonstration of the convergence of the growth rate on the rate of growth of population becomes heuristic rather than rigorous (though it can be established mathematically).

Its intuitive plausibility is reinforced by the consideration that if gross saving is assumed to be a fixed proportion of gross income, the proportion of it required to make good the collapse of capital installed in the past will increase as the rate of growth falls towards the long-run equilibrium level, and vice versa; whereas if net saving is assumed to be a fixed proportion of net income, net income, and therefore the amount of net saving, relative to gross output will fall as the rate of growth falls towards the equilibrium level (because the proportion of the capital stock collapsing will rise), and vice versa. The use of a gross or net savings curve to demonstrate convergence, however, implicitly compresses the implications of the growth history of the economy for contemporary replacement requirements into the form of the savings curve, and ignores some possible complexities in the dynamic process of convergence on the equilibrium growth rate.

Diagrammatically, the conditions for maximization of consumption per head are the same as in the previous case: equality of the net rate of return on capital with the rate of population growth or of the gross rate of return on capital with the sum of the rate of population growth and the rate of depreciation, and equality of the share of capital with the savings ratio, either gross or net. These statements, however, conceal a complication that is of economic importance, concerned with the meaning of depreciation. In the previous case, depreciation by assumption corresponded exactly with the reduction in the contemporary productive capacity of the existing capital stock and the associated loss in its value. In the present case, depreciation represents the disappearance of capital constructed in the past, and is not directly connected with the loss of value of capital equipment as it ages, a loss which is associated not with a reduction in its current productivity but with a shortening of the period over which it will be productive. In other words, depreciation in this model is the real loss of capital through wearing out of parts of the capital stock, not the depreciation allowance that business firms would charge to permit the replacement of the present stock when it wears out. Similarly, net income is conceived as gross income less replacement cost of worn-out equipment, not as gross income less replacement allowances for the existing stock. The "golden rule" conditions must be interpreted in accordance with these concepts of depreciation and net income; they would appear much more complex if framed in terms of accounting concepts of depreciation and net income and the corresponding definition of the rate of return on capital.

(c) Technical Change

The model assumes only one exogenous source of economic growth to which the economy adjusts, the rate of population increase, and does not allow for the possibility of growth through exogeneous technical change. Customarily in growth theory it is assumed that technical change occurs at a constant rate, but that it may be neutral, biased towards labour-saving or biased towards capital-saving, "neutrality of innovation" being capable of definition in two major ways. One is Hicksian neutrality, defined as innovation that raises the marginal productivity of both factors in the same proportion. The other is Harrodian neutrality, defined as innovation that, at a constant rate of return on capital, would keep the capital-to-output ratio constant and raise output per man at the same rate as technical progress occurs.

The diagrammatic model can easily be extended to take account of technical progress of the Harrod-neutral type, since such progress can be equated to an increase in the effective supply of labour (the quantity of labour measured in "efficiency units") at a rate equal to the rate of technical progress. All that is required is to re-label the abscissa of Figure 1 as the ratio of capital to efficiency-units of labour, and to re-define n as the sum of the natural rate of growth of the labour force (p) and the rate of growth of efficiency-units supplied per man associated with Harrod neutral technical progress (t). The diagram can then be used to demonstrate the convergence of the rate of growth of the economy on the equilibrium rate ($p + t$), determined by the exogenously given rates of population growth and technical progress. The conditions for maximum consumption per head are alternatively that the rate of return on capital should be equal to the sum of the rates of population growth and (Harrod neutral) technical change, and that the proportion of income saved should be equal to the share of capital in national income, as before. Cases of biased technical progress (biased by reference to the standard of Harrod neutrality) cannot be readily analysed diagrammatically, however; nor can cases of technical progress defined in terms of the Hicksian concept of neutrality (except in the case of a Cobb-Douglas production function, where Hicks-neutrality and Harrod-neutrality are the same thing).

III. APPLICATIONS TO DEVELOPMENT THEORY

The model developed in Section I can be applied readily to illustrate some propositions in the theory of economic development.

One such proposition is the possibility of a "low-level equilibrium trap," and the associated conclusion that what is needed to start a country on the path of self-sustaining economic growth is some sort of "big push" or "minimum critical effort," designed to raise capital and income per head above some initial level beyond which the economy will grow automatically, in the sense of steadily raising capital and income per head.

Two alternative possibilities of a low-level equilibrium trap are illustrated

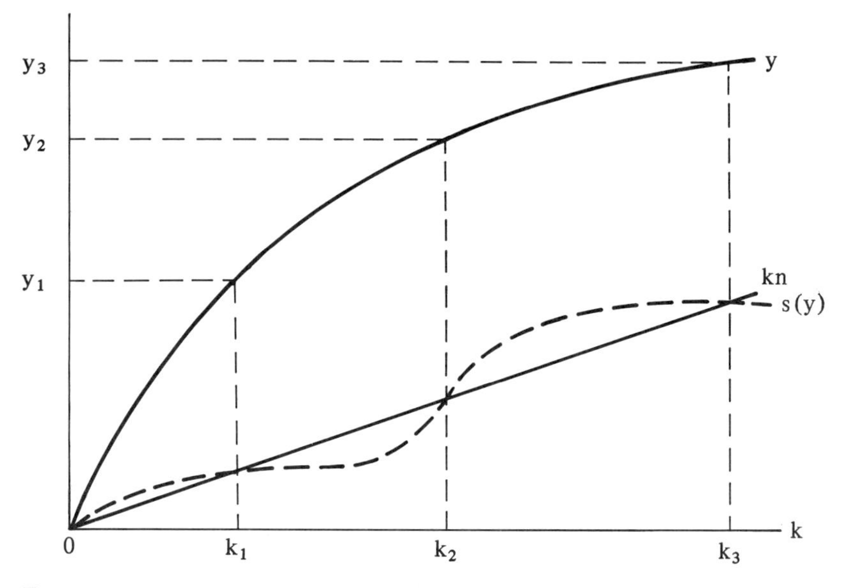

Figure 5.

in Figures 5 and 6. In Figure 5 it is assumed that at low levels of income per head the savings ratio is low, whereas after some critical level of capital and income per head the savings ratio begins to rise, approaching a new higher level as the economy becomes richer; the rate of population increase is assumed constant, independent of the level of income per head. In Figure 6 the savings ratio is assumed either to be constant (the dashed curve $O.sy$) or, more realistically perhaps, to vary inversely with the rate of population growth (the initially dashed, then dotted, function $O.s(y)$); the rate of population growth is assumed to be a function of income per head, being zero for low income levels, then rising rapidly as income per head rises, then gradually falling to a constant rate at high levels of income. In both cases there is a stable low-level equilibrium, with income per head and capital per head constant respectively at Oy_1 and Ok_1; an unstable intermediate-level equilibrium with income and capital per head constant respectively at Oy_2 and Ok_2, from which any chance divergence would cause the economy either to grow in income and wealth towards y_3, k_3 or retrogress towards y_1, k_1; and a high-level stable equilibrium with income and capital per head respectively constant at Oy_3 and Ok_3, which may be interpreted in the present context as the stage of full development. Starting at y_1, k_1, a small once-for-all injection of additional capital per head would produce only a temporary rise in income per head, the economy being unwilling to save enough from the higher

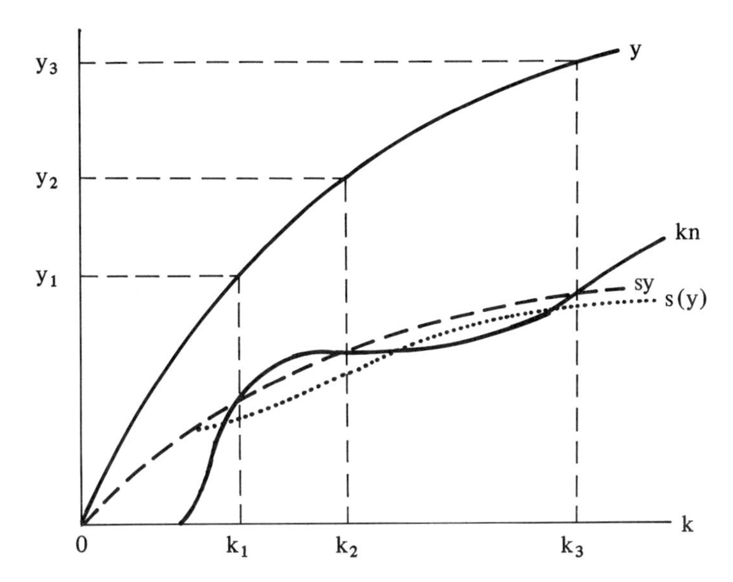

Figure 6.

income to prevent the capital per head available to future generations from declining as income grew. In order to move the economy onto a path of self-sustaining economic growth, enough additional capital must be provided to raise the capital-labour ratio above Ok_2. Similarly, a slight rise in the savings ratio would not suffice to move the economy out of the neighbourhood of its present income per head; in order to start it on a self-sustaining growth path, the savings ratio must be raised sufficiently so that it lies completely above the capital requirements curve at the left-hand side of the diagram.[8]

The diagrammatic apparatus can also be used to explain the seriousness of the handicap to development of rapid population growth, and the growing importance currently being attached to programmes of birth control. Figure 7 depicts two economies, equipped with the same aggregate production function and saving the same proportion of national income, but differing widely in their rates of population increase (n_1 and n_2). The growth of country 1, the country with the low rate of population increase, converges on the income level Oy_1 and capital stock Ok_1 per head, while the growth of country 2, the country with the high rate of natural increase, converges on the lower levels of income and capital per head Oy_2 and Ok_2. More significantly, the

[8]A third possibility of a low-level equilibrium trap could be constructed by assuming a constant savings ratio but allowing increasing returns to increases in the capital-labour ratio for low levels of capital-intensity.

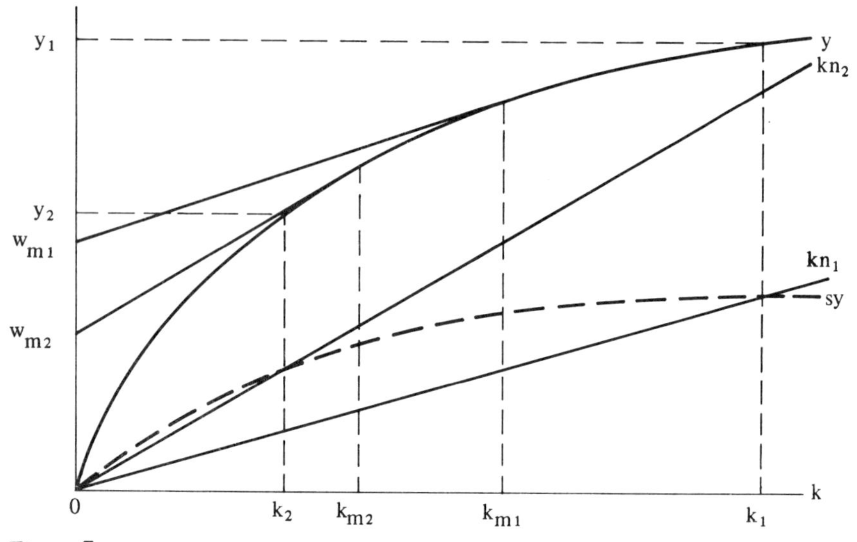

Figure 7.

maximum consumption per head obtainable (on a sustained basis) by country 2 is Ow_{m2}, whereas country 1 can obtain the substantially higher consumption per head Ow_{m1}. Moreover, as the diagram is drawn country 2 must raise its savings ratio to achieve the maximum consumption per head available to it, while country 1 must actually reduce its saving ratio. In general, however, the relation between the savings ratios in the two countries required to maximize their respective levels of consumption per head at all points of time depends on the characteristics of the aggregate production function: by the golden rule, the required savings ratios are equal to the shares of capital in national income, and as previously explained this share rises or falls with income and capital per head according as the elasticity of substitution between capital and labour is greater or less than unity (alternatively, as the elasticity of output per head with respect to capital per head rises or falls as capital per head increases). Whatever is required of the shares of income saved in the two countries, however, it remains true that the maximum obtainable level of consumption per head must be lower in the country with the higher rate of population increase. It is also evident that its rate of population increase may be great enough to confine that country to a poverty level of consumption per head, whatever it does with its savings ratio and whatever donations of foreign aid it receives—unless foreign aid is provided on a permanent basis and its amount increases at the rate at which the country's population is growing.

VII

Inflation

Full employment, rapid growth, and price stability compose a very familiar trio of major macroeconomic goals. What is probably just as familiar is the fact that the U.S. economy has not enjoyed all three of these economic blessings simultaneously in recent years. If we take as a starting point 1953, the year of the ending of hostilities in Korea, we find that the period to 1962 was one of unusually slow growth, that the years to 1966 were years of less than full employment, and, for a single blessing, that the years to 1965 (apart from 1955–57) were years of remarkably stable prices.

However, while slow growth and unemployment had both ceased to be major problems by 1966, in that year inflation was well on its way to becoming such a problem. By 1968–69 it had fully achieved this dubious distinction—one had to go all the way back to the 6.7 percent increase of 1951 to find a more rapid annual rate of price advance. In the late sixties, inflation had thus become as much *the* domestic economic issue as growth had been the issue a decade earlier.

This most recent inflation, like its predecessors, is not a process that can begin to be explained by simply labeling it with one or another of still another familiar set of terms: demand-pull, cost-push, and mixed causes. This set of terms, however, does provide a simple but useful theoretical framework from which analysis can begin. The first selection in this part is an excerpt of two short sections from an article by Martin Bronfenbrenner and Franklyn D. Holzman, the first of which, with the aid of a basic graphic apparatus, sets out the framework noted, although it is identified here by the less familiar but equivalent terms: pure demand, pure supply, and mixed sources.

The second of these two sections considers the definition of inflation. Although it obviously can be defined as a rising price level, the selection shows that this obvious definition needs considerable expansion and clarification before it can really be considered meaningful.

In the second selection of this part, Fritz Machlup takes as his point of departure the standard conceptual framework set forth in the first selection, identifies its limitations, and develops a more adequate framework in terms of the concepts of autonomous, induced, and supportive demand inflation and aggressive, defensive, and responsive cost inflation. On the basis of these concepts, model sequences of the inflationary process are developed and applied briefly to what may be the most perplexing problem in the study of inflation–identifying whether any concrete inflationary experience was "initiated" by cost-push or demand-pull forces.

Machlup's focus is primarily on the dichotomy of demand-pull and cost-push. The final selection in this part, by Charles L. Schultze, introduces what is now the best-known model of mixed inflation: the sectoral, or demand-shift, model. Schultze grants that excess demand has been the cause of our *major* inflations and that cost-push has played a role in some of our inflations, but he also holds that, even in the absence of pure demand-pull or cost-push forces, mild inflation can be expected in a dynamic economy whenever rapid, sizable changes in the composition of demand take place. In our recent experience the 1955–57 period of rising prices was accounted for primarily by demand-shift, according to Schultze's detailed study of the inflationary forces at work during this period.

23

SOURCES AND DEFINITIONS OF INFLATION

MARTIN BRONFENBRENNER
and FRANKLYN D. HOLZMAN

A. SOURCES OF INFLATION

One key issue is the identification of the fundamental source or sources of inflationary pressure. Does inflation arise from the demand side of the goods, factor, and asset markets, from the supply side, or from some combination of the two—the so-called mixed inflation? Does the answer differ in the short and the long run, in developed and under-developed economies, with differences in countries' economic structures, in creeping, trotting, or galloping inflations, in the 1950's and the 1940's?

Answers to such questions are not only academic, but have important policy implications. Thus, if an inflation is due to excess demand, it is generally considered controllable by demand-reducing fiscal and monetary policies. If it is due largely to forces of cost and supply, it may not yield to such easy therapy. Fiscal and monetary policies, that is to say, may cure a cost inflation only at the price of unemployment and slower growth, either temporary or permanent. Many cost-inflation theorists therefore propose mitigation rather than elimination of inflation. Others rely on voluntary restraints in pricing and bargaining. Still others propose disequilibrium systems of direct control (wage- and price-fixing, rationing, allocations) if

Reprinted from Part I, pp. 594–600, of Martin Bronfenbrenner and Franklyn D. Holzman, "Survey of Inflation Theory," *American Economic Review* (September 1963), pp. 593–661, by permission of the authors and publisher. Martin Bronfenbrenner is a professor at Carnegie-Mellon University, and Franklyn D. Holzman is a professor at Tufts University.

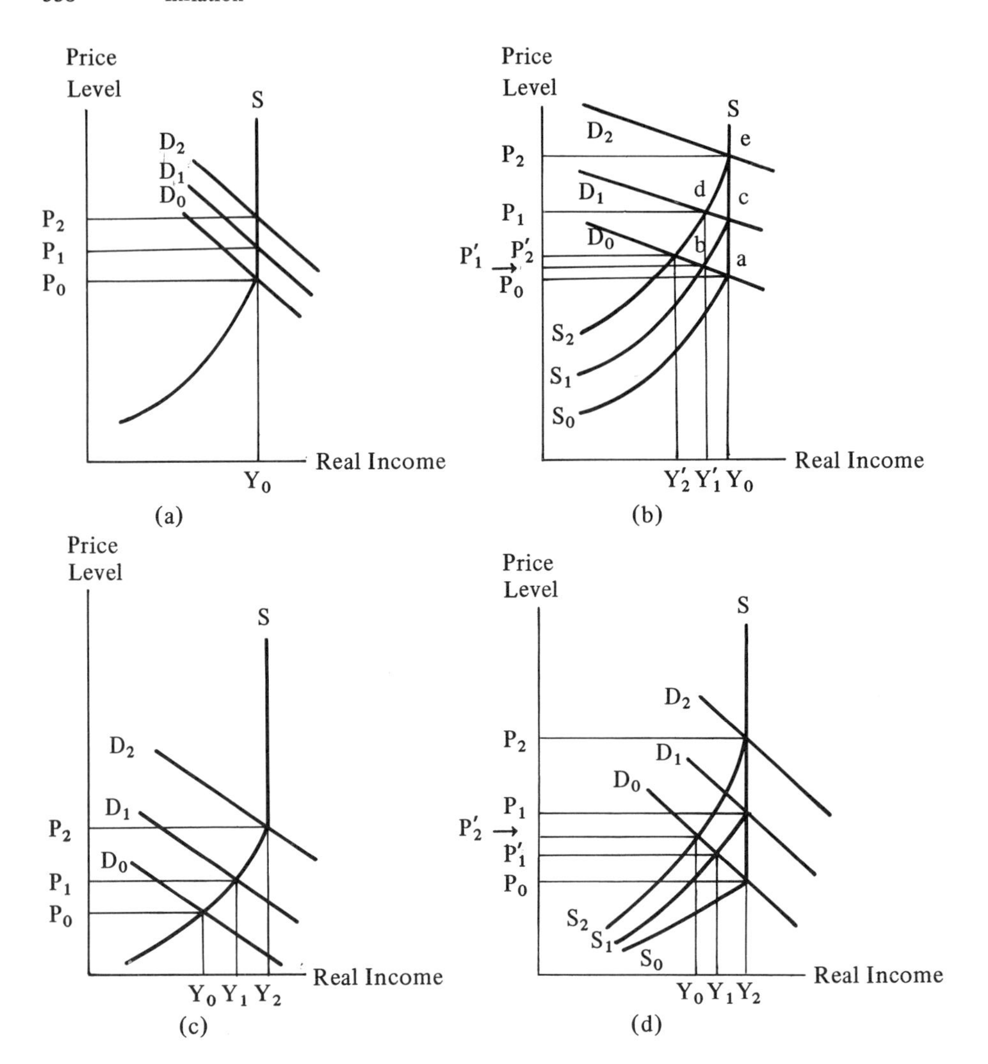

Figure 1.

high levels of employment and growth are to be reconciled with price stability.

The four diagrams of Figure 1 illustrate different types of inflationary positions in a closed economy.[1] The horizontal axes all represent real national income or GNP; the vertical axes represent "the" price level with no

[1]More extended classifications of inflation theories are found in several sources, such as Holzman [4], Machlup [7] [this article appears in the volume as Selection 24], and Phelps [8].

direct controls. Aggregate demand curves D are drawn sloping downward. This slope illustrates Patinkin real-balance effects with a constant nominal money supply and static price expectations. In some circumstances inflation-engendered redistribution of income and wealth also leads to a downward slope of D. Aggregate supply curves S are drawn sloping upward—in some full-employment cases, as vertical lines. Shifts in aggregate supply functions result from changes in money-profit margins and money-wage rates. Interdependence between D and S functions may exist; it is considered explicitly in Figure 1d.

Pure-demand-inflation theorists tend to assume that at some income level Y_0 (Figure 1a), corresponding to full employment, the aggregate supply function becomes completely inelastic, as drawn. No income level lower than Y_0 is a full-employment one, and increases in demand beyond D_0, as to D_1 and D_2, raise the price level from P_0 to P_1 and P_2.

Pure-supply-inflation theorists, on the other hand, maintain that, in societies of oligopolies, unions, and other pressure groups, the aggregate supply curve moves upward, as from S_0 to S_1 and S_2 in Figure 1b,[2] whatever happens to aggregate demand. The full-employment real-income level Y_0 is then maintainable only at rising price levels (P_0,P_1,P_2). Unemployment is the cost of holding prices closer to P_0 or to any previously achieved level. If aggregate demand, for example, is held at D_0, real income falls to Y_1' and Y_2'. Even so, the price level rises from P_0 to P_1' to P_2'. If the government is committed to full employment, the path of temporary equilibrium points will be something like *a-b-c-d-e*.

One variety of mixed-inflation theory denies for several reasons, one of them money illusion,[3] that aggregate supply is price-inelastic at full employment. In Figure 1c, (Y_0, P_0), (Y_1, P_1), and (Y_2, P_2) are all full-employment positions in that no involuntary unemployment exists. The first corresponds to A. P. Lerner's "low full employment" with substantial voluntary unemployment [5, Ch. 13], and the last to his "high full employment" with little or none. The region between low and high full employment was called by Keynes "semi-inflation" in contrast to the true or full inflation of Figure 1a. Mixed-inflation theorists usually think society prefers the couple (Y_2, P_2) to the other alternatives, even when all three are full-employment positions. In this type of mixed-inflation theory, inflation does not continue after (Y_2, P_2) is reached. In this respect, the solution is related more closely to demand than to cost inflation. . . .

Another mixed theory is illustrated in Figure 1d, where interrelated shifts in S and D induce unemployment inflation. This differs from the pure cost

[2]Supply shifts might also result from rising import prices in an open economy.

[3]We define money illusion as an unjustified expectation that price levels will remain constant or that short-run changes will be reversed in the longer run.

inflation of Figure 1b in that the extent of the shift in supply increases as unemployment declines. Whether demand rises from D_0 to D_1 and D_2 or remains at D_0, supply moves from S_0 to S_1 and S_2; the shift is larger, the closer the economy approaches full employment at Y_2. In this version full employment is a more unstable position, and more difficult to achieve by rapid inflation than under pure cost-push, because the induced supply shifts are larger at low levels of unemployment. On the other hand, price stability may be possible at the cost of less unemployment in this model than in the one represented in Figure 1b. The model represented in Figure 1d may also be more realistic than that of Figure 1b; casual empiricism suggests that cost-push is often moderated by the level of demand. . . .

B. DEFINITION OF INFLATION

In the preceding diagrams and discussion, inflation has meant a rise in "the" price level, i.e., a depreciation of the monetary unit. This is the most obvious, but by no means the only, definition. Indeed, disagreement over the definition of the term is symptomatic of the confusion in inflation theory. We list some issues slurred over by definitions in terms of "the" price level. (No such list can be exhaustive.)

1. Which of an infinity of possible price levels is meant? An implicit national income or GNP deflator has recently come into favor. Such deflators were largely unknown before 1939, and reliance was usually placed on wholesale price indexes. In many cases price indexes will show widely differing rates of change, and the differences may become a political issue.[4]

2. What allowance should be made for new products, quality changes, shifts in consumption habits, and other factors considered in the utility analysis of price index numbers? In the United States, an AFL-CIO task force relied on these factors during World War II in alleging that the official indexes understated the magnitude of wartime inflation. This was the Meany-Thomas Report [11]. In the late 1950's, a National Bureau of Economic Research task force, headed by Stigler, suggested on similar grounds that the indexes have overstated the magnitude of U.S. inflation subsequent to the Korean War [9].

3. When price controls are in effect, should the indexes be based on black

[4]The Ikeda Government in Japan, for example, relied on wholesale price indexes to show that the rapid economic growth of 1960–62 was not inflationary, while the Opposition relied on consumer price indexes and national income deflators to show the reverse. Quite generally, quoting the U. S. Council of Economic Advisers [2, p. 167], "a period of stability in the wholesale price index tends to be a period of slow rise in the consumer price index and in the implicit price index for GNP." This is because of rises in prices of services and in public payrolls.

market as well as official prices? Even in the absence of organized black markets, what allowances, if any, should be made for lessened availability of goods under control? The terms "repressed" and "suppressed" inflation have been used to refer to these cases,[5] as distinguished from "open" inflation when no anti-inflationary direct controls are in effect. Are "repressed" and "suppressed" inflation types of inflation or alternatives to inflation?

4. Assume that commodity taxes and subsidies are used widely, as in contemporary France. Should prices be taken gross or net of such taxes and subsidies? Suppose also that, as in France before 1959, subsidies are used to hold individual prices down, with commodities in the official indexes being given larger subsidies (or lower taxes) than others. How reliable are price indexes under this sort of *a posteriori* sampling bias?

5. Assume that, following destruction and disruption due to war, flood, or earthquake, there is a sharp fall (i.e., shift to the left) in the aggregate supply curves of Figure 1. Is the result to be called inflationary when no increase in aggregate demand has occurred? Does it make any difference if the same destruction and disruption simultaneously create unemployment?

6. Consider Figure 1c, where a rise in the price level leads, at least in the short run, to an increase in real output and employment. Is this really inflationary, or should the term be limited to instances in which no significant increases in output or employment occur?

7. Suppose that, as probably happened in the 1920's, technical progress has brought about a widespread reduction in production costs with no corresponding reduction in prices. Were the resulting increases in money wages and gross profits inflationary?

8. Does it make a difference whether price increases have been anticipated correctly (so as to minimize their effects on the distribution of income), or whether they are unanticipated or anticipated incorrectly? As an extreme case of Lerner's [6] "expectational" definition of inflation, suppose that prices fell by 5 per cent when a fall of 10 per cent was anticipated generally. Is this inflation?

9. Does it make a difference, as suggested by James [3, p. 3], whether a price level change is or is not regarded as permanent and irreversible?

Our answers to these questions may be affected by extraneous issues such as whether or not we consider inflation, or tight money, or direct controls to be Good Things. If one considers inflation, for example, a Bad Thing, it is difficult to avoid a question-begging definition which will render Good

[5]These terms, due to Ropke, are often used synonymously. Where they are differentiated, we suppose that direct controls remain effective only in the short run when an inflation is *repressed,* but that these controls remain effective indefinitely when an inflation is *suppressed.* Compare Charlesworth [1].

Results somehow noninflationary, even when accompanied by price increases.

For those unwilling to accept the evidence of price indexes per se, a number of alternative definitions are available. By no means all of these are new, and, once again, the list is not intended to be exhaustive.

1. Inflation is a condition of generalized excess demand, in which "too much money chases too few goods."

2. Inflation is a rise of the money stock or money income, either total or per capita.[6]

3. Inflation is a rise in price levels with additional characteristics or conditions: it is incompletely anticipated; it leads (via cost increases) to further rises; it does not increase employment and real output; it is faster than some "safe" rate; it arises "from the side of money"; it is measured by prices net of indirect taxes and subsidies; and/or it is irreversible.

4. Inflation is a fall in the external value of money as measured by foreign exchange rates, by the price of gold, or indicated by excess demand for gold or foreign exchange at official rates.

An unusually comprehensive definition (including cost-push in the factor markets and excess demand in output and factor markets) is Turvey's [10, pp. 534 ff.]. He calls inflation "the process resulting from competition in attempting to maintain total real income, total real expenditure, and/or total output at a level which has become physically impossible, or attempting to increase any of them to a level which is physically impossible." . . .

References

1. Harold K. Charlesworth, *Economics of Repressed Inflation,* London, 1956.
2. *Economic Report of the President*, Washington, Jan. 1962.
3. D. C. Hague, ed., *Inflation*, Proceedings of the Conference of the International Economic Association held at Elsinore, 1959. New York, 1962.
4. Franklyn D. Holzman, "Inflation: Cost-Push and Demand-Pull," *American Economic Review*, March 1960, *50*, 20–42.
5. A. P. Lerner, *Economics of Employment,* New York, 1951.
6. A. P. Lerner, "The Inflationary Process—Some Theoretical Aspects," *Review of Economics and Statistics*, Aug. 1949, *31*, 193–200; reprinted in A. P. Lerner, *Essays on Economic Analysis,* London, 1953.
7. Fritz Machlup, "Another View of Cost-Push and Demand-Pull Inflation," *Review of Economics and Statistics*, May 1960, *42*, 125–39.

[6]These definitions, generally in disfavor in the period since World War II, are associated with the neutral-money theorists of the 1920's and 1930's, particularly in Austria.

8. Edmund S. Phelps, "A Test for the Presence of Cost Inflation in the United States, 1955–57," *Yale Economic Essays*, spring 1961, *1*, 28–69.
9. George Stigler, *et al.*, *The Price Statistics of the Federal Government,* National Bureau of Economic Research, New York, 1962, pp. 35–39.
10. Ralph Turvey, "Some Aspects of the Theory of Inflation in a Closed Economy," *Economic Journal*, Sept. 1951, *61*, 532–43.
11. U. S. Office of Economic Stabilization, *Report of the President's Committee on the Cost of Living*, Washington, 1945, pp. 25–32 (R. J. Thomas), 32–39 (George Meany).

24

ANOTHER VIEW OF COST-PUSH AND DEMAND-PULL INFLATION

FRITZ MACHLUP

It is with some hesitation that I join the discussion and thus contribute to the galloping inflation of the literature on the creeping inflation of prices. My excuse is probably the same as that of most of my fellow writers: dissatisfied with much of what others have written, I have, perhaps presumptuously, decided that my way of thinking would be more successful. Hence, I am presenting another view of cost-push and demand-pull inflation.

THE CURRENT DEBATE

Before I set forth the controversial issue and the most widely held views, I shall indulge in a few preliminaries by referring briefly to the old squabble about what should be meant by inflation.

Inflation of What?

Some people regard "inflation"as a *cause* (explanation) of a general rise in prices (and of some other things too), while others use the word as a *synonym* (equivalent) for a general rise in prices. In times when governments undertake to control prices by prohibitions with threats of sanctions against unauthorized price rising, many writers realize how awkward it is to use the

Reprinted from the *Review of Economics and Statistics,* (May 1960) pp. 125–39, by permission of the author and publisher, Harvard University Press. Copyright 1960 by the President and Fellows of Harvard College. Fritz Machlup is a professor at Princeton University.

term inflation to signify price increase, because then they want to discuss the "latent" or "repressed" inflation—one that does not show up in a general price index, or does not show up adequately. Also when one talks about inflation and deflation as apparent opposites, a definition in terms of general prices is quite inconvenient, inasmuch as the problem of deflation is so serious largely because it shows up in falling volumes of production and employment instead of falling prices.

One solution would be to use the word inflation always with a modifying word that tells exactly *what* is blown up: currency, credit, spending, demand, wages, prices, etc. This would be a great help; indeed some controversial problems would disappear, because the disputants would find out that they were talking about different things, and other problems would be greatly clarified. The most lively issue of our times, whether "our" inflation in the last four years has been due to a demand-pull or to a cost-push, would lose some of its muddiness if the analysts had to qualify all their pronouncements with regard to the inflation of credit, spending, demand, wholesale prices, consumer prices, and so forth.

A search of the learned literature would yield scores of definitions of inflation, differing from one another in essentials or in nuances. A search of the popular literature, however, reveals no realization of the differences in the meanings experts give to the term. The differences apparently have been reserved for the treatises and the quarterlies; the daily papers and the weeklies were not to be encumbered with "technicalities." Now that inflation has become such a widely debated topic, with many scholars participating in the debates, the popular meaning of inflation, denoting an increase in the consumer price index, has been increasingly adopted by the professional economists. Although this is probably bad for analysis, we may have to accept it. But at the risk of appearing pedantic I shall continue to speak of various kinds of inflation and to specify which I happen to be speaking about.

The Controversial Issue

Opinion is divided on whether consumer prices in recent years have increased chiefly (1) because industry has invested too much and government has spent too much (relative to the nation's thrift) or (2) because big business has raised material prices and/or big labor has raised wage rates too high (relative to the nation's increase in productivity). The issue is partly who is to be "blamed" for the past rise in consumer prices, and partly what policies should be pursued to avoid a continued increase.

If demand-pull inflation is the correct diagnosis, the Treasury is to be blamed for spending too much and taxing too little, and the Federal Reserve

Banks are to be blamed for keeping interest rates too low and for creating or tolerating too large a volume of free reserves, which enable member banks to extend too much credit.

If cost-push inflation is the correct diagnosis, trade unions are to be blamed for demanding excessive wage increases, and industry is to be blamed for granting them, big business may be blamed for raising "administered prices" of materials and other producers goods to yield ever-increasing profit rates, and government may be assigned the task of persuading or forcing labor unions and industry to abstain from attempts to raise their incomes, or at least to be more moderate.

Not everybody draws the appropriate conclusions from the theory which he espouses. And not everybody is willing to adopt policies to correct the undesirable situation. (Nor does everybody find the situation sufficiently undesirable to get seriously worried.)[1] The ambivalent position of many partisans of labor unions is noteworthy. They reject the wage-push diagnosis because, understandably, they do not wish to take the blame for the inflation. But they also reject the demand-pull diagnosis, because this diagnosis would militate against the use of fiscal and monetary policies to bolster employment. They want effective demand to be increased at a rate fast enough to permit full employment at rapidly increasing wage rates; but they do not want to attribute increasing prices either to the increase in demand or to the increase in wage rates. The only way out of this logical squeeze is to blame the consumer-price increase on prices "administered" by big business; but in order to support this hypothesis one would have to prove that the profit margins and profit rates of the industries in question have been rising year after year—which they have not.[2] But we shall see later that matters are not quite so simple and cannot be analyzed exclusively in these terms.

Our first task is to deal with the contention that the distinction between cost-push and demand-pull inflation is unworkable, irrelevant, or even meaningless.

"Cost-Push No Cause of Inflation"

There is a group of outstanding economists contending that there cannot be such a thing as a cost-push inflation because, without an increase in purchasing power and demand, cost increases would lead to unemployment and depression, not to inflation.

[1] *Cf.* "Argument for Creeping Inflation," *New York Times,* March 3, 1959; "Slow Inflation: An Inescapable Cost of Maximum Growth Rate," *Commercial and Financial Chronicle,* March 26, 1959; "Inflation—A Problem of Shrinking Importance," *Commercial and Financial Chronicle* April 23, 1959—all by Sumner H. Slichter.

[2] "The period 1947 to 1958 was a time of decreasing profit margins. This fact is important because it shows that the initiative in raising prices was not being taken by employers. In the

On their own terms these economists are correct. The rules of inductive logic say that if A and B together cause M; and if A without B cannot cause M, whereas B without A can cause M; then B, and not A, should be called the cause of M. Make A the wage-raising power of the corporations; make B the credit-creating and money-creating power of the monetary system; make M the successive price increases. It should be quite clear that without the creation of new purchasing power a continuing price increase would be impossible. Hold the amount of money and bank credit constant (relative to real national product) and all that the most powerful unions and corporations can do is to price themselves out of the market.

Having admitted all this to the economists who reject the possibility of cost-push inflation, we can shift the weight of the argument to the question whether, given the power of the monetary system to create money and credit, this power would be exercised to the same extent if strong trade unions and strong corporations desisted from raising wages and prices as it actually is exercised when wages and prices are being pushed up. There would probably be quick agreement that, given our present system, the exercise of the wage-raising power of strong unions and the price-raising power of strong corporations induces, or adds impetus to, the exercise of the ability of the banking system to create purchasing power.

The point then is that an increase in effective demand is a necessary condition for a continuing increase in general prices, but that a cost-push under present conditions will regularly lead to an expansion of credit and to that increase in effective demand which will permit the increase in consumer prices.

There remains, however, an important question of fact. Assume it is decided not to exercise the power to create money and credit—more than is needed to maintain a constant ratio to real national product—even at the risk of severe unemployment that might result if wages and prices increased; would we then have to expect that the strong unions and corporations would continue to make use of their wage-raising and price-raising powers? Some economists are convinced that unions and business firms would adopt much more moderate policies if they had to fear that any lack of moderation would lead to unemployment and stagnation. This does not mean that a considerable level of unemployment would be required to impress industry and unions with the desirability of moderation. Industrial firms would know that, under an unyielding monetary policy, they could not hope to pass increases in labor

four years 1947 to 1950 inclusive the net income of non-financial corporations after taxes per dollar of sales averaged 4.45 cents. In the next four years the average net income was 4.10 cents per dollar of sales; and in the three years 1955 to 1957 inclusive, it was about 3.3 cents per dollar of sales." Slichter, *Commercial and Financial Chronicle,* April 23, 1959.

cost on to consumers and they would therefore refuse to yield to union pressure. Unions, in turn, would not strike for higher wages if they were sure that industry could not afford to give in. Hence, no cost-push and no extra unemployment.

Acceptance of this view by any number of economists would not yet make it a practicable policy. It could not work unless the monetary authorities embraced it without reservation, since any indication of a lack of faith and determination on the part of the authorities would remove the premise: unions could hope that industries would hope that an eventual relaxation of the monetary brake would "bail them out" and by means of an expansion of demand avert the business losses and the unemployment that would threaten to arise in consequence of wage and price increases.

"Demand-Pull No Cause of Inflation"

Having shown that there is a sense in which the contention is correct that "cost-push is no cause of inflation, it takes a demand-pull to produce it," we shall now attempt to show that the opposite contention may likewise be correct. There are indeed assumptions for which it would be appropriate to say that "demand-pull is no cause of inflation, it takes a cost-push to produce it." What are these assumptions and how do they differ from those of the traditional model?

In the traditional model, prices rise or fall under the impact of anonymous market forces. They rise when at their existing level the quantity of goods demanded exceeds the quantity supplied. Not that producers, noticing the increased demand, would decide that they could do better if they "charged" more; rather the mechanism of a "perfect market" would automatically lift prices to the level where the consumers would not want to purchase any more than was supplied. Sellers, in this model, don't ask higher prices, they just get them. The same thing happens in the model of the perfect labor market. When the demand for labor increases, workers don't ask for higher wages, they just get them as a result of competition.

In a large part of our present economy, prices and wages do not "rise" as if lifted by the invisible hand, but are "raised" by formal and explicit managerial decisions. Assume now that prices and wage rates are administered everywhere in the economy in such a way that changes in demand are not taken into account; instead, they are set in accordance with some "rules of thumb." Prices and wages may then be so high (relative to demand) that inventories accumulate, production is cut, and labor is unemployed; or they may be so low (relative to demand) that inventories are depleted, production is raised, customers must patiently wait for delivery or their orders are rejected, and there are plenty of vacancies, but no workers to fill them. If the rules of thumb are universally observed by producers, distributors, and labor unions and take full account of increased cost of production and increased cost of living, but disregard all changes in demand, then there can be no demand-pull upon prices. In such circumstances an increase in effective demand leads to unfilled orders and unfilled vacancies, but not to higher prices.[3]

One may object, of course, that such a model cannot possibly apply to all markets; that there exist numerous competitive markets in which no producer has enough power to "set" or "charge" a price; that in many markets in which prices are administered the would-be buyers, in periods of increased demand, offer higher prices in order to be served and sellers are glad to accept them even though they exceed their list prices; and that this regularly happens when the demand for labor is brisk, so that wages paid can be higher than the rates agreed in collective bargaining. Thus, demand-pull is likely to work despite the existence of administered prices and wages.

Although the objection may be sustained on practical grounds, this does not destroy the value of the model. If there are, in actual fact, *many* industries where backlogs of orders accumulate while prices fail to rise and where job vacancies grow in number while wages fail to rise, then the model has some relevance, and it is legitimate to speculate about the functioning of an economic system in which *all* prices and wages are administered on the basis of cost calculations and held at the set levels even in the face of excess demand. It is not easy to decide whether on balance the institutions in our economy are such that a model featuring "market-clearing prices" or a model featuring "cost-plus prices" fits better the purposes of speculating about the over-all performance of the entire economy.

In any case, the contention must be granted that there may be conditions under which "effective demand" is not effective and won't pull up prices, and when it takes a cost-push to produce price inflation. But this position disregards an important distinction, namely, whether the cost-push is "equilibrating" in the sense that it "absorbs" a previously existing excess demand or whether it is "disequilibrating" in the sense that it creates an excess supply (of labor and productive capacity) that will have to be prevented or removed by an increase in effective demand. Thus we are back at the crucial issue; a "monistic" interpretation cannot do justice to it.

Statistical Tests

It is possible to grant the usefulness of the distinction between cost-push and demand-pull in building theoretical models for speculative reasoning, and yet to deny its usefulness in identifying the causes of general price increases in

[3] ". . . if all prices were administered on the basis of markup over direct cost—then excess demand might exist in all markets, yet without effect on the price level." Gardner Ackley,

concrete situations. It may be that the concepts are not operational, that statistical tests are either unavailable or unreliable.

Some have proposed to answer the question, whether wage-push or demand-pull had "initiated" the upward movement of prices, by looking to see which has *increased first,* prices or wages. But "first" since what time? If prices and wages have risen in turn, in successive steps, the choice of a base period is quite arbitrary, and a conclusion assigning the leading or initiating role to one factor or the other would be equally arbitrary. (This is especially so if our statistical information is limited to annual data.)

Not much better is the idea of looking to see which of the two, money-wage rates or consumer prices, has *increased more.* The arbitrary choice of the base period for this comparison is again a serious difficulty. But even more important is the fact that the annual rise in productivity (out put per labor hour) normally secures increases in real wages over the years. Hence it is to be expected that wage rates increase relative to consumer prices regardless of whether there is inflation, and regardless of whether prices are pulled up by demand or pushed up by wages. Even some highly-seasoned economists have fallen victim to another logical snare: that any increase in money-wage rates that *exceeded the increase in labor productivity* was a sure sign of wage-push. Yet, even if there were no labor union in the country and no worker ever asked for higher wages, a demand-pull inflation would eventually pull up the wage level; and if the demand-pull were such that prices and wages rose by any percentage above two or three a year—and it may well be five or ten or twenty per cent—money-wage rates would be up by more than the rate of increase in productivity. This, then, would have been the result of demand-pull only, without any wage-push at all. Hence the proposed statistical test is completely inconclusive.

A test which is based on a fundamentally correct chain of reasoning would compare profit rates with wage rates, and diagnose demand-pull when *profit rates increase faster than wage rates.* A slight variant of this test uses the relative shares of profits and wages in national income. The theory behind these tests is simply this: when an expansion of effective demand—without a wage-push—pulls up product prices, an increase in profits and profit rates would result until wage rates are pulled up by the derived demand for labor. On this theory, an increase in consumer prices associated with increased profit rates, but with wage rates lagging, would reliably indicate the existence of a demand-pull inflation. The operational difficulties with a test based on this theory are the same as those connected with other statistical tests: the arbitrary selection of the time periods. The theory, moreover, applies to an economy in which most prices are the result of anonymous market forces, not

---

"Administered Prices and the Inflationary Process," *American Economic Review,* Papers and Proceedings, XLIX (May 1959), 421.

of administrative decisions. If most prices were administered and the price setters decided to raise their "profit targets" (perhaps at the same time that trade unions were out to engineer a wage boost, but a little faster or by a bigger jump) we could find—given the present monetary regime guided by the high-level-employment goal—that prices and profit rates increase ahead of wage rates even though the movement was not started by an autonomous expansion of demand. Hence, the lead of profit rates is not a reliable indication of demand-pull; it may occur also in conjunction with a cost-push in which price setters take a leading part.

Widely accepted as reliable symptoms of demand-pull inflation are over-employment and over-time payments. The statistical operations proposed to establish these symptoms are, for over-employment, to see whether *job vacancies exceed job applications* and, for over-time pay, to see whether *average hourly earnings have increased faster than wage rates.* Some critics rightly point out that the presence of these symptoms does not rule out that some cost-push has contributed to the inflation of prices. Indeed it would have been possible that a cost-push actually initiated the process and that the compensatory monetary injection, expanding demand to avoid the threatening unemployment, turned out to be heavier than necessary. Thus while these tests can verify the existence of an inflation of demand, they cannot prove that it was excess demand that precipitated the inflation of consumer prices.

PROPOSED CONCEPTS AND DISTINCTIONS

The diversity of expert opinion and the absence of any good statistical tests to support a diagnosis may in part be due to the lack of precise definitions. It is clear that an inflation of effective demand is a necessary condition not only for a demand-pull inflation of consumer prices but also for a cost-push inflation. Without an expansion of demand the cost boost would result in less production and less employment, not in a continuing rise of the level of consumer prices. Should one then speak of a demand-pull inflation only when the expansion in demand is clearly the initiating factor and any administrative cost increases are clearly induced? Or should one also speak of a demand-pull inflation if administrative wage and material-price increases start and lead the procession of events, but are then joined and overtaken by induced or compensatory expansions of demand?

Autonomous, Induced, and Supportive Demand Inflation

It is useful to distinguish autonomous from induced and supportive expansions of demand. *Autonomous* would be expansions which are not linked to previous or to expected cost increases; hence, disbursements which would also occur if no cost increases had been experienced or anticipated. *Induced* expansions of demand are direct consequences of a cost increase, in that those who receive the increased cost-prices or those who pay them will make larger disbursements than they would have made otherwise. For example, the industrial firms yielding to union pressure for a wage increase may borrow from banks (or dig into cash reserves) in order to pay the higher wage bill; or the recipients of higher wages may increase installment purchases and induce an expansion of consumer credit. *Supportive* (compensatory) expansions of demand would be those which are engineered by monetary or fiscal policy designed to reduce the unemployment arising, or threatening to arise, from cost increases. For example, the monetary authorities may reduce reserve requirements or create reserves in order to allow banks to extend loans, or the fiscal authorities may increase government expenditures in an attempt to expand effective demand and employment.

Without wishing to restrict the freedom of choice of those who formulate definitions, I submit that the choice should be appropriate to the purposes for which the concept is used. If the concept of a demand-induced inflation, or demand-pull inflation, is to serve for diagnostic and prognostic purposes in the development of economic policies, it would seem preferable to confine it to autonomous expansions of demand. This would not obstruct but rather aid the analysis of instances in which cost-induced expansions or supportive expansions of demand should turn out to be excessive in the sense that they create more employment opportunities than are destroyed by the cost increases, and hence give rise to some of the symptoms of a demand-induced inflation.

Aggressive, Defensive, and Responsive Cost Inflation

Similar obscurities due to a lack of essential distinctions surround the concept of the cost-induced inflation. Perhaps so much is clear that the term refers to increases in consumer prices that are the (direct or indirect) result of cost increases—labor cost, material cost, or any other cost. But it is not clear whether these cost increases have to be *autonomous* in the sense that they would not have come about in the absence of any monopoly power (price-making power), merely as a result of competitive demand. For it is quite possible that formal administrative decisions are behind cost increases which, however, do not go beyond what would have occurred without such decisions. For example, a trade union may achieve a "victory" in its negotiations with an employer group bringing home the same raise in pay which the individual employers would have offered (without collective bargaining) in trying to get or keep the labor force they want. Let us decide to call these cost increases *responsive* (or competitive) to distinguish them from those that could *not* be obtained in a purely competitive market.

It would be misleading to denote all non-responsive (non-competitive) price or wage increases as "autonomous," since they may well be "induced" by some changes in the economic situation. (And the adjectives "autonomous" and "induced" are usually used as opposites.) A wage-rate increase, for example, is not responsive unless it is in response to an excess demand (short supply) in the particular labor market; but an increase which is not "demand-induced" (and which therefore presupposes some "autonomy" with respect to competitive market forces) may yet be induced by (a) an increase in the employer's profits, (b) an increase in wage rates obtained by other labor groups, or (c) an increase in the cost of living. I propose to call (a) a "profit-induced" wage increase, (b) an "imitative" (or "spill-over") wage increase, and (c) a "defensive" wage increase. Any one of these increases may act as either an "impulse" or a "propagation" factor in the inflationary process.

Profit-induced and imitative increases as well as spontaneous increases may be called *aggressive* because they are designed to achieve a net advance in the real wage rate. A *defensive* increase merely restores real earning which the group in question has long been enjoying; an aggressive increase raises real earnings above that level. The specification of a time interval is necessary in the definition so that one avoids calling "defensive" what really is a battle to defend the ground just gained in an aggressive action. For example, an aggressive wage-rate increase of ten per cent is likely to be partially eroded within less than a year through the resulting cost-push inflation (aided by induced and supportive expansions of demand). If the same trade unions then demand "cost-of-living raises" to restore their real wages, it would be somewhat ironic to call these new wage adjustments "defensive." But there will always be a wide range in which cost increases may as legitimately be considered defensive as aggressive, especially since trade unions take turns in their actions, each defending the real earnings of its own members that have suffered in consequence of the aggressive actions of other unions, and at the same time attempting to obtain a net improvement.

Administrative price increases by industries producing materials and other producers goods which enter as significant cost items into the prices of many other products can likewise be characterized as responsive (competitive), defensive, or aggressive. Purely responsive increases cannot occur in an industry with much unused productive capacity; only when plants are working at capacity and orders are piling up can administrative price increases be merely responsive; in such circumstances it is economically irrelevant that these prices are administered. Defensive increases leave real profit rates substantially unchanged; these increases take account of increased production cost and no more. Needless to say, the rates of return must be calculated on the basis of the reproduction cost of the required capacity; that is to say, the book values of the fixed capital may be too low if reproduction cost of building and equipment is higher than at the time of their acquisition, or too high if assets are included which are not required for current production. Thus, price increases designed to defend, in periods of falling production, a profit rate that is calculated on the basis of the value of assets inclusive of unused capacity are really aggressive; and price increases designed to raise the money rate of return on capital just enough to take care of increased replacement cost are really defensive.

Should all kinds of wage increase and price increase be included in the concept of a cost-push inflation whenever they are collectively negotiated, unilaterally announced, or otherwise the result of administrative action? I submit that increases which are merely responsive (competitive) do not belong there at all. Defensive increases do of course play an important role in the process of price inflation and the economist will surely not leave them out of his analysis. But in an explanation of an inflationary process going on year-in year-out the aggressive increases have a more substantive role to play than defensive increases; and when it comes to assign "blame" for an inflation of consumer prices, the aggressive cost boosts will obviously be the more eligible candidates.

The Basic Model Sequences

With the help of the proposed concepts the two basic model sequences of consumer-price inflation can be easily described.

(A) *Demand-pull inflation:* Autonomous expansions of demand (government spending, business spending, consumer spending) are followed by responsive (competitive) price and wage increases.

(B) *Cost-push inflation:* Aggressive increases of wage rates and/or material prices are followed by induced and/or supportive (compensatory) demand expansions.

Cost-push models are relatively simple as long as they contain only a single impulse—either wage or price increases—with all sequential changes in the nature of adjustments.

(B-1) *"Pure" wage-push inflation:* Aggressive increases of wage rates are followed by induced and/or supportive demand expansions, and by responsive increases of material prices and other wage rates.

(B-2) *"Pure" price-push inflation:* Aggressive increases of material prices are followed by induced and/or supportive demand expansions, and by responsive increases of other material prices and wage rates.

Models become more complicated as more discretionary actions are included in the sequence of events, especially imitative and defensive increases of cost elements, or even aggressive increases, requiring further adjustments. For example, an autonomous demand expansion may be followed by administered wage and price increases more drastic than merely competitive increases would be; thus, the increases would be partly responsive and partly aggressive, requiring further demand expansions, induced or supportive, if unemployment is to be avoided. Or, aggressive wage and price increases may be followed by excessive demand expansions, perhaps because a nervous government rushes in with overdoses of supportive injections of buying power; some of the effective demand thus created would then be in the nature of an autonomous expansion, resulting in further (responsive) upward adjustments of costs.

ATTEMPTED APPLICATION

Even the most complicated model sequence will probably still be much simpler than the actual course of events as reflected in the data at our disposal. Since reality is so messy that no neat and simple model will fit at all closely, whereas various complex models will fit approximately, it is not surprising that even impartial analysts arrive at divergent interpretations of the so-called facts.

The Postwar Inflation

In the narrow scope of this article no attempt can be made to sift the data, to assess the comparative applicability of the various models, and to award first prize to the best-fitting model. But I shall not dodge this question and shall indicate briefly what impressions I have derived from the data presented by governmental and private researchers.

I believe that for an explanation of the consumer-price inflation from 1945 to 1948, and from 1950 to 1952, the basic model of the demand-pull inflation does as well as, or better than, any of the other models, simple or complicated. On the other hand, for the period 1955–59 several cost-push models appear to do better, and I am prepared to regard the consumer-price increases of these four years as a result of a cost-push inflation.

The choice among the various cost-push models is a hard one, especially in view of the controversy about the behavior of administered material prices. The periodic increases in steel prices have sometimes been regarded as the most strategic impulse factor in the inflationary process. A special theory of "profit-target pricing" assuming "periodic raising of the target" has been devised in support of this diagnosis and an array of empirical material has been added in its support.

Wage or Profit Push?

Neither this theory nor the statistical data seem to me to make the model of the "material-price-push inflation" a plausible explanation in the period in question. While many of the administered price increases may have hampered the performance of our economy and accelerated the inflationary process, I doubt that all or most of them have been "aggressive" in the sense defined. The reported data on profit rates and profit margins do not, in my judgment, indicate that the price increases were aggressive. Of course, few, if any, of the increases since 1955 have been in the nature of responsive adjustments to excess demand—but probably most of them were defensive in nature, taking account of cost increases without raising real profit rates. I cannot verify this impression of mine to everybody's satisfaction, and perhaps not even to my own. But my impression is strengthened by the deduced consequences of certain assumptions, which I consider plausible, concerning the policies and objectives of business managers.

There is, in my opinion, nothing invidious in contending that there are essential differences between most wage increases obtained by strong labor unions and most increases of material prices announced by strong corporations. Nor is it meant to be critical of union policies or uncritical of business policies if many wage increases are held to be aggressive, and many administered price increases defensive. The point is that the situation of most businesses is such that a series of aggressive price increases would be either injurious to them in the long run or down right impossible. A series of aggressive wage increases, on the other hand, may be both possible and beneficial to the labor groups concerned.

To hold that most administered price increases have been defensive rather than aggressive, does not mean (a) that the prices in question were not too high—they probably were, (b) that the increases did not speed up the inflationary process—they certainly did, or (c) that they were "justified"—which they were not if a competitive marked model is used as the standard. But if the question is only whether these price increases were the "impulse factors," the "initiating forces" of the price inflation, then I believe the answer is negative.

WAGE INCREASES AND PRODUCTIVITY

I do not expect serious exception to the proposition that most of the wage increases obtained by strong trade unions in the last four years, whether spontaneous or profit-induced or imitative, have been aggressive in the sense defined. (This is in contrast to most wage increases between 1945 and 1952, which were responsive.) We must now inquire whether aggressive wage increases are inflationary if they do not exceed the relative rate at which productivity increases.

Aggressive Wage Increases to Capture Average Productivity Gains

According to accepted doctrine, the consumer price level can be held approximately stable, and full employment maintained, if the average increase in money-wage rates does not exceed the average increase in productivity in the economy as a whole. Some of the necessary qualifications to this proposition are not relevant to the issues under discussion. For interested readers they are presented in a footnote.[4] One qualification,

[4]There is the first qualification for the sacrifice of fixed-income recipients. The existence of contractual payments in fixed money amounts makes it possible for wage rates to increase a little more than productivity. Assume, for the sake of a simple arithmetical illustration, that of a national product of $1,000 a share of $700 is distributed in the form of wages, $100 in the form of profits, and $200 in the form of fixed interest, rent, and pension payments. If now net national product rises by $20 (or 2 per cent) and the recipients of fixed money incomes get no share in the increased product (because prices are held stable), 20 per cent of the increased product, i. e., $4, becomes available as a possible bonus for labor in addition to their 70 per cent share of $14. Total wage payments can thus increase by $18 or 2.57 per cent.

A second qualification relates to possible improvements in the terms of trade. Assume that the price of imports (relative to the price of exports) falls by 2 per cent and that imports had amounted to 10 per cent of the net national product, of $100. If the entire gain of $2 is seized as another bonus for labor, wages can rise by $20 or 2.86 per cent.

A third qualification concerns the possible effects of increased tax revenues. Assume that the effective tax rate on profits (distributed plus undistributed) is 50 per cent while the marginal tax rate on wages is 20 per cent. The additional profits are (10 per cent of $20 =) $2 and the taxes on this are $1. The taxes on additional wages are (20 per cent of $20 =) $4. If the government kept expenditures constant despite increased revenues, another bonus of $5 could be distributed in the form of wages, bringing the total addition to $25 before taxes, or more than the entire increase in net national product. (We neglect now the tax on the third bonus.) Wages before taxes could with all three bonuses be increased by 3.57 per cent, compared with a 2 per cent increase in national income.

The second and third bonuses, however, cannot be counted upon; the second bonus may just as likely be negative since the terms of trade may deteriorate rather than improve. Even the first bonus is likely to disappear in an economy with perpetual inflation, because contractual incomes might gradually be made subject to automatic cost-of-living adjustments. All three qualifications are probably less important than the one presented in the text and this one works in the opposite direction.

This exposition has been freely adapted from Friedrich A. Lutz, "Cost- and Demand-Induced Inflation," *Banca Nazionale del Lavoro,* No. 44 (March 1958), 9-10. The adaptations were necessary because I believe Lutz's argument to be partly erroneous.

however, that may matter here to some extent concerns the additional profits needed as returns on the additional investments required for the increase in national product. It is sometimes possible for total product per worker to increase thanks to a progress of technology, organization, or skills, without any increase in capital investment. More often, however, it takes some additional investment to achieve an increase in productivity. If such investments were not allowed to earn a return, progress might be stopped short; but if they are to earn a return, total profits must increase lest the rates of return on capital are cut, which could lead to reduced investment and employment. Hence, as a rule, wage increases must not absorb the entire increase in output. And if the additional investment were so large that capital per worker has increased at a percentage rate greater than that of output per worker, wage rates cannot even increase by as much as output per worker and still allow price stability with full employment.[5]

The following formulation will steer clear of such technicalities and express the essential points. Apart from a few modifying influences, such as a squeezing of quasi-rents in stagnant industries, a whittling down of the real claims of recipients of contractual incomes, or a lucky improvement in the terms of foreign trade, real wages per worker cannot increase faster than product per worker. If *money*-wage rates are raised faster than productivity, and the monetary authorities supply the money needed to pay the increased wages without unemployment, prices will rise enough to keep *real*-wage rates from rising faster than productivity. To say that the price inflation has the "function" of keeping the increase in real wages down to the rate at which productivity increases may help some to understand the mechanism. But it is not really an appropriate expression, for nothing has to "function" to "prevent from occurring" what cannot occur anyway. Either prices rise (with the help of supportive expansion of demand) to cut the real wage rates to the level made possible by the productivity increase, or unemployment occurs (if demand expansion is prevented or restrained) and cuts total real wages even lower.

If money wages were not increased at all and all increments to the net national product that are due to technological progress were distributed to consumers in the form of lower prices, *all* income recipients–wage earners, owners of businesses, and fixed-income recipients–would share in the increased product. If money wages all over the economy are increased approximately by the rate at which average productivity has increased, prices

[5]If wage rates were to increase as much as output per worker while prices were kept from rising, total output would not be large enough to allow any return to be earned by the new capital; employers, then, might not want to maintain the level of investment and employment. See Lutz, *loc. cit.*, 4.

on the average will neither fall nor rise and hence the fixed-income recipients (bondholders, landlords, pensioners, perhaps also civil servants, teachers, etc.) will be cut out of their share in the increment. Thus, aggressive money wage increases which, on the average, equal the average increase in productivity in the economy will improve the relative income share of labor at the expense of the receivers of contractual income.

Aggressive Wage Increases to Capture Individual Productivity Gains

The "rule" that price stability and full employment can be maintained if all money-wage rates are increased by the same percentage by which average productivity has increased in the economy as a whole is frequently misunderstood and mistakenly applied to advocate increases in money-wage rates in individual firms or industries by the same percentage by which productivity has increased in these firms or industries. In other words, the rule is perverted to the proposal that the benefits of advancing productivity should accrue to the workers in the industries in which the advances take place. It is twisted into a proposition justifying

> . . . union demands in those industries, which, because of improved technology and consequent cost reductions, can afford to pay higher wages without charging higher prices for their products. This proposition is thoroughly unsound. It misses completely the economic function of prices and wages; its realization would sabotage the economic allocation of resources without serving any purpose that could be justified from any ethical or political point of view. [6]

A sensible allocation of resources requires that the same factors of production are offered at the same prices to all industries. It causes misallocations if industries in which technology has improved are forced to pay higher wages for the same type of labor that gets lower pay in industries where technology has not changed. Wage rates should be temporarily higher in fields into which labor is to be attracted, not in fields where labor is released by labor-saving techniques. It is economic nonsense to advocate that wage rates should be forced up precisely where labor becomes relatively abundant.

> One might accept an economically unsound arrangement if it were ethically much superior. But no one could claim that the proposition in question satisfied any ethical norm. If five industries, let us call them A, B, C, D, and E, employ the same type of labor; if any of them, say Industry A, develops a new production process and is now able to make the same product as before with half the amount of labor; then this Industry A could afford to raise its wage rates without raising its selling prices. Should now workers in Industry A get a

[6]Fritz Machlup, *The Political Economy of Monopoly* (Baltimore, 1952), 403.

> wage increase of 100 per cent while their fellow workers in Industries B, C, D, and E get nothing? Should the coincidence that the technological advance took place in A give the workers there the windfall of the entire benefit, raising them above the rest of the people? I can see no ethical argument that could be made in favor of such a scheme.
>
> But as a matter of practical fact, apart from economics and ethics, the scheme could never be consistently applied, because the workers in other industries would not stand for it, . . . similar wage increases would have to be given in all . . . firms and industries regardless of their ability to pay, regardless of whether their selling prices would remain stable or go up slightly or a great deal. It simply would not be fair if a favored group were to be the sole beneficiary of progress while the rest of the population would have to sit back and wait for better luck.[7]

No fair-minded person would ask them to sit back and wait; every labor union with any power at all would press the claims of its members, and where no unions existed workers would eventually appeal to their employers and to the public to end the injustice. Yet, any "equalizing" wage increases would be clearly of the cost-push type and would, if unemployment is prevented, lead to consumer price increases which take away from the originally privileged worker groups some of the real gains they were first awarded (with the approval of short-sighted commentators and politicians).

This spill-over of money-wage increases and the cost-push inflation which it produces (with the help of a supportive demand inflation) serve to redistribute some of the productivity gains first captured by the workers in the industries where the gains occurred. This redistribution by means of consumer-price inflation cuts back the real wages of the first-successful labor groups, whose unions will then complain about the erosion of their incomes and will call for seemingly defensive wage increases to regain the ground lost through inflation (though they rarely lose all of their gain in real income and often keep a large part of it).

In short, a policy that condones wage increases in industries which, because of increased productivity, can afford to pay increased wages without charging increased prices, is actually a policy that accepts a rising cost-price spiral without end.

PRICE REDUCTIONS ESSENTIAL FOR STABILITY

A wage increase obtained by a particular labor group may initiate an inflationary process, but the speed of this process will depend largely on the

[7] *Ibid,* 404–5.

incidence of defensive price increases and of imitative and defensive wage increases. If nothing but responsive (competitive) price and wage increases were to occur, the rate of inflation initiated by an isolated wage boost would be very small, perhaps negligible. It is, nevertheless, interesting to examine models of price inflation that include neither defensive nor imitative increases.

Inflation Without Spill-Over Wage-Push

In the inflationary process described in the last section, the industries that were forced to pay the increased wages (out of the economies provided by improved techniques) were assumed for the sake of the argument not to increase their selling prices. The price inflation was chiefly the work of a spill-over of the wage increases into fields where productivity had increased less or not at all. But even in the absence of any spillover, even if no worker in the country were to receive a raise that did not come from economies in production, some degree of consumer-price inflation would be inevitable in an economy in which (a) wage rates are never reduced in any sector, even in the face of unemployment, (b) wage rates are increased to capture productivity gains entirely in the industries where they accrue, and (c) full employment is secured, if necessary, through expansion of effective demand. Now when workers are released in the industries where productivity increases, but production, with unchanged prices and unchanged demand, is not increased, it will take an inflation of demand to create employment for the workers set free by the advance of technology. In other words, the "technological unemployment" will have to be cured by an expansion of demand, which in turn will cause a rise in consumer prices.

Does not this argument overlook the increase in demand on the part of workers who receive wage increases? It does not. Since the wage increases were granted just to offset the cost reduction made possible by the increase in output per worker, the workers who stay employed received their raise out of funds no longer paid out as wages to the workers who lost their jobs. A little arithmetic may clarify this point. If 90 workers can now produce the output previously produced by 100, and are now paid the total wage that was previously paid to 100, the total purchasing power in the hands of the workers stays the same. The 10 workers who were released get nothing, and what was saved on them is being paid to the "more productive" 90. The firm, paying the same wage bill (though to fewer workers), finds its costs neither increased nor reduced and keeps its selling prices unchanged. Since at these prices demand is the same as before, the firm has no use for the 10 workers; nor has anybody else if wages rates are nowhere reduced. If the authorities want them reemployed, a demand inflation has to be engineered. True, the

10 workers will produce something once they are employed, but only after increased prices have created incentives for employers to use more labor; or they will have to be employed (and paid for with new money) in the production of public services not sold in the market.

The assumptions built into the model underlying this chain of reasoning have excluded growth (of labor force and capital stock) and excess capacity. If there were adequate excess capacity in each and every line of production, the demand created (in order to re-employ the labor released by the more productive industries) could be satisfied without price increases anywhere. But no inflation model can reasonably include the assumption of ubiquitous excess capacity; limited facilities (bottlenecks) are implied in any explanation of inflation. Thus, no exception should be taken to the assumption that the new wages paid to the re-employed workers will not all be spent for their own products, but largely for other things, and that prices will be bid up in the process.

The exclusion of a growing labor force and a growing capital stock have served merely to simplify the reasoning. When inputs and outputs are increasing, a certain increase in the money supply and in aggregate spending will be required to manage the increase in output and trade at given prices. An expansion of money demand to effect a re-absorption of technological unemployment would be over and above the money demand required to take care of the growth in labor force and capital stock. To combine the analyses of such growth and of technological unemployment would be an unnecessary complication; the other growth factors can be disregarded without vitiating the conclusions derived in an isolated treatment of technological unemployment.

The price inflation to be expected from a demand inflation engineered to absorb "technological unemployment" will of course be quite moderate in this case, where all the spill-over wage increases are ruled out. Here is a type of inflation that cannot be characterized as a cost-push inflation, and not as a demand-pull inflation either, if that term is reserved for autonomous expansions of demand. To be sure, aggressive wage increases are involved in the process, but these increases, merely offsetting the growth of productivity, will push up only the cost per labor hour, not the cost per unit of output, and thus no price increases can be said to result from cost increases.

Inflation Without Any Wage Increases

One may easily jump to the conclusion that technological unemployment, and the need to resort to demand inflation as its only cure, is entirely due to the aggressive wage increases, giving to the workers in the technically advancing industries the entire benefit of the productivity gain. This conclusion would be wrong. The consequences will be the same if in the absence of any wage increase the firms in question find their profits increased but for some reason fail to let consumers benefit in the form of lower selling prices.

Does this argument rely on lower marginal propensities to spend, or on insufficient investment opportunities, or on excessive liquidity preferences? It does not. Even if it is assumed that corporations spend all of their retained profits and stockholders spend all their dividends—just as the workers would have spent their wages—the workers released in the industries where technology has advanced will not be reemployed without the help of demand inflation unless prices to consumers are lowered. The case is almost the same as that in which the workers captured the productivity gain, except that now the corporations and their owners pocket the entire benefit.

Why "almost" the same, why not exactly the same? Because there is the possibility that an increase in retained earnings, as an increase in capital supply, raises the marginal productivity of labor and thus the demand for labor at given wage rates. But it would be absurd to expect that this would suffice to re-employ all the released labor. Assume that the entire amount saved on the wage bill is spent on new machinery; this new demand for machinery (and indirectly for the labor that goes into its manufacture) merely takes the place of the former workers' demand for consumer goods (and indirectly for the labor that went into their production). Thus the spending of the retained profits—earned by reducing the wage bill—constitutes no increased demand for labor. Only the resulting increase in productive facilities may eventually help the demand for labor to the extent of a small fraction of the technological unemployment created by the (labor-saving) increase in productivity. Hence the conclusion is the same as it was in the case of wage increase: only if consumers get a chance through lower prices to buy more product with their given money incomes will the released workers get a chance to find jobs in the absence of demand inflation.[8]

But why should firms refuse to lower their prices when production costs fall? The well-known theoretical models of a monopolist responding to a lowering of his cost curve show with no reasonable exceptions that he would reduce his selling price and increase his output. If firms can be observed acting otherwise, what is wrong with the model or what is wrong with the

[8]This does not mean that the entire increase in productivity must be passed on to consumers in the form of reduced prices. Technological unemployment will neither be perpetuated nor require a price-inflating demand expansion for its cure if wage rates are raised by the national average increase in productivity. This will still permit price reductions in the industries where productivity has increased. The money the consumers save in buying these products at reduced prices will be spent on other goods and will drive up some other prices, without however raising consumer prices on the average.

firms? One possible hypothesis would be that the firms of the real world had been in "disequilibrium," charging less than profit-maximizing monopoly prices and waiting for a good occasion to adjust their position. If now their costs are reduced, inaction, failure to reduce their prices, may be an easy way to adjust. Another hypothesis would be that the firms of the real world are in positions of not firmly coordinated oligopoly, where the safest rule is always "not to rock the boat," that is, never to reduce prices lest a rival mistake it for an outbreak of price competition. A third hypothesis would be that the "administered" prices in modern business cannot be explained by any models based on intelligent considerations, but are set by some fixed rules of thumb, and that one of these rules is never to reduce a price. There are perhaps still other hypotheses to explain the fact of "downward inflexibility" of prices–if indeed it is a fact. But no matter which hypothesis is accepted, the conclusion remains valid that if prices are not reduced when productivity has increased, technological unemployment arises and cannot be absorbed except through demand inflation and consequent consumer-price inflation.

Stabilization of Individual Prices Necessitates Inflation

The argument of the preceding pages was designed to demonstrate that the failure to reduce prices in industries where productivity has increased will result in an inflationary increase of general prices, which

(a) will be most rapid if the productivity gains are captured by the workers of these industries by way of wage rate increases–because of the practically inevitable spill-over of the wage increases to other worker groups; but

(b) will also occur, though much more slowly, in the absence of such spill-over, because it will take a demand expansion to re-employ the workers released when the wage bill of the progressive industries is distributed over fewer workers; and

(c) will not be avoided even in the absence of any wage increases, because a demand expansion will be required to re-employ the workers released when the entire part of the wage bill that is saved through the technological advance is transformed into profits without giving consumers a chance to buy more product.

An economist willing to rely on the most abstract and general principles of economic theory can derive this "inevitability" of inflation from a simple set of theorems. He can deduce from the equilibrium conditions in a system of general equilibrium that general prices must rise if individual prices are maintained in industries where productivity increases. For a fall of production cost in one industry will call forth a reduction of the price of its product relative to the prices of all other products; this adjustment of relative prices will, in a money economy, proceed either through a fall in the money price of the product that now requires less labour per unit than before or through an increase in all other money prices (or through a combination of both); hence, stabilization of the money price of the more economically produced product implies that equilibrium will be restored through a general increase in money prices.

I do not propose to use this technical way of reasoning to convince trade union leaders, business executives, or members of Congress. But the previous argument was, I trust, understandable before I added the sophisticated demonstration of its conclusion.

The O'Mahoney Plan to Check Inflation

It should now be clear that the only way to prevent inflation of consumer prices, and prevent unemployment too, is to make prices more flexible in the downward direction and, in particular, to encourage price reductions in industries where productivity has increased. Senator O'Mahoney's plan, partly incorporated in Senate Bill 215 of April 1959, and receiving serious consideration by several members of Congress, would achieve exactly the opposite. According to the preamble of the Bill, its author believes that "inflation will be checked if the pricing policies of these [dominant] corporations are publicly reviewed before increased prices may be made effective." On this theory the Bill provides for public hearings and investigations of large corporations whenever they want to raise prices. But the harder it is made for firms to raise prices the more surely will they avoid ever reducing their prices.

If a nation is committed to a full-employment policy, that is, to a policy of using demand inflation to create employment, it can avoid inflation only by avoiding anything that may create unemployment. Since economic growth proceeds chiefly through technological progress, and technological unemployment can only be avoided through price reductions, the prime requirement of a non-inflationary full-employment policy is to prevent the workers, owners, and managers of the progressing industries from capturing all the productivity gains accruing in these industries in the form of increased money wages and increased profits, respectively, and to encourage the dispersion of most of these gains to consumers in the form of reduced prices.

The O'Mahoney policy in effect encourages the trade unions in the industries in question to get out and capture the entire productivity gains for their workers. It does so implicitly because, if the firms are prevented from raising prices after the aggressive wage increases have absorbed "only" the new economies, the labor unions will no longer be blamed by the public for causing or precipitating higher prices. The "visible link" between these wage increases and price inflation is removed, and the union leaders will have even less compunction in pressing for these supposedly non-inflationary wage increases. The firms, losing all or most of the productivity gains to their workers, will hardly be eager to reduce prices. But even if they should, by means of tough bargaining, succeed in keeping a good deal of the gains, they will surely not dream of sharing any part of them with the consumers, because they would consider it foolish to reduce prices that cannot be raised again except after expensive, cumbersome, and perhaps embarrassing public inquisitions.

The O'Mahoney plan to check inflation would actually tend to make inflation perennial and perpetual. The only thing that can be said for the proposed policy is that it might in the short run, perhaps for a couple of years, slow down the progress of the price inflation. But even this is doubtful since, apart from encouraging trade unions to fight for the productivity gains accruing in their industries, it does nothing to check the spill-over wage increases, which in genuine cost-push fashion engender many chains of defensive, "approvable" price increases and necessitate continual resort to supportive demand inflation.

CONCLUSION

It was not the purpose of this article to lead up to a critique of a proposed policy; this was a mere by-product. The intention was to examine the conceptual framework employed in recent discussions and, in view of its inadequacies, to propose some improved theoretical tools that may serve better in the analysis of the inflationary process of our time.

Analysis requires the following distinctions: an administered cost increase may be "equilibrating" in the sense that it merely "absorbs" a previously existing excess demand, or it may be "disequilibrating" in the sense that it creates an excess supply that may be prevented or removed only by an expansion of demand. To facilitate the analysis, three kinds of demand expansion are distinguished: *autonomous, induced,* and *supportive.* Likewise three kinds of cost increase are distinguished: *responsive, defensive,* and *aggressive.* Any one of these cost increases may be "administered"; but the responsive ones would also occur in a fully competitive market. Neither defensive nor aggressive increases are in response to excess demand, and both therefore presuppose monopolistic power; defensive increases, however, attempt merely to restore previous real earnings of the group concerned, while aggressive increases raise real earnings above previous levels.

With the aid of these new concepts one can construct models of the inflationary process of various degrees of complexity. It may be possible to develop empirical tests for the choice of the model that fits best the recorded data of particular periods. The author believes that the price inflations of the periods 1945–48 and 1950–52 were of the demand-pull type, but that for 1955–59 a cost-push model would fit better. He tentatively suggests that wage-push was more effective than profit-push.

Finally the relation of inflation to increases in productivity was examined. The popular idea of a "non-inflationary" distribution of productivity gains by way of wage increases to the workers employed in the industries in which technology has advanced was found to be untenable. Imitative wage increases would lead to a brisk inflation. But some degree of inflation would occur even without such "spill-over" wage increases, because the distribution of the productivity gains to the workers or owners in the progressing industries would result in technological unemployment, and remedial full-employment measures would inflate the price level.

25

RECENT INFLATION IN THE UNITED STATES

CHARLES L. SCHULTZE

THE CURRENT CONTROVERSY: DEMAND-PULL VERSUS COST-PUSH

The purpose of this study is to examine the nature of the gradual inflation to which the American economy has been subject in recent years. There is relatively little controversy over the basic features of a wartime or reconversion inflation; rising prices are attributed to an increase in the effective demand for goods and services over and above the capacity of the economy to furnish them. There is wide disagreement, however, about the nature of and remedies for the more gradual rise in prices which has occurred during the postwar period. Most of the discussion has centered on the merits of the "cost-push" versus the "demand-pull" theories of inflation. Proponents of the cost-push thesis attribute the major blame for the price increases, particularly those of the 1955–57 period, to autonomous upward movements in either wage rates or administered prices or both. The demand-pull theorists on the other hand, assert that price increases currently, as always, are the reflection of aggregate excess demand for goods and services, including the services of the factors of production.

We have been and shall be using the concept of excess demand throughout this study in a dynamic sense. In an economy characterized by steadily

Reprinted from "Recent Inflation in The United States," Joint Economic Committee, *Employment, Growth, and Price Levels,* Study Paper No. 1, 1959, pp. 4–16, by permission of the author. Charles L. Schultze is an economist with the Brookings Institution.

improving technology and substantial net investment, the supply of goods and services forthcoming at full employment is continually growing. Hence an absolutely stable demand could only be consistent with full employment if prices declined. Excess aggregate demand, in a dynamic context, only exists, therefore, when monetary demands for goods and services are rising *faster* than the constant dollar value of supplies of goods and services at full employment. The degree of excess demand will, of course, be influenced by the composition of the aggregate: an increased output in some industries can more easily be supplied than in others. Moreover, as Chapter 4 points out, we can have a situation in which output is below its potential even though the labor force is fully employed. If, for example, there is large-scale hiring of salaried employees, those employees may be retained even when output does not rise as expected–we have underemployment. But these refinements aside, the essential point to remember is that the term "excess aggregate demand" is used throughout in the context of a growing full employment supply.

In analyzing the process by which price increases are generated there are two major sets of factors to be considered:

1. The impact of rising prices and wages on aggregate demand for goods and services.
2. The impact of changes in the demand for goods and for factors of production on prices and wage rates. Put more simply, how does the growth of excess capacity and unemployment affect prices and wages?

Prices and wages have a dual nature when considered in the aggregate: they are costs to buyers and incomes to sellers. Thus an increase in the general level of prices does not automatically mean a reduction in the quantity of goods and services demanded as it normally would in the case of a single commodity. The increased cost of purchasing any article or any factor of production is matched by the higher incomes received by the seller. So long as the increase in prices is accompanied by an equal increase in money expenditures, *real* purchases of goods and services will not be affected and employment will not be reduced. There are, however, indirect influences on the level of real demand exerted by a rising price level. If the tax system is progressive, the higher money incomes lead to a higher proportion of income taken in taxes. With a constant money supply, higher prices normally lead to a tighter money market, which in turn has some depressing influence on investment demand. If these and other indirect effects are important, their depressing influence on demand must continually be offset by demand increases from other sources, if the rising price level is not to result in rapidly growing unemployment. If, on the other hand, these indirect effects are relatively unimportant, then a rising price level will not bring about excess capacity and unemployment, or at least will do so only very slowly.

If prices and wages are *sensitive* to changes in demand, then no inflation can continue unless aggregate excess demand is constantly being renewed. The appearance of unemployment and excess capacity would quickly halt any price rise. Consequently the strength of the indirect influences discussed above determines how large an inflation will result from a given initial excess demand. There can be no inflation without the excess demand, however. Hence monetary and fiscal policy, appropriately handled, can achieve full employment and price stability; all that needs to be done is to prevent the excess demand, without which wages and prices would cease to rise. If, on the other hand, wages and prices are relatively *insensitive* to changes in demand, then the indirect influences of the price level on aggregate demand will determine not how large the price rise will be but how much unemployment it will generate. For if prices and wages do not respond to growing excess capacity and unemployment, then the limitation of aggregate demand will not halt the inflation–it will only lead to unemployment.

The responsiveness of prices and wages to changes in demand is thus the central issue. Let us call prices and wages which are sensitive to changes in demand "flexible" and those which do not respond to demand, "cost-determined." The latter category includes both those cases in which prices and wages adjust solely to changes in costs[1] and those in which there occur autonomous increases in prices and wages. We can distinguish four types of situations, depending on the nature of price and wage behavior and the impact of rising prices and wages on demand.

I. Rising prices and wages tend to reduce demand and employment:
   1. Prices and wages *flexible.*
   2. Prices and wages *cost-determined.*

II. Rising prices and wages do not tend to reduce demand and employment:
   1. Prices and wages *flexible.*
   2. Prices and wages *cost-determined.*

So long as prices and wages are cost-determined, then a cost-push inflation is possible, regardless of whether case I or case II holds. If the direct effects of a cost-push inflation are relatively weak, so that real aggregate demand is not reduced (case II), then the inflation is self-validating–a cost-push inflation will not, of itself, lead to unemployment. If the indirect effects of rising prices and wages on aggregate demand are significant (case I), then unemployment and excess capacity will result. But since prices and wages are not flexible, the inflation will continue. In this situation, the maintenance of

[1]Changes in consumer prices are equivalent to changes in costs for the purpose of wage determination.

full employment requires a positive Government monetary and fiscal policy to provide the validating demand. In either situation the failure of aggregate demand to keep pace with a growing full employment output would not eliminate the inflation, so long as price and wage decision making does not respond to demand conditions.

If, on the other hand, prices and wages vary in response to changes in demand as well as costs, then the failure of demand to match full employment supply will quickly bring an inflation to a halt. The effect of rising prices and wages on aggregate demand determines how much of an inflation will result from a given initial excess demand. If a general price and wage rise leads to a large reduction in demand, then the economic system has a built-in self-correction factor. The Government need only exercise self-restraint; so long as excessive deficits and money supply increases are avoided, inflation is not a serious problem. If, on the other hand, the self-corrective influence of a rising price level is weak, then positive government counterinflationary policy may be a recurrent necessity. In either event, the flexibility of prices and wages implies that full employment can be maintained without price inflation. If prices and wages start to rise, a restriction of aggregate demand will lead to a cessation of price and wage gains rather than a growth in unemployment.

The controversy between the demand-pull and cost-push theorists is in reality, therefore, a debate about the consistency of full employment and price stability.

> Given an appropriate monetary-fiscal policy, the answer to the question whether we can continue to enjoy a large, growing, and reasonably stable volume of production and employment . . . lies in the relations of prices, costs, and profits.[2]

Do labor unions and monopolistic firms largely disregard the state of the market in setting prices and wages? Are prices marked up as costs rise with little regard for demand conditions? Does a rise in the cost of living lead to an equivalent wage increase even in periods of unemployment? Few would take an extreme position on these questions. There is rather a spectrum of opinion. Toward the one end of the spectrum are those who feel that prices and wages do respond rather quickly to changes in demand. The possibility that strongly organized groups can push up their cost prices in the absence of ex ante excess aggregate demand is not "an empirically important possibility,"[3] according to these demand-pull theorists. Further, according to this theoretical approach, the existence of inflation implies that the excess

[2]Edward Mason, "Essays in Honor of John H. Williams," p. 189.
[3]Milton Friedman, in "The Impact of the Union," edited by D. M. Wright, p. 244.

demand must be an *aggregate* excess. If prices and wages are responsive to demand conditions, excess demands in particular areas of the economy, balanced by deficient demands in other sectors, will merely lead to a realignment of relative prices. Only if demands in the aggregate are too high will the general level of prices rise.

Toward the other end of the spectrum are those who feel that prices and wages are, within a substantial range, set independently of demand conditions. No one would deny that there is some level of unemployment and excess capacity which would halt a price-wage spiral. But the cost-push theorists feel that the degree of unemployment and excess capacity required to break through the cost-determined nature of wages and prices is quite large. The power of big business and big labor to determine prices and wages is so great, that under conditions of relatively full employment even without excess demand, a secular rise in the price level is unavoidable.

The validity of either approach in this controversy cannot be discovered from the historical relationship of a few large aggregates. The fact that in recent years wages have risen faster than productivity, for example, is often cited as evidence that we have been experiencing a cost-push inflation. But this relationship tells us absolutely nothing about the nature of inflation. In the purest sort of demand-pull inflation, wages would also rise more rapidly than productivity. By the same sort of "reasoning" we could cite the fact that money expenditures rose more rapidly than output as a proof of demand-pull inflation. An equally strong condemnation applies to demonstrations which point to the rise in the money supply or its velocity as proof of the demand-pull nature of inflation.

Even the timing of wage and price increases cannot be offered, by itself, as evidence of the nature of the inflationary process. Suppose, for example, that prices are marked up mainly in response to rising wages. Then an excess demand inflation will first lead to a rise in wage rates through its impact on the labor market, and only thereafter in a price rise. The historical data would indicate that the increase in wages preceded the rise in prices, yet the inflation would be one which was initiated by excess demands.

A cost-push inflation need not arise solely from an *autonomous* upward push of administered wages or prices. If prices are set by applying a constant margin to costs, and if wages are determined by movements in the level of consumer prices, then an initial general price rise, stemming from any source, can perpetuate itself, as wages and prices successively adjust upward to each other. The greater the insensitivity of the price and wage "markups" over cost to unemployment or excess capacity, the greater the inflationary possibilities. The shorter the lag between the mutual adjustment of prices to wages and wages to prices, the faster the inflation will proceed.

The response of prices and wages to changes in demand cannot, in reality, be forced into the simple categories of "flexible" and "cost-determined." The most important fact about their behavior, for the purpose of analyzing creeping inflation, is its asymmetry. Prices and wages tend to be more flexible upward in response to increases in demand than they are in a downward direction in response to decreases in demand. As a consequence, the composition of demand as well as its aggregate magnitude, takes on a central role in the generation of inflation. The further development of this point is one of the major features of the present study.

THE NATURE OF THE RECENT INFLATION

An examination of recent economic history suggests that creeping inflation is not a phenomenon which can be dealt with in aggregate terms. In particular the price increases from 1955 to 1957 stemmed, in the main, neither from autonomous upward "pushes" of administered prices or wages nor from the existence of an aggregate excess demand. Neither of these explanations can satisfactorily account for a number of apparent paradoxes during this period: The dissipation of a relatively modest 5 per cent per annum rise in money expenditures in a 3½ per cent price rise and only 1½ per cent output gain; the apparent correlation of price increases with demand increases industry by industry, but with an upward bias, so that the overall level of prices rose while the overall level of demand was not excessive; the fact that prices rose more rapidly than unit wage costs, while at the same time net profit margins were shrinking; and finally the high level of investment activity followed by disappointing gains in productivity and consequent increases in unit costs.

The theoretical and empirical analysis of the economic processes which lead to creeping inflation is not easily summarized. It is not a relatively simple matter which can be condensed into a short formula, like the popular "too much money chasing too few goods." Nor is it a "devil" theory in which abound the villains of most cost-push theories—the union boss and the greedy monopolist. We shall attempt in the remainder of this chapter however, to sketch the characteristics of economic behavior which lead to creeping inflation and indicate briefly the application of the analysis to the 1955–57 period.

The Importance of the Composition of Demands

Prices and wages in the modern American economy are generally flexible upward in response to excess demand, but they tend to be rigid downward. There is, as we noted earlier, an asymmetry in their behavior. Even if demands in the aggregate are not excessive, a situation of excess demand in some sectors of the economy balanced by deficient demand in other sectors will still lead to a rise in the general level of prices. The rise in prices in markets characterized by excess demand will not be balanced by falling prices in other markets.

Excess demand in particular industries transmits its impact to the rest of the economy through its influence on the prices of materials and the wages of labor. Crude materials prices are normally quite sensitive to changes in demand, and are unlikely to rise significantly unless demands for them in the aggregate are excessive. Prices of intermediate materials, supplies, and components, on the other hand, are more likely to be rigid downward, but flexible upward in response to an increase in demand or costs. Prices of those materials chiefly consumed by industries with excess demand rise, since excess demand for the final goods usually implies excess demand for specialized materials. Materials used mainly in industries with deficient demand will not fall in price, unless the demand deficiency is quite large. Thus excess demand in particular sectors of the economy will result in a general rise in the prices of intermediate materials, supplies, and components; industries which are not experiencing excess demands will find themselves confronted with rising materials costs.

Wages will also be bid up in excess demand industries. Wages in other industries will tend to follow. Even though demand for labor is not excessive, firms cannot allow the wage differential between themselves and other firms to get too large; this is not because they fear the wholesale desertion of their work force, but because they do not wish to experience the inefficiencies and lowered productivity which result from dissatisfaction over widening differentials. Rising wage rates, originating in the excess demand sectors, thus spread throughout the economy. Because productivity gains in the short run are greatest where demand and output are increasing, firms in those sectors where demand is rising slower than capacity will often be faced with even larger increases in unit wage costs than firms in the areas of excess demand. In some cases the size of wage increases will be determined by long-term contracts concluded in earlier periods. Except as such increases are modified by changes in the cost of living (through escalator clauses) they will have little relationship to the current state of the market.

The spread of wage increases from excess demand sectors to other parts of the economy accentuates the rise in the price of semifabricated materials and components. Thus the influence of rising costs and the resistance of prices to declining demands will be larger at the later stages of the production process, other things being equal. The opportunities for rigidities to build up and for rising costs, particularly labor costs, to affect prices are multiplied as products approach the finished state.

Producers of finished goods will be confronted with a general rise in the level of costs, even when the demand for their products and their own demands for materials and labor are not excessive. The more cost determined are the pricing policies of the industries involved, the greater will be the price rise. In competitive sectors of the economy the rising costs will be at least partly absorbed. But in very many industries they will be more fully passed on in higher prices. Markups will of course be shaded when excess capacity begins to rise. As inflationary pressures spread out from excess demand sectors, their force will be somewhat damped in the absence of excess aggregate demand. Similarly the tendency of wages to follow the pattern set in the rapidly expanding industries will be modified as unemployment rises. But so long as markups and wages are more sensitive in an upward than in a downward direction, a rise in the general level of prices can be initiated by excess demand in particular industries.

This kind of inflationary process cannot be neatly labelled. It arises initially out of excess demand in particular industries. But it results in a general price rise only because of the downward rigidities and cost oriented nature of prices and wages. It is not characterized by an autonomous upward push of costs nor by an *aggregate* excess demand. Indeed its basic nature is that it cannot be understood in terms of aggregates alone. Such inflation is the necessary result of sharp changes in the composition of demand, given the structure of prices and wages in our economy.

The downward rigidities and cost-oriented nature of prices and wages act like a ratchet on the price level. Most maladjustments of prices relative to each other and of prices relative to wages tend to be corrected by upward movements in the out-of-line prices or wages rather than by a mutual adjustment to a common center. The short-run inflationary mechanism which we have been describing thus imparts a long-run secular bias to the price level. A floor is placed under each higher level, from which later increases take off. During earlier periods in our history, the recurrence of substantial and lengthy depressions broke through these rigidities and forced large declines in the levels of prices and wages. The widespread bankruptcies and reorganizations of depression periods also led to massive writedowns in the value of fixed assets. This removed an additional feature of the ratchet mechanism. Moreover, a much larger proportion of total value produced originated in the demand sensitive raw materials industries—particularly agriculture. Even if rigidities in the industrial sector were as great then as now, they played a smaller role in the overall economy.

Overhead Costs

A second major factor influencing the determination of prices and the movement in the general price level in recent years has been the rapid growth in the proportion of overhead or fixed costs in total costs. This development played a particularly important role in the 1955–57 period.

Between 1947 and 1955 a very large part of the rise in total costs was accounted for by the rise in relatively fixed costs. Of the total increase in employment during those years, 65 per cent represented employment of professional managerial, clerical, sales, and similar personnel. Only 20 per cent of the increase was accounted for by operatives, laborers, and craftsmen. In manufacturing, nonproduction worker employment rose 40 per cent and production worker employment only 2 per cent. During this same period fixed capital costs per unit increased very rapidly. Prices of capital goods rose relative to other prices, and the proportion of short-lived equipment to long-lived plant rose sharply. Depreciation charges thus expanded very substantially. Depreciation and salary costs per unit, taken together, accounted for more than 40 per cent of the increase in total unit costs in manufacturing between 1947 and 1955. Adding profits per unit we account for two-thirds of the cost increase.

The period between 1955 and 1957 was characterized by a very sharp rise in investment outlays accompanied by a quite modest growth in aggregate demand and output. Not only was capacity expanded rapidly but there was a continuation, indeed an acceleration, of the postwar growth in the number of overhead employees. Unlike earlier postwar booms however, the expansion in these relative fixed inputs was not matched by a corresponding rise in output (Table 2). Fixed costs per unit of output therefore rose sharply, not because output was falling but because it did not rise rapidly enough. Prices were raised almost, but not quite enough to cover these higher costs. Of the total rise in unit costs (including profit margins) some 55 per cent was accounted for by higher salary costs per unit as compared to 40 per cent by higher wage costs. Book depreciation charges are unreliable for most purposes; neverthe-

Table 1. Changes in Manufacturing Costs and Prices
(in per cent points)

	1947–55	*1955–57*
"Price" of value added in manufacturing	29.8	9.6
Unit wage cost	9.0	3.9
Unit salary cost	7.7	5.6
Depreciation per unit	4.2	1.0
Profits per unit	7.2	-2.2
Indirect taxes per unit	1.6	1.3

Source: App. A [not reprinted here].

Table 2. Indexes of Capacity, Employment, and Output in Manufacturing Industries *(1947 = 100)*

	1955	*1957*
Capacity:		
A[a]	156	175
B[b]	146	163
Nonproduction worker employment	140	155
Production worker man-hours	103	100
Output	140	145

[a]A–McGraw-Hill Department of Economics estimates.
[b]B–Fortune magazine estimates.

less, in combination with other costs, they put pressure on profit margins and to some extent on prices.

The fact that a large part of the increased employment during the period was in the nature of overhead employment helps explain why the general price rise, during a period in which monetary demands were not excessive, did not lead to significant unemployment. By the same token the lack of rise in output relative to fixed inputs accounts for the disappointing gain in productivity. The rise in prices was accompanied by a relatively moderate increase in money expenditures. Real expenditures and output rose by substantially less than the "normal" postwar rise to be expected from growth in the labor force and productivity gain. Yet instead of a rise in unemployment, there occurred a shortfall of productivity below its potential. Output per production worker man-hour continued to increase fairly sharply throughout the period–indeed production worker employment declined. But the failure of output to match the rise in overhead labor input substantially moderated the overall gain in productivity. In general, the more important fixed costs become, the more sensitive productivity will be to changes in output.

The failure of output to rise toward the levels implicit in the expansion of fixed inputs was partly due to the fact that declining demand in particular sectors of the economy–housing and automobiles–largely offset the rising demands for investment goods. But in addition the attempt to recapture in prices a substantial expansion in fixed costs at existing levels of output tended to raise the level of prices relative to any given money income; the gross saving rate at any given level of output was increased. This in itself damped the rise in output, so that the process tended to be self-defeating. Had output risen along with capacity, overhead costs would have been spread over a larger volume of output. But, by restricting the growth in real demand, the very pricing policies which attempted to recover fixed costs at low levels of output, led to a rise in fixed costs per unit. To some extent a kind of "vicious circle" occurred. The failure of aggregate output to increase raised fixed costs per unit. Insofar as prices were marked up relative to wage and salary rates in order to recover these higher unit costs, the forces impeding the growth in output were strengthened. This kept fixed unit costs high, and so on around the circle again.

The major part of the general rise in prices during recent years may thus be attributed to two sets of factors:

1. The downward rigidity and cost oriented nature of prices and wages in most of industry. During a period in which dynamically stable *aggregate* demand veils a fairly violent shift in the composition of demands, such market characteristics will result in a general rise in the level of prices. This rise cannot be said to result either from excess *aggregate* demand or from autonomous upward adjustments of administered prices and union wages. Rather it stems from excess demand in particular markets, and is propagated throughout the rest of the economy by a cost mechanism.
2. The attempt to recapture in prices at least some of the increase in fixed unit costs which occurred when a vigorous investment boom and a rapid substitution of fixed for variable labor input impinged on a situation of sluggish growth in output. Further, the fact that most of the employment rise was in overhead labor helps explain why the subnormal growth in output did not involve a rise in unemployment. It did however lead to the growth of excess capacity.

None of the foregoing is designed to indicate that all inflations are mainly the result of these processes. Excess aggregate demand has been the basic cause of all of our *major* inflations, including the postwar reconversion inflation. And for a short while in late 1955 there seemed to be some excess aggregate demand. But the major thesis of this study is that the creeping inflation of 1955–57 is different in kind from such classical inflations, and that mild inflation may be expected in a dynamic economy whenever there occur rapid shifts in the mix of final demands. It is, in effect, a feature of the dynamics of resource adjustment where prices and wages tend to be rigid downward. Moreover, it gives a secular upward bias to the price level so long as the major depressions which "broke" the ratchet in the past are avoided in the future.

Similarly there is no attempt here to prove that *autonomous* upward pressures of wage rates have had no impact on the price structure. Such pressures may have played a role in recent inflation. But the role was not a major one. The mere showing that wage rate increases exceeded productivity gains proves anything at all with respect to the magnitude of this role. (It is interesting to note, however, that the substitution of overhead for direct labor implies that wage rates cannot rise as fast as the statistical number called output per production worker if total unit costs are to be stable.)

A DETAILED ANALYSIS OF THE 1955–57 PERIOD

. . . In this summary it is impossible to do more than list some of the more important characteristics of the general rise in prices which occurred during those years.

Demands and Prices

1. As the economy recovered from the 1954 recession it reached a situation of aggregate excess demand in late 1955. Demand in all sectors of the economy were high and rising. The three major volatile sectors–capital goods, automobiles, and housing–were expanding particularly sharply. Production rose even more rapidly than sales, as inventory accumulation speeded up. Raw materials prices, which are especially sensitive to the state of existing and expected demand, rose steeply during the last half of the year. This aggregate excess lasted only briefly however. After the end of the year purchases of automobiles and houses fell rapidly, and remained at reduced levels in 1956 and 1957. Business demand for capital goods, on the other hand, continued to boom throughout the period.

2. On balance aggregate money outlays, after mid-1955, rose at a rate of about 5 per cent per year. Prices rose at a 3½ per cent annual rate and output by only 1½ per cent. The normal postwar rate of growth in output during prosperity periods has been about 4 per cent per year.

3. The slow rate of growth in output and productivity cannot be explained by the "indigestion" hypothesis–(i.e., the very size of the investment boom itself caused such dislocations that normal productivity gains were temporarily impossible). Output per man-hour of production workers *did* rise significantly; producers *were* able to substitute overhead for fixed labor; most importantly there was a strong interindustry correlation between output and output per man-hour. Those industries whose output rose also achieved substantial productivity gains.

4. Thus the difference between the rise in aggregate money expenditures and output did not represent aggregate excess demand. The output rise was clearly less than the economy's potential. The growth of widespread excess capacity is a good commonsense indicator of this.

5. The magnitude of price rises among different sectors of the economy and among different industries was associated with the magnitude of the rise in demand in each sector or industry. On the average, however, prices rose, even though demand, in the aggregate, was not excessive. There was, in other words, a substantial upward bias in the relationship of price changes to demand changes.

6. The magnitude of price rises among industrial commodities was related to two major factors: In general, commodities which experienced the largest price rises were those which had the largest increases in demand. With some important exceptions, most commodities with large price rises were those associated with the boom in capital goods. The frequency of price declines and the magnitude of average price increases among different groups of commodities differed also according to the stage of fabrication. Very few finished commodities were reduced in price; price increases were, on the average, somewhat smaller and the evidence of price flexibility slightly greater for semi-manufactured materials; the smallest average price rise, after late 1955, and the most flexibility occurred among crude materials.

7. Steel and automobiles were the major exceptions to the pattern described in the preceding paragraph. Relative to the change in demand and output price increases were much larger than those associated with similar changes in demand and output in other industries.

Wages

1. Wage rate increases were fairly uniform among different industries. Wages in industries with stable or declining output rose by the same amount as they did in rapidly expanding industries. A United Nations study has found this uniformity of behavior to exist among industrial countries generally.

2. Productivity gains were closely associated with the degree of rise in output. Industries with rising output tended to have larger productivity gains than other industries, and vice versa.

3. As a consequence of these characteristics of wage and productivity behavior, wage costs per unit of output rose less in expanding than in contracting industries.

4. Price increases in the capital goods and associated industries accounted for two-thirds of the rise in the industrial wholesale price index between 1955 and 1957. Their prices rose 15 per cent compared with an average increase of 4 per cent for all other industries. Yet wage rate increases in the two groups were almost identical. Because of the relationship between productivity and output mentioned above, unit wage costs in the industries with large price increases averaged less than in other industries. Prices in industries which accounted for the bulk of the overall inflation also rose substantially more than wage costs. In other industries unit wage costs rose proportionately (but not absolutely) more than prices.

Overhead Costs

1. All of the employment rise during the period was in overhead type employment. In fact the employment of direct labor fell substantially.

2. More than 50 per cent of the rise in total units costs in manufacturing

was accounted for by rising unit salary costs, and an additional 20 per cent by rising depreciation. Net profit margins declined from the high levels reached in late 1955.

3. The rise in salary costs per unit was not only due to an increase in salary rates—which rose by about the same amount as wage rates—but also by the rising ratio of salaried employment to output. The increase in this ratio stemmed chiefly from the failure of output to rise along with capacity. Had it done so, evidence from other postwar years indicates that the salaried employment-output ratio would not have increased.

4. Since productivity of both direct and overhead labor is output sensitive, it is clear that, within moderate limits, a further rise in output could have resulted in lower unit costs. The data suggest an elasticity of minus one-half; i.e., a 1 per cent further rise in output in industries operating below capacity could have yielded a one-half per cent decline in total unit costs.[4]

Consumer Prices

1. In the Consumer Price Index, food, nonfood commodities, and services each account for approximately one-third of the total weight. Even among nonfood commodities manufacturers' prices make up not much more than half of the total price, the rest being transportation, wholesaling, and retailing costs. The service component of the CPI is made up of a long list of heterogeneous items, including such things as auto, real estate, and medical insurance, public utility rates, haircuts, postage, and interest rates. Thus it would seem that the direct impact of changes in industrial prices and wages on the Consumer Price Index is relatively limited. Yet an increase in the prices of manufactured products diffuses itself throughout the economy by many indirect routes. Steel prices rise, school construction costs go up, and property tax rates are adjusted upwards; an initial rise in the CPI on account of an increase in industrial prices leads, with some time lag, to rising wages in the service industries and, e.g., auto-repair charges rise; and the examples could be multiplied ad infinitum.

2. About one-third of the rise in the Consumer Price Index was contributed by increasing food prices. In turn, half of the rise in food prices was attributable to rising farm prices for livestock and half to increased marketing costs. The livestock rise chiefly reflected changing supply conditions. But an examination of the details of the increase in marketing costs shows that the same factors were operative as in the industrial sector generally.

[4]This assumes that the additional demand for production labor would not have led to even more rapid wage increases. Considering the reductions in production worker employment during the period, this is a most reasonable assumption.

3. The heterogeneity and institutional character of service prices make any simple characterization suspect. The rise in consumer prices generated in other sectors of the economy, and the general rise in wage rates, however, did lead after some time lag to a significant speedup in the rate of increase in service prices after mid-1956. And the rise in service prices in turn had repercussions on the increase in wages and prices in the industrial sector of the economy.

SOME IMPLICATIONS

Although it may not be obvious at first, this analysis is fairly optimistic with respect to its implications for the magnitude of the potential secular upward drift in the price level. In particular the size of the price increases between 1955 and 1957 are not a good indicator of the kind of problem which may be confronting us (assuming, of course, we do not allow classical excess aggregate demand inflation to get started).

The magnitude of the shifts in demands between mid-1955 and mid-1957 were unusually great, even for a dynamic economy. We should not be continually subject, for example, to a 2-year increase in expenditures for fixed business investment of some 25 per cent (and a much larger rise in order backlogs) accompanied by 20 per cent decline in residential construction and automobile sales.

The upward price pressure arising out of attempts to recapture fixed costs at reduced "standard volume" is not a continuing phenomena. It is unlikely, indeed impossible, for the average operating rate at which entrepreneurs attempt to recapture fixed costs to fall indefinitely. Indeed the very size of the current ex ante profit margin, at full utilization of capacity, which resulted from this reduction in standard volume should become a moderating factor, offsetting price pressures from other sources as output rises toward full utilization of capacity.

This study does not attempt to evaluate the policy aspects of creeping inflation. It does, however, lead to certain general conclusions which are relevant in the formulation of anti-inflationary policy.

In the first place it is quite obvious that monetary and fiscal policies designed to combat an inflation arising out of excess *aggregate* demand are not suitable to a situation in which demand in the aggregate is not excessive. When, as in recent years, a rise in the general level of prices accompanies a growth in excess capacity, further restriction of the general level of demand may be positively harmful. Since productivity is sensitive to changes in output when output is running below capacity, a general reduction in demand is more likely to raise unit costs by its effects on productivity than to lower them by its effects on wage rates. This will be particularly true if the restriction of aggregate demand continues to leave the booming sectors of the economy relatively unaffected.

Monetary and fiscal policies which do not restrain aggregate demand, but impinge only on the sectors where demand is excessive may indeed limit the inflationary forces during a period of creeping inflation. Had investment demand risen more slowly between 1955 and 1957, and automobile and housing demand more evenly, we would have experienced a larger rise in aggregate output and a smaller rise in prices. The question of selective tax and credit controls is far too broad to be discussed here; their application involves a host of economic and social questions which cannot be casually answered. At the same time however, our analysis does indicate that counter-inflationary monetary and fiscal policies must take into account the composition as well as the magnitude of demand. The use of monetary and fiscal policy to prevent the emergence of aggregate excess demand can prevent one type of inflation–indeed the most harmful type. But inflation can still arise in a situation of dynamically stable aggregate demand. Under these circumstances we can either attempt to alter the composition of demand by using *selective* monetary and fiscal policy or we can accept the moderate price increases which take place. This is our choice. We cannot solve the problem, indeed we shall do positive harm, by a further restriction of aggregate demand through *general* monetary and fiscal restraint.

There is one final implication of this analysis. The moderate inflation of recent years was part of the process of resource allocation. Simply because it is called inflation, one cannot attribute to it the dire consequences associated with classical hyperinflation. It does indeed benefit some individuals and harm others–like many other aspects of the resource allocation process. In fact it is, in part, a reflection of the attempt by individuals and groups in society to ease the adjustments in relative incomes which result from a shift in the composition of demand. Such an inflation probably disturbs the social structure less than do the rapid changes in technology, the shift of income between industries, and the movement of industries from one region to the other, which we take to be the marks of a dynamic economy.

VIII

Macroeconomic Policy

Although, conceptually, macroeconomic policy encompasses more than monetary and fiscal policies, by far the most important of the governmental actions that have the economy-wide impact needed to qualify them as macroeconomic are monetary and fiscal in nature. The selections in this part are limited to this particular area of policy and, furthermore, to only a few of the many issues that arise in what is, despite this limitation, still a huge policy area.

The first selection in this part is taken from the last chapter of the 1966 *Annual Report* of the Council of Economic Advisers. The year 1966 marked the twentieth anniversary of the Employment Act of 1946, which, among other things, gave birth to the Council of Economic Advisers. In this chapter the council reviews these first two decades of experience with monetary and fiscal policies under the act and thereby provides an introductory overview to this general area.

The next three selections, 27–29, focus specifically on some issues in monetary policy. Probably the most important and surely the most discussed of the many issues under this heading is that of the criterion or criteria for monetary policy. Which among a long list that includes interest rates, industrial production, unemployment percentage, volume of bank credit, and stock of money should be the guide or guides to monetary policy? Milton Friedman, in his presidential address before the American Economic Association (which appears here as Selection 27), repeats what has come to be a familiar prescription: The best guide to monetary policy is the total money supply, and the monetary authorities should publicly adopt the policy of achieving a steady rate of growth in this total. According to Friedman, which of a number of definitions of the money supply is chosen is relatively unimportant in comparison with the need to maintain a steady rate of growth in the money supply, however defined. Although this basic prescription is the same one reached in some of Friedman's earlier writings, the road he follows here to his destination differs somewhat from the roads he traveled earlier.

Although Friedman and others who favor a monetary rule remain a minority, it appears that by 1968 their position could not continue to be disregarded as it had been in certain circles during earlier years. The Council of Economic Advisers saw fit to discuss the question of a monetary rule for the first time in its *Annual Report* for 1969, and this discussion appears as Selection 28.

The council, at least the last one in the Johnson Administration, which wrote the 1969 *Annual Report,* remained in favor of the discretionary type of monetary policy that has long been followed by the monetary authorities. The many other economists who also argue in favor of discretionary policy over policy determined by a rule do not thereby argue that discretionary policy is without its shortcomings. However, unlike the Friedman group, which finds such policy so likely to be destabilizing in practice that there is virtually no alternative to its outright abandonment, other economists in a more traditional line find a degree of effectiveness in discretionary monetary policy in the face of what are recognized as its considerable limitations. Such is the approach taken by Howard S. Ellis in his selection, which is the last of several specifically on monetary policy.

The three remaining selections, 30–32, take up some related questions in the area of fiscal policy. The first of these is a chapter from a popularly written book by John M. Culbertson in which he sets out in nontechnical language the meaning of fiscal policy, its measurement via the concept of the full-employment surplus, and some problems encountered in its implementation.

The next selection, by Wilfred Lewis, Jr., summarizes the results of his study of federal fiscal policy during the four recessions since World War II. For each recession and recovery period, Lewis attempts to determine the dollar amounts of change in federal expenditures and receipts attributable to the operation of the automatic fiscal stabilizers and those attributable to discretionary fiscal actions. His estimates suggest that the automatic fiscal stabilizers made a substantial contribution to the stability of the economy over the period in question and that discretionary fiscal actions were relatively less helpful. Actually, as measured by the implicit federal surplus at full employment (which is similar to the full-employment surplus that is met in the Culbertson selection), discretionary fiscal actions of the federal government were found by Lewis to be expansionary in only one of the four recessions, approximately neutral in two, and contractionary in the remaining case.

Discretionary fiscal actions are influenced by political considerations, prior governmental commitments, and various other factors, in addition to the state of the economy. These other factors could be such that it would not be too surprising to find neutral or even contractionary discretionary action taken in the face of a future recession. One can only be fairly confident that action will be in the right direction when that action is of the kind that follows from the operation of the automatic, or built-in, stabilizers. The final selection, by M. O. Clement, provides a thorough analysis of the concept of automatic stabilizers (monetary as well as the more familiar fiscal), including the criteria that any device must satisfy to qualify as such a stabilizer.

26

THE EMPLOYMENT ACT: TWENTY YEARS OF POLICY EXPERIENCE

COUNCIL OF ECONOMIC ADVISERS

There were great expectations and not a few qualms when the Employment Act was signed into law on February 20, 1946, following enactment by heavy bipartisan majorities in both houses of Congress. This year, which marks the 20th anniversary of that enactment, is a suitable occasion to review our experience under the Act, to take stock of where we stand today, and to consider the challenges ahead.

THE ACT AND ITS BACKGROUND

The legislation of 1946 set forth the following declaration of policy:

> The Congress declares that it is the continuing policy and responsibility of the Federal Government to use all practicable means consistent with its needs and obligations and other essential considerations of national policy, with the assistance and cooperation of industry, agriculture, labor, and State and local governments, to coordinate and utilize all its plans, functions, and resources for the purpose of creating and maintaining, in a manner calculated to foster and promote free competitive enterprise and the general welfare, conditions under which there will be afforded useful employment opportunities, including self-employment, for those able, willing, and seeking to work, and to promote maximum employment, production, and purchasing power.

In making this declaration, the Congress recognized that the billions of independent spending and saving decisions of a free economy could well

Reprinted from the *Annual Report of the Council of Economic Advisers* (1966), pp. 170–86.

result in levels of total demand either short of full employment or in excess of productive capacity. Furthermore, it took the view that Government policies could play a constructive role in improving the stability and balance of the economy.

The Act was a product of the experiences of the Great Depression and World War II. The Depression shook but did not destroy the faith in an automatic tendency of the economy to find its proper level of operation. In the early 1930's, public works and other antidepression programs were justified as temporary "pump priming," to help the private economy get back on its track after an unusual and catastrophic derailment. And the departure from orthodox fiscal principles was made with regret and without complete consistency. The Government expenditures explicitly designed to combat depression necessarily increased budget deficits; but this implication was veiled by financing these outlays through an "extraordinary" budget. Meanwhile, taxes were raised, and salaries and housekeeping expenditures cut in the regular budget, thereby reducing the over-all stimulation of Government measures.

The relapse of the economy in 1937 into a sharp decline from a level still far below full employment gave rise to conflicting interpretations. To some, it proved that pump priming and Government deficits had undermined the confidence of the business community and thereby only worsened the situation. Others, however, concluded that it pointed to the need for larger and more sustained fiscal and monetary actions to revive the economy. In drawing this conclusion, economists were buttressed by the writings of J. M. Keynes, who offered a theoretical explanation of the disastrous depression. The Keynesian conclusions received additional support during World War II because they offered a satisfactory explanation of why the high deficit-financed defense expenditures of that period not only wiped out unemployment but went beyond to create inflationary pressures.

Memories of the disastrous 1930's were very much in the public mind as World War II was drawing to an end. Many active proponents of "full employment" legislation in 1945 and 1946 feared a relapse into depressed levels of economic activity like those of the 1930's, once military spending ended. They looked toward Federal public works spending as a peacetime replacement—at least, in part—for the wartime defense outlays.

The opponents of "full employment" legislation had several reservations and objections. Some feared that it would mean a statutory blessing for perpetual budgetary deficits, soaring public expenditures, and massive redistribution of income from upper to lower income groups. There were doubts that Government actions could and would on balance raise employment; and there were fears that these actions would lead to regimentation and would jeopardize the free enterprise system. The proponents of legislation, on the other hand, argued that the Act would merely provide a setting essential to the proper functioning of the free enterprise system because a depressed economy heightened social tensions, discouraged innovation and initiative, dulled competition, and undermined confidence.

The legislation which finally emerged from this discussion wisely abstained from diagnosing depression as the disease and public works as the cure, but instead concentrated on establishing the principle of continuing Government responsibility to review and appraise economic developments, diagnose problems, and prescribe appropriate remedies. And it placed major responsibility squarely upon the President, who was asked to discuss his execution of that responsibility in an Economic Report to be transmitted to the Congress at the start of each year.

The Act also established two agencies–the Council of Economic Advisers in the Executive Branch and the Joint Committee on the Economic Report (later named the Joint Economic Committee) of the Congress–with interrelated but separate responsibilities. These institutions have each filled a vital and previously missing role in their respective branches of Government–they have provided a coordinated overview of the economic impact of the entire spectrum of Government tax, expenditure, monetary, and other activities. To maintain the emphasis on advice and coordination, the Joint Economic Committee was not given any substantive legislative responsibility nor the Council any policy-executing duties. Both agencies have participated actively in the counsels of Government; both have conscientiously striven for a thoroughly professional economic competence and approach in their respective reports and recommendations; and both have contributed to the public understanding of economic issues.

Today's economic policies reflect the continuing impact of the Employment Act in all the years since its inception. And our accumulating experience is certain to be reflected in the policies of the future. This chapter reviews the development of policy in the past 20 years and outlines the present relationship between economic analysis and economic policy.

AVOIDING DEPRESSIONS AND BOOMS

The Congress proved wise in its decisions to state goals broadly and to concentrate on continuing review, analysis, and proposals, since the specific problems that actually arose were somewhat different from those which many supporters of the Employment Act had anticipated.

Although an important part of the impetus for the Employment Act derived from the prolonged depression of the 1930's and the resulting fear of stagnation in the American economy, this problem did not prove to be the primary challenge to economic policymaking under the Act. Indeed, immediately after World War II, excess-demand inflation proved to be the key problem. Subsequently, policy was focused on the age-old problem of limiting the size and duration of cyclical swings. Only much later and in a much different and milder form did stagnation arise as a live issue.

Thus, much of our experience under the Act consisted of policy actions to combat recession—lest it turn into depression—and to contain excess demand pressure—lest it generate inflationary boom.

Combating Recessions

A series of relatively short and mild recessions required Government attention in the postwar period. The problem of cyclical declines was not unexpected by the framers of the Employment Act, nor was it new to the American economy. In the period between 1854 (the beginning of the business cycle annals of the National Bureau of Economic Research) and World War II, we had experienced 21 periods of recession or depression. Our postwar record is blemished by 4 additional periods of contracting economic activity—1948–49, 1953–54, 1957–58, and 1960–61.

Compared with the previous cyclical record, the postwar recessions have been far shorter, considerably milder, and substantially less frequent. Postwar recessions ranged in duration from 8 to 13 months; the average duration of previous declines had been 21 months, and only 3 had been shorter than 13 months in length. Measured by the decline in industrial production from peak to trough, postwar recessions ranged in magnitude from 8 percent to 14 percent. By comparison, in the interwar period, the declines ranged from 6 to 52 percent; three of the five contractions exceeded 30 percent and only one was less than the 14 percent maximum of the postwar period. During the past 20 years, the economy has spent a total of 42 months, or 18 percent of the time, in periods of recessions, far less than the 43 percent applicable to the 1854–1939 era.

Discretionary Policies. This improvement in the postwar record of the economy was aided by the deliberate discretionary steps taken by the Government to modify the impact of business downturns and thereby to prevent cumulating declines into depression. The speed and force of these actions—in both the fiscal and monetary areas—varied among the recessions. Thus, in 1949 little new fiscal action was taken, partly because inflation was viewed as a key problem even during the decline, and partly because Government measures taken the previous year were expected to have a considerable impact on the economy: the tax reductions of 1948 were supplying large refunds, and large expenditure increases were forthcoming under the recently enacted Marshall Plan. The Federal Reserve did act to reduce reserve requirements in a series of steps during the spring and summer of 1949, reversing a two-year rise in short-term interest rates.

In 1953–54, as military outlays declined and aggregate activity retreated, the principal expansionary influence came from previously scheduled reductions of corporate and personal income taxes. But some new action was taken to reduce excise taxes and to speed up expenditures. All three major instruments of monetary policy–reserve requirements, the discount rate, and open market operations–were used to encourage the expansion of credit-financed expenditures. Meanwhile, the Administration planned larger fiscal steps that might be taken if the recession seemed likely to be prolonged. Significantly, in 1954, the bipartisan character of expansionary fiscal policies was established for the first time, as the Republican Administration of President Eisenhower adopted measures that had previously been linked to the New Deal and Keynesian economics.

In 1958, the recession was considerably deeper than its two postwar predecessors and both the Eisenhower Administration and the Congress were more vigorous in taking action. An important concern of earlier years–that business confidence might be disturbed by Government recognition of a recession–seemed insignificant since the sharp recession was obvious to all.

Several important measures were taken. The benefit period for unemployment compensation was temporarily extended. Grants to States under the Federal highway program were enlarged and accelerated, and other programs in the budget also were expanded or rescheduled to provide an earlier stimulative effect. The Government also acted to spur housing activity by financial operations in the mortgage market and by altering terms on Government-guaranteed home mortgages. The important measures were launched near, or after, the trough of the recession. Thus, in retrospect, policy helped most to strengthen the early recovery rather than to contain or shorten the recession. Nevertheless, in view of the general recognition that the Government would be running a substantial deficit in any case, these additions to Federal outlays were a significant reflection of changed attitudes toward the role of fiscal policy.

Monetary policy also played a constructive role in the 1957–58 recession, once the monetary authorities moved to ease credit 3 months after the peak in economic activity. Thereafter, Federal Reserve actions contributed to a revival in housing and other investment by promoting a sharp reduction in interest rates, both short- and long-term.

The first fiscal measures to deal with the 1960–61 recession were taken with the inauguration of President Kennedy in January 1961, when the recession had just about run its course. Nevertheless, improvements in the social insurance system, rescheduling of Federal expenditures, and expanded programs (including defense and space) were an important stimulus to the recovery during 1961. In contrast to the delay in taking fiscal measures, the Federal Reserve reversed a tight money policy early in 1960, prior to the downturn.

Not all discretionary changes in taxes or expenditures have contributed to economic stability. Indeed, some steps taken to pursue national security or social goals had destabilizing economic impacts, which were not always appropriately offset. Previously scheduled payroll tax increases took effect in 1954, 1959, and 1962, and drained off purchasing power in recession or in initial recovery. In 1953, defense outlays declined and triggered a recession before offsetting expansionary policies were adopted.

Structural Changes for Stability. On the whole, discretionary fiscal and monetary actions made a distinct positive contribution in limiting declines. Even more important in this respect was the strengthened inherent stability of the postwar economy.

In large measure, this can be traced simply to the greater size of the Government relative to the total economy: that is, the increased importance of Government expenditures—both purchases of goods and services and transfer payments. Government outlays do not participate in the downward spiral of recession; because of its borrowing capacity, the Federal Government—unlike businesses and households—can maintain its spending in the face of declining income receipts. Although State and local governments do not have equal immunity from the need to tighten their belts, they have been able to maintain their growing spending programs relatively unaffected during the mild postwar recessions.

The increased relative importance of Government outlays is shown in Chart 1. Social insurance and national defense have added especially to the postwar totals of Federal outlays. State and local outlays have been rising rapidly in an effort to catch up with neglected needs and to keep up with the desires of a wealthier society for improved public services.

The contribution to the stability of the economy resulting from a high level of Government expenditures, insulated from revenue declines, has been augmented by the cushions to private purchasing power provided by the built-in fiscal stabilizers.

When private incomes and employment decline, purchasing power is automatically supported by both a decline of Federal revenues and an increase in unemployment compensation payments. Transmission of the virus of deflation is thus impeded. During postwar recessions, the progressive Federal personal income tax has not had to demonstrate its full stabilizing effectiveness because of the mildness of dips in personal earnings. There have, however, been sharp declines in corporate incomes; the Federal Treasury has shared about half of the drop in profits, thereby helping to bolster dividends and to cushion cash flow, and hence investment outlays.

Chart 1. Role of Federal and State and Local Governments in the Economy

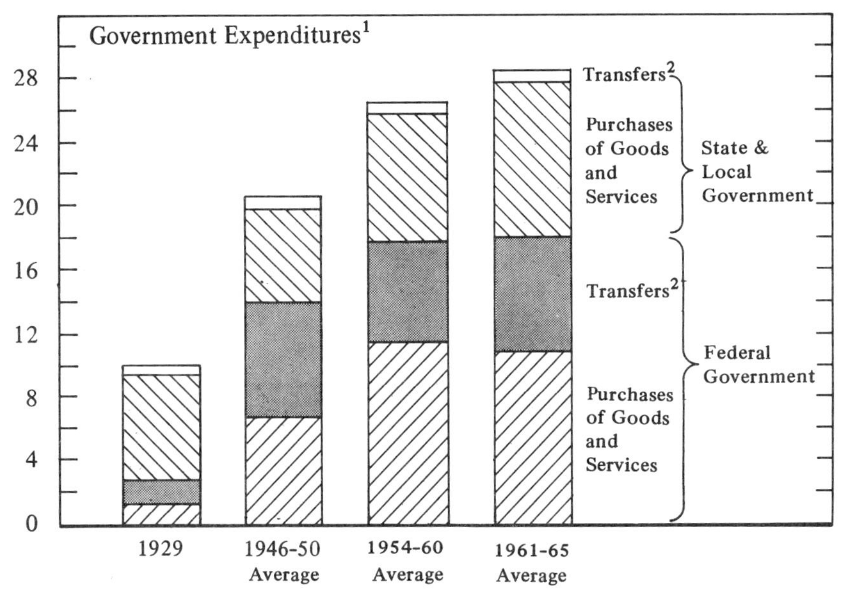

[1] National income accounts basis.
[2] Transfer payments, net interest, and subsidies less current surplus of government enterprises.
SOURCE: Department of Commerce.

A number of improvements in our financial structure were developed in the 1930's to assure that financial collapse and declines in economic activity would not generate a vicious downward spiral as they did after 1929. These important financial mechanisms include Federal insurance of private deposits; the separation of commercial and investment banking functions; the Federal Reserve's increased ability to provide banks with reserves in time of crisis; and the joint work of the Federal Reserve and the Securities and Exchange Commission to reduce harmful speculation in the stock market. The very existence of these structural changes has contributed to stability by improving confidence.

With the help of the more stable structure of the economy, recessions in the postwar era have been limited to declines in investment spending (and, in 1953–54, Federal outlays). Consumer incomes have not declined significantly, and hence households have maintained their spending in recession. With the nearly two-thirds of GNP represented by consumer expenditures insulated from decline and with a solid foundation of public outlays, declines in private investment have not cumulated. In contrast, the Great Depression generated a decline of consumer outlays of 40 percent from 1929 to 1933, and the shrinkage of consumer markets aggravated and reinforced the collapse in investment spending.

Containing Inflationary Pressures

The desirability of price stability was clearly recognized in the legislative discussion of the Employment Act. But few considered the danger of postwar inflation nearly as great as the opposite danger of relapse into depression. The legislation itself emphasized the objectives of using resources fully and attaining high employment. It did not explicitly label price stability an objective of policy, although this was implicit in the Act and fully reflected in the policies of every Administration. Nevertheless, concern has been expressed at times that policies for "maximum employment" might allow demand to press too hard on available resources, thus biasing the American economy toward inflation.

In the wartime environment, inflationary pressures of excess demand had been suppressed by direct controls on prices and by rationing. It turned out, however, during the years immediately following World War II that these measures had served partly to postpone–rather than to eliminate–significant demand pressures. Substantial backlogs of demand emerged in the 1946–48 period. Consumers and businesses possessed large accumulations of liquid assets to finance the rebuilding of their depleted stocks of household appliances, machinery, and equipment, and their houses and plants.

Thus, contrary to expectations, the initial years of the postwar era were marked by excessive rather than inadequate demand. In this environment, living standards of consumers, the productivity of labor, and the capacity of businesses rose rapidly. But so did the price level, with a jump of 31 percent in consumer prices from June 1946 to August 1948. Automatic fiscal stabilizers helped to contain the growth of private after-tax incomes, and were reflected in budgetary surpluses during the period. The economic policymaking machinery set up under the Employment Act may have moderated pressures to cut taxes drastically. Meanwhile, monetary policy was tied to a policy of supporting Government bond prices and was not free to combat inflation.

During the Korean war, however, the Government acted vigorously to counter inflationary tendencies close to their source. The March 1951 Federal Reserve-Treasury "accord" unleashed monetary policy. Selective controls on consumer installment credit and on home mortgages were instituted. The enactment of three large increases in income and profits tax rates in 1950 and 1951 is one of the better examples of timely fiscal policy. These actions reflected, in part, recommendations by the Council of Economic Advisers and hearings and reports of the Joint Economic Committee.

Right after the outbreak of hostilities, prices had risen sharply in a flurry of consumer and business buying and, as a result, prices and wage ceilings had been imposed early in 1951. Once the restraining influence of over-all fiscal and monetary policies was fully felt, there was little pressure on the ceilings, and the economy was able to meet the peak defense demands of the emergency without inflationary strain.

The immediate postwar period and the early months of the Korean war are the two blemishes of clearly excessive demand on our postwar record. Apart from these two intervals, wholesale prices have shown a net increase of only 2 percent in the postwar era. In 1956 and 1957, the only other periods of marked price increases, over-all demand was not generally excessive. That inflation raised new issues, which are discussed below. In view of the whole postwar record, it can hardly be said that the Employment Act has biased policy toward inflation.

EVOLVING PROBLEMS AND POLICIES

During the postwar era, the American economy has remained free of the malignant diseases of depression and run-away inflation. And the rate of economic growth has considerably exceeded its long-term average. The objectives of the Employment Act, however, have not always been fully met. In particular, experience has demonstrated that the avoidance of depression did not guarantee the achievement of "maximum employment" and the avoidance of excess-demand booms did not assure the maintenance of price stability.

Inadequate Demand in Expansion

The strength of private demand in the early postwar years and then again immediately after the Korean war led to a reassessment of the tasks of stabilization policy. After a decade of postwar experience, suspicions arose that the typical problem would be to contain rather than to stimulate private demand.

Any such conclusion was soundly refuted by the facts of the ensuing years. With the backlogs met, and with a marked decline in the rate of family formation, private demand weakened in the late 1950's. The economy's performance weakened correspondingly because Government did not act to compensate. Thus, while unemployment had averaged 4.2 percent of the civilian labor force in the first postwar decade, it remained above that level every month between late 1957 and October 1965, averaging 5.7 percent.

The problem of inadequate demand in expansion, which became the primary focus of fiscal action in the 1960's, was a new challenge to policymaking under the Employment Act. In the first postwar decade, each time the economy advanced or rebounded from a recession, it reached the neighborhood of full employment. The policymakers had been ready in the early postwar years to deal with noncyclical problems of submerged prosperity or stagnating production. They had seen maximum employment as a moving target which could be maintained only through a substantial growth of output. Both the Council of Economic Advisers and the Joint Economic Committee had given these issues repeated attention in the late 1940's and early 1950's. But until the late 1950's, no experience had been encountered to distinguish the problem of full employment from that of cyclical prosperity.

Then came a sequence of disturbing events: the 1957–58 recession followed a year of slow advance; the 1960–61 recession began from a peak far below full employment; and the expansion that began in 1961 seemed to be running out of steam after little more than a year.

During the initial years of this period, Government policy maintained vigilance against excessive buoyancy of demand when that was no longer the problem. Restrictive fiscal and monetary actions choked off the recovery of 1958–60. The shift to an expansionary fiscal policy by the Kennedy Administration early in 1961 was designed primarily to initiate a thriving recovery. A determined policy strategy to assure complete recovery was first formulated when the economy faltered in 1962.

The combination of fiscal stimuli to consumer demand and direct tax incentives to investment, together with monetary actions permitting an ample rise in credit, promoted a vigorous and sustained expansion after 1963. The inherent strength of both consumption and investment demand appeared in a new light, once the Revenue Act of 1964 exerted its invigorating influence.

Inflation at Less than Full Employment

Another problem encountered at times during the postwar era has been the tendency of prices to rise even in the absence of over-all excess demand pressures. This tendency reflects structural characteristics of the American economy. The economy is not made up of fully competitive labor and product markets in which large numbers of buyers and sellers interact and respond passively to prices. On the contrary, in many industries both unions and businesses exercise a considerable degree of market power. As a first result, wages and prices are both somewhat rigid in downward direction. To the extent that prices rise more readily in response to excess demand than they decline in the face of excess supply, the price level is given an upward bias, which can become particularly acute if there are sharp shifts in demand among various sectors of the economy. Secondly, because of market power, some firms augment increases in costs originating elsewhere and unions can escalate their wage demands if prices begin to rise. Third, firms can use a strong market position to widen margins in a period of prosperity even if there are no upward pressures on their costs. Fourth, in the nature of the collective bargaining process, key wage bargains in some industries may tend to establish a pattern applied elsewhere. In particular, if the industries with key wage bargains happen to have excess demands and very strong profits, the pattern will tend to pull wages upward more rapidly throughout the economy.

An important, broadly oriented study by the Joint Economic Committee analyzed the workings of these important influences in the 1956–57 inflation. In that period, excess demands that were present in machinery and equipment, automobile, and metals industries led to price increases that were not offset elsewhere. Large wage settlements in these industries with high demand and high profits had pattern-setting effects on many other contracts, thus adding to costs on a broad front.

Rising prices that originate from such a process can affect expectations, jeopardize the stability and balance of an expansion, and create inequities and distortions just as readily as demand inflation. But measures to restrain these price increases by reducing over-all demand will enlarge unemployment and impair the productivity record so important to cost-price stability over the longer run. Policies to improve the operations of markets, increase resource mobility and accelerate technical change can help to increase the economy's resistance to rising prices. But in a world where large firms and large unions play an essential role, the cost-price record will depend heavily upon the responsibility with which they exercise the market power that society entrusts to them.

The need for responsible private action was brought to public attention in the Economic Reports of President Eisenhower's second Administration. Through the major innovation of the guideposts in the Kennedy and Johnson Administrations, this need has since been focused and developed into a national policy to enlist the force of public opinion to maintain cost-price stability. The emergence of such a policy has been all the more important in recent years because of the balance of payments problem that has persisted alongside the domestic need for more expansion.

ECONOMIC POLICY TODAY

Two decades of economic analysis and policy experience have shaped the development of a revised economic policy. By some, current policy has been labeled the "new economics." It draws heavily on the experience and lessons of the past, and it combines both new and old elements. Current policy represents a coordinated and consistent effort to promote balance of over-all supply and aggregate demand—to sustain steady balanced growth at high employment levels with essential price stability.

This approach to policy has several key aspects, not entirely novel by any means. First, it emphasizes a continuous, rather than a cyclical, framework for analyzing economic developments and formulating policies. Stimulus to demand is not confined to avoiding or correcting recession, but rather is applied whenever needed for the promotion of full-utilization and prosperity. Second, in this way, it emphasizes a preventive strategy against the onset of recession. Third, in focusing on balance of the economy, this policy strategy cannot give top priority to balance in the budget. When private investment threatens to outrun saving at full employment, a Government surplus is needed to increase total saving in the economy while restrictive monetary policy may also be called for to restrain investment outlays. When, as in recent years, private saving at full employment tends to outrun actual private investment, the balance should be corrected by budget deficits and expansionary monetary policy. Fourth, it considers the budget and monetary conditions in the framework of a growing economy, recognizing that revenues expand and thereby exert a fiscal drag on demand unless expansionary actions are taken; similarly, it recognizes that money and credit must expand just to keep interest rates from rising. Fifth, this strategy emphasizes the use of a variety of tools to support expansion while simultaneously pursuing other objectives. Manpower policies, selective approaches to control capital outflows, as well as general fiscal and monetary measures, are all part of the arsenal. Sixth, it calls for responsible price-wage actions by labor and management to prevent cost-inflation from impeding the pursuit of full employment. Finally, it makes greater demands on economic forecasting and analysis. The job of the economist is not merely to predict the upturn or the downturn but to judge continuously the prospects for demand in relation to a growing productive capacity.

The Nature of Cyclical Instability

An industrial economy is vulnerable to cumulative upward and downward movements in activity, so evident in our long-term record. While they can have diverse specific causes, these cyclical fluctuations can be explained as the result of imbalances between the rate of growth of productive capacity and the rate of growth of final demands that make use of productive capacity.

During periods of prosperity, a considerable part of the Nation's output is used to increase productive capacity through investment in plant and equipment and business inventories. If demand keeps pace, sales expand and the new capacity turns out to be profitable. Businessmen find that their decisions to increase capacity have been validated and they continue to pursue expansionary investment policies. If, on the other hand, inventory stocks are built up far in advance of need—on the basis of overly optimistic sales forecasts or as an inflation-hedge—businessmen will subsequently wish to cut back their rate of accumulation. Similarly, if outlays for business fixed investment add to productive capacity faster than demand expands, overheads on new capital cut into profits, inducing business firms to trim their capital outlays. Even if businessmen continue to add somewhat to their productive capacity, the mere decline in the rate of expansion can mean an absolute reduction in the demand for capital goods and for output to go into inventories. Payrolls and purchasing power are thereby curtailed and a decline in total demand can result. Thus a slowdown in economic activity is converted into a definite downturn—a recession or depression.

Imbalance can arise because businessmen in the aggregate invest too much and overbuild, creating more capacity than the economy can—even at best—put to productive use. Or alternatively it can stem from "underbuying," a growth of final demand too slow to make use of even moderate additions to capacity. In principle, cyclical movements can also be triggered by overbuilding of new homes and consumer durables.

Overbuilding of inventories—partly encouraged by expectations of rising prices—was probably the key factor in the first postwar downturn, which occurred in 1948. That experience demonstrated that a situation of high total demand could deteriorate rapidly into recession without any change in the basic underlying factors in the private economy or any restraining shift in public policy. In 1953, the sharp decline in defense outlays reduced final demands and precipitated recession; productive capacity became temporarily excessive and investment spending declined. In 1956–57, rapid growth of productive capacity was associated with an investment boom; meanwhile, final demands grew very slowly. It is not possible to deliver a clear verdict on whether more vigorous growth of final demand would have justified the high investment levels then obtaining. But with the slow growth of demand that actually occurred, there was an abrupt decline in plant and equipment spending as well as inventory investment in 1957. In 1959–60, the rate of expansion of capacity (including inventories) was not excessive measured against the capabilities of the economy; the failure of the economy to support that growth of capacity must be attributed to "underbuying," the inadequate expansion of final demand, in an environment of restrictive fiscal and monetary policies.

In the future as in the past, policies to avert recession cannot wait until imbalances develop and the signs of a downturn are clear. The fact that economic activity is rising cannot be an assurance of continued growth if the expansion is too slow to match the growth of productive capacity. Nor can a strong level of investment be relied on to sustain expansion if it threatens an excessive growth of productive capacity. Recognizing these tasks, Government must apply its fiscal and monetary policies continuously to sustain and support a balanced expansion, sometimes by moderating the strength of an excessive investment boom, sometimes by adding to the strength of lagging final demand. The best defense against recession is a policy to sustain continued expansion. In a free economy, fluctuations in private demand will inevitably occur, and the Government will not always have the wisdom or the ability to counteract them. Continued expansion cannot be guaranteed, but recurrent recession need not be accepted as a necessary fact of economic life.

Policy for a Growing Economy

In order to achieve the goal of maximum employment, the Government must coordinate all its policies to take account of the persistent growth of the economy's potential output.

The Problem of Fiscal Drag. One consequence of economic growth is that budgetary policies become more restrictive if they stand still. If tax rates are unchanged, Federal revenues will grow continuously as the economy expands. Meanwhile, if Federal expenditures are held constant in the face of growing revenues, the Federal budget will exert a continuing "fiscal drag" on private demand.

Either increased expenditures or reduced tax rates can offset this influence. A total of these two types of stimulative actions which exactly matched the dollar amount of normal revenue growth would provide a precise offset to fiscal drag (and would leave unchanged the high-employment surplus). . . .

A simple mechanical offset to fiscal drag is not, however, a satisfactory rule for fiscal policy. When aggregate demand threatens to exceed the supply capacity of the economy, some fiscal drag should be allowed to operate. On the other hand, waning strength in private demand points to fiscal action that would more than offset the drag, effecting a desirable decline in the high-employment surplus.

Furthermore, tightness or ease of monetary policy is important in determining appropriate fiscal actions. There is an analog to drag in the monetary area: A growing economy generates rising demands for liquid assets and increasing needs for borrowing. If monetary policies stand still in the sense of holding supplies unchanged, continually tighter credit conditions and higher interest rates will be the result.

Accelerating Growth. The growth of the economy is a major influence on policy; the opposite side of the coin is the major role of policy in influencing potential economic growth. The larger the amount of current output invested in physical and human resources, the more rapidly productivity and the productive capacity of the economy will increase.

A number of policy choices can speed growth by shifting resources into various types of investment. Public investment in human and physical resources can yield rich returns in more rapid economic growth. Some public investments, such as those on research and development, encourage complementary private investment. Outlays for manpower training improve labor skills and productivity. Throughout our history, investment in education has been one of the key contributors to growth. Private investment in plant and equipment is a key determinant of our industrial capacity. It can be stimulated by easing monetary policies. It can also be encouraged by selective tax reductions, such as the investment credit and depreciation reform of 1962 and the reductions in corporate tax rates in 1964 and 1965.

When the economy is below full employment, any stimulative measure is likely to add to private investment, thereby contributing to the growth of potential, as well as to actual, output. But, at full employment, more resources can be devoted to capital formation only if current consumption is restrained. A policy strategy to accelerate growth may therefore point to higher personal income taxes or similar measures to hold consumption below what would otherwise be appropriate.

Choices of Tools. Economic policy has many tools available in pursuing the goals of full employment, rapid growth, price stability, and balance of international payments. The full range of economic objectives must be reflected in the selection of policies to meet particular circumstances.

Policy instruments differ in their impact. Sometimes policy tools can advance the economy toward more than one goal. For example, manpower policies help to maintain price stability at high employment and to promote economic growth. Conflicts may occur, however. For example, high interest rates impinge particularly on investment both at home and abroad, hence somewhat reducing foreign capital outflows but also reducing aggregate demand and slowing economic growth. In the case of potential conflicts, instruments must be used more selectively; for example, moderate changes in interest rates can be supplemented by taxes on foreign investment, like the Interest Equalization Tax.

The potential for timely results differs for various policy instruments. Monetary policy can be altered readily, although its full economic impact will not be immediate. While some restraint or speedup in Federal outlays can be applied by Executive authority alone, tax rate changes must, of course, be approved by the Congress. The speed of congressional action on tax changes has varied. It acted rapidly to increase taxes in 1950, and to reduce excise taxes both in 1954 and 1965. On the other hand, it took 13 months to enact the comprehensive Revenue Act of 1964. Tax revision can help to avoid the necessity for abrupt changes in Federal expenditures, which could require stopping a project before its conclusion or starting a new one with inadequate planning.

Given the possibility for achieving needed short-run stimulus or restraint through changes in taxes, transfer payments, or monetary policy, decisions on expenditures for public services can rest on basic judgments of costs and benefits of public and private spending. The availability of this choice permits resources to be devoted to the highest priority uses.

PREREQUISITES OF SUCCESSFUL POLICY

Choice of the right policy action demands full information about the state of the economy and understanding of its workings. And execution of stabilizing policy requires public understanding and acceptance.

Information

An important requirement of economic policymaking is a firm and timely knowledge of where the economy stands. Spurred by the need for prompt and enlightened decisions, the Federal statistics program has made rapid forward strides in the postwar period, and now provides a much better gauge of current economic developments. Of the 369 monthly series now carried in *Economic Indicators,* the statistical summary prepared by the Council and issued by the Joint Economic Committee, only 60 percent would have been available by the monthly publication date at the time *Economic Indicators* was launched in the late 1940's.

In addition to the information on current developments, a number of anticipatory surveys have been instituted which provide important information on the probable future course of the economy. Outstanding among these is the Commerce-Securities and Exchange Commission survey on plant and equipment; additional important clues to future developments come from the Commerce inventory survey and the Census quarterly survey of consumer buying intentions. Important information also is obtained from private sources including the University of Michigan's Survey Research Center, the National Industrial Conference Board, and McGraw-Hill, Inc.

Yet, our data are not completely satisfactory. The revisions of the national accounts last summer gave evidence of how much we learn later that could have been helpful on a current basis. There are any number of areas—capital stock and capacity, productivity, employee fringe benefits, job vacancies, among them—where there are important gaps and weaknesses in our quantitative information which can be remedied only by expansion of our statistical programs.

Not all the information useful to the Council comes from published sources or takes the form of numbers. The Council, as enjoined by the Act, finds it most useful to consult regularly with business and labor. These consultations provide valuable information and opinions, and also allow the Council to explain and clarify Administration views.

Professional Knowledge

Facts are the essential raw materials for analysis, but they require intelligent processing to be useful in guiding policy. The ability of economists to diagnose and forecast on the basis of current facts and to evaluate the impact of alternative policy measures is a key determinant of what policy can do to maintain stable balanced growth.

Our economic knowledge has made great advances in the past generation, but many important questions remain, answers to which should be and can be improved through further research.

There are many quantitative uncertainties in forecasting the strength of private demands. Some of these were illustrated in 1965 when the improvement in profits and sales—coupled with the shifting defense picture—generated a more rapid and greater surge in investment demand than was foreseen initially. Furthermore, the linkage between monetary policy actions and changes in ultimate spending also require more exploration. And even in areas that are more readily quantified, such as the impact on GNP of changes in Government purchases and personal tax reductions, there remains a considerable range of doubt about the timing of the impacts and the specific influences on consumption and investment.

Departing from the domain of aggregative output effects, we need a better understanding of many more specialized problems, such as the functioning of labor markets—how job vacancies are filled, how skill shortages are met, and how excess supplies in one area are ultimately absorbed elsewhere. Such knowledge can be a useful guide to the possibilities for expanding output and employment while avoiding bottlenecks.

But while much remains to be learned about our economy, it would be a disservice to understate the power of economic analysis, and to underrate the substantial contribution of the profession to the successful course of our economy in the postwar period. The Employment Act provided the framework in which this professional contribution could be rendered and be given its proper place in the framing of public policy.

Public Understanding

Not all of the needed improvements in knowledge and understanding are of a technical character. Even though viewed as correct by the professional analyst, policies cannot be applied effectively unless the Congress and the public at large understand how the proposed measures intend to further desirable objectives.

If policy proposals of the Administration are to be converted into legislation, they must be convincing to the Congress. Twenty Annual Economic Reports have explained the rationale for the programs of four Presidents. And the Joint Economic Committee has rendered invaluable service in contributing to an understanding of general economic policy and specific proposals. The principles of fiscal policy and their implications for tax and expenditure legislation have been central to the Nation's economic education in the past 20 years. The great increase in understanding is best seen in the sophisticated current level of public discussion.

Proper understanding of policies by the public, moreover, contributes to the very success of the policy measures. In the absence of public understanding, there can be perverse reactions. If people read policies to maintain price stability as an announcement that inflation has arrived, rather than an exercise of determination to avoid it, destabilized prices may be the result. If people see steps to combat recession as a sign of panic rather than a support to the economy, this too can have adverse psychological effects. In particular, a firm appreciation by the American people of the rationale of wage-price guideposts is essential to make them effective and to limit the need for active participation by Government. It is the public that gets hurt by irresponsible wage-price decisions, and public reaction can be the best reminder to those with market power of their social responsibility.

CONCLUSION

As the primary objective set by the Employment Act is being reached, new problems move to the fore and are receiving increasing attention in public policy. These include the efficient use of the Nation's human and natural resources, the conquest of poverty and suffering, the reconstruction of our cities, and the many other tasks set forth in the preceding pages of this Report. And undoubtedly in the pursuit of the goals of the Employment Act during the next 20 years, policymakers will encounter a new range of problems, no more completely foreseeable now than were the issues of today in 1946.

While important problems remain, we are nonetheless at an historic point of accomplishment and promise. Twenty years of experience have demonstrated our ability to avoid ruinous inflations and severe depressions. It is now within our capabilities to set more ambitious goals. We strive to avoid recurrent recessions, to keep unemployment far below rates of the past decade, to maintain essential price stability at full employment, to move toward the Great Society, and, indeed, to make full prosperity the normal state of the American economy. It is a tribute to our success under the Employment Act that we now have not only the economic understanding but also the will and determination to use economic policy as an effective tool for progress.

27

THE ROLE OF MONETARY POLICY[1]

MILTON FRIEDMAN[2]

There is wide agreement about the major goals of economic policy: high employment, stable prices, and rapid growth. There is less agreement that these goals are mutually compatible or, among those who regard them as incompatible, about the terms at which they can and should be substituted for one another. There is least agreement about the role that various instruments of policy can and should play in achieving the several goals.

My topic for tonight is the role of one such instrument–monetary policy. What can it contribute? And how should it be conducted to contribute the most? Opinion on these questions has fluctuated widely. In the first flush of enthusiasm about the newly created Federal Reserve System, many observers attributed the relative stability of the 1920s to the System's capacity for fine tuning–to apply an apt modern term. It came to be widely believed that a new era had arrived in which business cycles had been rendered obsolete by advances in monetary technology. This opinion was shared by economist and layman alike, though, of course, there were some dissonant voices. The Great Contraction destroyed this naive attitude. Opinion swung to the other

[1]Presidential address delivered at the Eightieth Annual Meeting of the American Economic Association, Washington, D. C., December 29, 1967.

[2]I am indebted for helpful criticisms of earlier drafts to Armen Alchian, Gary Becker, Martin Bronfenbrenner, Arthur F. Burns, Phillip Cagan, David D. Friedman, Lawrence Harris, Harry G. Johnson, Homer Jones, Jerry Jordan, David Meiselman, Allan H. Meltzer, Theodore W. Schultz, Anna J. Schwartz, Herbert Stein, George J. Stigler, and James Tobin.

Reprinted from the *American Economic Review* (March 1968), pp. 1–17 by permission of the author and publisher. Milton Friedman is a professor at the University of Chicago.

extreme. Monetary policy was a string. You could pull on it to stop inflation but you could not push on it to halt recession. You could lead a horse to water but you could not make him drink. Such theory by aphorism was soon replaced by Keynes' rigorous and sophisticated analysis.

Keynes offered simultaneously an explanation for the presumed impotence of monetary policy to stem the depression, a nonmonetary interpretation of the depression, and an alternative to monetary policy for meeting the depression and his offering was avidly accepted. If liquidity preference is absolute or nearly so—as Keynes believed likely in times of heavy unemployment—interest rates cannot be lowered by monetary measures. If investment and consumption are little affected by interest rates—as Hansen and many of Keynes' other American disciples came to believe—lower interest rates, even if they could be achieved, would do little good. Monetary policy is twice damned. The contraction, set in train, on this view, by a collapse of investment or by a shortage of investment opportunities or by stubborn thriftiness, could not, it was argued, have been stopped by monetary measures. But there was available an alternative—fiscal policy. Government spending could make up for insufficient private investment. Tax reductions could undermine stubborn thriftiness.

The wide acceptance of these views in the economics profession meant that for some two decades monetary policy was believed by all but a few reactionary souls to have been rendered obsolete by new economic knowledge. Money did not matter. Its only role was the minor one of keeping interest rates low, in order to hold down interest payments in the government budget, contribute to the "euthanasia of the rentier," and maybe, stimulate investment a bit to assist government spending in maintaining a high level of aggregate demand.

These views produced a widespread adoption of cheap money policies after the war. And they received a rude shock when these policies failed in country after country, when central bank after central bank was forced to give up the pretense that it could indefinitely keep "the" rate of interest at a low level. In this country, the public denouement came with the Federal Reserve-Treasury Accord in 1951, although the policy of pegging government bond prices was not formally abandoned until 1953. Inflation, stimulated by cheap money policies, not the widely heralded postwar depression, turned out to be the order of the day. The result was the beginning of a revival of belief in the potency of monetary policy.

This revival was strongly fostered among economists by the theoretical developments initiated by Haberler but named for Pigou that pointed out a channel—namely, changes in wealth—whereby changes in the real quantity of money can affect aggregate demand even if they do not alter interest rates. These theoretical developments did not undermine Keynes' argument against the potency of orthodox monetary measures when liquidity preference is absolute since under such circumstances the usual monetary operations involve simply substituting money for other assets without changing total wealth. But they did show how changes in the quantity of money produced in other ways could affect total spending even under such circumstances. And, more fundamentally, they did undermine Keynes' key theoretical proposition, namely, that even in a world of flexible prices, a position of equilibrium at full employment might not exist. Henceforth, unemployment had again to be explained by rigidities or imperfections, not as the natural outcome of a fully operative market process.

The revival of belief in the potency of monetary policy was fostered also by a re-evaluation of the role money played from 1929 to 1933. Keynes and most other economists of the time believed that the Great Contraction in the United States occurred despite aggressive expansionary policies by the monetary authorities–that they did their best but their best was not good enough.[3] Recent studies have demonstrated that the facts are precisely the reverse: the U. S. monetary authorities followed highly deflationary policies. The quantity of money in the United States fell by one-third in the course of the contraction. And it fell not because there were no willing borrowers–not because the horse would not drink. It fell because the Federal Reserve System forced or permitted a sharp reduction in the monetary base, because it failed to exercise the responsibilities assigned to it in the Federal Reserve Act to provide liquidity to the banking system. The Great Contraction is tragic testimony to the power of monetary policy–not, as Keynes and so many of his contemporaries believed, evidence of its impotence.

In the United States the revival of belief in the potency of monetary policy was strengthened also by increasing disillusionment with fiscal policy, not so much with its potential to affect aggregate demand as with the practical and political feasibility of using it. Expenditures turned out to respond sluggishly and with long lags to attempts to adjust them to the course of economic activity, so emphasis shifted to taxes. But here political factors entered with a vengeance to prevent prompt adjustment to presumed need, as has been so graphically illustrated in the months since I wrote the first draft of this talk. "Fine tuning" is a marvelously evocative phrase in this electronic age, but it has little resemblance to what is possible in practice–not, I might add, an unmixed evil.

It is hard to realize how radical has been the change in professional opinion on the role of money. Hardly an economist today accepts views that were the common coin some two decades ago. Let me cite a few examples.

[3]In [2], I have argued that Henry Simons shared this view with Keynes, and that it accounts for the policy changes that he recommended.

In a talk published in 1945, E. A. Goldenweiser, then Director of the Research Division of the Federal Reserve Board, described the primary objective of monetary policy as being to "maintain the value of Government bonds. . . . This country" he wrote, "will have to adjust to a 2½ per cent interest rate as the return on safe, long-time money, because the time has come when returns on pioneering capital can no longer be unlimited as they were in the past" [4, p. 117].

In a book on *Financing American Prosperity,* edited by Paul Homan and Fritz Machlup and published in 1945, Alvin Hansen devotes nine pages of text to the "savings-investment problem" without finding any need to use the words "interest rate" or any close facsimile thereto [5, pp. 218–27]. In his contribution to this volume, Fritz Machlup wrote, "Questions regarding the rate of interest, in particular regarding its variation or its stability, may not be among the most vital problems of the postwar economy, but they are certainly among the perplexing ones" [5, p. 466]. In his contribution, John H. Williams–not only professor at Harvard but also a long-time adviser to the New York Federal Reserve Bank–wrote, "I can see no prospect of revival of a general monetary control in the postwar period" [5, p. 383].

Another of the volumes dealing with postwar policy that appeared at this time, *Planning and Paying for Full Employment,* was edited by Abba P. Lerner and Frank D. Graham [6] and had contributors of all shades of professional opinion–from Henry Simons and Frank Graham to Abba Lerner and Hans Neisser. Yet Albert Halasi, in his excellent summary of the papers, was able to say, "Our contributors do not discuss the question of money supply. . . . The contributors make no special mention of credit policy to remedy actual depressions. . . . Inflation . . . might be fought more effectively by raising interest rates. . . . But . . . other anti-inflationary measures . . . are preferable" [6, pp. 23–24]. *A Survey of Contemporary Economics,* edited by Howard Ellis and published in 1948, was an "official" attempt to codify the state of economic thought of the time. In his contribution, Arthur Smithies wrote, "In the field of compensatory action, I believe fiscal policy must shoulder most of the load. Its chief rival, monetary policy, seems to be disqualified on institutional grounds. This country appears to be committed to something like the present low level of interest rates on a long-term basis" [1, p. 208].

These quotations suggest the flavor of professional thought some two decades ago. If you wish to go further in this humbling inquiry, I recommend that you compare the sections on money–when you can find them–in the Principles texts of the early postwar years with the lengthy sections in the current crop even, or especially, when the early and recent Principles are different editions of the same work.

The pendulum has swung far since then, if not all the way to the position of the late 1920s, at least much closer to that position than to the position of 1945. There are of course many differences between then and now, less in the potency attributed to monetary policy than in the roles assigned to it and the criteria by which the profession believes monetary policy should be guided. Then, the chief roles assigned monetary policy were to promote price stability and to preserve the gold standard; the chief criteria of monetary policy were the state of the "money market," the extent of "speculation" and the movement of gold. Today, primacy is assigned to the promotion of full employment, with the prevention of inflation a continuing but definitely secondary objective. And there is major disagreement about criteria of policy, varying from emphasis on money market conditions, interest rates, and the quantity of money to the belief that the state of employment itself should be the proximate criterion of policy.

I stress nonetheless the similarity between the views that prevailed in the late 'twenties and those that prevail today because I fear that, now as then, the pendulum may well have swung too far, that, now as then, we are in danger of assigning to monetary policy a larger role than it can perform, in danger of asking it to accomplish tasks that it cannot achieve, and, as a result, in danger of preventing it from making the contribution that it is capable of making.

Unaccustomed as I am to denigrating the importance of money, I therefore shall, as my first task, stress what monetary policy cannot do. I shall then try to outline what it can do and how it can best make its contribution, in the present state of our knowledge–or ignorance.

I. WHAT MONETARY POLICY CANNOT DO

From the infinite world of negation, I have selected two limitations of monetary policy to discuss: (1) It cannot peg interest rates for more than very limited periods; (2) It cannot peg the rate of unemployment for more than very limited periods. I select these because the contrary has been or is widely believed, because they correspond to the two main unattainable tasks that are at all likely to be assigned to monetary policy, and because essentially the same theoretical analysis covers both.

Pegging of Interest Rates

History has already persuaded many of you about the first limitation. As noted earlier, the failure of cheap money policies was a major source of the reaction against simple-minded Keynesianism. In the United States, this reaction involved widespread recognition that the wartime and postwar pegging of bond prices was a mistake, that the abandonment of this policy was a desirable and inevitable step, and that it had none of the disturbing and disastrous consequences that were so freely predicted at the time.

The limitation derives from a much misunderstood feature of the relation between money and interest rates. Let the Fed set out to keep interest rates down. How will it try to do so? By buying securities. This raises their prices and lowers their yields. In the process, it also increases the quantity of reserves available to banks, hence the amount of bank credit, and, ultimately the total quantity of money. That is why central bankers in particular, and the financial community more broadly, generally believe that an increase in the quantity of money tends to lower interest rates. Academic economists accept the same conclusion, but for different reasons. They see, in their mind's eye, a negatively sloping liquidity preference schedule. How can people be induced to hold a larger quantity of money? Only by bidding down interest rates.

Both are right, up to a point. The *initial* impact of increasing the quantity of money at a faster rate than it has been increasing is to make interest rates lower for a time than they would otherwise have been. But this is only the beginning of the process not the end. The more rapid rate of monetary growth will stimulate spending, both through the impact on investment of lower market interest rates and through the impact on other spending and thereby relative prices of higher cash balances than are desired. But one man's spending is another man's income. Rising income will raise the liquidity preference schedule and the demand for loans; it may also raise prices, which would reduce the real quantity of money. These three effects will reverse the initial downward pressure on interest rates fairly promptly, say, in something less than a year. Together they will tend, after a somewhat longer interval, say, a year or two, to return interest rates to the level they would otherwise have had. Indeed, given the tendency for the economy to overreact, they are highly likely to raise interest rates temporarily beyond that level, setting in motion a cyclical adjustment process.

A fourth effect, when and if it becomes operative, will go even farther, and definitely mean that a higher rate of monetary expansion will correspond to a higher, not lower, level of interest rates than would otherwise have prevailed. Let the higher rate of monetary growth produce rising prices, and let the public come to expect that prices will continue to rise. Borrowers will then be willing to pay and lenders will then demand higher interest rates—as Irving Fisher pointed out decades ago. This price expectation effect is slow to develop and also slow to disappear. Fisher estimated that it took several decades for a full adjustment and more recent work is consistent with his estimates.

These subsequent effects explain why every attempt to keep interest rates at a low level has forced the monetary authority to engage in successively larger and larger open market purchases. They explain why, historically, high and rising nominal interest rates have been associated with rapid growth in the quantity of money, as in Brazil or Chile or in the United States in recent years, and why low and falling interest rates have been associated with slow growth in the quantity of money, as in Switzerland now or in the United States from 1929 to 1933. As an empirical matter, low interest rates are a sign that monetary policy *has been* tight—in the sense that the quantity of money has grown slowly; high interest rates are a sign that monetary policy *has been* easy—in the sense that the quantity of money has grown rapidly. The broadest facts of experience run in precisely the opposite direction from that which the financial community and academic economists have all generally taken for granted.

Paradoxically, the monetary authority could assure low nominal rates of interest—but to do so it would have to start out in what seems like the opposite direction, by engaging in a deflationary monetary policy. Similarly, it could assure high nominal interest rates by engaging in an inflationary policy and accepting a temporary movement in interest rates in the opposite direction.

These considerations not only explain why monetary policy cannot peg interest rates; they also explain why interest rates are such a misleading indicator of whether monetary policy is "tight" or "easy." For that, it is far better to look at the rate of change of the quantity of money.[4]

Employment as a Criterion of Policy

The second limitation I wish to discuss goes more against the grain of current thinking. Monetary growth, it is widely held, will tend to stimulate employment; monetary contraction, to retard employment. Why, then, cannot the monetary authority adopt a target for employment or unemployment—say, 3 per cent unemployment; be tight when unemployment is less than the target; be easy when unemployment is higher than the target; and in this way peg unemployment at, say, 3 per cent? The reason it cannot is precisely the same as for interest rates—the difference between the immediate and the delayed consequences of such a policy.

[4]This is partly an empirical not theoretical judgment. In principle, "tightness" or "ease" depends on the rate of change of the quantity of money supplied compared to the rate of change of the quantity demanded excluding effects on demand from monetary policy itself. However, empirically demand is highly stable, if we exclude the effect of monetary policy, so it is generally sufficient to look at supply alone.

Thanks to Wicksell, we are all acquainted with the concept of a "natural" rate of interest and the possibility of a discrepancy between the "natural" and the "market" rate. The preceding analysis of interest rates can be translated fairly directly into Wicksellian terms. The monetary authority can make the market rate less than the natural rate only by inflation. It can make the market rate higher than the natural rate only by deflation. We have added only one wrinkle to Wicksell—the Irving Fisher distinction between the nominal and the real rate of interest. Let the monetary authority keep the nominal market rate for a time below the natural rate by inflation. That in turn will raise the nominal natural rate itself, once anticipations of inflation become widespread, thus requiring still more rapid inflation to hold down the market rate. Similarly, because of the Fisher effect, it will require not merely deflation but more and more rapid deflation to hold the market rate above the initial "natural" rate.

This analysis has its close counterpart in the employment market. At any moment of time, there is some level of unemployment which has the property that it is consistent with equilibrium in the structure of *real* wage rates. At that level of unemployment, real wage rates are tending on the average to rise at a "normal" secular rate, i.e., at a rate that can be indefinitely maintained so long as capital formation, technological improvements, etc., remain on their long-run trends. A lower level of unemployment is an indication that there is an excess demand for labor that will produce upward pressure on real wage rates. A higher level of unemployment is an indication that there is an excess supply of labor that will produce downward pressure on real wage rates. The "natural rate of unemployment," in other words, is the level that would be ground out by the Walrasian system of general equilibrium equations, provided there is imbedded in them the actual structural characteristics of the labor and commodity markets, including market imperfections, stochastic variability in demands and supplies, the cost of gathering information about job vacancies and labor availabilities, the costs of mobility, and so on.[5]

You will recognize the close similarity between this statement and the celebrated Phillips Curve. The similarity is not coincidental. Phillips' analysis of the relation between unemployment and wage change is deservedly celebrated as an important and original contribution. But, unfortunately, it contains a basic defect—the failure to distinguish between *nominal* wages and *real* wages—just as Wicksell's analysis failed to distinguish between *nominal*

[5] It is perhaps worth noting that this "natural" rate need not correspond to equality between the number unemployed and the number of job vacancies. For any given structure of the labor market, there will be some equilibrium relation between these two magnitudes, but there is no reason why it should be one of equality.

interest rates and *real* interest rates. Implicitly, Phillips wrote his article for a world in which everyone anticipated that nominal prices would be stable and in which that anticipation remained unshaken and immutable whatever happened to actual prices and wages. Suppose, by contrast, that everyone anticipates that prices will rise at a rate of more than 75 per cent a year—as, for example, Brazilians did a few years ago. Then wages must rise at that rate simply to keep real wages unchanged. An excess supply of labor will be reflected in a less rapid rise in nominal wages than in anticipated prices,[6] not in an absolute decline in wages. When Brazil embarked on a policy to bring down the rate of price rise, and succeeded in bringing the price rise down to about 45 per cent a year, there was a sharp initial rise in unemployment because under the influence of earlier anticipations, wages kept rising at a pace that was higher than the new rate of price rise, though lower than earlier. This is the result experienced, and to be expected, of all attempts to reduce the rate of inflation below that widely anticipated.[7]

To avoid misunderstanding, let me emphasize that by using the term "natural" rate of unemployment, I do not mean to suggest that it is immutable and unchangeable. On the contrary, many of the market characteristics that determine its level are man-made and policy-made. In the United States, for example, legal minimum wage rates, the Walsh-Healy and Davis-Bacon Acts, and the strength of labor unions all make the natural rate of unemployment higher than it would otherwise be. Improvements in employment exchanges, in availability of information about job vacancies and labor supply, and so on, would tend to lower the natural rate of unemployment. I use the term "natural" for the same reason Wicksell did—to try to separate the real forces from monetary forces.

Let us assume that the monetary authority tries to peg the "market" rate of

[6]Strictly speaking, the rise in nominal wages will be less rapid than the rise in anticipated nominal wages to make allowance for any secular changes in real wages.

[7]Stated in terms of the rate of change of nominal wages, the Phillips Curve can be expected to be reasonably stable and well defined for any period for which the *average* rate of change of prices, and hence the anticipated rate, has been relatively stable. For such periods, nominal wages and "real" wages move together. Curves computed for different periods or different countries for each of which this condition has been satisfied will differ in level, the level of the curve depending on what the average rate of price change was. The higher the average rate of price change, the higher will tend to be the level of the curve. For periods or countries for which the rate of change of prices varies considerably, the Phillips Curve will not be well defined. My impression is that these statements accord reasonably well with the experience of the economists who have explored empirical Phillips Curves.

Restate Phillips' analysis in terms of the rate of real wages—and even more precisely, anticipated real wages—and it all falls into place. That is why students of empirical Phillips Curves have found that it helps to include the rate of change of the price level as an independent variable.

unemployment at a level below the "natural" rate. For definiteness, suppose that it takes 3 per cent as the target rate and that the "natural" rate is higher than 3 per cent. Suppose also that we start out at a time when prices have been stable and when unemployment is higher than 3 per cent. Accordingly, the authority increases the rate of monetary growth. This will be expansionary. By making nominal cash balances higher than people desire, it will tend initially to lower interest rates and in this and other ways to stimulate spending. Income and spending will start to rise.

To begin with, much or most of the rise in income will take the form of an increase in output and employment rather than in prices. People have been expecting prices to be stable, and prices and wages have been set for some time in the future on that basis. It takes time for people to adjust to a new state of demand. Producers will tend to react to the initial expansion in aggregate demand by increasing output, employees by working longer hours, and the unemployed, by taking jobs now offered at former nominal wages. This much is pretty standard doctrine.

But it describes only the initial effects. Because selling prices of products typically respond to an unanticipated rise in nominal demand faster than prices of factors of production, real wages received have gone down–though real wages anticipated by employees went up, since employees implicitly evaluated the wages offered at the earlier price level. Indeed, the simultaneous fall *ex post* in real wages to employers and rise *ex ante* in real wages to employees is what enabled employment to increase. But the decline *ex post* in real wages will soon come to affect anticipations. Employees will start to reckon on rising prices of the things they buy and to demand higher nominal wages for the future. "Market" unemployment is below the "natural" level. There is an excess demand for labor so real wages will tend to rise toward their initial level.

Even though the higher rate of monetary growth continues, the rise in real wages will reverse the decline in unemployment, and then lead to a rise, which will tend to return unemployment to its former level. In order to keep unemployment at its target level of 3 per cent, the monetary authority would have to raise monetary growth still more. As in the interest rate case, the "market" rate can be kept below the "natural" rate only by inflation. And, as in the interest rate case, too, only by accelerating inflation. Conversely, let the monetary authority choose a target rate of unemployment that is above the natural rate, and they will be led to produce a deflation, and an accelerating deflation at that.

What if the monetary authority chose the "natural" rate–either of interest or unemployment–as its target? One problem is that it cannot know what the "natural" rate is. Unfortunately, we have as yet devised no method to estimate accurately and readily the natural rate of either interest or unemployment. And the "natural" rate will itself change from time to time. But the basic problem is that even if the monetary authority knew the "natural" rate, and attempted to peg the market rate at that level, it would not be led to a determinate policy. The "market" rate will vary from the natural rate for all sorts of reasons other than monetary policy. If the monetary authority responds to these variations, it will set in train longer term effects that will make any monetary growth path it follows ultimately consistent with the rule of policy. The actual course of monetary growth will be analogous to a random walk, buffeted this way and that by the forces that produce temporary departures of the market rate from the natural rate.

To state this conclusion differently, there is always a temporary trade-off between inflation and unemployment; there is no permanent trade-off. The temporary trade-off comes not from inflation per se, but from unanticipated inflation, which generally means, from a rising rate of inflation. The widespread belief that there is a permanent trade-off is a sophisticated version of the confusion between "high" and "rising" that we all recognize in simpler forms. A rising rate of inflation may reduce unemployment, a high rate will not.

But how long, you will say, is "temporary"? For interest rates, we have some systematic evidence on how long each of the several effects takes to work itself out. For unemployment, we do not. I can at most venture a personal judgment, based on some examination of the historical evidence, that the initial effects of a higher and unanticipated rate of inflation last for something like two to five years; that this initial effect then begins to be reversed; and that a full adjustment to the new rate of inflation takes about as long for employment as for interest rates, say, a couple of decades. For both interest rates and employment, let me add a qualification. These estimates are for changes in the rate of inflation of the order of magnitude that has been experienced in the United States. For much more sizable changes, such as those experienced in South American countries, the whole adjustment process is greatly speeded up.

To state the general conclusion still differently, the monetary authority controls nominal quantities–directly, the quantity of its own liabilities. In principle, it can use this control to peg a nominal quantity–an exchange rate, the price level, the nominal level of national income, the quantity of money by one or another definition–or to peg the rate of change in a nominal quantity–the rate of inflation or deflation, the rate of growth or decline in nominal national income, the rate of growth of the quantity of money. It cannot use its control over nominal quantities to peg a real quantity–the real rate of interest, the rate of unemployment, the level of real national income, the real quantity of money, the rate of growth of real national income, or the rate of growth of the real quantity of money.

II. WHAT MONETARY POLICY CAN DO

Monetary policy cannot peg these real magnitudes at predetermined levels. But monetary policy can and does have important effects on these real magnitudes. The one is in no way inconsistent with the other.

My own studies of monetary history have made me extremely sympathetic to the oft-quoted, much reviled, and as widely misunderstood, comment by John Stuart Mill. "There cannot . . ." he wrote, "be intrinsically a more insignificant thing, in the economy of society, than money; except in the character of a contrivance for sparing time and labour. It is a machine for doing quickly and commodiously, what would be done, though less quickly and commodiously, without it: and like many other kinds of machinery, it only exerts a distinct and independent influence of its own when it gets out of order" [7, p. 488].

True, money is only a machine, but it is an extraordinarily efficient machine. Without it, we could not have begun to attain the astounding growth in output and level of living we have experienced in the past two centuries—any more than we could have done so without those other marvelous machines that dot our countryside and enable us, for the most part, simply to do more efficiently what could be done without them at much greater cost in labor.

But money has one feature that these machines do not share. Because it is so pervasive, when it gets out of order, it throws a monkey wrench into the operation of all the other machines. The Great Contraction is the most dramatic example but not the only one. Every other major contraction in this country has been either produced by monetary disorder or greatly exacerbated by monetary disorder. Every major inflation has been produced by monetary expansion—mostly to meet the overriding demands of war which have forced the creation of money to supplement explicit taxation.

The first and most important lesson that history teaches about what monetary policy can do—and it is a lesson of the most profound importance—is that monetary policy can prevent money itself from being a major source of economic disturbance. This sounds like a negative proposition: avoid major mistakes. In part it is. The Great Contraction might not have occurred at all, and if it had, it would have been far less severe, if the monetary authority had avoided mistakes, or if the monetary arrangements had been those of an earlier time when there was no central authority with the power to make the kinds of mistakes that the Federal Reserve System made. The past few years, to come closer to home, would have been steadier and more productive of economic well-being if the Federal Reserve had avoided drastic and erratic changes of direction, first expanding the money supply at an unduly rapid pace, then, in early 1966, stepping on the brake too hard, then, at the end of 1966, reversing itself and resuming expansion until at least November, 1967, at a more rapid pace than can long be maintained without appreciable inflation.

Even if the proposition that monetary policy can prevent money itself from being a major source of economic disturbance were a wholly negative proposition, it would be none the less important for that. As it happens, however, it is not a wholly negative proposition. The monetary machine has gotten out of order even when there has been no central authority with anything like the power now possessed by the Fed. In the United States, the 1907 episode and earlier banking panics are examples of how the monetary machine can get out of order largely on its own. There is therefore a positive and important task for the monetary authority—to suggest improvements in the machine that will reduce the chances that it will get out of order, and to use its own powers so as to keep the machine in good working order.

A second thing monetary policy can do is provide a stable background for the economy—keep the machine well oiled, to continue Mill's analogy. Accomplishing the first task will contribute to this objective, but there is more to it than that. Our economic system will work best when producers and consumers, employers and employees, can proceed with full confidence that the average level of prices will behave in a known way in the future—preferably that it will be highly stable. Under any conceivable institutional arrangements, and certainly under those that now prevail in the United States, there is only a limited amount of flexibility in prices and wages. We need to conserve this flexibility to achieve changes in relative prices and wages that are required to adjust to dynamic changes in tastes and technology. We should not dissipate it simply to achieve changes in the absolute level of prices that serve no economic function.

In an earlier era, the gold standard was relied on to provide confidence in future monetary stability. In its heyday it served that function reasonably well. It clearly no longer does, since there is scarce a country in the world that is prepared to let the gold standard reign unchecked—and there are persuasive reasons why countries should not do so. The monetary authority could operate as a surrogate for the gold standard, if it pegged exchange rates and did so exclusively by altering the quantity of money in response to balance of payment flows without "sterilizing" surpluses or deficits and without resorting to open or concealed exchange control or to changes in tariffs and quotas. But again, though many central bankers talk this way, few are in fact willing to follow this course—and again there are persuasive reasons why they should not do so. Such a policy would submit each country to the vagaries not of an impersonal and automatic gold standard but of the policies—deliberate or accidental—of other monetary authorities.

In today's world, if monetary policy is to provide a stable background for the economy it must do so by deliberately employing its powers to that end. I shall come later to how it can do so.

Finally, monetary policy can contribute to offsetting major disturbances in the economic system arising from other sources. If there is an independent secular exhilaration—as the postwar expansion was described by the proponents of secular stagnation—monetary policy can in principle help to hold it in check by a slower rate of monetary growth than would otherwise be desirable. If, as now, an explosive federal budget threatens unprecedented deficits, monetary policy can hold any inflationary dangers in check by a slower rate of monetary growth than would otherwise be desirable. This will temporarily mean higher interest rates than would otherwise prevail—to enable the government to borrow the sums needed to finance the deficit—but by preventing the speeding up of inflation, it may well mean both lower prices and lower nominal interest rates for the long pull. If the end of a substantial war offers the country an opportunity to shift resources from wartime to peacetime production, monetary policy can ease the transition by a higher rate of monetary growth than would otherwise be desirable—though experience is not very encouraging that it can do so without going too far.

I have put this point last, and stated it in qualified terms—as referring to major disturbances—because I believe that the potentiality of monetary policy in offsetting other forces making for instability is far more limited than is commonly believed. We simply do not know enough to be able to recognize minor disturbances when they occur or to be able to predict either what their effects will be with any precision or what monetary policy is required to offset their effects. We do not know enough to be able to achieve stated objectives by delicate, or even fairly coarse, changes in the mix of monetary and fiscal policy. In this area particularly the best is likely to be the enemy of the good. Experience suggests that the path of wisdom is to use monetary policy explicitly to offset other disturbances only when they offer a "clear and present danger."

III. HOW SHOULD MONETARY POLICY BE CONDUCTED?

How should monetary policy be conducted to make the contribution to our goals that it is capable of making? This is clearly not the occasion for presenting a detailed "Program for Monetary Stability"—to use the title of a book in which I tried to do so [3]. I shall restrict myself here to two major requirements for monetary policy that follow fairly directly from the preceding discussion.

The first requirement is that the monetary authority should guide itself by magnitudes that it can control, not by ones that it cannot control. If, as the authority has often done, it takes interest rates or the current unemployment percentage as the immediate criterion of policy, it will be like a space vehicle that has taken a fix on the wrong star. No matter how sensitive and sophisticated its guiding apparatus, the space vehicle will go astray. And so will the monetary authority. Of the various alternative magnitudes that it can control, the most appealing guides for policy are exchange rates, the price level as defined by some index, and the quantity of a monetary total—currency plus adjusted demand deposits, or this total plus commercial bank time deposits, or a still broader total.

For the United States in particular, exchange rates are an undesirable guide. It might be worth requiring the bulk of the economy to adjust to the tiny percentage consisting of foreign trade if that would guarantee freedom from monetary irresponsibility—as it might under a real gold standard. But it is hardly worth doing so simply to adapt to the average of whatever policies monetary authorities in the rest of the world adopt. Far better to let the market, through floating exchange rates, adjust to world conditions the 5 per cent or so of our resources devoted to international trade while reserving monetary policy to promote the effective use of the 95 per cent.

Of the three guides listed, the price level is clearly the most important in its own right. Other things the same, it would be much the best of the alternatives—as so many distinguished economists have urged in the past. But other things are not the same. The link between the policy actions of the monetary authority and the price level, while unquestionably present, is more indirect than the link between the policy actions of the authority and any of the several monetary totals. Moreover, monetary action takes a longer time to affect the price level than to affect the monetary totals and both the time lag and the magnitude of effect vary with circumstances. As a result, we cannot predict at all accurately just what effect a particular monetary action will have on the price level and, equally important, just when it will have that effect. Attempting to control directly the price level is therefore likely to make monetary policy itself a source of economic disturbance because of false stops and starts. Perhaps, as our understanding of monetary phenomena advances, the situation will change. But at the present stage of our understanding, the long way around seems the surer way to our objective. Accordingly, I believe that a monetary total is the best currently available immediate guide or criterion for monetary policy—and I believe that it matters much less which particular total is chosen than that one be chosen.

A second requirement for monetary policy is that the monetary authority avoid sharp swings in policy. In the past, monetary authorities have on occasion moved in the wrong direction—as in the episode of the Great Contraction that I have stressed. More frequently, they have moved in the right direction, albeit often too late, but have erred by moving too far. Too late and too much has been the general practice. For example, in early 1966, it was the right policy for the Federal Reserve to move in a less expansionary direction—though it should have done so at least a year earlier. But when it moved, it went too far, producing the sharpest change in the rate of monetary growth of the postwar era. Again, having gone too far, it was the right policy for the Fed to reverse course at the end of 1966. But again it went too far, not only restoring but exceeding the earlier excessive rate of monetary growth. And this episode is no exception. Time and again this has been the course followed—as in 1919 and 1920, in 1937 and 1938, in 1953 and 1954, in 1959 and 1960.

The reason for the propensity to overreact seems clear: the failure of monetary authorities to allow for the delay between their actions and the subsequent effects on the economy. They tend to determine their actions by today's conditions—but their actions will affect the economy only six or nine or twelve or fifteen months later. Hence they feel impelled to step on the brake, or the accelerator, as the case may be, too hard.

My own prescription is still that the monetary authority go all the way in avoiding such swings by adopting publicly the policy of achieving a steady rate of growth in a specified monetary total. The precise rate of growth, like the precise monetary total, is less important than the adoption of some stated and known rate. I myself have argued for a rate that would on the average achieve rough stability in the level of prices of final products, which I have estimated would call for something like a 3 to 5 per cent per year rate of growth in currency plus all commercial bank deposits or a slightly lower rate of growth in currency plus demand deposits only.[8] But it would be better to have a fixed rate that would on the average produce moderate inflation or moderate deflation, provided it was steady, than to suffer the wide and erratic perturbations we have experienced.

Short of the adoption of such a publicly stated policy of a steady rate of monetary growth, it would constitute a major improvement if the monetary authority followed the self-denying ordinance of avoiding wide swings. It is a matter of record that periods of relative stability in the rate of monetary growth have also been periods of relative stability in economic activity, both in the United States and other countries. Periods of wide swings in the rate of monetary growth have also been periods of wide swings in economic activity.

By setting itself a steady course and keeping to it, the monetary authority could make a major contribution to promoting economic stability. By making

[8]In an as yet unpublished article on "The Optimum Quantity of Money," I conclude that a still lower rate of growth, something like 2 per cent for the broader definition, might be better yet in order to eliminate or reduce the difference between private and total costs of adding to real balances.

that course one of steady but moderate growth in the quantity of money, it would make a major contribution to avoidance of either inflation or deflation of prices. Other forces would still affect the economy, require change and adjustment, and disturb the even tenor of our ways. But steady monetary growth would provide a monetary climate favorable to the effective operation of those basic forces of enterprise, ingenuity, invention, hard work, and thrift that are the true springs of economic growth. That is the most that we can ask from monetary policy at our present stage of knowledge. But that much—and it is a great deal—is clearly within our reach.

References

1. H. S. Ellis, ed., *A Survey of Contemporary Economics,* Philadelphia, 1948.
2. Milton Friedman, "The Monetary Theory and Policy of Henry Simons," *Jour. Law and Econ.,* Oct. 1967, *10,* 1–13.
3. ——, *A Program for Monetary Stability,* New York, 1959.
4. E. A. Goldenweiser, "Postwar Problems and Policies," *Fed. Res. Bull.,* Feb. 1945, *31,* 112–21.
5. P. T. Homan and Fritz Machlup, ed., *Financing American Prosperity,* New York, 1945.
6. A. P. Lerner and F. D. Graham, ed., *Planning and Paying for Full Employment,* Princeton, 1946.
7. J. S. Mill, *Principles of Political Economy,* Bk. III, Ashley ed., New York, 1929.

28

SOME ISSUES OF MONETARY POLICY

COUNCIL OF ECONOMIC ADVISERS

The record of the past 8 years demonstrates that flexible, discretionary monetary policy can make an effective contribution to economic stabilization. The economy's gradual return to full productive potential in the early 1960's was partly attributable to a monetary policy which kept ample supplies of credit readily available at generally stable interest rates. And in early 1967, the prompt recovery of homebuilding after the 1966 slowdown was the direct result of timely and aggressive easing of credit conditions by the Federal Reserve.

The most dramatic demonstration of the effectiveness of monetary policy came in 1966, however, when a dangerously inflationary situation was curbed primarily by a drastic application of monetary restraint. Credit-financed expenditures at the end of that year appear to have been as much as $8 billion below what they might have been had monetary policy maintained the accommodative posture of the preceding 5 years. And there were substantial further "multiplier" effects on GNP as these initial impacts reduced income and consumption spending.

THE CONDUCT OF MONETARY POLICY

The primary guides for monetary policy are the various broad measures of economic performance, including the growth rate of total output, the relation of actual to potential output, employment and unemployment, the behavior

Reprinted from the *Annual Report of the Council of Economic Advisers* (1969), pp. 85–93.

of prices, and the Nation's balance-of-payments position. Extensive research, together with the experience of the last few years, has increased our knowledge of the complex process by which monetary policy influences these measures. While there are still major gaps in our knowledge of the precise chain of causation, some conclusions seem well established.

Like fiscal policy, monetary policy affects economic activity only after some lag. Thus actions by the Federal Reserve must be forward-looking. In considering the prospects ahead, however, an assessment must be made of both the expected behavior of the private sector and of the likely future course of fiscal policy. The inherent flexibility in the administration of monetary policy permits frequent policy adjustments to take account of unexpected developments in either the private or the public sector.

Sectoral Impacts

Monetary policy can affect spending through a number of channels. To some extent it works by changing the terms of lending, including interest rates, maturities of loans, downpayments, and the like, in such a way as to encourage or discourage expenditures on goods financed by credit. There may also be market imperfections or legal constraints and institutional rigidities that change the "availability" of loans as monetary conditions change—that is, make it easier or more difficult for borrowers to obtain credit at given terms of lending. Under some circumstances, purchasers of goods and services may finance their expenditures by liquidating financial assets, and changes in the yields on these assets produced by a change in monetary policy may affect their willingness to engage in such transactions. Changes in monetary policy may also, on occasion, change the expectations of borrowers, lenders, and spenders in ways that affect economic conditions, although these expectational effects are rather complex and dependent upon the conditions existing at the time policy is changed.

Monetary policy affects some types of expenditures more than others. The extent of the impact depends not only on the economic characteristics of the activity being financed but, in many instances, on the channels through which financing is obtained and the legal and institutional arrangements surrounding the financing procedures.

Residential Construction. The sector of the economy most affected by monetary policy is residential construction. Although the demand for housing—and for mortgage credit—does not appear to be especially responsive to mortgage interest rates, the supply of mortgage funds is quite sensitive to several interest rate relationships.

The experience of 1966 clearly demonstrated how rising interest rates can sharply affect flows of deposits to banks and other thrift institutions and thereby severely limit their ability to make new mortgage loans. In the first half of that year, the net deposit gain at savings and loan associations and mutual savings banks was only half as large as in the preceding 6 months. These institutions could not afford to raise the rates paid on savings capital to compete with the higher rates available to savers at banks and elsewhere because of their earnings situation—with their assets concentrated in mortgages that earned only the relatively low rates of return characteristic of several years earlier. Commercial banks experienced a similarly sharp slowing in growth of time deposits in the second half of the year, as the Federal Reserve's Regulation Q prevented them from competing effectively for liquid funds. This forced banks to make across-the-board cuts in lending operations.

In addition, life insurance companies had a large portion of their loanable

Table 1. Net Funds Raised by Nonfinancial Sectors, 1961–68

Nonfinancial sector	*1961–65 average*	*1966*	*1967*	*1968*[1]
Total funds raised (billions of dollars)	59.2	69.9	83.1	97.1
Percent of total raised by:				
Private domestic nonfinancial sectors	84.5	88.7	79.9	80.4
State and local governments	10.8	9.7	12.6	11.7
Nonfinancial business	34.6	48.1	44.8	37.0
Households	39.0	30.9	22.5	31.7
Mortgages	25.5	18.6	13.7	17.1
Other	13.5	12.3	8.8	14.6
U.S. Government	10.6	9.0	15.3	16.7
Rest of world	5.1	2.1	4.8	2.9
Percent of total supplied by:				
Commercial banks	35.1	24.7	43.6	39.1
Nonbank financial institutions	43.6	32.2	39.0	29.7
Savings and loan associations and mutual savings banks	22.1	9.9	19.5	14.0
Other	21.5	22.3	19.5	15.7
Federal Reserve and U.S. Government	10.1	16.3	11.2	12.9
State and local governments	6.8	8.9	9.4	7.7
Foreign lenders	1.2	–2.0	3.9	–.3
Nonfinancial business	2.7	4.6	.5	5.1
Households, less net security credit	.5	15.3	–7.5	5.8

[1] Preliminary.
Note.—Detail will not necessarily add to totals because of rounding.
Source: Board of Governors of the Federal Reserve System.

funds usurped by demands for policy loans, which individuals found attractive because of relatively low cost. High-yielding corporate securities also proved an attractive alternative for some institutional investments that might otherwise have gone into mortgages.

Table 1 provides some indication of the extent of these various influences. As can be seen, savings and loan associations and mutual savings banks together supplied less than 10 percent of total funds borrowed in 1966, well below their 22 percent share in the preceding 5 years. This was the main factor limiting the availability of household mortgage loans. The effect on homebuilding was quick and dramatic, as the seasonally adjusted volume of new housing units started fell by nearly half between December 1965 and October 1966.

In 1967, as interest rates in the open market retreated from their 1966 highs, the thrift institutions were able to regain their competitive position in the savings market. A good part of their funds was fairly quickly channeled into the mortgage market. By fall, housing starts had recovered nearly to the level of late 1965.

Many factors–including several significant institutional reforms, sharply improved liquidity positions, and the widespread expectation that monetary restraint was only temporary pending passage of the tax bill–helped to moderate the adverse effects of renewed monetary restraint on mortgage lending in 1968. But the thrift institutions again experienced some slowing of deposit inflows when market interest rates rose to new heights, and mutual savings banks switched a good part of their investments away from the mortgage market to high-yielding corporate bonds.

State and Local Governments. State and local governments also felt the effects of monetary restraint in 1966. These governments cut back or postponed more than $2.9 billion, or nearly 25 percent, of their planned bond issues that year.

It is difficult to determine precisely what caused these postponements. In cases involving more than half the dollar volume, the reasons given related to the prevailing high level of interest rates. In some instances, the interest costs simply exceeded the legal ceiling governments were permitted to pay for borrowed funds. In other cases, finance officers decided to delay bond issues for a few months in the expectation that interest rates would decline.

This sizable cutback in borrowings had a relatively small effect on State and local government expenditures. Larger governments apparently were able to continue most of their projects about as scheduled by drawing down liquid assets or borrowing temporarily at short term. Smaller governmental units, however, cut their contract awards by a total estimated at more than $400 million.

Because of the problems State and local governments often face in raising funds, the Administration is proposing the establishment of an Urban Development Bank, which could borrow economically in the open market and then lend in the amounts needed to individual local governments. The Bank could lend at federally subsidized interest rates, with the Federal Government recovering the cost of the subsidy through taxation of the interest income earned by holders of the Bank's securities.

Business and Consumer Spending. The 1966 credit squeeze undoubtedly also had some effects on business and consumer spending, though the amount of impact is not easily determinable. Most theoretical and empirical studies find that business firms in some way balance the cost of borrowed capital against the expected returns from their capital projects. Some small firms may also simply not be able to obtain funds during tight money periods. In 1966, bank lending to business did slow sharply during the second half of the year. Many of the larger firms shifted their demands to the open market—and paid record high interest rates for their funds—but some of the smaller ones probably were forced to postpone their projects.

Household spending on durable goods—particularly automobiles—has been shown to be affected by changes in the cost and availability of consumer credit, as reflected in the interest rate, maturity, downpayment, and other terms. While it is difficult to sort out cause and effect, households borrowed only two-thirds as much through consumer credit in the second half of 1966 as in the preceding half year. Capital gains or losses on asset holdings accompanying changes in yields may also induce consumers to spend more or less on goods and services.

Active and Passive Elements

Monetary policy, like fiscal policy, has what might be termed active and passive components. Recognition of this distinction played an important role in formulating the accommodative policy of the early 1960's. In the 1950's, economic expansion had generally been accompanied by rising interest rates, which tended to produce an automatic stabilizing effect somewhat similar to the fiscal drag of the Federal tax system discussed earlier. The large amounts of underutilized resources available in the early 1960's made such restraint inappropriate and credit was expanded sufficiently to prevent it from occurring.

It is especially important to distinguish between these elements in monetary policy at cyclical turning points. If, for example, private demand weakens and causes a decline in economic activity, interest rates will generally fall as credit demands slacken, even without any positive action by the Federal Reserve to push rates down. This induced fall in interest rates can help to check the decline in economic activity but may not, by itself, induce recovery. Similarly, as the economy rises above potential, the induced rise in interest rates may only moderate the expansion but may not bring activity back into line with capacity.

An active monetary policy during such periods requires positive effort by the Federal Reserve to produce further changes in interest rates and in availability of credit beyond those that would occur automatically. Since expectational responses may either accentuate or moderate the effects of the initial action, it is sometimes difficult to know in advance precisely how much of a policy change is needed. But the main point is clear—at such turning points, interest rate movements alone are not likely to provide an accurate reflection of the contribution of monetary policy to economic stabilization. Careful attention must also be paid to credit flows, particularly those to the private sector of the economy.

MONETARY POLICY AND THE MONEY SUPPLY

Examination of the linkages between monetary policy and various categories of expenditures suggests that, in the formulation of monetary policy, careful attention should be paid to interest rates and credit availability as influenced by and associated with the flows of deposits and credit to different types of financial institutions and spending units. Among the financial flows generally considered to be relevant are: the total of funds raised by nonfinancial sectors of the economy, the credit supplied by commercial banks, the net amount of new mortgage credit, the net change in the public's holdings of liquid assets, changes in time deposits at banks and other thrift institutions, and changes in the money supply. Some consideration should be given to all of these financial flows as well as to related interest rates in formulating any comprehensive policy program or analysis of financial conditions.

Much public attention has recently been focused on an alternative view, however, emphasizing the money supply as the most important—sometimes the only—link between monetary policy and economic activity. This emphasis has often been accompanied by the suggestion that the Federal Reserve can best contribute to economic stabilization by maintaining growth in the stock of money at a particular rate—or somewhat less rigidly, by keeping variations in the rate of growth of the money stock within a fairly narrow band.

There are, of course, numerous variants of the money view of monetary policy. The discussion below focuses only on the simple version that has captured most of the public attention.

Money and Interest Rates

In a purely theoretical world, abstracting from institutional rigidities that exist in our financial system and assuming that relationships among financial variables were unvarying and predictable, it would make little difference whether monetary policy was formulated in terms of interest rates or the money supply. The two variables are inversely related, and the alternative approaches would represent nothing more than different paths to precisely the same result. The monetary authorities could seek to control the money stock, with interest rates allowed to take on whatever values happen to result. Or alternatively, they could focus on achieving the interest rates that would facilitate the credit flows needed to finance the desired level of activity, allowing the quantity of money to be whatever it had to be.

But financial rigidities do exist that often distort flows of credit in response to swings in interest rates. And financial relationships have changed steadily and significantly. Just since 1961, several important new financial instruments have been introduced and developed, including negotiable time certificates of deposit and Euro-dollar deposits. Attitudes of both investors and lenders have also undergone marked shifts, with sharp variations in the public's demand for liquidity superimposed on an underlying trend toward greater sensitivity to interest rates.

There is, to be sure, enough of a link between money and interest rates at any given time to make it impossible for the Federal Reserve to regulate the two independently. But this linkage is hardly simple, and it varies considerably and unpredictably over time. The choice between controlling the stock of money solely and focusing interest rates, credit availability, and a number of credit flows can therefore make a difference. This choice should be based on a judgment—supported insofar as possible by empirical and analytical evidence—as to whether it is money holdings alone that influence the decisions of various categories of spending units.

Money and Asset Portfolios

The Federal Reserve conducts monetary policy primarily by expanding and contracting the supply of cash reserves available to the banking system. Such actions seek to induce an expansion or contraction in loans and investments at financial institutions, with corresponding changes in the public's holdings of currency and deposits of various kinds. The proportions in which the public chooses to hold alternative types of financial assets depend upon a complex set of preferences, which, in turn, depend upon interest rate relationships.

The process of expansion and contraction of money and credit stemming from Federal Reserve actions is fairly complex. But one aspect of it should be clearly understood: The money so created is not something given to the public for nothing as if it fell from heaven—that is, it is not a net addition to the public's wealth or net worth. There can be an immediate change in public wealth, but only to the extent that changes in interest rates generate capital gains or losses on existing assets.

Any change in the money stock is associated with a change in the composition of the public's balance sheet, as people and institutions are induced to exchange—at a price—one asset for another or to increase (or decrease) both their assets and their liabilities by equal amounts. Since all the items in the public's balance sheet might be changed as a result of these compositional shifts, the change in the public's liquidity is not likely to be summarized adequately in terms of any single category of financial assets.

It is, of course, possible that decisions to spend on goods and services are affected more by the presence of one type of financial asset than another in a spending unit's portfolio. But there is only scattered evidence of such behavior in various sectoral studies that have been undertaken to analyze the factors affecting the spending decisions of consumers, businesses, or State and local governments. Indeed, to the extent these studies do find spending decisions systematically affected by financial variables, it is often through changes in interest rates and availability of credit.

Money and Income and a Monetary Rule

One problem with the money supply as a guide to monetary policy is that there is no agreement concerning the appropriate definition of "money." One definition includes the total of currency outside commercial banks plus privately held demand deposits. A second also includes time deposits at commercial banks, and even more inclusive alternatives are sometimes used. On the other hand, there is a more limited definition, sometimes called "high powered money" or "monetary base," which includes currency in circulation and member-bank reserve balances at the Federal Reserve banks.

These different concepts of money do not always move in parallel with one another—even over fairly extended periods. Thus assertions that the money supply is expanding rapidly or slowly often depend critically on which definition is employed. In the first half of 1968, for example, there was a sharp acceleration in the growth of currency plus demand deposits, but growth of this total plus time deposits slowed considerably.

On the other hand, relationships between movements in GNP and any of the money concepts have been close enough on the average—especially when processed through complex lags and other sophisticated statistical techniques—to be difficult to pass off lightly.

There is, of course, good reason to expect some fairly close relationship between money and income. This would be true even in a completely abstract situation in which it was assumed that the money supply per se had no direct influence on GNP, and that monetary policy worked entirely through interest rates. Since interest rates and the money supply are inversely related, any rise in GNP produced by a reduction in interest rates and increased credit availability would be accompanied by at least some increase in the money supply.

The relationship also exists in a sort of "reverse causation" form—that is, as income goes up so does the demand for money, which the Federal Reserve then accommodates by allowing an increase in the actual money stock. This is precisely what happened during the 1961–65 period of accommodative policy, and it is always present to some extent as the Federal Reserve acts to meet the economy's changing credit needs. The problem of sorting out the extent of causation in the two directions still challenges economic researchers.

A one-sided interpretation of these relationships is sometimes used to support the suggestion that the Federal Reserve conduct policy on the basis of some fixed, predetermined guideline for growth of the money supply (however defined). Given the complex role of interest rates in affecting various demand categories and the likely variations in so many other factors, any such simple policy guide could prove to be quite unreliable.

The experience of the past several years illustrates the kinds of difficulties that might be encountered in using the money supply (defined here as currency plus demand deposits) as the exclusive guide for monetary policy. As described previously, high interest rates in 1966 began affecting the nonbank thrift institutions, the mortgage market, and the homebuilding industry soon after the start of the year. But during the first 4 months of that year, the money supply grew at an annual rate of nearly 6½ percent, well above the long-term trend. Later that year, the financial situation of major mortgage lenders improved somewhat and housing eventually rebounded despite the fact that growth of money supply plus bank time deposits was proceeding at only a snail's pace.

Growth of the money supply in the second quarter of 1968 was at an annual rate of 9 percent. The reasons for this acceleration—to a rate almost double the growth in the preceding quarter—are not fully apparent. The Federal Reserve could have resisted this sizable increase in the demand for money more than it did, but interest rates in the open market would then have risen well above the peaks that were in fact reached in May. Whether still higher rates would have been desirable is another issue, which cannot be settled merely by citing the rapid growth of the money supply.

These illustrations suggest that any simple rigid rule related to the growth of the money supply (however defined) can unduly confine Federal Reserve policy. In formulating monetary policy the Federal Reserve must be able to take account of all types of financial relationships currently prevailing and in prospect and be able to respond flexibly as changing economic needs arise. In deciding on such responses, especially careful consideration must be given to likely changes in interest rates and credit availability, in view of the effects of these factors on particular sectors of the economy—especially the home-building industry.

29

LIMITATIONS OF MONETARY POLICY

HOWARD S. ELLIS

Since all conceivable economic policies have their limits, the task of appraising any specific policy, in a world that falls short of perfection in a number of ways, implies an estimate of how important its limitations are when compared to available alternatives.

Bearing in mind this relativism, I shall approach the subject of the limitations upon monetary policy from three angles: the effectiveness of its operation, the desirability of the ways in which the policy works, and the value and mutual compatibility of its aims. These three categories cannot always be completely separated, but they will serve well as an ordering device for the appraisal.

THE EFFECTIVENESS OF MONETARY POLICIES

The limitations ascribed to the effectiveness of monetary policy may be divided for purposes of study into two major groups. One of these groups embraces objections or limitations of a general theoretical nature. The shortcomings of monetary policy are supposed to be inherent in the nature of things, including the normal reactions of individuals and firms. The other group is concerned with institutional developments, particularly recent

Reprinted from Neil H. Jacoby, ed., *United States Monetary Policy,* rev. ed. (Praeger, 1964), pp. 195–214, by permission of the publisher. Howard S. Ellis is a professor at the University of California at Berkeley.

developments in the United States. The limitations of monetary policy are due to historical and specific reasons, and not necessarily to the operation of the monetary mechanism. Perhaps the two groups can be designated as "general" and "institutional" limits on the efficacy of monetary policy.

"General" Limits upon the Efficacy of Monetary Policy

1. *Income, assets, and spending.* J. M. Keynes lent the great authority of his name to the idea that *income* is the central economic phenomenon and that the influence of varying rates of investment upon economic activity can be traced by exclusive attention to the division of *income* between consumption and investment. Some of Keynes's followers have deduced from this that government tax and expenditure policies are potent because they bear directly on income. But monetary policy, they believe, at best exercises a milder, more circuitous, or slower effect on economic activity because its impact is primarily or originally upon the value and composition of *assets.*

More recent followers of Keynes, such as Don Patinkin, in *Money, Interest, and Prices,* have repudiated this idea. Every money outlay, they argue, involves the individual person or firm in a decision as to how much money should be retained; and every retention or holding of money involves a decision as to whether it is best to hold wealth in this form or in the form of securities or productive equipment that yields income. Thus the background of asset holdings may be as important and pervasive as income in determining expenditures. If this is true—and it seems impossible to avoid the logic of the position—then monetary policy through its effect upon *assets* may abstractly have just as strong and immediate results on spending, employment, and prices as does fiscal policy through its effect upon *income.* Whether fiscal or monetary measures have, in fact, the greater potency depends upon a variety of factors that differ considerably from one situation to another.

2. *Interest elasticity of the demand for and supply of capital.* One of the channels—it will later transpire that it is not the crucial one—by which monetary policy is supposed to be able to influence economic activity is the effect of central bank discount policy on market rates of interest and thus on investment. But just how elastic the demand for capital may be with regard to interest rates has been debated for decades without producing a simple or conclusive answer. Econometric studies of investment behavior have yielded unsatisfactory results.[1] We can be fairly certain that long-term borrowers—for residential and industrial construction and for public utility investment—are more sensitive to interest cost, borrowers for investor purposes less so, and

[1]Cf. Karl Brunner, "The Report of the Commission on Money and Credit," *Journal of Political Economy,* December, 1961, p. 613.

consumers and all types of "speculative" borrowers least so. These conclusions reached in 1952 by the Chairman of the Board of Governors of the Federal Reserve Board[2] were reflected a decade later by Samuelson, who added that "the evidence does seem inescapable that increases in the cost and tightening of the availability of credit do have substantial effects on investment spending."[3] Recent attempts by the Federal Reserve to raise short-term interest rates for the sake of the foreign balance, while holding down long-term rates for the sake of domestic investment (the so-called twist operation) must rest on a conviction of the Board that interest cost is significant for investment.

In the early 1950's, John H. Williams and Robert V. Roosa expounded a theory that central bank action operated only secondarily upon borrowers and savers, but primarily upon the positions and decisions of lenders. This effect, which has been known popularly as the "freezing-, pinning-, or locking-in" of bank holdings of government securities, was thought to follow from a reluctance of banks to sell securities at less than par values when interest rates advance. Thus the rise of the Federal Reserve discount rate was believed to have an immediate and potent effect in restricting bank lending.

Subsequently, however, doubts arose as to the strength of the "Roosa effect." Banks, it was pointed out, feel an obligation to take care of their regular customers and may accept some losses in order to extend loans and retain patronage. Furthermore, the federal income tax provision peculiar to banks that permits them to deduct full net capital losses in calculating taxable income reduces the penalty on taking losses from the sale of securities. Statistical studies by John H. Kareken and Warren L. Smith bear out the scepticism regarding locking-in.[4] It has been pointed out, however, that a substantial *de facto* locking-in exists for some banks in the requirement of collateral for public deposits and uninvested trust funds.[5] While this explanation of the lock-in is new, it operates, as Roosa had argued, to transmit Federal Reserve discount policy to the market without much slack. The really residual quantity for the banks thus locked-in is not government securities but mortgages. Obviously, the rapidity with which mortgages can

[2] *Monetary Policy and the Management of the Public Debt,* Joint Committee Print, Joint Committee on the Economic Report, 82d Cong., 2d sess. (Washington, D.C., 1952), Part I.

[3] Paul A. Samuelson, "Reflections on Monetary Policy," *The Review of Economics and Statistics,* August, 1961, p. 267.

[4] Cf., respectively: "Post Accord Monetary Developments in the United States," Banca Nazionale del Lavoro (Rome), *Quarterly Review,* September, 1957, pp. 344–45; "On the Effectiveness of Monetary Policy," *American Economic Review,* September, 1958, pp. 588–607.

[5] As of June 29, 1963, all commercial banks held government deposits of all categories of $31,341.2 million, but held federal, state, and local securities of $94,533.7 million, or three times the amount of deposits. However, it is reported on good authority that some important banks have a rather narrow leeway between collateral required and securities actually held for this purpose.

be shifted to nonbank owners is limited when compared with government securities, particularly in view of the lack in this country of a well-developed secondary market for mortgages.

Beside the somewhat narrower meaning of locking-in as applied to the commercial banks, the term has been given a broader meaning: high rates of interest operate to lock-in *any* owner of a bond, and the longer the maturity the greater the leverage exercised by the high rates. This universally recognized and by no means novel fact reported by the Radcliffe Committee has become the keystone of central banking and of monetary control. In the United Kingdom, the Bank of England apparently no longer controls the volume of bank reserves through the traditional channels of open-market operations and the discount rate. It has taken on the obligation, presumably as a consequence of the increased role of government in the total of investment, to provide the Exchequer with residual finance according to need.[6] In place of the usual controls over bank reserves, the authorities have attempted to limit liquidity (in general, not simply money) by funding short- into long-term debt, i.e., into "consols," the key securities in the gilt-edged market. Thus the Radcliffe Committee has come to rely almost exclusively upon debt management and to regard the supply of money as merely incidental; and it has not hesitated to endorse whatever high interest rates might be supposed to be necessary to control private liquidity in this way.

Against this "Radcliffism" even Professor Gurley, whose philosophy the committee undoubtedly thought they were espousing, is compelled to protest that the "money income ratio, modified by the presence of other liquid assets, and within the context of real variables, was the principal determinant of the level of interest rates in Britain during the postwar period."[7] In fact, the attempt in the United Kingdom to put the opposite view into effect, by operating on interest and leaving the money supply to the "needs" of the Exchequer, failed to control liquidity. "Credit was dear but not scarce," and inflationary pressures prevailed. The upshot of the British experience is that "what happens to the money supply is much more significant than what happens to interest rates."[8] This conclusion, which would seem to be unavoidable, does not say that interest elasticities are completely unimportant, but it does sign the death warrant of Radcliffism in its attempt to control spending through interest rates alone.

[6]Samuel I. Katz, "Radcliffe Report: Monetary Policy and Debt Management Reconciled," Banca Nazionale del Lavoro (Rome), *Quarterly Review,* June, 1960, pp. 148-70.

[7]John G. Gurley, "The Radcliffe Report and Evidence," *American Economic Review,* September, 1960, p. 680.

[8]Katz, *op. cit.,* pp. 165, 168. It is interesting to observe what Alfred Marshall said long ago: "I do not myself put the rate of discount in the first place; my own way of looking at it was rather to lay stress upon the actual amount of money in the market to be loaned." ("Evidence Before the Gold and Silver Commission [1887]," *Official Papers* [London, 1926], p. 48.)

Commercial bankers and central bank authorities have always attached as much significance in a tight-money policy to what they call "availability" as to the interest rates. Now "availability" may be variously interpreted, with corresponding variations in its significance. In the Radcliffe view, the quantity of lending (or at least of long-term lending) is uniquely related to the interest rates on gilt-edge; in this view availability plays *no role*. But in the bankers' view, lending is always associated with more or less risk, and the lender always decides not only whether he is prepared to lend, but also whether he is prepared to lend as much as the borrower wants. Unlike potatoes, loans are not available to the single demander in unlimited quantity. Thus an "unsatisfied fringe" of borrowers appears as a permanent feature of credit markets; lenders never offer unlimited sums to individual borrowers, whatever the rate of interest may be.

This rationing of credit, or what may be called the "quality of credit" varies in intensity in the course of the business cycle; the variation is greater than customer loan rates, but because it does not lend itself easily to quantitative reporting, it is ignored in econometric models. At the close of the 1955–57 tight-money episode, a survey of bankers on the effects of Federal Reserve policies elicited the response from only 1 per cent of those replying that the increased cost of borrowing "appreciably" discouraged borrowing, 42 per cent said the effect was "very little," and 57 per cent stated that they were giving more attention to the past records of applicants; 42 per cent said they paid increased attention to maintaining balances on account; 38 per cent required faster payment schedules; 25 per cent scaled down the size of loans from amounts requested.[9] The full effect of a tight-money policy can never be shown by the behavior of interest rates. Still more important is the reduction of availability, and the outcry against the the Federal Reserve policy of tight money during 1956–57 and still more in 1959 seems to bear eloquent witness to the fact that the policy "took hold" on the conditions of commercial bank lending.

3. *Perverse reactions of the market.* The increase of monetary velocity during periods of business expansion and its decline during contractions is a natural consequence of changes in certain main economic variables that operate in one direction. Dishoarding in boom periods occurs naturally as the result of improved investment prospects, rising prices, increased employment and output, and rising interest rates, which increase the cost of holding idle balances. A procyclical behavior of velocity is clearly observable throughout the present century; as long ago as 1936, it led Professor J. W. Angell to

[9]E. Sherman Adams, "Monetary Restraint and Bank Credit," *Banking* (Journal of the American Bankers Association), September, 1957. The poll covered 1,400 banks with two thirds of the total assets of commercial banks of this country.

conclude that greater stability in the money supply would result in greater stability in velocity and money incomes.[10] It was generally recognized that induced changes in velocity rendered efforts at stabilization through monetary devices more difficult, though not impossible if complemented by appropriate fiscal measures.

The general tenor of the Radcliffe Report in England and the Eckstein Report in the United States, however, has been to regard induced velocity changes in the course of economic fluctuations as rendering monetary controls impotent or virtually so.[11] This extreme conclusion seems to result from (1) the confusion of secular with cyclical developments, and (2) the altogether human weakness, to which economists have always been vulnerable, of projecting a recent trend into the indefinite future.

With regard to the first point, there can be no doubt that velocity has increased secularly since 1946 under the influence, first, of a gradual dishoarding of cash balances accumulated under rationing during the war, and second, of a gradual increase in the volume of near-moneys called into being through the growth of nonbank financial intermediaries. But even the doubling of income velocity, from about two to four per annum, should not swamp a monetary authority when distributed, as it has been, over nearly twenty years. The *cyclical* variations of velocity, which are of more immediate concern in both the Radcliffe and Eckstein reports, do not appear more formidable than in earlier periods. Indeed, an important conclusion of Milton Friedman's massive statistical enquiry into United States monetary history is that, "In response to cyclical variations, velocity has shown a *systematic* and *stable* movement about its trend, rising during expansion and falling during contraction."[12] With regard to the upward trend of velocity since 1946, the conclusion of the Commission on Money and Credit seems warranted:

> . . . this does not mean that a restrictive monetary policy does not have a restrictive influence. It means only that to restrict lending by a given amount, the growth of the money supply must be more limited than if velocity did not rise. The increase of velocity need not negate the effectiveness of monetary policy.[13]

[10] J. W. Angell, *The Behavior of Money* (New York, 1936), pp. 162–63.

[11] *Report of the Committee on the Working of The Monetary System* (London, 1959), pp. 132–33. *Staff Report on Employment, Growth, and Price Levels,* Joint Committee Print, 86th Cong., 1st sess. (Washington, D.C., 1960), pp. 343–61.

[12] Milton Friedman and Anna Jacobson Schwartz, *A Monetary History of the United States, 1867–1960* (Princeton, N.J., 1963), p. 682. It should be noted that a "*stable* movement about its trend" is a somewhat different matter from simple stability of velocity, which is attributed by Lawrence S. Ritter to "quantity theorists." Cf. *Banking and Monetary Studies,* Deane Carson (ed.) (Homewood, Ill., 1963), p. 150.

[13] *Money and Credit: Their Influence on Jobs, Prices, and Growth,* The Report of the Commission on Money and Credit (Englewood Cliffs, N. J., 1961), p. 49. Cited henceforth as CMC Report.

With regard to the second point, against two decades of secularly rising velocity are to be set the preceding seventy-five years of declining velocity. Prediction is a hazardous business; but the least that can be said is that a reversal of the upward trend since 1946 is a distinct possibility, and some rational grounds exist for expecting it. More important, however, is the reflection that if cyclical velocity variations around the trend do not appear to be growing larger, the trend would merely influence the relative difficulty of controlling booms compared with depressions. In either event the gradualness of the change scarcely appears to be a menacing limit to the efficacy of monetary policy.

4. *Lags in effects of monetary policy.* The conventional view concerning lags has been that, while they impair the efficacy of monetary policy, they take effect within a sufficiently short time to be at least contracyclical in operation. Professor Friedman has, indeed, taken the position that the lags are so long and so variable that monetary policy does not necessarily stabilize, but may as often contribute to the violence of economic fluctuations.[14] The Eckstein Report reaches the somewhat more conservative conclusion that the lags are long and "create difficult problems";[15] and the Commission on Money and Credit concludes that general monetary controls since the war have required from six to nine months to produce a change in the direction of ease and a further six months for their maximum effect.[16] Actual evidence concerning lags is scant and the judgment of informed observers fails to provide the policy-makers with much illumination. In this uncertain state of affairs, it is well to recall that other stabilization devices, such as changes in taxes and in government expenditures, also involve serious lags, particularly in the United States where the absence of responsible cabinet government forces the Congress to undertake the laborious task of determining fiscal policy. The history of the tax reduction proposed in 1963 is a case in point.

Uncertainty concerning timing has caused Professors Friedman and Shaw to abandon discretionary monetary control altogether, and they are joined in large measure by Professor Angell. Not many other economists, however, have been able to convince themselves of the merits of the alternative they propose—a fixed annual increment to the money supply. This is particularly difficult to accept in view of the plurality of objectives of monetary-fiscal policy and the necessity for adapting to new situations as one or other of these goals seems, for the time being, to be more important from a national viewpoint.

Rather than abdicate monetary policy altogether, which would seem to

[14]Milton Friedman, *A Program for Monetary Stability* (New York, 1960), p. 87.
[15]*January 1961 Economic Report . . .*, p. 394.
[16]CMC Report, pp. 244–45.

leave a vacuum into which direct controls would be bound to rush, it would seem preferable to concentrate upon devices to reduce the lag of monetary-fiscal measures, and to improve the setting in which these policies operate. . . .

Institutional Developments Adverse to Effective Monetary Policy

The preceding sections have considered difficulties encountered by monetary controls arising out of the economic behavior patterns of households or firms. By contrast, certain other difficulties arise from institutional developments, and these are constantly changing. In the early 1950's, the member banks' resort to borrowing from the excess reserves of other member banks—the use of "federal funds"—was usually mentioned as a source of embarrassment to monetary control. In the course of a decade, this has largely dropped from view, following the general realization that these borrowings represented a "once-over" increase of the commercial bank credit superstructure on a given amount of Federal Reserve deposits. Monetary policy could easily take account of this fact and compensate for it. Currently, commercial banks are making extensive use of "certificates of deposit" as a means of increasing the volume of lendable funds. The "negotiable CD" has enhanced the substitutability of time deposits for demand deposits, with the result that a greater amount of total deposits, and lendable funds, is related to a given level of primary reserves. In this sense, further "economy" in the use of reserves has been achieved.[17] This is also a once-over change and also does not present a progressive source of difficulty for the monetary authorities.

Another institutional limitation, the "bills only" rule, which the Federal Reserve created for itself, has now apparently passed into desuetude after a short life extending from 1953 to 1958. Economists outside the Board of Governors generally regarded this rule as a gratuitous narrowing of the field and efficacy of open-market operations. Eventually the Board, without formal retraction, disavowed the rule in deeds, for instance, in the late summer of 1958 to "correct a disorderly market,"[18] and thereafter to hold down long rates for domestic purposes while raising the short rate to aid in coping with the loss of gold abroad.

Another institutional obstacle that faded away was the belief, held in the

[17]According to a special survey conducted by the Federal Reserve, negotiable time certificates of deposits outstanding at 410 member banks amounted to $6.2 billion by December 5, 1962, compared to about $1 billion at the end of 1960. At the end of 1963, the total of these certificates outstanding was $9.92 billion. Mr. Charles F. Haywood, Director of Economic Research, Bank of America, San Francisco, called to my attention the parallel of this phenomenon with the growth of the use of federal funds in the early 1950's. I am indebted to him for a number of valuable suggestions and criticisms.

[18]Ralph A. Young and Charles A. Yager, "The Economics of 'Bills Preferably,'" *Quarterly Journal of Economics,* August 1960, pp. 364–65.

first postwar years, that a large national debt placed limits on monetary policy. Reactivating monetary controls after the support of the government security market during the war would, it was feared, spell a collapse in their values and usher in a depression. Federal Reserve action in cautiously easing the supports and finally, after the Accord of 1951, in abolishing them, produced no such effect. Nowadays the *size* of the debt is not regarded per se as causing difficulties for monetary policy. There would probably be a consensus among economists that the maturities are too short for desirable leverage effects from Federal Reserve discount rates; and the interest ceiling on long-term securities is a nuisance for effective policy. But these are relatively less important matters than those we are about to consider.

1. *The growth of nonbank financial intermediaries.* More important, at least in the current literature, is the discussion of the growth in recent decades of financial institutions other than commercial banks. Resting upon earlier researches by Goldsmith into financial intermediaries in general, Shaw and Gurley proclaimed the superior importance of the "state of liquidity of the whole economy" over the supply of money, which was only one component of liquidity and a dwindling one at that. While monetary theorists had for many years spoken about near-money, the challenging presentation of Shaw and Gurley led to extreme reactions. On the one hand, some people were (and some still are) prepared to argue that monetary stringency calls new financial intermediaries into being or activates the economizing of cash through the creation of near-moneys, making velocity indefinitely extensible and rendering monetary controls impotent.[19] On the other hand, orthodox economists continued to insist on the uniqueness of money as a means of payment, however much the securities of nonbank institutions might contribute to liquidity.

Appeal in these circumstances to *a priori* arguments as to whether other intermediaries are like or unlike banks are apt to be bootless. It is clear that money and near-money are within certain ranges and under certain circumstances substitutable assets, and the practical problem is the empirical investigation precisely of this substitution.

It is probably too early to look for conclusive results, but a substantial number of investigations, such as that of Warren L. Smith, point to a greater degree of substitution between the demand and time deposits of the commercial banks than between demand deposits and money on the one hand, and accounts with savings and loan associations and mutual savings banks on the other.[20] The implication of this finding is, fairly clearly, the

[19] Cf. Radcliffe Report, *passim;* H. P. Minsky, "Central Banking and Money Market Changes," *Quarterly Journal of Economics,* May, 1957, pp. 171–87, Ritter, *op. cit.* pp. 148–50.

[20] Warren L. Smith, "Financial Intermediaries and Monetary Controls." *Quarterly Journal of Economics,* November, 1959, pp. 542–46; similarly, David Fand, "Intermediary Claims and the

greater importance of being able to cope with the destabilizing portfolio adjustments of commercial banks than with controls over other financial institutions. One device, suggested by Professor Alhadeff, for securing greater stability in bank holdings of governments would be to make all bank-eligible government securities nonmarketable. Compared with the complexities of regulation of nonbank intermediaries, this device is simpler, but would entail a drastic reduction in the bank demand for government securities as secondary reserves. General monetary controls are probably the best answer to bank portfolio adjustments.[21] The time could conceivably come when the nonbank intermediaries can be shown to contribute so much to the short run instability of velocity as to require regulation akin to the banks. This would not appear to be highly probable, however, because commercial banks "specialize in providing the marginal fluctuating portion of the financial requirements of the private sector of the economy. Intermediaries are more specialized in providing long term funds for mortgage finance, fixed capital investment, and capital improvements by state and local governments."[22]

Meanwhile, however, there would be a good case for more extensive and more stringent supervisory control over nonbank financial institutions, trust, and private pension funds, as recommended by the Commission on Money and Credit.[23] This move can be recommended not only on grounds of equity and equalizing in some measure the conditions of competition among financial intermediaries, but also in removing an existing institutional bias toward investment in real estate. In the interest of economic growth, this bias is unfortunate.

2. *Federal lending policies.* As long ago as 1912, the Aldrich Commission had discussed the problem of an effective coordination of various federal departments and agencies concerned with credit, but without concrete results. In 1957, three economists again examined the theme, with particular reference to federal lending and guaranteeing agencies, concluding that these activities were then "at least as influential as determinants of total demand as were federal fiscal operations," and that these operations were often in direct conflict with Federal Reserve policy.[24] Since the Treasury-Federal Reserve

Adequacy of our Monetary Controls," *Banking and Monetary Studies,* pp. 234–53; H. G. Johnson, "Monetary Theory and Policy," *American Economic Review,* June, 1962, pp. 373–74; David A. Alhadeff, "Credit Controls and Financial Intermediaries," *American Economic Review,* September, 1960, pp. 655–71.

[21] The so-called Heller Report (*Report of the Committee on Financial Institutions to the President of the United States* [Washington, D.C., 1963]) recommends the imposition of reserve requirements on mutual savings banks and savings and loan associations; but this is explicitly said not to be necessary for effective monetary policy, but is justified on the basis of equity.

[22] Smith, *op. cit.*, p. 550.

[23] CMC Report, pp. 174–80.

[24] R. J. Saulnier, Harold G. Halcrow, and Neil H. Jacoby, *Federal Lending: Its Growth and Impact,* Occasional Paper 58, National Bureau of Economic Research (New York, 1957).

Accord of 1951, the coordination of credit policies has improved, not only in that area, but generally. Nevertheless, it is probably true that the lending agencies have a natural expansive bent, based on their interests in a particular segment of the economy. While this is not a matter of immediate concern, it would be well to follow the recommendation of the Commission on Money and Credit in making explicit provision for some kind of consultative machinery to secure unified credit policy. The responsibility lies with the executive branch of the federal government.

3. *Cost-push inflation.* The prevalence of periods of general expansion and inflationary pressure in the United States (and elsewhere) since the war has led to widespread concern with the problem and to the identification of and emphasis upon cost-push types of inflation, in contrast to older theories which ran—at least implicitly—largely in terms of demand-pull. As is frequently the case, the inruption of a new theory produced extreme views. The pure cost (or wage) explanations of price-level behavior took root first in Europe—for example, in England, with Abba Lerner, and in Denmark, with Jorgen Pedersen. Perhaps its most straight-forward advocate in the United States is Sidney Weintraub.[25] The opposite extreme is represented by the "Chicago School" economists, who have generally denied that trade unions significantly raise real wages and who have attributed inflation to monetary factors rather than to the influence of wages.[26] Our analysis rejects both of these extremes, as well as extremes in another sense, namely, that all cost inflation devolves into demand inflation, or vice versa, or that it is conceptually impossible to separate the two. One good reason for admitting or insisting upon the presence of both cost and demand elements is the plausibility attaching to another somewhat new approach—Schultze's demand-shift, theory of inflation—which involves both sides of the market.

The masterly review of inflation theory, in general and in all important varieties, written by Bronfenbrenner and Holzman makes it undesirable to repeat the performance here in an unsatisfactorily sketchy fashion.[27] From this review it seems clear that most economists (including the present writer) consider cost-push inflation to be important in the contemporary scene, and that most economists assign active roles to both labor unions and to oligopoly and monopoly pricing of commodities. Most economists (again including the present writer) consider cost-push to be a most serious limitation of or threat to the efficacy of monetary control. Although some die-hard "monetarists" believe that the Federal Reserve could break the cost-push by a sufficiently

[25] *Classical Keynesianism, Monetary Theory and the Price Level* (Philadelphia, 1961).
[26] E.g., Richard T. Selden, "Cost-Push *versus* Demand-Pull Inflation, 1955–57," *Journal of Political Economy,* February, 1959, pp. 1–20.
[27] Martin Bronfenbrenner and Franklyn D. Holzman, "Survey of Inflation Theory," *American Economic Review,* September, 1963, pp. 593–661.

tough restrictive monetary policy, this seems to be completely unrealistic from any practical view of the political scene, particularly with a background of a persistent 5 or 6 per cent residual unemployment rate.

Despite the critical importance of cost-push, there are good reasons, both theoretical and practical, for insisting upon the *admixture* of cost and demand that characterizes the inflations of the late 1950's and the early 1960's. Most important, the facts seem clearly to point that way: ". . . the inflation appears to have been due to excess demand in certain sectors, notably capital goods, together with sharp increases in wages at a time when productivity was rising only very slowly."[28] Moreover, cost inflation, though economically distinct, does indeed pass rapidly into demand inflation and vice versa; statistically they are difficult to disentangle. Also, the "new" kind of demand-shift inflation is—despite the author's denial of the relevance of either cost-push or demand-pull to the 1955–57 inflation—actually a compound of both.[29] Thus the evening-up of wage differentials, markup pricing, and the existence of oligopolistic product markets are given as reasons why wage-push can flourish. But these same factors figure prominently in making demand changes inflationary in Schultze's exposition. Indeed, in a purely competitive situation it is doubtful whether demand-shifts would be inflationary.

A practical reason for emphasis on the *de facto* mingling of cost-push, demand-pull, and demand-shift inflation is that a large part of the remedies against one type are—simply by reason of the mutually reinforcing character of the different types of inflation—effective against each and every one: Antitrust may hold down monopoly and oligopoly profits and thus restrain the push for higher wages; antitrust applied to gratuitously restrictive labor practices would reduce the inflationary effect of demand-shifts, and so forth. Possibly most important, however, is the fact that restrictive fiscal and monetary policies act not only via demand-pull, but on the other types as well.

While these reflections may be somewhat reassuring, they do not suffice to guarantee that monetary (and fiscal) measures may not break down from sufficiently strong pushes on the cost side. There is a definite need for *wage policy*; and the most generally available and defensible policy is resistance against wage increases exceeding the national *average* increase in productivity. Despite the fact that this criterion has been derided as ridiculous,[30] it

[28] Warren L. Smith, "Monetary Policy, 1957–1960: An Appraisal," *The Review of Economics and Statistics,* August, 1960, pp. 269–72.

[29] Charles L. Schultze, *Recent Inflation in the United States,* Joint Committee Print, 86th Cong., 1st sess. (Washington, D.C., 1959). Demand shift as a cause of expansion and price-rise figures in D. R. Robertson, *Banking Policy and the Price Level* (London, 1926), chaps. ii and iii; and William Fellner, *Monetary Policies and Full Employment* (Berkeley, Calif., 1946), chap. iv.

[30] Bronfenbrenner and Holzman, *op. cit.* p. 639.

quite properly commands widespread respect, is understandable to the layman, and can with equal justice be applied to profits.

Authoritarian wage determination would be repugnant to the traditions of democracy and freedom in this country, but this does not preclude an administration wage policy. The mere announcement of such a policy would presumably exercise some influence on collective bargaining. But government influences upon wages are in fact manifold: legal minimum wage legislation, the adjudication of wage disputes, the scale and duration of unemployment compensation, the prices paid government contractors, and the wage and salary scale of an ever-increasing number of government employees. It is scarcely to be expected that a wage policy would be perfectly achieved, but it would supply a powerful support to fiscal-monetary measures and a logical complement to antitrust.

THE DESIRABILITY OF MONETARY CONTROLS FROM THE ANGLE OF THEIR "MODUS OPERANDI"

Does Monetary Policy Discriminate Unfairly?

Some economists, such as Leon Keyserling, J. K. Galbraith, and S. E. Harris, have argued that the incidence of monetary controls is discriminatory and that this limits their usefulness and should limit their use. These economists have objected to what they consider unfair discrimination, as evidenced in the tight-money policy of 1955–57, against residential construction and borrowing by local governments, small business, and consumers. They lament what they regard as the social injustice of limiting the credit available for building homes, schools, and small business premises and equipment, and for the durable consumers' goods required by low-income families, which are insensitive to interest charges.

Moved by criticisms of this sort, the Federal Reserve conducted a full-scale inquiry in 1957 and 1958 into the financing of small business;[31] and subsequent investigations have extended the coverage to other fields supposed to be at a disadvantage from tight-credit policies.[32] These extended empirical studies have reached the conclusion that "Discrimination amongst borrowers was apparently largely on traditional banking standards of credit-worthiness and goodness of borrowers."[33] To those who basically do not

[31] *Financing Small Business,* Report to the Committees on Banking and Currency and the Select Committees on Small Business, U.S. Congress, by the Federal Reserve System (Washington, D.C., April 11, 1958), Parts I and II.

[32] Cf. G L. Bach, "How Discriminatory Is Tight Money?," in *Banking and Monetary Studies,* pp. 254-90; James R. Schlesinger, "Monetary Policy and Its Critics," *Journal of Political Economy,* December, 1960, pp. 608–12; CMC Report, pp. 57-60.

[33] Bach, *op. cit.*, p. 289.

believe in the allocation of capital by its cost in interest, there is nothing to recommend the meeting of inflation by screening out the less important uses of capital by its price. This position would then necessarily involve the allocation of capital by authoritarian decision, which in some quarters would be feared as potentially more discriminatory than allocation by price.

Interest Cost to the Treasury of Flexible Monetary Policy

Another objection to monetary controls (opposed to the way they operate rather than to their efficacy) is the complaint that tight money raises the cost of borrowing to government itself. This factor seems to assume importance in contemporary conditions in which, in the United States, the service of the publicly held national debt runs to nearly $8 billion annually, or less than 7 per cent of the federal budget.

The truth in this matter lies somewhere between one extreme view, which would assess the cost of debt service simply at its face value, and another extreme, which counts the real cost of internally held public debt at nil, i.e., a pure transfer cost. The real costs of the $8 billion service on the publicly held debt—assuming that the loss in want-satisfaction of those taxed approximately equals the gain to those to whom interest is paid—are the costs of the processes of tax collection and interest disbursement and the impairment of production incentives through taxation. In addition, if government securities are held preponderantly by the well-to-do, and if the tax system is not correspondingly progressive, there may be a loss in aggregate utility in the transfer. But these costs, which are by-products of the $8 billion debt service, will strike many persons as modest, when one considers one of the two or three available stabilization mechanisms for the $600 billion-income economy of the United States.

The rational attitude is that the payment of interest is the cost of avoiding inflation. Concerning the coupon rate on a security of given maturity, the higher interest rate presumably results in firmer holding in the hands of the public. Concerning contrasting costs of different maturities, shorter term debt is generally cheaper, but—being more liquid for the holder—less restrictive upon spending.[34] But, of course, varying the mix of debt maturities is only one way of raising or lowering the average rate paid on the national debt.[35]

[34]Earl R. Rolph, "Principles of Debt Management," *American Economic Review*, June, 1957, pp. 302–20. If long-term rates are lower than short, then both economy and restraint of inflation would be best served by a complete shift to long; but these situations (e.g., 1957) are generally too brief to be significant.

[35]It is undoubtedly true, as Warren L. Smith contends, that marginal changes in the maturities of the debt do not have important consequences; cf. his *Debt Management in the United States*, Study Paper No. 19, Joint Economic Committee (Washington, D.C., 1960). Here we are not concerned with these changes per se, but with the absolute height of the interest structure.

THE STRENGTH AND WEAKNESS OF MONETARY POLICY VIEWED FROM THE ANGLE OF PLURAL GOALS

Whether and in what sense monetary policy is to be regarded as effective depends upon the purposes it is supposed to serve, and upon the mutual compatibility of these purposes. Is it possible to discern some priorities among imaginable goals? In what respects are the goals complementary or contradictory?

From the history of central banking, it is evident that the regulation of the balance of payments came very early—in the case of the Bank of England, not later than the first quarter of the eighteenth century. Price stability as an objective lagged not far behind, although the Federal Reserve was loath to recognize this as a responsibility long after Irving Fisher elevated it to a primary aim. High-level production and employment were certainly emphasized in the business-cycle theories of the twentieth century, though it remained for Keynes and the Employment Act to make them parts of the economists' creed. Finally, the emphasis on growth, though no more novel than the *Wealth of Nations,* received its current impulse from the Cold War and from the aspirations of the poorer peoples for economic development.

To these objectives of monetary policy, recognized fairly generally as basic,[36] others have been added, such as preserving or securing equity in the distribution of wealth and income, providing adequate support to national defense, and the encouragement of economic freedom and private enterprise. To avoid an impossible overload on one set of control instruments, however, these latter goals generally have to be regarded as ancillary. True enough, inflation and deflation, overly full employment and unemployment undesirably bias the distribution of wealth and income. But monetary policy can, at best, avoid these distortions of distribution; it cannot be expected to achieve equity, which depends basically upon real factors, modified in some measure by fiscal arrangements. Much the same can be said concerning economic freedom and private enterprise. They flourish in a relatively stable economic setting to which monetary policy can contribute; but they are not themselves its product. With respect to national defense, the larger its claims the more difficult is the task of monetary control, but the marshalling of resources is primarily a problem for public finance and for government administration in general. We therefore relegate these objectives to other control mechanisms, or make them paramount for monetary objectives in unusual circumstances only.

Among the four basic objectives—price stability, high and stable output and employment, growth, and balance-of-payments equilibrium—it is cur-

[36]E.g., by the Commission on Money and Credit; cf. CMC Report, pp. 12–13, and chap. viii.

rently fashionable to assign to the first and fourth an importance subordinate to the others; but there are good reasons for caution on this score. In the first place, rather substantial attention must always be given all four and special circumstances can make any one for the time being the great national issue. Second, within certain limits the attainment of each of these objectives may condition the realization of the others or of another. Third, it may be that a certain purpose which seems to be an overriding one from a national viewpoint is not primary among the objectives to which *monetary* control may reasonably aspire. This is the case with the objective of growth. I proceed in reverse order with these points.

Fostering Economic Growth

Economic growth or progress is frequently given an honorific place in the objectives of monetary policy, and it would certainly be folly to deny that monetary controls do have such a purpose. But how does monetary policy promote progress? As ordinarily understood and practiced, monetary control does not and should not involve the authoritarian direction of resources into particular uses, including those most intimately conjoined with progress. How then does monetary control make a contribution in this direction? The answer would surely have to include that this control makes whatever contribution it can to high-level employment and price stability. In this way, the tempo of progress is accelerated through the avoidance of the wastes of speculation and of misdirected production. If, in addition, a liberal or free enterprise system is desired, either for the sake of freedom itself or for the sake of the economic progress that has been linked with capitalism, then monetary control may be viewed as making a further contribution toward progress by facilitating the operation of a liberal economic regime. Nevertheless, the mainsprings of economic advances do not lie in the monetary system but in saving, investing, innovating, trading, organizing, etc. Active policies to further growth and development are oriented toward these (and possibly other) "real" factors. When we have covered the aims of promoting a free-enterprise economy, securing full employment, and maintaining price stability, we have exhausted the contributions of general monetary policy to progress.

Stable Prices and Stable and High-Level Output

It is common in current discussions to say that the choice between stable prices and stable and high-level output presents a dilemma: Indeed, this idea has been formalized into a "dilemma model" in theory.[37] There are

[37]Cf. Bronfenbrenner and Holzman, *op. cit.*, p. 627.

important elements of truth in the idea of a dilemma in the face of these two objectives, but it is not *all* a matter of dilemma. Both sides need to be understood.

In the first place, it should be emphasized that stabilizing prices in some contexts serves also to stabilize output and employment. Thus, if the choice is between strong cyclical ups and downs and marked abatement of these fluctuations through monetary policy in a matrix of proper complementary policies, there is no dilemma. Similarly it would be difficult to deny that the stoppage of marked and chronic price inflation or deflation could improve output and employment. Thus by no means all actual cases involve a policy dilemma between stable prices and stable output.

In the second place, there can be no dilemma for monetary policy in choosing whether to affect prices or output. As Paul Samuelson has cogently pointed out, if an expansionary monetary or fiscal policy is pursued:

> . . . the resulting change in $P \times Q$ will get distributed between expansion in Q as against P, depending upon how much or how little labor and capital remains unused to be drawn on, and how strong or weak are the cost-push upward pressures that come from the institutional supply conditions of organized and unorganized labor, of oligopolistic price adminstrators, and more perfectly-competitive enterprises.[38]

The monetary authority cannot face a dilemma of choice as to the impact of its action if there is no choice. Furthermore, it is generally recognized that in deep depression an expansionary monetary policy might not increase either P or Q, but go in large part to the graveyard of idle cash balances.

The real "dilemma" of the monetary policy-maker is thus not the question of whether to direct his efforts more in one of these two directions than the other, but rather how much of a sacrifice of one objective to accept for a gain in the other, in case of incompatibility. A statistical study by Dewald and Johnson has reached the conclusion that monetary policy in the United States in the decade following the Treasury-Federal Reserve Accord did not sacrifice high employment and growth to price stability or balance-of-payments equilibrium.[39] But the fact that a substratum of unemployment persisted through the greater part of 1962, 1963, and into 1964, accompanied by a tendency of prices to rise rather than fall, seems to show that monetary policy had for the time being reached the end of its string. Since *aggregative* fiscal policies do not operate in a far different way from general monetary

[38]Paul A. Samuelson, "Reflections on Central Banking," *National Banking Review*, I, No. 1 (September, 1963), p. 23.

[39]W. G. Dewald and Harry G. Johnson, "An Objective Analysis of the Objectives of American Monetary Policy," *Banking and Monetary Studies*, pp. 171–89.

measures, the same conclusion must be reached here also, though the *tax reform* approach to growth and lessened unemployment has yet to be fully tested.

Balance-of-Payments Equilibrium

Much the same considerations as those treated in the preceding paragraphs apply to this objective in comparison with others. But in this case, the foreign balance is a less vital matter for the United States than for many (probably for most) other countries, and the foreign balance can be influenced by many measures other than monetary policy. During the closing months of 1963 the outflow of gold decreased, and part of the credit for this improvement should probably go to the rise of short term interest rates without corresponding increases in long rates. But the vigorous use of restrictive monetary and fiscal policies scarcely seems to be indicated by the domestic or international situation. If these policies can restrain the rate of inflation in this country behind the one abroad, the effect will be favorable on the gold situation. For the rest, a variety of other measures of a remedial character are available.

A judicious summing up of the evidence would seem to indicate that monetary controls are neither so potent as its most zealous advocates in the past decade have believed nor so limited as has been argued by the skeptics, particularly those of the Eckstein and Radcliffe committees. Debt management directed toward the behavior of long term gilt-edged securities does not suffice: The quantity of money has to be controlled. Fiscal policy in the more general sense is an indispensable and powerful complement of monetary policy; but in the United States today there is not sufficient flexibility in taxes or expenditures to make fiscal policy a dependable, unique channel for stabilization.

The review of supposed limitations on monetary policy points to an upward cost-price spiral as the only really insurmountable obstacle to the effectiveness of conventional monetary controls when combined with appropriate fiscal measures. Skeptics of monetary policy seem to be torn between the beliefs that they are too potent and too little effective; sometimes both ideas are combined into the contention that controls fail to operate until a certain point, at which they "take hold" with sudden violence. But a discrete or "all or none" operation of monetary controls has in fact been conspicuously absent in recent history.

30

THE USE AND ABUSE OF FISCAL POLICY

JOHN M. CULBERTSON

If we are to diagnose the state of our economy and prescribe for its future health, we must know what medicines its physicians have been pouring into it and what medicines we have on the shelf if we wish to change the prescription. The medicines referred to are the actions of the government that are interventions in the organized processes of the economy. . . .

For fiscal policy and then for debt management and monetary policies, we must ask ourselves four questions: "How do we define and measure the policy actions? Just how do the policy actions affect the economy? How should we define a policy that is neutral or passive? How should we define one that is actively stabilizing in the sense of combating disturbances arising elsewhere?"

THE MEANING AND MEASUREMENT OF FISCAL POLICY

Fiscal policy—the policy of the fisc, or treasury—is government policy toward its expenditures and revenues, which is reflected in its net deficit or surplus. Specifically, the variable that is controlled by policy, that is an impinging force on the economy, is the expenditure programs and the tax programs of the government as these are determined by legislation and administrative actions.

Reprinted from John M. Culbertson, *Full Employment or Stagnation?* (McGraw-Hill, 1964), pp. 83–94, by permission of the publisher. John M. Culbertson is a professor at the University of Wisconsin.

Government expenditures inject money into the economy, adding to total demand either directly or through increasing incomes. Government receipts pull money out of the economy, reducing total demand. Thus, it is reasonable to net the two against each other and to think of fiscal policy as measured by the net excess of government expenditures (the net deficit) or the net excess of receipts (the net surplus) of the government.

This involves some awkward measurement problems, especially the question of just when transactions are measured (at the time of placing of government order, receipt of goods, making of payment, and so on). The measure of most interest to us is the consolidated cash budget of the government, which includes all types of inflow and outflow, recorded at the time that they involve cash transactions with the public. The traditional measure, the administrative budget, is inferior in that (1) it does not include the activities of trust funds and some other government agencies, and (2) some transactions are not included on a cash basis. Another competing concept is that involved in the national income accounts. This is useful for economic analysis and can be used to supplement the cash budget.

Thus, we take as the primary measure of fiscal policy the net cash deficit or surplus of the government. If as between two years the cash deficit is increased, it seems to be indicated that the net injection of funds into the expenditure-income stream by the government is enlarged and that fiscal policy has shifted in the direction of expanding total demand.

However, a bit of reflection discloses a serious ambiguity in this measure. Suppose that as between our two years the economy had slipped into a recession. Even though the government did not change its tax and expenditure programs, tax receipts would automatically decline because of reductions in incomes of individuals and businesses. Some kinds of government expenditures would just as automatically increase, such as unemployment compensation. Even though the government did nothing, the fiscal position would shift toward a deficit. Do we want to characterize this as an expansive change in fiscal policy? If we do this, how shall we distinguish between (1) an enlarged deficit resulting from reductions in tax rates or increases in expenditure programs in an effort to prevent recession and (2) an enlarged deficit reflecting the fact that a recession exists, and thus was not prevented?[1]

We should never be so naïve as to judge the management of a corporation on the basis of its profits without taking account of the effect on profits of a change in economic conditions. We surely should distinguish between the effects upon profits of changes in management policy and the effects upon profits of changes in the state of the economy. This is just as necessary in the

[1]These are distinguished as "active" and "passive" deficits in *Annual Report of the Council of Economic Advisers,* January, 1963, pp. 66–74.

case of government fiscal policy. A failure to do so we may label the *deficit fallacy*.

We get some odd results if we apply the deficit fallacy. In a very bad depression such as that of the 1930s, the decline in revenues and the pressure for government expenditures may be so great that even fanatic efforts to raise taxes and limit expenditures, i.e., to do the wrong things, would not prevent an increase in the deficit. Is a government that in a depression tries its utmost to raise taxes and reduce expenditures to be credited with an expansive fiscal policy? Are we to say, on the basis of such an experience, that fiscal policy as a weapon against depression has been tried and failed? A criterion according to which fiscal policy is always right, even when the government does all the wrong things, obviously does not make any sense.

To avoid such foolishness, we must define fiscal *policy* as the change in government tax and expenditure *programs*. To measure these, we can take the change in the surplus (or deficit) that it is estimated would exist at a *given level of income*. In a static economy, we could do this by always computing what the deficit or surplus would be with the given tax and expenditure programs at a fixed level of income. However, in a growing economy, we must take as our reference point, not a stable income, but rather an income growing at a rate sufficient to maintain full employment in the economy. Thus, the most useful measure of fiscal policy is the cash deficit or surplus that it is estimated would result from the given tax and expenditure programs at the full-employment level of income.

TARGETS FOR FISCAL POLICY

On this basis, what do we mean by a fiscal policy that is unchanged, neutral, or passive? Evidently, in the short run it is one that keeps the expenditure and tax programs of the government unchanged. If this is done, in a recession government receipts will automatically fall, some expenditures will automatically rise, and the fiscal position will move from surplus toward deficit. However, the full-employment cash surplus of the government, computed on the basis of the estimated full-employment level of income of the economy, will not change. Thus, we divide the change in the actual recorded deficit into that part caused by the recession and that part (in this case, none) caused by a change in policy.

Over longer periods of time, there is another interpretative problem. With the sort of tax system that we now use, unchanged tax rates in a growing economy would result in rising government tax receipts. There is no such automatic tendency for government expenditures to rise (although, in fact, they have risen on balance). If government expenditures stayed unchanged while economic growth raised tax receipts, the government surplus would grow steadily larger. This would have a restrictive effect upon the economy. It would limit growth in total demand. To learn whether this is, or is not, happening, we can use the same measure, the full-employment cash surplus of the government. So long as this is kept unchanged, we know that the tendency toward a rising government surplus is being offset either through increase in government expenditures or through reductions in tax rates.

On this basis, the most meaningful measure of a fiscal policy that is unchanged, or neutral, as between two periods of time is one that keeps the full-employment surplus of the government unchanged.[2] A change in fiscal policy designed to increase total demand is one that through increases in government expenditures and/or reductions in tax rates reduces the government's full-employment cash surplus (or increases its deficit, as the case may be). To change fiscal policy in a restrictive direction, the full-employment cash surplus should be increased by reducing government expenditures and/or raising tax rates, or simply by keeping expenditures and tax programs unchanged over a period of time long enough for economic growth to raise the full-employment surplus.

To maintain a neutral, or noninterventionist, fiscal policy would take careful management. A change in government expenditure programs, say, for international reasons or because some new program is introduced, must be accompanied by a corresponding revision on the tax side if fiscal policy is not to be a haphazardly disturbing element in the economy. Also, if expenditures do not increase over the years as rapidly as estimated full-employment tax receipts, frequent adjustments must be made to lower tax rates to keep the full-employment surplus from growing restrictively large. These things cannot be done without very close and responsible attention to the government's fiscal position, perhaps with some delegation of authority for flexible adjustment of taxes to keep them in line with expenditures. Also required is agreement to focus attention on the full-employment surplus of the government, that is, avoidance of the deficit fallacy. The formation of United States policy meets neither of these requirements. We should not be surprised, therefore, to find that actual fiscal policy has been haphazard, if not positively misguided.

The level at which the full-employment surplus is set involves a separate policy decision. If it is set high, this will involve more government saving and promote lower interest rates and more investment (or consumption

[2]In this context, "unchanged" really ought to mean unchanged as a percent of gross national product rather than in absolute amount. Because it simplifies the story and because in the short run the difference is negligible, we ignore this point in the remainder of the discussion.

The conceptual and computational problems of measuring fiscal policy are discussed in Michael E. Levy, *Fiscal Policy, Cycles and Growth,* National Industrial Conference Board, New York, 1963.

financed by borrowing). Of course it also will involve higher taxes for a given level of expenditures, and it will be more economically restrictive. Since we take for granted that the overall package of policies must bring forth a full-employment growth in total demand, a more restrictive fiscal policy must be accompanied by a larger cash ratio and liquidity ratio for the economy—through more expansive financial policies—in order to avoid strangling the economy.

A reasonable policy for most times is to plan for a small full-employment surplus, so that if the economy is kept prosperous on the average over a period of years, the government debt will change little. Deficits during recessions will be offset by surpluses in prosperity. A fiscal policy thus fixed, however, must be accompanied by monetary and debt management policies such as to assure that the economy actually is kept prosperous. If policy drives the economy into economic slack, then even though fiscal policy is restrictive and involves a large full-employment surplus, the actual budget will show a deficit because of weak economic conditions. Then the traditionalists will cry that prudence requires reducing government expenditures, raising the full-employment surplus still higher, and strangling the economy with a vengeance.

THE EFFECTS OF FISCAL POLICY

How does fiscal policy affect the level of total demand? Why does a reduction in tax rates tend to increase total demand for the output of the economy? We can give a simple, common-sense answer that makes the effects of fiscal policy seem quite definite, but when we consider matters more searchingly, the outcome becomes somewhat more uncertain.

We can think back to the simple conception of a self-sustaining flow of money expenditures and income through the economy. When we add taxes to this picture, it is as a drain of funds out of private incomes, a loss that would cause the flow of private expenditures to diminish. However, offsetting this are the government expenditures, which we must add to private expenditures in order to determine total demand for the output of the economy. If government expenditures increase relative to government receipts, which is to say that the government deficit increases, then there is a net additional injection of funds into the expenditure-income flow. This tends to cause an increase in total demand.

We can extend our analysis to consider the indirect effects of this injection of funds into the expenditure-income flow by using the concept of the fiscal multiplier (or investment multiplier). Suppose the government increased its purchases of goods and services by $1, which increased total incomes in the economy by $1. If additional income resulted in additional spending equal to four-fifths of its amount, then GNP would go up by another 80 cents. But this would raise income by another 80 cents and result in additional expenditures of another 64 cents, and so on. It can be shown that the total increase in the income-expenditure stream resulting from a continued $1 injection of government expenditures under the conditions assumed would amount to $5. The multiplier is the reciprocal of the fraction of any additional income that is not spent, in this case the reciprocal of 1/5, or 5.

Such calculations make fiscal policy seem a powerful and precise tool. Unfortunately, the true picture is not quite so simple. In the first place, the multiplier process takes time to work itself out, and before it gets fully worked out, a great many things may have changed, including fiscal policy itself. Secondly, the attitude of people toward spending additional income is not entirely stable or precisely predictable; in the short run it varies rather widely. Third, the implicit assumption of the multiplier analysis that other things are unchanged is not really applicable.

We can illustrate this by contrasting two cases. In one case, additional government expenditures are financed by sale of liquid short-term securities and creation of new money, and are thus financed in a way that does not crowd out any private borrowers by increasing the cost or reducing the availability of credit to them. Neither does it weaken their balance-sheet financial positions. Thus, the additional government spending constitutes a net addition to total demand. The expansion of output then induces private investors to increase their investment expenditures because of greater optimism and fuller use of their plant capacity. Thus, an increase in private investment amplifies the expansive effect of the government expenditures. In the other case, the increased government expenditures are financed by long-term securities that are competitive with those of private borrowers. Thus, they crowd out of the market some private borrowing, and the resulting reduction in private investment substantially offsets the increase in government expenditures.

Evidently, there are several elements of uncertainty as to the immediate effects of a change in fiscal policy. An important element in this uncertainty arises from financial considerations. An increase in the government deficit must be financed in some way. Ordinarily this is done by the sale of some sort of securities, but then it is important what kind of securities are used. The sale of securities may be accompanied by an increase in the money supply, which also will alter the story. On certain very special assumptions, none of these things will matter because interest rates and credit conditions are firmly fixed. But these assumptions are seldom, if ever, applicable.

Thus, a change in fiscal policy in the direction of producing a smaller full-employment cash surplus clearly promotes economic expansion if other things are equal. However, other things are not usually equal, and the timing and extent of effect of a change in fiscal policy are uncertain. The type of government expenditures and receipts involved alters the outcome somewhat, and financial considerations are crucially important, especially as concerns the more lasting effects of fiscal policy. Indeed, fiscal policy may be thought of as simply involving the immediate flow effects of a change in money supply or in the structure of government debt.

There are no government stabilization policies whose results are precisely predictable. These limitations on our ability to predict the effects of a change in fiscal policy limit the sort of things that we can hope to do with it, but it remains a powerful and important weapon. Even if we do not aspire to use fiscal policy in any carefully calculated way to promote economic stability, considerable efforts are required just to keep inadvertent changes in fiscal policy from being a cause of economic problems.

HOW POWERFUL IS FISCAL POLICY?

How much power do we have in fiscal policy? What could we expect to accomplish with it in the event of extreme need?

Fiscal policy makes sense only if accompanied by supportive debt management and monetary policy. It would be absurd to run a government deficit in an effort to increase total demand and then finance the deficit by selling long-term securities. This would simply minimize its favorable effect, and might nullify it entirely.[3] If we treat fiscal policy as an ally of an expansion of the economy's liquid assets or money supply, we have an extremely powerful weapon. An expansive fiscal policy will inject funds into the expenditure-income stream, financing them in a way that does not interfere with private borrowing and that increases the economy's cash ratio or liquid-asset ratio, which eases the web of financial constraint and increases total demand in the usual way. In other words, fiscal policy is a way of positively injecting into the economy funds accompanied by favorable financial effects. This can be done on a larger scale than will ever conceivably be needed. If the government deficit is financed in this way, the continuing effects of the increase in the economy's cash ratio and liquid-asset ratio will assure that large deficits will not continue to be needed for long. Thus fears of prolonged deficits and continued growth in the government debt will not be relevant.

[3]Traditionalists, however, when they reluctantly consent to a government deficit, are likely to insist that it be financed "soundly," i.e., not by money creation or short-term debt. Thus, they manage to get the worst of all worlds: government deficits but little economic expansion, so more government deficits.

Government surpluses used to retire short-term debt or money are strong contractive medicine. Again, there is not likely to be a problem of insufficiency of power.

If fiscal policy is used in opposition to, rather than in concert with, monetary and debt management policies, then we have a different story. Achieving the desired effects under such conditions may require extremely large government deficits or surpluses, and there is some doubt about how long even these could succeed. In view of the questionable political feasibility and uncertain psychological repercussions of really extreme fiscal policies and the uncertainty about how much fiscal policy it takes to offset a given amount of opposing monetary policy, the potentialities of such policy packages seem much more limited and difficult to estimate.

FISCAL FALLACIES

On the way to an orderly fiscal policy, which is the only sort consistent with a secure prosperity in the future, there are many roadblocks. The government's processes for controlling its expenditures and receipts would have to be rationalized. The Congress doubtless would have to give the President some discretionary power over receipts just to maintain a controlled fiscal policy, not to speak of an anticyclical fiscal policy. People in government would have to learn to think of an adjusted surplus, the full-employment surplus, rather than the recorded fiscal position as the measure of fiscal policy. This seems a rather complex and slippery concept, although in truth it is no more difficult than those that we are accustomed to apply to evaluation of the position of a business.

The danger of an extravagantly destabilizing fiscal policy arises from application of the ideas of the economic traditionalists. Their conception of the matter is simple. Government deficits are inherently bad, irrespective of economic conditions. They are unsound, imprudent. They constitute "living beyond our means," "spending money we haven't got," "mortgaging our future," and so on. Thus, the prescription is to balance the budget or run a surplus every year if possible. But since what is taken as the measure is not the full-employment surplus but the actual recorded surplus, it is implied that the weaker the economy gets, the more taxes must be increased or government expenditures reduced. Such policies clearly are restrictive. They may increase the full-employment surplus drastically. Thus, policy may play a potent role in aggravating a recession, or a prolonged period of economic slack. The market economy has no protective mechanism against this. This is sabotage from within.

Although the traditionalist position is usually presented as reflecting the sound application of the wisdom of business financial practice, it does not stand inspection even on these grounds. A business that was hit by an assuredly temporary reduction in sales and profits would not be regarded as farsighted if it tried to maintain its reported profits by abandoning its research, halting its investment, or decimating its trained labor force. Indeed, if the business were in a strong financial position and had some concern for its goodwill, it might feel some social obligation to try to run a cash deficit, to maintain its investment program, to minimize layoffs. It would do this on the theory, which is too obviously true to be disputable, that by reducing its expenditures and the incomes of its workers it would immediately cause additional economic hardship and through this worsen the general economic situation of the country.

Thus, one approach would be to argue that the government ought to behave like a large, financially strong business with a social conscience, only more so. After all, for the government to contribute to the maintenance of full employment is not merely a matter of *noblesse oblige* but a matter of national policy, embodied in the Employment Act of 1946. Further, while the financial resources of any business are limited, those of the government are much greater than any conceivable peacetime need. The government has great future taxing power, immense borrowing power, and potentially unlimited access to funds by borrowing from the Federal Reserve and the banks and thus creating money (which in any case would be the proper thing to do in the event of severe unemployment).

Thus, for the government to apply to itself in a responsible way the standards used by business would require that it be willing freely to run deficits during periods of economic weakness and unemployment.

The position of the traditionalists, then, cannot really be supported by any sort of reasonable analogy from principles of business or personal finance. It has about it a mystical or superstitious temper that seems to defy attack by reason.[4] It is a brand of economic know-nothingism. If it were applied to business affairs, to medicine, to almost any other line of activity, it would readily be recognized as the primitive thought that it is. Unfortunately, with

[4]The traditionalist approach was in a position of unusual dominance in the 1920s and early 1930s and had much to do with making the Great Depression what it was. Here is a sample of the orthodox advice of that time:

> With the monotony and persistency of Old Cato, we should make one single and invariable dictum the theme of every discourse: balance budgets. Stop spending money we haven't got. Sacrifice for frugality and revenue. Cut government spending—cut it as rations are cut in a siege. Tax—tax everybody for everything. . . .

Bernard Baruch, testimony before the Senate Finance Committee in February, 1933, quoted in Marriner S. Eccles, *Beckoning Frontiers,* Alfred A. Knopf, Inc., New York, 1951, p. 100. Other similar examples are given in this source.

regard to economic policy, primitive thought is much with us.[5] For an economy beset with economic slack resulting from deficient total demand to set about laboriously to reduce needed government expenditures—this seems to reflect the quality of thought that would lead a besieged and starving city to burn its food to appease the Gods.

Of course, if enough people are captured by a superstition, then it becomes, in a perverse sense, true. If people believe that integrity and confidence require that in a recession government expenditures must be reduced, then perhaps to do so is the lesser evil. If the people of a besieged city believe that they can only be saved by burning their food to appease the Gods, then perhaps this is what must be done. Superstition is a real force, and it can be a crucially important constraint upon policy. But to say this does not convert bad policy into good policy or error into truth. It merely explains why error is committed. It explains how a nation can build a structure of beliefs that makes successful policy impossible.

[5]A symptomatic episode was that in which the Chamber of Commerce of the United States made a movie in which a group of eighth graders in Mitchell, South Dakota, expressed their ideas on the government deficit, evidently for educational use. The basis for such use seemed to be this belief, as expressed by the Chamber's president: "These youngsters in South Dakota made better economic sense than many of today's adults." It is not customary, in this day and age, to seek advice from eighth graders on questions of medicine, military strategy, or business management. That it seemed appropriate to the chamber of commerce to represent them as authorities on fiscal policy casts light on only one thing, the intellectual state of the leaders of the chamber of commerce. *The New York Times,* Western Edition, May 16, 1963, pp. 11, 16.

31

FEDERAL FISCAL POLICY IN THE RECESSIONS OF 1948–50, 1953–55, 1957–59, AND 1960–61: A SUMMARY

WILFRED LEWIS, JR.

THE IMPLICIT FEDERAL SURPLUS AT HYPOTHETICAL HIGH EMPLOYMENT

Because the level of national income determines the amount of revenue collected from given tax rates, the size of the actual budget surplus at any particular time depends passively on the level of economic activity as well as actively on discretionary tax and expenditure actions. In using the budget surplus to indicate whether discretionary fiscal behavior has neutral, expansionary, or contractionary effects on the economy, it is essential to distinguish between active and passive changes in the surplus. The distinction is made at several places in this study by the use of an analytical tool of fairly recent development–the implicit federal surplus.

The implicit federal surplus, as used in this study, is the difference between federal receipts and expenditures calculated for existing programs and tax rates, but assuming the economy is at high employment so far as the fiscal effects of the built-in stabilizers are concerned. The basic idea underlying this concept of implicit federal surplus is not new. It bears a close kinship, for example, to the "stabilizing budget" policy which has been recommended by

Adapted from *Federal Fiscal Policy in the Postwar Recessions,* by Wilfred Lewis, Jr., The Brookings Institution (1962), pp. 12–24. Reprinted by permission of the publisher. Wilfred Lewis, Jr., is an economist with the National Planning Association.

the Committee for Economic Development (CED) since early in the postwar period.[1] The CED's suggested policy would set discretionary taxes and expenditures so as to yield some surplus at high employment and would tolerate deficits caused by induced declines in tax collections if economic activity fell below high employment. However, until recently there have been few attempts to draw fiscal policy conclusions or recommendations from quantitative estimates or judgments about the size of the federal surplus at hypothetical high employment.[2]

If a decrease in the *actual* federal surplus in recession represents nothing more than the automatic drop in revenues or increase in unemployment compensation caused by the drop in economic activity below a high employment trend, the *implicit* federal surplus will remain unchanged in size. With tax rates and government expenditure programs unchanged, fiscal policy can be regarded as neutral in an important sense, rather than compensatory or expansionary. This does not mean that the income-generating effects of a deficit caused by built-in stabilizers are any less than if the deficit were the result of discretionary factors. Rather, it refers to the fact that a purely passive federal offset to private expenditure reductions would be self-reversing with the start of recovery and self-terminating with the return of the economy to high employment. A budget policy which is neutral in this sense is consistent with a return to high employment and recovery of the pre-existing rate of utilization of other factors of production only if the original cause of decline in private spending is removed, or if it is offset by increases in other categories of private spending.[3] A decrease in the size of the implicit federal surplus, on the other hand, can be taken as indicating that the income-generating effects of the budget have increased relative to high employment GNP.

A neutral budget policy can be successful only if the recession is caused by a temporary and self-correcting decline of private expenditures. Even more important, unless fiscal policy makes use of calculations on a fairly current basis of the size and effects of the implicit surplus, there is danger of perverse fiscal behavior which would aggravate the decline in private spending—or, more likely, slow or prevent complete recovery. This is because actual figures on the budget surplus may give misleading signals during recession about the income-generating effects of the budget. The passive drop in revenues can

[1]See *Taxes and the Budget* (Committee for Economic Development, 1947).

[2]See statement of Charles L. Schultze in *Current Economic Situation and Outlook,* Joint Economic Committee Hearings, 86 Cong. 2 sess. (1961), pp. 120–22; statement of Herbert Stein in *Hearings on the Economic Report of the President,* Joint Economic Committee, 87 Cong. 1 sess. (1961), pp. 209 ff.; and CEA, *Economic Report of the President, January 1962,* pp. 79–84.

[3]"Neutral" in this sense can be viewed as short-run neutrality. In the long run, the degree of built-in flexibility in the budget must be viewed as a variable which can be changed as a matter of public policy.

produce a decrease in actual surplus large enough to hide an increase in the implicit surplus.

The foregoing possibilities are not idle speculations. The record of discretionary fiscal policy during the postwar recessions and recoveries has left something to be desired. And misleading budget signals given off by actual, rather than implicit, surpluses and deficits are a part of this story.

. . . .

THE FINDINGS IN BRIEF

Since the major focus of this study is on fiscal policy, much attention is given to distinguishing among and, to the extent possible, determining separate amounts involved in automatic built-in fiscal stabilizers, discretionary antirecessionary actions, and expenditure and tax changes occurring primarily for reasons other than recessions. An overall summary of federal receipts and expenditures during the four postwar recessions and recoveries, as shown in Table 1, provides a useful point of departure.

Automatic Stabilizers

. . . .

The built-in fiscal stabilizers have made a substantial contribution to the stability of the postwar economy. They have pushed the federal budget strongly toward deficit when that was needed in each postwar recession, thus helping to slow the economic decline. The resulting change in the surplus has been large relative to the change in total output, ranging from 40 percent of the fall in GNP from peak to trough in 1948–50 to more than 100 percent in 1960–61. Moreover, in spite of a lagged impact on the federal cash budget, the economic effects of the built-in stabilizers have been timely with respect to contraction. It appears likely that the built-in stabilizers have limited the duration as well as the severity of postwar contractions. Of course, after the trough is passed and employment and output rise, the built-in stabilizers reverse direction. Then they increase the surplus or reduce the deficit, and thus retard recovery.

The built-in fiscal stabilizers are of two general types: some have direct effects; others, indirect effects. Those having a direct effect on disposable personal income–individual income tax, unemployment compensation, and employment taxes–have become somewhat more important for several reasons. Increases in payroll tax rates, mainly for old-age and survivors insurance (OASI), have so promoted employment taxes as a built-in stabilizer that their effects on government receipts are now about a third as large as the variations in the yield of the individual income tax. At unchanged tax rates,

Table 1. Summary of Federal Receipts and Expenditures, Postwar Recessions and Recoveries[a]

(In billions of current dollars)

Recession and recovery	*Peak quarter*	*Trough quarter*	*Terminal quarter of recovery*	*Change, peak to trough*	*Change, trough to recovery*
1948–50	**1948–IV**	**1949–II**	**1950–II**		
Receipts	42.6	38.5	47.3	–4.1	8.8
Expenditures	38.8	42.4	39.0	3.6	–3.4
Surplus or deficit (–)	3.8	–3.9	8.3	–7.7	12.2
(Change in surplus due to built-in fiscal stabilizers)	...	...	...	(–3.7)	(6.1)
1953–55	**1953–II**	**1954–II**	**1955–II**		
Receipts	72.3	63.3	71.7	–9.0	8.4
Expenditures	79.4	68.7	68.1	–10.7	–0.6
Surplus or deficit (–)	–7.0	–5.4	3.5	1.6	8.9
(Change in surplus due to built-in fiscal stabilizers)	...	...	...	(–6.6)	(10.4)
1957–59	**1957–III**	**1958–I**	**1959–II**		
Receipts	82.5	75.4	91.6	–7.1	16.2
Expenditures	79.9	83.5	91.1	3.6	7.6
Surplus or deficit (–)	2.6	–8.1	0.5	–10.7	8.6
(Change in surplus due to built-in fiscal stabilizers)	...	...	...	(–8.7)	(17.4)
1960–61	**1960–II**	**1961–I**	**1961–IV**[b]		
Receipts	96.9	92.5	103.1	–4.4	10.6
Expenditures	92.5	98.0	105.2	5.5	7.2
Surplus or deficit (–)	4.5	–5.5	–2.1	–10.0	3.4
(Change in surplus due to built-in fiscal stabilizers)	...	...	...	(–6.8)	(10.8)

[a] On basis of national income accounts, seasonally adjusted annual rates. From . . . U.S. Department of Commerce, *U.S. Income and Output* (1958) and *Survey of Current Business,* July 1961 and February 1962. Figures . . . may not add because of rounding.

[b] The last quarter for which data are available is 1961–IV, although 1962–II is considered the terminal quarter of recovery in this study.

the individual income tax grows faster than gross national product and seems to have acquired somewhat increased sensitivity to cyclical changes in GNP. Finally, there is some evidence that private consumption has become more responsive to cyclical changes in disposable personal income, and this promotes the importance of the stabilizers which directly cushion declines in such income.

The indirect stabilizers–corporation income tax and excises–account for larger portions of the change in federal surplus or deficit than the direct stabilizers. However, at least for minor recessions, they are inefficient because they probably add substantially less to private spending than they subtract from federal budget receipts. This effect might be a net disadvantage if the public and political response were so opposed to budget deficits that expansionary fiscal action of a discretionary nature were thereby inhibited. Moreover, concern about budget deficits is strengthened by the lag in the collection of corporation income taxes, which produces a cash budget deficit after recovery is under way.

Discretionary Fiscal Actions

. . . . Compared to the automatic stabilizers, deliberate actions to counter recessions generally have been less helpful. Recession is never the only factor, and seldom the most important factor, shaping federal fiscal and budgetary policy. As a consequence, specific antirecession actions have been subject to numerous constraints which have limited their effectiveness from a stabilization standpoint.

As a rule, the government has favored countercyclical actions that could be justified, at least in part, on other than purely stabilization grounds. This is perhaps the major reason why countercyclical actions on the expenditure side of the budget have had more appeal than tax cuts, which would have required justification primarily on counterrecession grounds. Under this "mixed motives" approach, expenditures which would have been undertaken anyway sometimes have been labeled "counterrecession." The converse is probably also true–some redefinition of long-term program goals undoubtedly has taken place in the heat of battle against recession. As a consequence, it is frequently difficult–sometimes impossible–to decide definitely whether or not the motive in particular actions was primarily to counter recession. But, insofar as a distinction is possible, those actions which appear to have been primarily counterrecessionary have been on the expenditure side of the budget. A possible exception is the reduction of excise taxes in 1954, for which the recession was a frequently advanced but not the only argument.

Measured by changes in the implicit federal surplus at high employment during the recession phase, discretionary fiscal actions of the federal government were sharply contractionary during the recession of 1953–54, were mildly expansionary in 1948–49, and were approximately neutral during the other recessions. The story during the recovery phases is less favorable, even allowing for discretionary antirecession actions. In the 1949–50 and 1954–55 recoveries, the implicit surplus increased even though the economy was still below high employment. In both these cases, however, a net increase in the implicit surplus in the terminal quarter compared to the prerecession peak proved not to be too restictive a budget policy in the light of later developments in the economy. In the 1958–59 recovery, the implicit surplus through the end of calendar 1959 was not much larger than it had been before the recession. However, a reaction to the very large fiscal 1959 deficit resulted in cutbacks in expenditures which, coupled with tax increases, caused a drastic increase in the rate of the implicit federal surplus in early 1960. The 1960–62 period of recession and recovery is the only one for which the implicit surplus declined from prerecession peak to terminal quarter (based on expectations in March 1962). However, the prospect in early 1962 was for a reversal of this behavior by the end of the year and prior to the achievement of what the administration had declared was its full employment target of 4 percent unemployed.

Interestingly, the general magnitude of counterrecessionary increases in expenditures has been roughly the same for the three recessions in which such actions took place, in spite of different mixtures of actions. . . . The 1954 recession featured an administrative speed-up which leaned heavily on the Department of Defense. In 1958, Congress was considerably more aggressive, but the administrative speed-up that year exempted the Department of Defense. The 1961 administrative actions included activities of the Department of Defense, and featured congressional action also, but less than in 1958. Although the President proposed some steps in 1949, no significant counterrecession actions were actually undertaken in that recession.

A direct comparison of the relative contributions of deliberate counterrecession actions and built-in stabilizers is somewhat misleading because of different timing. Discretionary actions have not been in effect before the trough month so that, except for possible anticipatory effects, they have not been a factor in cushioning the decline or in causing turning points. On the other hand, discretionary actions have made a contribution during the recovery phase, which is a time when the built-in stabilizers reverse direction and operate to slow recovery. However, the fiscal effects (and reasonable estimates of economic effects) of discretionary actions during the recovery phase have been considerably smaller than the contribution of the automatic stabilizers during the recession phase.

It has not been difficult to reverse discretionary actions, at least for those identified as primarily counterrecessionary. Such actions generally have been self-terminating, or were terminated by discretionary action prior to full recovery. Actions that might be more difficult to reverse, such as new public works starts (as distinguished from speeding work in progress) generally have been avoided.

While expenditures could be, and were, justified in part on other than stabilization grounds, tax cuts would have required (or at least were so viewed) an admission by public officials that a recession was serious enough to call for corrective action not otherwise justifiable. This made the expenditure side more attractive to public officials, particularly in the early stages of recession when the extent of need for corrective action was still uncertain. In addition, tax cuts faced a serious obstacle on those occasions when they were considered or recommended because they involved controversial questions of equity and the distribution of tax burdens by income groups.

Constraints on Antirecession Policy

Some of the constraints under which discretionary actions have operated recur with enough frequency to command more attention than they generally get from economic analysts.

A major category of constraints on counterrecession policy can be described as "prior commitments and long-range goals." It would have been most difficult for President Truman, just re-elected in a campaign featuring charges of Republican "fiscal irresponsibility" for having cut taxes in 1948, to have proposed tax cuts in January 1949. Similarly, it would have been difficult for the newly installed Eisenhower administration, pledged to reduce spending and the budget deficit, to propose expenditure increases in 1953–54; or for newly elected President Kennedy, having pledged expenditure increases and possibly tax increases to meet the Soviet threat, to ask for tax cuts in 1961. Such commitments are not necessarily inconsistent with counterrecession action, but certainly limit the range of policy alternatives.

Short-run uncertainty about whether the economy was or was not in recession, or about to be in recession, has been a limitation on counterrecession action, but not so serious as public statements and appearances might suggest. Concern over the need to maintain public and business confidence has sometimes limited public acknowledgement of recession and delayed the initiation of corrective actions. As a rule, administrations have delayed public acknowledgment of recession until the evidence was overwhelming–well into the period of decline–but have called the turn promptly, and started to reimpose fiscal restraints, as soon as the trough was passed and recovery started. Uncertainty about whether the economy might not a year or so hence be faced with the problem of inflation has been a greater limitation than inability to make short-term forecasts. Lack of certainty about the government's own requirements for defense expenditures has been a factor in this. In at least three of the four postwar recessions, there were, at times which were critical for purposes of antirecession decisions, strong feelings that defense expenditures might have to be increased by unknown, but potentially inflationary, amounts. As a consequence, there has been a high—probably too high—premium on reversibility, and often actions that were judged not reversible were avoided. The feeling that tax cuts might prove irreversible, for example, was a definite factor against their use.

Concern over balanced budgets in one form or another has been an active constraint in each postwar recession. There have been only brief interludes around the trough when the desire for balanced budgets has been suspended temporarily in favor of deliberate additions to the budget deficit. The 1946 Employment Act probably stimulated more aggressive antirecession actions than might otherwise have been forthcoming. However, there is little in the record to support the contention sometimes voiced that this legislation has biased public policy toward inflation by promoting more aggressive action to combat unemployment than inflation. Sentiments for balanced budgets and fiscal responsibility are still strong; discretionary antirecession actions have been reversed sharply during recovery. And it can be argued that any strengthening by the Employment Act of the linkage in public attitudes between the budget and the state of the economy applies to inflation as well as unemployment. Neither major party has shown a monopoly on "fiscal responsibility," and it has not been the exclusive property of either the executive or legislative branches. Anxiety over rising prices during some of the contractions and some of the recoveries has also operated as a constraint on expansionary fiscal actions, and balance of payments difficulties also played this role at the time of the 1959 recovery and the 1960–62 recession and recovery.

Recurring attention to the geographical distribution of expenditures by surplus labor areas has not enhanced overall stabilization goals, and the attention given to such attempts may have delayed action on other more effective measures. There have also been repeated suggestions to raise minimum wages—an ambiguous antirecession action at best.

Concern with "efficiency" aspects of budgeting by both the executive branch and Congress has sometimes served as a constraint on counterrecession expenditures. For example, the Department of Defense was left out of the 1958 procurement speed-up partly because it was felt that this was inconsistent with program objectives. In 1961, when consideration was being given to a list of public works projects which agencies could start within six months and complete within two years if additional funds became available, the point was made that several of the projects on the list were needed less than other larger and slower projects. Further, the starting of additional military public works for purely counterrecession purposes was questioned as possibly inconsistent with defense goals.

Other constraints have been present in the principle of trust fund financing and earmarked revenues for highways, social security, and unemployment. There is evidence that expenditures for highways have more potential flexibility than most other federally financed public works. However, under present arrangements, highway expenditures are closely geared to earmarked highway-user charges, so that any speed-up requires offsetting increases of tax rates immediately or within a short period. (In 1958, highway expenditures were accelerated, but the condition of the trust fund at that time was fortuitous and temporary.) This forestalled using highways as an antirecession action in 1961. Similarly, social security and unemployment expenditure proposals often have had to be matched by early payroll tax rate increases, the timing of which has not been helpful from a stabilization standpoint. There has been at least one increase in OASI payroll tax rates–in support of the trust fund principle–in each of the four recession-recovery periods.

Considering their timing and generally modest proportions, it seems doubtful that the discretionary counterrecession actions can be assigned much importance in limiting the duration or severity of the postwar recessions. The fact that accomplishments were as great as they were suggests that equity, national needs, or other arguments than recession could be marshalled in behalf of the actions that were taken.

Given the many constraints that have been operative, and the general absence of detailed contingency plans, it is somewhat problematical whether fiscal programs which were more expansionary could have been put together on short notice if, in fact, they had been needed. The variety of *ad hoc* expenditure proposals, and the ingenuity with which these were defended, suggest that the government may have come close to reaching the full potential of the flexibility that exists on the expenditure side of the budget. Also, the political sensitivity of equity aspects of tax cuts, and the failure to reach advance political consensus on which tax cuts would have been most desirable in recession, make it unlikely that quick action could have been taken on the tax side.

Federal fiscal actions undertaken primarily for reasons other than the recession on some occasions have been perverse; on other occasions, they have been more helpful in stimulating the economy than actions taken primarily to counter recession. Drastic tightening of federal fiscal activity for budgetary reasons or long-run program goals was a major initiating factor in the 1953–54 and the 1960–61 recessions, and an aggravating factor during the early stages of the 1957–58 decline. A large well-timed tax cut in 1948 helped greatly to cushion the 1948–49 decline, but was undertaken for quite different reasons. Increases in defense outlays at one stage or another of the 1949, 1958, and 1961 recessions were fortuitous since they reduced the need for discretionary counterrecession actions that might not so easily have won approval.

By concentrating on the effectiveness or ineffectiveness of particular fiscal proposals and actions, and on cataloging the constraints which have operated on public officials, it is hoped that this study will help to define the policy problems which are likely to be faced in future recessions. However, this approach makes it easy to lose sight of the real progress that has been made over the postwar period in improving the fiscal response to recession. In 1948–49, both the Congress and the executive branch initially had appeared so opposed to unbalanced budgets as to pose a threat of quite perverse fiscal actions. By the middle of 1949, at least a passive budget deficit was accepted and even defended by President Truman as the proper policy. In 1954, President Eisenhower's administration was willing to accept a limited number of discretionary increases in public spending. By 1958, Congress and Eisenhower's second administration both undertook a wide range of antirecession actions, although with some reluctance on the part of the administration and some regret on the part of both branches afterwards. And in 1961, the Kennedy administration proposed promptly and publicly a coordinated attack on recession—still, however, with signs of regret about the deficit financing this entailed, and a rather hasty reversal after the initiation of recovery was assured.

There are many remaining constraints, however, and a great deal of work is needed to sharpen the fiscal tools to be used in combating recession, and in improving the skill and timing with which they are used. It is especially important that the deficits generated automatically during recession shall not be allowed to provoke fiscal reactions that impede the return of the economy to high employment.

32

THE CONCEPT OF AUTOMATIC STABILIZERS

M. O. CLEMENT

Since World War II there has been a growing conviction that the great economic convulsions of past experience are no longer likely. This persuasion is based in part on recent historical evidence, which is in turn reinforced by changes in the institutional structure of the economy. The adoption of the Employment Act's mandate, the acceptance of the counter-cyclical efficacy of an unbalanced budget, the rejuvenation of monetary policy, the relative growth in the government's contribution to economic activity, and the increased progression of the over-all tax structure are examples of these institutional changes. Additional optimism is derived from the improvement of economists' knowledge and experience with respect to countercyclical policy. Still, historical extrapolations have proved unreliable before; economic forecasting is an art rather than a science; Congress jealously guards its fiscal prerogatives; as recent popular controversy has amply demonstrated, discretionary countercyclical weapons are considered too blunt, excessively time-consuming, and apt to backfire (even assuming a consensus on effective action can be obtained); monetary policy is likewise blunt and likely to be decisive in only one direction—and then, perhaps, too decisive! Clearly, there is little justification for optimism on the basis of these developments alone.

There is, however, another related institutional change that is stressed by many who feel that future cycles in economic activity will not be severe. During the latter stages of the war, economists, on the basis of theoretical

Reprinted from *The Southern Economic Journal,* January, 1959, pp. 303–14, by permission of the author and publisher. M. O. Clement is a professor at Dartmouth College.

arguments, proposed that the fiscal system exerted an automatic countercyclical impact.[1] With no change in tax rates, revenues from the existing tax system would expand and contract in positive relation to changes in national income and probably more than proportionately; federal outlays would exhibit an opposite tendency, although quite likely to a lesser degree. It was also on this favorable operation of the expanded system of automatic stabilizers that hopes for less severe business fluctuations in the future were pinned. Indeed, the refusal to lower tax rates during the 1957–58 recession is, in part, an illustration of government belief in considerable built-in stabilization potential.

The realism, or lack thereof, of placing hopes on the countercyclical effectiveness of the built-in stabilizers has been subjected to more or less extensive examination. The studies of Hart,[2] Egle,[3] the Committee for Economic Development,[4] the Universities-National Bureau Committee for Economic Research,[5] and White[6] stand out, although this listing is by no means exhaustive. These assessments of the countercyclical efficacy of the battery of automatic stabilizers, however, have been based on a definition of built-in stabilization which is unnecessarily restricted in its operational elements. The purpose of this article is to spell out in greater detail a more realistic conceptualization of the compensatory scope of automatic stabilizers.

THE CONCEPT OF AUTOMATIC STABILIZERS

In discussions of the role of automatic stabilizers in counteracting cyclical swings it is usually assumed that the impact of these devices is fiscal in nature.[7] This rather limited interpretation of the scope of automatic stabiliza-

[1] This dating, of course, is an oversimplification which does not do justice to an impressive number of perceptive scholars. Norman F. Keiser, "The Development of the Concept of 'Automatic Stablizers,'" *Journal of Finance*, December 1956, XI, pp. 428–37, provides an extensive list of authors who had considered at least some aspects of this question prior to the mid-1940's.

[2] A. G. Hart, *Money, Debt, and Economic Activity* (2d ed. New York: Prentice-Hall, 1954), chaps. 27 and 28. See also the 1948 edition of the same work.

[3] Walter P. Egle, *Economic Stabilization: Objectives, Rules, and Mechanisms* (Princeton: Princeton University Press for the University of Cincinnati, 1952).

[4] Numerous pamphlets, but see especially *Problems in Anti-Recession Policy* (New York: CED, 1954).

[5] *Policies to Combat Depression* (New York: National Bureau of Economic Research, 1956). The papers by Joseph A. Pechman and David W. Lusher treat the issue of the efficacy of automatic stabilizers.

[6] Melvin I. White, "Personal Income Tax Reduction in a Hypothetical Contraction," *Review of Economics and Statistics*, February 1949, XXXI, pp. 63–68, and his more comprehensive study, of which the article just cited is in the nature of a summary, *Personal Income Tax Reduction in a Business Contraction* (New York: Columbia University Press, 1951).

[7] This is explicit in a 1947 symposium on reconversion problems. See S. Norris Livingston, "Economic Policy in Transition," *Review of Economic Statistics*, February 1947, XXXIX, p. 21.

tion measures runs throughout the literature. A few economists, however, have visualized built-in flexibility as having a broader impact than the term "fiscal" would suggest. Hart proposed several criteria by which to judge the automatic stabilization qualities of a particular countercyclical measure. Any device which begins its compensatory effect without waiting for a new policy decision and which also (1) tends to produce budget deficits during slumps and surpluses during upswings, or (2) expands the community's stock of cash in slumps and reduces it in high prosperity, or (3) tends to lower the public's demand for cash balances during slumps and raise it in high prosperity, or (4) any combination of these would, according to Hart, be designated a built-in stabilizer.[8] In view of recent research in the theory of income determination this set of criteria should probably be amended. "Stock of money and near monies," i.e., stock of "moneyness," should be substituted for "stock of cash" in the second test above. This is in keeping with the current attitudes on the determinants of the level of effective demand which have evolved from emendations and additions to Keynes' concise formulation.[9] From a purely practical standpoint it also seems reasonable to delete the third condition above from the set of criteria. Policy measures which have the effect of altering the nature of the drive for liquidity must work through expectations and habitual responses. The degree of indirectness involved means that little operational certainty can be attached to devices of this nature. Completeness demands, nevertheless, that this test be included.

While Hart's set of criteria establish minimum conditions which automatic stabilization devices must fulfill, as will be argued subsequently, it is inadequate in several respects. No doubt the most obtrusive and certainly greatest impact of the built-in stabilizers is their effect, through budgetary imbalances, on income levels. Nevertheless, this facet of automatic stabilization has been unduly stressed. Such over-emphasis is doubtlessly derived in part from the hold that the interaction of the multiplier and the acceleration principle has gained on the explanation of cyclical movements. But to a large extent it is also due to the fuzziness of the theory which tries to relate

---

Alvin H. Hansen (*Business Cycles and National Income* [New York: W. W. Norton and Company, 1951], pp. 144–45) and James A. Maxwell (*Fiscal Policy: Its Techniques and Institutional Setting* [New York: Henry Holt and Company, 1955], pp. 100–109) implicitly endorse this viewpoint. Of course, fiscal policy includes monetary effects but most writers do not stress this. Milton A. Friedman, "A Monetary and Fiscal Framework for Economic Stability," *American Economic Review,* June 1948, XXXVIII, pp. 245–64, reprinted in *Essays in Positive Economics* (Chicago: University of Chicago Press, 1953), pp. 133–56, is a major exception.

[8] A. G. Hart, *Money, Debt, and Economic Activity* (2d ed.), p. 462. These same tests appear in the book's first edition also. Egle, *op. cit.,* p. 47, subscribes to these criteria too, but, as will be seen, Egle extends the tests into an important area that Hart only concedes by implication.

[9] See, for example, James Tobin's appeal in his article, "The Business Cycle in the Post-War World: A Review," *Quarterly Journal of Economics,* May 1958, LXXIII, pp. 286–88.

changes in the stock of money and near monies and the drive for liquidity to variations in aggregate demand. Not only is this theory vague and ill-defined but, what is worse for economists, the relationships deduced by *a priori* arguments are poorly suited to quantification and hence are not ideal subjects for empirical confirmation.

The above reasons offer little justification for neglecting the monetary side of automatic stabilization measures. It is not necessary to invoke the Pigou effect, as Friedman does,[10] in order to admit this possibility. Clearly, changes in income level and rates of change in income are not the only determinants of changes in the level of effective demand. Other economic magnitudes—liquidity positions, expectations, habits, to name a few general categories—while quantitatively less significant in impact and knowable with less precision, frequently assume critical importance. Discussion of these sorts of relationships cannot be shunned if the countercyclical efficacy of automatic stabilizers is to be properly evaluated. Whether or not these monetary and attitudinal relationships can be quantified, their effects must somehow be assessed.

Be that as it may, it must be acknowledged that built-in stabilization devices which elicit automatic responses in government budgets counter economic fluctuations more effectively than automatic devices which give rise solely to variations in the stock of moneyness or the demand for cash balances. Government surpluses and deficits have a relatively more direct impact on total effective demand than do variations in the supply of moneyness or liquidity demands. Increases in the supply of moneyness may serve merely to satisfy an enhanced drive for liquidity. Only when this thirst for liquidity is sated can increases in moneyness have even an indirect bearing on the income level. To some extent, however, this discussion is academic. All current automatic stabilization devices operate reasonably close to the income stream. Since the gold standard has been abandoned there have been no built-in stabilizing measures which have directly produced variations only in the quantity of moneyness. There are no measures which evoke automatic variations in the demand for cash balances as distinct from automatic tendencies to saturate this demand. Nevertheless, in all cases where automatic stabilizers cause swings in the government surplus or deficit, variations in the stock of moneyness or in ability to satisfy liquidity are also involved. The monetary aspects of automatic countercyclical devices reinforce the fiscal aspects.

While Hart's criteria posit the minimum conditions by which it is possible

[10]See Friedman, "A Monetary and Fiscal Framework . . ." *op. cit., passim.* Also, George L. Bach, "Monetary-Fiscal Policy Reconsidered," *Journal of Political Economy,* October 1949, LVII, p. 391, n. 20.

to determine whether a particular stabilization measure is automatic in its operation, they do not constitute the conditions which a relatively *effective* system of automatic stabilizers must satisfy. In order to have the maximum anticipated favorable economic impact, both direct and indirect, an automatic countercyclical device must not detract from the possible beneficial results.[11] Negation of the beneficial results could be incurred by an adverse impact on expectations. Persons responsible for making economic decisions must be able to anticipate a fairly definite pattern of action from the stabilization policies and from the economic system. In the absence of this "predictability of action"[12] the expectations of decision-makers will vacillate, the stability of the economy's internal response mechanism diminishes, and what may have been an effective stabilization policy becomes less satisfactory, if not damaging.

An automatic stabilization arrangement which possesses predictability of action must fulfill criteria in addition to those already set forth. Decision makers cannot adopt reasonably stable responses to economic change, influenced as it is by a system of automatic devices, without a relatively extended period of adaptation. Consequently, one of the additional requisites of an efficacious automatic countercyclical program is that the devices must have enough permanence to become part of the economic milieu of decision-making units. Once a set of built-in stabilization measures is instituted, however, the arrangement need not be unalterable. The aspect of permanency is a relative matter. What seems necessary is that once an automatic countercyclical arsenal is built-in its expected tenure must be such that its impact can be amalgamated into the multitude of considerations which enter into business and consumer decisions. While it is not feasible to attach a specific duration to the time period for which these devices must seem permanently installed, the length would vary with the horizon of the private planning period and with the countercyclical mechanism of the specific type of device. Moreover, the magnitude of the anticipated change in the stabilization system is an important consideration. If expected changes are to be relatively minor then undoubtedly the changes could be undertaken more frequently. On the other hand, a major adaptation of the system should be inaugurated very rarely.

In this respect the purely fortuitous nature of the present arsenal of automatic stabilizers may have been a blessing. These stabilizers became a part of the economic response mechanism without fanfare and the public

[11] Egle, *op. cit.*, especially pp. 45–47, dwells on this issue. The next few paragraphs lean heavily on his exposition. See also A. G. Hart, "The Problem of 'Full Employment': Facts, Issues, and Policies," *American Economic Review*, May 1946, XXXVI, pp. 283–86.

[12] The term is Egle's. *Op. cit.*, p. 46.

unconsciously adjusted its thinking to take them into account. When economists ultimately became cognizant of the existence of a considerable amount of built-in stabilization and made their awareness known, the public's economic adjustment was already an accomplished fact. Had the government overtly instituted a system of automatic stabilization measures for the express purpose of decreasing cyclical instability, expectations would have been grossly revised. By the unplanned and, for the period that mattered, unknown intrusion of automatic countercyclical devices the additional dislocations attendant to the revision of expectations were minimized.[13]

An additional requirement for an effective set of automatic devices is that the objectives and important provisions of the stabilization complex must be clearly defined. The stabilizing effect as such need not be blueprinted; rather the essence of this requirement is procedural. If there is to be predictability of action, automatic stabilizers must preclude the possiblity of administrative discretion and recourse to new legislative enactments. To some extent this is not entirely possible.[14] Yet an effort must be made to minimize substantially the area in which discretion can be exercised. Otherwise, human vagaries and frailties would unnecessarily aggravate the difficulties already attendant to the assimilation of the effects of automatic devices into the private planning process.

The true merit of the built-in stabilizers is their automatism. The operation of an automatic mechanism for providing changes in tax revenues, therefore, is likely to be more effective than tax adjustments of equal value magnitude which are dependent on legislative or administrative decisions regardless of the punctuality of the action. An increase in tax payments will be more

[13]This, perhaps, would be one way to rationalize the greater acceptability of the Committee for Economic Development's stabilizing budget policy and the current obscurity of Friedman's well-reasoned proposal. In large part the CED found that the contemporary economy provided substantially effective automatic measures whereas Friedman's plan called for rather revolutionary restructuring of existing economic institutions.

The CED's program was first comprehensively elucidated in CED, *Taxes and the Budget: A Program for Prosperity in a Free Economy* (New York: CED, November 1947). Subsequent CED pamphlets provided restatements, amplification, and emendation of this program. The original CED scheme, its subsequent development, and its fortunes are capably analyzed in Walter W. Heller, "CED's Stabilizing Budget Policy After Ten Years," *American Economic Review,* September 1957, XLVII, pp. 634–51. Friedman's proposal is presented in his essay, "A Monetary and Fiscal Framework . . ." *op cit.*

[14]For example, the countercyclical impact of one of the traditional automatic measures, the unemployment insurance program, depends on a low-level administrative decision regarding the qualifications of the prospective beneficiary. The same sort of determination is frequently necessary with respect to allowable deductions for income tax purposes. The farm price-support program, should it qualify as a built-in stabilizer, requires annual appropriation bills from which the funds to service the price-support obligations are drawn. Should Congress fail to pass these bills, the price-support program would rapidly atrophy.

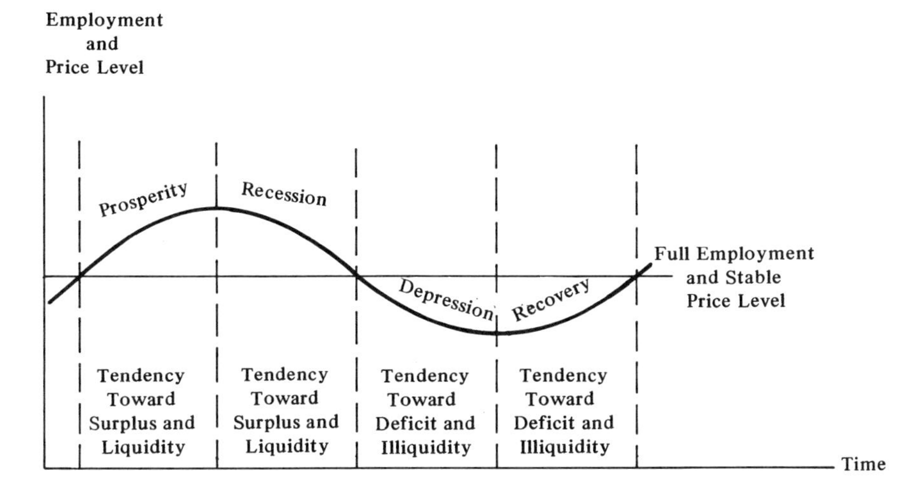

Figure 1. Ideal Countercyclical Action of Automatic Stabilizers

effective in inducing expenditure responses if the taxpayer can, with each prospective income rise, anticipate the increase in tax payments and relative fall in liquidity than if he must wait until the appropriate government authority revises tax rates. However, should the automatic mechanism elicit reactions which, while automatic, do not conform properly to movements in economic activity it may be worse than useless. Thus the issue of proper conformity is of some moment.

Accepting the dual stabilization goals of a relatively stable general price level and relatively full employment and giving neither pre-eminence, and also recognizing that neither of these is perfectly attainable under any foreseeable system of countercyclical measures, what is the ideal timing of the compensatory contribution of the automatic stabilizers? Figure 1 caricatures the business cycle, following the Schumpeterian model of the four-phase cycle. Letting the trendline represent the achievement of the joint stabilization objectives, an ideal countercyclical mechanism would abet cyclical movements toward the trendline and tend to cancel movements away from it. During Schumpeter's prosperity and recession, therefore, the compensatory devices should tend toward a government surplus and a diminution of liquidity; during his depression and recovery periods the opposite should be true. If the countercyclical impact of the built-in devices were instantaneous then rigidly tying their activation to variables that conform perfectly with the turning points in economic activity would provide the desired compensatory effect only during Schumpeter's depression and prosperity. However, Friedman has correctly observed that even for automatic stabilizers the passage of time between the device's initial reaction to economic change and its economic impact is of significant duration.[15] While reliable empirical evidence of the duration of this impact lag is lacking, it seems likely that the weighted average impact lag is of such length that, in fact, automatic stabilizers that are linked to cyclically conforming series do approximate the desired compensatory performance. Ideally, therefore, the automatic stabilizers' countercyclical action should be rigidly fixed to conforming variables and, of course, variables which at the same time exhibit a wider amplitude than the cycle itself. Hence, the final requirement of effective built-in stabilizers is that they be closely tied to operational variables that are sensitive to and conform with economic fluctuations.

If these conditions are met—if a stabilization device is relatively permanent, well defined, and linked to cyclically sensitive and conforming series, i.e., if it possesses predictability of action—and at the same time Hart's amended criteria are fulfilled, a countercyclical measure may be said to be automatic and, chances are, relatively effective. It should be noted that these requirements almost certainly exclude formula flexibility from consideration as an element of built-in stabilization policy. An important facet of inherent stabilization in the economy is that decision-making units should be able to adopt reasonably certain expectations concerning the operation of the economic response mechanism, given the arsenal of countercyclical measures. Where the stabilization arsenal contains large elements of formula flexibility the adoption of reasonably certain anticipations requires a higher order of sophistication and precision of knowledge than would expectations involving the types of stabilizers here being discussed—the so-called fixed or constant automatic stabilizers. Furthermore, unless the formula were kept secret and, in fact, could not be surmised by the public, a stabilization arrangement which entailed rate changes in the tax system for different phases of the cycle would create opportunities for injurious speculation.

Consequently, another important, although not necessarily distinguishing, feature of the type of stabilization device here defined as automatic is that its automaticity be of a by-product nature and not the resultant of purely countercyclical considerations. Its operation should not be derived from a separate, external formula which was instituted for compensatory purposes. All of the current potential automatic stabilizers are of this type—there are no stabilizers possessing formula flexibility unless the merit-rating provisions of the unemployment insurance programs can be so considered.

[15] Friedman, "A Monetary and Fiscal Framework . . ." *op cit.*, p. 146. This "impact lag," of course, will be of varying length depending upon the mechanism through which the particular stabilizer imparts its countercyclical influence.

THE CURRENT BATTERY OF AUTOMATIC STABILIZERS

What are the currently operating federal stabilization devices which qualify as automatic countercyclical compensators? As has been mentioned, most economists would classify as automatic stabilizers those devices which, without the necessity of new policy decisions, tend to render budgetary deficits in slumps and budgetary surpluses in booms. Hart's criteria broaden this classification somewhat but the inclusion of his tests concerning the supply of and demand for moneyness do not in practice admit a larger number of existing measures to membership. The commonly accepted automatic stabilizers must be included in either case, Hart's additional criteria serving simply to underline another dimension of the mechanism of the stabilizers. The insistence that automatic stabilizers must have predictability of action, however, may filter out some of the countercyclical measures which are conventionally accepted as being automatic. Hence a brief enumeration of the measures which qualify according to the complete set of criteria postulated above is warranted.

The three major sources of federal revenue—personal income and corporate income taxes and excise taxes—clearly meet the tests. The current collection features, cyclical volatility of the base, and progressive rates of the personal income tax combine to make it a powerful automatic stabilizer. Excise taxes and the corporate income tax possess countercyclical flexibility because of the volatility of the tax base alone, although in the case of the latter there is rudimentary progression due to favorable treatment extended small corporations. The lagged quarterly payment provision is not too damaging since, in practice, corporation managements seem to operate on the principle of accruing tax liabilities.[16] There can be little debate that these taxes satisfy Hart's conditions, nor can it be convincingly denied that they are clearly defined, of a by-product nature, tied to cyclically sensitive and conforming variables, and possess an aspect of permanency.

The techniques by which the above forms of government revenue exert their automatic countercyclical influence are certain enough. Because of the sensitivity of the tax base and, where applicable, due to the progression in the structure of rates, these built-in tax devices permit the retention of a larger share of income. At the same time, because of their impact on the budget's balance, they tend to alter the supply of moneyness. The mechanisms of automatic flexibility in budgetary expenditures, however, are less precise since there are no expenditure concepts directly analogous to the

[16]This is supported by E. Cary Brown, "Pay-As-You-Go Corporate Taxes," *American Economic Review*, September 1947, XXXVIII, pp. 641–45, and Hart, *Money, Debt, and Economic Activity* (2d ed.), p. 464. The spreading of losses under the corporate income tax, since it is discretionary with management, seems likewise to have little pertinence to the issue at hand.

revenue concepts of "base" and "structure of rates." This, however, is not a major hurdle in an attempt to list the government spending activities qualifying as automatic stabilizers. None of the criteria postulated above make reference to the specific mechanism by which the countercyclical impact must be achieved. All that was proposed was that built-in stabilizers should (1) possess predictability of action, (2) go into effect without the need for fresh policy decisions, and (3) have the proper effect on the government's budget and on the supply of or demand for moneyness.

Not many government expenditures programs qualify on the basis of these three criteria, but certainly the social security schemes fit. The countercyclical effect of the Old Age and Survivors Insurance program depends upon the variation in aggregate contributions growing out of fluctuations in the "covered" payroll base with the flexibility of benefit disbursements coming from the withdrawal out of or entry into the "covered" labor force of insured persons over the requisite age level for eligibility.[17] The unemployment insurance program is probably the most direct and automatic of the various built-in devices.[18] As with the OASI arrangement, the countercyclical sensitivity of contributions to the unemployment insurance trust fund is a derivative of the volatility of the covered wagebill upon which employers' contributions are based.[19] The compensatory workings of the benefit payment provisions are obvious. Thus, the countercyclical effect of both these types of social security legislation is twofold: a drop in the level of economic activity tends to lower employers' and employees' aggregate contributions and to increase the amount of benefit payments from the trust funds; an increase in economic activity tends to raise the aggregate amount of contributions and to lower the total value of benefit payments. Unlike other expenditures programs, such as public assistance schemes, the OASI and unemployment

[17] *Survey of Current Business,* July 1947, XXVII, p. 46, points out the conformity of the withdrawals of covered employees from the labor force during cyclical contractions. See also R. A. Dahl and C. E. Lindblom, "Variation in Public Expenditure" in Max F. Millikan (ed.), *Income Stabilization for a Developing Democracy* (New Haven: Yale University Press, 1953), pp. 378–80.

[18] Of course, the unemployment insurance system operates under state laws rather than by federal legislation. Nevertheless, Philip E. Taylor, *The Economics of Public Finance* (rev. ed.: New York: Macmillan Company, 1953), p. 534, suggests that there is, in general, substantial uniformity among the state systems. Additionally, the federal Treasury acts as a depository and disbursing officer for state funds accumulated under their unemployment insurance programs. There is therefore some justification for considering the insurance system a "federal" program.

[19] Merit or experience rating provisions complicate the picture. The average contribution rates move anticountercyclically because of the merit rating provisions. Nevertheless, the volatility of the payroll base effectively compensates so that, on balance, the revenue operations of the unemployment insurance programs impart a favorable stabilization impact. See Charles A. Myers, "Experience Rating in Unemployment Compensation," *American Economic Review,* June 1945, XXV, expecially p. 341, and W. A. Andrews and T. A. Miller, "Unemployment Benefits, Experience Rating and Employment Stability," *National Tax Journal,* September 1954, VII, pp. 193–209.

insurance programs permit little administrative discretion. The determination of the amounts contributed, of the amounts payable as benefits, and, to a large extent, of eligibility for benefits is taken out of the hands of individual officials; rather the tax and benefit formulas and conditions of eligibility are clearly stated in the enacting legislation.

One other government expenditure program deserves consideration. It has been fashionable to accord the status of built-in stabilizer to the federal farm price-support programs. According to the arguments presented in favor of their inclusion it is immaterial whether support payments are designed to maintain agricultural prices during a deflationary period or to provide parity incomes for producers of certain important products. If the price-support programs are fashioned to maintain farm prices, the amount of payments made to producers will increase as deflation progresses. Contrastingly, government support payments during periods of high prices will presumably slacken. If, instead, the support program is planned to provide parity prices, only a fall in farm prices proportionately greater than the drop in non-farm prices will increase the government's subsidies to agricultural producers and so contribute a net increase of government funds to the income stream. Historically the normal migration of labor from farming to industry has tended to reverse itself during depressed periods and farmers have tended to increase agricultural output as prices fell. Consequently, there is a natural inclination during a depression for the prices of farm products to decline more rapidly and further than nonfarm prices, bringing about an increase in support payments as the contraction develops. Thus, the farm price-support programs, according to this line of reasoning, contain a substantial measure of built-in flexibility.[20]

At one time these arguments may have possessed validity. During the first term of the Eisenhower administration, however, rigid price supports gave way to a flexible farm price-support system in which not only the support levels can be altered, within a range, at the discretion of the executive branch of the government but also the parity prices themselves are calculated on a more flexible basis. This encroachment of flexibility into the price-support system is a telling blow to its automatic stabilization potential. The program is still, in a way, capable of satisfying the criterion of being well-defined. Congress has only given the Administration discretion to alter support levels within specified limits. But in a fundamental sense, the discretion of the executive branch creates a situation in which it is difficult to hold expectations with relative certainty. The devices are no longer as assuredly installed on a relatively permanent basis and, because of the discretionary element, they

[20]Maxwell, *op. cit.*, pp. 123–24, and Taylor, *op. cit.*, p. 538, rely on this argument. See also F. V. Waugh, "What Sort of Price Policy is Practical in the U.S.A.?" *Journal of Farm Economics,* December 1952, XXXIV, p. 608.

are no longer closely tied to cyclically sensitive and conforming variables. Hence, the farm price-support programs lack an essential element of effective automatic stabilization—predictability of action—and, therefore, do not qualify as automatic stabilizers.

IN SUMMARY

No one, including Friedman whose automatic stabilization proposal is most innovationary, believes that built-in stabilizers can prevent a major cyclical movement, once under way, from causing severe hardships. The prevailing professional assessment is that the existing automatic compensatory arsenal is not very effective. The CED, in the present institutional environment, places more faith than most economists in the countercyclical strength of automatic stabilization measures.[21] Aside from the CED's position, Hart seems more favorably disposed toward automatic countercyclical efficacy than the remainder of his colleagues. Although he provides no analytical basis for his belief, Hart contends that built-in stabilizers can be counted on to set a floor to contradictions.[22] Most economists are unwilling to go even this far. They assert that automatic devices "can only *temper*, but never *prevent* or fully counteract, a fluctuation in economic conditions."[23] An intuitively compiled weighted average of economic opinion on the efficacy of the existing battery of automatic stabilizers might be the following: the automatic stabilization features of the current fiscal system cannot be relied on alone to dependably stabilize the economy. They are capable, certainly, of reducing the amplitude of the relatively mild swings in economic activity, they might conceivably provide a floor and a ceiling to these fluctuations, but in no event can they initiate an actual reversal of cumulative movements. The so-called Princeton Manifesto, indeed, seems to provide such a weighted average.[24]

It is possible that this "weighted average" opinion gives an overly pessimistic appraisal of the countercyclical potential of the built-in stabilizers—a pessimism stemming from the failure to consider two important facets of the operating mechanism of the automatic devices. Most analysts do

[21] This faith apparently extends to the hope that built-in flexibility may be able to initiate the reversal of a minor-cycle contraction. See Herbert Stein, "Budget Policy to Maintain Stability," *Problems in Anti-Recession Policy,*" pp. 88–89.

[22] Hart, *Money, Debt, and Economic Activity* (2d ed.), p. 492.

[23] Hagen, *op. cit.*, p. 173. A vast number of similar statements can be found in the literature, of which the following seem representative: Maxwell, *op. cit.*, p. 114; Gerhard Colm, "Fiscal Policy and the Federal Budget," *Income Stabilization for a Developing Democracy,* p. 246; and Egle, *op. cit.*, p. 54.

[24] U.S. Congress, Subcommittee on Monetary, Credit, and Fiscal Policies, Joint Committee on the Economic Report, *Monetary, Credit, and Fiscal Policies: Hearings,* 81st Cong., 2d Sess., 1950, p. 91.

not consider the monetary element in the operation of the stabilizers. The ability of automatic stabilizers to alter the liquidity of the economy, while sometimes included in the list of criteria that automatic stabilizers must satisfy, has usually been omitted from the theoretical and empirical analysis of their compensatory role.[25] Nevertheless, monetary phenomena are essential to a realistic assessment of the capabilities of the existing built-in stabilizers.

The other neglected facet of the mechanism of automatic stabilization devices is their impact on the cyclical response pattern through their ability to cause adjustments in expectations. In view of the importance attached to expectations by the major cycle-minor cycle format,[26] there is a possibility, because of the stabilizers' effects upon anticipations, that an unappreciated measure of success is available to the built-in stabilization arsenal. Should the liquidity and expectational aspects of the automatic stabilization mechanism be given a deserved place in the analyses of the countercyclical role of the automatic stabilizers it may be found that there is indeed some justification for believing that the less severe of the future fluctuations in economic activity will be remedied without recourse to discretionary measures and without undue economic hardship. At the very least a more realistic and theoretically up-to-date assessment of the efficacy of the automatic stabilization arsenal will be made available to policy makers.

[25]Colm has recognized the potentialities of this omission. *Op. cit.*, pp. 245–46.

[26]R. A. Gordon's most complete development of his major cycle-minor cycle hypothesis is found in "Investment Behavior and Business Cycles," *Review of Economics and Statistics,* February 1955, XXXVII, pp. 23–34.